Stepmoms on a Mission

Stepmoms on a Mission
A Compassionate Exploration to Find Answers, Options and Hope

CATHRYN BOND DOYLE

Edited by Katharine Trussler
Cover Design by Katharine Trussler
Back Cover Photo by Fred Glasser, S18Photography, New Jersey

Copyright (c) 2018 Cathryn Bond Doyle
All rights reserved. This book may not be reproduced in whole or in part, stored in a retrieval system or transmitted in any form or by any means—electronic, mechanical or other—without written permission from the author, except in the case of brief quotations embodied in critical articles and reviews. For information or request, please contact Cathryn Bond Doyle, P.O. Box 7, Medford, NJ 08055, (609) 206-2009 or cathryn@smoms.org.

ISBN-10: 0998263605
ISBN-13: 9780998263601

Library of Congress Control Number: 2016917590
Stepmoms on a Mission, Medford Lakes, NJ
BISAC: Family & Relationships/Parenting/Stepparenting/Self-Help/Personal Growth

Stepmoms on a Mission
Medford Lakes, New Jersey

Dedication

This book is dedicated to all the Stepmoms I've ever worked with and to every other Stepmom seeking to become wiser, more loving and closer to her partner.

Heartfelt Thanks and Acknowledgements

My personal study and work with Stepmoms is only possible because of the long-standing generosity of my wise, loving and resilient husband. He has also been through a lot as part of a stepfamily. I'm forever grateful to him for supporting me and my work right from the beginning of my stepmother journey. He provided the resources which enabled me to devote the time and get the training I needed to help myself and so many other stepmothers and their partners. Our shared belief that there is wisdom and value to be gleaned from upsetting situations has kept us on the same team all these years and I'm so thankful we weathered the storms together.

Jeanette Pasqua is my amazing soul sister. She's been a continual source of laughter, lovingkindness, healing and encouragement for me since before the idea of this book was born in 2004. She always believed this book would one day be published—even when I couldn't see the pathway forward. Jeanette, you and your loving support are a treasured gift! Thank you to the moon and back.

Katharine (Kate) Edwards Trussler is the editor of this book. Kate is a courageous stepmother who I met a few years ago when she took one of my workshops. When I mentioned I was trying to edit my own manuscript, she shared that she is a communicator by profession and could help me with the edits. She is an answer to my prayers. This book is better because of her knowledge of my work and her tremendous writing talents. She also found the perfect photo *and* designed the beautiful cover for this book. Thank you for your ongoing encouragement, rewrite after rewrite. Each moment has been a pleasure, Kate!

I'm deeply grateful to all my wonderful teachers with a special mention of the late Christopher (Kit) Carson and the late Moriah Marston. Kit, Moriah and the other professionals I had the pleasure of learning from have been so generous with me, sharing their own particular areas of expertise. They were patient with my questions, kind to me along my learning curve and wonderfully supportive of my insistence that there must be new approaches to find or develop to heal myself, then help other Stepmoms deal with the challenges and complexities that arise in stepfamily life. You'll read many of their ideas throughout this book.

Finally, a special thanks to the twenty Stepmoms (SMOMS), members of smoms.org, who contributed their stories to this book. They wanted each of you to know that no matter how you're feeling right now, you're not crazy or alone in your feelings and—perhaps more importantly—that things can get better when you're willing to change. Sharing this deeply personal work together has resulted in a nourishing and empowering sisterhood among us Stepmoms on a Mission. Ladies, I'm grateful our paths crossed and so proud of you all and the work we've done together.

Foreword from a Veteran Stepmom on a Mission

When I was a young and single working girl, a vice president many rungs above me on the tall corporate ladder complimented my work on a massive project. I thanked him, but uncharacteristically admitted that I was a bit steamed because another colleague was taking credit for my hard work. He responded that I was not to worry because, "Those who know, know, and those who don't know, don't know that they don't know."

Since I later got the coveted promotion, while my colleague did not, I knew that those who mattered knew the truth. His adage stuck with me, and later when I married a man with children, I found that friends and relatives whom I asked for advice on how to best thrive might give all sorts of suggestions, but really, "they didn't know, and didn't know that they didn't know," so their ideas generally just fell flat.

Trying to find some answers on handling children who weren't my own, and dealing with a bio-mom who seemed intent on making the lives of my darling husband and me a rollercoaster of loud angry phone calls and nastily worded emails, I trolled the internet for articles. Fortunately, I found a community of Stepmoms who were on a mission to make their lives, marriages, and families as positive as possible. These women were part of smoms.org, under the guidance of founder Cathryn Bond Doyle. The timing was fortunate for me as Cathryn had just opened her website days earlier and I was the first internet member of a group that had been meeting weekly in person for two years. We were a small group at the beginning and even though thousands of women have passed through the site over the years, the one thing that is consistent is the compassionate, non-judgmental, creative support we all receive.

Over the last 16 years, I've turned to smoms.org and Cathryn countless times for advice, insight, inspiration, and sometimes just a good chuckle. Surely, my former VP would agree that it is good to get your guidance from those who get what you're feeling and who've already been through the challenges you're facing. In the following chapters, you will find a virtual first aid kit on handling all varieties of issues—both big and small—that risk becoming infected wounds on your psyche, the children, and your marriage.

Cathryn, with all her wisdom, and the voices of thousands of ladies who've been in your shoes behind her, will advise on the challenges of knowing when and how to properly step up to assist your beloved in parenting responsibilities, and when to step back. These children, as much as you love them, are not your own, and the drama that often accompanies them can be their parents' and not yours.

At times as a Stepmom you will be stepped upon, but Cathryn's sage counsel will advise you how to best protect yourself from that repeatedly happening, and to brush yourself off and move forward—more aware and skilled from each experience.

With great affection, I thank my dear friend Cathryn for being there for me and for so many of us. I am confident her advice will be of assistance to you too.

Ali
Stepmom since 2001
SMOM since 2002

Letter from the Editor

When I first met Cathryn Bond Doyle in 2010, I was a new Stepmom with stars in my eyes. As an optimistic and creative person with lots of love to give, I thought I could figure out what to do, no matter what challenge came my way. And yet as a stepmother, I was wrong over and over and over again. Sometimes I couldn't even SEE the map home and I was getting so lost! Thank goodness I stumbled upon smoms.org in one of my darkest, most confused hours. Over the past eight years, Cathryn's website has been a lifesaver for me, and her virtual workshops have helped empower and energize me to embrace the possibilities in my life and relationships. I'm so fortunate to say that Cathryn and her guidance have been my saving grace, time after time.

I can't explain why, but from the very beginning, I felt I'd be Cathryn's editor someday, although I am not a book editor by profession. (I'm an internal communicator in the corporate world, so I plan, write, revise and distribute all kinds of material—just never books!) What a dream it would be to help Cathryn spread her talents and message even more widely throughout the stepmother community, I thought. And then for many years, I kept that dream to myself. Now, for the past 18 months, I've witnessed first-hand the construction of this exceptional resource, and have watched Cathryn herself grow beautifully through this work. I am blessed to call her a friend, and I'm so proud of what she has assembled within this purple book jacket.

This book you are holding in your hands appeals to the stepmothers who want to make a difference in the world as human beings. It is teeming with advice about how to understand your own motivations and tendencies, and how to control what you can control and let the rest go in mindful, self-respecting ways. Cathryn discusses boundaries (SO important!) and she challenges you to revisit your personal beliefs and child-created strategies. Whether you're best friends with your stepchildren's bio-mom or on the other end of the spectrum, your interactions with her can be better. Whether you're treated as a second mother by your stepkids or dismissed as a non-person, you can optimize your role in your own household, recognizing and rewarding your own worth. And best of all, you can strengthen and nurture your relationship with your partner, achieving your own (new?) happy family dream together!

The material in this book is based on Cathryn's decades of study, plus her interactions with specialists and eighteen years of working with thousands of other stepmothers. As a person, Cathryn is honest and caring, and you'll find that this comes through in her every word. She has written and rewritten chapter after chapter in an effort to make it the best it can be for YOU. If a topic speaks to you, I recommend you read the material and sit with it for a while, as its meaning in your life may take some time to unfurl, like the petals of a flower in the first hours of morning. As Cathryn will say, you may also experience resistance to some of her revelations or ideas. The resistance itself will be meaningful for you! Take it in, think about it some more and see where it takes you.

I've told Cathryn I believe this book is her gift to the universe. And whether you can see it yet or not, you are a gift, too. You are loved. You are valued. You are worth it. You are not alone. In these thoughtful, insightful pages, Cathryn can help you find your own map home.

Katharine Trussler
February 2018
Stepmom since 2010
SMOM since 2013

Preface

As is true for many women before me, becoming a stepmother was a catalyst for an unplanned journey of new experiences, challenges and growth. Along the way, I gradually addressed my own issues and went on to work with thousands of women across the country and around the world. I became a Stepmom in 1996 at age 40. By then I'd already spent eighteen years in the field of retail banking, the last twelve of those as an independent consultant. With an extensive background in human behavior, creative problem-solving, sales and communications, I felt qualified for (and excited about) my new role as a Stepmom. I wholeheartedly believed it would be fun and that I'd be good at it. Since I didn't have my own kids, my heart warmed at the chance to participate in the joys of parenting. Ready for a break from life on the road, I shut down most of my consulting practice so I could get to know my stepson. I was delighted to care for this bright five-year-old boy who was with us half the time. I was also happy, even eager, to help my partner with the logistics of stepfamily life, confident that four adults working together could create a super-duper life for one child.

I thought everyone involved would want me to be an active member of the parenting team—I was wrong. I thought I was prepared (even read a lot of stepfamily books) to seamlessly fit into life with my partner, my stepson, his bio-mom and her new partner—I was mistaken. I considered myself aware, good at self-care and very good in relationships and problem-solving—but once under situational stepfamily stress, I discovered I wasn't skilled enough at any of these things.

In addition to having seemingly relevant experience and abundant, genuine enthusiasm for my new role, it turns out I was also naïve and often jolted by the complex power struggles, unforeseen conflicts and unimaginable emotional traumas that can crop up in stepfamily situations. The harsh reality that people don't always want to get along or resolve problems showed itself immediately. Still, for reasons unknown to me at the time, it took me *way* too long to remove my Pollyanna-powered rose-colored glasses to see this truth. I strongly resisted accepting that my glorious happy family fantasy was not going to materialize as I'd initially believed and so joyfully imagined. That lengthy delay in my recognition and full acceptance of our stepfamily reality caused my husband and me immeasurable stress. I was unaware I was blinded by my own hopes, beliefs and desires.

While I brought my own personal beliefs, needs and personality to the table of our stepfamily life, so did my husband, stepson, his bio-mom and her new husband. We didn't share enough common goals so things didn't work out the way I hoped. Naturally, I had brought many assumptions and expectations into my role as a Stepmom and—you guessed it—I was wrong about virtually all of them. I was unable to resolve our stepfamily differences, and I was exhausted, hurting and out of ideas. So one day I made a new choice. I turned my attention away from trying to change others and focused on learning how to change myself. From that new perspective, I did two things for my own well-being.

First, I began what turned out to be an unexpected seven-year quest seeking the advice and instruction of several experts that included more than 1,100 paid consultation hours. The men and women I encountered changed my mind and my life in so many ways. You'll read many of their specific suggestions in this book.

Second, I sought out a local stepfamily support group. And in November 1999, after attending three monthly meetings, I was politely asked to leave that group. They awkwardly but firmly suggested I *not* return, saying I was too focused on helping other attendees craft creative strategies to resolve their issues. They told me I could return only if I agreed to sit quietly and offer no suggestions to others. While I know the listening-quietly approach has been a winning formula for many, it just wasn't what I needed and wanted as a Stepmom under duress. I wanted to talk with someone who knew how I felt. I wanted compassion, encouragement and new ideas for reducing the stress my partner and I were feeling. I wanted to be a part of a proactive and honest community and to strengthen my overall sense of well-being. Driving home that night, somewhat discombobulated by what had just happened, I was stopped at a traffic light when something inside me shifted. The energy started to flow and I blurted out my sudden realization, "Holy cow, I'm a Stepmom on a Mission!" That was the moment I realized I needed to start my own group for women who loved their partners, who wanted to love their stepkids and who were creative, curious, action-oriented, like-minded individuals in the role of stepmother. So I did.

On March 1, 2000, eighteen women showed up for the first official weekly meeting of Stepmoms on a Mission. Two years later, smoms.org opened as a free, anonymous resource for Stepmoms across the globe.

Preface

This book is a collection of ideas, insights, tactics and strategies gathered from my own experiences and drawing from my private work with hundreds of Stepmoms and continued interactions with thousands of other Stepmoms through the website. I have learned that the ingredients that work for Stepmoms on a Mission of all backgrounds and circumstances are compassion, support, creativity, courage, open-mindedness, a willingness to learn and a commitment to lovingkindness.

I wrote this book with two main goals in mind: First, to give you information to help you feel better, stand up for yourself more effectively, eliminate your resentments and reclaim your personal power. Second, to give you (and your partner) approaches you can use to strengthen your loving relationship. These approaches can empower you both to handle whatever happens as an indivisible, consciously aware and loving team.

This manual, like a guidebook, points out new ways for you to look at and handle many common stressful stepfamily situations. It gives you more choices to consider, explains why you might want to make those choices and provides alternative routes (even detours) to help you get to your personal destination. This is a book about finding new ways to take responsibility for your well-being, and it is not about reinforcing the feelings of victimhood, nor about blaming or bashing others. It contains practical, hard-earned, field-tested wisdom that stepmothers can use to shorten the sometimes long, lonely, steep and costly learning curve they may experience in uncharted stepmothering territory.

The challenges of being a Stepmom can be unlike anything many of us have faced or could even imagine. We often start out enthusiastic, generous and willing to do whatever it takes to create our happy family dream. Sooner or later, we may find we are unprepared for the intense and often chronic stress that can wear us down and damage our relationships. I know how difficult it can be to be a Stepmom. I have also been fortunate enough to experience and witness, over and over again, the triumph and the lasting happiness that come from feeling self-aware, understood, supported, competent and empowered. May you find in this book the answers, options and hope you need to create a fulfilling life with your beloved partner.

Cathryn Bond Doyle
March 2018
Stepmom since 1996
SMOM since 2000

Introduction

Since you're reading this book, it's likely you're looking for some relief, or maybe you're just looking for new ideas. Whatever brought you here—welcome. Through my experiences I've learned that feeling better starts with honoring your feelings, becoming more conscious of your beliefs and needs, being willing to see things differently and gaining new skills so you can make wise, personalized, empowered choices. If you're up for that, this book can help!

Begin Wherever You Are

My first question for each new client is this: *"What can we work on right now to bring you an immediate sense of relief or inspiration?"* She tells me, and we go to work to give her a breath of emotional fresh air and a chance to see how she can feel better and help herself in new ways—right away. Since you can't tell me what you need today, this book is written and organized so you can find the right support and guidance for you, wherever you may be on your journey as a Stepmom. As eager as I am to have you learn everything you need to know, I recognize your individual needs and feelings. I also respect that the energy, time and patience you'll need to do this work will vary from day to day. With that in mind, I wrote this book like a reference and instruction manual, and you can seek out and return to its contents as needed.

This book can be read cover to cover but it doesn't need to be. Use the Table of Contents as your map. Trust your heart and gut reactions to the titles of the chapters and go to the ones that call to you or that address whatever is happening in your stepfamily life. For example, if you and your partner are at odds over how to handle an urgent issue, go to Chapter 18. If your resentments are tearing you up inside, go to Chapter 12. If you're eager to gain more empathy for your partner, go to Chapter 27. If you're looking for ways to help your stepkids feel more empowered, go to Chapter 37, Tip #25. If your stepkids' bio-mom is driving you nuts, go to Section Six and jump right into the material. You get the idea. The chapters are grouped into topic-based sections, so if you're unsure of exactly what you want or need, you can choose a section that looks interesting to you.

Because each chapter is written to stand on its own, there is some repetition of content throughout the book. If you decide to read the book from the beginning, by the time you finish it you'll be well-versed in the concepts, approaches, tactics and skills I recommend. Within some chapters you'll see references to other chapters—these are more guideposts as you explore each topic.

You will notice I use a lot of words to explain *how* and *why* my suggestions work. I take the time to do this because my mentor, Kit Carson, taught me this is the best way to help others truly understand new things. He wanted me to understand vs. mimic or memorize on blind faith alone. His approach made it easier for me to learn new things and more importantly gave me the knowledge I needed to confidently customize something (if needed) to better fit my own personality, values and circumstances. I always appreciated this approach, and it has been a component of my teaching since 1986 when I first began leading workshops.

While each stepfamily situation is complex and unique, it has become clear that regardless of the differences in our life circumstances, stepmothers share many of the same issues. Beginning at our very first SMOMS support group meeting in 2000 and continuing with Stepmoms ever since, I've noticed that once feelings are expressed, understood, acknowledged and supported with judgment-free compassion, some kind of natural emotional shift occurs for the Stepmoms involved. It feels like some kind of expanded inner space is created along with a renewed sense of enthusiasm. This usually results in excitement, and bolsters a newfound readiness to seek answers, acquire new skills and get to work on feeling better. This is what I hope I've created for you with this book: a resource you can turn to that will remind you you're not alone, crazy or oversensitive in whatever you're feeling. Plus, it is a guidebook you can consult—at anytime!—to find new ideas to help you handle any stepmother challenge, puzzle or opportunity.

Material on smoms.org

In addition to what you'll find in this book, there are seventeen bonus chapters available on the SMOMS website at smoms.org/BonusChapters. These include six additional chapter topics and eleven follow-up comments and discussions with Stepmoms about chapters contained in this book. A list of the bonus chapters and discussion topics can be found in

Chapter 39. This particular website address is *not* viewable by the public nor on the site navigation bar so you need to type it into your search engine. In addition to the bonus materials for readers of this book, there are several public-access stepmother articles posted under "Cathryn's Articles" on smoms.org. You can see a list of these articles in Chapter 40.

Abbreviations in the Book

- DH can stand for dear husband or divorced husband. It's your partner (of either sex) and is interchangeable with the terms of husband, fiancé, boyfriend (BF) and future dear husband (FDH). In all cases a partner refers to the one you love who is the bio-parent of your stepkids.

- SS and SD are shorthand for stepson and stepdaughter, respectively. DS and DD are shorthand for your biological dear sons and dear daughters. A number after any of these initials refers to his or her age. For example, SD9 is a nine-year-old stepdaughter.

- Bio-mom refers to the biological (or adoptive) mother of your stepkids. We conceptually classify bio-moms into three groups—kind, civil and uncooperative—to help us better understand and address general situations when sharing our stories and asking for support. We acknowledge and honor that there are many amazing bio-moms in stepfamily situations. In fact, about half of the tens of thousands of women passing through smoms.org over the years are both stepmothers *and* biological mothers. These terms are meant to be descriptive, not judgmental, and are based on bio-mom behaviors and interactions with you, your partner and your stepkids.

- Mother-by-marriage is the term we use for a Stepmom who doesn't currently have any bio-kids.

"Yeah, Buts"

I believe every resistance, doubt, objection and question about a new idea is important and worthy of further investigation. While it might be tempting to push your way past them or just stop reading, I encourage you to pay attention each time you find yourself thinking, "Yeah, But…" in reaction to what you read in this book. Any resistance you may experience holds a key to some important personal insights. Make note of them. If you're interested in digging more deeply, see if you can figure out what a "Yeah, But" might be trying to distract you from by asking yourself, your partner or a trusted friend what they think. Could it be a possible future experience, awareness or feeling? These insights can be transformational. Chapter 11, and Bonus Chapter 2 called "Understanding Emotional Resistance" (see smoms.org/BonusChapters) offer you more about emotional resistance and the benefits of honoring it with your time and attention.

Stepmother vs. Stepmom on a Mission

In my mind, a stepmother is any woman in an intimate relationship (married or not) with a man (or woman) who has children from a previous relationship. Any stepmother willing to invest her precious time and energy to explore her feelings, learn new ideas and relationship skills, and bravely own her contributions to difficult situations—all with the goal of improving her own well-being and her life with her partner—is a Stepmom on a Mission, or a SMOM, for short. SMOMS is also a one-syllable acronym for the name of our group and our website, smoms.org.

Even though there's not a one-size-fits-all formula for Stepmom success (darn it), there are many emotional and relationship dynamics that all stepmothers can apply to their situations to get positive results. As Stepmoms on a Mission, we've learned the power of a few basic day-to-day behaviors and attitudes. As a preview to my approach, here are a few fundamentals that have proven significant to our success:

- Striving to be awake (consciously aware in the present moment) as much as possible, to get clear on our thoughts and feelings so we can honor and learn from them.

- Reminding ourselves, and each other, to mute the harsh inner critic and replace its messages with gentle, unconditionally friendly and supportive self-talk.

- Doing our best to pause, breathe and resist the urge to lash out when we feel emotionally triggered, or when trauma or melodrama strike.

- Cultivating compassion for ourselves, our partners and our stepkids in every situation *before* taking action.

- Making our own well-being and our connection with our beloved partner our highest priority.

Introduction

We do these things because we've learned it makes us feel better and because we love our partners and want to feel empowered in our ever-evolving role as stepmothers. Last but not least, we all want a happy life, even if it looks a little (or a lot) different than the one we originally envisioned when we first became stepmothers.

As you become more conscious about what you're thinking, feeling, believing, needing, saying and doing, you will feel more capable and confident about any stepfamily situations you're facing. This ever-growing calm competence will make you feel less anxious, less resentful, less hurt by others, less angry and, thankfully, more capable of helping yourself process any of these feelings in healthy ways so you can get on with your life with your beloved partner.

SMOMS Stories

In addition to my teachings, you'll see that twenty SMOMS have written about their experiences for you. When they learned I was finally writing this book, they wanted to support the journeys of other stepmothers in a tangible way. With this in mind, they openly share their feelings, struggles and lessons learned with you in these pages. We sister SMOMS are united in our desire to support each other and now you. We want to give you the support, tools and wisdom you seek as you learn new ways to nurture yourself and your relationship.

On behalf of myself, the twenty sister SMOMS who share their stories and the thousands of other determined women who have been part of this work with me since 2000, we hope the difficulties we faced, the lessons we learned and the skills we developed on our journeys benefit you in some way. We're glad you're here—as a Stepmom on your own personal mission toward empowerment. Let's get started.

Table of Contents

Heartfelt Thanks and Acknowledgements · · · · · · · · · · · · · · · · vii
Foreword from a Veteran Stepmom on a Mission · · · · · · · · · ix
Letter from the Editor · xi
Preface · xiii
Introduction · xvii

Section One
A Stepmom and Her Self-Awareness

One	Practical and Empowering Expectations for a Stepmom on a Mission · · · · ·	3
	Daisy Mae's Story ·	13
Two	Honoring vs. Shaming Your Feelings · · · · · · · · · · · · · · · ·	17
	Sharon's Story ·	23
Three	Healthy Boundaries vs. Hurtful Blockages · · · · · · · · · · · ·	25
Four	The Pros and Cons of Catastrophizing: Imagining Worst-Case Scenarios to Help Yourself ·	30
	Chloe's Story ·	37
Five	Thinking of Leaving Your Partner? ·	40
Six	Ten Suggestions for Creating an Enjoyable Mother's Day · · · · · ·	48
Seven	Potential Stepmom Missteps: Understandable, Unintentional, Common and Correctable ·	56
	La Belle Reine's Story ·	69
Eight	The Birth of Beliefs and Resentments: Discover How Your Beliefs Impact You ·	72
	Susan's Story ·	94
Nine	Use Your Stressful Experiences to Find Relief, Healing and Empowerment · · ·	101

Section Two
A Stepmom Working with Resentment

	Calla's Story · 130
Ten	Are You Over-Giving to Your Partner and Stepkids? · · · · · · · · · · 133
Eleven	Why You Might Resist Giving Up Your Resentments · · · · · · · · · · 145
	A Happily Ever After SMOM Story · 153
Twelve	Understanding Resentment: The Basics of This Painful Form of Anger · 154
Thirteen	Eliminate Ongoing Resentments and Feel Great About It · · · · · · · 161
Fourteen	Processing a Resentment in Real Time: A Stepmom Example · · · · · 168
Fifteen	Resolving Resentments from the Past: Get What You Need to "Let It Go" · 175
	Ava's Story · 183
Sixteen	Embittered or Empowered?: Working with the Unchangeable Facts of Your Stepmom Life · 186
Seventeen	Feeling Like a Victim?: Reclaim Your Freedom with a Creative Choice · 202

Section Three
A Stepmom's Relationship and Her Partner

Eighteen	Resolve Conflicts in How You and Your Partner Handle Trauma: Acquire Super Powers as a Couple · · · · · · · · · · · · · · · · · 219
	Hopeful Stepmom's Story · 233
Nineteen	His Kids: His Call: Transform Your Relationship and Radically Reduce Stress Between You and Your Partner · · · · · · · · · · · · · · · 237
	Gracie Lu's Story · 267
Twenty	Nobody's Right/Nobody's Wrong: A Tactical Approach for Intimate Relationships · 269
	Jackie's Story · 287
Twenty-One	Understanding Defensiveness: Finding Compassion for the Defense Strategies You and Your Partner Bring to the Relationship · 289
Twenty-Two	Stop Being Defensive with Each Other So You Can Listen and Talk Openheartedly · 298
Twenty-Three	Three Yucky Relationship Projections Possible Between You and Your Partner · 313

Table of Contents

Section Four
A Stepmom's Partner

	Serenity Now's Story	322
Twenty-Four	Emotional Callousing: Why Your Partner May Not Be Able to Understand What Upsets You	323
Twenty-Five	Supporting Your Partner Through Divorce Guilt and Fears	331
Twenty-Six	Your Partner's Relationship with His Ex-Wife Impacts Your Partner's Behavior: Learn More to Improve Your Relationship	342
Twenty-Seven	Empathy for Your Partner: Stepfamily Stress from Your Partner's Perspective	355

Section Five
A Stepmom and Her Stepkids

	Robin's Story	370
Twenty-Eight	The Loyalty Wars: When Stepkids Feel Stressed About Loving Their Stepmom	373
Twenty-Nine	Ever Get Angry When Your Stepkids Get Away with Things?: Discover the Reasons for Your Strong Reactions	395
Thirty	Caring For vs. Catering To Your Stepkids	407
	Jersey99's Story	412
Thirty-One	The "Stop Trying So Hard and Start Lovingly Ignoring Your Stepkids" Plan	415

Section Six
A Stepmom Dealing with Her Stepkids' Uncooperative Bio-mom

	Diane's Story	428
Thirty-Two	"Sounds About Right": Use This Approach When Bio-mom's Actions Upset You	430
	Courtney's Story	446
Thirty-Three	When Your Stepkids' Bio-mom Doesn't Want to Get Along with You	448
	Diana's Story	459
Thirty-Four	Feeling Hatred?: Redirect These Intense Feelings to Reclaim Your Power	465

	Pandora's Relief's Story · · · · · · · · · · · · · · · · 477	
Thirty-Five	Is Your Stepkids' Bio-mom Consistently Uncooperative?: Shifting Your Attitude and Approach Brings Relief · · · · · · · · · · · 479	
	Christine's Story · 497	
Thirty-Six	Managing an Uncooperative Bio-mom (and Stepkids): Reduce Stress Almost Immediately · · · · · · · · · · · · · · · · 499	

Section Seven
Stepfamily Tips, Closing Comments and Additional Materials

Thirty-Seven	Thirty-One Tips to Improve Your Well-Being and Stepfamily Relationships · · · · · · · · · · · · · · · · · · · 515

- Tip #1: Cue Cards for Your Partner—An Effective Way to Teach Him What You Need to Hear · · · · · · · · · · · 515
- Tip #2: Refer to Your Partner's Ex-wife as the Stepkids' Mother (or Mom) · · · · · · · · · · · · · · · 518
- Tip #3: Ten Ways to Feel More Loved by Each Other · · · · · · · 518
- Tip #4: The Power of One Thing · · · · · · · · · · · · 521
- Tip #5: A Satisfying Response to the Accusation, "You're Not My Mother!" · · · · · · · · · · · · · · · 522
- Tip #6: Pause Before Doing Anything for Your Stepkids · · · · · 525
- Tip #7: Create Stress-Free Zones with Your Partner · · · · · · · 525
- Tip #8: Learn to say "NO" · · · · · · · · · · · · · · 527
- Tip #9: "Make It OK" for Your Partner to Change His Mind · · · · · · · · · · · · · · · · · · 528
- Tip #10: Ask Your Stepkids If They Want You to Clarify You're Their Stepmom · · · · · · · · · · · · · 529
- Tip #11: Get a Letter for Authority with Your Stepkids · · · · · · 529
- Tip #12: Think Big Picture · · · · · · · · · · · · · · 530
- Tip #13: R-E-S-P-E-C-T · · · · · · · · · · · · · · · 531
- Tip #14: Establish a Secret Support Code with Your Partner · · · · · · · · · · · · · · · · · · 533
- Tip #15: When the Bio-mom Doesn't Return Stepkids' Clothes—Try This · · · · · · · · · · · · · · 535
- Tip #16: Create a Calm Re-Entry Ritual When Stepkids Come to Your Home · · · · · · · · · · · · · 536
- Tip #17: Reminisce About Loving Times with Your Partner · · · · · · · · · · · · · · · · · · 537

- Tip #18: A Third Alternative to Right/Wrong and Good/Bad Judgments · 539
- Tip #19: Responding to "You're Being Over-Sensitive!" · 541
- Tip #20: Complain Consciously · · · · · · · · · · · · · · · · · · · 542
- Tip #21: Reframe the Comments Your Stepkids Make About Their Bio-mom · 545
- Tip #22: Use an Email Program to Communicate with Bio-mom · 549
- Tip #23: Encourage Yourself with a "Nice Job!" · · · · · · · · · · · 550
- Tip #24: Ask Your Partner for His TLC · · · · · · · · · · · · 552
- Tip #25: Give Your Stepkids Some Genuine, Positive Power · 553
- Tip #26: A Mistake Allowance—Help Kids Enjoy Learning · 558
- Tip #27: Lessen Your Power Struggles with Teenage Stepkids · 559
- Tip #28: Honor and Process Your Anger · · · · · · · · · · · · · · · · 560
- Tip #29: Remember a Moment of Feeling Like Your Best Self! · 563
- Tip #30: Rituals and Traditions to Honor All Family Members · 566
- Tip #31: Bring Compassion to Yourself · · · · · · · · · · · · · · · 568

Thirty-Eight	Closing Comments: Do You Want to Be Right or Happy?	570
Thirty-Nine	Bonus Materials at smoms.org/BonusChapters	575
Forty	Cathryn's Public Articles on smoms.org	577
Forty-One	About the Author	580

Section One

A Stepmom and Her Self-Awareness

The SMOMS's Serenity Prayer

*"May I have the patience and humility to believe things can get better, the willingness and courage to avoid blaming, the wisdom to pause, to look at my contribution to each situation and...
the energy and flexibility to keep trying new ways to create more love and less stress in our lives."*

~ Adapted from Original Serenity Prayer by
Charter Members of SMOMS
Medford, NJ, 2000

One

Practical and Empowering Expectations for a Stepmom on a Mission

I have yet to have a woman tell me she grew up wanting to be a stepmother. In fact, no one—male or female—has ever said to me that they grew up imagining a happy life with a partner who has kids from a previous relationship. Whether you've been a Stepmom for years or days, being aware (and wise) about your expectations is going to support you and your partner through stressful situations. Expectations are an important emotional component of achieving a goal, yet it's common to hear experts and family members telling stepmothers under stress to lower their expectations. They act as if it is a simple task without negative impact. That's not been my experience.

Initially the advice to lower our expectations seems sensible, but as a Stepmom myself, I found it depressing and a little annoying to think I had to give up my dreams of a happy family to supposedly reduce disappointments and temper stressful situations. So, I went to work to study the topic of Stepmom expectations believing I could find some that are realistic, achievable, supportive and even empowering.

Picture this scenario: A man with children from a previous marriage and a woman willing to embrace them all fall madly in love. With a strong sense of connection, the couple believes and fully expects that the power of their love will get them through the tough times. These positive aspirations make them feel very good as they begin their lives together. It's an exciting time. It's a time when passion, confidence, empathy and mutual support are palpable for these two committed people. However, if there are difficulties with the stepkids or their bio-mom, couples like this one—no matter how strong, committed or prepared—can begin to feel tension between them. It's uncomfortable. It can even be a bit scary. This is when action-oriented and energetic Stepmoms often seek out information for how to make things better and build further on the connection they share with their partner. With this book as a supportive resource, I want to help you and your partner.

You Don't Have to Accept a Lower Standard

The idea that we shouldn't expect too much in the future isn't an easy one to swallow, and for good reason. Many of us cling to our bright expectations because we fear that lowering them means we have to give up on what we've hoped for—specifically, our dreams of a happy stepfamily life. Who wants to imagine their future with flat or pessimistic expectations? Who wants to accept that emotional turmoil is going to become a way of life? Who wants to be told that the pain of being excluded, disregarded or disrespected is just something we have to live with? Not me, and hopefully not you! There is another way to approach the stepmother experience, and in this book we'll walk through it together, beginning with acknowledgment of your hopes and expectations.

So make your list: What are your expectations as a Stepmom? Do you know what your partner's expectations are? How do your expectations differ from your partner's expectations? It's helpful to take a moment to jot them down. Have you two actually shared expectations with each other out loud? Expectations, like beliefs, are very powerful influences on our choices and reactions to life situations. It is a valuable exercise to make them conscious, share them with your partner and make the adjustments that best suit your lives together.

How Expectations Impact Your Well-Being

At some point we create an expectation (positive or negative) about an upcoming situation. From that point forward we compare our present reality with the future we expect. Interestingly, expectations for our future have a lot more influence over the present than most people realize. When our view of the future is positive, we feel better in the present moment, even though our future hasn't happened yet.

The mere thought of a positive future event creates an immediate sense of happiness and well-being. Conversely, when we expect a sad, painful or scary event in the future, it makes us feel terrible immediately. That's how impactful our expectations of the future are in our daily emotional lives. Good and bad expectations for the future impact our feelings in the present. That's why expecting good things feels great, right now, and expecting difficult circumstances in the future doesn't feel very good, right now. Given the choice, we can understand the desire to have and hold on to good expectations. When current circumstances conflict with our imagined goals, we can feel sad, angry, disappointed and anxious. When people tell a stepmother to lower her expectations, it's treated as a magic formula for avoiding upsetting feelings. In my view, people say that because they don't know what else to say or how to help us, or that's what they've always been taught. But does that make it true? I believe there's another way.

Here's a thought: What if the answer *isn't* in lowering your expectations but *is* in creating wiser, broader, deeper, new expectations? Let's look at some common expectations and then review some new ones that have proven more realistic, achievable and supportive of a happy, balanced stepmotherhood.

Rookie Stepmom Expectations

1. My stepkids will get used to having two homes. They'll eventually get used to two different sets of rules and enjoy being with each parent and their partners.

2. My stepkids' bio-mom will get over her anger/bitterness/neediness if we just give her some time. Eventually she'll become at least civil and cooperative with us so one day we can be parenting allies.

3. My stepkids' bio-mom will follow the agreed-upon rules and guidelines just as we will.

4. My stepkids' bio-mom will respect any differences she and her ex-husband have. They will not bad-mouth each other or any stepparents involved because that's the right thing to do for the children's emotional health.

5. If applicable: One day my stepkids will realize that their bio-mom has waged a Loyalty War against me and they'll stand up to her, realizing that they have the right to love their stepmother without being punished by their bio-mom.

6. My stepkids will grow to love, respect and appreciate me for all I do (and have done) for them.

7. My partner will appreciate all I do for his kids and express his gratitude regularly.

8. We'll have lots of fun family parties, events, vacations and experiences together.

9. Once the shock of the divorce or remarriage wears off, everyone is going to want to make an effort to get along so we can all be involved in the stepkids' school activities, celebrations and other important life events. It will be worth all my efforts to achieve this goal.

10. My partner will no longer be influenced or manipulated by his ex-wife.

11. My partner will make decisions about his kids without being influenced by any fears or guilt from the divorce and I will find it easy to support his decisions.

12. My partner will seek and value my opinions whenever he's not able to see things objectively and he'll appreciate my wisdom and perspective. Together we'll do the best we can for his kids.

13. If we have to go to court, everything will work out fine because we're honoring the divorce and any co-parenting and custody agreements. We keep our promises and an accurate log of events. We pay for professional and expert opinions and always act in the children's best interest even if it's difficult for us. We expect the court system will be fair and side with the dad when the facts and evidence support that decision.

14. As I take on more responsibility for my stepkids' care, I will be included in more childrearing decisions and given appropriate authority where needed.

15. My partner is going to be compassionate, patient and supportive about how his ex-wife and children impact me. He'll take action on my behalf whenever I need him to and he'll stand up for me as his partner.

16. Teachers, coaches, friends, members of my partner's family and the community will eventually come to treat me as a respected and important member of the stepkids' parenting team.

Because you're here, chances are good that some of these expectations are on your list and that you're not seeing the results you had hoped for when you first created them. I know how disheartening these unfulfilled expectations can be for stepmothers. But what are the options? What are some realistic, healthy and wise expectations for stepmothers? What's the alternative to having low (or no) expectations?

Recommended Expectations

1. Expect to do your best (and be your best self) when you face each new situation. Recognize that your best will vary under different circumstances. Mute the voice of your inner perfectionist. Turn on the faucet of kindness and expect to shower yourself regularly with huge doses of patience and compassion. Expect challenges to your self-esteem and use that emotional stress to become stronger so you can count on yourself when necessary. Do your best in a thoughtful, respectful and fair way so you can feel good and be proud of yourself at the end of each day and in hindsight.

2. Expect that your partner will stand up for you to the best of his ability within the reality you've inherited. Imposing impossible-to-live-up-to superhero powers onto your partner really isn't fair. Remember he only has control over his own actions and not those of his kids or ex-wife.

3. Expect that due to the complexities of childrearing issues, you and your partner are likely to have differing views on how to handle and deal with his kids and previous partner. When this happens, do your best to defer to his decisions and ask for (and expect) your partner to appreciate you for this consciously loving choice of making your connection with him and your own well-being more important than getting your way or pressuring him to do things your way.

4. Expect that your partner may not be willing (or able) to abide by some of your wishes and suggestions if he has a strong need to minimize conflict and any retribution from his ex-wife or if his childrearing beliefs disagree with yours. As you and your partner begin your life together, find out what he is (and is not) willing to do to support your involvement in his kids' life, public and private. Talk specifics even if it's uncomfortable, and even when you're both under stress. See Chapter 18 for an approach to deal with any conflicting needs and strategies when handling stressful situations.

5. Expect that your partner's beliefs, experiences and feelings about the divorce will impact how he believes he should treat his children and their bio-mom. His fears and guilts may unintentionally and intermittently blind him to the impact of his choices on you. This is not personal. Be as supportive and compassionate as possible because this is very painful for many dads. Expect that you can find ways

to help yourself and your partner deal with these stressful feelings. See Chapter 25, Supporting Your Partner Through Divorce Guilt and Fears.

6. Expect to change and revise your childrearing beliefs so you can create a more powerful, applicable, customized version that better suits your present stepfamily situation and enables you and your partner to handle stepfamily situations as a conscious, loving team.

7. Expect that there will be times when you have to find new ways to stand up for yourself because sometimes your partner will not be able do so to your satisfaction.

8. Expect to defend your personal boundaries *and* expect that sometimes you may need to completely defer to your partner's needs, wishes and fears about his children, for the sake of your relationship and well-being. This is the dance of intimacy. See Chapter 19, His Kids: His Call.

9. Expect that your experience with your stepkids' bio-mom at the beginning of your relationship is how things are going to be between you. If your stepkids' bio-mom is angry or vengeful with your partner or upset he has another partner, expect that this will be reflected in her interactions with you. Listen to your partner. He can help you save time so you can approach her from a wise, self-protected and powerful position. If she comes around over time and decides to be cooperative, terrific. Treat this change of behavior as a bonus, rather than an expectation. See Chapter 32, Sounds About Right.

10. Expect to seek and find comfort in the compassion, validation, camaraderie and ideas from other stepmothers. There will be times when your partner can't relate to your feelings or support you in the ways you need—not because he doesn't love you—he does love you. It can be a Mars vs. Venus thing, an innocent misunderstanding or a case of two different perspectives unable to see common ground—yet. Getting the support you need from other stepmothers who understand what you're feeling will help you get back into your adult self, find your own balance and create a plan to feel better. Helping yourself in this way takes a lot of pressure off your partner, non-stepmother friends and family who want to help but just don't know how.

11. Expect that your partner will need your help because he may not always understand—nor be upset about—the same things that concern you. Take responsibility to teach him more about your feelings. When you don't understand why he does what he does, interrupt the urge to judge and instead have more empathy for him.

As Marianne Williamson teaches from *The Course in Miracles*, which I paraphrase, *"give to him that which you're looking for from him."* This approach is very impactful and can help a couple increase compassion for each other.

12. Being a stepmother may turn out to be the most difficult job you'll ever have. With this in mind, expect that you're going to have moments when you question your sanity about getting into, and staying in, this relationship.

    Know that having these thoughts is usually an attempt to numb present pain or anger. Questioning your own judgment about getting into a relationship when you're feeling out of control, outraged and/or in deep emotional pain is a reactionary pain-numbing tactic. It's a judgment so it numbs your feelings—temporarily. Numb feels better than pain, rage, hurt, etc. This is not bad or wrong, just important to recognize and honor. When you have this feeling it's an indication that some things need to change.

13. Expect that you may feel out of control, angry, resentful, hurt or left out at some point. Being a stepmother gives you an opportunity to deal with unprocessed feelings that you brought into your relationship. By expecting these feelings you can look for ways to support yourself faithfully every time something happens that triggers a strong reaction.

    There's so much to be learned from the stepfamily situations that upset you. Be proactive. Learn healthy ways to process your feelings and to heal from emotional wounds. Seek support resources and get excited about learning new ways to respond to recurring situations that upset you. Find ways to make yourself feel better and use your creativity and energy for self-care strategies and tactics.

14. Expect that there will be power struggles between:

    - You and your partner

    - Your partner and his kids

    - Your partner and his kids' bio-mom

    - You and your stepkids' bio-mom

    - You and your stepkids

By expecting them, you can watch for them and stay out of (or step away from) any power struggles, saving yourself immeasurable stress. If you realize you're caught in a tug-of-war power struggle, make your well-being and commitment to your partner more important than the allure of winning or the desire to avoid losing. Make the conscious choice to let go of your end of the figurative rope so you can refocus your attention, time and energy on your highest priority—feeling good and having a loving connection with your partner.

15. Expect that your relationship with your stepkids is impacted by their bio-mom's willingness or resistance to allowing them to have a relationship with you. Depending on their bio-mom's attitude and behaviors about your existence in their lives, your stepkids may balk at your requests or ignore your instruction, claiming you have exceeded your authority as the "woman of the house" or their father's partner. Be willing to do your part to have a relationship but if they're unwilling or disinterested in getting along, do your best to accept this reality. See Chapter 28, The Loyalty Wars, and other chapters in Section Five for more about dealing with your stepkids in effective, empowering ways.

16. Expect that your stepkids are going to be emotionally shaken up (to varying degrees) by the divorce and perhaps by your presence on the scene.

    The younger stepkids may soak up your lovingkindness. This gives you a wonderful opportunity to get to know them and help them through difficult changes they had nothing to do with or any choice about. However, they may also misdirect their anger at you when they're feeling upset or powerless about their circumstances. When this expected possibility happens, redirect your attention to supporting yourself, your own well-being and your relationship with your partner.

17. Expect there may be times when you become the rage target for angry, hurt stepkids. Stepmothers are sadly often the parental figure stepkids feel they can most easily afford (or desire) to lose. As hurtful as that can be, when you expect this reaction from them and realize it's just the best they can do as kids, you're less likely to be caught off guard or feel crushed when it happens. Understanding that your stepkids are under tremendous pressure, even if you can't see it or don't understand it, will help you have more compassion for them. Do your best to take their actions less personally. See the Second Agreement in *The Four Agreements* by don Miguel Ruiz for a description of how to take nothing personally.

18. Expect there will be grief, rage and other feelings to handle if you're unable to have the relationship you desire with your stepkids or their bio-mom. Get the help you need to release these powerful emotions and process the loss of the happy family memories you will not get to experience so they don't have to cause you illness or stress in your relationship. For more support on this, see Chapter 31, The Stop Trying So Hard and Start Lovingly Ignoring Your Stepkids Plan, and Chapter 33, When Your Stepkids' Bio-mom Doesn't Want to Get Along With You.

19. Expect to be flexible and creative with the details of your own personal happy family dream with your partner. "*This or better*" is a philosophy that can help you keep the faith when things are not working out as you originally envisioned. Cultivating and maintaining a positive attitude about your ability to find solutions to each situation makes it easier for you to keep your heart and mind open to new ideas.

20. Expect you and your partner can love and appreciate each other through any situations that occur by doing your best to stay in your adult self vs. your unconscious child-self. Agree to share whatever you're thinking and feeling in honest, compassionate ways. Expect that you will each have different emotional hurdles to get through and that it will be easier if you work as a team.

    Being in a stepfamily can create many emotional hooks of distraction that can test and strain a loving couple, especially when they're already under previously unexperienced forms of stress and trauma. As you and your partner continually affirm your overarching goal of maintaining a loving connection, you'll be inspired to make choices that may surprise you. You and your partner can avoid untold stress, pain, rage and anxiety with this strategy.

21. Expect that you and your partner will be challenged by experiences you're unprepared for. When this happens, stay positive, look for sources of new skills, new ideas and emotional support. Expect that you and your partner can figure out ways to handle everything that happens to you as long as you make your relationship and your well-being your highest priority. This is a repetitive theme because it's often forgotten when you're under stress *and* because it's also the key to the greatest success as a Stepmom/Divorced Dad couple.

22. Expect that you can (and will) handle whatever happens. Be confident. Expect that you'll become a stronger, wiser, more aware, more skilled and more compassionate

and more empowered woman as a result of dealing with (and learning from) all the difficult stepfamily situations you face with your partner. Keep a positive attitude that things are going to work out, even if you can't yet see how. Keep looking for new ideas and more answers. It's easy to get swept up and blown away by all the stress and intense emotions being a Stepmom can bring into your life. When you expect these situations and frame them as learning, healing and growth opportunities, you're going to have quite a life-changing adventure with your beloved.

Your Expectations

As you become wiser and more awake, you will be less impacted by "EX-ternal" forces. As you handle outside influences more quickly and confidently, it's easier to hold on to the love and joy you share with your partner. You're trying to do the right thing for everyone involved. These intentions are a powerful force.

In spite of what many experts tell us, you can have your expectations *and* be realistic too. How? You can do this by looking into the specifics of each expectation. You can be realistic and optimistic. You can place a higher value and more attention on what you can do to stay connected to your partner. You can consciously nurture your self-esteem and well-being while events involving your stepkids and their bio-mom occur. Ideally, you have expectations that make you feel prepared *and* positive about your future. I don't believe it's about raising or lowering your expectations. I think it needs to be less about the ideal family fantasy you may have initially imagined and much more about the feelings, experiences and journey you take with your beloved partner one day at a time.

What expectations are you and your partner holding for your family? For each other? Where have they been unmet or caused you stress? How do your expectations compare with potential expectations outlined in this chapter? Wise expectations can make you feel realistic and optimistic. Instead of trying not to be disappointed, you can feel prepared, open-minded and confident that you can handle any inevitable challenges (whatever they are) and still create a joyful life. This confidence helps you feel better about your future and therefore better each day.

A Stepmom and Her Self-Awareness

Daisy Mae's Story

July 2016

My story with Stepmoms on a Mission begins on a cold January night in 2013, about eight months into my relationship with an incredible man and his son. I have to say relationship with the man AND his son, because Stepmom life—for me—is about my life in this family. I entered into the relationship cautiously but once I entered, I dove in head first. I was excited to find a man who not only loved me, but was already a good dad. I had an instant family.

As time passed, the struggles of step-life presented themselves in full force. Dealing (or not dealing) with my stepson's bio-mom, raising a child who's not mine and who knows it, dealing with a man who is supposed to love me the most—but is always afraid to anger his ex or his kid—is a LOT. And add to that the adjustments from having a young kid appear in my life out of nowhere and learning to deal with kids and kid things. Very few of my friends had kids, and all who did were the bio-parent. The things that were driving me crazy, no one seemed to understand, not even my FDH (future dear husband). I felt nuts and alone. So, on this cold night in January, I Google searched "Stepmom support." There were many forums and articles that I signed up for. The only subscription I kept was to smoms.org.

Simply stated, working with the founder, Cathryn Bond Doyle, and applying her practices has changed my life. It has changed my life, my FDH's life, my stepson's life and even my parents' lives vicariously. I had no idea how "asleep" I was to this world. I was literally just floating through, and allowing other people to dictate my joy, my well-being and my priorities. I have since woken up. In doing so, my partner has risen with me. He is not as conscious of what's happening—yet—but he knows he feels better. He knows he's happier. My stepson has been spared many potentially hurtful moments because I learned to be awake to my surroundings and to choose to be an adult when dealing with stressful things, rather than reacting as I did in my youth. The most surprising benefit of all is that my parents listen to me now when I speak. I have been able to give them advice and compassion and understanding, not so much as their daughter, but as a wise, awake, adult woman. I see different suggestions I've made to them come into play.

I started my journey as a SMOM the day after I joined smoms.org, with a post on the boards. I posted about how every move I made, I felt judged by my partner and others as not being a good enough "mom." I felt very lost, alone, angry and confused. I was trying to please everyone and do everything right. I was trying to prove I was the best Stepmom I could be. If it wasn't good enough for anyone else, I felt it wasn't good enough for me.

One of the many things Cathryn has taught me is how to take back my power. She taught me how to be good enough for ME and to not let the judgments of others hurt me. She calls it being emotionally "stung" when others hurt us. She taught me how to use my energy like an imagined "beekeeper's suit" to protect myself from the invisible bee stings. Well, it works. Mine's purple by the way.

I took resentment courses with Cathryn. In those workshops I learned to explore my childhood beliefs and survival strategies, and to recognize I was still using them as a grown-up, but didn't need to. I was delighted to realize that I could create new adult strategies with all the skills and talents that I have today. I learned to analyze my choices and decipher whether I was making this choice as my awake adult self, or as my younger self. This helped me a lot dealing with a child—my stepson (SS). In the beginning (and sometimes now still) I would get sucked into the childhood mentality of things and forget that I am a powerful adult who can make other choices. I know that my shift in approach has taught him that there is more than one way to do things. I've shown him that people can choose other paths. We've grown closer because of my ever-expanding compassion and wisdom. It's like he knows that I see him—really see him.

The milestones I've reached in my journey with Cathryn and SMOMS over these past three years are truly noteworthy. I look back at my posts and it's like watching myself grow up before my eyes. My posts in the beginning were all from an angry, confused girl with too much weight on her shoulders looking for justice. I saw my rants about bio-mom, rants about FDH, rants about SS, society, kids, bio-mom again—all from a place of fear, hurt and mistrust. Slowly the titles change from "Bio-mom Rant" and "SS is driving me up the wall" and "This Hell I'm living" and "I can't take anymore" to "Had a good day." and "Wow. Awake today" to "MAJOR BREAKTHROUGH."

The point is that my current posts are less about what others are doing TO me and more about what I am manifesting for myself by standing up for myself in new ways.

My initial story at smoms.org speaks of pain and anguish. It speaks of confusion and tears. Once I realized something had to change and that it was going to be me, the story grows into one of increasing confidence and comfort. It grows into love. It grows into a story of discovery and joy. A story worth telling. A true love story. My story grows into learning about my authentic true self so well, that the people in my life have risen to the occasion, or eventually fade away. FDH has a saying: "Lead and the rest shall follow or fall behind." I never really understood that until SMOMS. It's not about leaving others behind, it's about not holding yourself back when others aren't ready. I'm my own woman now. I know that when I stand beside my FDH, we're complementing, not completing each other. We complete ourselves and complement each other's strengths.

Oh, don't get me wrong, others still do things that upset me, break the "rules" or are just thoughtless. The difference is that now I recognize what's happening very quickly. What used to upset me for days, I can now process in hours or sometimes minutes. Why? Because I have a bunch of skills and am able to see what's really going on. Nowadays, I realize I can make new choices. Choices that honor me and my needs in a thoughtful way, without prompting me to feel guilty. What a relief. I even surprise myself sometimes.

This is a story that would have been very different without Cathryn. I don't know if I ever would have gotten past the pain and anguish. I am certain my relationship would have been much harder. I would be a very heartbroken, wounded woman. But I am not.

While there's so much more I could say, I credit Cathryn Bond Doyle with these things:

- For seeing my potential and coaxing it out of me.
- For listening to the same story told 15 ways until I finally "got it."
- For offering advice, even when she knew it made me mad to hear it—because I asked her to tell me the best of what she had to share with me.
- For getting mad WITH me when people hurt me and didn't seem to care or take responsibility for their impact.
- For celebrating my successes with me.
- For teaching me that I am freaking awesome and deserve to feel joy, always.

This whole Stepmom thing is a real tried-and-true roller coaster. I don't think anyone is prepared for it or knows what they're getting into until they're on it and moving. What Cathryn does is give you the seatbelt and safety harness to be able to keep your eyes open and your heart strong. We all slip sometimes—maybe we punch the seatbelt clip and it comes loose, and we have to buckle it back up again—and that's OK. Life is a learning process. But with the tools Cathryn provides you can learn with all the battle armor required to face this world of being a Stepmom.

I am awake now. Being awake frees me from so many old patterns and choices that used to hurt me or make me angry. I've been helping other members of smoms.org lately and it feels great to be able to help others wake up like I did. If you want to be a Stepmom on a Mission, join us, and I'll see you there.

Daisy Mae
Stepmom since 2012
SMOM since 2013

Two

Honoring vs. Shaming Your Feelings

With all the negative societal stereotypes about stepmothers, it can be easy to unknowingly soak up some false beliefs and hurtful attitudes about ourselves. As any member of smoms.org will attest, this job is hard. But take heart! There are tools presented in this chapter (and throughout this book) that you can use to support yourself emotionally in many different ways.

Life is so much more pleasant when a Stepmom brings conscious compassion and lovingkindness to herself in each moment. It can be surprisingly hard to do this during stressful times. The good news about this self-care practice is that the more you do it for yourself, the easier and more positively impactful it becomes. The goal? To be consciously kind, patient, attentive, loving and supportive of yourself when reflecting on what you did, said, think or feel in any given situation.

When you're experiencing intermittent or unrelenting downpours of emotional stress, it's easy to lose track of how you're treating yourself and your own feelings. I hope this chapter gives you a new awareness and some kinder options when you're working with difficult emotions like resentment, rage, hatred, anger, sadness or grief.

Being aware of whatever you're feeling is a different experience from being immersed in your feelings. When you can name your feelings, you're still at least partially standing in your conscious, adult, wise-woman self. This is a good step. Being aware of whatever you're feeling, vs. being in a reactive, lash-out, unconscious mode, gives you a better chance to look at your feelings in one of two vastly different ways:

(1) You can have a loving, curious and compassionate approach or (2) a harsh, judging, controlling, hostile, martyred, blaming, shaming approach. Quite a choice with impactful results on you and your daily life.

After reading this chapter, I hope you'll make the conscious choice to lovingly explore whatever you're feeling in self-honoring and self-respecting ways.

Shaming vs. Honoring?

In a nutshell, shaming your feelings is the opposite of honoring your feelings. When you choose to honor each and every thing you're feeling with loving curiosity and the intention to learn from your feelings, then there's really no space for judging, numbing and shaming your feelings. You will feel the difference almost immediately and once you realize you have control over this choice, it's an easy one.

What can be confounding is realizing that whenever you're not honoring your feelings, you're usually somehow shaming, judging, ignoring or reacting to them. This can be very hurtful to your well-being. It's not bad or wrong—just hurtful—and if you're doing this, I'm going to assume you're only doing so because of your beliefs or out of habits learned in childhood. That harshly critical internal voice is extremely dishonoring to you as a human being. While this is a familiar approach which many believe is an effective way to control unwanted behaviors, I believe that nothing good can come of it. Many of us have done this to ourselves because this is what was done to us as children. We keep doing it because we're unaware of any other options.

Geneen Roth calls this tactic "the voice of shame" in her book, *Women, Food and God*. She explains this voice is trying to negate your value, make you shrink and completely obliterate all the goodness you feel about yourself. The voice of shame is usually a composite of all the criticisms you had to endure as a child from parents, caregivers, teachers, religious leaders and others who had genuine power over you at the time. Until you realize it, this voice becomes the anti-compassionate force within you, commenting negatively on your every thought, feeling and activity.

Next time you find yourself being harsh with whatever you're feeling, you can now make another more loving choice. Yes, it can be that fast and that straightforward. The birth of these hurtful comments can often be tracked back to something that was said to you, witnessed by you or imposed on you as a little one in truly disempowered situations.

Negative Self-Talk

"Shame on you for expressing your anger."

"How dare you think of yourself over another! You're so selfish."

"Shame on you for talking back to the teacher." (Even though you were falsely accused.)

"How disappointing that you question my orders. I'm going to have to punish you." (And they did.)

"That's an unkind thought or feeling. God isn't going to like that at all."

"Shame on you for making me angry. You do as I tell you."

"What you want or feel is unimportant compared to what I tell you to do." (Spoken or non-verbal, both are equally torturous.)

"What a cry-baby. We're tougher than that in this family. Get over yourself."

As you wake up to the negative impact on your well-being whenever you shame yourself for anything you think or feel, you now have the ability to silence that harsh inner voice. You can choose to stop listening to it, hitting the metaphoric mute button. You can counter the reflexive inner shaming voice with a tender, soothing voice of patience and compassion. Think of the tone of voice you would use with a precious toddler or your most beloved friend—use that tone for self-talk. Can you imagine how your life experiences would change if you talked to yourself like this? Give it a try—experience it for yourself.

This awareness of and the ability to end any inner shaming, judging, numbing voices can be the beginning of a whole new daily life experience for you. The chant, "Ding dong the witch is dead" comes to mind. With conscious awareness, you can separate your present, wise, adult self from the past and your childhood influences by making the conscious choice to treat yourself in new ways—kind supportive ways that you choose. This is a tremendous shift and one of the greatest benefits of becoming more conscious. You have complete control over how you talk to yourself. Do you have any beliefs that tell you otherwise?

As you begin to be more aware of your true feelings and needs, that shaming voice may initially get louder. It's just trying to keep you small because the strong implication in the original shaming messages is that they are there for your own good or are trying to keep you safe. It's important to realize that while this may have been true for you as a child, it's no longer true for you as an adult.

As the adult, wise woman you are today, you can now begin, from moment to moment, to consciously separate yourself emotionally from the little girl you used to be. You can decide to acknowledge that you're quite capable—now—to handle yourself in your present life situation. You can reinforce to yourself that you no longer need to be kept in line or controlled with shame, judgement or numbing your feelings in order to survive. You can now choose to honor whatever you're feeling and work with this new information and the power that flows with it. There's a lot of power to be reclaimed. The child you used to be and all your younger selves are looking to you to choose a stance of self-kindness.

A Kinder Approach

Below is the process I use. Tailor it to your personality and try it the next time you notice you're not being very kind to yourself.

If you find yourself shaming your own feelings, the first thing to do is to recognize it. *"Oh my goodness, I'm being pretty darn mean to myself. I'm going to stop that right now and start being kind to myself."*

With this awareness you're interrupting a life-long habit. Congratulate yourself. Pat yourself on the back—it really helps. See Chapter 37, Tip #23. Look at yourself in a mirror, smile at yourself and give yourself a virtual high five. This is also a good time to ask yourself some probing questions.

1. *"Why would I put myself down in this painful way?"*

    Often, without realizing it, your shaming voice may be trying to keep you from owning more power and a truer sense of self. As children, many of us were told to be quiet after we said something bright or wise because the adults weren't interested or felt they should be smarter than a child. They may have told you, *"Shut up"* or *"Be quiet, who do you think you are?"* or *"You're too big for your britches. Off to your room."*

2. *"If I didn't shame myself, and instead honored and paid attention to these feelings, is there any part of me that fears becoming too powerful (in a not-so-good way) in this situation or relationship?"*

Do you see any patterns of putting yourself down when you're on the verge of becoming your more empowered self? Do you hold any beliefs or fears that your partner or others may not love you—as much or at all—if you're being as powerful as you could be? This is a common experience for many little girls. Those little girls grow up to be women and without realizing it, retain those false beliefs and fears. What limiting beliefs, or "shoulds," might you hold about shaming vs. honoring feelings? What limiting beliefs are you willing to change?

3. *"What if I begin to honor whatever I'm feeling, even when I don't have an explanation for it?"*

As you identify any limiting or false beliefs from your past, they lose their power over you. The very process of becoming conscious and aware is transformative. As you look for false beliefs, you can become conscious of them and therefore able to change or replace them with something that feels better. You can consciously change any limiting beliefs and say something like this to any harsh inner voices:

"You're done here. I choose to ignore you. You're retired now. Thanks for trying to help but I'll take it from here. I'm choosing to respond to whatever I'm feeling or thinking with compassion."

This is a wonderful moment of self-empowerment. Each time you bring your attention back to yourself and choose to treat yourself with gentle lovingkindness, you heal a little bit, or a lot, and things shift inside you in good ways. I wish it for all stepmothers everywhere. Heck, I wish it for everyone everywhere.

Honoring Feelings Is Worthwhile

Honoring your feelings, whatever they are, and giving them your loving attention will give you tremendous amounts of information about what you truly want and need. As you give yourself permission to have wants, needs and rights in your life, something we all deserve, you can also use some of the energy from your newly honored anger and rage to help you establish and uphold new boundaries internally and in your life situations.

You can choose to refuse to shame yourself going forward. You can promise yourself that you'll do your best to treat your feelings and yourself differently—with honor instead of shame. It's not about being perfect, just about being aware and intending to do things differently going forward.

You can give any painful memories that may come forward your intensely loving attention. You can tell all those younger You's that *everything* you have ever felt is worthy of respect and honoring. You can make time to experience those feelings and comfort yourself, the way you would another human being who may tell you about the very same thing. As you make these commitments to yourself, you're probably going to feel lots of emotions. This is the chance to honor all of them as the newly aware, increasingly loving, talented adult woman you are today. Emotions are timeless. You can acknowledge your feelings the way you always wished someone else would. It changes your everyday life experience of your world. In one sentence, it's about being your very own best friend, from moment to moment.

Honoring vs. shaming your feelings is the beginning of a whole new inner life. Learning from whatever you're feeling makes you more powerful as a responsible, emotionally self-supporting, compassionate, resourceful adult. As you read these words, can you imagine how that would feel? What would your life be like if you used your feelings, your energy and your attention to become your most wise and empowered self? Can you feel confident being in your full power in your life and relationships? If not, what would need to change so you can give yourself permission to feel empowered?

I believe that our feelings are always trying to give us some valuable feedback about our needs, rights and boundaries, and so honoring them is a shortcut to increased well-being and happiness. Now that you know all this, shaming your feelings is like injuring yourself or sending yourself to an emotional prison camp. On behalf of all your younger and future selves—please choose to honor your feelings.

For more about how your beliefs are formed in childhood, see Chapter 8.

For a follow-up discussion on this chapter, go to smoms.org/BonusChapters and click on the chapter title, "Honoring vs. Shaming Your Feelings." See the complete list of additional chapters and follow-up discussions in Chapter 39.

A Stepmom and Her Self-Awareness

Sharon's Story

July 2016

Dear Cathryn, I want to take a moment to let you know that working with you over the past year has made such a difference in my life. When I called you last year, I was desperate to reduce the stress in my life as a stepmother. I felt overwhelmed, alone, unprepared, and unappreciated by my new family. Little did I know that I was partially to blame for putting myself in a situation where I was doing things for others that they probably should have been doing for themselves. My tendency to "over-give"—as you call it—is one of the many things I've learned about myself while working with you, as well as the far-reaching impact of being raised by a narcissist. It's been interesting—and quite unexpected—to see how the emotional wounds of my childhood are being revealed and healed as I become a more conscious stepmother and wife. You've helped me dig deep and find the courage to face a lot of feelings; doing so has led to several deep realizations. My eyes have been opened and it feels great.

My husband and stepkids impact me differently now that I am—as you would say—"awake." Thankfully, I'm much less reactive. I now feel empowered to make different creative choices and it's helped me feel good about myself in a whole new way. I feel so much more excited about our future as a family. I now know that I was put into this family—at this time—in order to bring healing to myself, my husband and my stepchildren. Like you, I'm now also a Stepmom on a Mission.

You've helped me learn how to see the meaning in the behaviors of others, even when I perceive it as hurtful. I now understand that much of what they've been doing is an unconscious reflex to survive and numb their own pain and fear. I can now see my own survival strategy and it explains so much of my past choices. This understanding has given me a newfound compassion for myself, my husband and my stepkids. It's now much easier for me to keep my heart open to them, even when we're upset with each other.

I want to tell you how much I appreciate your ability to truly stay with me when I get overcome with emotions or push back with my survival defense strategies during our private sessions. It's helpful for me in a few ways. You're so patient and kind and I don't feel judged so I feel safe to express my thoughts and feelings, many of which have surprised me. You've shown me I no longer need to judge myself but that it's much more productive to be gentle and curious with myself. And on those days when I'm just too tired or emotional to take notes or integrate all the insights you're explaining in a session, I feel relaxed knowing I can listen to the recorded sessions whenever I'm ready. It's been really interesting listening to myself with fresh ears—another surprising source of insights.

While I enjoy reading the forums online on smoms.org, our private sessions have made the biggest impact on my shift from victim to victor. I'm now more confident than ever that I can move through the challenges I'll face with my stepfamily. I also feel a new sense of calm competence about using my new skills with people outside of my family. I'm thrilled to say that today I feel like an empowered woman who's getting wiser every day. Yes, I know there will still be issues but now I feel prepared. What a difference from this time last year!

Cathryn, most importantly, you've taught me how to value myself even when no one else does. I've learned how to set up boundaries to ensure that any attempts by others to put their issues onto me are quickly rebuffed. I call it my force field and it works like a charm. I can't say enough about the positive impact our working together has had on my life. Thank you from the bottom of my healing heart.

Sharon
Stepmom since 2013
SMOM since 2015

Three

Healthy Boundaries vs. Hurtful Blockages

Whenever you're in a situation that upsets you, it's helpful to look at your personal boundaries to see if any present boundaries have been violated or need revising. Maybe you need a new boundary. When a boundary is clear and strongly upheld with a grounded action plan for any violations, you can be confident, knowing that this particular piece of your emotional territory is safely protected. It's a calm feeling knowing that you're ready to respond to just about anything.

However, whenever you think you've set a boundary but realize you still feel angry or like you just can't let go of the situations from the past, you may actually have a blockage, not a boundary. Blockages keep everything out and prevent love from flowing as well. That's hurtful. Not wrong or bad, just hurtful and definitely not achieving the desired goal of supporting your well-being.

What's the difference between a healthy boundary and a hurtful blockage? A healthy boundary is like a screen door. A screen door keeps out dreaded bugs and other yucky things. The screen lets in the light and air and also allows you to see clearly what else is on the other side of the screen. With a good screen door you can relax knowing you don't have to spend time or energy worrying about unwanted things getting into your space.

A hurtful blockage is like a solid steel vault door. It keeps out the unwanted things for sure. It also keeps everything else out. With a good steel vault door you don't have to worry about dreaded things getting past it. The bad news is that it also stops the light, the air and anything else good from getting to you. This can be upsetting to a kind person on the outside of the door trying to get your attention. It's also hurtful to you because inside the steel vault door you can't see what's on the other side or what goodness you may be missing out on.

You can apply this analogy to many things you experience on your stepmother journey. So much of the stress is about boundaries being violated, beliefs being trampled, needs going unmet and feelings being ignored, disregarded or judged as wrong. With strong, clear boundaries, you can open your heart again, knowing that whenever the boundary is violated you know how you'll respond. Happily, an effective boundary gives you the freedom and confidence to relax. It creates the circumstances that allow for more joy, love, respect and other unexpected good things to flow both ways through the screen of your healthy boundary and a blueprint for handling future boundary violations.

If your boundaries have been repeatedly ignored, dented and violated to the point where you lash out or push back in not-like-you ways, you may think you're setting boundaries but you're more than likely using blockages to try to stop the stressful situation from happening again. Sometimes there's so much rage or hurt that you feel the need (consciously or not) to slam a steel door in the face of the one who's violated your boundaries. We all can relate to that feeling. It's a lot like a *"Take that!" "Get out of my face!" or "Screw you!"* kind of shut-down feeling and action.

It's so necessary to express this anger because chances are good you've been enduring emotional pain "for the good of the cause" for far too long, or you may be expressing anger without being conscious of the cause, so it's just bluster or vitriol and nothing gets processed or protected. Expressing anger provides you with energy to make changes and to set up either a new boundary or blockage. This feels good immediately because you're giving yourself permission to protect yourself. Nothing like a good steel vault door to stop the incoming pain, right? Well, at least this can be true at first. Sometimes it's necessary but it's not meant for long-term use unless we're talking about protecting you from abuse or harm.

Sooner or later you're going to realize that steel doors block out the very things you need to have flow through to you: lovingkindness and compassion. When the emotional steel door keeps out the love, support and comfort from the ones you love so much, it can hurt you all.

When you realize you're still feeling pain even behind your steel door/blockage, what choices do you have?

1. At first, you may try to talk yourself out of needing whatever can't get through the steel door/blockage to reach you. Since there's no emotional pain in the mental plane, thinking about stuff like this actually does feel less painful. The only catch is that you have to continually think and think about it to stay numb. This is one of the allures/benefits of obsessive thinking.

2. Maybe you pump up your rage and pain to justify the steel vault door's presence. You could rationalize your right to put up and keep up that steel door, right? When this happens, you can get swept up in any number of defensive or controlling patterns, creating a delusion that you're free or at least making progress. Instead, you're really just distracting yourself with activity and perpetuating more rage. This isn't stupid or wrong, just not very helpful and can cause even more personal and relationship pain.

3. Perhaps, and more than likely, you don't even know that there's a screen door/ boundary option that will prevent, reduce or stop the negative impact of painful situations. You may understandably think the steel door is your only option. If this is the case, you end up feeling like you only have one choice because the pain, fear, rage, etc. are now unacceptable or unbearable.

When you feel exhausted by pain or rage, it can be wise to put up the steel door/blockage just to get the pain to stop, even for a little while. When you're in a lot pain, feeling nothing is very appealing. It's very understandable. It makes sense to shift into survival mode. While you may feel relieved to *not* be in as much pain, you can end up mistakenly believing that you're powerless over the actions of others and that can lead you to feelings of blame, self-pity or martyrdom. It's also disempowering when you feel you have no choices and are stuck with only one option.

When I was exhausted or in deep pain, I made choices to put up blockages because what I did know (and tried) wasn't working and I didn't know what else to do. Sometimes I felt at the end of my emotional rope. It can be scary to think you may have to choose to erect a steel door between yourself and your beloved partner just to stop the pain, rage, fears, shame, disrespect or anything else that is just too much for you. This is a horrible choice to ponder. Recognizing that you *do* have other choices and that you can protect yourself with a screen door boundary option, even if you have no idea what it is yet, is an empowering shift.

How do you know if your new choice is a boundary or a blockage? Being conscious enough to ask yourself this question is a terrific start. Reflect on this question, *"Now that I've made this decision to set this new boundary, how do I feel—right now?"*

1. Do you feel satisfied and relaxed about establishing this new boundary?

2. Can you give everyone a clean slate and move on as your naturally good-natured self?

3. Now that you've got a good, clear boundary that your loved ones understand and will respect, can you authentically love those who will be affected by your new decisions?

4. Do you have a clear plan for responding and reasserting your new boundary in case it gets violated? How did you feel about the reactions of others when you explained your new boundary and consequences.

5. Knowing you have a new boundary in place for future events, do you feel ready to compassionately turn your attention to yourself and to what you need to do to heal from the negative impact of whatever happened in the past?

If you can reply *"yes"* to most of these questions, chances are very good you have yourself a screen door boundary and can now turn your attention to healing wounds and getting future needs met. Yahoo! However, what if you feel good about the new boundary you've just imagined but feel some fear about announcing it to your partner or stepkids? This fear makes a lot of sense, especially if you've been over-giving or hesitant to ask for what you need. It's important to look at any fear you have about your rights to stand up for yourself in your relationships. I call it fear of "rocking the relationship boat." If you feel this fear, see the chapters about defensiveness for more support.

If you replied *"no"* to most of the questions above, you may have a steel vault door/blockage masquerading as a boundary, so ask yourself:

"As I imagine the future, am I still feeling angry about this situation and its past impact on me?"

"Have I found a solution that allows me to feel better so I can move on as my happy self? Or am I looking to make sure that the people on the other side of the door feel shut out every day until I decide they have paid for their violations?"

If you realize you've created a passive-aggressive-style blockage and are intending to punish others instead of establishing a new boundary, take a moment to be very understanding and patient with yourself. Hey, you were under a lot of pressure! You tried everything else you could think of. You did what you had to do at the time. Now you realize you have another choice and a renewed sense of hope.

For more about this topic, see my public articles on smoms.org, "Are Your Choices Based on Courage or Fear?" and "Hostility is Not Fine!"

Creativity is an excellent skill for determining new boundaries. Creativity can flow more freely when you feel safe from scary interactions or confrontations. You can place effective barricades between you and the things you want to keep out of your life, including relationship-related and life-threatening issues. When you need to revise old boundaries and establish new ones, it's time to put on your creative thinking caps. It's amazing (and really exciting) what options come to mind with the single intention to find hurtful blockages and replace them with healthy boundaries.

For a follow-up discussion on this chapter, go to smoms.org/BonusChapters. Click on the title "Boundaries vs. Blockages." See the complete list of Bonus Chapters in Chapter 39.

Four

The Pros and Cons of Catastrophizing
Imagining Worst-Case Scenarios to Help Yourself

Stepmothers face many unknowns and a whole lot of uncontrollable issues that are unique to stepmotherhood. Unknowns and uncontrollable issues can impact people negatively, causing us to feel fear, anger and all kinds of stress. As human beings, we can choose to handle the unknown, the unclear and any loss of control in a variety of ways. A common reaction is to experience anxiety. Another is to try to control (or counter-control) people and situations. Some people put on blinders and avoid facing these issues as much as possible. Sometimes total surrender is all we have to offer, which can be peaceful or terrifying. Sometimes we consciously (and unconsciously) employ various combinations of strategies as we try to bring a sense of order and safety into our lives.

When a woman becomes a stepmother, she inherits more than just the children of her beloved partner. In addition to her stepkids, many stepmothers are impacted by their partners' ex-partners and former in-laws who may try to overly impose their authority or demonstrate a sense of entitled involvement in every choice or activity. Trying to get non-stepfamily folks to understand our situations and resulting feelings can be frustrating to say the least. The impact of these inherited people and situations that seem out of our control can range from mildly annoying to enraging. Our thoughts, feelings and reactions can be triggered without warning, which can also cause stress with our partners.

One tactic for dealing with the anxiety and stress of unknowns and uncontrollables is catastrophizing. Catastrophizing is the art of taking in what has actually happened and then imagining worst-case scenarios of what could happen in great detail. It's thinking (sometimes obsessing) about all the bad things that could happen next as we imagine outcomes and corresponding strategies.

We're not always aware we do this. If a stepmother has been through a series of emotional, logistical, legal or financial nightmares with another person (oh, let's just say someone's ex-wife or stepchildren) it's natural for her to imagine future events will unfold like the past ones and lead to negative outcomes. For this and many other reasons, she may believe she's making a smart choice to catastrophize whenever something out of the blue happens and triggers her anxiety. Let's look at the pros and cons of this choice and then review some other options.

The Pros of Catastrophizing

1. It provides a relief of sorts. It's something to do with the energy that anxiety and worry generate in your mind and body.

2. It's practical. The more bad things you can imagine happening, the better prepared you can be for whatever does happen. Preparation can give you the illusion of control and safety.

3. It creates a cheap and fast thrill. Ever notice how when someone you don't like does something wrong, dumb, stupid or mean, there's a part of you that secretly enjoys it? When they do this particular thing, you may feel "better than" them even if just for a few moments. If a person has caused you pain in the past, imagining ways this person might cause more problems in the future can give you a strange, brief respite from the fear and pain of the past. Talking about and thinking, *"There she goes again, now this ridiculous thing and that inconvenient or unfair thing will happen too"* just feels inexplicably good or maybe even makes you feel superior. Through catastrophizing, you manifest in your imagination more evidence of that person's overt wrongness and that feels better than anxiety, even if only for a little while.

4. Listing and explaining all the possible bad things that might happen—as a result of something that did or is about to happen—can sometimes justify getting the attention (and time) from someone who you may feel has ignored or neglected you in some way. Perhaps your partner, a parent or a friend? Bringing them an

upsetting and urgent issue, along with all the horrible possible things that could result, can give you a valid reason (excuse?) to work together to avoid or solve any problems before they get too bad. That's what you tell yourself anyway, in the hope that this special someone will give you their full attention and, if you're lucky, will validate your feelings and support your ideas. Working together on the same side of an issue feels good, and therefore appears reasonable and beneficial.

5. You may get lots of attention from others when you quickly mention what has just happened but then spend the majority of the time explaining all the horrible, frustrating, unfair, annoying, expensive, time-consuming and inconvenient consequences that could happen. As a result of your detailed story, sometimes you get lots of much needed TLC, compassion and indirect anger expressed on your behalf. This particular benefit of catastrophizing can be truly nourishing when you're at the end of your rope physically, emotionally and/or financially. This kind of acknowledgment can even help you pull yourself back from the ledge when you feel you can't take any more stress.

With all these perceived benefits, it's easy to appreciate the seductive qualities of catastrophizing. It makes sense that someone would catastrophize to feel better and more prepared to respond to the imagined or real hostile actions of others. However, there's another side to this tactic. Let's take a look at the negative consequences of catastrophizing.

The Cons of Catastrophizing

1. It takes a lot of energy to think about all the bad things that could possibly happen. In fact, catastrophizing can waste a tremendous amount of energy and ruin lots of otherwise happy and peaceful hours, days or longer.

2. It can spoil your good mood. It gives others the ability to steal your well-being from afar. I call it emotional terrorism. Catastrophizing is a way of upsetting yourself as you imagine how the next letter, email, text, voicemail or phone call could ruin your day with all its possible negative impact. You know how to imagine this because you've already lived through many upsetting situations caused by others. Thinking about these things doesn't usually make anyone feel happy or relaxed.

3. It's painful—physically and emotionally. When you catastrophize you usually take things to the worst-case scenario in your mind. Your subconscious mind doesn't

know the difference between a memory and an imagined experience, so when you think about bad things happening you're actually mentally and emotionally torturing yourself. Thinking thoughts of bad things possibly happening not only generates frightened or angry feelings, but also triggers physical reactions like adrenal stimulation, increased stomach acid, sore throats, chest pains, headaches/migraines, back and muscle pain, insomnia and stress of all kinds. You may experience all this real stress even though nothing has actually happened yet. This is a heavy price to pay to feel that you're prepared. There have got to be more empowering ways for you to prepare for unexpected and uncontrollable situations without harming yourself in the process. Are you willing to believe this could be true?

4. It alters your view of the world in a negative way. When you catastrophize and imagine something bad happening (or a whole bunch of somethings), a part of you begins to watch for signs that you're right. As I like to say, this is not a wrong thing—it's a human thing. You may lose perspective, get caught up in the negative possibilities or lose your ability to see the big picture when you catastrophize. You can miss good things that actually do happen while you're looking for evidence of bad things that might happen. A funny example of this is the famous BB-gun narrative in the movie "A Christmas Story." The mother continuously voices the catastrophe she imagines by repeating, *"You're gonna shoot your eye out."* This fear causes her real worry. It also blinds her (pun intended) to anything good about the gift of the BB gun to her dear son. The father tries to express the positives, while she can only see the negative. Like this mother, you're not likely to notice the good stuff and pleasure you miss when catastrophizing, but it's a price you pay with this strategy.

5. It can waste a lot of time. Most of the things you worry about never happen, and when you spend time catastrophizing, you lose those hours forever.

6. It causes stress in your loving relationships—often with the people you love the most. This is natural, but what a costly price to pay. When you're catastrophizing, you often put yourself in a heightened state of nervousness, fear or agitation and let's face it, none of these states of mind is all that adorable or fun to be around. When you've been repeatedly hurt or upset by someone in the past, there's often self-pity and hostility present that can leak out onto the ones you love the most. Focusing attention on possible bad things that might happen in the future can cause even more stress, arguments and pain for you and your loved ones right now. At the

very time you need (and want) your loved ones to be on your side so you can draw strength from each other, they may pull away from you. They may also be exhausted from trying (and failing) to assuage your anxiety. Eeyore, Winnie the Pooh's friend, comes to mind.

Under pressure, it's easy to forget your powerful, wise strengths and sophisticated resources. When you're feeling and thinking about all the bad things that could happen, you may lose your confidence and your loving good nature. You also can lose access to positive creative solutions and your intuition because your focus is solely on the negative. There's got to be a more empowering way to deal with your anxiety. Without question, your fears are founded on real possibilities. How can you help yourself be prepared in healthy, productive ways without giving away your power to all those scary (potential) future happenings and the people creating them?

If Not Catastrophizing, Then What?

1. Do your best to focus on what's happening—right now. Do everything you can to stay with what has actually happened, right in the present moment. It's a chance to practice the power of now in a real way. Eckhart Tolle's book, *The Power of Now*, is a great read filled with wisdom and effective suggestions.

2. Consider distracting yourself by using that stirred-up energy in productive ways. Try something physical like cleaning out a closet or the garage, starting that craft project or doing whatever you need to do to stay focused on your life—today.

3. Call a friend who will listen and help you by giving you lots of support. Ask her to help you create an action plan for what's actually happened instead of all you fear for the future.

4. Create a first aid anxiety/self-care kit for yourself. Customize your own kit with things that help you remember who you are and give you instant support and distractions. Consider making a list of positive affirmations, inspiring quotes and music that you can enjoy at a moment's notice to help you regain your balance and sense of adult self. Make a list of things you can do when you have 15-30 minutes. Create a personal self-care list of things that soothe you, support you and remind you that you're not alone.

5. Practice feeling consciously calm and capable. Use affirmations, meditations, music, breathing techniques and anything else that helps interrupt the old panic patterns. Take a moment to imagine how you would feel if you believed you could handle whatever happens whenever it actually happens. If you believe in yourself and your abilities, you'll feel better right away.

6. Practice the SMOMS C.O.D. (collect on delivery) technique. This is about you choosing to refuse to accept anything that you don't want to accept, think about or bring into your home—as if it were a package from UPS or FedEx. If something comes to your emotional door and it's from someone or about something that's not your responsibility, remember you have choices. Refuse to take it into your mind. Return it to the sender, energetically and metaphorically. Resist your curiosity and the allure of the melodramatic. Send it back or perhaps forward to the person who is responsible for handling it. This takes some self-discipline at first and yet it's so liberating and can work wonders for your daily well-being.

7. Bring self-compassion to each situation. Yep, turn your newly found energy and attention to supporting your needs. Put some time and energy into giving yourself whatever you need in this moment. What could that be? Detach from the situation? Process any fear that comes up? Write an anger letter? Leave the room? Go for a walk? Take a bath? Watch funny YouTube videos? Listen to a playlist compiled to comfort you? Finish reading (or writing) that article or book? Do research for your next vacation with your partner? Do something fun with a child or pet? Help a friend? Do whatever you need to do. Taking care of yourself in any conscious way is a great action step that's never risky, rarely causes more stress with your partner and is a valuable use of your precious time and energy. No regrets are likely with this approach.

8. Choose to have faith and trust in your partner. Maybe just trust in your relationship if you can't trust him right now. This is easy to say and sometimes hard to do if in the past, he hasn't reacted to situations as you would have liked. In her book, *The Surrendered Wife,* Laura Doyle (no relation) talks about how hard it can be to trust. She also shares specifically how positive it can be for a relationship. As you step back and let your partner handle a situation his way—as the bio-dad and ex-husband—he's likely to feel more "manly," less pressured and less defensive with you. At first this may involve some acting on your part as you lovingly disengage from the drama of the situation. I urge you to stick with it so you can reap the

rewards. Chapter 19, His Kids: His Call, will elaborate on this approach for stepmothers.

9. Have a back-up plan, then put it in the drawer (so to speak) knowing that you are prepared. Ask and answer for yourself, *"if the thing I fear actually happens, how can I help myself?"*

For most of us, learning new and healthy ways to deal with unexpected and usually uncontrollable issues and events is a good use of our time. It helps us preserve our sense of well-being and it develops our confidence in ourselves and our relationship with our partner. Catastrophizing isn't bad or wrong—it just has some big downsides and can create more pain and suffering than other options. Becoming conscious of this tempting and common reaction, and how you may engage in it when you're under stress, is often all that's needed to motivate you to make another choice.

Making new choices to support yourself in healthy, effective and kind ways can feel like a breath of fresh air with a dose of renewed hope and energy tossed in for good measure. If catastrophizing is your reactive strategy of choice, that's a good thing to realize. If this feels right for you, make a promise to yourself that the next time something upsetting happens that triggers the urge to catastrophize, you'll try one of the ideas in this chapter. Consider it an experiment or a field test. You're always invited to let me know how it goes and share your experience with me too!

A Stepmom and Her Self-Awareness

Chloe's Story

July 2016

My name is Chloe. I became a SMOM and joined the website group in 2007. I was desperate for knowledge about what seemed to be happening to my little family, and every other website I visited was full of condemnation for someone in the stories. I wanted ideas for solutions and support. Smoms.org was the ONLY place I found that. My situation is different from that of most SMOMS but there were always one or two who would speak up and give me ideas and support. Cathryn's ability to understand and help was truly the lifesaver I so desperately needed.

In addition to being a member of the site bulletin boards, I participated in Cathryn's Resentment Workshop in the fall of 2014. When I decided to participate, my husband (DH) and I were almost two and a half years into a court fight with his ex—in two states simultaneously—about visitation issues with my teenaged, long-distance stepson (SS). This was the second time in our 10-year marriage we had gone through a long and complicated court fight in two states at the same time. We had literally spent five of our 10 married years in unnecessary legal battles trying to maintain our relationship with my SS. We started none of it. The ex lost every legal battle in every state but it cost us about $30K, almost cost us our marriage, and definitely cost me more of myself than I'd like to admit.

In 2014, I was in as bad a place personally as I'd ever been during the last 10 years. I had just about resigned myself to the fact that my marriage wasn't going to make it. We'd fought long and hard but it just wasn't going to be enough. The level of vindictiveness from my DH's ex was taking its toll. I was so angry and depressed all the time that I was beginning to think about how to give up on both my marriage and myself. I changed from an energetic, enthusiastic, happy person and began giving up on everything. That scared me. My DH had begun to give up on everything too.

Then one day, out of the blue, Cathryn sent me a private email. She said she'd been thinking about me and wanted to invite me to participate in her upcoming workshop. Wow! That was a surprise. I struggled with thinking it was a waste of time and that I was beyond help from such an unlikely place. I certainly wasn't ready to accept that a change in my perspective about my own resentments would help anything in my real life struggles, much less in my marriage or the current court case. I think I thought about it for a week or two. I even told my husband about it over coffee one day. I knew he was slipping away from me.

I also knew from Cathryn that there would be homework and things I might need/want to discuss with him if I took her workshop. I wanted his support and his participation but I didn't think I'd get it in the way I wanted it. But I blurted out about the workshop anyway like a verbal "Hail Mary" and said I thought I needed to do something for myself before I was lost. I got his attention but a half-hearted level of support. It seemed to me at that moment that DH was happy I was admitting I was the one with the problem and that he was off the hook.

Very gradually, over the course of the workshop, my DH became more interested and supportive of the things I discussed with him. He even read some of the workshop materials. Even more gradually, my own thoughts became less angry, less hopeless. Even when I didn't know what to think anymore, I was less negative. DH responded to that in his own way with more positivity toward me and our struggles. We even changed our strategy with the court cases. Some might say we gave up. In a way, we did. I prefer to say that we took a good hard look at reality and what we wanted in the future and made decisions based on those positive thoughts for ourselves and our own future together.

It wasn't easy. In fact, the workshop is very hard work. You have to be brave and I felt anything but brave. However, the only place I felt safe and not judged at that time was in this workshop, and after I shared my struggles for the first time, I actually felt completely safe. It was the compassionate responses from Cathryn and the others that brought me back each week.

I feel lucky that the more I looked at myself, the more tools I learned from Cathryn and the other women in the workshop. DH and I gradually had more and more to discuss and

A Stepmom and Her Self-Awareness

we both slowly learned to do things differently. We're still learning how to use the skills I discovered. Without Cathryn's one-on-one support and the resentment workshop, I feel certain I'd be divorced from my DH today. I'm not saying Cathryn and this workshop fixed everything that was wrong in my marriage or my life. Life is a challenge. I will say that my life is so much better because I took the chance and the time to open up and listen to Cathryn and the other SMOMS in the workshop.

To make a long story short, life is better now. I didn't think it was really possible for a long while. I'd lost hope. But now DH and I feel things changing every day. We catch ourselves smiling, even laughing. We had lost that. We're just beginning to do tiny little projects around the house and talk about dreams of the future again. We had stopped doing that—completely stopped. I don't think we believed in a future together for a while and then when we started to believe again, we were afraid to give it a voice for fear it would disappear again.

So to my dear sister Stepmom who might be at the end of what she believes she can tolerate: I want you to know—you can handle more. You're stronger than you think you are. You have an entire community of sister Stepmoms at smoms.org who understand what you're going through and who will be there for you like no one else will be there for you. They'll even be there for you if you decide to stop being a Stepmom. "Once a SMOM, always a sister" is their belief.

You have access to the founder, Cathryn, who's not only going to be your biggest cheerleader, but who can help you learn about yourself and your situation in a way that's safe, empowering and helpful—and at your own speed. I've learned there's always a choice you can make about how to handle a situation. Let Cathryn and these sister SMOMS help you identify those choices so you can be your best self, for yourself and for your families. I can't say enough about how Cathryn and my sister SMOMS helped me.

Chloe
Stepmom since 2004
SMOM since 2007

Five

Thinking of Leaving Your Partner?

While the passion you likely felt when falling in love with your partner was amazingly strong, at times you may find this relationship to be excruciating and infuriating. You're not alone—most of us have felt this way for a few moments, or perhaps many. You may find that occasionally mulling over the possibility of leaving your partner is the only way to imagine alleviating the pain or rage you might be feeling in that moment. This can be stressful on so many levels *and* it's important to acknowledge and honor any feelings that result from this daunting idea.

Giving yourself permission to explore your feelings about possibly leaving your relationship can lead you to surprising and unpredictable insights that can actually bring you a sense of relief, like emotional breathing space. You're not acting on your feelings, just allowing them to show themselves and be explored. Sometimes you may imagine futures and how you'd feel if they happened, just to help you endure a present situation—not because you intend to act on your thoughts but because some of your pain can be relieved through the act of imagining a different future. I encourage you to be courageous enough to explore what you're thinking and feeling so you can discover more about what you need.

A while back, one SMOM found herself in this situation, and had come very close to the difficult decision to leave her partner and move on with her life in a new way. She announced on one of our site's bulletin boards that she was seriously considering leaving her partner after years of trying her very best, and upon realizing he seemed unwilling to open his mind to explore new options. She wanted some support and here's what I wrote to her:

Dear SMOM,

First I want to offer you my compassion and full support for whatever you decide to do. So often, the stressful circumstances between a Stepmom and her partner result in feeling like every single unhealed emotional wound you have is being trampled on. You may feel like you're both stepping on each other's most tender, painful and vulnerable places (because you are), often causing you both so much pain, rage and fear that you can't see things (or each other) very clearly. It can seem—and you can end up believing—that it's your partner's fault you're feeling such deeply upsetting feelings. If you say words and do things that hurt each other's feelings, it's usually because you're both so busy defending yourself that you can't understand or see each other's perspective, have compassion for each other's wounds or find any other way to look at a situation that's OK for you. However, from what you've written, I see this as a potentially eye-opening opportunity for a transformational experience for you and your partner if you try some new approaches.

While I only know what you've written and not all the details of your personal story (how can we know the complexities of another person's life?) I've worked through these scary feelings with many other Stepmoms and their partners over the last several years. It may be helpful to realize how much our perspectives can change once we've been through it and are now on the other side of waking up to so many previously unconscious thoughts, feelings, beliefs and defensive patterns. Perhaps knowing that there are new ways to seeing things that you've not yet tried may encourage you—maybe even your partner.

I believe that there's a potential pathway back to the intense depth of love you two once shared—and I believe this is true for all Stepmom/Divorced Dad couples who started their relationships with an intense knowing they were to be together, as you described in your situation. From what you've written, and in spite of all you've tried, he's still unwilling to participate with you in this relationship work—that does make it much harder and scarier. The love you once shared may (or may not) still be there, but it can be extremely difficult to feel that love when it's buried under the heavy rubble of unprocessed anger and hurt that couples spew (both intentionally and unintentionally) on each other and as well as emotional debris built up from being under extended periods of extreme stepfamily pressures. Ironically and sadly some of the rubble and wounds seem to have been created when you were both trying hard to solve problems and connect with each other.

This is common. It can be complicated *and* it can also be untangled if you're both willing to stop what you're doing and realize that it's actually because your hearts were once so wide open to each other that you've been able to impact each other so deeply and now painfully.

Perhaps unbeknownst to you and your partner, you both brought emotional wounds and rigid beliefs into the relationship (everybody does) and now it's about deciding if you're both willing to do the personal growth work to heal those wounds and regain and ideally increase the depth of love between you two. The key word is both. From what you wrote it sounds like your partner is still stuck in blame, blinded by his defense strategies and refusing to open his mind to your feelings, insights and options. When our partners are unwilling to wake up, own their impact and learn new skills, they often shut down or lash out, causing even more distractions and damage to our relationships. It's not about judging him as a bad person, just acknowledging that it's hurtful, un-loving and not helpful for the healing of your relationship.

Your planned time apart could be a good thing for you. You've tried so hard for so long and given him so many invitations to work with you. I'm so sorry for the pain you're feeling. I can tell you're hurting so much. On the far extreme of feelings, I also completely understand the wave of euphoria and sense of freedom you mentioned at the thought of being free of the stress. This happens when you imagine an end to all the pain and rage that seem to be caused by your partner, the stepkids or their bio-mom. It's very understandable to want the pain to stop. It also makes sense that you want to do everything you can to give that love you once felt a chance to break through any impasses and disagreements. You're being very courageous.

If you can work through your own tangle of misunderstandings, resentments and hurt feelings, it may give you a chance to see each other in a new light. Maybe it will also dissolve some layers of defensive armor you've needed in the past, making it possible to reconnect and find a new place of trust and empathy, and finally revealing how your differing wounds, conflicting beliefs and even varied cultural upbringings were the source of so many of your very real and intense relationship difficulties.

How have other Stepmoms made it past all this pain, blame, rage, fear, shame and guilt? Many are able to do this because for some reason, the couple decides to stop defending themselves and blaming and judging each other. Some agree to start taking more responsibility for their impact on each other and agree to seek help for healing their individual emotional wounds. Out of this work can come strong waves of empathy for each other as couples begin working together to look at issues, past and present, in a new way and on the same side.

I had help on this from a gifted therapist, the late Moriah Marston, who was also a stepmother with challenges. It can be difficult (yet worth the effort) to find a therapist who truly understands the unique dynamics among a Stepmom and her partner, stepkids and their bio-mom. If you decide to work with a therapist, refuse to settle and keep looking until you find someone who feels confident he/she can help you with the uniquely complex issues that face stepfamilies. What works for traditional family dynamics is rarely effective with Stepmoms under duress. More and more resources are available every year—thank goodness. The reality is that relationship progress is much easier, quicker and often more lasting and substantial when both people are willing to do the work. If we Stepmoms could handle all the relationship issues ourselves, there would be a lot of amazingly happy Stepmom/bio-dad partnerships out there. Why? Because we've already invested a tremendous amount of love, energy, time, money and pure life force to try to make things work with our partners and their kids. It takes two to have a successful intimate relationship, which makes both parties vulnerable to being hurt. It takes two of you working together, instead of in opposite corners of the emotional boxing ring, to make things truly wonderful between you so you can build more trust in the love you share going forward. If your partner is not willing to work on his issues with you, it can be a difficult and disheartening reality to accept.

Sometimes our partners can be so defensive, numb, hurt or exhausted from their past relationships and the stress from the current situation that it's difficult for them to see the long-term benefits of this personal growth work. It can feel overwhelming to recognize, feel, process and learn from all the emotional wounds and the impact they've had on you both. As you know, it takes great strength and commitment to take responsibility for your feelings and your impact. When your partner refuses to do any work, it's an incredibly painful reality deserving of whatever time it takes you to process the sadness, anger and grief.

If you choose to move on and not try anymore, I certainly respect your choice. Sometimes relationships need to end so we can heal and move on to new happier, healthier ones. No judgments here. As many feelings and issues that we Stepmoms share, there are so many unique variables involved for you and your situation. While it's impossible to force anyone to do their own personal growth work, there's a lot you can do while in a situation like this one. When your head, heart and gut are all in alignment over a particular course of action, it's green lights all the way. The key is to find ways to become more conscious so you can see situations, your feelings and his feelings more clearly. That's always where the mystery, the challenge and the answers reside.

Whatever you decide to do, please invest the time and energy in healing the very real wounds that have surfaced in this current relationship. Make this pain and rage, and all your hard work in this relationship, mean something positive and help you become more authentic and empowered by taking the time to heal your emotional wounds, revising the limiting beliefs you've uncovered and reclaiming all the power you have lost because of them. None of the wounds that have surfaced are your fault. None of them. As hard as it may be to believe, your partner's wounds are not his fault either. I believe we're attracted to the one whose love will bring our wounds to the surface and who has the power to heal us and teach us about who we really are. This is a difficult road to travel. Whether or not you stay with your partner, this is a powerful path of personal transformation. Either way, this is a life-enhancing opportunity to become wiser and stronger—more of your true self.

Many couples have unintentionally trampled through each other's emotional wounds, triggering defenses, and doing so without the awareness, willingness, ability or intention to see and take responsibility for their own individual issues and impact on each other. This is not an accusation but more of an observation and explanation. It can get so painful that it feels like torture to be in each other's presence. However, it's not that you two caused the wounds, but that your wounds somehow overlap or more likely dovetail with each other. Sometimes we're each so hurt we can't see the other clearly, other than to think, *"How can my partner say he loves me and continue to do something that causes me so much pain?"* This is also how many partners feel, wondering how the women they love can do things that cause them to suffer.

Here's a suggestion—to the best of your ability, the next time you two feel like you're in this painful place of stepping on each other's wounds, interrupt yourself. Stop in your tracks (freeze frame) so you can see it, own it, apologize for it (or ask for an apology) and get curious about whatever issue either of you has just become conscious of. It's about deciding together that you're willing to make your painful issues "we" problems that both parties work on without blame and with equal commitment to a mutually agreeable solution. Unfortunately, all this emotional work is invisible and therefore so much harder to see, diagnose and care for than physical injuries. If you stepped on each other's toes or knocked one another down, hopefully you'd immediately and sincerely say, *"I'm so sorry, you OK? How can I help you feel better?"* without any sense of defensiveness or anger. You'd both know it was an accident. You'd be quick to apologize, truly sorry you hurt the other and eager to make amends. You'd also be likely to accept a sincere apology and move on, believing it was unintentional and knowing a bit more about each other. When you can look at hurting each other's feelings as emotional invisible toe stomping, everything can change in the dynamic between you and your partner. There's so much more space to love each other and usually a greater willingness to receive love as well. This is where you two can reconnect as a team.

Some couples are lucky enough to avoid this excruciating experience. Some agree to deny the existence of any problems. From what I've seen since 2000, a Stepmom simply can't do all this relationship work by herself. Many couples make it through the intense tangles of emotional wounds because the Stepmom is willing to do the work. She's willing to feel any feelings that have been covered up by a lifetime of over-giving, numbing judgments, blame, self-pity or limiting beliefs and imprisoning defensives strategies, and her partner eventually sees the value and benefit of this relationship work. Even though it takes two people willing to believe the benefits of this work are worth the effort and courage required, when a Stepmom turns her attention away from her partner and starts working on herself, she changes. As if by magic, her partner may decide to make changes as well. When we let go of trying to change others, people feel that freedom and it creates a new space for positive change.

Whatever you decide to do, new levels of awareness, wisdom, power and healing can come from this experience. You're already on the path to heal those painful places in your psyche and heart so you never have to experience them again. It's true that with or without your partner, you have the ability to make this experience mean something priceless for your future. You have the power to make this relationship—and all these years of trying so hard—the catalyst for your healing and awakening. Nothing you have invested in this relationship is wasted. I truly believe loving someone is never a waste of time or energy.

By learning from each issue and healing the wounds and defensive patterns that have surfaced and caused you so much pain or rage, you will not want—nor be compelled—to repeat this experience in your relationships. This particular truth was all I had to hear to choose to dig in and do more deep personal work. It's also important to do whatever you can to take care of yourself and get the rest you need so you can begin to feel good about yourself and your life. Remember that joyful love-filled energetic woman you were before you began to feel crushed, drained, resentful and maybe even bitter? Everyone needs and deserves to claim the freedom to make her own choices and timetable. I certainly want you to respect yours—whatever that means for you.

I send you my very best wishes during this very difficult time. May you look back on this phase of your life and realize that it was the gateway to tremendous growth and healing—preparing you, through the fire of so much pain, for decades of future joy and love.

[End of my reply]

Having thoughts about leaving your partner is an emotional red flag that calls for change. It means that something in the relationship needs to end, not necessarily the relationship itself. Paying attention to what's going on in your world and your feelings when these "I need to leave" thoughts occur to you will reveal the circumstances that need to change.

Explore Your Responses to These Questions

- If there's a sense of aloneness or feeling left out, what would need to change for you to feel better?

- Where do you feel you are on your partner's priority list? What does he say when you ask him about his priorities? What would need to change for your wishes and his actions to line up?

- Do you need any unfairness or inequity of rights in your home to change and get re-balanced? How would things be different and what would need to change to create a sense of equality for you in your relationship?

- What feelings do you envision will go away if the relationship ends? Make a detailed list.

- What negative impact from the stepkids or their bio-mom would need to be changed or eliminated entirely for you to feel good about staying and working on your life with your partner?

- What actions and feelings do you need more of from your partner?

- What words do you need to hear from your partner to feel more known and loved?

The more specific you can be about what needs to be different, the more likely you are to find a way to make it happen for you. If your partner is willing to do any of this work, miracles can happen. I believe our partners want us to be happy and are so relieved when we can help them find us (and the love we felt at the beginning of our relationship) once again. It's about knowing you've tried your best and explored all your options. Perhaps you're now aware of some new avenues you can pursue, perhaps not. Sometimes, even with all the forces of your lovingkindness, you may prove to yourself that leaving the relationship actually is the wise, well-thought-out best decision for you. It's never about right or wrong. It's about what's best for you. When you follow your feelings and trust in your heart and gut as you make choices going forward, it will be what's right for you and everyone else impacted, even if they don't thank you at the time. I wholeheartedly believe this to be true and wish you the courage and support you need to handle whatever choices are best for you.

Please see Chapter 18 and the other chapters in Section Three for specific strategies and tactics you can use to improve your relationship with your partner.

Also see the chapters in Section Four, A Stepmom's Partner. So many of our partners are also overwhelmed by stepfamily situations and because they are often hesitant to seek support or understanding, they simply hunker down more deeply into their child-created survival strategies, unaware they have options other than enduring or expressing their rage at their imagined powerlessness. The partners of stepmothers suffer with much of the same anger, pains, fears, guilt and isolation that stepmothers do—they long for joyful loving connections with their partners, just like we do. These chapters may help you see your partner and your situation in a new light.

If you are looking for some ideas about how to help yourself with sadness, see smoms.org/BonusChapters and click on the chapter titled "Honoring and Supporting Your Feelings of Sadness." For a complete list of bonus chapters and follow-up discussions, see Chapter 39.

Six

Ten Suggestions for Creating an Enjoyable Mother's Day

As Mother's Day makes an appearance on our calendars every year, I thought I'd share a few things that can enable you to create a more enjoyable occasion for yourself. These ideas are in no particular order of importance. Sift and sort through this list for ideas that make sense for you, your life situation and personal preferences.

Suggestion #1: Get clear about any expectations and assumptions you may have about this holiday, recognizing that Mother's Day can be emotionally charged for some stepmothers. This is true whether you're a stepmother and a bio-mom or a mother-by-marriage (no bio-kids). This annual Sunday focused on bio-moms can be an emotional magnet—it can bring all your unhealed emotional wounds, outstanding resentments and any unmet needs related to being a stepmother to the surface of your awareness.

Knowing this, you can help yourself and avoid painful moments by being conscious of what you're expecting to happen on each approaching Mother's Day. There are no right or wrong expectations, just met or unmet ones. Being honest is very important as you search your head, gut and heart for answers to these questions:

"What am I expecting to have happen on Mother's Day?"

"What do I believe should happen for me on Mother's Day?"

"What would I like to have happen on this Mother's Day?"

Suggestion #2: Look at your beliefs about what makes a happy Mother's Day for you. Resentments, emotional wounds and rage triggers are caused when your reality conflicts with your needs and your beliefs. Until you start to uncover and identify your beliefs, you're unaware of the vast majority of them. Yes, it's true. Time spent exploring your beliefs is a true act of self-respect and usually a fascinating experience. There's tremendous wisdom and power in discovering your personal set of beliefs. Most of your beliefs were formed when you were very young. They were promptly filed away into your subconscious minds. You forget that you created them as little ones and that you can change them at any time.

Answer and Share With Your Partner

- How do you believe you should be treated by your stepkids right before, on or right after Mother's Day?

- Specifically, what do you believe they should do, say, not do or not say?

- What do you believe your partner should do, say, not do or not say to you on Mother's Day?

- What do you believe your role is in creating a good Mother's Day for yourself?

- What role, if any, do you believe you should play in helping your stepkids honor their bio-mom for Mother's Day?

Suggestion #3: Do you have any past Mother's Day-related emotional bruises that still bother you? This is a gentle reminder to bring the power of your own lovingkindness to yourself in this process. Review your needs and hopes with the same compassionate attention you would naturally offer your best friend when helping her prepare for a big event in her life.

Consider These Questions

- What's going on in your life right now?

- What happened last year on Mother's Day?

- What's your history with your own mother on Mother's Day?

- What are your tender emotional buttons on this topic?

- How can you provide extra TLC for yourself during this holiday?

- Is there an imbalance between the way Mother's Day and Father's Day are celebrated in your home? What changes could be made, going forward, so both of you feel both holidays are honored in a satisfying way?

Talk with your partner, a trusted friend or another stepmother about what you're feeling and about what you've discovered about your feelings. This can help you feel understood, supported and prepared for any possible planned activities over this weekend. The key here is to be conscious of what you need and expect so you can eliminate any unconscious, self-sabotaging experiences.

Suggestion #4: Assume your partner's mind-reading license has expired. Have a Mother's/Father's Day conversation with your partner in March or April to avoid feeling hurt, unappreciated or disregarded on Mother's Day. With some conscious planning, you can avoid any trauma and emotional ricocheting that can generate more resentments. You can also avoid creating an emotional wedge between you and your partner caused by misunderstandings or mistaken assumptions.

Disappointing Mother's Day Feelings

"Why didn't my partner know what I wanted, needed, expected, deserved and would love on Mother's Day?"

"Why didn't my partner make an effort to teach my stepkids (maybe even your shared children) how to express appreciation and acknowledge me on Mother's Day?"

"Why didn't the stepkids express gratitude for all I do for them?"

"Why didn't my partner prompt the stepkids to take actions I would have liked?"

You can avoid experiencing these by talking with your partner at least a couple of weeks before the holiday. A disappointing, hurtful, upsetting Mother's Day can result in a diminished, vengeful or otherwise uncomfortable Father's Day experience. Both partners lose in this scenario. My vision for Stepmom/partner couples is for both partners to stay lovingly connected by successfully enjoying both holidays, even if it means creating non-traditional plans. As long as you two are good with it, that's all that really matters. Right? Right!

Use your talents and skills when taking responsibility for your own well-being on Mother's Day. Make being happy more important than being surprised. Talk with your partner and see if you can agree on how to handle both Mother's and Father's Day holidays. Often the stepmother is the do-er, the lover of holidays and the energetic creator of fun experiences for her partner and any children in her life. The women who find smoms.org often do more for their partners on Father's Day than their partners do for them on Mother's Day. Depending on the couple and the state of the relationship, this can be a breeding ground for martyrdom and resentments. Resentments can blow up into intimacy-impacting disconnections between a Stepmom and her partner. This disconnection feels terrible. If unresolved between you, it can also have a significant negative impact on the expectations and plans for a happy summer.

You can avoid all this distress by having an honest conversation with your partner. Find a balanced way to handle both occasions as a "we" experience with a shared challenge—as one team with the same goal. This may mean the Stepmom needs to agree to do less and her partner needs to agree to do more while there's still time to plan for both holidays. If you enjoy surprising others and being surprised this is a place for potential self-sabotage. Creating a specific plan with your partner can take the potential disappointment, possible pain and emotional shrapnel out of both holiday experiences.

Suggestion #5: Take a look at any emotional ledger you may be keeping with your partner or stepkids. It's human to keep track of how others treat you. If your partner, your stepkids and their bio-mom have let you down, hurt your feelings, disregarded you and angered you, a Stepmom's emotional ledger can involve a long list of very real and hurtful situations.

Because of the commercial and social hype around Mother's Day it can be tempting to hope that a fabulous Mother's Day might balance or erase some of that ledger. Become aware if you're holding any outstanding emotional accounts receivable that you may hope or assume will get paid up on Mother's Day. Acknowledging and interrupting this unspoken expectation can spare you, your partner and your stepkids painful emotional eruptions that can occur when a stepmother feels disregarded or disrespected on Mother's Day. Whatever you can do to avoid this upsetting experience is very self-loving and good for your connection with your partner. Balance and settle your past issues in other ways—and on other less charged days. See the smoms.org article called "Are You Keeping an Emotional Ledger?" for ways to process your list.

Suggestion #6: Take responsibility for having a happy Mother's Day by getting creative. I understand that this might be a sensitive and potentially anger-triggering suggestion for you. Why? Many of us have the belief that a happy Mother's Day is an occasion where our partners are supposed to dazzle us with their understanding of what we need, want and like. We want to be delighted that they make the effort and that they do, say, buy and arrange things that make us feel treasured, at best—or appreciated, at least—by our partner and stepkids. This is another potential set-up for feeling awful and creating pain for you and your relationship with your partner.

What if you made a new choice this year? Consider reframing Mother's Day as a day for you to acknowledge your own worth as a mothering figure in the lives of any children you care for. What if you decided that your well-being and peace of mind are so important that you're not going to leave your enjoyment of the day to chance or at the mercy of any unconscious issues that might cause you stress? What if you plan your own Mother's Day?

This is not about becoming controlling. The urge to control is a common fear-based reaction to past bad experiences, unbalanced emotional ledgers and painful resentments. This could just be an experiment. You may have the belief that if you participate in the planning, you're ruining the special surprise or squashing any heartfelt intent from your partner or the kids involved. This is a limiting, false belief—a set-up that puts your happiness at risk. Who wants that belief in your personal book of beliefs?

Keep your mind and heart open to new ideas. Choose to make having a great Mother's Day more important than any old beliefs. Make a new belief—*"I do whatever is needed to make sure I have a fabulous Mother's Day because I deserve to have a fabulous day."* If you feel your heart harden in this planning process, take note and look at what you're thinking, believing and imagining about the future. What are you expecting? How are you feeling about taking care of your own happiness on this holiday?

If you're feeling anxious about it, remember this: Anxiety is often the anticipation of anger or the fear of a future boundary violation. If you feel anxious, use that energy in a positive way to create a fun day for yourself where you can relax, knowing you're going to be A-OK.

Mother's Day is intended to be a happy, nourishing, honoring day for all the women who mother others. Giving yourself permission to use some of your energy to find fun, peaceful, creative options that are doable in your life situation is a great way to take care of yourself. The good news? The odds of this approach creating happy memories and a more loving connection with your partner are excellent.

Suggestion #7: Start a new tradition for yourself with your partner, your stepkids and any bio-kids you have. Talk with your partner and invent your own day for being honored in your family. Create something that doesn't compete with Mother's or Father's Day. Kids love fun rituals and traditions. What fun ideas can you start for your family? This is a place for your uniqueness to be honored. How about creating a [insert your name here]'s Day. What do you love to do? Pick a day each year when everyone does it, eats it, listens to it, plays it, makes it, watches it and experiences it. The sky's the limit and the memories of those shared experiences can fuel you through a lot of other situations. How does it feel to challenge yourself to create something joyful on your special day?

Suggestion #8: Mute your harsh and critical inner voice—we all have one, and Mother's Day is no place for it. Here's a short, straightforward way to protect yourself from any crushing, hypercritical self-talk and to distinguish the unforgiving introjected voice from your loving inner guidance. Ready? If whatever you're thinking makes you feel less good about yourself *in any way*, hit the mute button, change the channel, shout, "*be gone*!" and move to another more loving inner conversation. Yes, it's that cut and dried. Refuse to ruin any more of your precious daily moments by listening to or engaging in not-so-loving self-talk.

Suggestion #9: Mothers-by-marriage, be especially kind to yourself. For those of us who, for a variety of reasons, do not have our own bio-kids, Mother's Day can range from being a non-event to a painful excavation of any as-yet unhealed wounds caused by not being a bio-mom. It's important you take responsibility for creating a nourishing day for yourself. Your partner may not understand what you need or are expecting from year to year. You may experience Mother's Day in a wide variety of ways—some of them upsetting and others challenging to process, and all of them valid.

- It can feel like the world is jumping up and down on your broken heart.

- It can be a time to focus on your own mother if she is still around.

- It can be a time to daydream with your partner about the future children you already love and look forward to bearing and raising.

- It can be a time to mourn the loss of the future dreams you didn't get to experience because you're not going to be a bio-mom.

- It can be a time to share a loving connection with your stepkids as you help them prepare to honor their mother, choosing to feel the joy from any love or appreciation they share with you as their Stepmom.

- If your stepkids are caught in the Loyalty Wars, it can be a painful and maybe no-longer-unavoidable time to acknowledge that you're paying a heavy price as a target of their wrath and confusion. It may be time to consciously and compassionately accept that your stepkids are caught in a terrible bind, unable or unwilling to acknowledge your role and effort in their lives due to the punishment they experience (and rightly fear) from their own bio-mom. As an adult, you can find ways to support yourself. In spite of how they're acting, your stepkids are doing the best they can, compelled and limited by their young brains to survive this painful circumstance while trying to gain/keep/earn their bio-mom's love and attention. See Chapter 28 for more about the Loyalty Wars.

- It can be a time to do something wild, fun and crazy with other non-bio-mom friends.

- It can be a time to do something special with your partner or your own kids, since this holiday will likely be stepkids-free.

- It can be a time to give yourself whatever you want. Loving, compassionate solitude to breathe, to rest, to hike, to shop, to travel, to craft, to read and to acknowledge your own worth in special ways is always a good option.

Suggestions #10: Holidays hold different meanings and varying degrees of importance for each of us. So it's about becoming clear about what you feel and what you want. There's no good reason to judge whatever you feel. Talk with your partner about whatever you think and feel about Mother's Day. Remember that as much as he loves you, he can't read your mind. Even though Hallmark, TV and the movies try to get you to feel holidays should be observed in certain ways, be courageous and tell him what this one means to you. Exercise your personal power—ask him to help you create *exactly* what you want for a happy Mother's Day.

There are so many unique circumstances in your life. I want to encourage you to use Mother's Day as a time to bring your attention back to yourself. Think about what you can do to honor yourself. You deserve a pleasant and happy Mother's Day, whether your stepkids do anything to honor it or not. You deserve to appreciate yourself and I believe your partner wants to as well. If the stepkids you care for also appreciate you, that's a terrific bonus. May your future Mother's Days be happy ones.

Seven

Potential Stepmom Missteps
Understandable, Unintentional, Common and Correctable

This chapter covers some Stepmom blunders, blindspots, false assumptions and limiting beliefs that lead to hurtful behaviors and upsetting situations that can be avoided with awareness. They're included here with the intention of sparing you as much stress, pain, wasted energy and unwinnable arguments with your partner as possible—as soon as possible. FYI: There's a "Lessons Learned" forum on the public section of the smoms.org website where dozens of Stepmoms share things they'd do differently if they could start over in their stepmother role. Reviewing these materials offers you additional chances to benefit from the experiences of veteran Stepmoms.

Being a Stepmom exposes you to situations you've probably not faced before, with people who may not want to get along with you no matter what you do or try. These situations and people can cause stress between you and your partner and evoke strong, high-intensity feelings no one ever taught you how to process. Being a stepmother involves mostly on-the-job training, presents a huge learning curve and often requires relationship, communication and emotion-processing skills you've yet to learn. Making mistakes is nothing to be ashamed of and, in my view, is an expected part of learning and mastering any new skill. I like what Harriet, Shirley MacLaine's character, says about mistakes in the movie, *The Last Word* (2017). *"You don't make mistakes. Mistakes make you. Mistakes make you smarter. They make you stronger and they make you more self-reliant."* Isn't that a super way to look at anything you consider to be a mistake?

I've also found it helpful, maybe even motivating, to reframe your stepfamily experiences as a curriculum of advanced-placement relationship courses where you're going to learn and master lots of new skills. This attitude can activate all kinds of inner strengths and make whatever you're facing easier to handle. You may even find the investigation, deciphering and acquisition of newfound insights and skills to be quite rewarding.

Hopefully you'll be kind to yourself whenever you trip up (or are tripped). Ideally, you'll choose to be determined to learn something useful from any missteps—this can make your journey feel more like an adventure. This attitude, perhaps occasionally accompanied by the uplifting *Rocky* theme song, can make you feel stronger, more skilled and better prepared for future challenging situations. Take advantage of any value you can glean from stepmothers who've gone before you. When I decided to go out on my own in 1984, leaving my secure banking job, my wonderful Gramps gave me a piece of advice that I'd like to share with you. *"Only listen to, and take advice from, people who've already successfully done what you're trying to do. Everyone else is just giving you opinions."*

If you realize you've been doing something featured in this chapter and you're open to doing things differently, take a deep breath and try this sequence, not original to me, for processing your feelings: Recognize, Acknowledge, Forgive (or Apologize) and Change. It's very effective and gives you an elegant way to dodge your own defensiveness so you can move on and learn all kinds of new things about yourself, others and life.

Emotion-Processing Technique

1. Recognize—in as much detail as possible—what you've been doing, feeling, thinking, saying.

2. Acknowledge—to yourself (and your partner as needed) the precise impact of the behavior in question. Admit the negative impact on yourself, your relationship and anyone else affected. This step is much easier with a humble attitude and honesty. I was taught that being honest is expressing the truth (the facts) in a way that takes the feelings of others (and yourself) into consideration. It's in line with the intention to be kind and authentic—I've always liked it for that reason. Tell yourself the truth in an honest, compassionate way.

3. Forgive—yourself and others. It may also be appropriate to apologize to someone or ask for an apology. This is the step that's often wrongly replaced with harsh judgments, impossible promises or self-hatred. Make no space for that in this process! When you don't feel sincerely ready (or able) to forgive yourself or another,

try breaking down the act of forgiveness into two parts: why it was done and what was done. Understanding the *why* of any behavior is incredibly helpful and oddly satisfying. For some reason, it can be easier to forgive why something was done and it's often all that's needed to feel better. As you and your partner learn more about why you each feel, think, say and do (or don't do) things, defenses usually drop and allow compassion to flow more freely, creating more space for love and authentic forgiveness to follow. Forgiving someone (and yourself) for why the behavior happened is usually good enough to allow you to move forward in the process. If wholehearted forgiveness occurs for both why and what was done, it's a true bonus for everyone involved.

4. Change—make a decision to be different going forward. Use any energy of anger, sorrow, regret or anxiety to compel and inspire you to be different. Rather than looking back, look forward and make a promise to yourself, your partner and even your younger selves that you'll change in a specific way. Some people don't really change, they just *hope* they won't do something again—which isn't much of a powerful covenant. When you learn there are ways you can be more loving and honest, make the commitment to do so and keep your word. It's not about being perfect but about sincerely doing your best.

When this process is accompanied by self-compassion, you can use it to move elegantly through the learning process. With all the emotions that can be triggered and evoked by stepfamily circumstances, following this sequence can save you a lot of time and misery. It offers you a structured way, like a ritual, to uncover and feel new things and move past your previous triggers or limitations with confidence and clarity—without shame, stress or tension—freeing you to move on to new situations, wiser from the experience.

Watch for Clues: If anything in this chapter makes you cringe, sigh, be defensive or feel embarrassed, it's a clue there's something valuable for you to discover. Addressing anything you may be doing, or did—in a new way—can save you a lot of future stress. Hopefully and perhaps surprisingly, you'll also feel some joy in each self-revelation. It takes humility to recognize and acknowledge the impact of your behavior. It takes courage to open to new ideas and implement changes. Trying something new can also result in more mistakes. The good news is that the sooner you realize that things can improve by changing your actions, the sooner you can reap the benefits and feel stronger, smarter and better about your life.

Understandable, Unintentional, Common and Correctable

Potential Misstep #1: A Stepmom mistakenly assumes her partner wants the same happy family dream she wants. She may make this assumption without talking to her partner about his own dream, or about what he wants from his life with her. It may never occur to her they don't share the same vision.

As a new member of a recently fractured family, it's natural for a Stepmom to want everyone to get along and move forward in ideally kind (or at least have civil) interactions. However, remember that your partner has chosen to end his relationship with his ex-wife for many reasons. The idea of interacting with her, sharing future events with her and acting like everything is fine between them may not be your partner's goal. Talk about it with an open mind. Find a dream you can agree to consciously create together. Getting clear on what you and your partner want to create going forward can make your life together much happier and more peaceful because you will be working toward the same goal.

Potential Misstep #2: A Stepmom mistakenly assumes her partner wants a particular custody or co-parenting agreement. She may think he wants to live near to (or far away from) his kids because *she* believes that's the right thing for him to do. She may not have asked what her partner would prefer or may even intentionally try to influence his decision.

She may have her own ideas about custody. She may want her partner to pursue/maintain a particular custody agreement or do other divorce-related things exactly the way she envisions. The stress occurs when a Stepmom assumes her partner agrees with her, instead of asking what he truly wants and supporting his wishes as the bio-dad. Enthusiasm can blind energetic stepmothers. With a sincere apology and the open-ended question of *"What do you want to create with your kids and ex-wife?"* you and your partner can identify/resolve conflicts and better understand and support each other.

Potential Misstep #3: A Stepmom mistakenly believes her partner has the ability to control his kids and his ex-wife and therefore gets angry at *him* when his kids or ex-wife do upsetting things.

Initially she may see her new partner as a superhero, so when he fails (which he always will) to get his kids and his ex-wife to do whatever she believes is the right thing, she may judge him as weak. Even worse, she may shame him for not bringing about the results she wants in the way she wants him to. This can hurt her partner and their relationship. It's an unfair expectation—a false belief—that needs to be adjusted. Once this impossibility is pointed out, hopefully the Stepmom can accept that neither she nor her partner can successfully control anyone other than themselves—and maybe, temporarily, very young children. Rather than giving away your power to your partner and unfairly expecting him to change or control others, make a new decision to learn from him and work together to find ways to address whatever's upsetting you in your stepfamily life. By getting clear on what you can and can't control, you can minimize any negative impact and protect your well-being in the future.

Potential Misstep #4: A Stepmom may believe (and fear) that if she goes along with her partner's approach to handling things with his kids and his ex-wife, it will be more painful than she can handle or accept.

This belief and fear deserve to be fully explored and addressed between a Stepmom and her partner instead of being unconsciously played out in response to the actions of the stepkids and their bio-mom. When a couple is conscious that the Stepmom's fears are triggered by her partner's strategy, they can combine forces to find new ways to comfort the Stepmom *and* honor her partner's approach with his kids. There are many times when the actions of your stepkids or their bio-mom will cause you genuine distress that really needs to be processed privately and not through your interactions with them. They may be vengeful and their actions may require you and your partner to make difficult choices or take creative actions to assuage your fears and anger. This is all possible when a Stepmom and her partner share their true feelings with each other and work together.

Tip: When the Stepmom feels her partner's approach or plan is not the one she'd select or she judges his plan as wrong, her wisest approach will be to recognize the intensity of her feelings and pause *before* expressing her criticism to her partner. If this happens to you, you can improve the situation by seeking to answer a few important questions about your own feelings before turning your attention to your partner for a discussion.

"What's my motivation for wanting my partner to take a specific action?"

"Why is it so important to me that my partner follow the advice I suggest?"

"What am I hoping/needing to get from the actions I recommend?"

"What am I afraid will happen if my partner doesn't do what I want him to do?"

"Does this situation impact me directly? If not, why am I feeling so strongly that my partner should do what I want instead of honoring his own opinions?"

"What would it take for me to shift my focus away from getting what I want and toward finding ways to support my partner?"

"Have I taken the time to truly understand and honor my beloved partner's feelings and opinions about this matter? Why am I assuming my needs and opinions are better or more important than his?"

Potential Misstep #5: A Stepmom takes on the role of championing her partner's parenting rights without being asked and is totally convinced she's being helpful. She makes it her goal to avenge the unfairnesses and grievances her partner has suffered at the hands of his ex-wife. This role eventually causes more problems than it may solve in the short-run.

A power struggle between a Stepmom and her partner's ex-wife puts her partner in a no-win, triangulated position that he probably didn't ask for and would prefer to avoid. It can be demeaning, disempowering and stressful for your partner to have to choose between accommodating the woman he loves now and giving in to whatever his ex-wife wants.

In this situation, the Stepmom is probably disregarding her partner's personal needs, acquired knowledge and opinions in the battle between the two women. This can be infuriating, excruciating and impossible for the Stepmom's partner to resolve. The Stepmom has the power to stop this complex and stressful situation by stepping back and giving up the role of her partner's champion—except when her partner specifically asks for her help.

In many cases, out of pure exhaustion or deep silent rage, the Stepmom's partner may give in to his present partner (the Stepmom) and give up trying to handle stepfamily situations, perhaps because the conflict with both women is too painful for him to handle or try to change. This situation will also risk triggering every childhood mothering wound that he has not yet addressed. On top of his pain, he may be criticized and shamed by his partner for not doing enough. This is a horrible, despairing situation for him. See Section Four for more about your partner's perspective.

A Stepmom may find herself fighting for her partner's rights without realizing that much of her emotional energy comes from her urgency for justice, her longing for a worthy role in her new family or a competition (conscious or not) with her partner's ex-wife. If this is true for you, you can stop this prickly relationship dynamic by redirecting your energy toward infusing your partner with your love, support and confidence. Process your feelings about the situation and your partner's ex-wife separately from the interactions between your partner and his ex-wife.

"Help is not help unless perceived so by the recipient." My mentor, Kit, told me this in 1984 and I repeatedly forgot it for the first 13 years of being a Stepmom. Perhaps you can remember it more often than I did. If you do, you'll stay more connected with your partner. You can be ready to help—all he has to do is ask. Strive to empower his confidence, self-esteem and self-respect.

Potential Misstep #6: A Stepmom mistakenly assumes the role of head negotiator with her partner's ex-wife instead of taking the much appreciated support role of her partner's cheerleader and biggest fan. A Stepmom may do this because she's impatient with the divorce process, co-parenting agreement and other negotiations and judges herself as more capable of handling this type of thing than her partner.

While this might be true in terms of efficiency or a particular skill set, there's a huge, often-overlooked disadvantage of your involvement in any negotiation or communication with a less than civil, uncooperative ex-spouse. Because your partner's ex-wife knows your partner's style, your influence, wording and suggestions are likely quite evident to her. If she's unhappy about your presence (or even existence in her children's lives), your participation could unintentionally fuel her vengeance. She may get a twisted thrill by causing your partner and you more stress. She may derive a greater sense of control by making it more difficult to finalize agreements or changes as a way to punish you and cause problems between you and your partner.

For the good of your intimate relationship, be aware of how any urgency to be involved in communications can trigger more problems than you're trying to solve. Whenever you possibly can, defer to your partner's negotiating style. Spend your time dealing with your valid feelings toward your partner's ex-wife in the privacy of your own life. Remember that your partner spent years developing a relationship with his ex-wife. This is easy to forget when a Stepmom is eager to get on with her new life with her partner but sees interacting with his ex-wife as an obstacle to that goal.

Potential Misstep #7: A Stepmom sees her strong beliefs in the important principles of doing the right thing and promoting justice as the only correct, absolute, black-and-white approach. She uses her beliefs to rationalize the need to be included in the relationship and communications between her partner and his ex-wife because she believes it's how she can help her partner. She's looking for a role and thinks she has found her value and purpose in this newly created stepfamily.

In reality, your partner may feel his greatest need is to relax when he gets home and stop feeling anxious when interacting with his ex-wife—no matter what the cost—preferring to give in to her and his kids to avoid conflicts or to settle outstanding issues. This can be infuriating to a Stepmom if she believes that giving in, failing to take a stand or accepting an unkept commitment represents quitting, losing or settling for something that's unfair or just plain wrong. Ideally, and for her well-being, a Stepmom will choose to suspend her personal judgments and choose to support her partner, his needs and his approaches.

However, realistically ignoring these situations is going to make many (most) stepmothers angry for a variety of reasons, perhaps just out of principle. Sadly, trying to control or get even with your partner's ex-wife is just going to create another unwinnable power struggle. Stepping off the competitive game board with your partner's ex-wife truly is a wise, loving and thoughtful yet counter-intuitive choice. This choice makes sense as a strategy when a couple agrees to make their own peaceful life together more important than fighting with the bio-mom over anything—yes anything. If your partner wants to take a stand for something and wants your help, that's a different situation. Get clear about any conflicts over what you believe should happen vs. what your partner wants to create with *his* ex-wife and *his* kids. How does it feel to make supporting your partner more important than superimposing your judgements. Chapter 19, His Kids: His Call, explains this important topic in detail.

Potential Misstep #8: A Stepmom refuses to believe her partner when he explains that his ex-wife is not likely to change her uncooperative behavior or ever want to get along with the Stepmom.

This hard-to-believe reality (if it's true for you) can be extremely difficult for an optimistic or enthusiastic Stepmom to accept. However, you'll be doing yourself a huge favor and you can save yourself and your partner immeasurable pain by accepting it now. This courageous empowered acceptance frees you to refocus your attention on other things that are achievable. This is a place to apply the Serenity Prayer on Section One's title page.

Without realizing it, a Stepmom may resist accepting her partner's opinion on this topic. She may set out to prove him wrong by trying to convince his ex-wife to change her ways and get along. Sometimes a well-meaning Stepmom's attempts to be nice and get along actually increase the hostility from an adversarial ex-wife, causing unimaginable stress for the Stepmom and her partner. The solution for this resistance to reality is to get curious, learn more and take advantage of your partner's experience co-parenting with his ex-wife. Rather than trying to change her, use your wits, wisdom and energy to focus on activities that sidestep or shield you from any negative impact. See the chapters in Section Four and Section Six.

Potential Misstep #9: A Stepmom may incorrectly believe it's her job to find ways for the stepkids and their bio-mom to get along with her and her partner. This Stepmom takes actions to reinforce this goal—even if she knows her partner would prefer to ignore disagreements and avoid conflict, and is actually OK not having everyone get along. He wants a calm happy life with his new partner more than he wants his present and past partners to get along. This surprisingly common misunderstanding between a Stepmom and her partner can be resolved with an honest and mutually respectful conversation.

Potential Misstep #10: A Stepmom may use some version of the phrase, *"If you love me, you'll do what I want."*

This hurtful controlling statement, sometimes used as a last resort or when logic doesn't support her desires, is a common misuse of the loving connection between a Stepmom and her partner. This statement may be fueled by the painful, infuriating feelings of being betrayed by her partner if the Stepmom feels like she's third or fourth on her partner's priority list.

By using this implied proving-and-testing-love ultimatum, a Stepmom may not realize that she's potentially disrespecting her partner's equally valid rights to try to get his own needs met. She's pressuring him to do what she wants so she can feel loved by him and better about the situation. He may initially reluctantly agree so he can avoid her wrath or her potential withdrawal of love, but he's probably going to resent it because it's an unloving manipulation. This is unfair to her partner and usually not a simple either/or situation, as a Stepmom may believe it to be. In my experiences with partners of stepmothers since 2000, chances are extremely high that her partner does love her—and deeply. He may just have different needs and values or a conflicting viewpoint about how to handle something that deserves to be honored just as much as the wishes and needs of the Stepmom. When under stepfamily pressures it can be difficult for a Stepmom to stay conscious of what's happening so she can avoid any painful reactions, but it's still a worthy goal. If you ever feel your only option is to give your partner an ultimatum, pause—the situation calls for more love, more shared empathy and the "Nobody's Right, Nobody's Wrong" approach. See Chapter 20. Also see smoms.org for an article called "Testing and Proving Love."

Potential Misstep #11: A Stepmom assumes that because she's a woman and new to the family group, she can see stepfamily issues more objectively than her partner. Therefore, when the Stepmom and her partner disagree, she believes she knows how to handle her stepkids and their bio-mom better (or more effectively) than her partner. Even if she's correct about her objectivity, this belief can become a lose-lose power struggle that's very draining and damaging to the couple and their relationship.

A Stepmom may disagree with her partner's suggestions for how to interact with his children or ex-wife in any given situation. She may even disregard his advice and act on her own. Worst of all, she may begin to lose respect for her partner and judge him as weak, wrong and a bad father because he disagrees with her and is unwilling to do whatever it takes to be right or to win. This common misunderstanding can lead to excruciating, seemingly impossible-to-resolve arguments and an ever-expanding invisible wall between a Stepmom and her partner that can severely impact their intimacy and trust.

More About this Situation

- Reality check: A Stepmom does *not* know her partner's ex-wife better than he does—unless possibly if the Stepmom and ex-wife have had a previous relationship.

- It can actually cause more stress when the Stepmom tries to change the relationship dynamic between her partner and his ex-wife. Things get much better for a Stepmom and her partner when a Stepmom uses her loving superpowers to help her partner avoid and contain any negative impact from his ex-wife instead.

- The Stepmom's partner and his ex-wife spent years working together to establish their relationship, yet it's common for a well-meaning Stepmom to truly believe she can manage or control her partner's uncooperative ex-wife into behaving in a civil, fair, honorable way. This is almost never true or realistic unless the ex-wife has a change of heart, which is rare yet can be wonderful.

- No happy family dream is going to be possible when the Stepmom refuses to listen, trust, support or respect her partner's opinions about his ex-wife and his kids.

- Rather than judging her partner, a loving Stepmom can choose to have faith in her partner and put her focus on working with what she can control—her well-being and life with her partner.

- For some reason, any version of the mistaken belief, "it's more important to get justice at any cost than it is to give in and lose," seems more common when a Stepmom doesn't have her own bio-kids. If this is you, be aware of this potential for avoidable stress with your partner. Be sure to honor all the feelings that arise for you and process them privately instead of on the battlefield of your stepfamily relationships.

Potential Misstep #12: A Stepmom may believe talking is the only way to resolve conflicts.

In her urgency or need to talk things out or to be heard, seen or included, a Stepmom may forget that sometimes keeping quiet and doing nothing can also be effective tools for resolving disagreements. Under pressure, a Stepmom may lose some of her listening skills and compassion for her partner's feelings. When stressful conversations are required, put a time limit on them. Ten to twenty minutes is usually enough. This brings mutual motivation for efficiency and the relief of knowing there's an agreed stopping point for the stressful topic of conversation. This limit has the tendency to make the conversations more productive. Combine this time limit with an agreement that after they finish their stepfamily business, the couple agrees to put aside the topic and spend the rest of their evening, day or weekend in happy, non-stepfamily-related peace together. This is often exactly what the Stepmom is looking for and what her partner craves. See Chapter 37, Tip #7, for an idea about creating a stress-free zone for you and your partner.

Suggestion: *Not* talking and *not* doing, even if you agree with the concept and adopt it as a strategy, can leave you with excess energy bubbling up looking for focus and direction. When you find yourself with this extra energy, use it for yourself. Give yourself permission to be the recipient of your own lovingkindness—not to numb or distract yourself, but in ways that truly support, nourish and comfort you. When doers and givers are stressed, they tend to automatically focus their energy on others. However when you decide not to do or talk to others, using that energy for yourself is the wisest choice for all. Hint hint!

Potential Misstep #13 (Expanding on Misstep #7): A Stepmom may believe that striving for justice, winning and fairness are worth all the energy, conflicts and stress required to accomplish these goals. This may include her making extra efforts, arguing and maybe even insisting (refusing to give up the belief) that there are ways to force her partner's ex-wife or kids to abide by rules and agreements.

When a Stepmom is driven (obsessed?) to seek justice, she can be so passionate that she acts in ways that unintentionally disregard and disrespect her partner's wishes and needs. Her partner may want peace over just about any conflict with his ex-wife. Ironically, feeling disregarded and disrespected is one of the common complaints of do-the-right-thing-at-any-cost Stepmoms, which is something to be mindful of. Could your actions be causing your partner to feel the same way you feel? Could you be accusing him of doing what you are doing? Hmmm? If so, this realization can bring new waves of compassion for a Stepmom when it comes to her choices.

From a Stepmom's perspective, there can seem to be a lot of unfair or "wrong" occurrences in stepfamily life, especially if both bio-parents aren't respectful, kind or at least civil to each other. While intention is a powerful force, the will of a Stepmom is not likely to impact or change the intention and attitude of an uncooperative bio-mom. Whenever possible, make the wishes of your partner more important than your need to try to force your partner's ex-wife to be fair, kind or civil or to do the right thing. If you feel strongly about injustice and get angry when others get away with not following the rules, look into your past experiences for examples where someone got away with not being fair and it hurt or angered you. You'll likely find something extremely important there from your past. Spending time processing your personal pre-Stepmom emotional wounds and experiences is a much more productive and beneficial use of your time. Hint hint!

See Chapter 9 for ways to use the energy stirred up by your emotions to find more empowerment for yourself.

Check out Chapter 37, Tip #26, and see if a mistake allowance might support your process.

A Stepmom and Her Self-Awareness

La Belle Reine's Story

July 2016

Dear Stepmom seeking support,

I've been stepmother to a (now 13-year-old) girl for the past 10.5 years. I have a very interesting and difficult past with my stepdaughter and her biological mother. I felt used, abused and completely exhausted from trying to juggle the demands of my ill husband, stepdaughter and her biological mom. I had no boundaries and was in a toxic and miserable situation. I had pictured a happy blended family but instead got quite the opposite.

About five years ago, I was on the brink of a nervous breakdown. I was so overwhelmed with feelings of obligation, fear, resentment, guilt and shame regarding my role in my stepdaughter's life and the difficulties I was having with her mother. I had no one to turn to who could really understand. One night I was on the internet and found Cathryn's site and my life has never been the same. After reading a few of her articles on smoms.org, I decided to send her a private message asking for help. When I wrote the letter, I really didn't think I'd get a response. But I did. Her response, our correspondence and the work we did together have CHANGED MY LIFE!

When I received Cathryn's lengthy response I sobbed tears of relief and gratefulness because I had finally found a beacon of hope. Below is an excerpt from my reply to her initial email. It truly describes how I felt, and still feel, about Cathryn and smoms.org.

"Cathryn…I just finished reading your email and I am in shock…that somehow you know me and can see into the depths of my soul!!! I felt like I was reading a letter from my future self. Does that make sense? It was as if my future, healthy self was sending me a message to help me become HER. That may sound crazy but THAT IS WHAT THIS FEELS LIKE!!!

"I don't know much about you but what I do know is that the LORD has sent me to you and I feel it in my soul that you were put on this earth to help people like me and you will be blessed beyond measure for your compassionate service...... I can't imagine the energy it takes to run this site and then to take the time to write such a sincere, insightful and loving email to me just blows my mind. THANK YOU isn't enough. I want to send you a hug and somehow let you feel my gratitude because my words aren't expressing what I am feeling. This IS MY TIME...I know that the reason I found your site is because I was preparing myself to finally take control of my life and GET OFF THE RIDE...the crazy roller coaster ride that I've been on my entire life. Every single word you wrote resonated with me so deeply that it shook me to the core..."

Ladies, I went from feeling sad, alone, defeated and confused to feeling hopeful, inspired, understood and relieved. It was as if Cathryn had been living in my home and observed all that I had been going through and could see right to the heart of all my problems. I couldn't believe that a woman I had never met could know and empathize with me more than my husband or best friend could.

Cathryn is sensitive, unbiased, accepting, gentle yet firm and passionate in her advice. I thank the Lord for finding her. She helped me push past a "wall" of false beliefs and faulty boundaries that had been keeping me from freeing myself from self-inflicted torment regarding my stepdaughter and bio-mom. She helped me tap into my own strength and somehow I found the courage I needed to finally make the changes in my life and take control of my life. Sharing my needs and feelings with her helped me to put my role as a Stepmom into perspective. I feel more awake, wise and good about being me than ever before. It's exciting to realize I can stand up for myself, honor my feelings and change my beliefs and boundaries—as needed—without any guilt.

It's 2016 now and believe it or not, my stepdaughter and her bio-mom are living with me and my husband. It's something I would never have believed possible. It's a miracle.

A Stepmom and Her Self-Awareness

I consider Cathryn a marvelous mentor and happily a very dear friend. I will be forever grateful for her support, concern and kindness in helping me. I know that anyone who is struggling in their role as a Stepmom, and who's in the right place to make the necessary changes, will 100% benefit from Cathryn's help.

She gave me the tools to free myself from a very unhealthy and damaging relationship and rebuild my life as a Stepmom with a peace, confidence and joy that I never knew existed. I really can't say enough about how much having Cathryn in my life has helped me. I urge each of you to allow Cathryn and her work to do the same in your life too.

A bunch of us from smoms.org have been urging her to write this book for the last couple years. It's filled with proven ideas and hard-earned wisdom that millions of Stepmoms can now learn about and use in their own lives. While we worked through this material over the years, you now have it all in one place. Wonderful.

Sincerely,
La Belle Reine
Stepmom since 2006
SMOM since 2011

Eight

The Birth of Beliefs and Resentments
Discover How Your Beliefs Impact You

The following is my viewpoint on the initial formation of resentments and beliefs. Understanding why you feel as you do and why you do what you do gives you the power to make new choices with greater wisdom and compassion. Feelings of resentment begin to emerge shortly after you are born—perhaps even the moment you're pushed and pulled, without regard for your wishes, from your mother's warm, cozy womb. As a baby, you're 100% disempowered. You're totally reliant on other people, unable to take a stand to meet your needs or set your own boundaries. You're completely vulnerable to, and at the mercy of, the actions of others. You have only limited ability to help yourself or express yourself to those who have your very survival in their hands.

From the moment you're born, you have only a few ways to communicate your feelings and needs:

- You can look toward or away from someone.

- When you're happy you can smile, coo and giggle.

- When you're calm or resigned you can remain quiet or sleep.

- When you're feeling anger, fear or pain you can make faces, cry, wave your arms and legs, scream or remain still.

As a baby, your needs and boundaries are honored only to the degree that others understand what you want or need and are willing and able to give it to you. This is true powerlessness.

This vulnerable state is also experienced by toddlers, by older children, and at times by those who are ill, injured or elderly and need daily care from others. If we define one form of rage as the realization of our powerlessness, being a baby and child offers many rage-inducing situations.

On the emotional front, from the moment you're born you have lots of feelings. Even if you don't understand the causes and forget the circumstances, they're still real feelings. Your emotions are made up of energy. My theory is that the foundation for resentment is forged the first time you're angry, perhaps for being slapped and stuck under harsh lights the moment you're born. At birth some part of your psyche realizes that you're completely incapable of helping yourself or of taking actions that would make you feel better. This same part of your mind protects you from emotions too intense for your baby mind to handle. You can certainly experience fear, rage, loneliness, cold, hunger, etc. even though you don't have the words to express them.

If a baby is hungry and no one addresses this, there's a moment when she realizes that she can't help herself get food when she needs it. She's physically incapable of obtaining nourishment to satisfy her genuine need. She may cry (and cry), and if food comes, she may decide the effort of crying is worth it. However if she cries and food doesn't appear, she experiences the rage of being disempowered. Unable to use her anger to bring about what she wants, this emotional energy morphs into something she can do. This is the moment resentment is born.

Just because you can't talk as a baby doesn't mean that you don't have thoughts and feelings, right? Every unacknowledged feeling is energy that exists and that has to move. This energy has to go somewhere, so if it can't be expressed and acknowledged, it goes into the unconscious mind and is forgotten consciously. It doesn't go away. It gets stored away and is no longer accessible by your conscious mind. This is why you have very few conscious baby memories. It's also why memories can come back to you—when the right questions are asked or the right circumstances generate feelings that line up with those shoved-away feelings. Stepfamily situations can trigger the same thoughts and feelings that you've been storing in your unconscious or subconscious minds from previous and similar situations.

As described throughout the book, as soon as babies are conscious enough to think, they begin to put things into their newly created subconscious "Book of Beliefs and Rules." Babies start accumulating rules and beliefs with the limited—but ever-increasing—awareness and knowledge available to them at each moment. Here's the important thing to realize about this process: once a belief is created and stored in our subconscious mind, it becomes a personal law of behavior until it's consciously revised or replaced with a new belief.

Baby-Created Beliefs

"The only way to get attention (or something I want) is to cry, scream and fuss until something changes or improves."

"In order to get what I want, I have to endure and wait."

"I have to force myself to smile and make happy sounds to get what I want or something bad will happen."

"No one responds to me when I cry so it's not worth the effort."

"When I scream or cry, I get ignored or hurt."

"I have to wait for others to help me."

"I'm powerless to help myself when I feel scared."

"If I smile, someone will be nice to me and good things will happen."

Whenever a baby's need goes unmet or a boundary is violated, she will experience some level of resentment, acceptance or even despair, based on her personality. The tactics she uses to successfully get whatever she can from others (or not) create the beliefs she brings into her childhood.

Children and Their Beliefs

As you grow, you learn more about the ways of your world. You gain more capabilities and have more ways to communicate with the people who have control over your life and well-being. As you learn things, you also become more conscious of what you want and don't want. You can make more conscious choices about your own needs. You also create more beliefs and rules to help yourself feel safe and make sense of your ever-changing world. As you grow and learn more, you automatically replace existing beliefs with new updated ones. The specifics of what you learn and the beliefs you add to your personal rulebook are based on your personality and your unique childhood circumstances and experiences.

As children grow up, they're better able to take actions to meet their needs. They're more capable of expressing specific feelings whenever their boundaries are violated. Ironically, they can become both empowered *and* frustrated when they can't help themselves get what they want. Why? Because they've had a tiny taste of being responsible for their own well-being through increased communications and physical skills. Their new abilities are empowering and exciting, while their inability to fulfill personal needs and wishes is both motivating and infuriating.

My Take on the Terrible Twos

1. As you realize you can express the word *"no,"* your frustrations, angers and rage suddenly have a powerful outlet that creates an impact on others. This can feel darn good to a child.

2. The choice between *"yes"* and *"no"* is something you begin to consciously understand. You've been at the mercy of other people's *"no"* your entire little life. You already have a lot of unprocessed anger, rage and resentments that have been shoved into your unconscious warehouses of emotional energy and experiences and saying *"no"* gives you some immediate relief and fuels your new strategy for helping yourself.

3. You attempt to empower yourself through terrible-twos behavior, mirroring maneuvers often used on you. Where do you think little ones get the idea for *"no"*? At this point, the only stand-up-for-yourself tactic your baby brain knows how to express (aside from crying) is to say *"no."* This exciting new capability makes you believe you can now do more for yourself. It may also be the time when you discover the power of passive aggression. Whether you use it to influence others will depend on the reaction you get when you say *"no."*

As you continue to grow into your teen years, you're better able to understand what you need and think of ways to get it. You can better express your desires to others and you have ever-increasing physical and verbal skills. As a result, you can more effectively get more of what you want. Still, you're unable to take care of yourself in all the ways you'd like to. If you're lucky, you have someone in your life who sees and respects your feelings and is able to teach you how to handle your feelings. However, by this time, most of us remain unskilled at processing our emotions and releasing the energy of our specific fears, pain, worry and stress. This is not because we did anything wrong or are dumbbells—our limited physical and mental capabilities have simply not fully developed.

Your awareness that you're still at the mercy of others generates natural rage, and this leads to resentment. All the unresolved, dishonored and unprocessed rage, pain, fear and anger from childhood continue to be redirected into your unconscious mind because they're too painful or too intense for you to handle or accept at this time in your life. When this happens, some mystical part of your psyche steps up and stores away that emotional energy until you have the skills to process, resolve, release and learn from it. The fact that you're reading this now tells me you're ready to do this work.

As you get older, resentment becomes more uncomfortable because you're now becoming more aware (conscious) that there are circumstances where you need to learn to repress or swallow certain emotions in order to, as you believe, survive. You may learn it's not safe to express certain feelings around certain people, as you'd risk being punished in some way. How do you learn that? Through the trial and error of expressing your feelings to the people who have power over you. You pay attention to the reactions you get each time you express yourself (or do something) in a specific way. If your actions result in your being hurt or scared, your instincts lock them into your subconscious mind as a dangerous and bad thing to do. Whether the people who teach you are kind or not-so-kind to you, you tell yourself stories about what happens around them that make sense to you and that you can accept. Then you create new beliefs for your personal rulebook.

As children, we all had different experiences, even children in the same family. We each created an array of personal beliefs shaped by the levels of awareness, kindness, compassion and attention we received (or didn't receive) from the people taking care of us. We learned which behaviors resulted in good experiences and which ones caused us pain. We locked in our child-created beliefs as laws and we follow them for the rest of our lives. Understanding this process, we can see what an awesomely impactful, daunting responsibility caring for a child is and how much our choices as caregivers can impact a child's life from day one.

Not all beliefs cause problems or additional stress for you as you become an adult. Below are some possible beliefs a child might create when trying to make sense of experiences associated with met and unmet needs. As you grow up, new beliefs will replace earlier formed, conflicting beliefs on the same topic because you're consciously choosing new and updating existing beliefs. You will keep a belief in place until it's changed, no matter what your chronological age. This is an important point to remember—one you'll see throughout this book.

Child-Created Beliefs

- *"I'm more likely to get what I want if I say please."*

- *"I never get what I want unless I say please."*

- *"The only way to get what I want is to cry, scream and be angry."* Until you realize this is your belief, you're likely to respond to discomfort in this singular way, unaware that there's any other way to get what you want. As a result, you may stay angry when something upsets you because you're unconsciously holding another impactful belief—that feeling angry is the only way to get what you want or bring about relief and change.

- *"I have to endure, deny and tolerate my anger and resentments because if I express my upsetting feelings, I'll get hurt in even more painful ways. I must find another way to get what I want without sharing my true feelings."* This is the logical beginning of the motivation to learn to tap dance, manipulate, lie or be passive-aggressive.

- *"I can't get (or do) what I want unless someone else agrees to do it for me."*

- *"I can't get (or do) what I want unless someone else gives me permission."* or *"When people are upset with me, it's my fault—it means I'm unlovable and I can't bear that."* or *"Staying connected to people is more important than getting what I want."* These beliefs are the kernels that birth approval-seekers and codependents.

- *"If I take a stand for my needs and try to make choices for myself, I get punished, don't get what I need or things get even worse."* Seeds of martyrdom, pessimism and despair are planted here.

- *"I have no power to create the changes that will help me feel better or safe."* This can be the beginning of victimhood.

- *"I have to be a good girl and not make anyone upset in order to get love and attention."*

- *"If I upset others, they'll reject me and I'll be devastated."* Free-floating anxiety arises from these beliefs.

- *"I have to serve others to earn my right to be here. I don't deserve anything unless I earn it."* Achievers and performers are created through this belief.

- *"Since I can't get what I want from others, I'll just hang on to my resentments. At least holding on to my angry feelings gives me a sense of power and it's something I can control."* Self-reliant rebelliousness and stubbornness protect this child from conscious pain as she chooses to feel anger over pain.

Homework: Think about your personal Book of Beliefs. Does anything resonate with you so far? The more conscious you can become of your feelings and beliefs, the better. As you become aware of the specific beliefs that are driving your opinions and actions, you can change them to be more appropriate for your life as an adult. With compassion for yourself, this can be a fascinating exploration and a liberating experience. There's no reason to be afraid of any beliefs you discover. Every belief that is no longer working for you can be revised or completely replaced with a new belief that's more appropriate for the adult woman you are now.

Do you believe that your beliefs can be changed or not? This is also a belief. It's one I hope you'll replace with a new, more empowering belief such as: *"I have the power to create and change any of my beliefs. I choose to customize my book of beliefs to serve me as the adult I am today."*

As a child, situations that hurt or scare you feel life-threatening and are therefore existentially terrifying beyond all logic and reason. Most grown-ups don't understand that children don't have the ability to discern lengths of time, the concept of sarcasm or the degree of grown-up anger and danger they may be facing. Children just feel the raw sensations, emotions and energy. Until someone explains what's happening, you'll determine the meaning of painful and scary moments by drawing on your past experiences. When the pain or fear becomes too much, your psyche once again steps in and helps you survive by shoving the energy of the feelings into your unconscious minds. You continue to make up beliefs that make sense to you. You're simply looking to assuage your fears and feel you're OK, unconcerned with accuracy or truth.

Hopefully, once you understand this dynamic, it is easier to be forgiving of any of your past behaviors and compassionate with the child you used to be. Your younger child self was very creative in helping herself survive—and she succeeded. Now you can help yourself in new ways as an awake, capable, adult woman. This is a repeating theme you'll see a lot in this book.

While the list of possible child-created beliefs about dealing with resentments and anger is virtually unlimited, the examples above may help you see that the vast majority of beliefs that grown-ups use to make sense of their lives are indeed now unconscious, child-created ones. The only difference is that presently these grown-ups are using more complex implementation strategies. Many (most?) grown-ups are stuck in their childhood or adolescent patterns because they don't realize they have a choice. You now know you have a choice. What beliefs do you want to change?

Why Children Run Away from Home

Running away from home is a common way for children to act on and process their angry feelings. When kids realize they have the option to run away, emotional energy flows from their unconscious warehouse that has been holding old anger. This gives them courage and energy to take a stand for themselves. The excitement of being able to express their anger propels them to take actions that they believe will make the people in charge of them take notice. They feel ever-increasing bursts of empowerment. It's along the same lines as the good feeling of saying "no," yet better because they get to take physical action. They feel free in those few glorious moments of deciding to leave and realizing that they have the capability to take need-fulfilling actions on their own behalf—like planning their getaway, packing stuff, storming or sneaking out, etc. In those moments, they touch on a new powerful feeling of being able to take charge of themselves. This is a magical, euphoric moment for a child.

However, sadly, the bliss often evaporates the moment they realize that they can't actually live independently. They realize they're not as empowered as they hoped. Resentment about the unfairness of the situation floods back as they're now undeniably aware of their own inability to help themselves. They also realize they have no choice but to return home and this puts them back into that familiar place of powerlessness. However, a new memory of their empowerment stays with them and it will build as they experience more and more self-reliance. Parental and caregiver reactions to a child running away from home will also impact the child's new beliefs and degrees of resentment.

The way parents respond when a child runs away from home and then returns can have a pivotal, life-changing impact on the runaway. I wonder how many parents are aware of the deep ramifications of their responses. Below are four possible parental choices when a child returns home from running away. While this information may be helpful to those of you with bio-kids or stepkids, I include it here to help you have more compassion for any of your childhood experiences that may need your attention and lovingkindness.

Parental Reaction #1: Punishing parents who greet the returning child with anger usually drive a child to create a belief that looks something like this: *"When I assert my rights and take actions to meet my own needs, I get punished by the people I love and need the most. I can't trust them anymore as a safe place for some of my feelings."* This angry reaction can be so jolting to some children that they can't process its truth. As a result, their shock and rage get shoved into their unconscious minds. Experiences like this one are one more reason so many of us have a large warehouse full of emotional energy.

Parental Reaction #2: If worried parents express that they are upset, thereby making the child's decision to run away all about the negative impact on themselves, the child might create a belief like this: *"When I take a stand for meeting my needs I hurt the people I love. That makes me a bad person who should be ashamed of putting her needs before those she loves."* This experience can also lead to the belief: *"When I'm told I'm bad, I can't feel good about myself until the other person forgives me."*

Parental Reaction #3: If parents ignore the running-away incident, plus the child's attempt at self-care and trying to take responsibility for her well-being in her own way, the resulting belief could be the following: *"When I try to help myself because I'm angry or upset, the ones I love ignore me and this means they don't care about my feelings."* This is rarely true, but all that matters is how the child interprets the parents' actions. This is based on the child's brain and limited understanding.

Parental Response #4: The most loving and respectful parental reaction to the child's courageous attempt at taking a stand to meet her own needs is a series of steps. Ideally, the parents express joy that the child is back safely and give the child lots of expressions of love. Next, the parents express their sincere eagerness to learn what the child was feeling that made her want to run away in the first place. Patient (vs. impatient) parents who listen and give their child empathy and loving attention because they want to better understand the child's feelings give her a tremendous gift.

When the parents make it clear the child's feelings are valid and respected, they can talk about ways to help her make new, creative changes to avoid the initially upsetting circumstances. They help the child realize (and soon believe) that there are always solutions possible, even if she doesn't know what they are. The trust and emotional safety between the parents and child increase as the parents consciously help the child get more of what she wants. This creates a life-empowering belief.

A child experiencing the gift of having her feelings be valued and respected might create these beliefs: *"When I'm upset, I can get my needs met by talking with the ones I love. They are happy to help me figure out a solution that honors my needs in a kind way."* Or maybe this one: *"I can express my upsetting feelings to the ones I love and they will still love me."* This is a wonderful parenting situation for this lucky child.

Your Childhood Survival Strategy

I learned about survival strategies from Dr. Alice Miller and cover this concept in more detail in Chapters 9 and 18. In case you haven't read those chapters yet, here's a synopsis: Somewhere in childhood (ages 4-8) you create and then lock in your childhood survival strategy. This strategy is a collection of beliefs and behaviors that enabled you to survive your childhood and that you continue to use now with varying degrees of ease and success—or not. To survive emotionally you *had* to come up with a strategy for reacting to upsetting circumstances and feelings—we all do this. We all have a survival strategy.

The beliefs and tactics you absolutely needed to get through your childhood are now firmly written in your subconscious rulebook of life. These include defensive behaviors and justifications for whatever choices you make. Unless you consciously change your beliefs as you become an adult, you'll operate on whatever beliefs are there from your childhood. You'll use this same strategy for the rest of your life. The tactics and logistics might change as you get older and wiser, but they will still be reactions to the same beliefs and chosen behavior patterns. When others don't abide by your beliefs, you're likely to judge them as wrong.

When couples have strong disagreements and can't find the way to a happy compromise, it's usually an indication that underneath whatever actually happened is a series of conflicting core beliefs about how to handle stressful situation from childhood. This is why uncovering and acknowledging your respective beliefs and strategies is so important when you're under stress in your relationship.

You follow the rules in your personal rulebook, whether you're conscious of those rules or not. When people are scared, get angry or feel pain, they usually go more unconscious, experiencing varying degrees of emotional shock and reverting to the childhood survival strategy, even if the tactics for implementation look grown up. See the referenced chapters and Section Three for more information about resolving relationship stress and getting closer to your partner.

A Teenager's World

As a teenager, you have more abilities than you did as a child and you're much more self-aware. You have more skills and independence. Maybe for the first time, you have friends, peers and other people that will be on your side when you're at odds with your caretakers. After a lifetime of being all alone against the will of the big powerful ones you love, becoming consciously aware of your new skills and options brings you a new and empowering sense of self. The teen self realizes that she can now survive in the world without her parents. You begin to form a new sense of how power can be expressed in your life. You may want to claim total power over your own life, even though you're probably not totally capable of this quite yet.

By the time you're a teenager, there are already vast warehouses of unprocessed emotions and energy stored in your unconscious mind. Your subconscious is filled with memories and your Book of Beliefs is filled with details that are no longer questioned nor retained in your conscious mind. Rebellion feels so good because it serves as an avenue of expression for the powerful, unconscious energy of rage to flow through you. When energy moves, it feels so good—even exhilarating. In the moment the energy is flowing, you can feel almost invincible. As you find more ways to express this energy through your conscious choices, you're likely to stand up for yourself and voice disagreements with or opinions that differ from those of your parenting figures.

The emotional energy a teenager expresses through acts of rebellion far exceeds the actual energy generated in the moment. This is because it is supplemented by energy from similar past experiences that has been unexpressed or unprocessed. A teen who expresses this energy may be perceived as a drama queen, belligerent or just plain difficult. I believe this behavior is an indication of the amount of as-yet unprocessed emotional energy that is within each child. Wouldn't it be amazing for conscious adults to help the teen learn how to honor and manage the forceful energy pouring through her, rather than for them to judge her? I'm not even addressing the powerful impact of hormones.

For all you "good girls" out there who gave your parents little or no trouble even as a teen, this behavior may be an indication of baby or childhood experiences that resulted in a belief something like this: *"In order to survive, I have to make my connection with the people I love more important than getting my own needs met."* Or: *"I have to contain my upsetting emotions or I'll lose the love of the people I need to survive."* There are many variations of this belief. This is one reason why some teens don't rebel. They want to be powerful and express themselves but the fear of being devastated by the loss of their parents' love is greater than the imagined benefit of being free.

If you have a parent who is an overt or covert narcissist, you're likely to have a belief that looks something like this: *"If I take a stand for my needs or uphold a boundary for my own well-being, I'm being rude, mean and selfish."* Someone with this self-punishing belief is easy for the takers of the world to manipulate if she doesn't want to be judged as wrong, rude, mean or selfish. Once this false belief is uncovered, it can be replaced with a healthier, empowering belief. What a relief!

A healthier belief: *"I have a right to set and uphold my personal boundaries. No connection with any other person is more important than standing up for my well-being and safety."* Replacing this one belief can change your world view in many positive, daily, life-enhancing ways. Hopefully by now you see that time spent looking into any limiting or false beliefs can bring about powerfully positive changes in your life.

Teenage-Created Beliefs

Teenage-created beliefs will override many baby and child-created beliefs as you realize you have new capabilities and ideas for interacting with (or avoiding) people, feelings and circumstances. Below are a few possible beliefs resulting from your teenage years.

For Fortunate Teens

"My expression of anger is respected when I present it in healthy ways. Positive change occurs when I express my feelings to the ones I love."

"The ones I love help me get my needs met and honor my boundaries—even when they disagree or see things differently."

For Many Teens

"My expression of anger is punished, shamed and disregarded without respect for the situation or my feelings. The punishment is too painful for me to continue standing up for myself."

"I can't create the change I need. Therefore I have to silence my anger and live with my resentment as best I can."

"I have no option but to rage at the world—to heck with the consequences. The emotions pouring through me are too strong to hold back. I have the right to express myself any way I want to."

"My expression of anger is denied or judged, so I have to find discreet ways to process these powerful feelings."

Hopefully, any alternative methods of self-expression that a teen chooses will be healthy. If not, the process of converting unhealthy expressions of anger and rage into healthy ones is part of growing up and becoming wise. The beliefs often relate directly to how much a person did or did not feel respected by the grown-ups in her life when she was a child. They also can indicate if the grown-ups in a child's life directed their anger at others or at her.

If you grew up in a family where expressing anger was not allowed or was judged as ignorant, or if you were made to feel wrong in any way for expressing your anger, you had to do other things with all the naturally occurring anger that arises in childhood. You found other ways to express your anger or deny it. Perhaps you did so passively or by numbing your anger with harsh self-judgements. Maybe you got sad instead of angry and let the tears dissipate your emotions because crying was OK in your family. Maybe anger was completely accepted and even excused from consequence—perhaps this was because at least one of your parents believed that whatever is said or done in anger doesn't really count or needs to be ignored or endured silently.

Every family has a set of beliefs about expressing anger, whether they are spoken or just understood without using words. What are your beliefs about expressing anger and how to process it? Do you know what beliefs your partner has about anger? Do they conflict in any way? Looking into this with your partner and then making a new set of beliefs as a couple can take some creative work. This work can dramatically reduce the stress between you two in many ways.

Thinking about feelings vs. *feeling* your feelings is another survival tactic preferred by some, often without intention or even knowing why. What's the benefit? There's no pain in the mental plane of thoughts and thinking, while there is pain in the emotional realm. It's why many people choose to stay in their heads rather than experience their own feelings. The thinking approach is truly less painful than feeling and therefore seems like a smart, conscious choice.

Another alternative to feeling is to judge yourself or others. Being judgmental freezes your feelings temporarily. It's like emotional novocaine. Self-pity and guilt provide the same temporary relief. Even though the benefits are temporary, many people prefer being numb and distracted to facing and feeling their emotions. For more insights on the dynamics of feeling judgmental, see the public article on smoms.org called "Feeling Judgmental?"

Note to Stepmoms with teenage stepkids: Can you figure out the beliefs influencing the behavior of your teen stepkids? It can be very helpful in your relationship (interesting, too) to do some emotional detective work with your partner to uncover what beliefs may be impacting their behaviors. It's never too late to change beliefs so your conscious work can help them find new beliefs as needed. This is especially true about relationship-related beliefs and the impact of divorce on their beliefs.

Rebellious Teenage Behaviors

Belief: *"My expression of anger is met with anger."*

Choice: *"I care more about asserting my rights as an individual than I care about keeping the connection with my parents."*

Belief and Choice: *"I feel so much rage, I choose to refuse to give them what they want because I believe if I go along with them I lose myself."*

This is where each teen makes a decision about what's more important to her—having power or being connected to loved ones.

Some beliefs help a teen make sense of the unconscious nuclear rage and angry energy that can well up within her without warning. These feelings can be so strong that they generate a sense of immortality. *"At last I'm free from the control of others."* Sadly, many relationship bridges will be damaged or severed if the adults in the teen's life are unwilling or unable to understand what's going on for her. Even though our bodies grow up, most of us are still being driven by our personal child-created survival strategy. Most of our choices and behaviors, until examined consciously, are determined by the teen or child we used to be. I got the term "child you/we used to be" from studying the work of Dr. Alice Miller and her groundbreaking book, *The Drama of the Gifted Child*.

Understandably, very few teens are conscious enough of their beliefs to understand that they have many more choices than what they see as obviously good/bad, right/wrong or what they want or don't want. Part of being an adolescent is living in these extremes and absolutes. Understanding the limitations of this phase of emotional growth makes it easier to have compassion for their actions. It may also help you understand *why* you did whatever you did as a teenager.

Liberate Yourself from Limiting Beliefs

Childhood strategies begin to imprison you as a teenager. If you have a belief that you'll get hurt if you express anger, you won't express it openly, even though you are quite capable of putting your feelings into words. You'll figure out other ways to get what you want to the best of your abilities. You'll do this unknowingly, and within the confines of your personal Book of Beliefs. Whether that takes the form of approval-seeking, conscious manipulation tactics (actively or passively aggressive), controlling or rebelling behaviors or giving up, the emotional energy is so strong that you may not feel like you have any choice about how you behave. At this point in your young teen life, you may stop trying to get approval or you may never take a stand, even though you have the ability, strength and intellectual creativity to do so. See smoms.org/BonusChapters for a chapter explaining your three states of consciousness.

As you become a grown-up, the successful childhood strategy that you believed you absolutely needed to survive your childhood now limits and can emotionally imprison you, especially in complex and never-before-experienced stepfamily situations. I've noticed that things rarely change for us until we take responsibility for building a new adult-created strategy for handling stressful events in life. As an adult you can move from survival to success strategies by consciously creating new approaches for the person and situations you face today. You'll want to consciously discover, revise and update your beliefs in line with your adult skills, wisdom and resources to better serve the woman you are NOW. The good news? Your adult-created strategies are always open to more changes based on feedback, new information and experiences. If you don't like a belief or your behavior, you now know you can change it. Accepting this will help you experience a lot less pressure to be perfect and you'll find that your options are without any limitations.

Homework: Your Beliefs

1. What beliefs are you now holding because they were true for you or made sense to you when you were a baby or child?

2. What beliefs have you been imposing on yourself which now interfere with your ability to meet your own needs, set or uphold your own boundaries or take a stand on your own behalf as the adult you are now?

3. What beliefs from childhood were drilled into you that you no longer agree with and that you want to change for your present situation?

4. What are your beliefs about what makes a woman a good stepmother?

Making this list of beliefs will serve you in many ways. Please note that the beliefs of being a good stepmother are not the same as being a good bio-mother and many stepmothers forget this. As you become more aware of how your beliefs directly impact your choices and experiences as a stepmother, you have the chance to validate, change or replace them.

Today, right now, you're an increasingly self-aware woman, consciously seeking new ways to handle your emotions, take care of yourself and create new, healthy boundaries for yourself. You have more resources, skills, talents, support structures and creativity than ever before—more than you had yesterday, last month or last year. You have more wisdom now than before you read this chapter. Recognize, Acknowledge, Forgive and Change. Make it OK for you to change your mind about any attitude, behavior or choice you have made in the past. *"That was then and this is now."* I love this mantra because it gives me the sense of relief that things can be different—better—going forward.

Reality check: We all have huge warehouses of unconscious emotional energy and unclaimed power that we can begin to consciously tap into and use to help ourselves in new ways. It can be a liberating, exciting and sometimes, like any adventure, a little bit scary with a tremendous upside to claim.

Application in Your Daily Life

Going forward, when an event occurs and your reaction feels bigger and more charged than the actual situation really deserves, see if you can stop yourself from reacting and give yourself time to think and feel. Sometimes a mysterious emotional charge, surge or compulsion to lash out or weep deeply occurs for issues that may seem trivial on the surface or trivial to others. Whenever this happens, it's a great opportunity to learn something about yourself. You can truly help yourself understand more about an event or feeling from the past that a younger version of you didn't know how to handle. If you are game to work with these feelings and go on this emotional exploration, give yourself some quiet time to reflect.

Ask Yourself

"What specific feelings were just triggered by this situation?"

"What's my earliest memory of feeling this same way as a child?"

"What can I remember about those circumstances?"

"How are those past circumstances similar to the present situation?"

Over the years of doing this exercise in workshops, it has been met with skepticism from some of the participants. However, over and over again, these questions would prompt a sudden rush of old memories, even among the skeptics. When you remember something from your past, lots of information, emotions and energy start to flow so it's important to be compassionate with yourself at this point. It often starts with an unexpected sense of hurt (sadness and anger) and then moves to anger—or vice versa, starts with anger and moves to pain. Remembering, acknowledging and validating any newly remembered feelings can give you a new empathy and appreciation for the child you used to be. You're also likely to begin to see things that happened to you in a new way with much more context, helping you better understand what you were up against and how creative you were to survive it. By doing this work and putting your attention on whatever you're feeling, all that energy can finally be expressed and released. Oh what a relief it is! This is a wonderful technique for your emotion-processing tool kit.

You can choose to learn how to work with your unconscious emotional energy in a conscious way. You can begin managing whatever emotional energy comes up for you with the new skills, talents and resources of a wise, adult woman, even when you're under stress. Yes, this is really possible. If you didn't know about all of this before reading this chapter, there was no way you could have handled anything in your past any differently than you did. Happily, one benefit of doing this work is that you can feel more love, appreciation and forgiveness for the younger versions of yourself. When you're compassionate toward yourself, this journey can truly be a loving and exciting exploration. This is a chance for you to make significant breakthroughs. This is a chance to bring your lovingkindness to the younger You's who often didn't get the support and guidance they needed and deserved. It's a very profound journey to help you reclaim your lost strength.

Child-Created Beliefs About Grown-Ups

As babies, children and teens we created some beliefs about what grown-ups did and why they did it. We created beliefs about how parents were supposed to be and about the power they had over young people. We thought these were rules and laws, unquestionable and unchangeable. There's not a child in the world who doesn't consciously think, *"When I'm a grown-up, I'm going to do X, Y or Z."* Or, *"When I'm grown up, I'm gonna do whatever I want."* Thinking and believing this helps children channel some of their angry energy into the future. There's tremendous emotional energy thrown into that belief about that future, like a time capsule we promise ourselves we'll open at a certain future time in our lives.

When a stepmother finds it difficult or even impossible to have compassion for certain childhood situations that our children or stepchildren experience, this can be related to a belief that grown-ups have—or should have—power over children in their care. A stepmother who believes this may not feel compassion for the protests and rebellions of her stepkids or bio-kids. If this is your experience as a Stepmom, it may be a clue that you have unaddressed related emotions to be processed. See Chapter 29.

Remember, you start out as a grown-up (not an adult) run by child-created strategies and beliefs. This is true until you wake up and become an adult who is conscious of your child-created beliefs, recognizing that you're driven by your beliefs about how parents are supposed to raise and treat the children in their care. When a stepmother running her home lacks that imagined power over the children living there, she's going to feel a lot of rage pour through her because she lacks the power she was raised to believe she has a right to have.

- Can you relate to that conflict between a belief and the reality of a situation?

- What examples of this kind of conflict are you aware of in your life right now?

- How many of your beliefs about childrearing are you conscious of now?

- When you look at your beliefs about what rights and choices a parenting figure should have, can you understand how that belief was created by the child you used to be?

- When you were growing up and your beliefs were being formulated, did being in a stepfamily or being a Stepmom ever cross your mind? If not, can you take a moment to acknowledge this reality and have compassion for yourself? Can you see that a nuclear family and a stepfamily are not the same thing, no matter what others tell you?

Write down your beliefs and keep a running list as you become more aware. The list can be very revealing. It's helpful to keep reminding yourself that your conscious mind has the power of choice. Remember as you identify the beliefs driving your present choices that you can now make new choices. This is one of the greatest things about being an awake, conscious adult.

So there you have it. That's my theory about the birth of beliefs and resentments. I know it's a lot to take in. I also realize that some of the things I've described may rub up against some of the beliefs you already have about this topic. I'm asking you to embrace the Fifth Agreement, which is a recent addition to the first four by don Miguel Ruiz—"*Be skeptical and listen more.*" Rest assured, you can always go back to your old ways. You won't forget. If you're willing to keeping moving past any resistance to defend your existing beliefs, you're going to add to your base of wisdom in profound and wonderful ways. Once you understand the concepts I'm presenting, then you have the power to define, choose, customize and adopt whatever beliefs feel right for you. This is my goal for you, to help you create an adult strategy for facing your stepmothering life challenges and to feel empowered and more like the loving, creative and talented woman you truly are, even when you're dealing with stressful stepfamily situations.

I'm asking you to be open enough to try out some of these concepts in your own mind. Test them. My intention is to expose you to new possibilities so that things within your heart, gut sense and mind can shift, flex and show themselves to your conscious mind. Remember that when you feel resistance, you know that you're on to something very good and helpful to your growth and well-being.

An Elephant Story
The Power of Beliefs

This true story illustrates how your early childrearing and resulting beliefs can impact and limit you until you consciously uncover and change them. As is the case with the elephant story I'm about to describe, the beliefs you adopt when you're very young have a continuing impact in your life when you're not aware they exist. On the other hand, once you are aware of any false beliefs you always have the power to change them and create more empowering beliefs.

When a baby elephant is born in captivity, a rope is tied around one of her back ankles and then fastened to the ground with a spike. When the sweet little thing tries to go with her mommy elephant or explore a new space beyond the length of the rope, she cannot. Because the elephant is just a baby, the rope holds even against her very best baby elephant efforts to free herself and go wherever she wants to go. Sadly, it only takes a little while for the baby elephant to give up, accept she can't free herself and stop pulling against the rope. From that moment on, for the rest of her life, as soon as the elephant feels the pressure of the rope on her back ankle, she automatically just stops in her tracks, no longer even bothering to tug at the rope, whether or not it is staked into the ground. For the rest of her long life, whenever she feels that pressure on her ankle, she stops trying to get to or get away from anything or anyone.

Think about how sad and unfair this training ritual is for the elephant. It's clear it offers handlers the ability to control this incredibly strong animal, but the elephant isn't free to use her own power to help herself. As soon as the elephant feels the pressure of the rope on her back leg, she stops herself from moving forward. If she realized what was happening or if someone helped her understand about (make her conscious of) her own increasing strength, she would realize that she had all the strength needed to easily pull that rope out of the ground and go anywhere she wanted to go. But tragically no one enlightens her and this beautiful, intelligent, powerful mammal is limited by something she learned as a baby and never thinks to question or test this as an adult.

For the rest of her life, she will be restrained if anyone ties a rope around her ankle, with or without a peg into the ground. The elephant believes she has no power over the rope because that was true for her as a little one. Because of her very real experiences as a baby elephant, it never dawns on her to test the rope again as she grows up.

I hope the truth of this story is churning things up within you. I hope it is awakening "ah ha's" as you begin to realize that you no longer have to abide by *any* of the beliefs created in your childhood—not a single one. As an adult woman, you're free to create your own rulebook of personal beliefs (yes really!) and free to change or delete any outdated beliefs that no longer serve your well-being. All this is possible once you realize you have this power and choice.

How does this story apply to being a Stepmom? Like the baby elephants, you've been conditioned by your parents, caregivers, teachers and other authority figures so that you were easier to manage and control as a baby and child. If there are situations where you find yourself feeling intense emotions (anger, pain, anxiety or fear) or recognizing certain patterns of feeling left out, powerless or disregarded, perhaps stopping yourself from speaking out or acting on your own behalf, chances are very good that you have some personal beliefs that compel you to impose these same limitations on yourself, without anyone saying a word to you. This elephant story is included because I've seen how power-limiting these child-created beliefs can be for stepmothers under stepfamily stress. I want you to know you have a choice. You have tremendous power when you're aware and conscious and I want you to know how to use it.

A variety of false and limiting child-created beliefs can result in stepmothers losing power, giving away power in exchange for being loved, or fighting for or denying personal rights just because of a belief that *"this is the way it's supposed to be in relationships or family life."* Because these foundational relationship beliefs are most often created when you're an infant or toddler, of course you forget them until you go looking for them. As a matter of fact, it may never occur to you to question these personal rules.

When something upsets you, do you automatically look to others as the cause of the problem? What would you find if you paused before blaming or judging and instead looked for the belief that may be contributing to your stress in a given situation? Maybe if you believed differently, the situation would not upset you. Maybe if you had a different belief, you would behave in a new way—confident in your ability to handle things well. Just like the adult elephant immediately stops moving forward whenever she feels the pressure on one of her back ankles, you may discover you're limiting or denying the full expression of your power, feelings and needs because childrearing circumstances taught you limits and you bought it. More than likely you unconsciously abide by these rules stored in your subconscious—no longer even thinking to test your strengths, adjust to the stepfamily circumstances or create new beliefs. Here are a few limiting, false beliefs that cause a Stepmom to lose or give away her power.

"The key man or person I love most in my life has the power to approve or disapprove of my actions."

"If someone I care about is upset, it's my fault. Or…it's none of my business."

"If the one I love most disconnects from me, I'm devastated and can't survive that happening."

"I give away my power so I can be included and connected."

"I believe that fighting for justice is worth the pain it causes my relationships."

"I honor my needs only after I take care of those around me."

"Honoring my needs or taking care of myself, particularly when others are upset by this, makes me a mean, selfish or rude person so I must not make choices that upset others."

How were the infant, toddler and "child you used to be" trained in an attempt to make you easy to manage? What beliefs can you uncover (make conscious) that might be causing you to silence your own voice or disregard your well-being in your stepfamily situation and your relationship with your partner? What current beliefs would you need to change in order for you to feel more empowered in your stepfamily life? How about creating new beliefs that better suit your adult needs today?

If you're interested in why you might resist the idea of giving up your resentments, please review Chapter 11.

If you want a refresher about understanding emotional resistance to increased self-awareness, go to smoms.org/BonusChapters.

Book recommendation for dealing with teenage stepkids: Anthony Wolf's fabulously insightful and practical book, *Get Out of My Life But First Could You Drive Me and Cheryl to the Mall?* It contains proven tactics for understanding and more effectively relating to any teens in your life. Even though it's not about stepchildren, it's the best book we've found so far for dealing effectively and compassionately with teens. If you have teenagers in your life, it's a treasure and a pleasure to read.

Susan's Story

July 2016

I entered my role as a stepmother with much enthusiasm, and with the deep, natural understanding that my husband's five-year-old twin sons both liked and trusted me. Even though my husband's ex-wife appeared to be full of anger and frequently acted out in emails and in court, I considered myself one of the lucky ones. Furthermore, and maybe most importantly, I was certain my love for and experience with other children in my life, plus lifelong guidance and love from my inspired parents and grandparents, would continue to help me sidestep the shadows of the suspicion and hate-talk I'd heard other stepparents so often experienced.

In those early days, I felt ready and willing to combat anything that could ever face our little family. My husband and I were on the same page when it came to handling his ex-wife—his email responses to her requests, attacks, and accusations were logical and matter-of-fact. We worked on them together, always doing our best to keep any emotion out of it. But even after years of us trying to ease the tension, she continued to shout at us in public, send harsh and irrational emails, speak cruelly about us in front of the children and their friends, and take my husband to court time after time after time.

With each court case, my husband and I put together huge black binders of correspondence and other documented evidence to demonstrate that her accusations were just more of the same exaggerated lunacy. Each time another wave of accusations came crashing down toward us, tens of thousands of dollars made their way from our paychecks to our lawyer. While we never initiated anything, we bravely stood our ground, working side-by-side to survive emotionally and financially, and to provide a warm, stable home for the boys.

By the time we'd been married for three years, and after a successful round of in vitro fertilization and the birth of a little girl, the pressure I felt to deal with my husband's ex had become unbearable. Although I knew my husband and I were a crackerjack team when it came to legal issues, I had nothing left to give when it came to our marriage. I was exhausted. On top of it all, my husband's nerves were raw, and he flinched at any provocation by his ex. I had started to say things like, "If you let her get under your skin the way you do, you might as well still be married to her," and "Let her go. Divorce her already." I was ready to move on and let go, no matter what venom came our way, and I was lonely and frustrated and feeling hopeless.

Day by day, I was accumulating mountains upon mountains of resentment toward my husband, and I wanted to get the heck away from it all. How could he still be giving so much energy and emotion toward a woman who wished us nothing but harm?

When no one was looking, I poked around the internet for any kind of help I could find. I can still remember my heart jumping into my throat when I stumbled upon a post about an upcoming stepparent resentment workshop through something called Stepmoms on a Mission, or SMOMS. I scanned the public-facing sections of the SMOMS website, hoping there was a nugget in there to help me feel a little more connected to hope. The more I read, the more I knew I wanted to register. But with all the legal debt we were facing, I thought, I had no right to even consider it. Every dollar was precious. What's more, I was too ashamed to tell my husband about the theme of the course. How could I tell him I was resentful? Would he think I wasn't trying hard enough? He'd be devastated, I thought. What a jerk I must be.

I thought about it for several days while I quietly devoured the conversations on the SMOMS boards. Eventually, I told my husband what I knew about the SMOMS group and asked if we could swing the small fee for the workshop. Could he watch the baby on Monday nights? He was both curious and supportive, thank goodness. I signed up.

Oh, how that workshop changed everything for me. On the call, listening to Cathryn's lecture and then joining in with her and the other participants for the live discussion, I felt like I was truly heard. I didn't feel like a whiner, or guilty for the resentment I was feeling. Instead, I got to know a small group of women who were facing their own challenges in the role of Stepmom. All the while, Cathryn stood by to help ground us in her firm belief that wherever each of us was, we could get to a better place. She challenged us to be vulnerable and then gave us the tools to build up healthy strength. She asked us to share the stories we were living, and then to imagine our ideal selves. On one particular Monday, when only a few of us could join live, I shared with the group that my husband's ex and her father had aggressively confronted me in person again and that I was frightened. The others had powerful stories to tell, too, and for the first time in several years, I experienced a breakthrough, suddenly feeling like there was still hope of a normal life no matter what was happening around us.

Thanks to Cathryn and my sister SMOMS, I realized that I could and should build boundaries to protect my sense of safety and my sanity, and to preserve my ability to be a good wife and mother. I regained my courage to face my marriage, and my resentment gradually faded. A year and a half or so passed and my family's challenges were beginning to become rather ordinary. I fell out of touch with the SMOMS group and pressed forward, feeling like I had the tools I needed for our day-to-day life.

But it wasn't over. In June 2015, our second little girl was born prematurely and my husband's ex filed a motion with the court claiming we were both abusing the boys. This was a first. In our most vulnerable time, with our newborn baby attached to monitors and oxygen and struggling to breathe, that crazy-making, selfish woman had attacked—this time, coming after me, too. Cathryn's voice was in my mind when I told my husband we could choose not to speak about court or his ex-wife while we were in the hospital. That baby needed us, I told him, and we couldn't afford to give any of our life force to his ex or her ridiculous accusations. We would fight it in good time, I said. And we would win—again. But not in that moment. Not until we were at home with our littlest one.

By the time our sweet fragile baby was released from the hospital, still on oxygen (as she would be for the next year), the ex had called Social Services on us several times, and the boys had started to act out toward us in ways we had never experienced. They shouted at us, cussed at us, and called us names. One of them began to speak cruelly toward his two-year-old sister, and my husband and I began to feel helpless again—this time in ways we'd never imagined. When Social Services came to our home, the boys told him that I'd hit one of them with a spoon. Fortunately, my mother and mother-in-law were in town to help with the baby, and they both attested to the truth.

Over time, speaking to various people, the boys' story changed several times—sometimes they said I had a spoon in my fist, sometimes I didn't, and sometimes it was a tablespoon or something else, striking a chest or a hip or a stomach—but the message was still the same: they were angry, and they believed what their mother told them about us being horrible people. I was crushed. How could they lie? How could they even believe me capable of what they were describing? In those awful days, with Cathryn's spirit beside me, I would often close my eyes to step outside of it all and regroup. I told the boys repeatedly that I loved them, no matter what, and I tried my best to push aside my desperate fear that someone would come and take my girls away. That old desire to run far, far away from the madness was back, only this time, what I was feeling wasn't resentment—it was black, dark, hopeless despair.

At the recommendation of the Social Services representative, my husband and I had cameras installed throughout our house. We then met with our attorney and requested a parental responsibilities evaluation, welcoming the chance to open our lives to strangers for an unbiased view. Surely someone, someday would see what we were going through and maybe we could get those poor boys the help they needed to feel balanced and whole again. We were surprised when my husband's ex-wife agreed to the evaluation.

Several months later, I sat outside of court while the proceedings went on behind closed doors. I was to testify, but not until several other witnesses had gone before me. The psychiatrist who had put together the parental responsibilities evaluation (which had proven to be squarely in our favor) testified on that first morning, and on his way out he said to me, "Be careful. [Her lawyer] is going to go for your jugular." I couldn't find my breath. Inspired, I sent an email to Cathryn from my phone, telling her I could use some positive thoughts, and she wrote back immediately, asking me to text her so we could chat. I did. She coached me through standing up there in the waiting room, breathing mindfully, and anchoring my feet in the ground in a position of strength. She then reached out to several of my sister SMOMS from the resentment workshop and reassured me that they were behind me. I could feel that they were. I felt sure-footed and empowered.

The next day, when I finally took the stand, opposing counsel asked me where I had gotten the list of books, articles, and videos about stepmothering, parenting, and personality disorders that we'd submitted into evidence. I told him I'd collected them over a period of several years. He asked me if I'd read or viewed all of them. I said I had. He asked if I knew anything about the psychiatrist's testimony from the previous day. I said I did not.

He said, "Almost all of these books are about borderline or narcissistic personality disorder, isn't that true?"

"No," I said.

"No? Yes they are, aren't they?" he insisted.

"The first third of the list is about being a stepmother or about parenting," I said.

"Well," he said, "many of these are about borderline or narcissistic personality disorders, aren't they?"

"Some are," I said.

"You believe that woman over there (indicating my husband's ex-wife) has one or both of these personality disorders, don't you?"

"I wouldn't know," I said. "I am not a psychologist or psychiatrist."

A Stepmom and Her Self-Awareness

"Isn't that why you consulted these resources? Where did you get this list?"

"I belong to a stepmothers' group," I told him.

In that moment, I could almost hear my sister SMOMS cheering. I could feel them circling behind me as I sat there in that wooden chair. "I talked with some of the other members about the behaviors I was seeing (the ex) display, and they recommended several of the books you see here. My husband and I wanted to get a better idea of what could be going on, what her perspective might be, and what we could do to help ameliorate our relationship with her."

I could tell the lawyer was getting flustered. He said to me, pointing to the ex, "You just wanted to blame her for everything, didn't you?"

But I didn't waiver. I continued, "As I said, we really wanted things to improve. So we read everything we could find and tried a million different approaches. Nothing worked. Her attacks and accusations just kept coming."

And then her attorney backed off. What I didn't know was that the psychiatrist who had evaluated our family environments had stated to the court that my husband's ex-wife was a narcissist and that she and her parents put constant pressure on the boys to believe that their father was a bad Dad, and that their sisters and I were awful too. I didn't need to diagnose her as a narcissist—it had already been done. The judge had heard it. And whether the ex could ever absorb or acknowledge it, she had heard it, too. This was the best my husband and I could do to shine a light on what we had been through, and to declare that enough was enough.

Before adjourning on that final day, the judge ordered the family therapy my husband and I were requesting, and with the therapist's help we are working on addressing the boys' confusion and anger. I am working on rediscovering my trust and love for them, too.

I still visit the SMOMS boards from time to time. Even when I'm not writing posts, I look up themes that reflect my own challenges and try to learn from others' experiences and responses. And I'm continuing to build upon what I learned from the resentment workshop—giving myself permission to feel, to tell my husband what I need, to create a safe space for myself and my thoughts, and to set and uphold those critical boundaries. Cathryn and my sister SMOMS changed everything for me, and whenever I've needed rescuing or even just a warm (virtual) hug, they have sent a light into those spaces where there was only blackness. I am more than I could have ever been without them – not just as a Stepmom, but as a human being, alive and awake and aware—and I am forever grateful.

Susan
Stepmom since 2010
SMOM since 2013

Nine

Use Your Stressful Experiences to Find Relief, Healing and Empowerment

While being a stepmother with challenging stepkids or an uncooperative bio-mom can be exceptionally painful and enraging, I've learned and seen that it's also a profound pathway to discovering and claiming your true power, and to healing your emotional wounds in the process. It can also lead to greater wisdom and the strengthening of your loving connection with your partner.

In this chapter, I'm going to explain the possible *why's* behind your intense feelings. Together, we'll explore how your beliefs and something called your emotional survival strategy contribute to your stress and your choices and can lead you to greater empowerment. I write this in hopes that it gives you a clearer understanding of what may be happening to you in your stepmother life situation. Ideally, may this give you a vision of the lifelong benefits that you can claim and embrace by understanding the sources of any crazy-making stress you're experiencing.

After hearing hundreds of stories and reading thousands more about how Stepmoms and their partners began their relationships, I'm convinced that we all fell in love with our partners for profoundly positive reasons. Most of us fell deeply in love, often quickly and beyond logic and reason, with a mutual knowing that we were meant to be a couple and trusting we can find value and lessons from each difficulty. My theory is that whenever we become more conscious of what we're feeling—and why—we have the chance to turn each stressful situation into a learning experience that makes us more aware, more empowered, more loving and more capable of honoring ourselves as we love and support our partners and stepkids. This is our mission.

I first drafted this chapter in 2014 in a spontaneous attempt to help a few sister SMOMS on the smoms.org bulletin boards who were really feeling at the end of their emotional ropes. They were eager to make sense of all the pain they were feeling. They were understandably furious that all their skills, energies, resources and good intentions weren't working or helping them feel better. And worse, they were tired of being blamed or judged as oversensitive for not being willing to let stepkid/bio-mom actions or issues go unaddressed. Many were feeling at odds with their partners and facing the heartbreaking possibility of losing their Happy Family Dream and maybe even fearing they might need to end their relationships with their beloved partners for their own emotional survival. If their relationships ended, it would not be because they fell out of love, but because they could no longer endure the excruciating pain, rage, drain on their resources, unending injustices, loneliness and despair that can set in from feeling unloved, neglected or even betrayed by their partners.

Like most of you, I've been down the whitewater rapids of many stepmother challenges right from the beginning of my Stepmom journey, which began in 1996. When Stepmoms make the efforts to wake up to new insights about themselves, learn new skills and realize their own ability to help themselves in all situations, miracles of lasting change and well-being spring up in their lives. I've seen it happen countless times. I have lived it, have helped others find it and believe you can find it also.

In order to understand why you may be feeling the way you do as a stepmother, it's essential to recognize the emotional coping strategies and beliefs you bring to the relationship. Your partner has his own set of issues, but for now, we're going to stay focused on you. So, let's start at the very beginning—your life as a little girl. While it may be initially unclear what this has to do with being a Stepmom, I ask you to settle in and think about this explanation and then decide.

The Foundation of Emotional Life

Every one of us comes into this world and experiences disempowerment. The degree of this disempowerment is inversely determined by the amount of attention, lovingkindness and respect our parents and caregivers give to us, our needs and our feelings.

Every one of us experiences the rage of feeling disempowered. We're all capable of feelings long before we can understand them intellectually or talk about them. Still, when we're babies and toddlers, many parents treat us like we're incapable of understanding what is happening or having feelings about things they assume we don't know. Silly in hindsight, but universally true. From birth, big people force little ones to do things *"for your own good,"* usually without regard for our feelings. Why? Because they believe they know better or it may be what their parents did to them, or maybe it's the opposite of what their parents did. Perhaps it's what the current childrearing experts tell them is best.

Growing up we have very little control over most of our circumstances. As a result, we all experience various degrees of rage, fear, neglect, disregard, manipulation, pain and many other upsetting things. Even if we have loving parents who are doing their best, when we're infants, toddlers, kids and teens we don't have the power to stop or change or determine most things in our lives. We're dependent on others and are impacted physically, mentally and emotionally by the way others treat us.

With amazingly keen insight, we somehow know we don't have the ability to help ourselves, right from birth. We instinctively and ingeniously use whatever skills we have available to create and endure circumstances as best we can. As babies, it may only be the ability to turn toward or away from something. It's the ability to cry, to scream, to smile, to sleep or to do nothing if some part of us gives up trying, resigned to a painful fate. As we grow, our capabilities become more sophisticated and we find new ways to express and help ourselves, again always doing the best we can. It's all about trying to feel safe, OK, loved and connected to other human beings.

When we're children, our sweet vulnerable baby/child self feels all these feelings but we usually don't have the ability to help ourselves as we would like to. Awareness of this inability to help ourselves leads to even more rage because it's caused by the awareness of our powerlessness.

The pain and fear we experience in these moments can be so excruciating that some wise part of our psyche knows when our baby/child brains and hearts just can't deal with it. At those times—and to keep us sane and alive—our psyche shoves those intense feelings into our unconscious minds where we don't have access to them at a conscious level. All that intense emotional energy waits in our unconscious until we become conscious enough to know it's there to be handled and are strong enough to feel it, learn from it and release all that pent-up emotional energy.

Every Child Creates a Strategy to Survive

Every. Single. Child. In order to survive any of the painful, scary, enraging, humiliating and despairing feelings that we experience in our childhood, we urgently search for ways to understand (explain to ourselves) our feelings to help us cope and find ways to live with these feelings. It is during these earliest moments of our lives when we begin to create beliefs about how things are, how things are supposed to be and why people do whatever they do. It's also when we begin to create beliefs about who we are, what love looks like and how we think, feel and talk about ourselves.

From birth to about 9 years old, we make ourselves the cause of any stressful circumstance because our little minds can't really understand how things can happen that don't have anything to do with us. Sometimes our little emotional hearts literally can't handle the truth (or impact) that the people we love and depend on for our lives aren't being loving, kind or respectful when we need them to be, or may not even want us there at all. It's just too much for a little one to let in and process. So to survive, we make up stories and create beliefs that make sense to us—drawing on natural creativity and whatever we know. We watch those around us and brilliantly develop a childhood survival strategy. Every human being does this to survive emotionally. Thankfully, because of their innate brilliance, most children survive their childhoods and become grown-ups. Here, I refer to grown-ups as an age-related term. I use the term adult to mean a grown-up who's conscious of her feelings, choices and actions to the best of her ability.

Think about this for a moment. A three-year-old child isn't equipped to handle the possibility that her mom or dad doesn't care enough about her to look after her with joyful lovingkindness. A five-year-old child can sense resentment and anger from a parent easily, but doesn't have the perspective and ability to understand that her parent might be angry at others, nor can she discern the degree of anger or danger. Because a child can't do anything to change her painful treatment, she convinces herself she somehow caused it all and therefore deserves to be treated this way. A child does this because making sense of circumstances feels somehow soothing.

At some deep level she also knows that she can't physically escape. She knows she can't survive without these giant powerful people. She also knows she has to find ways to get what she needs by getting their attention, to the best of her ability, so she won't die. Yes, it can feel that dramatic to a little one. She creates her survival strategy a little bit at a time based on trial and error, feedback and results. These experiences are also the cause of many fears and anxieties that can stay with us until we intervene by becoming conscious and more aware or until we wake up and see things clearly.

As children, in order to hold on to the hope of surviving, we may decide to believe that we're the one at fault for anything that upsets us. We may believe we're the reason others act as they do. We feel we're the reason they ignore or mistreat us or else we give up trying and decide that people treat us like they do because this is the way it is. For some reason, we feel compelled to invent explanations that make sense to us. For many, it's believing that it's our fault our parents aren't always kind, are unaware of our needs or don't take good care of us because it's too emotionally devastating to let in the truth or admit that we're out of control. To our baby/child's mind, if others don't treat us well, we end up feeling (then believing) we're not lovable or worthy or good enough. We also may believe that if we change somehow or in some ways, we'd feel OK, safe, connected and happy.

As we grow, we begin to realize that we have more abilities to do things for ourselves—things that may get us seen, fed, noticed, loved, touched, talked to or even out of harm's way. Perhaps we realize that we need to perform or pretend to get others to do things for us. Common goal? Survival! With each new option or ability we try everything we can think of at each stage of our development. We try our best because we believe it's the only way to survive physically and emotionally. We either keep trying in order to maintain hope that a pain-free, rage-free, anxiety-free life is possible or we may give up and endure life with a sense of resignation.

We Create Beliefs to Make Sense of Our Lives

As we find some success with our varying tactics, we usually forget that we're carrying beliefs we invented. We forget that we're the ones who decided, for example, that we're unlovable or need to earn love or avoid pain. We focus on doing more and more of the things that seem to be working for us with the people in our lives. Every time a tactic works, this reinforces our original false beliefs and strengthens our belief in the need for and effectiveness of our strategies.

By the way, beliefs like *"I'm not lovable"* or *"I can only get attention if I serve others"* or *"I have to give others whatever they want or I'll be rejected"* or *"I can't count on anyone but myself"* are all false absolutes, but even as grown-ups we're often so busy trying to feed our emotionally starved psyches that we don't realize they're only beliefs we made up. Unknowingly we reinforce patterns that we've continually repeated in our childhood and adolescence because we're unaware of any alternatives. As we grow up we also forget—or never realize—that we can change our beliefs anytime we want to. It's important to realize that as adults, we can absolutely create new beliefs—anything that's no longer working for us can be rewritten exactly the way we want it to be now. Adult-created beliefs always replace and override child-created beliefs. This is one of the most unknown and underutilized rights of adulthood. Chapter 8 explains my view of how beliefs and resentments are created.

So to summarize, as children we're all doing our best to survive. We're making decisions to the best of our abilities, and anytime we need to make sense of something we create a story or belief. These beliefs are in control of our choices until we become aware of them and decide to change them. As we grow up, we craft strategies that allow us to make sense of the way we're raised and treated. We're told by our parents, our relatives, our cultures, our schools and society how we're supposed to be, think and feel to avoid judgments, shunning, shame and punishment. We're told what behaviors and choices make us a good or bad child. We learn what gets us more (or less) of what we want or don't want. We're also forced, conditioned and even brainwashed to accept certain things as if they're the law or we'll face what feels like potentially life-threatening punishment. As children, we don't have the ability to discern degrees of punishment. If we don't comply, we can experience discomfort in many degrees of pain or rage. It's what happens to all of us. We remember when we were punished, and we make new decisions about what we need to do to survive. These tactics quickly become reflexes that we rely on, whether we're aware of them or not.

The good news? Your childhood survival strategy was successful. You made it to being a grown-up. The important thing to know now is this: it's time to retire your child-created strategy. Why, since it got you this far? Because until you wake up and realize that you're being driven by your childhood survival strategies, especially when under stress, you will repeatedly make decisions and react to upsetting situations in the same way you did as a child, just with more resources and more sophisticated tactics. If you look back at some of your reactions to stressful stepfamily situations, can you see (or feel) that some part of you is anxious and/or enraged that you can't seem to control and cope with things successfully, the way you used to before becoming a Stepmom?

It Worked Then, Why Not Now?

The statement below may be a shock to you at first. When I first read Dr. Alice Miller's books and learned about her theories, this statement startled me too. However, as soon as I began to explore this concept and apply it to myself, then to others, I found it to be true and remarkably helpful. In fact, this concept is one of the most important points of this chapter, maybe of this book.

The very same strategies that allowed you to successfully survive the disempowering and hurtful experiences of your childhood become the imprisoning, limiting and ineffective strategies you unconsciously employ (or default to under stress) as you face more complex situations in life as a grown-up.

The confounding thing is that many of the skills you used successfully growing up, or right up until you became a stepmother, now fail to bring you the same results when you face complex and difficult stepfamily life situations with your partner. The pain, rage, fear, loneliness and grief that you may be experiencing as a stepmother often runs deeper than the present-moment circumstances you're facing. Have you ever noticed that? The depth of so much emotion is due to many things that are built on and around two primary factors:

Factor #1: As stepmothers we often find ourselves feeling disempowered in our family situations. This creates feelings very similar to those we experienced as babies, kids and teens, and that were shoved into our unconscious minds way back when. I see our unconscious minds as giant warehouses of emotional energy waiting to be reclaimed. When feelings about a particular current situation align with and then tap into similar feelings held in your unconscious, these feelings can rush forcefully into your conscious mind and express themselves as extremely intense feelings. Sometimes they may even blast through you like emotional energetic projectiles. At first, it can be scary and shocking how much genuine emotional intensity you can experience from an event that may seem minor, even to you. It may seem initially illogical but only because no one has explained what's going on. However, on the day you understand what's happening, this very real emotional energy begins to make complete sense and reveals valuable personal insights. That day of understanding can be today. You can learn how to process your feelings practically and compassionately. Your feelings are real and don't just go away because someone judges you or tells you to "let it go."

Factor #2: The authentic rage of disempowerment or feeling disregarded, along with whatever else you're experiencing, goes to the heart of some very deep, very real emotions you're probably unaware you're carrying around. Hatred, rage, pain and fear become even more intense because you can't seem to figure out how to make them go away or use them to get what you want. The strategies that got you through childhood don't work anymore—what the heck? The same strategies that used to work—even right up to the time you became a stepmother—don't seem to work in your stepfamily situations. Have you noticed this? It's enraging, depressing and sometimes both. In our stepfamily world, it's upsetting when our defenses, distractions and strategies that we use to keep ourselves safe simply don't stop, fix or force our stepkids, their bio-mom, our partners (or the courts) to do the loving, fair or right thing that we believe they are supposed to do. Our tactics can't seem to make them do what they said they'd do or what we want them to do. This is the stuff of temper tantrums.

Whatever the causes, we may feel like we're tapping into a nuclear power plant of emotional energy. Something can happen and out of nowhere we react as if we're on fire. Maybe we become our version of the Incredible Hulk with very little compassion for anyone. Maybe we break something or maybe deep, gut-wrenching sobs wrack our bodies because we can't figure out why things are happening as they are. It can be confusing, scary, heartbreaking and sometimes damaging to our relationships.

What's a Stepmom to Do?

Thankfully there are many ways you can respond to your emotional experiences calmly, compassionately, competently and without judgment. Once you digest this chapter, it can be the beginning of a whole new life experience as a Stepmom *if* you're open to embracing this new understanding and overall approach.

Experiencing your feelings and facing the truth and insights about your reactions without self-compassion can set you up to be judged by those you love. When you're not caught up in feeling hatred or blaming others, you may feel the urge to harshly judge yourself. *"How could I do this? Why am I being so emotional?"* Not really a question, just a cruel dose of self-judgment. The following is a list of potential emotional states you may experience as a Stepmom under duress until someone shows you there are other more positive, empowered choices:

- Depression can set in when dozens (or hundreds) of upsetting experiences, like layers of unprocessed anger, get frozen within your psyche. Combined with self-judgment, these emotions can become too heavy to bear, weighing you down physically, mentally and emotionally.

- Anxiety can become a factor—and can even overcome you—if you're fearful of what (or who) might violate your boundaries next or hurt you at any moment. Living with this fear can feel like experiencing emotional terrorism. It can come out of nowhere, at anytime, and you don't know how to stop it.

- Eating, drinking, going onto the internet, shopping or working too much can feel like the only ways to give yourself relief or a feel-good moment. With food (often my go-to emotional supplement), you may be trying to feed your starving sense of self (or value) that's been neglected by others. Ironically it's also common that you may have also neglected yourself along the way because you were paying more attention to others than yourself. You may choose other addictive ways to feed yourself. It's not bad, wrong or stupid. It's human nature. It's survival. It's worthy of your loving compassionate awareness so you can find new healthy ways to help yourself get more of whatever you need.

- The numbing temptations of blaming, judging, feeling "better than" or self-pity can all be a substitute (conscious or not) for making responsible, adult, loving choices. You may choose these options when you don't believe you can handle (or free yourself from) your true grief, pain or sadness.

- The temptation to engage in controlling, hostile or even "wicked" behaviors can take over and harden your heart. This can happen because you don't know what else to do to protect your vulnerable core self and no one has ever shown you how.

- You may revert back to childhood tactics of isolation, withdrawal or silent rage because you don't know what else to do. You may do this now because some part of you believes it worked for you when you were a child. See the repeating pattern?

- Physical illness can manifest because the feelings are backlogged, compressed and denied, and can't find any emotional avenue of expression and release. Since it's all energy and energy has to move, it can show up in your body and try to get your attention in that form. Ideally you want to process this energy when it's still in your emotional realm and before it gets to your physical body. Wherever the tension is now, acknowledging, directing and releasing the energy will help you feel better in several impactful ways.

When you want to be a good Stepmom but nothing you're doing is working, it can be difficult to stay positive. Doing, trying, helping, doing more, trying harder, suggesting options and trying to help others can figuratively drive you into the ground. Why do you keep doing what isn't working? Probably because you're unaware that you're repeating the same patterns. You may feel that if you stop trying you'll be rejected, abandoned, disregarded or ignored—which some part of you thinks is too painful to handle or even survive. Further, if you accept the situation and stop trying, part of you may fear failure is the only option, which engenders more fear, rage, pain and maybe guilt and shame. One thing's for sure: all these feelings are too painful for *"the child you used to be."* The good news is that now that you're an adult, these feelings are *not* too painful to be handled by the woman you are now.

Tapping into your unconscious warehouses of unprocessed emotions can be fraught with discomfort, especially when you're not conscious of what's happening. But my ongoing message for all stepmothers is that when you choose to make conscious contact with your feelings and do the work to release all of your backed-up emotional energy, you'll be freed up to handle yourself in new ways. This allows you to be the relaxed, confident, talented, resourceful adult you naturally are when this unconscious warehouse of emotions is not triggered. It's about upping your game, becoming wiser and increasing your skill set—and it feels so much better than the old ways of handling things.

When I first learned about this process, it gave me great hope because of the immediate positive impact. Thankfully it also gave me an unexpected boost of energy to do the work I needed to do to get through my list of charged stepfamily experiences and reclaim my power over my own well-being. What can you do now? Below is a short list that may take a lifetime to master or maybe only days, weeks or months to get really good at. Whatever your timetable, you can begin to make changes now and feel better in your everyday life.

Be "Awake" as Often as Possible

- Learn to be more aware of what you're thinking and feeling in each moment by getting into the habit of asking yourself *how* you're feeling from moment to moment. Yes, it can be as simple as that. If you need a reminder, take advantage of technology to set timers or alerts to help you stay aware of your feelings. "Am I aware of how I feel now?" is an effective question.

- It's easy to feel like the wise, loving, adult version of your best self when you're comforting or solving a problem with a dear friend. Many women experience this adult feeling when we're in our "Mother Bear" energy as we stand up for our loved ones or an animal, or when we stare down a threat to something we value. Remember how it feels to be truly awake and competent, then tap into this whenever possible.

- Get good at separating the feelings of your present self from the feelings of the child you used to be and even the feelings of any other younger versions of yourself as well— including that newbie stepmother with a happy family dream or even the version of you from before you read this chapter. Curiosity is a great asset in this work.

- Begin to acknowledge, honor, love and have unconditional compassion for the feelings of the child you used to be in a new and respectful way. This is probably the single most self-respecting thing you can do to help yourself right now. In my view, when you embrace this approach you shift from being a stepmother to becoming a Stepmom on a Mission of empowerment. Giving yourself and your feelings this loving attention can make you feel differently (better) about yourself, your situation and your relationship with your partner. Many SMOMS feel this impact when they first find the website, talk with other members or work with me. Even doubters and skeptics discover and experience inner strength and relief when they give themselves the emotional support they've been lacking—and looking for—from others.

A Doable Challenge

Get clear about the components of your unique childhood strategies for dealing with stressful situations. Pick a current stepfamily situation that's upsetting. Now think about it in a new way. Slow down your thought process so you can learn about the sequence of each one of your thoughts and feelings. This is such a rich source of personal insight. As you reflect on your behavior in this situation, ask yourself these questions:

"Would I recommend that my best friend act this way if she were in the same scenario?"

"Was I feeling wise, awake and like an empowered adult when I reacted as I did?"

"If I were going to go through this situation again—if I had a do-over—where could I make different choices?"

"How could things have worked out differently, if I'd been different?"

If you do this work, you'll begin to see you've made many choices without realizing that you were making a choice or had any options. Slowing down your thought process and becoming aware of how it operates—and how it could operate differently going forward—is like discovering gold under your own chair. Who knew you were thinking and feeling so many things? Who knew you had so many choices? As you get curious and lovingly examine the choices and tactics you've selected, you'll also begin to see evidence and examples of how some of your past behaviors (when under stress) now look more like the work of a sophisticated, hard-working child.

In this new place of increased self-awareness, it's easy to feel foolish, embarrassed, ashamed or even pathetic or guilty about past behaviors and choices. This is why it's important to be even more compassionate, reminding yourself to make this a loving exploration rather than an exercise in self-judgment. It's the difference between having a nightmarish experience and creating a fascinating, sometimes magical personal growth adventure that results in a lot of new, useful information about yourself, enabling you to create a happier future. The more you know, the more powerful you'll feel, whatever the circumstances. I encourage you to make it a compassionate, fascinating adventure.

What Triggers Your Childhood Survival Strategies?

Here are a few questions you can use to uncover more about your childhood strategies. If you want more input, ask a trusted friend or loved one because their insights can be very helpful. Ask someone who you're certain will be loving and who truly wants to help you learn more about yourself.

- How do you handle it when people are angry with you? What do you automatically think? Feel? Do?

- When another person gets what they want (let's say your partner, stepkids or their bio-mom) but you don't get what you want, how do you feel? What do you say to yourself about the situation? How do you react?

- What do you do when someone violates one of your personal boundaries? Do you have different reactions to a boundary violation based on who the person is in your life? Do you rationalize or endure the violations of those you love?

- Think about a personal belief or boundary that was recently violated. How did you react? Do you have a consistent reaction? Did you speak up or stay silent? Did you express your feelings directly or assume the person involved would get the message based on your upset or angry behavior? Do you need a new boundary? What needs to change so you're willing to uphold it in the future?

- When your partner doesn't do as you want, what meaning do you give his actions? How do you explain his actions to yourself? How much effort do you (or don't you) invest to try to understand your partner's point of view?

- How do you initially react when someone wants you to do something that you don't want to do?

- Wtow do you handle the situation? How important is it to you to resolve the situation?

- Do you believe a mutually satisfying solution is possible for every situation? Is finding a solution worth the effort or not?

- Do you see disagreements as a battle where there's a winner and loser? If so, are you open to new viewpoint that results in win-win? Hint: look at your personal beliefs about right and wrong. See Chapter 20, Nobody's Right/Nobody's Wrong: A Tactical Approach for Intimate Relationships.

- Do you believe you're worthy of having equal rights in each of your relationships? If not, what are you telling yourself about a situation when you settle for less-than-equal rights? What beliefs keep you from expecting equal rights in each relationship?

Uncanny Similarities

You can push this exploration of your feelings and survival strategies even further if you're curious. Think back to what was going on for you when you were the same age as your stepkids—particularly the stepchild whose actions upset you the most. Time and time again, Stepmoms who do this exercise find themselves flooded with new memories that they didn't previously recall from their lives when they were that age. This is the magic of your mind. This is what happens when feelings and experiences move from your unconscious to your conscious mind.

When you ask yourself the previous questions and consider your limited perspective and survival mechanisms from when you were a child, the insights and "ah ha's" you discover/remember can bring you relief almost right away. This relief can border on miraculous, and it comes from no longer feeling crazy and having some (or many) of your past choices now make new and complete sense to you. As you remember feelings from your past experiences, compassion for the child you used to be can now flow freely, accompanied by even more feelings and often tears. Tears play an important role in emotional healing. Give yourself permission, space and time to cry. Grief and rage often release in waves. You will not cry forever—even if it feels that way or you fear that will happen. There will be lots of emotions to feel and honor and thankfully plenty additional waves of relief, even peace. If you're open to the possibility that this approach could be valuable to you, try it out. Be confident your psyche will only let you remember and retrieve emotions that you're ready to process.

Find the Value in Your Stress!

With a new awareness of the source of your intense feelings from the past—feelings that now make more sense and no longer make you wonder if you're going crazy—you're likely to feel a bit (or a lot) differently the next time that charged situation occurs. Yes, you'll still have feelings about each situation, but you're much more likely to stay awake and not let your reactions come between you and your partner. With ever-expanding self-awareness, new options and insights may start occurring to you right away, saving you countless hours of unproductive rage, pain, anxiety and anger that only intend to keep you upset without resulting in any actual release or relief.

By understanding that many (if not all) intense feelings generated by current circumstances are coming from as-yet unprocessed feelings from your past, you may find yourself being calmer about the situation. *"Oh my, there must be something important here for me to discover and process. I can handle my feelings privately. Right now I want to give my full attention to the current situation."* You can use your feelings as guideposts to exploring more about your own needs and unhealed issues—for your own benefit. One day you might even be able to silently thank your stepkids, their bio-mom or your partner for pushing you to your limits because it helped you to bust out of old patterns and discover more about your own strengths. If you're willing to work with your feelings, you'll find ways to improve your relationship with your partner and expand your self-awareness in more ways than you may be able to imagine right now. Hopefully knowing about these potential benefits makes it easier to choose to support yourself, dig in and discover the reasons for your feelings.

Take comfort and rest assured—there are very good reasons why you're feeling every single thing you feel as a Stepmom. When you stop unconsciously reacting to stressful stepfamily situations and start interrupting your childhood strategies and behaviors (which probably aren't working anyway and take a lot of your time and energy) you can begin to look at feeling upset as an emotional red flag that is trying to say to you, *"Hellooooo, please stop and look into this more deeply. There are some important emotions here that need your attention, acknowledgement and love. It's time for some new beliefs and boundaries and you have the power to make these changes."*

Unfortunately, until we realize that a loving path of self-discovery even exists, many of us just keep trying slightly different versions of the same childhood strategies over and over again. In the 1970's, Dr. Alice Miller called it "the unconscious compulsion to repeat" and describes it in her groundbreaking, phenomenally insightful and still controversial book, *The Drama of the Gifted Child*. (The book was originally titled, *The Prisoners of Childhood*.) I recommend it to those of you who want to know more about how this works.

Before selecting a potential therapist to help you with stepfamily issues and your personal growth, ask him or her if they're aware of Dr. Alice Miller and her work with healing childhood emotional wounds. If not, I strongly urge you to keep looking—that's how important and impactful her work (this work) can be on your healing and self-discovery process.

When we're under stress, most of us continue to do what we always did, even though it's not working. We may try a different flavor of the same thing, but do so with a child-like stubbornness and refusal to listen to anyone who suggests we stop or try something else. With the determination to get things to change, we continue to try in vain, which can lead to exhaustion, bitterness, resentments, martyrdom, depression, despair and a heartbreaking, invisible, ever-growing emotional wedge between us and our partners. This emotional barrier can make it very hard for us to feel the strong and powerful love that drew us into becoming a Stepmom in the first place. From my experiences and observations over the years, the love is still there, just buried under heavy, unacknowledged and unprocessed emotions that need your attention.

Is There Any Good News?

Yes! The good news is that you have the freedom and ability to learn from all the upsetting experiences you face as a Stepmom. Instead of going unconscious and deferring to your childhood strategies, you can now choose to stay awake, get curious, learn more about yourself and find new solutions that really can bring about more positive changes and lasting results. The benefits can start today!

More good news is that you have the choice to identify your childhood survival strategies with great compassion instead of with numbing judgment, shame or blame. Let's give your strategy some credit. Your childhood strategies worked. They are unique and ingenious, just like those of your partner. They helped you survive childhood situations. They got you this far and, in my view, deserve your respect and gratitude and now your farewell. Once you retire your childhood survival strategies, you can begin crafting a new adult strategy that almost effortlessly leads you to new choices, beliefs and skills, bringing about a greater sense of well-being and greater effectiveness in relationships.

Even more good news is that the most difficult part is almost over once you uncover the specifics of your childhood strategies. You've probably already felt so much pain, rage and fear—and you're still here. You've had to be very strong and brave for so long. You can now consciously redirect your energy toward finding more effective, healthy, self-respecting ways to feel better and more competent as the Stepmom you want to be going forward.

And some important good news—you can give your younger selves lots of kudos, compliments and respect as you retire your childhood survival strategies with gratitude. Your younger selves soak up praise and appreciation as much as anyone. Doing this in your imagination, as described in detail in other chapters, can have an immediate mood-boosting impact. It bears repeating—you can now replace the old child-created strategies with a new, consciously adult-crafted set of strategies for addressing stressful stepfamily situations that utilize your many wise gifts, talents and strengths.

A Stepmom Works This Empowering Process

The following is a true story of a Stepmom willing to try out this approach to get to the bottom of her rage toward something that occurs fairly often in her stepfamily life. She has since gotten to the bottom of several other upsetting experiences and as a result finds herself spending more of her waking hours feeling like her empowered adult self. Since she acknowledges and supports several younger versions of herself as part of this work, she feels much more compassionate (less harsh and judgmental) with herself and, surprisingly to her, more patient and empathetic with her own young children. This is an unexpected and welcome bonus of her excellent work. I hope this gives you a sense of how you can apply the process I explain in this chapter (and refer to elsewhere in the book) to any situations in your life that deeply upset you.

Step #1: Identify the Intensely Upsetting Event

Well in advance of each month, the Stepmom and her husband email a proposed custody schedule to bio-mom for her changes or approval. The Stepmom and her husband follow all agreements and then wait to hear back from bio-mom. They wait and wait—not feeling they can make plans until the schedule is agreed to by both parties. Days and sometimes weeks pass after the deadline and there is still no word from bio-mom. Grrr!

This lack of response (and waiting) makes the Stepmom angry and anxious while it only slightly annoys her husband. He keeps saying it "sounds about right" to him. After the bio-mom misses the one-week-to-reply deadline specified in their agreement, the Stepmom starts pressuring her partner to get an answer from bio-mom. He doesn't do anything because he knows it won't help. He knows his ex-wife and knows that reaching out will only extend their wait. Every time this happens (it happens a lot) the Stepmom feels a rage that even she knows is over the top, but when her partner tells her to "let it go and relax" she feels a sense of betrayal, alone in her feelings, criticized and even more angry at her husband. She doesn't know how to free herself from all this emotion. She wants to get to the source of these feelings.

Step #2: What Happened to Cause a Disproportionate Reaction?

Thinking about it, Stepmom realizes she has always felt upset whenever someone doesn't get back to her and keeps her waiting for a reply. She feels an intense anger and anxiety that keep building the longer she hears nothing from the bio-mom. However, her feelings reach new levels of intensity when the bio-mom repeatedly refuses to reply to them. To Stepmom's further frustration, when the bio-mom does respond, she either delivers bad news or gives no answers.

Step #3: What Are the Specific Feelings You're Experiencing?

The Stepmom wants to get to the bottom of this rage and anxiety so she decides to refocus on her own feelings. In that moment she realizes, much to her dismay, that most of her attention has been on judging and blaming others. So, what exactly is she feeling? She makes the following list:

"I'm feeling angry that the bio-mom is not following the rules about getting back to us within a week, as per the custody agreement."

"I'm feeling angry that she keeps doing this to us without any consequences to her."

"I feel angry at my husband because he won't even try to fix the situation."

"I feel sad and alone because my husband doesn't seem to care about how upset I am about this situation."

"I feel powerless (at her mercy) and that's enraging to me at a temper-tantrum level." (Her actual words at the time.)

"I feel hatred for this bio-mom for having the ability to impact (control) our personal plans by simply not replying."

Step #4: Identify a Younger Version of Yourself Feeling as You Do Now

Just checking in with herself, if she could imagine all her younger selves, starting with yesterday and back to being a baby, how old does she believe she is emotionally when she feels all this anger and anxiety today? As she sits there, pondering this question with her arms crossed and sort of pouting with her lip out, she realizes she feels about three or four years old.* She finds herself chuckling because she has a four-year-old son and now feels like she can better relate to his feelings.

*The age may be a guess and that's OK.

Step #5: Go Back Even Further in Your Memory

Once you identify an earlier age when your circumstances generated these same feelings, keep tracking back and search your memory for being even younger and feeling this same way. This conscious choice to seek out more info is when the conscious part of your mind (the only part of your mind with the power of choice) can seek info from the subconscious and unconscious parts of your mind and bring it back into your consciousness.

In searching her memory, Stepmom remembers hearing about her temper tantrums from her mother. She decides to call her mother and ask her more about these tantrums. After their conversation, Stepmom sits there a bit stunned at what she has just learned. Because she's newly aware of the issues of childhood survival strategies and the unconscious compulsion to repeat from being part of our workshop, she begins to realize the source of her seemingly disproportionate rage when someone leaves her hanging, so to speak, without replying. Her anxiety now makes sense to her. She begins to sigh a lot. By the way, sighing can be a healthy physical release of emotional tension when done consciously. This Stepmom learns the following things:

- Her mother tells her that when she was about three, she began having tantrums whenever she was asked to wait for something she wanted.

- Her parents' response, based on what they believed was the best way to handle it, was to send her to her room, lock her in and ignore her pleas and cries to be let out, never telling her when she could come out.

- Sometime after she stopped crying, her parents would come into her room, scold her (perhaps shame her) again and deny her a treat or activity as her punishment.

- Immediately after dolling out the punishment, her parents would say that it was time to move on, granting her a clean slate and acting like it never happened—refusing to acknowledge any of her feelings about the incident and requiring her to put on a "happy face."

- Her mother tells her this with the still-confident attitude that this is what good parents do. They did it for her own good.

As the Stepmom sits there thinking about this, she is flooded with memories of feeling exactly the same way about her parents (then) as she feels about her stepkids' bio-mom (now). She is angry her parents wouldn't give her something her three-year-old self believed she deserved, when she wanted it. She is enraged because she knows she was at the mercy of her parents and powerless to help herself—she couldn't open the door or get what she wanted without them. She suddenly remembers sitting on her bed staring at the door, feeling alone, without any sense of time, not knowing when they would come back in or, even worse, how she would be punished. For a child, this waiting and isolation is excruciating emotional stress, and this experience was repeated throughout her childhood over and over again—"for her own good"—without compassion or regard for her feelings and the impact of this behavior on her.

It now makes complete sense to her that every time she was sent to her room, there were a lot of feelings that were never processed or acknowledged and comforted. That's a lot of emotional energy she now realizes was sent into her unconscious, just waiting to be felt and processed. She sees how the circumstances were different but the feelings she has are the same. With her new awareness, it now makes sense to her why bio-mom's behaviors, just annoying to someone without a history like Stepmom's, is much more explosive for her. She finds herself relieved that she isn't crazy and that she is just beginning to understand herself and her emotions in new ways— ways that explain a lot to her.

Step #6: Comforting the Child You Used to Be

This next step, which she knows to do and already senses is going to be emotional, turns out to be a big deal for this Stepmom. As suggested, she closes her eyes and goes to a safe place in her imagination where she can invite that three-year-old version of herself to join her. She is skeptical about this part but is willing to give it a try because she has listened to other Stepmoms in the workshop describe their experiences.

To her surprise, she easily imagines seeing herself at age three. As this younger version of herself comes running toward her, she flings herself into the adult arms of this Stepmom. It is now like watching a movie for the Stepmom, even though she knows she is imagining this. The little girl is alternating between being angry and sobbing deeply about how scary it was to be left alone in her room not knowing when she was going to be let out and afraid of her punishment. This little girl is furious and so the Stepmom reflects her anger and understanding with words like, *"Of course you're angry, no one likes to be trapped!"* and *"That was so mean of them!"* The sensation of solidarity and power is palpable. This little girl was still furious, waiting to be acknowledged, and now her feelings are being respected and responded to as the most important issue of the moment. The Stepmom gives "the child she used to be" her complete loving attention. This is what children don't always get when the events actually occur.

This Stepmom is doing her best to validate and comfort this imagined younger self by encouraging her to keep talking and sharing her feelings. All the while, this adult Stepmom continues to make supportive comments and comforting sounds—all within the realm of her imagination.

Sadness follows the anger and the child begins sobbing. As the Stepmom holds her in her imagination, she realizes she is crying too. The tears seem to be coming from a very deep place and it feels like a relief and a release. For the first time, she becomes aware she is experiencing the ability to feel the feelings of the "child she used to be" *and* also consciously offering support as the adult woman she is now. It is initially odd but as she keeps her eyes closed, staying in her imagination, she finds she can consciously go back and forth between the thoughts and feelings of both her younger self and her present adult self. It is a profound moment for her to feel the two different sets of feelings.

Once the child stops crying and is only sniffling, the Stepmom begins to talk, offering her words of validation and support—words she'd needed to hear but had never heard from anyone. She wipes away the tears from her younger self's cheeks, looks into her eyes and begins to talk with her in a very loving tone.

"Oh Honey, you've really been through a lot. I'm so, so sorry this happened to you. It was scary and I can see why you're really really mad about feeling trapped and alone. I understand how you feel. I really do. It's awful. I want you to know that, starting today, I'm right here for you if you ever need me. It must have been so hard but it's going to be OK. I'm here for you now. You're not alone in your feelings, not anymore, not ever again."

As the Stepmom offers her comforting words, she becomes aware of how confident, strong and wise she feels while she comforts this younger part of herself—much like she did her own children. She becomes aware of how protective and compassionate she feels toward this little girl she used to be. She realizes that in all the stepfamily situations that upset her so much, it has never occurred to her to honor or comfort any of her younger selves. She feels a wave of remorse about that and makes a promise to herself to change that part of her emotional life.

As she finishes up, she is also aware that the child in her imagination seems to be comforted. After expending so much energy, the child in her imagination calms down and brightens up while being listened and talked to, understood and given loving attention. She realizes that she can help herself this way anytime she, the adult, needs support. The Stepmom has a brief moment of wondering if she is crazy, but the deep resonance of her feelings tells her this was real—just a brand new way of sorting out, experiencing and processing her feelings.

Just before ending her session, she promises her younger self that she will check in and pay attention to her, going forward. Then she gets the idea to ask her younger self if she would like to have a treat before they say good-bye. With a joyful look on her face, the child asks for a giant bowl of ice cream as her dinner. Ha ha! They both laugh and the Stepmom realizes she is actually laughing out loud. The Stepmom pulls a giant bowl of ice cream out from behind her (it's your imagination so things like that can happen), gives it to the child and sends her off with a kiss and a wave. As she watches the child move out of sight, she takes a few deep breaths, tries to remember everything that has just happened and opens her eyes. Wow! All that in 20 minutes of imagining.

Step #7: Back to the Present: How to Respond?

After this incredible session, all in her imagination, the Stepmom really feels like she has changed. Something has definitely shifted. She realizes that she is now feeling a lot more empathy and compassion for both her adult and younger selves over this issue of not hearing back from people. She now understands why she feels both angry and anxious when this situation occurs. Even though she knows she has more work to do with her past warehouse of feelings, it feels so freeing to realize that she can do this work consciously instead of needing to be so reactive to current events. It feels like she has reclaimed more control over her feelings and her well-being. She even surprises herself by thinking she can handle this situation when it happens again, this time in a new—dare she even think it—relaxed way.

A bit hesitant yet very excited, she tells her husband what she has done and all she has learned. When she is relaying her experiences with her three-year-old self, she begins to cry again and this time her husband pulls her into his arms and holds her until the tears stop on their own. It is another wave of healing and relief the Stepmom had not expected. Afterwards she feels even better and closer to her husband for supporting her so lovingly. This new shared knowledge and resulting compassion seem to dissolve the tension between them from past experiences and somehow an unspoken forgiveness, later expressed, happen naturally for both of them. It feels like a triumph for the couple.

Now that she realizes the important *why's* of her behavior when others don't reply to her, what can she do differently in the present to better support herself? How can she help herself feel more empowered when the actions of others trigger this tender place? To her surprise, she also realizes that it doesn't feel as tender to her anymore. She knows she is free of old emotions and believes she can now handle the situation as a conscious adult. Part of her is even eager to test her theory—that is another surprising feeling.

Step #8: What Can You Do Differently Now That You're Aware of Your Feelings?

After sharing all her feelings with her husband, he comes up with an idea for future emails about the schedule requests. He suggests they add a line to the end of each proposed schedule that goes something like this: *"Please give us your feedback in the next two weeks (twice the allotted timeframe in our agreement). If we don't hear back from you by then, we'll assume the schedule is OK as suggested."* Wow! The relief that this Stepmom feels at this suggestion is like a wave of joy flowing through her. Yes! She can wait two weeks to know the schedule. Her husband is coming to her rescue (from the little girl's viewpoint) and she is very grateful. No more fighting about delayed responses. No more anticipating fighting about delayed responses from the stepkids' bio-mom. It is a relief for both of them.

She decides not to make any plans for the coming month until the monthly schedule is finalized, overtly or by default. She realizes that in the past she used to plan things for the time they were supposed to have the stepkids (according to the agreement) but that this has only ever set her up to be anxious or potentially upset if things change, which they almost always do. It is another smart move that saves her lots of future anxiety.

She makes a promise to herself that anytime someone doesn't get back to her in a timely manner, she will honor her feelings by comforting herself and any younger version of herself who is also triggered or upset. As an adult, she knows that everyone isn't trying to upset her by not replying immediately. She knows, again as her adult self, that everyone has their own timetable for replying and that she is not going to be punished whenever they do reply. She also knows that the child she used to be is not an adult and doesn't understand these things so she can use comforting self-talk or go into another session in her imagination whenever needed. She is also conscious that when she feels those old twinges of anger and anxiety, she simply needs to picture that little girl she used to be and comfort her, which comes very easily to her now that she can differentiate between her adult self and her younger selves.

As a result of her new awareness and skills, the first thing she does is to pause when someone doesn't reply in a timely manner and she begins to feel upset. She then works to get clear on the difference between what she's feeling about the current situation and what's coming up from her past (recent and childhood). This conscious step saves her from so much reactionary anger and she makes a point to congratulate herself for staying "awake." She and her husband are delighted (and relieved) to discover that the intensity of her anger and anxiety is drastically diminished whenever the bio-mom doesn't reply.

Step #9: Epilogue—How Things Change for This Stepmom

The next few schedule requests include the new tagline at the end of the email. The stepkids' bio-mom never comments on it nor gets back to them with an OK before the deadline. She only replies when she wants a change, and that is OK for the Stepmom and her husband.

Stepmom feels back in control of her life again. No more giving the actions of the bio-mom—or in this case, inactions—her attention, energy or the power to rob this Stepmom of her well-being. It is an emotional victory.

From this point forward, this particular non-replying behavior almost never upsets her—at least not too much or for too long. Each time it occurs she brings her attention to herself, then comforts herself and her younger selves very quickly until one day, many months later, she realizes she is almost neutral about this behavior. Her husband is very impressed (and appreciative) with the change in his beloved wife since he knows this behavior from his ex-wife and others will continue. The Stepmom is also excited because since doing this work she is finally able to fully embrace the "sounds about right" approach that she once actively resisted in the SMOMS workshop. Maybe she resisted it because she needed to figure out what was going on with her younger selves first? Whatever the reason, she now feels free of any negative impact from this behavior. This is great work by this determined and open-minded Stepmom on a Mission.

Use Your Imagination to Process Your Feelings—A Recap

The previous example illustrates how this process can be effective when you're willing to explore your feelings and look into your childhood to find the unprocessed emotional energy that needs your attention. It's a chance to honor those old yet intense feelings and help yourself in new ways. If you feel drawn to this work and you want to get to the bottom of your own charged emotional situation, here's a review of the process:

1. Identify the intensely upsetting situation or behavior. Precisely what occurred to move you from feeling OK to not feeling OK?

2. What exactly is it about the specific circumstance that generates this disproportionate reaction?

3. What are the very specific feelings you're experiencing?

4. When can you remember feeling exactly the same way as a child or teen? How old were you? What can you remember about the circumstances?

5. Now go back even further in your memory. What is the earliest memory you have of feeling this way? Ask older family members for more info if you can trust they will be truthful and kind—in other words, honest.

6. Create some private time (30-60 minutes at first) to have a meeting in your imagination with that young child you used to be. Make it as vivid as possible. Find a photo of you at that age to make the visualization even more realistic. Meet that child in your safe place, her childhood bedroom or anywhere that feels right and safe. Ask her how she's feeling about the situation, then listen. Give her your full attention, seek to understand and validate her feelings.

7. When the child stops talking or asks you for help, speak to her in your most loving, supportive, comforting, protective voice. Comfort the child you used to be the way you wish you had been comforted. At some point, as hard as this may be to believe, she will cheer up, get happy, relax and be ready to go off.

8. Bring your attention back to the present situation. Review what happened so you can get clear about the difference between feelings from the past and those generated in the present. What can you do differently to better support yourself when this circumstance occurs in the future? What can you change in your choices? How can you support the younger versions of yourself?

9. Going forward, what can you do to help yourself remember to stay conscious of differentiating between your adult feelings vs. the feelings of the child you used to be? Sometimes it's enough to interrupt the intense reactions by simply asking yourself, "What am I feeling about this situation as the adult? What is the child I used to be feeling?" As you get good at this, answers will come naturally and quickly.

Mobilizing the emotional energy stirred up by your feelings in this new way will change things for you in many positive ways. It will change how you respond to the actions of others. It will change how you relate to your partner, your stepkids and the actions of their bio-mom. You will realize that you have the ability to craft a new happy family dream with your partner that you can implement and experience. It may not look like the original one, but it will be glorious and achievable. You will also become your most awesomely wise version of yourself, getting better with each new self-revelation.

I've been consciously following this specific strategy since 2007 and teaching it to stepmothers since 2009. With countless stories like the example I've shared with you, I passionately believe that being a stepmother can provide an amazing opportunity for healing emotional wounds that we have brought into our relationship—wounds that are reactivated by stepfamily situations and relationships. I believe stepmotherhood gives us experiences we can use to claim our authentic gifts and reclaim lost power, while clearing the way for a happier life with our partners.

See Chapters 14 and 29 for two more examples of this process. See Chapter 18 to learn how to work with your partner when your individual strategies for handling stepfamily-related stress conflict with each other.

The Ultimate Goal

This emotion-processing concept and approach can help you better understand your reactions to certain situations so you can face these same situations in the future with less anxiety, less bracing for an argument with your partner and more compassion for yourself. When you become more aware of the emotional energy you've not yet acknowledged or processed (and that you have held in your unconscious), you can give yourself relief and newfound emotional strengths that are tremendous—really beyond words. You'll know it when you feel it and it's a thrill! While going into the safety of your imagination to experience long-forgotten feelings, you also learn new and effective ways to support yourself by becoming your own best friend, mothering yourself the way you wished you were mothered and benefiting from your own wisdom and kindness. Can you imagine how that could feel?

From what I've learned personally and experienced with so many SMOMS, it's now my strong belief that if you do this work, you'll eventually be able to handle whatever's going on in your stepfamily life. This will be possible when you go to work with your best, most creative and most adult skills, resources and strengths. You'll find yourself responding to the previously upsetting actions of others from a wiser, calmer and more confident perspective. This ever-growing competence and compassion replace the old reactions of anxiety, fear, anger and rage. Instead of needing others to change so you can feel less stress and more peace of mind, you'll begin proving to yourself that you're capable of helping yourself in all situations. This is the reward for your hard work. This is self-empowerment.

Please see smoms.org/BonusChapters and click on the title "Your Three States of Consciousness." In this chapter, I review my understanding of how we can use the terms Conscious, Unconscious and Subconscious when working with our thoughts and feelings. For a complete list of additional free bonus chapters on the website, see Chapter 39 in this book.

Section Two

A Stepmom Working with Resentment

A student of Shantideva, an eighth-century Buddhist monk, was upset by how traveling the roads and terrains of the world were hurting his feet and causing him great pain. The student came up with a solution to end his suffering and wanted to share his idea with his teacher. He explained that if he covered the entire surface of the world with leather his feet would never be hurt again. With a kind smile, the monk replied, *"Your idea requires much time, effort, expense and leather. What about just wrapping your own feet in leather? With this approach you can walk on whatever surface you encounter without pain or suffering."*

~ Author Unknown
Quotes paraphrased

Calla's Story

July 2016

When I became a Stepmom in 2007, I was determined to be the best one ever. I went to a blended families class and read many books about blended families and parenting in general. I didn't have my own children yet and I was excited to jump right into a mothering role. My little two-year-old stepdaughter was sweet and amazing, and I naïvely thought I could step right into this family and live happily ever after. However, I soon found out that being a Stepmom was not like I imagined, and difficult situations began to arise with my stepdaughter and her bio-mom.

I realized that I had absolutely nobody to turn to for advice. I was in my twenties and none of my friends had children, let alone stepchildren. I searched for online forums where I could get support from other stepmothers while I learned how to navigate this new life. It turned out that all I found online were very angry stepmothers very hatefully complaining about their stepchildren, but unwilling (or not knowing how) to change things. That's not how I felt. I loved my stepdaughter but wanted to learn how to get through some of the trickier blended family situations. I ditched those groups and felt alone. I was on my own and found my own way.

Years later, I found myself overwhelmed. I was working part time with my stepdaughter living with us half the time. I now had three young children of my own and a husband who wasn't much help when it came to anything with the kids—yet. At the time, my husband and my stepdaughter's bio-mom both consistently dropped the ball on encouraging completion of homework and self-care. This left me feeling as though I was solely responsible for teaching my stepdaughter how to follow a morning routine, such as getting dressed in the morning, brushing her teeth and putting her shoes on. If she got a bad grade or a cavity, I felt that I had failed her.

As the years went on and I was spread thinner and thinner, I began to feel resentful. I was resentful of my husband who could sit around while I took care of everything. I was resentful of my stepdaughter because no matter how many great things I did with her and how many skills I taught her, her vastly different life at her mom's house seemed to erase any influence I had. Also, my relationship with her was suffering because I had all of the parenting responsibility for my stepdaughter without the reward of her love. Even though I had been stable in her life since she was under two years old, to her, I was not a parent. It didn't matter how many special outings we went on together, how many games we played or how much time I spent playing with her. She only saw me as the person who made her brush her teeth, change her underwear, brush her hair and pick her clothes up off the floor.

In the fall of 2014, I was broken. I searched online again for help—for some glimmer of hope—and somehow I stumbled across Stepmoms on a Mission (smoms.org). I have no idea how I didn't find them in 2007. Based on past experiences with stepmother forums, I was hesitant to join, but when I did, I instantly felt at home with the other forum members, my fellow SMOMS. These were women who cared about their families, including their stepchildren. They didn't want to complain. They wanted to make changes. Shortly after I joined, I had the opportunity to take Cathryn's resentment workshop. It was nine weeks of hard but fulfilling work with several other women determined to find ways out of the stressful situations of being a Stepmom. I was determined to learn how to take back control of my life.

Cathryn taught me things that I didn't even know I didn't know. She taught me how to break down problem areas so that I could tackle the root of the problems instead of just putting a bandaid on top. Cathryn also taught me how to figure out which things in my life are worth my energy and which things can't be changed and need to be let go. She then taught me how to let those things go and feel empowered in making it my choice. I am still a work in progress in this area—letting go of control tends to be hard for me. Since the resentment workshop, I still have issues that come up that I need help with, but I have never again reached the point of despair. I have skills in my pocket now. When I come across situations I've not yet learned how to handle, I know where to go for help: Cathryn's articles or Cathryn herself.

I've been a SMOM for two years now, and while being in a blended family is still difficult, I am much happier than I used to be. One of the biggest lessons that I learned from Cathryn is that although we can't change other people, we can change ourselves and our perceptions. With Cathryn's guidance and my determination to do the work to make changes within myself, I now have a husband who helps out with the kids and the housework. I also decided I needed to take a big step back from my stepdaughter's daily routines and schedule.

When I talked to my husband about my new role, my husband agreed to step forward. He now reminds my stepdaughter to start homework each night and checks it when it's finished. He makes sure he knows her school and vacation schedules and makes alternate arrangements when they are needed. He finally started noticing if she brushed her teeth or hair or had the same dirty clothes on as the day before. Since he is her dad, she loves him unconditionally, even though he is expecting the same out of her that I used to. Now that I have someone to share the responsibility with, my resentment toward my husband and stepdaughter has passed. I no longer have to spend my energy worrying about things out of my control and I can focus on enjoying my time with my kids and stepdaughter.

I would like to continue to strengthen my relationship with my husband. We don't argue about much, but when we do argue, it's often about the same issues over and over again—all relating to stress and high emotions over my stepdaughter's bio-mom. I've come a long way, but I'm not finished yet. I still have work to do with Cathryn. I would like to strengthen my relationship with my stepdaughter. I would like to have neutral feelings about my stepdaughter's bio-mom, rather than anger and bitterness when I hear her name. It's so much better than it used to be, and now I believe I can learn more skills and truly get past all these uncomfortable feelings.

I'm grateful that I became a SMOM and met Cathryn and all my wonderful fellow SMOMS. These women are an amazing source of support in my life. Without finding smoms.org I would still be struggling with no light at the end of the tunnel. Those of us who are Stepmoms understand that being a Stepmom is hard work, even when everything is going relatively well. At smoms.org we help each other remember that we're strong, capable, loving women and that we have the tools to tackle any obstacle that gets in our way.

Calla
Stepmom since 2007
SMOM since 2014

Ten

Are You Over-Giving to Your Partner and Stepkids?

One trait Stepmoms on a Mission share is being generous in so many ways, to so many people. Generosity is expressed by giving time, attention, money, possessions, effort, patience and compassion to others. Giving to others has been viewed as a positive quality for as long as most of us can remember. The bad news is that giving too much to others, what I'm calling over-giving, can lead us down a painful path of feeling resentful, financially stressed, taken for granted, alone, without resources to take care of ourselves. We may even be treated unkindly by recipients of our acts of giving and doing.

When you're feeling resentful or drained of your own life force and resources, taking some time to consider your motivation to give—with honesty and compassion—can bring valuable insights. Over-giving is a pattern that begins in childhood that usually starts as a belief about needing to do something to get love, be seen, to feel like a good person or to avoid getting in trouble. Sorting through your personal "shoulds" will show you where you can stop over-giving and start crafting your own personal sense of what I'm going to call "natural giving."

Natural giving brings you balance, joy, energy and a sense of well-being. It's sustainable giving because even though you're expending your resources and energy, these acts of giving bring you a self-fueling, self-satisfying feeling and sometimes a genuine return of energy from others. Natural giving is an antidote to resentment.

Over-giving is on the other end of the giving spectrum. When you over-give, there's an imbalance of exchange that depletes you. Over-giving creates resentments and upsets your physical, emotional and mental energy and health. It's a bummer and sadly a common one for a Stepmom who was once genuinely eager to give and do so much for her new stepfamily. It's also a slippery slope to martyrdom and self-pity, which is bad news for everyone involved.

The purpose of this chapter is to offer you encouragement and methods to engage in less over-giving and more natural giving. To shift this balance, you can start by examining your conscious (and discovering any unconscious) reasons for giving and doing. As you look into your many possible motivations, the goal is not to judge or criticize yourself, but to become more conscious of the answers to these questions:

"Why am I doing this?"
"What am I expecting in return?"
"How do I feel after I give (or do) this?"

There are many possible answers to consider. There are also revealing and helpful insights to learn about yourself in the process. Let's get started. It's empowering when you make a conscious choice to do something vs. when you act out of an impulse driven by habit, reflex, fear, beliefs or a sense of obligation. The more aware you are of your motivations *before* actually giving or doing for others, the more likely you are to interrupt old patterns and make different, wiser choices. As you become clear about your expectations for your giving, you'll experience more calm and less distress. The more you understand about why you act as you do, the less likely you are to be hurt, disappointed and resentful. Also, chances are greater that you're going to feel better, more balanced and happier in your life. That's a lot of good reasons to get good at natural giving.

Homework: If you're up for it, start a list of all the things you're giving and doing for others. The more detailed the list is, the better. You may be surprised by all the ways you're giving of yourself and your precious life resources. When you reflect on your list, check in with yourself to see which acts of giving or doing make you smile and feel energized and which ones make you feel upset in any way. Doing a gut check is also a very effective gauge of how your giving impacts your well-being. There's something about looking at a list vs. just thinking about it that can help you see more clearly where you may want to make some changes to feel better.

Why Do You Give to Others?

There are lots of possible motives for giving to others. The actual things you do are far less important than the reasons *why* you do what you do. It's also important to understand any expectations you hold about what you should receive in return for your giving or doing. What are your motivations for giving (and doing) for others? Here's a list of several possibilities:

1. Giving with the expectation of getting something back, or in exchange for your giving.

    The power and impact that this type of giving has on you is in the hands of the recipient. Balanced giving and receiving is a satisfying exchange and a positive experience. Not getting back what's expected, even if it's just wanting and not getting a simple "thank you," can be very upsetting.

2. Giving because of any kind of "should" belief you hold.

    In your mind, a good Stepmom should do—x, y, z. Or, you feel implied or spoken pressured to give. Or you're competing to keep up with bio-mom or other mothers. Maybe you want to avoid negative judgments by others or even the wrath of harsh self-talk.

3. "Giving in" to avoid consequences you fear or dread in some way. This kind of giving almost always leads to resentment and feeling pain and rage.

4. "Giving up something" with the expectation of eventual reciprocal giving up.

    "I gave up something I wanted for you, now you have to give up something you wanted for me." This is a common tactic I call testing and proving love. It is hurtful and has been creating martyrdom and resentment since the Stone Age.

5. Giving in response to unspoken, tacit requests that you assume, know, believe or sense are being asked of you—without ever checking it out. This request can come from lots of places: cultural and religious customs, family traditions and societal pressures to give and do for others as a woman, wife, mom, daughter, friend, homemaker and stepmother. This is one of the most straightforward causes of over-giving. Just because others want you to do for them or because it was done like that for generations does not make it the law in your world. Seriously. You're an adult now. Are you willing to believe you can break old rules and make your own? How would your choices differ if you did only what you wanted to do?

6. Giving to avoid, compensate or cover for any guilt or the belief that you owe a debt to another.

Many stepmothers start out doing too much because they're unaware they feel guilty for being happy, while the stepkids, bio-mom and even their partner may still be grieving or suffering because of the divorce. Often stepmothers want to help and give, give, give of themselves because they want their partner and stepkids to be as happy as they are. Stepmoms want to start living their version of the happy family dream as soon as possible. This is completely understandable *and* can be very draining. Furthermore it rarely works and is a breeding ground for resentment when the giving is not balanced with receiving.

7. Natural giving of yourself and resources is an expression of who you are, because the act of giving is self-fulfilling or self-satisfying in some way.

    This kind of giving is not driven by fear or expectation. It's an expression and sharing of your authentic feelings. Natural giving doesn't require external feedback. Sure, feedback is appreciated, yet viewed as a bonus—nice but unnecessary. Natural giving is powerful and sustainable because it's a self-contained, fulfilling (not draining) experience of giving and receiving energy for the giver.

What about you and your motivations for giving? As you review this list of possible motives and then review the list of things you're doing and giving to others, can you assign a motivation to each act of your giving? As you think about your motivations, do you see a pattern? Can you see—or maybe even feel—the difference between when giving is natural and when it crosses into over-giving?

Your giving and doing is often habitual, well-worn or reflexive. Because of this, you often can't see what's going on until you slow down your thoughts, stop reacting and consciously explore your intentions, beliefs and expectations. As you bring your attention to each act of giving and doing, it will be a much more interesting adventure if you suspend your judgments as best you can.

Behavior Has Meaning

We do and say whatever we do and say for darn good reasons. Your reasons are worthy of your curiosity and consideration. As you take responsibility for your past choices, you can also own that you made the choice to do or give to others. Whatever you discover was your motivation—it's OK. You were doing your best at the time and hopefully you can have compassion for yourself as you learn new things. You can also become conscious of, and honest about, how your choices have impacted you. Getting clear on your feelings may require slowing down your thought process even more. You can declare out loud or just to yourself that you're now reassessing all your choices to do for and give to others. This conscious acknowledgment and intention open the door to virtually unlimited changes, personal insights and possibilities. The more aware you are of why you're doing what you're doing, the more new options come to mind. Thinking about these new choices can help you feel better, right now, even if you haven't yet changed a single thing in your life situation. That's the power of conscious choice. It's really exciting to realize you have more power over your own well-being than you may have thought you did before reading this.

How Enthusiastic Stepmothers Become Bitter

Becoming a new stepmother is a lot like starting a new job. You're enthusiastic. You want to do a great job. You want to be liked and accepted and feel that you're good at what you're doing. This makes sense, right? However, society doesn't have a very clear or fair job description for being a stepmother and your enthusiasm can cloud your ability to see the healthy boundaries you need to sustain your giving, doing and well-being.

An Illustration of This Dilemma

Imagine the plight of the new enthusiastic substitute teacher. She's very excited to be in the classroom and so when she's asked to chip in elsewhere on the job, or wherever she sees a need or gap at school, she's truly happy to help, giving her time, energy and resources where needed. She finds herself very busy and excited about her involvement. It feels good to be included.

In addition to doing her own job in her classroom, she soon agrees to help the PE teacher, then assists the janitor when asked, then takes notes at a meeting for the principal whose secretary calls out sick. She fills in for an absent lunch lady (missing her own lunch break) and then helps the school nurse. She is given lots of responsibility because she's very good at what she's doing. But even with this added responsibility she gets little or no authority in any of these areas.

She doesn't mind at first because she feels happy to be included as part of the school family. However, after a while, this once-eager substitute teacher becomes exhausted, and her original happy enthusiasm to volunteer is now replaced with a heavy feeling of obligation. All those nice extra tasks now feel like part of her job. All the initial spontaneously expressed appreciation for her help is now replaced with an attitude of expectation. It also really hurts her feelings when people remind her she is only a substitute teacher whenever she expresses an idea about new ways to improve something or solve a problem.

She's now feeling resentful, but the others make it clear she's expected to carry on. No one tells her *"thanks for helping me and I'll take back my responsibility now."* The reality is that the only person who's going to help her out of this situation is—you guessed it—the substitute teacher herself. She's going to have to set some new boundaries. She's going to have to start saying *"no,"* make some changes, take a stand for her rights and honor her physical, emotional and financial limits. She also needs to accept the possibility that some of the people she's been doing things for might get upset if she stops. She wonders if she has the strength to endure any criticisms or shunning from her fellow school employees.

You might ask, *"Why does she do all this over-giving?"*

She's not so different from an eager-beaver newbie stepmother, is she?

There are several stepmother-specific reasons for over-giving that I've uncovered over the years. Because society seems to subtly hold stepmothers as unequal to bio-moms in relation to the stepkids, there's a lot of pressure on a stepmother (particularly one who wants to be active in her new stepfamily) to over-give. Each of us needs to find our balance of natural giving. There's no healthy map—yet. Whether conscious or not, a desire to be included and have the happy family dream, added to the powerfully expansive joy of falling in love, can propel many stepmothers beyond their comfortable and sustainable levels of giving. Over-giving is fertile ground for resentments, martyrdom, self-pity and blame-fests.

A Stepmom may take on too many tasks within her newly formed family because she wants to:

- Fill a logistical gap in support and chores.

- Be helpful to her partner.

- Try to claim equal rights as the woman of the house, along with her partner, to feel they're both parenting in the home.

- Feel like a good stepmother, as judged by her conscious and unconscious beliefs.

- Be included and create a role and a new space/place for herself in the pre-existing family.

- Stand up for justice and try to bring fairness and correct any wrongs against her partner and stepkids brought on by bio-mom, the divorce process or society.

- Overcome and change the wicked stepmother image.

- Avoid imagined (or verbalized) judgments from family, friends, community, school and her partner that she's not doing enough.

- Avoid potential anger or emotional withdrawal from her partner. If she fears her choices to reduce or stop giving or doing might upset her partner or trigger his fears and guilt regarding his kids or their bio-mom, she'll often continue doing and giving to avoid this anticipated relationship stress without ever discussing the matter.

- Avoid rocking the boat that everyone else seems to be enjoying, perhaps because she lacks the courage (or doesn't believe she has the rights) needed to take a stand on behalf of her own needs when that means doing less for others.

Anything on this list ring any bells of truth for you? Please be compassionate with yourself now and with that newbie stepmother you used to be. Look for giving-related choices you might want to change. Maybe you need to be doing less in order to restore your personal, emotional and physical balance of natural giving. Remember, there's no right or wrong about any of this. Be aware of any tendency to judge yourself as stingy, bad or selfish when what you're actually doing is taking better care of yourself. These self-judgments may be another way you get "hooked" or bully yourself into giving even when it goes against your often-ignored inner sense of natural giving. Sometimes you may feel you have to do something, yet upon reflection you realize that no one ever actually asked you to do these things. Oh how we Stepmoms pressure ourselves!

Once you're aware of why it is you're giving to others, you can begin to reevaluate your actions and give yourself more choices for creating a balance of giving and receiving. This is the personal, unique process of figuring out what's natural for you and your well-being.

Changes to Consider

Option #1. You could continue giving or doing, but now do so for different reasons. For instance, you could decide to continue doing a certain thing around the house because it makes you feel like a good homemaker even if others don't say *"Thank you."*

Option #2. What if you want to stop your giving altogether in a certain area? This can bring up a lot of rocking-the-boat fears. That's OK. Be supportive and kind to yourself. Right now, you're just opening up to the options. Sometimes relationship boats need rocking. Promise yourself that you'll create an implementation plan to honor your personality and situation.

Reassure yourself, as often as necessary, that your well-being is your responsibility and that your feelings are valid indicators of what you need. You're making a new map for your life. Making conscious choices is a very loving and empowering act of self-care. There's no time pressure—just the promise that sometime in the near future you will feel resentment-free about what you're giving and doing in a natural, sustainable way.

When I did this work, I had a huge *"Ah-ha"* moment. I saw clearly that I was so busy trying, doing and giving to make everyone happy and trying to solve our problems that it didn't occur to me to ask myself *why* I was doing anything. Keeping busy giving/doing was always what I did. Things needed doing and I was used to being the one to fill in the gaps. It was who I was, wasn't it? Nope. My liberating wake-up call was realizing that "doing" wasn't the only possible reaction to every situation and that I didn't have to rush in to do things all the time. What a relief to pause before giving and doing.

Beliefs That Perpetuate Over-Giving

"When I'm anxious, I should do something—anything—as soon as possible."

"When someone has a problem, I need to drop whatever I'm doing and help them immediately to the best of my skill set and resources to show them I care."

"When something bad or wrong happens to someone I love, jump in immediately and do, do, do on their behalf."

"If I stop doing for others, they will think I'm being selfish, lazy or unsupportive."

"If I stop trying to make things better, no one will jump in to improve my situation."

Giving and doing—or the other side of that pattern: taking, using and feeling entitled—can easily become a habit. It's usually deeply programmed within you when you are young, like saying please or thank you. Fortunately, when you shine your attention on what you believe, do, say or choose, you can always make new conscious choices going forward as needed. This is a pathway to freedom and the good news is you have complete control over these new choices.

Since doing this work, whenever I begin to feel bad about an interaction or an act of giving or doing, it's now a signal I respect. It's a clue for me to take time to question what I'm doing and why. So often you may be so busy doing that you don't stop and focus on yourself and what you're feeling. You may feel so pressured to keep up with your schedule that you forget you have a choice each time you decide to give or do. You may hardly ever consider that you also have the choice to *not* give or *not* do. This is a powerful choice that can occur to you when you pause to think before giving or doing.

Want to give it a try? Let's say you now realize or admit to yourself that you're over-giving or doing some things that you don't want to give or do anymore. Are you willing to trust your feelings and make your needs more important to you than your habits or old beliefs? Chances are good that if you resent what you're doing, you didn't really feel you had another choice. How does it feel to give yourself permission to make new choices? Can you believe that you have the right to make new choices that better fit your needs and new boundaries for your current life situation? If not, why not?

With a particular situation in mind, and firmly in the mindset of your adult self, consider these questions about each act of giving or doing:

"Is it really my responsibility to do this?"

"Am I still doing this because I now feel obligated to continue even though I don't want to anymore?"

"Was I actually asked to do this? If not, was it an unspoken, tacit agreement with my partner?" This is where cultural, religious and family rules can compel you to do and give in all kinds of situations. If this is true for you, it will continue to be the case until you interrupt these unconscious instructions and give yourself permission to make your own personalized choices. The conscious change can be both nerve-wracking and liberating.

"Am I doing this because I feel guilty that I'm happy while the stepkids are still grieving over their parents' divorce?"

"Am I doing this because I think I can do it better than the person actually responsible for doing this?"

"How would I feel if I stopped doing this?" Give yourself a chance to imagine not doing it anymore. Ahhhh. Open up to the possibility of change and see how that feels. Give yourself the chance to notice how you feel when considering this option.

"Can I give myself permission to stop doing this?" If not, why not? Whose permission do you believe you need?

"Do I believe my relationship can survive this new choice?"

"How many options can I come up with for new ways of giving/doing so that I don't feel resentful, but instead feel good about what I'm giving/doing for others?"

This is the time when creative problem-solving and taking a stand for *your* rights come into play. Use your imagination and do some brainstorming with trusted friends to find other ways to support what you know could work for you. While you may encounter resistance or rebellion, particularly from those who will now need to do more for themselves or the family, I can promise you that you'll feel better, stronger and more powerful, as you're no longer prisoner to the beliefs or expectations from the past. It feels very good to take a stand for maintaining your own personal, sustainable choices about doing and giving.

As I write this, Halloween is coming up, so let's use this holiday as an experiment in creating a plan for natural giving. Holidays are always a chance to become extra conscious of the difference between natural giving in your own unique way and the potential of over-giving for all kinds of reasons. Remember there's a list of motivations at the beginning of this chapter if you need a reminder.

There are so many ways to give and do for others during any holiday. Add in cultural, religious and family traditions and rituals, and maybe some competition between bio-parents about who gives the stepkids the best time, and it's potentially an over-giving festival of stress and discomfort between you and your partner or you and bio-mom or you and your stepkids. Goodness that's a lot of opportunity for potential stress.

Potential To-Do List

- Make stepkids' costumes

- Buy stepkids fabulous costumes

- Throw a party

- Do Halloween makeup

- Hire a party planner to help you have a fabulous party

- Decorate the house and yard

- Pay for someone else to decorate

- Make your own costume and be part of the fun

- Accompany the stepkids while they go trick-or-treating

- Stay home and hand out candy to trick-or-treaters

- Carve award-winning pumpkins

- Bake fabulous homemade treats

- Give out great treats you bought to impress

- Participate in the school holiday party

What other ideas come to mind?
What other choices could you make for giving and doing?
Would you prefer to avoid giving out candy and instead go out that night?
Would you rather go away and skip the whole holiday?

The key here is honoring *you* and *your* personality, talents, wishes, physical state, energy levels, finances and feelings about the specific holiday. What can you offer to your stepkids and your partner that feels fun and generates energy within you when you think about doing/giving it? Go through this list and as you consider doing each thing, take a moment to check in with your feelings about anything that doesn't inspire an excited "Yes!" Ask yourself how you feel about each possibility. What makes you smile? Snarl? Cringe? Dread? Feel energized, happy and creative?

Important Questions: When making decisions, can you make *your* well-being and feelings about each holiday be a higher priority than the expectations, beliefs or pressures from others? (Maybe you want to read that question again.) If you gave yourself the freedom to do whatever you wanted to, what would you do/give? Would you just as soon sleep through it, cruise through it or ignore it all together? Everyone has different feelings about each holiday. What are your feelings about this one?

If you honored your feelings and made conscious choices about your giving and doing for others this Halloween, would your partner support you? Can you give yourself permission to respect your uniqueness and only give and do what creates the experience of natural giving?

While it's often infuriating how unfair society is toward stepmothers and your role in your newly formed families, this lack of a clear map can also be your opportunity to create your own model of conscious stepmothering. When each holiday comes around, how about trying this exercise for yourself? How would it feel to forget about how society defines you (as a Stepmom) and instead create your own to-do list of giving and doing?

When you over-give, you deplete and give up a piece of yourself. This in turn causes resentments, resulting in dents and bruises to your own well-being. You may have good reasons for doing and giving whatever you're doing and giving, but that doesn't mean it's good for you or has to continue. You have the power to make new choices—ready to exercise it?

When you become conscious of making choices that honor the loving, caring, unique, adult woman you are now, your well-being is immediately impacted in a positive way. Finding your own ways to express your natural giving is a powerful way to reinforce who you really are, at your very best. Natural giving is a liberating, self-respecting, customized expression of yourself as an individual. It's an approach you can sustain over time with joy and maybe even an inner knowing of feeling good about who you are in each moment. The people around you will most likely adjust (some sooner than others). When you realize how much better you feel when you value your own giving, it's much easier to make conscious choices that are good for you. It's a self-supporting plan. Going forward, what changes do you need to make to ensure your giving is natural giving?

For a follow-up discussion about this chapter, go to smoms.org/BonusChapters and click on the title "Over-Giving."

Eleven

Why You Might Resist Giving Up Your Resentments

With all the pain, fear and rage that resentments cause you, do you ever feel hesitant to give them up or get past them, even once you realize you have the option to do so? This is a great question that deserves attention. Since there's power in feeling resentful, it makes sense you might be resistant to giving up any sense of power in situations where you already feel somewhat powerless. On the surface, it doesn't make sense to hold on to issues that cause you emotional discomfort. Still, you may willingly do this. You may even vigorously defend your reasons for doing so—consciously when questioned or unconsciously when feeling threatened in some way.

It's human nature to use logic to rationalize emotional reactions and decisions. Consider the saying my mentor, Kit, taught me at our very first consultation, *"We make decisions emotionally and rationalize them with logic."* Look at the list of issues you resent in your life and ask yourself:

- Can you see anywhere you could stop being resentful but something tells you you'd be losing something if you did? Letting others off the hook? Admitting defeat of some kind?

- Ever feel it would cost you too much emotionally or make you vulnerable if you stopped feeling angry and resentful?

- Can you figure out any future consequences you might fear (or not like) that could trigger resistance to letting go of your resentments?

- Can you uncover any logical and emotional benefits for staying resentful in spite of the obvious negative impact on you?

I can assure you there are good reasons for what you're feeling and doing. You're trying to keep yourself feeling emotionally safe, and achieving that goal takes many forms. Nothing wrong with this approach, it's just painful and blocking you from greater happiness and relief that you might not be able to see at this time. Resisting making changes and giving up feeling resentful can intertwine and tangle up your thoughts and feelings. Let's talk about what may be happening when you feel resistance to giving up your resentments.

Resistance is trying to tell you there's something beneficial for you to learn or experience if you move forward. With this in mind, what if you believed that the insights or healing that resistance signals will not go away just because you ignore it? Personal growth is not a one-day-only kind of offering or experience. If it doesn't feel like the right time to learn, heal or become aware of something, then you'll have more chances in the future. The only downside of not pursuing whatever you're resisting is that you will needlessly accumulate more unpleasant or painful experiences—experiences that could be avoided if you opened to your new awareness now. It's not wrong to avoid or delay your personal growth—that would be a judgment—but it's valuable to acknowledge that your choice will delay you changing, healing or learning something important. It's a trade-off of now or later. You may or may not know what the issue is that's causing you to feel resistant. Sometimes it's clear, and other times it requires some emotional detective work. While this chapter addresses specific resistance to giving up your resentments, you can also go to smoms.org/BonusChapters for an additional chapter that explains the general concept of emotional resistance. Click on the title "Understanding Emotional Resistance."

Brief Explanation of Resentment

- Resentment is trapped, unresolved anger indicating some sort of boundary violation, some unmet need or an imbalance between the energy you're giving out and the energy you're receiving.

- Anger is trying to tell you what is and isn't OK. Resentment is telling you something needs to change.

- Anger is trying to get your attention, urging you to set new boundaries, make new choices and somehow adjust your circumstances to improve some aspect of your own well-being.

- Anger also provides you with the energy to take action, make choices and implement changes that will honor your needs and help you keep yourself safe.

If for whatever reason, this energy is not able to complete the process—meaning you can't create those new boundaries, meet those needs or balance the energy of giving and receiving—your unresolved anger has to go somewhere, so it morphs into resentment. This energy gets stored as resentment, building up and negatively impacting your happiness, health and relationships.

Victim or Victor?

When you hold on to your resentments instead of taking action to resolve them, you're abdicating responsibility for your well-being. This naturally triggers disempowering rage within you, often without you understanding the cause of the additional rage.

Not taking action to help yourself resolve your resentments can be the result of the not-yet-conscious belief that your well-being depends on someone else doing or changing something. I say "not-yet-conscious belief" because you're likely unaware you're making this trade-off. Until you become aware of what you're feeling and doing to yourself, the resulting disempowered rage commonly manifests itself as righteous anger, blame, self-pity, martyrdom, depression, anxiety and physical illness or pain.

If you find yourself waiting (or pleading) for others to change so you can feel better or get what you want, you're not free or empowered. This state of helplessness can trigger all kinds of untapped feelings from childhood, when you truly were at the mercy of others. If resentments continue to build up within you, this can lead to resignation and feeling like a victim. Victims feel trapped, believing they have no options. As an adult, you always have options! If your approaches and decisions stem from your child-created strategies, you may vigorously defend the belief that you have no options and no power to bring about the changes you deem necessary. *"I've done everything I can and nothing will work"* is a common belief and defense of an unconscious victim.

While you often don't have the ability to stop others from doing whatever they're doing (like whatever your stepkids' bio-mom might do) or are unable to compel others (like your partner) to do something they're not doing that you think is important, you—as a conscious, adult woman—can always find solutions to improve your situation. Yes, always. Do you believe this? If not, why not?

It's important to be aware of the difference between not having control over what happens to you and having control over how you respond to whatever happens to you. While you may not be able to convince or force others to bend to your will, you can absolutely identify creative ways to meet your needs. You may not like the options available to you.

They may strike you as a waste of time, too scary, too risky or too difficult because you're exhausted or tired of being enraged. Still, as an adult, it's helpful to continue to remind yourself that choices are *always* possible.

Thankfully, in the long run and sometimes in the short run, assuming responsibility for your own well-being actually requires less energy and brings more rewards than becoming entrenched in your resentment or victimhood. You may need to experience this to believe it. I urge you to give it a try. In spite of these truths, some people are still believers in the power and benefits of being a victim.

Why Choose Victimhood?

1. It's often easier and less risky to wallow in resentment than to take a stand for yourself.

2. It's less scary (more familiar) to feel like a victim than to explore your possible feelings of not deserving to stand up for your rights, needs and wishes—for example, wanting to be treated like an equal member of the family but not actually feeling that way in your family.

3. It's easier to keep your focus on others than to explore the possibility that you don't feel you have a right to say *"No"* in your relationships without painful consequences.

4. When you rationalize your victimhood by choosing to believe you're helpless to help yourself, you're distracted from that still, small voice that might be telling you there are things you can do. Sometimes it's hard (scary) to hear that message. Telling others how helpless you are (in a given situation) can also reinforce your belief that there's nothing you can do to change things so you don't have to feel badly or guilty about not trying. This is a false belief that feels like the truth.

5. Feeling resentful can create a false sense of power that feels better than fear. It can create a brief sensation that you're safe from more pain, fear or wounds. This stirs up emotional energy but doesn't offer a release valve. Therefore, it ultimately engenders more disempowerment, rage and bitterness, and intensifies your need to blame others. This is an exhausting and vicious cycle I call the Vortex of Victimhood. See Chapter 17.

6. You might fear that if you stop feeling resentful and like a victim, and instead take actions to improve your well-being, bad things (worse-than-now bad things) will happen. This dark cloud of vague fear might stop you right in your tracks, causing you to swallow, stop or ignore any anger you feel. This unresolved anger can become more self-justified resentments, which can keep you from claiming or exercising your own power. Deep down, you may also believe the price of empowerment is too great and not really worth it—maybe, as a child, you were punished when you tried to assert your opinions, needs or boundaries. Once you remember that you're not a kid anymore but a wise, skilled, adult woman with resources and talents, your fears will likely lessen and maybe dissipate completely.

7. Giving up being a victim means you can't play the self-pitying *"Oh Poor Me"* manipulation card anymore. Sometimes you may believe that this is the only way to get what you want, and that giving it up leaves you with no way to get what you need. Sadly, this belief may come from very real childhood experiences. No judgments about this survival strategy coming from me—just something I've seen a lot over the years. Self-pity is punishing to those around you so choosing a new belief about your ability to help yourself has tremendous benefits to you and those around you.

You can improve your sense of well-being almost instantly by consciously shifting from believing that you are at the mercy of circumstances to believing that you can be victorious by creating a positive solution. This can bring you a wave of hope and joy even if you don't know what you're going to do—yet. This is how powerful your intention and beliefs can be in your life.

Resisting Releasing Resentments?

1. Could you be afraid that if you stop being resentful, nothing will ever change or things will only get worse? Perhaps you are carrying some version of the child-created belief, *"I have to be angry to get attention—otherwise I'll be ignored, rejected or neglected."*

2. Could you feel afraid that if you let go of your resentments, you'd become invisible and left out of the family dynamics? Being left out hurts. This is a common and sometimes valid fear for stepmothers.

3. Could it be too scary to take a stand on your own behalf for a number of valid reasons? You may have had experiences—perhaps in your childhood—proving that bad things may happen as a result of trying to stand up for yourself. The key here is to remind yourself that you're not a child anymore. Taking a moment to remind yourself that you're a capable adult woman—right now—usually helps. If you can have the presence of mind to imagine your best friend facing this same challenge, just watch the ideas start to pour out of you. It can really be exciting. Learning not to move forward until you're standing consciously in that wise, adult version of yourself will save you and your partner countless hours/days of stress. Learning to recognize when you're being your best adult self—and when you're not—becomes easy with a bit of practice.

4. You could discover an uncomfortable inner conflict: *"Is it really OK for me to take a stand for my own well-being? Do I have equal rights with everyone in my home?"* If rocking the boat by speaking the truth was frowned upon, punished, shamed or judged as selfish when you were growing up, this belief can feel tattooed on your subconscious and be very imprisoning.

5. Could you be afraid that if you stop feeling resentment and get to work figuring out what healthy boundaries you need, you might want or need changes that you fear your partner won't support? Is any part of you afraid your partner can't look beyond his own wounds and fears to support what you need?

6. Do you fear your personal growth process might threaten your relationship? Yikes, that's a scary one! It can be hard to trust in your partner's willingness to love you as you grow stronger, especially if he hasn't been willing to take a stand for you in the past. If this is the case for you, it's about choosing to stand up for yourself in ways you wish others would.

7. Believe it or not, some people resist letting go of resentment because they like the drama of it all. Peacefulness and calm can feel boring to those raised in a home where drama equals connection and excitement, or where proving and testing love is the only way love is measured.

8. Could you be holding onto your resentments because keeping the situation in your consciousness gives you hope that things could get better one day? Do you believe your resentment shields you from resigning yourself or accepting your circumstances or the actions of others? Does it protect you from experiencing any related grief or loss? This is a big one.

Try a New Attitude

The next time you detect your resistance to making a change to let go of resentment, please try this—give yourself the gift of time and look more deeply at what you're feeling. If you are, in fact, experiencing resistance, I hope that you'll welcome it gently and support yourself by saying something like, *"I'm feeling resistance. I know there's something valuable for me to learn from this."* I hope you'll choose to embrace what I call the Christmas Eve Theory of the Unknown. Believing that even though you don't know what you'll get, there will be a gift of positive insight just around the emotional corner of awareness. There will be something to learn that's going to help you in some way. With this courageous attitude, proceed with alert, loving attention.

Once you recognize resistance, take a deep breath, step into your aware, adult self and say as confidently as possible, *"I can honor, support and handle whatever comes up in this process or change. I'm going to take this at a pace that's right for me, even if I feel a bit afraid. I can do this."*

My goal is to encourage you to challenge your old beliefs and open up to the possibility that resentments *can* be resolved in a way that leaves you feeling better and more powerful. In spite of your past experiences, beliefs, wounds or fears, you're now a more awake, adult woman. You're wiser than you were before you read this chapter. There are many new ways to stand up for yourself when you believe in your right to do so. When you know you have the ability to learn whatever new skills you need, you can take a stand for your own well-being and happiness.

- Do you believe that you deserve to be happy in this stepfamily situation? If there are conditions required for this to be *"Yes,"* what are they?

- Do you believe that you deserve to have the final say about your well-being? Or have you given that power to someone else?

- Do you believe that you have equal rights with everyone else in your home? If not, why not?

- Can you open up to the possibility that you and your partner can find loving ways to change things in a mutually satisfying way? If not, why not?

- Are you willing to believe that feeling resistance is actually a sign that you're ready and able to change, even if it includes a proceed-with-caution warning? If not, what reasons or beliefs come up as *"Yeah, Buts"* or road blocks for you?

Imagine you feel fearless and convinced that there's great value in moving forward immediately. Now ask yourself, *"What are my next steps for increasing my personal power, well-being and wisdom?"* The answers will show themselves when you ask the question.

The willingness to believe that things can change for the better (and that you're no longer helpless) is a powerful state of mind even when you don't have the answers yet or even know where to start. Holding on to resentments is painful and exhausting, even if you're well-trained at enduring emotional hardship. The good news is you now have options that can lead you to feeling stronger, happier and more capable of creating a balanced exchange in your giving and receiving, while you find creative ways to meet your needs. When you do this work, resentment becomes a temporary emotional alert pointing out a place for you to have more happiness. What new solutions and insights are waiting for your attention just beyond any resistance you might be feeling?

The next several chapters (12-17) go into detail about resentments, teaching you how to process your feelings and free yourself from them in healthy, lasting ways.

A Happily Ever After SMOM Story

June 2016

A note to all struggling Stepmoms out there,

I found Cathryn Bond Doyle and smoms.org at three o'clock in the morning when I was teary eyed and unable to sleep over being cast as the evil stepmother. My dreamy relationship with my new spouse had become a nightmare. His "adult" children shunned me but used my energy, home, money and spouse to their advantage. My husband changed focus from being a new spouse to being a Super Dad who never said "NO" to his kids.

My health was suffering, my sanity was questioned, and I hated the person I had become. Was I evil? I did a Google search, and I think I typed, "Help, I hate my stepkids." I was guided to smoms.org and spent the next hour reading stories and words of hope from other Stepmoms just like me.

What a flood of relief to know I was not alone. I joined the group right on the spot. I was welcomed and nurtured by Cathryn and a heavenly host of other SMOMS (Stepmoms who join smoms.org). I worked privately with Cathryn and I worked in group seminars. I cannot tell you how valuable this experience was for me and for my marriage. I was able to make more personal growth in a single year than I had in 40 years.

I learned to set boundaries. I learned how to banish resentment. I learned how to be heard and respected by my new family. I have my wonderful husband back and my marriage is great beyond my expectations. I will be forever grateful to Cathryn and my fellow SMOMS.

Happily Ever After SMOM
Stepmom since 2006
SMOM since 2013
Woke up in 2014
Living the Dream since 2015

Twelve

Understanding Resentment
The Basics of This Painful Form of Anger

Resentment is hard to ignore. Have you noticed that? When we're actively resenting something we can often perceive a prickly, cold venom running through us. We may feel we're out of sorts, and may even judge ourselves as angry, mean, unloving people. We're usually justified in our feelings and can't seem to get them to go away. Resentment can churn up energy that we don't really know what to do with. This can result in us lashing out or shutting down or it can compel us to use controlling or hostile behavior to try to get the discomfort to stop.

Another important thing about resentment is that it rarely, if ever, goes away over time. It stubbornly refuses to be digested. This explains why the *"I'm going to ignore these feelings, stop talking about them and act like things are OK"* strategy rarely works without great negative impact. Time can help us heal and resolve hurt and grief, but not resentment or any other form of anger. Judging ourselves for feeling resentful doesn't help either—it only turns the negative energy against us in an attempt to numb or distract our feelings.

Resentment wants you to make changes in order to create and restore a healthy, self-sustaining, balanced flow of giving and receiving energy. Believe it or not, resentment is trying to help you. Who knew? None of us veteran SMOMS did until someone explained it to us. Today I want to explain it to YOU so that you also understand resentment's important function.

Homework: Make a list of your resentments. Write out every big and little thing you resent. Once you have your list, see if you can put each resentment into one of these categories:

- Resentments in your present life

- Resentments from unchangeable facts in your stepfamily situation

- Resentments from past experiences in your stepfamily situation

This exercise will help you see your patterns and decide what changes will make the biggest impact on your life. The good news about doing this work is that the insights you gain while resolving any present resentments will make it easier for you to understand and resolve other resentments in your life.

My View of Resentment

1. It's *always* stuck, unprocessed, unresolved anger from the present or from the recent or distant past. It's unresolved because the active process that anger tries to set in motion to bring about change somehow gets cut short, detoured or stopped before the change is achieved.

2. It's a form of anger indicating that you have unmet needs or that a personal boundary is being violated.

3. It indicates an imbalance between the energy you're giving out and the energy you're receiving in a certain activity.

4. It's trapped emotional energy that builds with each re-telling. If you don't do something consciously with this energy, unaddressed resentment can become like radioactive energy inside you. It can build up so intensely that you may lash out illogically, sometimes unintentionally, at others or at situations. Energy denied doubles in force—that can be a lot of energy running through your emotional and physical body.

5. It's the recognition, at some level of awareness, of a "lousy deal" that you feel stuck with. You may sense you are unable to address this without experiencing scary, negative consequences that may not feel worth it.

6. It's a disguised attempt to voice the *"No"* you don't actually think you can express safely. Whenever you think you have no good choices or options, you feel disempowered and maybe even disheartened, and that can lead to varying degrees of despair and depression. While some women act out to express their anger, others choose silent rage or a *"Why bother? What's the point?"* attitude to endure uncomfortable and almost impossible-to-ignore feelings.

7. It can indicate that there's a conflict between a belief you hold and an unmet need or a gap between that belief and your reality.

8. It's an emotional alert system—it's trying to tell you that something's wrong and that your attention is required. When you feel resentful, your attention is generally focused on another person, instead of on yourself and what you need. In those moments when you're focusing on how to change another person, you're actually experiencing another painful, enraging, usually unconscious feeling—a form of self-abandonment. You may realize that the more you focus on the other person (outside of yourself), the more disempowered you feel. This may lead to obsessive thinking about the other person or the situation, and you may believe changing that person is the only way to help yourself. Although you feel intensity building, you may not realize that you're abandoning your feelings and needs while thinking of others. This is a vicious cycle that you can stop right now with your awareness.

9. It can be your emotional teacher—giving you clues about what you need to change to be more empowered, well cared for and emotionally safe. Making the choice to bring your attention back to yourself can be fascinating, revealing, healing and comforting. One thing's for sure: working with your resentment in a constructive way will bring insights that you can do something about, unlike trying to change the behavior of others.

10. It can motivate you to look honestly at the level of responsibility you have (or haven't) taken to bring about a change in the past. It gives you a chance to make a new choice. Your awareness of the resentment you feel begs the question, *"To what degree do I believe I can take a stand for myself vs. abdicating responsibility and*

blaming others?" Resentments can be a catalyst for you to own and implement the changes you want and need, and when you embrace this task, you create a fundamental shift in your psyche—in a good way.

11. It's an emotional signal that you're ready (and able) to make some new choices. When you're resentful, you can be confident you have energy available to fuel your actions. Mobilizing and consciously directing your bottled-up, anger-generated energy is good for your health and well-being in many ways. Trying to ignore these feelings takes a lot of energy.

The Negative Impact of Resentment

1. It can eat away at your good nature, sadly poisoning the joy in your daily life.

2. It can putrefy into self-pity, martyrdom, bitterness and an uncharacteristic lack of compassion for others. This may harden your heart in ways you may later judge yourself for harshly, which can hurt you even more and become a painful vicious cycle you don't know how to interrupt.

3. It can taint your world view. It can extinguish your natural optimism. You can certainly understand why stepmothers-of-old have behaved in wicked ways. Maybe they felt like disregarded emotional nuclear time bombs of bitterness and rage. Maybe they felt trapped because, well—they were trapped. They didn't know how to help themselves. They were not prepared, trained or supported. Until the last decade or so, stepmothers had very little, if any, peer support or societal compassion. Shockingly, but all too commonly, I've heard therapists advise stepmothers to back off or even move out of their houses if they felt upset or if they wanted their stepkids or partners to change or be more respectful. Yikes! Grrr!

4. It can express itself as a low-level emotional malaise. Resentment may slip over you like a fog. It's much less frenetic than other forms of anger. It's something that can overtake you, putting you in an emotional resentment coma. Without realizing what's happening, you can find yourself sighing a lot and feeling irritated, tired, impatient and depressed.

5. It often triggers defensive behaviors between a Stepmom and her partner as beliefs and needs conflict. Without realizing the cause of (or cure for) the conflicts,

couples can slip into bitter power struggles that leave them each convinced they are right and the other wrong.

6. It can become a growing invisible wedge between a stepmother and her partner. This wedge impacts intimacy, attraction to each other and levels of trust. It's probably one of the most painful prices you can pay for not resolving your resentments.

7. It impacts your physical body. It's toxic for your spirit, heart and body. Your body is hardwired to let you know when a boundary is violated or a need goes unmet, even if you're fully conscious of what's going on. How does resentment get your attention in your body? Does your throat close or does your tummy get upset? Do you have trouble sleeping, tightness in your chest, sinus infections, headaches, backaches or neck pain? If you're unsure, pay attention to your body next time you're feeling resentful.

Society's View of Resentment

Many people believe that resentment is unavoidable. *"Learn to live with it"* is a common reaction to hearing about someone's resentment, especially when no solution is clear or the options for resolution are perceived as too risky.

Do you believe you need to build a greater tolerance for resentment? Some people are proud of their ability to endure this awful feeling. This cynical reaction to your resentment and other similar unsupportive ones can stir up personal survival beliefs and behaviors. For example, you may also believe you're supposed to become tougher and endure because there's nothing else you can do. Thankfully, this is false. As a wise, adult woman, there's always something you can do to help yourself resolve your resentments. I repeat the phrase, "wise, adult woman" to remind you that it's important to be conscious of when you're awake as your best self vs. unconscious and driven by child-created beliefs and survival strategies. See Chapter 9 for a thorough explanation of this dynamic and the relationship between the adult and child-based states of conscious awareness.

While society finds feeling resentful quite acceptable for some people—maybe even expected—this is strangely not the case when it comes to stepmothers. Have you ever noticed this? People can be quite cold, with varying degrees of hostility, toward a stepmother who expresses her resentments. Ever have anyone tell you to just *"get over it"* or stop complaining and accept things because supposedly you knew what you were getting into? In my experience, people who say things like this don't know how to help you, are running out of patience with you or are already living with their own resentments. Their comments reveal their own strategy for dealing with resentment. They endure. They suffer. They're resigned. They've given up on being able to change things and expect you to do the same. Stepmother/stepfamily stress is rarely supported by society outside of the occasional attempt at support, *"I don't know how you do it"* or *"You're the best thing that ever happened to those stepkids"* or *"I couldn't do what you're doing."*

As a stepmother, you may feel isolated, overwhelmed, judged and unsupported at the time you need compassion and new ideas the most. When your family and friends don't know how to help you, they can resort to hurtful judgments and actions just to get you to stop complaining, usually not intentionally but because they don't know how to help you or resolve their own resentments. Sometimes they may leave you feeling that resentment and pain are the price you have to pay to stay with your partner and honor your relationship commitments.

A New Approach

Can you imagine how differently you'd feel about your life if you knew that you could learn from every resentment, resolve them and feel better afterwards? Can you imagine how motivating it would be to work with your resentments if you truly believed it would lead you to relief, peace and empowerment? Even if you're skeptical, that's OK—give it a try. Consider adopting don Miguel Ruiz's Fifth Agreement: *"Be skeptical and listen more."* Can you open your hearts to a new way? You don't need to give up or resist addressing your resentments—you don't have to suffer emotionally, physically and in your relationships. There *is* another option!

Society and the Rights of Stepmothers

This could be a whole chapter but instead let's just look at it for a few moments. Unfortunately, society has created a "less than" status for stepmothers in the realm of families, expecting them to defer rights and authority to either or both bio-parents, and even to their stepkids. While stepmothers are often given a lot of responsibility for the care of stepkids in their home, there's clearly an imbalance of power, authority and status, and a lack of role definition.

You can bet that when the first shared societal beliefs about stepmothers came into being, there were many, many more bio-moms in society than stepmothers. Motherhood has been held sacred for eons and this view tipped the scale against stepmothers for many reasons. In spite of the growing population of stepmothers, society still hasn't created an equal place, a unique role or much-deserved compassion for them. It's remarkably unfair.

I believe that it's time for us to create a non-competing, non-conflicting, new and unique equal parenting role for stepmothers in today's families. We SMOMS can be the mapmakers to do this—even if it's one stepfamily at a time. When we reject old limiting beliefs and get clear on appropriate new beliefs for our situations, change is possible, inevitable and long-lasting. The following two views are common, core beliefs worthy of reflection. They impact you as a stepmother and in all your relationships. Where do you stand and how do you feel about the following?

First: Do you believe you have a right to balance the units of giving and receiving that you exchange with the people in your life? Or do you believe that you need to give more than you receive? Do you believe that others owe you because of what you've already done?

Second: Do you feel that you have equal power, rights and authority in your relationship with your partner and in your home? How would your life be different if you truly believed that you had absolutely equal rights with everyone else in your home? How would having equality change your attitudes, choices and behaviors in your life situation?

Sit with these questions to see how you feel about each one. How you answer these questions will be helpful and interesting as you move into the specifics of resolving your resentments. Remember, your beliefs impact every choice and moment in your life.

The next chapter explains a specific process for resolving your current resentments. The most important thing to know about feeling resentful is that there are important, valid reasons for these feelings. They impact your well-being on several levels. They are resolvable and will change your life for the better once you discover and make the changes needed. Imagine how different your life would be as a Stepmom without resentments. How would you feel if you knew resentment was only temporary, and that once it is addressed it will lead you to feeling happier and more respected, honored and empowered? This is a doable reality for you *if* you're willing to do the work. The next five chapters give you details about working with your specific resentments from the past and present so you can get very good at learning from and resolving them. This information will even help you avoid developing resentments in the future.

Thirteen

Eliminate Ongoing Resentments and Feel Great About It

This chapter covers details about how to resolve and dissolve your present-day resentments. We will also address the fears that may come up when you make changes and set new boundaries—or even when you just imagine changing. Maybe you fear rocking the relationship boat—a legitimate concern! This can be unsettling at best and terrifying at worst so we'll talk about that as well. When something's happening right now and you're aware you're feeling resentful, this chapter will give you a process you can follow to take action and feel better, like the title says. This chapter will make more sense if you review Chapter 12, Understanding Resentment.

Whenever you realize you're feeling resentful, you should pause and consciously acknowledge this feeling, perhaps saying to yourself, *"Oh my, I'm feeling resentful about this."* It may seem silly but making this conscious observation about your feelings makes it easier to step into your wise adult self. You want to remind yourself that you have a reliable process to change this feeling and that you're not powerless. Can you imagine Helen Reddy's song, *I Am Woman*, playing in the back of your mind? How about some power posing anytime you begin this new process? Knowing there are options can breathe hope, life and energy into a previously despairing situation.

Resentments try to draw your attention to your feelings about a particular circumstance. They help you become aware of an imbalance in the exchange of your giving and receiving with others. After acknowledging feeling resentful, ask yourself, *"What can I learn from these feelings?"*

When you're ready to resolve a specific current resentment, ask yourself any or all of the following questions and explore your answers. Not every question will apply to every situation. However, one or more will lead to you interesting places. I used to have these seven questions written on a notecard to help me remember. Never fear—after a while it'll become an automatic sequence in your mind. Want to try it? Think of the situation that you resent.

Understand, Then Eliminate Resentments

1. "What personal boundary, if any, is being violated?'

2. "Which of my needs, if any, is not being met?'

3. "What's the conflict between what I believe should happen and what is actually happening?"

4. "What's the conflict between what I believe and what I now realize I need?"

5. "Is there a conflict between how I feel about what's happening vs. what I believe I should do?"

6. "What beliefs are compelling me to do things even when I don't want to?"

7. "Where's the imbalance in my giving and receiving? What feels like a lousy deal for me? What specific new ideas can I come up with to create more balance?"

The following is an example of an imbalance in giving and receiving and a conflict between a Stepmom's beliefs and her needs. While there are countless examples, I want to work through this one to show you how it can work for you. There's another example in Chapter 14. Once you read through this scenario, plug in your personal resentment, go through the questions and see what you can learn about yourself and your new options.

Resolving a Present Resentment

The Situation: A Stepmom feels resentful about fixing breakfast for her stepkids because they're no longer kind to her during breakfast time, and do not act appreciative of her efforts. She realizes now that she's giving more than she's getting back in return for her giving.

First, she acknowledges, *"Wow, I'm feeling resentful getting up each morning and fixing a hot breakfast for my stepkids."* She's aware—a good start.

Next, she goes through the resentment questions to look for sources of imbalances and conflicts.

She asks herself, *"What personal boundary is being violated?"* Maybe no boundary is being violated at all, but considering this question is always a good place to start. She decides that it's not OK for her to feel disrespected by these children and treated like a disliked servant. Her boundary of expecting to be treated with respect is being violated.

Next, she asks herself, *"Which of my needs is not being met?"* She recognizes it's the need to feel appreciated and treated kindly in her own home. As she thinks about this, it feels correct and she realizes, *"This present situation has become a lousy deal for me"* so she knows she's on the right track for addressing the resentment.

She continues down the list of questions: *"OK, what's the conflict between what I believe should happen and what's actually happening?"*

This comes to her right away, *"I believe children should be polite and grateful to the adults who are taking care of them—especially when someone goes out of their way to do a nice thing for them."* Then with a twist of anger, she realizes that her stepkids are not abiding by this belief *and*, to make it worse, she appears to be the only one upset about this situation.

Next question: *"Is there a conflict between what I feel about what's happening vs. what I believe I should do?"*

She realizes she has a belief about what it means to be a good stepmother. She currently believes a good Stepmom fixes breakfast (the most important meal of the day) for the children in her care, and that means her stepkids. She used to be happy doing this when they were younger and excited to start their day with her, but lately they've been grumpy, short-tempered and sometimes even downright rude to her.

A conflicting need: *"I need people I care for to be nice to me, and at least respectful. I know I had to be respectful to adults when I was a kid. Even if I was angry or cranky, I had to be polite or I would've been punished. I want to feel valued and at the very least need to be respected in my own home. When they disregard me or refuse to thank me or express appreciation, their behavior conflicts with my needs."*

The second conflicting need that's causing an imbalance: She's not a morning person so getting up early has cost her many units of giving energy, not to mention sleep. To balance her giving, she's looking to receive more from her experience.

What Has This Stepmom Learned?

1. Presently she's pushing (bullying) herself to continue to get up and fix a hot breakfast because her beliefs are driving her actions. She sees that she has been the recipient of her own judgments anytime she ponders not fixing them breakfast. She's been telling herself she'd be a bad stepmother if she doesn't do this important morning task for her stepkids. She's punishing and coercing herself into action with her own inner harsh judgments.

2. She realizes, with a bit of a start, that no one had asked or required her to make the children's breakfast. In reality, she had joyfully volunteered, as if it were an expected, unspoken part of her job as woman of the house. That is an *"ah ha"* for her and she wonders what else she is doing without being asked.

3. She used to like to do this chore. The stepkids used to be happy about her attention but things have changed over the past year. Now she resents that the energy she puts out is not being balanced in the present situation.

4. She's tired of feeling badly and is ready to make some changes because her resentment is impacting how she feels about the stepkids, her partner and herself.

Her Options?

Remember: When you're looking to make changes, the more choices you can come up with, the better. Even if the choices are wacky and far-fetched, and even if you'd never actually choose them, they're still choices. Having the ability to pick from a list of options gives you a greater sense of freedom. Why? Because you feel more empowered when you have the freedom to choose. This is better than feeling as if you have only one (or no) option or are at the mercy of someone else. A lack of options can leave you feeling trapped and upset.

In order to transform this perceived lousy deal into a balanced exchange, this stepmother needs to get creative. She begins to look for new options—ways to reduce her giving, increase her getting back, build a better sense of balance and/or create new boundaries. Any of these can help her resolve her resentments. For the sake of this example let's assume her stepkids are all eight years old or older. Certainly her options will vary if they're younger.

Choices to Resolve Her Resentment

1. She could honor her needs and sleep in, not making breakfast at all.

2. She could honor her needs and sleep in, putting out cereal, cereal bowls or breakfast bars before she goes to bed.

3. She could decide that her belief about making a good breakfast is so strong that she's no longer going to expect her stepkids' appreciation. Instead, she'll give herself more personal kudos to balance her giving. This is an internal reframing, as opposed to an outward change—equally effective.

4. She could ask for more support in making breakfast to balance out her giving with more receiving. If she gets help that's meaningful to her, her resentment will likely dissolve.

5. She could decide that she's going to experiment with cooking because she loves cooking. If the stepkids don't want to eat her food, she could offer them self-serve options. This would increase her sense of receiving because she's going to have more fun and not expect anything from the stepkids. If they like it, it'll be a bonus.

6. She could speak to her partner and ask him for more help (or ask him to take over completely). She could trade another chore so she won't have to make breakfast in the future.

7. She could teach the stepkids how to fix their own breakfast, showing them where the supplies are, letting them choose some favorites and having a rehearsal to feel she's being responsible and that they're capable of helping themselves.

8. She could hire someone to come in early and fix the family breakfast. (Oooh just imagining this extravagance puts a smile on her face.)

9. She could send the stepkids out to breakfast with a neighbor or her partner for a new family or father/kids ritual.

10. She could start a breakfast club with the neighbors or the stepkids' friends and only make breakfast every third or fourth morning. Her new, expanded audience would more than likely appreciate her actions, even if her own stepkids say nothing.

11. She could leave things as they are but decide to give herself a new treat, activity or prize of some sort to create an emotional balance for this breakfast situation. She could talk with her partner about what that reward might be. It would have to be something that truly makes her feel like the deal is now a fair (ideally, even good) deal for her. Hmmm, what could that treat be in her life?

Can you feel how just imagining choices gives you a greater sense of power, freedom and potential relief? The more choices the better. Once you brainstorm for least three but ideally 8-10 options, take a look at each one and imagine how it would feel to implement it. Reject the ones you know you won't choose, even if it is fun to imagine them. Look more deeply at the ones that feel good, right and OK to you. Yes, this is about honoring and trusting your feelings as feedback for your well-being. No right or wrongs here—that would be a judgment. Since judgments hurt, suspend them and instead check in with your feelings.

When you choose the option you like best, move into the implementation part of your plan. How do you feel about making those changes yourself? Do you feel any anxiety or fear related to your partner's potential reaction? How supportive will your partner be in helping you get your giving and receiving back into balance or in helping you get your needs met? Does your partner need to read these chapters to gain an understanding of what you're trying to accomplish so you can feel less resentful? FYI: I've found guys to be quite supportive of this approach. It makes sense and most of them genuinely want their Stepmom partners to stop feeling resentful—for a whole bunch of valid reasons.

Keep These Questions in Mind

"Am I willing to make my own well-being and needs more important than any of my limiting beliefs that conflict with my current needs?"

"Am I willing to make my own well-being important enough to face my fears of being judged as a bad stepmother by my stepkids, partner or others?"

"How much courage and perhaps outside support do I need to begin making changes that can eliminate my resentments?"

"I'm feeling like the changes I want to implement need to happen over time. How can I break them into stages so everyone can get used to them and I can feel good about making this happen?"

With new awareness of your feelings, needs, intentions and now a new idea that feels good to you, create a comfortable action plan for making the changes. While others may initially resist your changes or voice objections, moving forward in a thoughtful way is one of the most respectful things you can do for yourself and your relationships. When speaking with your partner about the changes you want to make, be sure to tell him that the benefit of eliminating your resentments is feeling happier and much better about yourself and your life together. This has a direct and positive impact on your relationship with him.

For the sake of making this initial exercise a good use of your time, select a current resentful situation with a small emotional charge so that you can get the hang of this work. The bigger issues will become easier to resolve once you understand the process. Either way, as you begin, imagine all the stress you can eliminate with changes that'll make you feel better, less resentful and more in charge of your own well-being.

If you sense some resistance or defensiveness in yourself or your partner, please see Chapter 22, Disarming Defensive Behaviors. At smoms.org/BonusChapters there's a free bonus chapter titled "Six Sample Situations for Disarming Defensive Behavior Between You and Your Partner." I urge you to read it and then customize the examples for your situation.

If you feel resistance to doing any work to eliminate your resentments, there's a very good reason for this feeling. Check out Chapter 11, Why You Might Resist Giving Up Your Resentments.

Fourteen

Processing a Resentment in Real Time
A Stepmom Example

When you understand how to respond to feeling resentful about a situation, you also have the power to resolve it and can make the choice to treat it as a loving exploration (or not). When you approach the situation with compassion and curiosity, there's so much to learn about yourself. There's also a lot of personal power you can reclaim in regards to your own well-being—what a worthy goal.

The following true story is another example of how to use the skills explained in Chapters 12 and 13. This Stepmom on a Mission participated in one of my resentment workshops and her process shows you how to pull together the techniques and inner dialogues you might experience when you work on resolving your own present resentments. She recognizes she's resentful and is tired of feeling this way. In her example, you'll see how she does her best to stay conscious. Throughout the process she questions her thoughts and feelings to discover what she needs to do differently to recognize and resolve her resentments. I've written her experiences from first person and am sharing her relationship experiences and lessons learned as if she's reporting to you after the fact.

This Stepmom is lucky because her partner is willing to support her process and participate in helping her feel better by supporting her changes *and* changing his own behavior. I love a happy ending and fortunately this is a more-common-than-not outcome for Stepmoms using similar tactics to what you'll read below. In addition to the earlier chapters on resentment, you may also want to share the story with your partner as an inspiration for how this process can help you both find new ways to deal with your resentments and feel closer as a couple.

Example of Excellent Work!

My husband and I were watching a movie at home one Sunday evening, happy and relaxed. His daughter, my stepdaughter (19), called from college. While I could only hear my husband's side of the conversation, it was delivered with the high level of enthusiasm I've watched him share with his daughter over the years.

My husband to his daughter: "That's great honey! What a break! Good for you! How about that! Sounds like you're in good shape. Great job! Wonderful news! Oh, don't worry. You're going to do very well, I'm sure of it. You can do it."

You get the picture. Already my curiosity was aroused but in a not-so-positive way. I began to feel bitterness rise and my heart hardened, bracing for the news. Then I realized what I was doing—I was not feeling loving—so I took a deep breath to get calm and be present with him as I waited to learn what happened.

My husband ended the phone call and told me that his daughter was lucky enough to get a good part-time job (that she didn't have to look for) and got into a much coveted class (that she didn't register for on time), blah, blah, blah. I'm not sure I even heard the rest of the words because it was like an inner explosion of teeny tiny sharp bits in my head and heart. I kept breathing and said nothing for a moment—which was unusual for me and something I'd been working on.

My husband noticed my restraint. While we'd experienced this kind of tension many times over the course of our relationship, it hadn't happened for a while, so we were both aware something was up for me. I watched my husband take a deep breath, turn to me and ask, "Sweetie, what's happening?" with the tentative approach of someone thinking, "Is she gonna blow?"

I kinda chuckled seeing his fear. This immediately made me feel good because I know that one can't smile or laugh when engaging in self-pity. I gained a surge of inner confidence feeling I still had one foot in my wise adult self. Then I smiled, patted his shoulder and told him I needed to take a few minutes to think about this because I could tell there was a lot here to learn. I told him my bitterness and resentment were up big time because of what I'd just heard him say to his daughter. So I took myself into the other room. My husband watched me leave the room then returned to the movie.

When I was alone, I started talking with myself. "I know this feeling of bitterness. It's crystalized resentment." I continued to talk, as kindly as I could. "OK, it's OK, I'm OK. I'm gonna figure this out. I know how to do this. Let's go through the resentment questions."

1. *What boundary had been violated?* None. What I'd observed didn't affect me directly at all.

2. *What beliefs were conflicting with what's happening?* Well, I clearly held the belief that kids should have to earn what they got. I believed they should be responsible for the consequences of their actions or inactions. I believed my husband had been making a bunch of fear-motivated parenting choices and I judged these choices as wrong. Hmmm? That's not very loving of me. I thought to myself that I'd better track back to these beliefs before going back to talk with him.

3. *What needs weren't being met for me?* Right away I felt some meatiness to this question. After thinking about this for a few minutes, I realized that I was feeling bitter because I was watching my husband give validation, support, reassurance and enthusiastic encouragement to his daughter even though, in my mind, she did nothing to deserve the effusive praise. I was resentful because a whole bunch of good things had happened to my stepdaughter without her doing anything to earn them—darn it all. Oh my, I felt the anger and bitterness creeping in like all the times I'd felt this way in the past.

I was definitely on to something here. As I continued to think about this, I reminded myself that we all come into intimate relationships with emotional wounds, unmet needs and unresolved feelings from the past. Most of us also hope, at some level of consciousness, that our partners will give us the things we didn't get from our parents or previous lovers. This is not their job (nor is it feasible) but when it happens, it sure is a loving gift.

Oooh! That thought caught me in the gut. I realized that I was bitter (experiencing intense resentment) because I was witnessing my husband give his daughter the things I didn't get as a child from my own parents. And the encouragement and validation he was giving his daughter on the phone were the things I wished he would give me more of. I really resonated with this realization.

Because of my child-created personal beliefs, I didn't feel his daughter deserved the praise and support of her father. I also felt angry on behalf of the child I used to be, because I didn't get that kind of support, even though I worked so hard and followed my parents' rules. It just wasn't fair. In my imagination I could see one of my younger selves sticking out her lower lip as I crossed my own arms in front of my chest and sighed deeply. OK, this was progress.

Next, I became newly conscious that some part of me wanted my husband's daughter to be forced to live under the same rules that I had as a child. These were rules my parents put into place and others I'd made up as a child to explain my situation to myself and enable me to emotionally survive my own childhood. Ah ha! I see the conflict here between my needs and my beliefs about how things were supposed to be, and my reality. Do you?

Because I'd had to adhere to the strict rules of "rightness" of my family, I kept trying to get my husband to treat his daughter the way my parents had treated me. Noteworthy! From my perspective and experience, I saw my stepdaughter as defiant, entitled, unappreciative of all her many advantages and hardly making an effort for anything in her life. She didn't have to try hard or earn things like I did. Things came easy to her and she got away with a lot. She had two parents vying for her attention—a dynamic intensified by divorce—and with her kid radar, she played them both successfully, as children do.

When I saw my husband giving his daughter unconditional support, love and enthusiasm for who she was and not for what she did—things I didn't get from my parents—it really stirred up and tapped into my unconscious warehouse of rage and pain. I was a hard worker. I was a good girl. I was one of those achieving type kids always trying to earn (in vain, it seemed) complete approval and attention from my parents but never quite getting that sense of being "OK."

Whenever my husband would praise or reward his daughter when I thought it wasn't deserved or when his daughter didn't have to abide by the same rules or consequences I'd endured, I actually believed that I'd feel better if I could just convince my husband to parent differently. As hard as it was, and still is, for me to admit, I actually wanted my husband to be less enthusiastically supportive, more of a teaching parent and more strict about consequences, making his daughter more responsible for her own behaviors. I used to try to persuade (actually pressure) my husband with logic, article clippings, books and expert opinions. We lost many weekends of closeness over this apparent impasse.

Unexpectedly, I began to see the situation in a new light. Here my husband was trying to give his daughter the support he himself didn't get as a child and I was trying to persuade him to be less unconditionally loving and was angry at him for refusing my requests. I saw that I had been using childrearing logic as an unconscious justification to deny her the very thing I desperately wanted but never got from my own father. The moment I realized what I'd been doing, I was horrified, embarrassed and truly sorry about my behavior. I was ready to change my attitude and approach.

Why was I acting so unloving? This was not like me. I knew there was more to discover. As I was seeking answers, it became clear to me that my unconscious, underlying and present emotional needs were screaming at me internally. What did I want more of? I wanted more support from my husband than I felt he was giving me. It wasn't really about my stepdaughter, like I believed all those years. It was that my issues with my stepdaughter were bumping up against a childhood wound and a presently unmet need—I just didn't understand what was happening until now. I believed I would feel better if my husband would change by giving her less attention—and now I could see that I was wrong. Helping me get my needs met in this area was something I could have explicitly asked for and worked through with my husband if I'd been clear about it. I was clear now.

Watching my husband give unconditional love to his daughter was often very painful for me, for reasons I was just now uncovering. I was unfairly attributing my bitterness to the actions of my husband and stepdaughter. The truth was that these feelings came from a lifetime of unresolved hurt (anger and pain) that was expressing itself as resentment toward my stepdaughter. Before this realization, I was convinced the actions of my husband and stepdaughter were the cause of my bitterness. In that moment of awareness, I felt awful and intrigued at the same time. What was the cause of all these intense feelings?

I resented that my husband was giving his daughter what he was not giving me. In order to make sense and survive the circumstances of my upbringing, I had created a belief that love and attention had to be earned. I was resentful that my stepdaughter received love without having to earn it. Ahhh…BINGO!

It was as if all the lights went on and all the window shades went up at the same time. I was very clear on what to do next. I went back to sit with my husband and eagerly told him what I'd realized about the source of my resentments. As I expressed myself and saw him take in my words, I could feel my bitterness evaporating. It was such a relief to become aware of this dynamic between us. I felt myself excited by all the future stress we weren't going to have to experience.

A recap of what I told my husband:

1. *I told him I was so sorry for all the times I'd tried to bully him with logic so he would give (and do) less for his daughter. I asked him if he could find a way to forgive me.*

2. *I told him, but this time from a position of remorse, awareness and full disclosure, that I felt resentful when I saw him give his daughter what I felt like he had not been giving me. For years I'd been trying my best and giving all I could to help him from the very beginning and it didn't seem fair that his daughter got unconditional love and support from him and I felt like I didn't.*

3. *I shared the details of how I felt when I observed him parenting in a way I didn't get to experience. Because he knows me he instantly understood my behavior in a new way. He started shaking his head. Then he shifted from seeming nervous to being incredibly loving toward me.*

4. *I told him I was now back into my adult wise-woman state of awareness and awake to the real source of the rage and bitterness I was feeling. I could now understand that he was always trying to do whatever he could to find something right with his daughter. He was determined not to have his daughter experience the pain he'd experienced growing up with a father who gave him very little. My husband was parenting his way, rooted in his own reasons and beliefs, and it really had nothing to do with me. It was like layers of defensive, self-isolating anger were melting off me (and from between us) with each new bit of awareness and understanding.*

5. *I told my husband I would stop asking him to do less for his daughter to make my wounded child-self feel better. I also promised him that he would no longer have to choose between (1) parenting his way and fearing (or knowing) he was going to face my hostility and pleadings, and (2) needing to appease me and feeling pressured, angry and guilty that he was not parenting as he believed he should, plus resenting me for not supporting him. That was lose-lose-lose. He was visibly relieved as he continued to listen compassionately and patiently—which I appreciated and told him so.*

6. *Next, feeling nervous and somewhat unprepared, I gathered my courage, reached for his hand and said gently, "I need more emotional support from you. Going forward, will you please give me more attention, validation and enthusiastic encouragement when I look to you for feedback?"*

7. *He surprised me by saying, "Thank you so much for figuring this out. I want you to know I'm so sorry. I now see what you're saying and I really do want to support you more." More high fives and "way to go's" have become a physical response to shared moments of insight, appreciation and support.*

8. *I learned that day that when I share my thoughts and feelings in my calm, adult, authentic and loving voice, he can listen without feeling criticized or defensive. It was a tremendous victory for my well-being and our relationship.*

Now, whenever my husband does something for his daughter and that familiar choking bitterness begins to grip my heart, I bring my attention, compassion and positive self-talk back to myself.

For a few moments, I give myself and the child I used to be, all the lovingkindness I can muster. I remind myself that he's doing the best he can to be a good father. Whenever he's talking or texting with his daughter, I talk to the imaginary child I used to be, giving her all kinds of support in the form of positive and loving self-talk. This new response to feeling resentful has taught me so much about myself. The resentment I felt for years toward my stepdaughter has virtually evaporated.

The bonus: Now my husband feels he can tell me what's going on with his daughter, without the fear of triggering my bitterness or bracing for an argument about a dreaded call for action. The emotional charge has thankfully left the building, so to speak. I'm free to be my naturally empathetic and supportive self and he's been making efforts every day and anytime he sees the chance to offer me kind words of support.

Your Reaction?

Can you relate to this Stepmom's thoughts and feelings? Any ideas come to mind for you and your life? By working on this one situation, the Stepmom in our story has learned so much about herself because she was willing to interrupt her emotional habits, get curious and explore her own feelings. She was willing to trust there were good reasons for whatever she was thinking and feeling. She was right! This is so important. By working on this one common resentful situation she ended up also resolving years of old similar unprocessed resentments. By recognizing that the feeling of resentment is an alert that needs her attention and by slowing down her reactions, she and her husband can now help each other whenever either of them feels the twinges of present and past resentments. They can avoid a lot of stress between them and now authentically love and support each other.

You can turn this story into a true story for you and your life. It's such a relief to have a proven action plan whenever resentment shows up. You and your partner can become free from the emotional poisons of resentment by doing this work together. If your partner is not quite up for (or into) this work, you can still figure out what's going on with you. Once you know more about the true causes of your resentments, there are many things you can do to meet your needs, change your beliefs and bring your giving into balance.

Over the years I've worked through many of my own resentments, past and present, using the skills in this book. Stepmoms who have learned these skills have reported so many positive insights and lasting changes in their relationships. You can have the same benefits for your life. Imagine knowing that as soon as you feel a twinge of resentment, you'll honor your feelings and get to work to make some changes so the resentment resolves and you feel even better than before. Unlike so many stepfamily situations, this process is something you have complete control over. This process really works.

Fifteen

Resolving Resentments from the Past
Get What You Need to "Let It Go"

When we feel resentful over something that's happened in the past, it can feel like a big lump of something in our gut that just won't go away. Sometimes it can even feel like an obsession or like a haunting. It can make us feel slightly crazy when we think about it. It probably makes our partner defensive, frustrated or even furious when we can't seem to help ourselves from bringing it up over and over again. It can rush up into our minds anytime we feel hurt or angry. Sadly, when we do bring it up, it often re-inflicts more of the same hurts and angers like when it first happened.

- What the heck? Why can't we seem to let it go?

- How do we reply when someone tells us to get over it?

- Why can't we talk ourselves out of these nagging, stubborn persistent feelings?

Even if the resented issue or event is long over and done with, when you're feeling resentful, it means there's something more you need to learn, understand or become aware of. It means the resentment will not go away until you figure out what you need (and still don't have) as a result of the experience. The resentment will not go away until you uncover "the lousy deal" or the conflict between the reality you experienced and your beliefs and needs.

Thankfully resentments from the past can be resolved with or without other people's participation. When the people involved are willing to help you get what you need and regain your balance, that's wonderful for your relationship with that person, especially when that person is your partner. However, if the person involved isn't aware of their impact, isn't willing to take responsibility for their impact or isn't someone you can trust enough to work with, then you can still find ways to resolve your resentments. Thank goodness!

Identify a Resentment

The first step for processing your past resentment is to get clear about what you're feeling resentful about. The more specific you can be, the more effective the process. While this will work for anything from your past, to get the most out of this chapter and help yourself learn these new tactics with an immediate benefit, pick one event you'd like to resolve from the past that's between you and your partner.

The goal is to untangle the emotions so you can better understand what you're feeling, what you need to be different and what you can do to heal from it *and* make future choices that ensure the same thing doesn't happen again in the same way. This isn't a science so there's no way to tell which of the questions on the list below will help you in each situation. However with a bit of practice, you'll get quite good at this process, reaping immeasurable present and future benefits.

Which situation to pick from your past? My suggestion is you take a deep breath and ask yourself the following question. Then trust the first situation that comes to your mind.

"Which resentment can I work on that will bring the most relief to the present tension with my partner?"

Once you've picked your situation from the past, read through the complete list of questions below before starting your process. This gives your head, heart and subconscious and unconscious minds a chance to begin the process and contribute to your work.

Ask yourself the following questions and give each one some patient, honest, open-minded space. Some questions will not apply. Some will be more relevant than others. That's A-OK. Given the complexity of life, there are lots of possibilities. The list is a guideline for starters. This can be a good time for journaling your answers, instead of just thinking about them, so you can reflect on them from a fresh point of view.

You'll know when you come upon the insight that will bring your feelings into resolution. You may even think of another question as a result of thinking about the answers to one on the list. This is all very good. Remember, there's no right or wrong, good or bad, this is about what's meaningful, relevant and true for you and your feelings. If possible, give yourself some privacy and quiet time for this exercise. Also, this can be something you do in snippets of time. You can sleep on it or let it cook for a day or two so that the information you're looking for has a chance to surface on its own. This is a process with its own timetable. With a specific resentment from the past in mind, compassionately explore these questions:

1. What happened that shouldn't have happened? OR What didn't happen that should have?

2. Who am I truly angry at or hurt by? Note: Sometimes we blame our stepkids or their bio-mom but it's really our partner who has let us down or angered us by his actions or through his refusal to own his personal issues or take responsibility for the situation. Think about this carefully. Look deeply.

3. Did I contribute to or have any role in the upsetting event? (If you didn't contribute, move to next question.) If so, what did I do (or not do) that contributed to the stress of the situation? Do I owe anyone an apology? Am I still waiting for an apology? What am I looking for in an apology that would make me feel that amends have been made?

4. What are the patterns of over-giving, conflicts in beliefs, needs and reality that have given birth to this resentment in the first place? Can I pinpoint the time when my feelings changed from comfortable to uncomfortable—where the situation switched from feeling like a good deal to feeling more like a lousy deal?

5. If I could have a do-over in my imagination, what are at least 2-3 different choices I could have made during or after the event to reduce my stress and resentment?

6. If I was hearing about this situation happening to another Stepmom—meaning I had no history or ledger weighing on me and could look at the situation objectively—how might I see this situation differently? How might I advise her to proceed? What would I tell her to do that I didn't do?

7. What needs of others did I miss or misinterpret because I wasn't consciously standing in my adult self and/or was feeling hurt, tired, angry or scared?

8. Where are the missed opportunities for me to have felt and expressed empathy? Be aware of any defensiveness so you can help yourself in new ways. See Chapters 21 and 22 for more about defensiveness. Go to smoms.org/BonusChapters to read the chapter called "Six Sample Situations for Disarming Defensive Behaviors Between You and Your Partner."

9. What do I feel I still need to say to my partner in order to feel truly heard and known about how this event/circumstance impacted me?

10. What words do I need to hear from him that he hasn't said or refuses to say?

11. If Cathryn was to interview my partner (and we're pretending that he's delighted to honestly chat with her), what would my partner say about the situation? What does *he* believe I need from him right now?

12. Regarding what I want my partner to say but he won't: If he's unwilling to say it to me, could it be that he still needs something from me? Do I know what it is? Have I asked him directly? Am I willing to say it to him now in exchange for his desired words?

13. Can I see any power struggle or impasse of mutually unmet needs or beliefs? If so, what might the two of us be silently (or overtly) struggling over or refusing to give or exchange?

14. Going forward, what understanding, agreement or promise would I like from my partner so I can believe that this situation will not happen again?

15. If the situation is outside of his control, what is he willing to agree to do differently in order to help me feel supported in a new way? What are the agreed-upon consequences if either of us fails to do what we agreed to do? Do I need to write them down based on past experiences to feel confident this will happen as agreed?

16. What do I need to promise myself that I'll do differently going forward so that I can believe we can avoid this same situation causing resentment again? This is NOT about ultimatums or threats but about agreed boundaries and understood responses in the future.

17. What do I need to explain and share with my partner so that we can learn from this past situation and become more aware of our individual needs, our beliefs and what each of us needs to move forward together in the "nobody's right/nobody's wrong, we can create a mutually satisfying solution" relationship approach? See Chapter 20 for a detailed description of this kind and powerful approach.

18. What's my creative problem-solving plan of at least 2-4 acceptable amendments or agreements for how things can be different going forward to rebalance and resolve

the impact of this past resentment? After explaining these options to my partner, can we agree on at least one of them?

19. How confident, anxious, afraid or excited am I about talking with my partner about this new solution to resolving this resentment? How is my adult woman self feeling? What is the "child I used to be" thinking and feeling about this plan? Note: Use your imagination to differentiate between the present and younger you.

20. What fears come up for me when I think about presenting this new plan to my partner?

21. In what ways can I consciously help myself, talk with myself and do something differently to better support, protect and stand up for the emotional child within me?

This is quite a list, huh? You're right, it is! As Kit, my mentor, used to say, *"when you get the questions straight, the answers and insights begin to flow"*—as if you're seeing the old situation with a new, keen clarity and perspective. It can really be a very exhilarating experience to realize that there might finally be a way to look at a situation and bring you lasting relief.

What Can You Expect?

- Sometimes you can resolve a resentment in the privacy of your own mind by changing your perspective as a result of what you learn from this act of self-reflection. It's hard to see things clearly when you're blinded by the viewpoint that revenge, punishment or justice are the only acceptable solutions. Hindsight can give you some wise gifts when you're open to new insights.

- You may realize that some people are never going to give you what you want or need. These are the times when it's important to make the empowered choice to look to yourself (or trusted others) to help you find new ways to help yourself feel better, find a new perspective about what was lost in the original event. Giving yourself permission to grieve, to express anger in healthy ways or to have a witness for whatever happened can give you the attention, compassion and validation that was lacking in the original event. Learning spiritual, personal and other valuable lessons from whatever happened can be something you receive from the process of reflection. Sometimes, that alone can bring you a new willingness to digest the past resentment in exchange for a newfound peace of mind. Really! Happily, this is true quite often.

- Sometimes you'll receive great value—even from the lessons learned the hard way. My husband calls this the *"baseball-bat-over-the-head method of learning."* Ha! I know it well myself. Insights like a new awareness of your negative impact that you can now change, or uncovering a previously unmet need that you can now meet, healing a childhood wound or learning how to take nothing personally are also things of value that you can receive from exploring a past situation. When you realize any of these valuable insights, it gives you the chance to re-evaluate the experience. Sometimes your newly gained perspectives and planned changes to help yourself may lead you to decide that the scales of giving and receiving are now acceptably balanced.

- Sometimes the pain caused by stepfamily relationships is so deep, you realize that the event itself isn't the only source of the pain you feel/felt. When looking at your feelings with a new perspective, you realize the situation touched an unhealed childhood wound. This can be one of those "hard to swallow," need to put your pride and ego on the shelf moments. Especially if you've got a well-worn reflexive path of blaming others and now need to own that it's really not totally their fault—maybe, just maybe, a combination of your wounds and their actions have painfully interacted. While this can feel yucky at first, it's really empowering. This is a "symptom vs. cause" kind of issue. As you get to the cause of your pain, you can learn from and heal that wound, and then (here's the great news) the very same circumstance will never impact you in the same upsetting way, or maybe not at all. You have the power to make this healing happen.

- Sometimes you realize that you and your partner need to sit down and work on resolving this past event as a conscious, loving team working together. Nobody's right and nobody's wrong is the strongly recommended agreement for this to be as successful as possible. Bring your insights to your partner when you can be your most loving authentic self and ask him, *"Will you help me put this event to rest so we can leave it in the past?"* Asking from this emotionally open and loving place is the best way to invite your partner to do this work with you.

Sharing memories about how great it felt when you two shared a happy moment is a helpful precursor to your request for your partner's participation. Remembering a time when you two felt so strongly connected is a very good way to open both your hearts before you start your sharing.

Good things can happen when a couple is on the same side of this goal—to turn resentment into resolution. If he's open to it, great. If he's still feeling defensive or angry or judgmental, keep your insights to yourself for another time. If it feels right, ask him what he needs from you so that *his* resentments can be resolved. I've found guys have their own resentments even if they don't discuss or even understand them. The work you do can inspire and teach your partner.

Whether or not your partner is open to working with you on any of your outstanding past resentments, you'll be changed by this process in many healthy ways. Your increased self-awareness and the attention you give to your feelings are valuable benefits in and of themselves.

Please Note: If you have any fear of (and experience with) your partner's defensive behaviors or if you have a sense about how he feels about this situation, this would be a good time to read the chapters about defensiveness to see how you can help your partner feel safe enough to open his heart to work with you. Defensiveness is caused by actual, really painful, scary past experiences, so the more you understand this behavior, the more effective you can be in creating mutual emotional safety in your relationship.

Whatever you learn from this process, and whatever you decide to do or view differently, there's always going to be the moment when you have to decide, *"Am I willing to let this resentment go and move forward all the wiser or not?"* Some things in life are a process and some things in life are a choice. It's very important to honor your feelings and not push yourself before it feels right for you. This choice is up to you. Nobody can (or should) talk you into it.

When you're ready, this choice to release your resentment has the power to free you from its treadmill. I don't encourage you to let go of anything until it feels right for you. I hope you'll trust yourself and the process enough to believe that if you can't let it go, there must be more to discover, get compassion for, learn from, heal or accept. You'll know. You'll feel the relief. You may sigh heavily several times. The tears are likely to flow. These things are all confirmation of your good work.

It is valuable to understand that when you give your attention to your resentments, they can be clues that lead you to changes that make you feel happier in your life. I hope there's something here to give you a new sense of excitement and empowerment over whatever has or is creating resentment in your life from the past. Old resentments are so draining and often lead to despair. I also hope that some part of you believes that your well-being is worth the effort to give this a try.

This is a life-changing skill you're about to start practicing. Please remember to be patient and compassionate with yourself and whatever feelings come up for you. Remind yourself (and any younger, angry, hurt versions of yourself) that your feelings are all trying to help you better understand your emotional wounds and needs. They are clues to point out any conflicts so you, as the wise, resourceful adult woman you are today, can give them the loving, kind and compassionate attention you did not receive originally. Resolving resentments from the past is so liberating for you and your partner. Good luck. From experience, you're very likely to surprise yourself with the insights that come from pondering these questions. What a relief it can be!

See Chapter 25, Supporting Your Partner Through Divorce Guilt and Fears, to get another example of a couple working through a past resentment.

A Stepmom Working with Resentment

Ava's Story

August 2016

Two years into dating my boyfriend and being heavily involved with his children, I recognized how much support I could use in the realm of being a stepparent, particularly a childless stepmother. My journey involved a lot of pain regarding childlessness and my identity as a woman in this newly formed family. I had questions of "identifying" what (who) exactly I was in the home, and the zone was somewhat gray at times. I questioned what I wanted to be, who I wanted to become, what parts of me I wanted to preserve, how I wanted to respond to difficult scenarios with the children and how my journey with my partner and the kids could actually be part of my healing. The list of questions went on.

I had spent several months shaming myself for the conflicting emotions and thoughts I'd feel in my role as a stepmother to two young children, as well as my identity as an unmarried woman with no biological children of her own. I was trying to navigate my life and spirit while running on auto pilot as the woman of the house. I was experiencing a lot of judgement within and was too embarrassed to share some of my deep emotions with any friends. I didn't feel that my peers—who were in different situations—could relate. I didn't want to hurt my partner or his kids. My parents were so supportive but I still felt like I needed someone who walked this path before. A mentor. A "sister" who got me.

I recall going online for immediate support. I came across Cathryn Bond Doyle and her work through smoms.org. For the next half year, I navigated through the site, reading Cathryn's articles, reviewing concerns written by fellow SMOMS and checking out suggested books. All were very helpful and yet I knew I needed to take the next step for some one-on-one counseling with Cathryn. From the beginning, Cathryn was encouraging, supportive and compassionate. I felt she understood first-hand many of my conflicts, my challenges, my triumphs and my questions.

Cathryn encouraged me to welcome all feelings without judgement and to reflect on my experiences. She was a huge advocate for being kind and caring toward myself to the same degree to which I approached my partner and stepkids. She reinforced the necessity to take care of myself. Through our conversations and sessions, she provided practical approaches to nurture myself, my relationship and my connection with my stepkids. She reminded me many times that we can love and care for others regardless of whether or not we are biological mothers. Working through my feelings with someone who had experienced them herself helped me move forward in a more compassionate, self-honoring way. I now feel equal and comfortable with myself as a Stepmom.

She encouraged me to see the complexity and insights in my experiences as well as potential for increased self-awareness and healing. Her messages were loving and always respectful of my ability to make my own personal choices. She often pointed out the big picture and the importance of recognizing that everyone in the home matters—a message that sometimes stepmothers forget as they desperately try to be superheroes or prove their worth and right to a place in their homes.

Cathryn pointed out the beauty that comes with giving and receiving. She encouraged me to welcome love, to reflect on difficult interactions and to also approach some scenarios creatively and playfully. Since I'm good at this and at creative problem-solving it encouraged me to realize that I did have many of the core skills needed to improve my situation.

Perhaps the most supportive exchange was on a trip I took to the States from my home in Canada. I took a leap of faith and emailed Cathryn telling her I thought I'd be somewhat near her hometown. I didn't realize it was two hours away. Cathryn drove to the hotel where I was staying and spent most of the day with me. We shared a lovely brunch, connected through shared stories and began our one-on-one sessions face to face. It was extremely powerful and provided a lot of strength and understanding that I was desperately seeking at the time.

Cathryn and I have remained in contact over the years. She's a woman who really did set out on a mission to help other women experience the joys, the heartache, the trials, tribulations, laughter, tears and a-ha moments that go with being a Stepmom on a Mission. I will always feel grateful for our exchanges and all that I have learned about my own strengths and abilities that now enable me feel empowered as a stepmother.

Ava
Stepmom since 2011
SMOM since 2013

Sixteen

Embittered or Empowered?
Working with the Unchangeable Facts of Your Stepmom Life

When your ability to be the stepmother you want to be is unsupported or denied, your reactions can range from mild annoyance to feeling hateful, devastated, resentful and more. When your beliefs about how to be a "good Stepmom" and your need to be treated with respect and fairness conflict with what's happening in your stepfamily life, resentments can spin out of control. They can build up until you blow up, break down or—become more conscious of what's happening and help yourself in new ways. When other people's actions and decisions prevent you from expressing yourself as the stepmother you'd like to be or believe you should be, how can you help yourself? How can you shift from feeling bitter about the circumstances (many or most of which you can't control) to being empowered in your stepfamily situation?

As you better understand your thoughts and feelings, learning new skills along the way, you can reduce the negative impact of the emotional roller coaster of feelings, or even stop it altogether. You can step into your adult self and create choices that can help you feel better. These acts of consciousness and personal growth give your innate sense of dignity and well-being a fighting chance to triumph over any uncooperative and unfair actions of the stepkids, their bio-mom and maybe even your own partner. The purpose of this chapter is to address some of the unchangeable realities and the resulting resentments you may be facing with the goal of showing you how the creative thinking process and some philosophical choices can empower you as a Stepmom on a Mission.

Dealing with Present Resentments

You may want to review Chapter 11-15 for a detailed understanding of resentments and how to work with them. As a very brief review, resentment emerges from unresolved anger or unidentified conflicts from some part of your psyche that are trying to give you an important emotional message.

Causes of Feeling Resentful

- Some boundary is being violated.

- Some need is not being met.

- Some belief is conflicting with a need or a situation in your life.

- You're over-giving and there's an imbalance that needs your immediate attention.

Figuring out the message behind your resentments—particularly when those resentments are freshly recognized—can save you an abundance of time, energy and emotional stress. Unfortunately, ignoring your resentments will not make them go away. Instead, they will often increase in intensity until you're compelled to act, perhaps expressing your anger in a misdirected way or, ideally, choosing to respond consciously. I'm hoping you'll choose to compassionately give your attention to your feelings and make the changes that honor you as the adult woman you are—ASAP. If you're reading this chapter, you've suffered enough. No good comes from being in emotional pain until you can learn from it. While you can't change some things in your stepmother life situation, dealing with upsetting feelings is something you can change to improve your well-being and feel more in control over your happiness.

Dealing with Resentments from the Past

This topic can be complicated. Resolving resentments is much easier when your partner is on board and equally eager to process your feelings (and his) with you. There are lots of invisible intimacy wedges that can grow from unresolved resentments. That said, many past resentments can be resolved even without your partner's conscious participation.

Balancing your over-giving is very helpful and freeing—see Chapter 10. In addition, new healthy boundaries will help you move forward in an empowered, conscious way—see Chapter 3. And then there's the issue of your partner's ability and willingness to hear what you have to say *and* embrace your feelings empathetically and open-heartedly instead of defensively. This is an amazing experience—nothing trivial, easy or enforceable.

One of the keys to successfully resolving resentments from the past is to consider yourself a kind and creative emotional detective. This includes resisting blaming, looking for right or wrong, good or bad. Instead, work to learn more about yourself and your partner and the dynamic between the two of you when one or both of you are triggered in some upsetting way.

Rarely, if ever, is something you resent from the past an isolated event. Usually it's part of a pattern and can reveal false beliefs or emotional wounds that have affected you for a long time. Exploring each resentment can help you uncover and discover more about yourself—the awesome, the not-so-good, the wounded, the not-so-loving, the defensive, the tender-hearted, the fearful and the Wonder Woman within. When you embrace this discovery process with compassion, patience, courage, curiosity and confidence, relief is inevitable, your happiness is virtually unlimited and your life adventure can become wonderful, regardless of the behaviors of others. Yes, really! See Chapter 15 for more specifics about processing resentments from your past.

Things You Can't Change

It can be oddly difficult to choose empowerment over feeling embittered. When you become aware that something in your life is unacceptable or unchangeable and you experience any related disempowering rage, you really have two pathways for dealing with this reality. You can get lost in the rage or you can take healthy wise steps to improve your situation and feel better as a result of your efforts. However, please be compassionate with yourself if you've been caught up in the rage. Why? Because whenever we're in the midst of emotional turmoil, it takes a deliberate intention or some outside support (like this book) to help us realize that there are healthy options. This can be the beginning of your choice to take new steps.

"That was then and this is now" helps me stay in the present moment so I can see (believe or convince myself) that things really can be different. It helps me separate and free myself from the past—like permission for a clean slate and fresh start. One of the conundrums for stepmothers working with their resentments toward unchangeable facts is not being able to understand why something they knew and thought they had accepted right from the beginning of the relationship is now making them feel awful. It is a really good question to investigate because there are good reasons for your change of heart and valuable answers to discover. For the sake of clarity, let's break down the stepfamily examples into these two categories: things you knew and now resent and things that have revealed themselves that you now resent.

Here are some of the common unchangeable stepfamily situations you probably knew about at the beginning of your relationship but now you may find exponentially upsetting without really understanding why things have changed:

- Your partner had kids with another woman before you, robbing you of many precious shared "firsts."

- You wanted kids but your partner doesn't want more children.

- You're forced into a burdensome financial agreement that inhibits your lifestyle while you witness the bio-mom having what she wants (or what you want).

- You've inherited challenging stepkids but always figured you could connect with them eventually and have a good relationship with them.

Stepfamily situations that become clear after you're committed to your partner and you now discover are unchangeable:

- You inherit an uncooperative bio-mom or in-laws that never got over the divorce as you hoped they would, and still make things difficult for you and your partner in ways you'd never imagined.

- You and your partner both wanted a baby but, for whatever reason, were unable to have one.

- You're forced into expensive, energy-draining court battles or judgments that take over your life and prevent you from doing things you wanted to do.

If any of these (or other difficult, unchangeable situations) are true for you, they may be difficult to live with and also aggravate old wounds from your past. This is a good time to jot down your lists so you can keep them in mind as we move through this work. These resentments hold a lot of emotional energy. It's a lot to manage while you're busy living your life. Rarely has anyone been taught how to manage all these feelings. It's painful and can lead to suffering, beating your head against the wall, hurting yourself and often those you love by misdirected expressions of your rage or frustrations. Alternatively, you can decide "today is a new day" and accept that you've done your best with your present strategy and skill set and now decide to make some new choices, gain some new skills and use your energy in new ways.

The Unchangeable Facts in Your Reality

One of the first things you can do is confidently declare the situation as *"unacceptable."* Disregard whether others agree with you or validate your feelings—your affirmation is enough. Remind yourself you always have the choice to rise above any circumstances and look at them from a more philosophical perspective. Paraphrasing Vicktor Frankl's book, *Man's Search for Meaning*, the only thing you have complete control over, and that no one can ever take away from you, is the attitude you choose toward anything. With this in mind, you can look at the unchangeable, unacceptable facts in your life and make a new conscious choice—I call this choice "empowered acceptance." When you choose to accept the unacceptable, you consciously, intentionally shift your attention away from feeling at the mercy of anything or anyone and toward new ways to help yourself and your partner.

Working with unchangeable facts is the most challenging form of disempowering resentments. I believe that empowerment really boils down to being willing and able to make growth-motivated (vs. fear-based) choices and taking responsibility for finding the choices that best meet your unique needs. Some of your beliefs can interfere with or limit your sense of freedom or power for dealing with your situations. When you think about the unchangeable facts in your stepfamily life situation, ask yourself the following questions:

- In addition to being loved and supported by your partner, do you believe that you're responsible for your own well-being? If not, why not?

- How would your life be different if you had equal rights with every single person in your home? Do you believe you have equal rights?

- Are you willing to make your well-being more important than making your point, being right or winning?

- When you can't be the kind of stepmother you want to be because your stepkids, their bio-mom, your partner or others get in your way, what comes up for you when you consider accepting this reality and making your well-being your #1 priority? What could you be doing with that time, energy and attention to help yourself feel happier?

Isn't it odd how difficult it can be to answer these questions? Jotting down your answers and the "Yeah, Buts" is always helpful as you make this journey.

What If You Choose to Stay Resentful?

Surprisingly, making this choice to accept the unacceptable means you're not disempowered anymore. Why not? Because now you're making a conscious choice—your choice—to accept a reality that you can't change, like you do the weather or the order of the days of the week. If you choose to remain resentful about unchangeable facts in your life, even when admitting you have other options, this is a noteworthy personal decision. When you feel enraged by unchangeable facts and consciously decide to hold on to that rage, even though it has a cost attached to it, you can take one of two forks in the road. You can follow the martyred, embittered path or the path of empowered acceptance. If you do choose to stay focused on feeling resentful about what's unacceptable, then at least do it compassionately. The self-talk could sound something like this:

> *"I'm making a conscious choice to stay focused on what's unacceptable to me. Even though I don't understand why I'm unwilling to resolve my resentment about this situation, I'm going to be supportive and compassionate with myself.*
>
> *Rather than experiencing all the negative toxic feelings that go along with resentment, I'm going to give myself permission to label this unchangeable fact as unacceptable and see what I can learn about myself and the situation in this state of unacceptable-ness.*
>
> *For whatever reasons, I'm unwilling to let go of this rage so I'm going to get curious and learn more about it."*

While this wouldn't be my first choice for any stepmother, it's a real option. And this is a more empowered option than feeling self-pity, martyred or lost in rage, victimhood or despair under the illusion that you shouldn't be facing what you're facing. Can you see that? If staying resentful feels like a better option for you (at this time) than shifting to the suggested empowered approach, then I truly believe there must be some important insight, lesson or feeling awaiting your discovery. May you find that pearl of insight and then move into the relief of empowered acceptance.

Focus on New Goals

I ask you to consider that there's a new way to approach and learn from unacceptable situations. You can choose to channel all your unresolved angry energy from the past into helping you find new options for the present and future. As I like to say, cue the Rocky music, power pose, take a stand on a table like Norma Rae and dance or shout at the future you're about to create with your newfound power. The self-talk could sound something like this:

> *"Today I choose to believe that I have the ability to find more of my power in this situation. Once I find it, I'm determined to use it in new ways, with new choices and attitudes that better serve me and my needs."*

You can choose to believe you can change and control (somehow, in some way) the unchangeable realities that aren't OK with you—or you can choose to put your attention elsewhere and create something new. It's not about right or wrong. This is a very personal choice. Instead of trying to control, dominate, judge or punish others for not doing as you want them to do, you can choose to believe that there are other life situations out there that allow you to have, get and do whatever you need—even if it means that others involved aren't happy about it or even included as you'd hoped. Rocking the boat is sometimes necessary and almost always leads you to something better.

Finding the humility to believe there really is something you can do differently to help yourself is the key to freedom from bitterly painful resentments. This is true even if you don't know what that something is or how you'll get there or what the new situation could possibly look like. As Eleanor Roosevelt said, *"It's better to light a candle than to curse the dark."* It comes down to being willing (or unwilling) to broaden your beliefs and skills and become happy as a stepmother and in your relationship with your partner, no matter what the circumstances. It's a choice many are unaware of.

Where to Go From Here

You can begin by looking at your needs and personal beliefs beneath the surface of your situation. Use the power of your awareness and curiosity. These talents can also be applied to your new intention, and it can help you find new ways to create what you truly need. You can mobilize anger from the past to fuel your courage and replace your fears with faith and excitement.

Questions and Examples

- How would it feel to stop trying to change anyone else and instead put your attention toward creating something new (for you) that you have the ability to implement?

- What other ways can you give yourself the experiences you desire, such as feeling included, honored, respected, safe and loved?

- What would be different if you directed your creativity and energy to create new options that could give you what you need?

Unchangeable Example #1

You can't go to school conferences with your stepkid's teacher because of bio-mom objections, complaints and threats to cause trouble between your stepkids and their father.

Look Deeper: Look underneath the unfairness you perceive and explore what it is you want that's being denied. I know it can seem obvious, and that's your starting point because there's more. Could it be that you want to be included, to be validated, to be seen as a member of the parenting team or to have your place at your partner's side for all stepkid events? We stepmothers can all understand those very reasonable goals. However, usually it takes another stepmother with an uncooperative bio-mom to really know how it feels. Find someone who will give you that compassion. Once you've felt understood by another (a critical prerequisite for moving forward), take a breath and begin looking for what you can do to help yourself find a way to be OK with this situation.

Possible Solutions: Contact the teacher and have a second conference, even if you partner goes to both conferences. If that's not possible, ask your partner to take notes and meet him right after the conference so his memories are fresh and you feel like you get all the information possible.

Unchangeable Example #2

Your stepkids leave your house with their clothes and things in their backpack but often return without the things you gave them or the clothes you bought them.

Here's a situation from a Stepmom in one of our resentment workshops. You'll see how she got clear on what was not going to change, worked with her partner to try a new tactic, processed her feelings and let go of needing unchangeable things to change and feeling resentment about her stepfamily situation.

"Last year, my stepkids were in the 2nd and 4th grades and their bio-mom never sent them back to our house in the clothes they came to her in. At first it was annoying but then it became so frustrating to me. It was so unfair!!! I always send her kids back to her in the clothes they wore when they came to our house. I was getting so angry about it that I started keeping a detailed list. I felt almost obsessed and furious that she was keeping the stuff her kids brought to her house and sending them back in old, nearly too small outfits. So many of the fun toys and cool things they got from us were never returned. We (hesitantly) let them take things to show their bio-mom because we felt like they were their things and we were trying to be respectful. When my partner asked the bio-mom about a specific jacket that was a gift from his family, she never answered him or returned the items. Crap!

I kept mentioning it to my partner and he kept telling me, 'Just keep replacing the stuff, it's better than fighting with her to try to get things back.' Well to me it was the principle of the thing. It was part of the co-parenting agreement. It wasn't right! My complaints fell on increasingly deaf ears. A couple of times he told me just to return the kids in the worn or ill-fitting clothes. I was horrified that the teachers would think I would send kids in my care in such clothing. The rift became bigger and bigger between me and my partner. I knew I was letting this get to me and over-reacting but I just couldn't seem to let it go.

Finally one day, after an internal temper tantrum, I sat down with him to try to come up with a new plan. He remained consistently (annoyingly) unbothered by the situation but to his credit he sat with me, listened to me and then said, firmly and patiently, 'Buy some new clothes for the kids that you don't care about ever seeing again. Go ahead and keep returning her clothes, like you've always done, but have them wear the new disposable clothes.' (We laughed at his term.) He was pleased and sincere with me, 'Honey, please accept this solution and let's put this behind us. Let's not let her get to us anymore. She's not ever going to change and I don't want to argue about it anymore.'

Well, OK. He was right. I thought about it. I remembered the 'sounds about right' approach I learned here at SMOMS. This sure seemed to qualify. I decided to process my anger and feel gratitude that we could afford to implement his approach. I ripped up and burned my list of lost items, went shopping for their new clothes and—we never fought about this issue again. We shrugged, rolled our eyes, I sighed, and we were compassionate with the kids when they missed their things. Most importantly, I decided to accept this unchangeable reality and stop losing my own happiness over her actions. My partner was so grateful for my new attitude about it. At that point, I decided to take that as a win for me—and us."

Make Well-Being a Priority

This is a common message throughout this book. You can choose to make your well-being more important than anyone else's desire to deny, diminish, criticize or belittle your role in your stepkids' lives. It may be counterintuitive, but sometimes being predictable about following the rules, honoring agreements, being respectful, fair and thoughtful can make a Stepmom an easy target for a vengeful bio-mom looking to cause drama/trauma for you. Think back and look for situations where your predictability may have been used against you, so to speak. If you're a practitioner of the Golden Rule, I urge you to add a new clause at the end. I think a Stepmom's revised Golden Rule should read something like this:

> *"Do unto others as you would have others do unto you—until those doing unto you are not being kind or respectful, then turn your attention to treating yourself the way you wish to be treated."*
>
> ~ Cathryn's Expanded Version of the Golden Rule

Becoming aware of how your actions and choices contribute to any stress you're experiencing is key to feeling better because it will give you clues and ideas about new empowered choices you can make to improve your life situation. With your thoughts and feelings firmly anchored in your adult state of mind, you deny anyone the opportunity to steal your power or quash your self-esteem. Yes, you can still uphold your values, it may just mean doing so in creative, non-traditional ways. Succeeding in this challenge is one reward of this work. It feels triumphant!

Trying to outsmart or manage a situation is very different from trying to control, defeat, manipulate, cheat or pull rank. Can you feel the difference? Outsmarting and managing are meant here to represent acting out of dominion not domination. Dominion is working to create circumstances that respect everyone involved, not controlling other people. Controlling, beating (figuratively), trying to make others lose, etc., are acting out of domination—power over another person against their will. Domination and controlling are an age-old tactics and not very kind, loving or effective in the long term. You'll be able to manage stressful stepfamily situations with more ease and a lot less personal angst when you come from your empowered, adult, wise, awake self and focus on creating solutions for your well-being. Play music that fuels your courage and energy and put on that creative thinking cap.

Are you willing to make your happiness, your intimate connection with your partner and your sense of well-being more important than whatever an uncooperative bio-mom says, does or threatens? I hope you reply with a heartfelt urgency, *"Yes. I want to do that."*

The more willing you are to believe there are acceptable and maybe even better options beyond the straightforward right/wrong, good/bad, control-or-be-controlled models of behavior, the more powerful "outside the social box" options you can create. This can be quite an unexpectedly energizing intellectual and emotional adventure and is sometimes just what a weary, tired-of-feeling-angry and willing-to-help-herself Stepmom needs.

A Personal Pep Talk

If you're dealing with an uncooperative bio-mom, it's time to take a stand for your own happiness. Refuse to engage or play the victim and instead choose to be victorious by limiting, avoiding and containing her negative impact on you and your relationship with your partner. The concept of "empowered acceptance," accepting the unchangeable or turning away from a fight, might initially feel like losing. But think about it—what are you really losing when you step off the unwinnable game board set up by others? Isn't it a solid win for you to take actions that move you into a more peaceful place with your partner?

I suggest that you're only losing in your ego's version of your reality. Perhaps you may feel you're losing in the eyes of society? What are you really losing when you turn your back on age-old woman-to-woman power struggles that don't hold a prize of joy, happiness, significance or lasting value? You might have a belief that trying to get others to change (or do the right thing) is your only pathway to happiness (or the end of stress). This only has to cause you stress until you decide to change your beliefs and consider new options. Once you do make the conscious choices, all kinds of light bulbs can go on. This book is written to help you decide to look for those new options and to believe it's worth the effort.

Stepping on my soapbox for a moment: One of the hardest things about being a stepmother today is that there aren't any equal, respectful, positive societally defined or accepted roles for devoted stepmothers. The myth of all natural mothers being fully and compassionately dedicated to the well-being of their children seems to dominate the stories and social trend-setters of the past and present. Sadly, society and Hollywood keep perpetuating the evil stepmother stereotype without being challenged very much—yet.

That said, while greater society may lack a positive definition of our role, we Stepmoms on a Mission have the opportunity to cultivate and negotiate a new place within our families and with our partners. We can shift our intentions and focus, refusing to be defined by storybooks and misguided assumptions and focusing on our right (and abilities) to make our life as happy as possible. We can be mapmakers for future stepmothers and it's exciting to think about how we can contribute to the end of so much pain, suffering and stress for our future sister stepmothers.

Yes, it's a well-reasoned but still unpopular choice to make being happy more important than being right. Yes, this probably means changing some familiar attitudes and long-held, child-created beliefs. And more good news: yes, you can continue to be the person you want to be, with the values you want to have. Choosing to be happy instead of resentful empowers and liberates you, even if your stepkids or their bio-mom choose not to get along with you.

If we could make how we feel in each daily moment more important than whatever others may be saying or doing, we'd be a whole lot happier, calmer and more cheerful. How different would your life be if stepfamily situations couldn't upset you for more than 5-15 minutes per incident? This is not just a pep talk—it's a vision and I believe a real possibility for you and your partner as well. If you have inherited an unkind or not-even-civil bio-mom, along with your stepkids, see Chapter 32 to learn about the "Sounds About Right" approach mentioned in the case study.

Reality Check: Has the stress of your stepfamily life already had exhausting, infuriating, health-changing and maybe bank-draining impacts on you and One? Hopefully, imagining not having to continue feeling this way is enough motivation for you to change and learn new ways to look at your reality.

Won't things get better if you just endure and hang in? Maybe, if you're lucky, but not likely. Until you consciously choose to change any personal beliefs that allow others' actions to have power over your well-being, you'll unconsciously create more painful realities. That's not a criticism. It's just the way we human beings create our realities. The past is likely to be repeated until you do something differently.

Are you willing to give this new approach a chance? As someone told me long ago, if this new skill doesn't work, you can always go back to your current strategy. Kind of comforting, sort of funny and true.

Questions for Your Journey

- What does it feel like (what comes up for you?) to give this new approach a chance to work for you?

- Any "Yeah, Buts"? Please write these down as they'll be helpful in your process.

- What if you acknowledge and appreciate that you did your best to change your unchangeable situation and now choose to move on to a new goal which *is* within your control? What thoughts and feelings come up for you?

- How does it feel to accept—without any self-shaming or self-judgments—that your situation is *not* going to change by you continuing the tactics you've been using so far? Can you look at it more as having spent time and energy on, and now retiring, old beliefs and patterns with gratitude for helping you get to today? Then you can welcome new ideas without any defensiveness or criticisms. Just remember one of my favorite sayings, *"That was then and this is now."* Today is a new day and you have control over your choices each day.

- How does it feel to reframe winning to now be measured by degrees of your happiness?

Brace Yourself and Imagine this One

- How would it feel to grant your stepkids' bio-mom amnesty, even when her actions have been wrong, hurtful, unfair or even in violation of the rules? This choice is not about forgiveness, just about choosing to remove the meaning and significance *you* choose to give to whatever she's done that upsets you—for *your* own good. This can really be a tough decision. Isn't it odd how difficult it can be to make the choice to be happy over being right? By the time you get to the end of this book and read my closing comments, Do You Want to Be Right or Happy?, I sincerely hope you'll choose happiness.

Most of you have probably already been through a lot of challenging stepfamily experiences with your partner and your stepkids. You've made it this far and that means you have a lot of strength, determination and staying power. Thankfully you can now use this new information and your creativity to create new options to escape the torment of any situation that's unacceptable. Instead of suffering, you can get to work to create a life that you love. This is doable when you choose to make your happiness more important than anything else. It's a powerful belief to trust that when you act out of your heart and in response to your true needs, you're serving the highest good for everyone impacted—even if some are initially upset or resistant.

Going forward, you can reclaim lost power, feel good about yourself and deal with any situation when you consciously choose to take charge of how (and what) you think, feel, say and do in response to stepfamily situations—in your life as a whole. When you choose to learn from all the feelings that come up for you as a result of the actions of others, you reclaim and hold your power in wonderful ways that many stepmothers can't even imagine—yet. When you choose to put your attention on yourself and use your creative problem-solving skills to give yourself what's missing from your life, you can make all kinds of good things happen for you and your life with your partner.

A Realistic Happy Family Dream

For many reasons, uncontrollable by you, you may not be able to create the happy family dream you originally envisioned when you became a stepmother. However, if you look underneath the specific forms of your dreams to find the feelings you had imagined you'd experience, you can usually generate those same desired feelings in other ways. You *can* create new dreams with your partner. There really are new goals you can focus your energy on that can invigorate instead of drain you. Think of all the things you could create if you redirected your time, energy and resources into forging your new future plans and new dreams. Crafting a fabulous new vision is much more achievable when you're willing to turn away from the roadblocks that cause you stress and turn toward something new and positive. An empowered life is where you:

1. Become more of your wise, empowered self, having learned how to respond to the actions of others in ways that no longer distract you from your true goals and intentions nor drain your resources and energy.

2. Become more aware of your true thoughts and feelings and step more solidly into your emotional adult self at the first inkling of stress. This gives you access to your adult skills, resources and wisdom to handle the present situation and help you heal all the emotional wounds from your past.

3. Look at the ages of your stepkids as clues to your own healing by looking at possible emotional wounds you may have experienced when you were their ages. This unexplainable synchronicity has resulted in many eye-opening "ah ha's" with SMOMS over the years.

4. Can be happy and close with your partner, even if his kids don't cooperate or want to connect with you.

5. Can recognize and let go of any unachievable happy family dreams that society and the Brady Bunch might have instilled, deciding to create a new dream that will make you happy beyond your imagination. Yes, it's really doable!

6. Give yourself the time and space to grieve over anything you lose due to your stepfamily situation. Do this whenever necessary and then move on to find new ways of expressing yourself in the world.

7. Learn from the saying, "*When God closes a door he opens a window, but we often look so longingly at the closed door that we fail to see the windows opening all around us.*" This quote also applies to any unresolved resentments caused by unchangeable realities in your life situations. Suggesting you abandon your original dreams and create a new dream may feel harsh or even disrespectful to your present feelings when you're still grieving, yet it does hold up a light for the end of your painful struggles. Looking for the windows (options) is a choice that only you can make for yourself. The timing is personal, as it should be.

8. Turn away from relationship power struggles, clearing a new space for you to have power to create your own happiness and well-being. It's a bit like an emotional version of the martial arts principle, "yield to overcome."

9. Claim the freedom to be yourself, even when others won't cooperate with you. Believe and now take a stand that you can always find creative ways around any obstacles that are in alignment with your personal values, healthy beliefs and boundaries.

Profound and Impactful Choices

As difficult as it may be to accept this approach of empowered acceptance at first glance, consider how it might be applied in your life situation. It makes complete sense to be angry, sad, hurt and even enraged when other people's actions have negative impact on you. This is not about denying their impact but about choosing to rise above it and have a great life anyway. Every stepmother has the ability to be empowered in her personal situation—whatever the circumstances. This can happen when you're willing to become more aware of your feelings and more conscious of your choices. It's not about doing this perfectly, just doing your best to stay awake and aware.

When you choose to believe you can find creative ways to have an incredible relationship with your partner while becoming the best person you were meant to be, no matter how anyone else behaves, this is an empowered place to be. Feeling bitter makes sense and you could make a case justifying it, but being empowered is a whole lot more fun. From a calm, competent, wise, awake, adult position, there's just no room for long-term bitterness or resentment because it doesn't feel good. You'll be too busy living your life, adjusting to whatever circumstances life brings you, learning from your feelings and loving your life with your partner.

These choices are totally within your control. Yes, you have the power if you'll exercise it. If you can maintain compassionate lovingkindness for yourself while you discover more about (and honor) your feelings, beliefs, wounds, needs and options, your journey can be a thrilling adventure. You really do have the choice to shift from embittered to empowered.

Seventeen

Feeling Like a Victim?
Reclaim Your Freedom with a Creative Choice

We're about to cover a sensitive, potentially defense-triggering topic. Whenever we cover this material in my Resentment workshops, I've received this feedback from participating Stepmoms. Even though this topic has initially stirred up resistances and defenses, they all agree (now) that learning how to step out of the awful feelings of being a victim or martyr is an energy-saving, stress-reducing, happiness-enhancing skill valuable for stepmothers dealing with challenging stepfamily situations.

If anything you read here upsets you, it's an opportunity to explore your feelings in more depth. Any self-criticism, anger or resistance you may feel give you a heads up that there's something valuable to be learned IF you're willing to suspend judgments and activate your curiosity. If you find yourself thinking, "Yeah, But…" this is also important and noteworthy. If you write down what you're thinking, you'll have a chance to learn more valuable things about yourself as you move through this material.

If you've been under stress for an extended period of time or you're facing situations that aren't getting any better in spite of all your efforts, your natural feelings of anger and resentment can morph into bitterness and hatred. When you're in those painful emotional states, it's easy to feel like a victim or martyr because you are being negatively impacted by other people. Most people never had anyone teach them how to process and get out of these exhausting, painful, relationship-damaging emotional places. Thankfully today is a new day and you're about to learn that this is totally within your control. Yes, it's a choice you can make as often as you need to. How? First by taking a deep breath (instead of acting or speaking out) and then by remembering that you're an adult, quite capable and creative who can find new ways to feel better. Let's explore more about what that means so you can consider it for your own situation.

Strategic Choices When You're Resentful

1. Choose to leave the situation: the room, the house, the relationship.

2. Choose to accept the situation with conscious reflection and reframing to make it acceptable for you.

3. Choose to take a half-full perspective of the situation and believe you can find the lessons to be learned and apply creative solutions to change the situation to your liking.

4. Choose to stay resentful. (Hold your horses—why would anyone choose to stay resentful?)

Reasons to Stay Resentful

1. While you may prefer different options or circumstances, you may see no alternatives other than giving in, resigning, quitting or admitting to losing. If you find none of these acceptable, staying resentful can seem to be the best choice. It takes courage to take this position and maintain your resentment, knowing it's going to be difficult and hurtful. When you make this choice, it's important to acknowledge and support your decision, not judge it or yourself.

2. You may hang on to your resentment because you don't want others to get away with their "crimes." You may look at resolving your resentments (and moving on with your life) as allowing someone to get away with something. You may not feel ready to exonerate others for their actions—especially the actions that are having (or have had) a direct negative impact on you.

3. You may hold fast to your resentment because you believe that no one understands your situation and or is interested in learning more about how you feel. Letting go feels like abandoning yourself without being known.

4. You may hang on to your resentment because you fear the alternative will feel even worse. You may imagine or believe that the familiar discomfort of your resentment is better than your potential underlying and unknown fears and feelings. "The devil you know is better than the devil you don't know," right? This is understandable.

Fears Worse Than Resentment

- Fear that the emotional price you've already paid will go unacknowledged.

- Fear that you'll discover your situation is unfixable, bringing on despair and resignation.

- Fear that your relationship with your partner can't survive the truth of the situation.

- Fear that you don't have a right to your feelings and, if revealed to others, your feelings will be judged, disregarded, denied or chided.

5. You could be choosing to stay resentful because you want to punish your partner. Whoa! Wait! Did you just read that right? Yep. This *might* be conscious but is more likely unconscious and could now feel accurate as you consider it.

Why a Stepmom Wants to Punish Her Partner

- Because she might want her partner to feel the way she's been feeling—frustrated and angry that there are no acceptable choices, or she may think she is unsupported and powerless over upsetting stepfamily situations.

- As a result of what's happened, a Stepmom may feel that her partner has disappointed her, betrayed her in some way or broken promises—spoken or assumed—about how the couple should work together and treat each other when under stress. She may feel her partner has demoted her from top priority to feeling she sometimes falls beneath his kids, his ex-wife, his job and maybe even his fears.

You May Wonder

- Do these behaviors mean your partner doesn't love you anymore?

- Is it possible he no longer offers you what you want/need in a partner?

- Could some part of you be thinking, and feel afraid, that you don't want to be in this relationship anymore if these things are unfixable?

- Do you fear that he doesn't believe your happy family dream is possible anymore?

You may decide that feeling resentment is preferable to facing the pain of your relationship possibly ending. Staying resentful may feel like your only option. The good news is that there are always new things to learn and new choices to make when you know how to process your resentments. With the new information you're learning in this book you can make changes that shift your circumstances from unacceptable and misery-inducing to an empowered acceptance of the unacceptable without compromising your dignity or connection with your partner.

All of the chapters here in Section Two deal with ways to resolve, end or make peace with the things you resent in your life situation. This chapter delves into the details of what can happen when you consider the options and now consciously choose to stay resentful. It is always a choice and being aware of this can provide a breath of emotional fresh air.

The Price of Staying Resentful

When you choose to stay resentful you risk being swept up by the strong pull of constricting emotional energy. This energy can trap you in martyrdom, blame and self-pity, the half-empty perspective of any resentful situation—what I call "the vortex of victimhood." As I see it, the opposite of being a martyr is being a magician. Both a martyr and a magician know how to use their skills to highlight and bring about circumstances that justify their feelings. But there's a huge difference. Do you want to feel like an awesome, powerful, loving and hopeful magician? Or do you want to feel like an unappreciated, misunderstood, helpless, hopeless victim/martyr who is burdened with too much responsibility? Do you want to have a positive impact on those you love or do you want to hurt them? (Martyrs always punish those around them.) This really is a choice you can make. It's not about never getting caught up in the trap of martyrdom or victimhood, but about recognizing that trap when it confronts you and knowing how to use the power of your conscious mind to choose a new positive, powerful state of mind.

Please Note: This chapter does not seek to trivialize the experiences of anyone who is a victim of horrific treatment, crimes, illnesses and abusive situations where her life is harmed or endangered or where she is unable to stop the events. On a broader level, I want to acknowledge that we truly are impacted by the actions of others. The concepts I'm presenting here apply in situations where you *feel* like you're a victim, but with new curiosity and consciousness you can now see your circumstances can be a catalyst to help you grow, change, heal and become more skilled and empowered.

Victim by Circumstance—Triumphant by Choice

As I mentioned in the note above, it's important to confirm that in some cases, you truly are impacted by and a victim of another person's actions without recourse or control. I like to look at victimhood as a potential impact, not as a role, the way Viktor Frankl describes it in his book, *Man's Search for Meaning*.

In short, after years in a Nazi prison camp, Dr. Frankl notices that no matter what people may do to each other, the one and only thing others cannot take away, control or destroy is the attitude a person chooses to take about a situation. He talks about realizing that we may be unable to stop feeling the impact of others but *always* have the ability to choose our attitude—and therefore our experience and approach—about whatever happens to us. To me, this sums up what I'm asking you to consider as a Stepmom on a Mission in regards to your stepfamily life situations.

Compassion Alert: As you're reading this, be on the lookout for judging yourself harshly in any way. If you notice any not-so-nice thoughts about yourself, pause and take a breath. Next, kindly remind yourself that you've done your best, even if your best has varied under stress. That's all a person can ask of herself, right? Right! Today, with this new information, you can make a new choice going forward. You can decide that starting now, you're going to open up to some new ideas and try some new things with compassion, lovingkindness and patience for yourself. While you may be going, "Yeah yeah, compassion, blah blah, conscious choice, blah blah, be a wise adult," I risk annoying you with these repeated comments because these things, like compassion, etc, are often forgotten when you're under stress—hence my reminders. Let's start this process by being more descriptive of what you might be feeling if you feel stuck in your resentments.

Feelings When Trapped in the Vortex

- Exhaustion and despair from believing things will never change or improve.

- Disempowered or disregarded, which taps into unconscious rage.

- Out of control, resigned and adopting an outward "why bother?" response to whatever's happening in your stepfamily world (which may be unusual for you).

- Participating in the informal "Ain't it Awful" club meetings every chance you get where your only enthusiasm comes from swapping who's-got-it-worse woes with others without any talk of doing something about it.

- Giving your power away to others, believing only others can help you—doing this consciously or unconsciously, maybe even out of habit.

- Depressed and feeling weighed down by what can feel like thousands of layers of unprocessed anger experiences—making it impossible to motivate yourself to action, feel joyful or be optimistic.

- Experiencing a sense of futility—you may have abdicated responsibility for changing your life situation through avoidance, denial or passive aggression. This compounds any powerlessness and rage.

The feelings of victimhood and victorious are experienced on a scale of powerlessness to empowerment. You and your situation are unique. Because each of us has our own unconscious warehouses full of unprocessed emotions, a custom-designed survival strategy and other unique life experiences, the same situation will impact each of us in different ways. Remember this is not about rules, smarts or right or wrong. It's about honoring how you feel in a new way and believing you can figure out what you need to change so you can feel better.

Realizing you can't successfully control the actions of others is a good place to start. This truth can help you accept (without any negative self-judgment) that you are sometimes a victim of others' actions. While others impact you with their actions, you can respond by choosing to take new actions that will lead you out of all the bad feelings and into new and empowering territory where others can't harm you. This work is about believing you can ultimately be victorious, happy and OK, no matter what happens to you. The sooner you realize you're in the vortex of victimhood (because of how you're feeling and thinking), the sooner you can get out of it and move on with your life. This is the goal of this approach, this chapter and really, this entire book and our mission.

The Emotional Vortex of Victimhood

I think a whitewater river kayaking trip is a good metaphor for our journey as Stepmoms on a Mission. You're in your own kayak for the first time and you've never been on this wild body of flowing water before. If you're lucky, a guide who's familiar with the river will take the trip with you, prepare you for what's ahead or ideally join you for the more difficult parts. Since she's been down the river before, she can teach you the skills you need for your journey. A pioneering spirit and the willingness for on-the-job training accompanied by compassionate encouragement is a winning combination when learning new skills. Practice and good results can add to your confidence to take on new and greater challenges along the way. Feeling this way also makes the journey more invigorating, even fun, as you conquer your fears and handle difficult situations with skill and even gracefulness.

On any whitewater river, eddies form in its curves and among rocks. These circling waters of strongly flowing currents can create whirlpools that suck everything into their centers. Without some kind of intervention, trapped objects—even boats and people—can spin endlessly with the force. Paddlers who know how to recognize eddies can get past them by staying aware and avoiding them, *and* they know how to escape if ever caught so they do not fear these powerful swirling waters.

If an inexperienced kayaker is caught in a strong whirlpool on a whitewater trip, she may panic and exhaust herself paddling and battling the current. Even with strength and effort, she'll have very little chance of escaping the large eddies unless she understands what's happening and has the skills to do so. She's not bad or wrong for not knowing what she needs to know. She just still has some learning to do—and in this case, is highly motivated when on the river in the clutches of this vortex. While learning various skills in advance of a crisis is preferable, it's not always possible.

So what should she do? Surprisingly, it's not about more paddling. Instead, she should put her paddle into the water and hold it tightly against the side of her kayak. The paddle will act like a rudder and the force of the current will fling her kayak out of the whirlpool, freeing her to continue down the river.

As a stepmother, you may find yourself facing a whirlpool from time to time, propelled and trapped into the center of the vortex by the choices and behaviors you or others make. You may choose to confront and try to change recurring and uncomfortable circumstances (that powerful current)—and are likely paying a huge personal price as a result. Your personal whirlpools may be powered by any number of stepfamily traumas, societal prejudices and even your own partner. Your partner, remember, may be caught up in his own vortex or distracted by his fears and guilt, therefore he may be unable to help you or maybe even see what you're dealing with.

Stepmoms Vulnerable to the Vortex

- When you believe what's happened is unfair, disrespectful, unkind or wrong in some clear-cut, indisputable way, but your partner doesn't share your view. This is a vulnerable entry point into the vortex.

- When a not-so-cooperative bio-mom and/or stepkids do (or don't do) something you consider a problem.

- Your partner wants to handle something differently than you'd like him to, or you do something that causes stress for him. This can create a painful disconnection between the two of you. It can also add stress to a situation that you may not have created, but that impacts you negatively.

- More stuff happens and in your hurt, rage or fear you lose energy, time, resources and sense of well-being. Your heart breaks or hardens a little bit more each time another challenging situation comes up.

- An upsetting event passes unaddressed or has some kind of unsatisfactory solution. You're told to "get over it and move on" but you find it impossible to let it go.

- Your emotions aren't fully addressed or digested so they stick around, putrefying into some form of resentment. Sometimes the upsetting actions of others are added to the emotional ledger you're consciously or unconsciously keeping.

- You find yourself bracing for the next situation or visitation period. Uncomfortable already, you look for ways to deal with all the upsetting emotional energy you're feeling and now expect to feel. It can feel overwhelming. See Chapter 4, The Pros and Cons of Catastrophizing.

- You may continue to try things. While you may feel better because you're active, you may also feel trapped, exhausted, enraged, isolated from your partner and scared the relationship can't survive. Sometimes it's hard to remember feeling like the happy, energetic, loving and optimistic woman you used to be, so you try harder.

These feelings can understandably lure you into the "half-empty" negative view of your situation. If you're unaware of any other empowered choices, you may continue to do the best you can, yet keep implementing the same unsuccessful strategies and getting zero or worse results. This is where all your good energy can get zapped—you go round and round, trying with all your might and with all your knowledge to influence change, but you remain trapped. You're a smart, caring, energetic and strong woman so why would you get trapped in an emotional vortex?

Reasons We Get Trapped

- Because no one has ever taught you how to navigate out of this powerful, emotionally charged set of new situations and feelings. Fighting hard or defaulting to being dragged around and around can give you a false sense of movement, but these actions keep you stuck, unable to get past your challenges and moving forward with your life.

- Because when you're under stress you go unconscious and draw on skills you learned as a child (we all do). You do this until you consciously learn of other options and choose to make new positive choices. To be clear, every single human being is unconscious about things until she becomes conscious of them. It's not wrong to realize you've been doing this, it's actually the first step to making things better.

- When your child-created survival strategies no longer solve your adult problems, you can feel furious, cheated, unfairly overpowered and even overwhelmed that whatever is happening is too much for you to deal with. When this happens, you naturally look for ways to numb, distract and avoid feeling bad so you can feel better. Sometimes you may be so upset that you even stop caring about your impact on others. This is rarely intentional for most of us—but intentional or not, when you're under chronic or intense pressure, you draw from the choices of which you're aware. Your need and instincts to survive can compel you to do things that, once seen with the power of clear hindsight, aren't your proudest moments and choices. Bring compassion to that younger self. You were doing the best you could at the time.

- When you've done whatever you can, and when everything you try fails, you'll probably go to great lengths to stop the pain. At first these radical stop-the-pain-at-all-costs tactics may make you feel a bit better. Why? Because they serve as avenues for expressing pent-up emotional energy or act as emotional anesthetics. Wanting to relieve the pain makes sense, especially when you aren't aware of other choices—however, the relief is likely only short-term and often unexpectedly compounds the problems.

Feeling trapped in a vortex of emotional energy can be kinda scary. Realizing things can be scary but not necessarily dangerous can be soothing self-talk to "the child you used to be" and the other younger versions of yourself. It can also help your own newbie stepmother self, who's been through a lot of painful emotional whirlpools since she started on her metaphorical whitewater kayaking trip.

We're all going to come upon emotional whirlpools and vortices of victimhood as we go through life. Knowing how to move through them efficiently and successfully spares you anxiety and gives you the confidence to enjoy the rest of the trip. With practice, handling the whirlpools with ever-increasing mastery can be fun. So let's learn more about this.

Possible Feelings When Trapped

- Self-pity: *"Oh poor me,"* with the insistence it's hopeless to try anything new.

- Guilt: Anger you think you'll get in trouble for or that you don't have the right to express. This could also be resentment in disguise.

- Blame: *"I'm not responsible, they are. End of story."* This is often partially true—however, you're the one responsible for your well-being.

- Plots for vengeance: Real or imagined.

- Self-silencing despair often leaking out as hostility (anger caused by pain).

- Obsessive thinking about trying to control or change or punish the other person: Often at great cost to personal peace.

- Martyrdom: Feeling unappreciated, misunderstood, responsible for too much, closed-hearted, overburdened and disrespected without recourse. Martyrs always punish others—always.

- Bitterness: A cold, inflexible, pessimistic, horribly lonely, self-isolating feeling.

- Arrogance: *"I'm better than (or less than) them."* These are extreme judgments that temporarily numb your feelings and separate you from (and hurt) the people you love.

- Controlling, proving and testing love: *"If he loved me he'd do what I want, or else."*

Anything sound familiar to you? Can you look back at the situation and see now that you had more options? It's so important to practice self-compassion and "make it OK" for you to see new things about past experiences. It's how we learn, change and grow wiser. Self-reflection like this, with the intention to learn and heal, is valuable time spent and can result in all kinds of new insights and ideas.

Evidence You May be Caught

- You keep repeating the same stories looking for others to concur that things are unfair and wrong and that you're blameless and right.

- You keep experiencing the same patterns of upsetting behavior, thinking, *"he never listens"* or *"they never do what I say"* or *"they always ignore what I want."*

- You use absolute words like always and never. This indicates you're coming from the emotional maturity of "the teen you used to be." Adolescents talk this way to justify their statements. This is noteworthy—when emotions emerge from your unconscious, the words you use to express your feelings can help you determine your age of wounding. Look further into any potentially wounding experiences in your teen years if you find yourself saying always or never about a situation.

- You defend your right to continue to feel badly, even when someone offers suggestions. Upon hearing a new idea, you tell them why they don't understand, why their idea will fail or why nothing will help your situation. (This is a symptom of being in self-pity.)

- You're using a lot of mental, emotional, physical and financial energy and yet nothing is changing. Can you see your imagined self spinning around and around in that choppy swirling whitewater?

- You're bone-deep exhausted or overwhelmed and unable to do things you want to do. "Why bother?" can pop into your mind. You may even abandon self-care and activities that used to bring you joy.

- You can't laugh or joke around. Nothing is funny when part of you is determined to feel miserable. (This is another symptom of self-pity.)

- You find yourself repeating stories and can sound like a broken record of complaints, even to yourself.

Warning! Warning! Anti-Judgment and Harsh Inner Voice Alert: Whatever you're now thinking and feeling about past choices, this is *not* a place to hit yourself over the head with comments like, *"I made my bed so I have to lie in it"* or *"I knew what I was getting into"* (whatever that's supposed to mean). These are things people say when they don't know what else to say or do, or are tired of hearing about your situation. It's hurtful so please stop yourself if you find yourself entertaining these thoughts. Be kind to yourself. You've been through so much. Be your own best friend and if you recognize yourself in these descriptions, become your best personal cheerleader for change.

Free Yourself

1. Be self-aware: *"I'm feeling like I'm trapped as a victim. I don't want to stay in this uncomfortable place."*

2. Bring conscious, compassionate lovingkindness to yourself. *"This is hard and feels terrible. I can do better than this. I'm going to make a new choice."*

3. Recognize that whenever you feel like a victim, you've found a place for potential change and personal growth that needs your attention, healing and creative genius. It's an emotional signal telling you, *"Here's a place where I can transform my emotional life in a way that will benefit me and my well-being."*

4. Realize you're at a crossroads (half-full or half-empty) and choose to look at the half-full upside of an upsetting situation. Redirect your attention from whatever or whomever is wrong to what you can do differently to help yourself feel better. (This is the figurative step of putting your paddle in the water and holding it there as you aim for the other side.)

5. Get to work on coming up with new ways to better understand and approach all aspects of your situation. There are unlimited options with this attitude.

6. Identify moments of choice in the situation you're working on. Test out new choices in your imagination—speak or not, write or not, do or not? Talk them through with your partner, a trusted friend or another stepmother. This is a tremendous skill to cultivate. When you do this, your gut, heart and head will all want a vote.

7. When you identify an option that feels right for you, make a new choice and see what happens. It will likely fling you out of feeling like a victim and into a sense of triumph. If it doesn't bring the results you want, try something else.

Why Shift from Victim to Empowered?

- It's emboldening and enlightening. The very moment when you make the choice to believe change is actually possible, you'll feel better—really! Don't believe me? No need to believe me, just try it for yourself. Your new attitude and expectations about the future will immediately change how you experience your present situation.

- It gives you hope, the antidote to despair.

- It's energizing—just what your empty emotional tank and exhausted heart, mind and body need to create a brighter future.

- It naturally taps into your unlimited inner source of positive creativity, curiosity and courage.

- It can reactivate new levels of self-respect and a stronger sense of feeling capable and being responsible for yourself.

- It can reignite the possibilities for all kinds of positive choices, even if you haven't figured them out yet.

- It gives you the chance to master a new, more loving problem-solving approach to work on with your partner. See Section Three for several chapters on improving your relationship.

Some aspects of self-development are a process and others are a choice. Shifting your perspective to that of an empowered (magical) Stepmom begins with a choice. You don't need to be perfect at this. The good news is that anytime you feel you've fallen back into a vortex of victimhood, you can consciously escape the vortex without judgments. You can have compassion, encourage yourself and make a brand new creative choice.

The next time you sense you're approaching the vortex, ask yourself, *"Am I going to continue to feel like a victim or am I going to make creative, empowered choices so I can feel better?"* Happily, it's really hard to resist the enthusiasm that this question can generate. You might want to write it on a note card. Post it on your bathroom mirror. Make it your screen saver. Give yourself lots of positive self-talk.

A Compassionate Challenge

When you find you're facing resentment about anything, and especially about unchangeable facts in your life, start the healing process with some self-reflection. You can learn all kinds of information about your current approach, your assumptions, your needs and your situation that you can use to help yourself going forward. This will also give you a chance to reevaluate some of your past decisions. The self-reflection itself can be a little (or very) uncomfortable. Usually the more repulsed you are about something you may have done, the more likely it is that you've done it for darn good reasons. This is when it's important to remember the steps to process your feelings: Recognize, Acknowledge, Forgive and Change. See Chapter 7 for a more detailed description of this process.

Your mission, if you choose to accept it, is to reflect on past choices that may have trapped you in an emotional vortex of victimhood, so you can grow stronger from having gone through them. Write them down on a list so you can see them all. Are there any places where you now see there were (or still are) other options available? There's so much to learn from examining past scenarios. Sports teams get better by watching their past game tapes, right? You can use your memories and imagination to glean the same advantages. You have all this information stored in your conscious, subconscious and unconscious minds. Now you can create a safe place to work on your skills and choices so you can deftly navigate the white waters of stepmotherhood.

Again, be kind when examining your past choices. You'll find it easier to understand why you did whatever you did if you treat yourself like you'd treat your best friend in the same circumstances. Your behavior has meaning. It's valuable to understand the "why" motivating your choices. This is how you grow, change and can become wiser in life. This exploration gives you a chance to discover any unmet needs and personal boundaries that may have been violated. It's also a chance to identify beliefs that may need your conscious revision.

There's no right or wrong here. It's about realizing that each time you're upset, you're also at a crossroads. It's choosing to be more responsible for your own well-being, more aware of your impact and more empowered to handle things with new choices that increase your self-esteem and self-respect. Once you become conscious of any potentially painful, self-defeating behaviors, you can learn to interrupt and replace old patterns and make new choices going forward. This creates more room in your life for all the good stuff you imagined when you became a stepmother. It also creates space for you to spend time on non-stepfamily related activities that make you happy. Being and feeling like a victim has been a well-worn path for women throughout time because no one showed them any alternatives. Realizing that you're not stuck—not anymore— and you now have the choice to use your emotional energy to find creative options is a valuable life skill. It's a skill that can lead you to magician-caliber solutions.

Section Three

A Stepmom's Relationship and Her Partner

It was the best of times, it was the worst of times,
it was the age of wisdom…
It was the spring of hope, it was the winter of despair,
we had everything before us…

~ Charles Dickens, *A Tale of Two Cities*

Eighteen

Resolve Conflicts in How You and Your Partner Handle Trauma
Acquire Super Powers as a Couple

A happy family dream is an optimistic, passionate, joy-filled, lofty and motivating fantasy. It envisions everything working out beautifully for a couple and any children in their care, and a Stepmom creating such a dream with a new beloved partner is natural and understandable. For a Stepmom, this happy family dream can also be—at least in its initial version—unrealistic, unachievable and maybe even naïve considering the people she's inherited in her life and the very complex dynamics of stepfamilies. That's not her fault. It's not bad or wrong. It's just what happens sometimes for an enthusiastic, deeply-in-love Stepmom. Often without much of a honeymoon period, a Stepmom and her partner hit the ground running, working hard together to solve logistical problems and doing their best to keep up with all the various issues that stepkids and their bio-mom bring into their lives.

When any bio-parents, stepparents or children in any stepfamily situation refuse to play their parts in getting along, it can seem impossible to achieve a happy family dream. In my experience, the bio-dad often sees (and accepts) this reality much sooner, and with less resistance, than his Stepmom partner. Energized and new to the pre-divorced family dynamics, an optimistic Stepmom may wholeheartedly adopt the approach, *"We can fix this together (whatever this is)—there's lots of stuff we can do to make things better."* In the meantime, her partner may already accept or even be resigned to endure the conflicts his ex-partner and kids bring to the table of their lives. This difference in outlook about what's achievable is noteworthy, impactful and seldom acknowledged or discussed between a Stepmom and her partner. It's also a source of complex pain. Both the Stepmom and her partner can experience a sense of betrayal, even without really understanding what's happening between them. So they each try harder.

If the stress of stepfamily traumas begins to cause a Stepmom and her partner to feel at odds with each other, their relationship can begin to wobble without either of them knowing what to do about it. Disagreeing, sometimes vehemently, over how to handle demanding stepkids or their not-so-cooperative bio-mom can uncover differences that can be surprising, overwhelming, confusing and enraging for both of them. As they are jolted back to reality, their original happy family dream can become damaged, destroyed or—more likely—buried by unprocessed layers of anger, hurt and disappointment.

What can you do differently to avoid this tension between you and your partner? If you and your partner have experienced this dynamic, you know it can involve some serious moments of pain and rage. Regardless of what's already happened between the two of you, and in spite of however your stepkids or their bio-mom behave, there is a way you and your partner can rebuild a customized happy life dream as long as the love between you is still alive. I know it can be hard to imagine how certain differences can be resolved. I assure you, they can be, as long as you and your partner are willing to expand your viewpoints and open your hearts to a new way of looking at things. The mysterious and sometimes excruciating tension between you and your partner can evaporate from a newly formed, conscious foundation of mutual support. No longer sidetracked or divided by painful disagreements and hurt feelings, you'll strengthen your connection so you can find new ways to live a happy life together, in spite of any stepfamily traumas.

In this chapter, I'm asking you to consider shifting your attention to reduce and ultimately eliminate your painful relationship conflicts and any resulting sense of betrayal. You can become closer with your partner by becoming aware of the different ways you each try to resolve conflicts and handle trauma, which may be at odds with each other. It is not about how much you love each other but about how well you handle stressful situations as a team. Under stress, a couple can become upset with each other and then distracted from working on a solution because of how different—sometimes diametrically opposed—their strategies are for addressing a given situation. Repeated unresolved conflicts can lead you both to adopt testing-and-proving-love tactics and other hurtful martyr-like behaviors that rarely resolve anything, so it's important to interrupt this pattern ASAP.

Think back and identify a couple of situations where you and your partner disagreed over how to handle a stepfamily situation. Can you and your partner articulate your individual strategies for dealing with trauma and stress? Can you explain how the approaches differ? Most couples can't. Why not? Mostly because no one ever taught them what a survival strategy is, why we all have one, how to create a new one or about new ways they can behave as a team. Becoming conscious you even have a survival strategy is a *huge* first step. This new awareness of the existence of our survival strategies often genuinely surprises couples—in a good way. Gaining an understanding of the origins, value and role of our individual survival strategies can replace the well-worn downward pathways of "here we go again" anger with new waves of soothing empathy for each other. Getting clear on your individual survival strategies—and then identifying where they conflict—makes it possible to make new decisions going forward to resolve situations, all the while protecting each other from any vulnerabilities during conflicts or trauma.

What Do I Mean by Survival Strategies?

I learned about the concept and impact of survival strategies from Dr. Alice Miller's groundbreaking, controversial and brilliant book, *The Drama of the Gifted Child*. In this book, Dr. Miller explains that each of us emotionally survives our childhood by adopting a set of very specific behaviors, based on our personalities, capabilities and role models, that enable us to endure our circumstances and the feelings provoked by our experiences. While the full extent of each person's strategies is as unique as a fingerprint, they all share many common characteristics. And although they help us when we're young, it's important to realize that these very same strategies limit and even imprison us emotionally as adults. They compel us to react to stressful adult situations the same way we responded to them as a child—sometimes in more sophisticated ways, yet still using the same approaches.

When a Stepmom and her partner have similar survival strategies, they'll experience less tension and fewer conflicts between them when they need to respond to trauma in their lives together. Stepfamily issues will not create as much additional tension between them. However, if the couple used differing strategies and behaviors to survive their own childhoods, their automatic reactions and proposed solutions for how to solve stepfamily traumas are likely to differ. The key to responding to this relationship stress in wise and loving ways, as already mentioned, is becoming aware of the existence and make-up of their survival strategies. Once a couple understands this, they can learn how to better support each other as a powerful intimate partnership.

As members of an adult couple, you're no longer alone like you each were as a child. This is something that's easy to forget once you're triggered by conflicts and crisis. A crisis is the most important time to find ways to remember you're no longer a child, nor alone, but an adult with resources and a partner. For some of you, this awareness will unfold quickly and easily with a lot of amazing "ah ha" moments. Once you know what you're looking for, it may be easy to see how arguments get started and how they can now be avoided. For others, this process may require a bit more emotional untangling, study and relationship-detective work. Wherever you are on this spectrum, I can assure you that your efforts will be worthwhile, as you learn about the specific causes of stress between you and your partner. There are very good reasons and logical explanations for your stress. There are things you can do to eliminate the stress so you and your partner can focus on solving the actual stepfamily situation. Can you imagine your lives without this stress? Ahhhhh! Let's get busy exploring the possibilities.

What Makes Up Your Strategy?

To begin to see your survival strategies, start by looking at your reactions and behaviors when you're first aware of a crisis or a conflict in approach between you and your partner. What's your first default reaction when something upsetting happens? What does your partner do the moment he realizes there's a problem to solve? This is not about right or wrong, you're just searching for behaviors that are triggered when under stress.

Recognize Your Survival Strategy Tactics

- Do you swing into action immediately?

- Do you want to talk, talk, talk?

- Do you need to express rage or other feelings in reaction to facing trauma?

- Do you get very quiet?

- Do you *not* act, but instead step back to think carefully before saying or doing a thing?

- Does your partner think through stepfamily issues in the same way he solves a crisis at work?

- Do you take action immediately and often end up feeling badly because you realize, in hindsight, that your initial actions caused more conflicts or trauma?

- Do you prefer to process feelings before responding to the situation?

- Do you believe that immediate action is always best? Never best?

- Do you like to talk about and create action plans that involve changing the viewpoints or behaviors of others?

- Do you naturally defer to others to come up with a plan to bring about peace or end conflicts?

How do you and your partner react when there's a crisis to deal with and you don't agree on a solution? How do you react to each other when you disagree about how to proceed?

- Do you judge your partner's suggestions because you disagree or fear the consequences of what he's suggesting?

- Does your partner judge your suggestions as wrong or inflammatory to the situation?

- Does he say (or act like) he already has an approach that works for him? Does he make it clear he's not interested in ideas from you? Does this offend you or hurt your feelings?

- Does he assume you will follow his lead?

- Do you dismiss each other's opinions and feelings when under stress? It's easy to dismiss each other (sometimes unintentionally) when under stress because defensive walls can blind us to our impact on others.

- Do either of you get defensive, withdraw, lash out in anger or blame when you disagree?

- Do you defer, feel resigned and seethe silently, perhaps misdirecting your anger at a later time over another issue?

- Can you identify the reasons (beliefs) that compel and justify your behaviors?

- How open are you about revising your beliefs to adjust to your stepfamily situation?

- Do you ever get caught up in rigid right/wrong thinking? Are you willing to acknowledge that there might be multiple right (vs. wrong) ways to handle a situation—or not? If not, why not?

These are some common components of survival strategies and reactions to conflicting strategies. What approaches do you and your partner agree on? Where do your strategies conflict? You can see that many of the approaches directly conflict with each other, creating a breeding ground for hurtful, judgmental accusations and blaming each other for being wrong. When you and your partner want to do conflicting things in response to an issue, it's logical fodder for an argument unless you're conscious enough to look at it in an emotion-honoring, insightful new wise way. This type of disagreement puts immense pressure on you both, on top of any stress already caused by the actual situation. Yikes! At times when a couple needs to be closer and more united, conflicting survival strategies can make things even worse. Does any of this feel applicable or true for you and your partner?

A Real-Life Stepfamily Example

Louise and Gordon* have very different strategies when it comes to responding to last-minute parenting schedule changes by Gordon's ex-wife. The first few times Gordon automatically agreed to a change, Louise went along with it because she wanted to be a good sport and the couple felt OK about the occurrences. Many months and many more changes later, Louise found herself raging at any little adjustment because she was out of patience. She was tired of feeling like she was always losing some kind of invisible battle with bio-mom whenever Gordon gave in to his ex-wife. Louise later admitted being aware of that feeling of pouting and crossing her arms defiantly, like she did as a child when she didn't get her way. Gordon repeatedly explained he gave in to avoid more serious problems. When Louise wanted to make a counter offer or trade to make a change feel fair, she and Gordon argued because it conflicted with his "avoid making his ex-wife angry at all costs" strategy. Louise felt hurt because she perceived that Gordon was betraying her by siding with his ex-wife, and that he didn't value her feelings.

The couple began to argue more and more about requests for changing the schedule. The wedge of resentment grew bigger and both of them felt betrayed by the other. They also knew that Gordon's ex-wife was aware of his strategy to give in to her demands to avoid her wrath. Louise and Gordon felt the tension getting worse. It was seriously affecting their relationship but neither of them knew what to do or how to help themselves bridge the gap between them.

After I explained the concept of survival strategies, Louise and Gordon were able to identify their own strategies and where they caused conflicts. It was clear to them where conflict originated when it came to schedule changes requested by Gordon's ex-wife.

* Using my grandparents' names for privacy of actual couple.

Conflicts Uncovered

1. Louise's default reaction to sudden or unexpected change was to immediately spring into action to try to fix things. She did this consciously "for the good of the cause." She was not aware, until she investigated more deeply, that she was also motivated by a child-created belief that if she didn't do something, only bad stuff would happen. She believed that taking action—any action—helped her feel better (less anxious) whenever there was a problem. Her survival strategy included holding onto the illusion (and belief) that there was always a way to resolve things and have folks get along if she just kept looking for the right solution. In spite of repeated failures, bad consequences from her past attempts and even more tension with Gordon over their disagreements, she continued to try to convince Gordon that they needed to stand up to his ex-wife. She believed he needed to be stronger and more assertive and should convince his ex-wife to change her unreasonable requests to make it a win-win situation.

2. Louise's ideas and her half-full, ever-optimistic attitude, while initially delightful, now blew Gordon's mind. How could Louise be so naïve? Stubborn? Blind? He became more and more angry at Louise whenever his ex-wife requested (demanded) a schedule change and Louise refused to support him. He found himself bracing for an argument with Louise every time his ex-wife contacted him. Gordon experienced both anger and despair that he was feeling controlled by his ex-wife. Even worse, he was feeling badly about himself in light of his partner's judgments. He felt powerless because he couldn't see a way out of this dilemma.

3. Gordon learned early in life that the only strategy that helped him survive stress and trauma was to avoid conflicts at all costs and always defer—in this case to his ex-wife. Deferring, feeling resigned, enduring and accepting a less-than-ideal outcome (the impact of a schedule change) was always better, in his mind, than making it worse by confronting his ex-wife and creating even more chaos. He knew his ex-wife thrived on melodrama, was good at it and would never back

down in her quest to have the last word (and win) so she could always feel in control. He really couldn't understand why Louise couldn't accept this obvious-to-him reality.

4. Louise felt like an injustice was occurring and she had no way to fix it. She couldn't seem to get Gordon to understand how unfair it was to always be the ones giving in, especially when Gordon's ex-wife rarely agreed to their requests or even followed the plan as originally agreed. Louise grew more resentful of Gordon each time his ex-wife made a request and he caved in. She believed there had to be a reasonable way to get Gordon's ex-wife to comply or change (she was wrong about that) and for some reason, she didn't believe that giving in was really better than the worse future that Gordon was trying to avoid.

5. When I spoke with them, it was clear to me that they each strongly believed that their own solution was the only "right" course of action. They each felt the tug-of-war power struggle and this made them both feel angry and sad.

Even though neither Louise nor Gordon was initiating the stepfamily situation, the conflicts between their strategies caused stress between them. They kept getting angrier and angrier with each other and couldn't figure out how to deal with these painful repeated experiences. What they couldn't see—at least not until we talked about it—was that their emotional needs were different. They learned this resulted in the creation of conflicting survival strategies, and that they'd never been aware of nor talked about them.

Do you see how conflicting survival strategies caused this couple unwelcome stress? How could they better support each other to avoid feeling upset with each other? We went to work. After we isolated the tactics of their survival strategies, we uncovered where they conflicted in response to the actions of the ex-wife. Next, we spent some time talking about why they each believed their approach was superior. This exercise not only addressed the current situation, but also explored and revealed why they each believed that their strategy enabled them to withstand the emotional stress in their childhoods.

This was a very touching and emotional discovery process. Louise and Gordon shared stories they'd never thought were relevant but that now made complete sense to them. They discovered they had different priorities when they were dealing with stepfamily situations. Gordon was willing to do whatever it took to avoid stress with his kids and ex-wife and Louise was willing to pay the emotional price and do whatever she could to get justice. It never occurred to them that their differing needs caused their conflicts, and this newfound information sure did explain their arguments. Another surprise came when they both realized that while their tactics were different, sometimes opposite, their most basic goals had been the same: *"Do whatever I have to do to feel safe (or OK) about myself."* This new knowledge generated much-needed waves of compassion and love for each other, which washed away a lot of resentment between them. Neither of their strategies were wrong, they were just using different tactics with the same underlying objective. They felt relief and both became willing to approach their stepfamily situations differently. This is when a couple really becomes a team.

Their Resolution

Louise and Gordon suggested some options and I encouraged them to consider all kinds of creative possibilities rather than agreeing to the first one they both accepted. After talking about the options, Louise agreed to accept that Gordon's assessment of his ex-wife was accurate and that she would stop arguing with him. This was an important step. Louise also was enthusiastic about coming up with two or three fun ways they could respond to the impact of any of his ex-wife's requested changes. It gave her something to do with her eager optimism and urgency to act. Eventually she began creating a Plan B for all stepkid-related events, preparing her for any changes and alleviating her anxiety about possible future requests. Gordon agreed to happily go along with at least one of her alternative ideas. He was grateful she was willing to wholeheartedly support his responses to his ex-wife. He was extremely relieved about all the future conflicts and consequences they could now avoid.

In this work, Louise and Gordon learned so much about themselves and each other. Together, they reclaimed their power to stay connected. From this point forward, they felt heard, known and supported by each other anytime a request for a change came in from Gordon's ex-wife. They no longer argued about this issue—what a relief—nor felt resentful of each other. They no longer felt the need to brace themselves in anticipation of the next requested change, and they were triumphant and closer than ever before.

Still Can't Identify Your Strategies?

If the components of your survival strategies are not clear, think about something upsetting from the past and slow the situation down from the beginning. Start with the moment you learned about a problem or trauma and move forward—one thought at a time—to identify the unconscious survival strategies and behaviors you and your partner each employ. Look for patterns in your disagreements on how to best address a situation. Look for repeated complaints and accusations in your arguments that start with *"You never…"* or *"You always…"* Once you recognize your individual strategies for dealing with trauma and then figure out where they conflict, they're no longer unconscious choices or reactions! Being conscious of your choices reclaims your power in these situations. With this new knowledge the real empowered teamwork can begin.

Remember that doing this work is not about figuring out ways to make either of you right or wrong. Do your very best to suspend any reflexive blame or judgments because they're hurtful and a waste of time. What can you expect once you and your partner acknowledge the components and conflicting aspects of your individual survival strategies?

- The tension between you and your partner will likely diminish quickly and significantly.

- The compassion may return and make you feel closer—such a relief.

- The interest and energy for finding a creative solution for the stepfamily situation can become the new shared focal point, now that you agree you'll work together to find a mutually agreeable solution.

- You may begin to think of new and creative tactics for solving stepfamily situations.

- You can become aware that between you, you have several different skills, each developed from decades of practice—behaviors that when used appropriately, make you a more capable, wise and effective team of two. No more he-vs.-she power struggles.

- You may realize you can handle stepfamily issues easily and (hallelujah!) without the dreaded or actual tension between you and your partner.

Figuring out the components and motivations of your survival strategies, plus understanding the priority of your emotional needs and where they seem to collide with your partner's, can help you both revive the loving and now more confident attitude of *"together, we can handle anything."* It's very empowering and usually a huge relief for the couple.

What to Do to Reduce the Stress Between You and Your Partner

1. You can do this relationship work together, mindful of respecting each other's differences. If tension or defensiveness arises, remind each other that there are no one-reaction-fits-all stepfamily situations. This is not about trying to convince each other about what's better or worse. It's about exploring, learning more about yourselves and sharing with each other so that you tailor your approaches and solutions as a true team going forward.

2. Share your strategies for handling conflicts and trauma when things are relatively calm so you can be more prepared for the next situation. Learn from your past. Turn past arguments into clues and a discovery process for how to handle tough situations differently, in a blame-free zone with lots of compassion and creative problem-solving.

3. Agree to examine challenging situations from your most conscious adult point of view. Agree in advance that it's OK to remind each other to be conscious/awake if you begin to feel stress between you. Becoming defensive and using survival strategies are well-worn unconscious reflexes until you make them conscious. Help each other stay awake with gentle reminders so no one feels criticized.

4. Agree that whenever a trauma or conflict arises, you and your partner will do your best to interrupt any old reflexes and not talk about the solution until you both get on the same page as a loving team. This is much more productive than bracing for an argument or digging in your heels to defend your position.

5. Look for and identify any differences in your immediate reactions or suggested solutions. When new components of your survival strategies or defensive behaviors are uncovered, make time to explore them together. Different stepfamily events and actions can trigger varying degrees of fear, rage, pain or anxiety. This is a process (it takes time) so be patient and consider writing down what you learn so it doesn't get lost in the conversation.

6. Patiently teach each other *why* you do whatever you do in your shared, private empathetic zone. Remind yourselves that each of you has your own preferences for action (or inaction) because, as a child, it's the only thing you thought would work. Ideally you'll both understand how this approach was helpful for you in childhood and agree it's time to expand your options as the adults you are today.

7. Deeply listen to each other. Sometimes it helps to visualize your partner as a child, all alone, doing his best. As you set down your defenses and open your heart, you're probably going to feel greater compassion flow in strong new currents between you. This can be so healing and energizing.

8. Agree that neither of you will take any action to solve a stepfamily situation until you both agree on the solution. Most issues don't require an instant response, yet some of you may have what I call an "urgency pattern" (part of your survival strategy) that propels you into action without thinking things through—out of anxiety. If this is true for you or your partner, help each other remember to stay awake, be conscious, be aware—whatever words resonate with you. It's also a great idea to pre-agree on a solution for those situations that require an immediate response.

9. Important: Your partner knows his kids and their bio-mom very well and has a lot of experience dealing with them. Remember this when your preferred tactics differ from his suggestions and see if you can find ways to add to the effectiveness of his recommendations, instead of opposing them. Sometimes it's best to support and endorse his opinion and ask him to help you find ways to feel better about his ideas. This is a place to offer and ask for compassion and lovingkindness.

10. Many guys are eager to stop the bleeding in an emotionally stressful situation—their version of the urgency pattern—and it can be an extreme deferral/endurance strategy that's not always necessary. This is where you can bring your compassion and a lot of creative options to the table that he would never think of without you. This is another place for patient teamwork that can bring relief to you both.

The positive impact of being compassionate when doing this work can't be overemphasized. None of us is conscious of having a survival strategy until someone tells us about it. That's just the way it works. Today may be the first time you've heard about this concept. Your partner may not know about it either. When you learn something new about yourself or your partner, it helps you make sense of past choices. Every action, word and behavior is a choice—it's the unconscious compulsion to repeat certain behaviors when under stress that you're now making conscious and interrupting. There may be some apologies to exchange and some actions to forgive. This is also an important gesture and skill for strengthening your relationship. For more specifics about offering and asking for forgiveness, check out Beverly Engel's wonderful book, *The Power of the Apology*.

Do you each have a ledger from past events and arguments? If so, it can be very healing to review old situations and have an imaginary do-over. Discuss how you would handle those past situations—as a team—if you both knew then what you know now. What a relief it can be to know you no longer need to have all those power struggles and arguments with your partner, often about things neither of you caused. Think about all the time and stress you and your partner will save! See Chapters 15 and 25 for more about how to resolve disagreements and resentments from the past.

Your Happy Life Dream

When you do this work together you learn how to respond better to traumatic situations and handle any stepfamily-related conflicts that you and your partner face. This will help you feel closer, be closer, know each other better and love each other more deeply—because you're working together, giving each situation your very best as a compassionate, wise, loving team. At some point you may realize that your original happy family dream is not achievable because of the people and relationship dynamics involved in your stepfamily situation. You may need some time to mourn the loss of that original dream. If you do, it's very important to honor your sadness and grieve the loss of those future memories that won't happen the way you had imagined.

When you're ready, and you'll know when that is in your heart, you and your partner can begin to form a new dream that is possible for you two. The old stress will be gone. You'll get stronger each time you handle more stepfamily issues gracefully. You and your partner can reclaim the power over your own future and look for new possibilities—they're out there waiting for you. The process of reducing your relationship stress and deepening your connection will enable you and your partner to live your dream life right now, each day, no more waiting. My husband called it "finding a new North Star to guide us." When you and your partner are clear about your overarching goal to stay connected as a couple, you can remind each other of this anytime you feel that familiar tension build between you. As a loving team, you can keep reminding each other to make choices that bring you both (and all the children in your lives) as much happiness and connection as possible.

Dealing successfully with conflict is deemed by many as the most important skill for a joyful, enduring, intimate relationship. The suggested approaches in this book and specifically this chapter (identifying your needs and values, understanding and interrupting your defensive reactions, giving each other empathetic, blame-free support, etc.) can truly help you and your partner stay lovingly connected through all kinds of stepfamily stress.

Doing this work together doesn't have to be heavy or upsetting when you choose to be sincerely curious, practice compassion for yourself and each other's past experiences, and stay conscious of—maybe state them repeatedly—your desire to support each other in more wise and loving ways.

See Chapter 9 for more about how to learn from and become empowered by the emotional energy that is generated through your stepfamily situations.

Hopeful Stepmom's Story

July 2016

It's my pleasure to spend a few moments reflecting on Cathryn Bond Doyle's huge impact on my journey as a Stepmom on a Mission. I first became a stepmother in 2009. It was overwhelming to take on my two stepdaughters, but even more so to take on what I later learned was their narcissistic bio-mom. I'd never considered nor imagined the insanity that would come along with marrying a man who had 50/50 custody of his children and a hostile ex-wife.

It didn't take long to get to the point where I felt I was nothing more than an indentured servant to the children. I was also feeling constantly undermined and berated by their bio-mom. As a narcissist, their bio-mom was determined to control our household and destroy our joyful times together. She seemed to make it her mission in life to turn her children against both me and their father. When that didn't work, she then attempted to obliterate our marriage by causing problems in my household that created tension between me and my husband. For instance, she insisted on coming over to our house every day of our custody time and visiting with the children at the front door. She was constantly interrupting and disrupting our lives. She would call incessantly and no matter where we were or what we were doing, she would insist on speaking to her children. When we refused to allow this, she took us to court and a judge actually sided with her and allowed her "unfettered" access to the children. This created a lot of turmoil and resentment in our household.

I began looking online for advice on how to handle a hostile ex-wife when I came across the smoms.org website and read one of Cathryn's articles. Everything she was describing was actually happening in my life. I read another article and then another until I had read every article she had written. I felt as if she had actually been witnessing what was going on in my life. It was such a great feeling to actually know that someone understood what I was going through. I posted a few issues on the site bulletin board and other members of the group (SMOMS) responded and gave advice and encouragement.

One day after I posted that I was in deep crisis mode, I received a surprise email reply from Cathryn. I was amazed that the actual founder of the site had personally emailed me after reading my post. Her email was full of compassion and understanding, but also full of ideas and solutions. Instead of looking at an entirely overwhelming situation, she was able to take each issue and offer a suggestion for how I could regain control over my own life and my own decisions.

Was this possible? I didn't HAVE to cater to every whim of my stepkids and their mother? I didn't have to feel resentful of my husband for what I perceived as him allowing me to be abused by his kids and ex-wife? I had a voice? Yes, I did. I've been surprised that working with Cathryn via email exchange has been so effective. It has been great. We've worked together on the phone as well and I can highly recommend both options.

Cathryn has written me detailed and caring responses in our work together. She takes each issue and makes suggestions on how to change the things I can and cope better with the things I can't change. She helped me realize that some things—meaning the actions of the people in my life—were not going to change. Happily, she also pointed out all the ways I can change myself and be more creative so I can deal with others in a less painful way. She shared her own personal struggles with being a Stepmom. That's really helped me. Perhaps because she lived through it, she never judged me and always had even greater empathy and credibility with me.

Her advice has always been beneficial. She has an uncanny knack for writing essays about topics that I am struggling with—right when I need it. They've been such life savers, just filled with explanations and solutions that can be applied immediately. Since not everything is a quick fix, there's a progression where successes can and should be celebrated on even the smallest level. I've been celebrating a lot of little shifts and a few big shifts, and it all feels great.

I remember feeling so stuck in what my life had become. I was painfully sad that I had chosen to become a Stepmom. I was struggling with temper tantrums being thrown by a stepdaughter (SD) who had become an emotional terrorist in my life. I was unable to escape her and was being forced—or so I thought—to tolerate her verbal abuse and lack of reality. One day when telling Cathryn about this, she said to me very kindly, "You're not a tree." It was a bit of a jolt. I still remember that on a daily basis and use it to get me through hard moments. I am not a tree—I can move. I am not STUCK. If I can't adapt to it, I am free to go. If SD is having a meltdown, I do not have to be her hostage, I can move. It was, and is, very empowering.

I'm also a huge fan of her approach, "His Kids: His Call." Now, that said, it often still becomes my problem but after so many years of Cathryn's guidance and support, I am better equipped. She offers creative methods that are easily incorporated into daily life, oftentimes just simple little ideas that make a world of difference. Often it's about changing my own attitude or taking a moment for self-care. In my view, she's an expert on narcissism and knows better than anyone how to deflect, disarm and manage a narcissist. I realized through working with Cathryn that my troublesome SD was as equally narcissistic as my SD's bio-mom. Cathryn taught me some creative techniques to deal with her so that I can set some boundaries without her even realizing it and save myself a lot of stress.

Cathryn has been and still is a mentor, teacher, confidante and friend to me. She is a selfless person who has a huge heart and gives so much of herself to others. It's her mission that all Stepmoms on a Mission who want or need help will find it. She gifts so much of herself in order to give all of us the support and guidance we need. She works tirelessly and is the epitome of what a true caring person is. She will often send an uplifting message or just a little "Thinking of you" which immediately gives me a boost of encouragement.

She has taught me how to identify my wounds and recognize where they came from. She has shown me how to not be critical of my younger self who once developed beliefs that I needed when I was a kid, and that are no longer needed as an adult. This awareness has helped me learn to allow myself to change those beliefs. What a difference. What freedom. Plus, Cathryn made me into a magician. She gave me a virtual magic wand and I can wave it whenever I need to and change what needs to be changed. I have told her that there have been times that I felt as if SD had snatched away my wand, broken it in half and poked me in the eye with it. All in all those moments are much fewer and far between than they used to be. I feel like my courage to change is being rewarded.

I'm still working with the challenges of being a Stepmom. The difference now is I'm so much more aware of all the choices that I do have control over: what I do—and don't do—and what I say—and don't say. I still struggle with teaching my younger self that I no longer need to cater to the world nor make up for the inactions of others. What a relief. I finally see that I have a right to look after my own well-being. I can choose to say "no" and still feel good about myself. Over this past year, I've been excited and frankly, sort of amazed at myself for all the new confidence, skills and boundaries I'm using to help myself feel good. I'm no longer feeling like I'm in a hopeless situation.

Hopeful Stepmom
Stepmom since 2009
SMOM since 2009

Nineteen

His Kids: His Call
Transform Your Relationship and Radically Reduce Stress Between You and Your Partner

When a Stepmom and her partner have disagreements over how to handle the stepkids or deal with the stepkids' bio-mom, they may experience disruptions in a previously happy, healthy relationship. Over time and even worse, it can feel like an unresolvable, ever-present conflict has erected walls between them. No matter how hard they try, they can't ever seem to agree on solutions to difficult stepfamily issues. This impossible-to-ignore stress can be overwhelming and lead to depression, defensiveness and a lot of snowballing arguments.

This chapter is about a strategy that can enable you to stay close and connected with your partner regardless of any differences you may have in handling stressful stepfamily situations. This approach involves making new choices, revising some long-held beliefs and arranging your priorities to support the overarching goal of strengthening your relationship with your partner and feeling good about yourself.

Warning for Stepmoms under extreme stepfamily stress: there is a potentially radical approach ahead! The mindset I'm about to propose is likely to raise your hackles like it did mine and those of other Stepmoms when we first considered it. However, just imagine for a moment—what if this could help you avoid stress with your partner when dealing with upsetting stepfamily situations? I urge you to keep reading to see if this strategy makes as much sense to you as it does to me and so many other Stepmoms who have found it effective. Some of these ideas will challenge your beliefs about being a Stepmom or the woman of the house. They may conflict with your childhood survival strategies, trigger some defensive patterns and maybe even irk your ego. The good news is this: just by considering these ideas, and whether or not you implement them, you'll get some clarity about yourself, better understand how your beliefs may be conflicting with your partner's beliefs and see the stressful relationship dynamics between you and your partner more clearly.

As you can see by the title, I'm talking about something I call the "His Kids: His Call" strategy. This is a positive, much more collaborative approach than the once-popular "not my kids, not my problem" concept that offered some relief to many Stepmoms in the early days of my support groups. The premise of His Kids: His Call is a Stepmom choosing to make her loving intimate connection with her partner and her own emotional well-being the two highest priorities in her stepmother role.

In addition to using these priorities as strategic guideposts for discussions and decisions with your partner, you're also deciding that any disagreement over your partner's childrearing strategy is no longer going to come between the two of you. Rather than getting into power struggles and feeling judged, betrayed, hurt or angry with each other when you disagree, you're going to set aside the urge to get your own way. Instead, you're going to remember your two top priorities and choose to support your partner's decisions when it comes to his children and their bio-mom. Gasp! Yep, you heard me correctly. In addition, if you have your own bio-kids from a previous relationship, you could certainly ask your partner for the same commitment in reverse, but my experience shows that's probably already happening.

In 2009, it all came together for me after many tough inner conversations and I began practicing the His Kids: His Call strategy in my own life. The difference was palpable in so many ways! In 2013, I began teaching other stepmothers in my workshops and we hashed out a lot of issues even more completely. Now, with so many years of this under my belt, here's what I've come to think about this topic: When another woman's children are living in a stepmother's home, a complicated dynamic is created that neither the Stepmom nor her partner is prepared to handle. As much as a Stepmom and partner love each other, the stress brought on by conflicting childrearing beliefs just doesn't seem to go away in the stepfamily circumstances they face. It doesn't appear to be overcome or resolved with talking, with silent power struggles, through controlling behaviors or by taking a desperate stand with your partner and saying, *"if you loved me, Honey, you'd do X."* While these age-old tactics may work temporarily, they *always* seem to result in some form of resentment and rarely bring about permanent change or increased happiness for a Stepmom and her partner. Making decisions and taking action using His Kids: His Call is a realistic way to step away from many predictable power struggles and build room for healthy new harmony between you and your partner.

Much of this book is about tactics and skills. Effective tactics are essential when addressing specific events or circumstances, but this chapter is different. This chapter is about an overarching strategy—a new lens to look through, as a couple, when dealing with stepfamily issues. Since every good strategy also needs effective tactics for implementation, Chapter 20, Nobody's Right/Nobody's Wrong Approach for Intimate Relationships, builds on this strategy by recommending new ideas and related tactical approaches.

As you consider the His Kids: His Call strategy, it's likely to bump up against a bunch of societal beliefs about family life that you may have grown up with, defended and argued for, perhaps at the high cost of losing time and a heartfelt, peaceful connection with your partner. Think about something you and your partner have recently disagreed over—your respective positions are most likely based on logical, deeply held, well intended reasons that may be fueled by waves of powerful and mysteriously inflexible emotional energy. Have you noticed that? When upsetting stepfamily things happen and your ideas are rejected, judged or disregarded by your partner, you can both feel a sense of betrayal by the other. You may feel betrayed because your partner didn't take your advice or doesn't appear to value or respect your point of view. Your partner may also feel betrayed because you're not supporting him. These painful feelings pile on top of whatever stress the stepfamily situation is already causing you both. Ugh! Relationship stress caused by disagreements about how to handle the stepkids and their bio-mom is probably the most common relationship-jolting dynamic between a Stepmom and her partner. If you're familiar with this painful, enraging experience and are open to a new way forward, His Kids: His Call may be your answer.

Next time you're in the midst of conflict with your partner and while scratching your head, stomping your feet or wiping away tears, step away from your partner and give yourself some time (at least a few minutes) to consider some questions.

"Why do I feel so angry about this?"

"Why is it so important to me that he handle this situation the way I want him to?"

"Why am I so hurt by his choices?"

"Why do I feel such resentment, rage and hatred toward him, her, them?"

"How can someone who says he loves me make choices that he knows hurt me so much?"

"How are we going to survive 10-20 more years of this stress? I didn't sign up for this!"

These are valid questions and there are important, insight-filled answers awaiting your discovery. The answers and feelings that come up for you will likely reach beyond your present circumstances and apply to experiences from your past. Your feelings are rarely logical or rational—which is totally OK because emotions, by their very nature, are not logical. However, they are very important. My mentor, the late Kit Carson, used to say, *"We make decisions emotionally and rationalize them with logic."* If you want to better understand a decision, look past the logic and identify the underlying emotions. I've noticed that people often justify their decisions, wishes and strong recommendations with the genuine, unquestioned belief and declaration, *"This is the right way to handle this."* They believe it so strongly and rarely ask, *"Is this really true and right or just a belief I accepted without ever questioning its veracity in this stepfamily situation?"*

When you explore your beliefs, you'll discover that upholding some of your child-created beliefs in your stepfamily situations can cause you and your partner confusion, great pain, resentment and loneliness. One day, at the end of my emotional rope, I thought, *"There's gotta be a way to honor my needs and values AND stay connected to the partner I love, while also respecting his needs and values."*

After some lengthy, profound conversations with my husband, we came up with the His Kids: His Call philosophy. Be advised that adopting this probably also means putting your original happy family fantasy on the back burner, maybe even into the trash. It also means identifying the beliefs you have about being a good stepmother, perhaps including concepts like what you see in the list below.

Beliefs About a "Good Stepmom"

- Stands up for her partner against anyone who has hurt him.

- Does whatever she can to compensate for the pain caused by her partner's divorce.

- Helps her stepkids recover from the divorce.

- Does whatever she can to make it easy for her stepkids to get used to her presence in their lives.

- Teaches her stepkids good manners and to be responsible, respectful, loving, caring people.

- Models and exercises all the "mothering" qualities and behaviors possible so her stepkids feel welcome in her home.

All of these elements (and likely many more) constitute quite a job description. Your beliefs represent a huge set of responsibilities that are often left unspoken and are rarely achievable without the cooperation of others. It's time to speak about this with your partner. It's time to consider a new belief that could look something like this: *"Instead of focusing primarily on my stepkids and trying to make up for their past, I'm going to do whatever it takes for my partner to feel loved and supported while also taking care of myself and my well-being."* How does that belief feel for you? Any "Yeah, Buts" come to mind?

Imagine a Peaceful Future

How different would your relationship with your partner be if you two always felt like a loving team, on the same side of stepfamily issues? Consider that this is achievable when you make some changes. How would it be different for you if you adopted any (or all) of the following beliefs?

"I lovingly support and endorse my partner in having full responsibility for making the childrearing decisions for his kids (my stepkids)."

"I choose to put aside any of my child-created beliefs and rules about what the woman of the house needs to do/say/be when they cause stress for me in my new stepfamily. Going forward, I'm going to live by a new, customized, adult-created set of beliefs, needs and boundaries that work for me and my partner—to heck with society. We want to be happy so we're willing to be creative."

"My partner promises to honor and defend my needs, including my right to be respected by his kids and to feel emotionally and physically safe in my own home. He agrees to support me in processing my feelings about the decisions he makes so I feel respected and loved."

"Starting today, I'm choosing to support the actions my partner takes when interacting with his ex-wife. I choose to trust that he knows her better than I do and is making decisions to keep the stress and conflict to a minimum."

> *"Whenever the interactions between my partner and his ex-wife trigger me (and I can expect that to happen), I'm going to take responsibility for my self-care, honor and process my feelings and expect my partner's compassion in return for my support."*

Can you imagine the tension that would evaporate through this new set of choices? Are you too shocked at the thought of this to be able to imagine it? Need a moment? I imagine there are a bunch of "Yeah, Buts" flying through your mind now. Maybe even a "no frickin' way" blasting through your mind. I get that. You're not alone. Initially, I had a lot of objections. I'll address many of them in the following pages. If you still feel *"no way"* after reading this chapter, at least you've given the concept a chance and it may inspire other potentially enlightening changes and possibilities in your future.

One of the things I've noticed about stepfamilies today is that the couples who find a way to make their lives work do so by giving themselves permission to make their own rules. Without a working set of proven guidelines for successful stepfamily couples, we're all left to be mapmakers. As most of you already know, the nuclear family models don't always apply to stepfamilies. You and your partner can be part of this new evolution—maybe revolution—by being a conscious, strongly connected stepfamily couple.

As mentioned, the His Kids: His Call approach may directly challenge your beliefs about your roles and what should take place in a family home. It contradicts many expectations and ideas that, as a child, you needed to imagine would be true for you as an adult. This is nothing trivial—it's huge! As circumstantially disempowered youngsters (as every child is) we may have invested tremendous amounts of emotional energy into believing that one day, as the "woman of the house," we'd be in charge of the rules and people in our homes—like many of us perceived our mothers to be.

Whenever beliefs are directly violated by reality, there's a release of old stored up and unprocessed anger and hurt from our past experiences. This emotional energy from the past can get tangled up with whatever's happening to us in the present moment. As a result, we can experience an overwhelming, confounding surge of emotional energy that surprises even us. Some people are quick to judge this as an overreaction. It's *not* an overreaction, but rather tells you there's more to learn. There's a lot of strength, personal power and wisdom to claim when you can look for the meaning and significance of those powerful feelings. Here are some possible beliefs about becoming a grown-up that may have helped you get through your childhood:

> *"When I grow up, the children in my home will have to abide by certain rules—my rules."*

"When I'm the woman of the house, kids will be respectful to me and other adults and display the proper manners. If not, there will be consequences to teach them to be responsible."

"Children will be disciplined in ways that I deem appropriate for their own good."

"As a child, I had to do X and Y so any child in my home will have to (or won't have to) do the following things…"

"As a child, if I'd misbehaved in certain ways, I would've been punished big time—that's the way it needs to be—for our own good. Look, I turned out OK."

Most of your beliefs were formed in childhood. Unless you've done some conscious searching, you've probably forgotten most of their origins or details and simply abide by them. Somewhere along the line, they became rules and may even seem like "laws of life." See Chapter 8 for more about how we form our beliefs. See Chapter 29 to learn how easy it is to become angry with your stepkids when they behave in ways that conflict with your beliefs.

Eye-Opening Homework

Get clear on your beliefs. It can be a very interesting, worthwhile exercise to make them conscious so you can examine them. It will explain a lot of your behaviors, reactions and feelings since your beliefs inspire your actions and inform your decisions, whether you're conscious of them or not. How about that for the impact and power of beliefs?

If you're up for this exploration, make three lists of the beliefs you hold about being a good Stepmom, the woman of the house and a supportive wife/partner.

Your lists will likely include dozens of items. If your partner is willing to work with you (give him a big hug) then ask him to make three lists of *his* beliefs about what makes a woman a good (1) stepmother, (2) woman of the house and (3) wife/partner. The fascinating part comes when you compare your two sets of lists. You'll find similarities and conflicts in your beliefs. The conflicts will explain many of your disagreements with surprisingly logical clarity. Another helpful benefit of doing this work together is discovering conflicting beliefs you didn't know you had or may never have discussed with your partner, and which you'd perhaps mistakenly assumed you shared. This can be very eye-opening. The revelations and corresponding benefits can be compounded if you and your partner come from different cultural, religious or socio-economic backgrounds. No matter your circumstances, discovering and talking about the differences you two uncover will likely help you generate more compassion for each other—and this can forge a new foundation for teamwork where there once was conflict.

The most important thing to remember about beliefs is that you can change them at any time once you know exactly what they are. This is excellent news. Beliefs can feel like laws until you examine them. Each belief can feel like the only right way to do something, so you may judge anyone who disagrees with your beliefs as wrong, dumb or misinformed. An unconscious adherence to your child-created beliefs (as if they are laws) can lead to hurtful judgments and infuriating arguments, especially with your intimate partner. When you recognize that tension is stemming from a conflict of beliefs between your partner and you, you can avoid stress and turn the experience into a learning opportunity—allowing you two to get even closer. When your partner is willing, you can better understand, negotiate and then create new, customized beliefs for the two of you.

Thankfully, choice supersedes choice. You have the ability to override any existing beliefs by creating new ones that work for you and the unique circumstances of your stepfamily situation. Sounds good in theory, right? In reality, there are probably a bunch of "Yeah, Buts" screaming at you. That's OK. Let's address some of those now.

Resistance to His Kids: His Call Approach

Yeah, But #1: *"How in the world could I give up so much of my voice to support my husband? I already feel unheard. I'm supposed to be his partner, his equal partner, not just his yes-woman."*

His Kids: His Call is about giving up your attachment to certain beliefs and *never ever* about giving up your power, dignity, values or self-respect. It's about agreeing to a new strategy—one where you agree that staying close as a couple is more important than defending conflicting child-created beliefs that were imposed on you. So, what's a Stepmom to do who already feels vulnerable or anxious about maintaining her own boundaries in her stepfamily? What can a Stepmom and her partner do when their childrearing, bio-mom-handling beliefs conflict? How can they move forward without either of them having to lose or feel disregarded? It's about being creative, freeing yourself from containing beliefs from the past and giving yourself permission to define and live by new beliefs that suit your needs and goals. Imagine how your life might be different with these possibilities in place.

Yeah, But #2: *"How would things be different between my partner and me if I stopped asserting my beliefs and insisting my partner do what I think is right for his kids and with his ex-wife? How would it be different if I made supporting my partner more important than my opinions?"*

When I became a stepmother in 1996, I was enthusiastic about all the ways I believed I could help my partner and create a happy home life as a new stepfamily. I did all the things I believed I needed to do to create a healthy loving home for my five-year-old stepson who was with us 50% of the time. I looked at any pushback from my partner about childrearing or house-running topics as situations we simply needed to adjust to—mostly on his part, not mine. I thought I was flexible and devoted but began to see that I was not willing to compromise any "woman of the house" beliefs. Yikes! Yes, even though I didn't have any of my own kids, I had lots of beliefs about how I would feel, be treated and be included, in exchange for joyfully contributing what I believed were my responsibilities for childrearing and homemaking in my own home. Does my experience sound familiar to you? What about the assumptions, reactions and feelings below?

- You may resist being flexible, perhaps because of your commitment to the happy family dream and your fear that if you back off (or back down) your dream is impossible.

- You can feel like you're starting a new family but fail to account for the pull and strength of the already established patterns, rituals, agreements and beliefs that your partner and his kids bring with them.

- You may feel like an outsider in your own home and get caught in an unconscious power struggle with your partner and stepkids. Maybe you find it hard to accept that things in this stepfamily home are not going to be as you had imagined and this can be very upsetting.

- You might have some strong beliefs about your role as the "woman of the house" and when others prevent you from having your way, you experience a powerlessness that feeds your rage—and leads to more infuriatingly unwinnable power struggles.

- You may feel angry and strongly believe you have a right to be in charge of and take a stand in your own home to have things exactly the way you want them to be. This anger is totally understandable and (please hear this delivered in a gentle tone of voice) much of it is coming from your past. Why? Because the home you dreamed about heading as a child was probably not a stepfamily home. It's very important to understand that as stepmothers, one of the prices we pay for loving a partner with children from a previous relationship is learning to accept we've also inherited some pre-existing behaviors we never imagined and have very little control over.

- You may feel rage or hatred when another woman has the power to impact and influence the rules in your home. This is completely understandable and is another thing that engaging in a power struggle will not resolve.

When tension arises between you and your partner due to conflicts in beliefs, things can get complicated very fast. Sometimes your partner can feel like he's caught between a rock (the ex) and a hard place (you—his beloved). Maybe he feels he's caught between pleasing his kids and pleasing you. It feels lose-lose-lose. I call this frustrating scenario *"Bad Option A and Bad Option B."* This can be understandably enraging and excruciating for your partner—in addition to experiencing the stress of the current situation, he's probably also tapping into unprocessed pain and rage from his old power struggles and emotional wounds that pre-date your relationship.

On your side, you may feel like you're second, third or even fourth on your partner's priority list, based on your interpretation of his actions and whose opinion he accepts or acts on. Ever feel like you're fourth after his kids, their bio-mom and maybe even his work? This feels awful. Despair can set in for both of you when the stepfamily issues seem unavoidable, unresolvable and unending.

What can you do? In my experience, finding clarity and understanding each other's beliefs lead naturally to more compassion. Conflicts in beliefs don't have to become power plays where someone has to lose. When you figure out the belief that's fueling—maybe even compelling—your opposing positions, you'll learn a lot about each other. No matter how long your stepfamily has been in place, today is a new day. This is a new way to better understand the reasoning behind your partner's choices so you can support him, without feeling that it is costing you anything. Keep in mind that it requires quite a bit of consciousness to see through the tangles of power plays. I believe you'll find the benefits surprisingly worthwhile.

The "If Only They Were Different" Delusion

If you and your partner have been dealing with a stressful stepfamily life, it's easy to fall into a temporarily pain-numbing, delusional, heart-hardening frame of mind. How many hours have you spent thinking about ways to say this (or do that) in order to get your partner to see the wisdom in your ideas and agree with you about this issue or that idea? *"If only the stepkids, their bio-mom or my partner would be different!"*

You may feel caught in a loop of believing that there *has* to be a way to get your partner (or his ex) to see the rightness and fairness of whatever you're suggesting. You may think, *"Why can't they see that my suggestions are for the good of their children? Why don't they give any credence to all the articles, books, videos and expert opinions I've shared that support my suggestions?"* Perhaps in your mind, whatever you're suggesting is always in the best interests of your stepkids. Your suggestions are probably correct and your efforts sincere, but if they ultimately cause more stress with your partner and wasted hours and days of your life, is it really worth it? Which is more important to you, being right or taking care of yourself?

Workshop Feedback from Stepmoms

"I decided to give it a try. Supporting my partner's childrearing tactics was really tough at first but then I began to notice the power struggle you mentioned—I was trying to feel needed or like I was somehow supposed to know better as my stepkids' stepmother. I realized I wasn't respecting my partner as the actual bio-dad. I'm happy to report he's so grateful for my new support and for being able to relax more when the kids are around." ~SMOM1

"If I could do it all over again, I'd trust in my husband and his decisions about how to handle his kids and ex-wife. We were exhausted from all the disagreements and this approach has saved us. We didn't even realize how angry we were at each other until I stopped my part of the stress. What a relief to be on the same side again. Even when I see I would have done something differently, it's getting easier to let it go and appreciate we're not arguing about it anymore." ~SMOM2

"After considering your suggestions, I decided to stop the unsolicited advice (OK, nagging) and instead be my husband's most loyal cheerleader and sounding board. I wanted to be on the same side—his side—and it's working, just like it did in the beginning of our lives together. After a few weeks, he started asking what I'd do. I'm being careful not to jump in like I used to. Before I offer my ideas, I ask him what he thinks and help him sort it out. It feels great." ~SMOM3

"I wish I'd known sooner that the things that really upset me, as a result of my partner's choices, were pointing out emotional wounds I brought into our relationship. I've blamed and judged him for my pain a lot in the past. He read the workshop handouts and he's been a good sport about understanding why I was so upset. I could've spent all that lost time helping myself and being a lot more fun to be around. My partner and those emotional wounds deserve my attention and compassion and they both have it now. Thanks." ~SMOM4

"I believe that if I'd known about this approach from the beginning, the love that had drawn my husband and me together in the first place could've been mobilized and strengthened through each experience, instead of weakened and strained by stress. What a relief!"
~SMOM5

Letting go of fighting for your beliefs and instead supporting your partner feels terrific, particularly as it means avoiding the pain of unwinnable arguments. Through exploring this approach, you and your partner can become a closer, stronger couple who can be confident you'll weather future stepfamily struggles together.

Yeah, But #3: *"What's my role in the family if I make the choice to put aside my child-created beliefs and rules related to being the woman of the house? How can I still be a good Stepmom if I create a new set of personal beliefs and boundaries that focuses solely on my partner's happiness and mine?"*

Imagine your response to the questions below. Does anything below ring true for you? Does any of it inspire you to explore a perspective you might not have considered before now? Here are some questions and comments that you may share and want to ponder to learn more about yourself, your beliefs and your needs.

1. How can I support my partner's childrearing decisions when I would raise (or am raising) my child differently? I know they're his kids but what if I think he's doing something that's bad for them? How can I support something that I believe is wrong? Is there another way to look at this situation instead of as right/wrong or good/bad?

    Hold on—am I being judgmental because I'm not getting my way? Am I trying to control this situation because I feel my voice should be heard and honored as the "woman of the house?" Is what he wants to do actually wrong (oh that's harsh) or is it just different from what I'd do? He is their father! Can I step out of right/wrong thinking and make room for differing ideas?

2. Why do I resist accepting that my partner knows his kids and their bio-mom better than I do and is better able to gauge their reactions to various circumstances?

3. What if I show my partner that even when I disagree with him, going forward I'll defer to his judgment and trust him to do what he thinks is best for his kids? He's their bio-dad. If they were my bio-kids, I would expect him to defer to me.

   Wait—could I let go of an issue and stop being angry at him if he'd listen to my thoughts and feelings with a compassionate, open mind? Am I looking for evidence that he has at least considered my point of view? Have I presented my viewpoint as a freely offered option or a demand? If I were watching myself as I presented my viewpoint, would I see someone treating my partner with respect or would I see someone being bossy, controlling and acting like she knew better than him? How do I think things would change if I shared my ideas in a kinder, more respectful, trying-to-help way, without the implied pressure that he needs to agree with me?

4. How would it feel to become a compassionate, non-judgmental sounding board for my partner—offering suggestions, but only when asked, so there's a mutually respectful, authentic, safe exchange of thoughts and feelings between us? What do I need from him that I'm not getting now to create this positive, on-the-same-team, problem-solving experience?

5. Can I actually find a way to be truly non-judgmental and accept my partner's guidelines when it comes to childcare-related decisions for his kids in my (our) house? What beliefs do I have in my rulebook that make me feel my opinions and beliefs should override his?

6. How can I *possibly* sit back and watch my partner's kids get away with disrespectful, hurtful or entitled behaviors? What's going on with me that makes me believe I need to act like the Manners Police or Hygiene Sheriff of the house?

   Check my list of beliefs for this answer. Look for more ways to take care of myself instead of trying to change others so I can feel OK.

7. What kind of stepmother would I be if I let the children in my home, in my care, act "that way" in front of me? In front of others? Toward me? Where's this rigid vigilance and insistence coming from? Am I acting like my mother? Like I thought my mother should have acted? Why am I making this issue so important? Am I actually being hurt by them or angry because they're not bound by the same childrearing rules I was forced to endure?

8. Do I notice any differences in my feelings or reactions when my stepkids' actions impact me directly vs. when I observe behaviors I believe are wrong? How would it feel to let go of all their behaviors that don't impact me directly? See Section Five to understand more about your relationship with your stepkids.

9. As a good, caring stepmother, how can I possibly stay behind the scenes and let my partner handle his own kids the way he wants to when I disagree? How is that approach respecting me, my opinions, feelings and needs as the woman of the house?

    Check my list of beliefs for this answer also. Do I believe that the views of a stepmother (or woman of the house) override a bio-dad's opinions?

10. How can I feel included in the family if I don't get to be in charge of the mothering, household rules and duties in my own home like my mother was? Shouldn't the woman of the house have a say? What's my role in this family if I just support my partner even when we disagree?

    Let me think about this—is it possible that I believe having a voice in the rearing of my stepkids and setting the house rules represent the only way I can feel included in this family? If I let all those issues go, is it possible I fear I'm not contributing enough or have no role—or that I might feel even more left out or disregarded? Hmmm?

11. How can I feel good about myself if I don't at least try to get my partner to do the things that I truly believe are in the best interests of his kids? Aren't I more objective than he is?

12. My partner is laid back and likes to avoid conflict with his kids. If I left the childrearing decisions to my partner, I really believe the following things would occur:

    - His kids wouldn't wear matching clothes.

    - His kids might not acquire the sense of responsibility and consequences I believe they should have.

    - Class projects, permission slips and homework might be late or incomplete or not as good as they could be.

- His kids wouldn't acquire the manners and personal hygiene I'd like them to practice.

- There'd be no consistent structure I believe children need in a good home.

- My partner would let his kids get away with anything just to avoid arguments. That means the kids would do as they please when at our house—including misbehave—and I'd be left with all the housework and chores and cleaning up after them. I don't want to feel like a maid or nanny in my own home.

- My stepkids would get away with behavior that I consider entitled, disrespectful, irresponsible, lazy, unhygienic or combative in front of my own bio-kids and this would influence them in a potentially negative or harmful way. What do I say to my own kids about that?

If your stepkids already treat you or your partner disrespectfully…

13. It's very hard to see my partner treated badly by his own kids. This hurts my feelings and sometimes makes me furious. Isn't it my job to stand up for my partner if he's too afraid to do it himself? Won't things only get worse if I do nothing?

    Wait a minute—am I catastrophizing to justify my involvement in raising my stepkids or to defend my right to control (stop) upsetting behavior in my home? Why am I making all this childrearing stuff more important than supporting, loving and being loved by my partner? See Chapter 4, The Pros and Cons of Catastrophizing: Imagining Worst Case Scenarios Believing It's Helpful.

    Alternative Big Picture Perspective: Instead of trying to control my stepkids, who've been parented by my partner (their father) for all these years, is there another self-respecting way that my partner and I can approach this situation that enables both him and me to feel OK about things, even when we differ and while we take each child's unique personality into account?

    Compassion Alert: Sometimes your partner may be caught in a massive set of power struggles, feeling alone and up against his kids, their bio-mom and now you. Keep in mind that anything you may try to impose that varies from the past could get back to bio-mom and stir things up even more. What can seem like a short-term correction to a well-intended Stepmom can become fuel for another battle between bio-parents. This, in turn, will produce more stress between you and your partner. Is the correction or consequence really worth all the additional problems it may cause you and your partner? The answer is probably *"no"* in spite of what your ego or child-self may think.

14. What would others think if my stepkids looked unkempt at school or acted in ways that I find unacceptable? How secure do I feel about being the stepmother in this family? Do I fear being judged based on my stepkids' actions? How does the community treat me as my stepkids' Stepmom? Are there areas in my life where I feel I'm being treated as "less than" because I'm not their bio-mom? Why am I making potential negative events and judgments (or even real negative events and judgments) so important to me?

15. Since I see that my partner suffers from divorce guilt and is often painfully manipulated by his kids and their bio-mom, isn't it my job to stand up for him, for his rights and for the best interests of his kids? Isn't this true even if my partner doesn't see it that way, is afraid of losing his kids' love or doesn't have the energy or courage to take a stand and confront his ex-wife?

    Note to Self: Is my partner asking for my help? Have I asked him what kind of support he needs from me? Am I willing to support him in the way he wants to be supported? What's going on with me when I step in and say or do or disagree with something without being asked, even when it causes more stress for him?

16. Aren't I being a good person and an excellent Stepmom if I'm willing to face conflict and the anger of my stepkids, their bio-mom or my partner for the sake of long-term benefits to my stepkids? What beliefs or experiences do I have that make me believe I need to stand up in this way at the expense of my own happiness or relationship with my partner? Would I take a stand over this issue with a neighbor's child? Hmmm? What exactly is my responsibility as a Stepmom to these kids?

Do you have any of these reactions when you consider giving up any perceived role and duties as the woman of the house and as your stepkids' Stepmom? Is this causing stress between you and your partner? It's helpful to remember that a lot of parent-child and parent-parent dynamics have already been established among your partner, his kids and their bio-mom. When you and your partner created your stepfamily, you weren't starting from scratch as you would with your own kids. Because of this, it's going to go a lot smoother for all of you if you'll follow your partner's parenting lead when it concerns your stepkids. Then redirect your energy and time toward your self-care, your bio-kids (if any) and strengthening your relationship with your partner.

Yeah, But #4: *"Aren't I at least partially responsible for my partner's kids growing up to be well-behaved, thoughtful adults? Don't I have something to teach them? If I see something lacking in the way the bio-parents are raising their kids, shouldn't I fill the parenting gap? What kind of Stepmom would I be if I didn't at least try? I mean they're kids and they deserve the best of all of us, don't they?"*

Through my personal experiences as a Stepmom and my professional work with stepmothers, I now strongly believe that right/wrong, good/bad absolute thinking severely interferes with lovingkindness in relationships. That kind of thinking is exemplified in the paragraph above—to which I used to totally relate, FYI. Well-meaning Stepmoms can make being right, doing the right thing or trying to get others to do the right thing much more important than being loving—all the time believing this is their only right choice. Why is this? Because their beliefs and their past experiences taught them (conditioned them) that doing the right thing should be their priority. Remember, this is only a belief—remember you have a choice and the freedom to make a new belief and therefore a new choice.

Yeah, But #5: *"If I stay quiet, I worry about my stepkids having terrible manners."*

This is certainly possible. However, I'm not sure anyone has ever needed therapy or counseling because their father didn't hold them accountable in their youth for table etiquette, or because they didn't brush their teeth three times a day, write thank you notes, complete chores or do many of the other things which you may argue about with your partner. Liberating News: Your stepkids are going to turn out exactly the way they choose to turn out. They can grow up to be OK even when "proper" childrearing protocols are not followed according to your rulebook. The important exception, of course, is if they grow up in abusive environments, but that's above and beyond the scope of this book. Stepkids can also be raised "correctly" and still have all kinds of problems. I've found that we Stepmoms often make childrearing rules super important because we want to be included in the process and know no other way to feel included. Could this be true for you in any way?

If your partner were a single father, he would have to find a way to protect and nurture his kids whenever they're in his care. He would allow them to do (or not do) all kinds of things for all kinds of reasons. Additionally, if he were a single dad he also wouldn't have to spend time and energy fighting with a partner and feeling hurt or inadequate as a result of her judgments. He wouldn't feel he let his new love down or—to make matters even worse—feel judged and shamed by two women, not just his ex-wife. *Gulp!* Somehow his kids would grow up with or without all the rules we believe should be imposed and upheld. Somehow they would learn what to do in order to get along with others. If your partner were a single father, his kids would grow up affected by all the adults in their lives—not just the bio-parents. Is this a possible creative opening for a conscious Stepmom?

Rather than trying to be a parenting figure in your stepkids' lives, what if you decided to model being the best possible adult version of yourself and the intimate partner of their father? Could making a map for having a loving connection—in spite of outside traumas or conflicting beliefs—be an even more positive, life-impacting model for your stepkids, especially given their experience with their bio-parents' painful divorce, which tremendously impacts their beliefs about intimate relationships?

What if you could look past your own childhood programming, toss out your child-created book of beliefs when it conflicts with your partner's approach, and instead decide to teach your stepkids—by way of your actions, attitudes and words—how to be loving, authentic and self-respecting individuals with healthy boundaries? I ask again: How would your life be different if you and your partner created a new book of beliefs that suited your current stepfamily situation, needs and wishes?

Yeah, But #6: *"How can I support my partner if I'm not helping him deal with his ex or trying to solve his childrearing crises? What else can I do with all my stepmother enthusiasm and desire to be included and involved in the lives of my stepkids?"*

Have you asked your partner these questions? So many Stepmoms admit they haven't, or that they haven't really listened to the answer. This is a great place to start. Perhaps you have your partner read this chapter and then you two talk about it? When you go in search of your beliefs, there are bound to be things you agree and disagree on. Once you can identify your areas of disagreement and isolate your conflicting beliefs, you can embrace your new strategy and consciously choose to supportively defer to your partner's approach—ideally resulting in more compassion for each other.

Hopefully your partner already acknowledges and appreciates everything that you contribute to his life and to that of his kids. Maybe your contributions entail a lot of logistical, financial and emotional support that's impossible to measure. I'm certainly not overlooking that aspect of your participation in your stepfamily life and I don't want you to either. However, when you explain to your partner what you're willing to do differently going forward—namely, supporting his approaches and decisions when it comes to your stepkids and his ex—the pressure on both of you can diminish almost immediately. Yes, almost immediately.

Yeah, But #7: *"If I'm not a childrearing resource or authority, then what can I do?"*

What if you could find other ways to bring value, love and positive impact to your stepfamily situation? The His Kids: His Call approach is not about silencing your voice, being disrespected or settling for hurtful experiences. While it can feel that way at first glance, it's truly about embracing a new strategy and then identifying the tactics that are most effective for you and your partner in your stepfamily situation. It's about refusing to get into power struggles over right and wrong because those experiences are painful, disconnect you and your partner and distract you from whatever situation needs your attention. It's about you, and ideally your partner, looking honestly at any rigid, inflexible beliefs you hold from your past that you didn't realize were changeable—and it's about being willing to change them so the two of you can be closer as a team. As already mentioned, much of the stress between a Stepmom and her partner can be eliminated by doing this work together.

Even if a Stepmom is the only one embracing this new strategy, a tremendous amount of stress will simply evaporate between you and your partner. When you do this work, at some point your partner is going to feel a positive shift. Based on the feedback I've received over the years, many partners get curious about the resulting lack of tension and often want to jump in to work with their Stepmom partners when they see the positive impact of this new strategy. For some bio-dads, this is a miracle they never even imagined was possible.

Yeah, But #8: *"I'm not willing to be blamed for all the stress between my partner and me. That said, I am willing to try something to end our painful arguments. Where do I start?"*

Good for you—and you're right! Rarely is a stressful relationship dynamic completely one-sided. However, when it comes to disagreements over childrearing and bio-mom issues, the Stepmom often carries a lot of responsibility for the stress caused in the relationship. Thankfully she also has the power to make the greatest contribution toward a positive change.

Implementation Ideas

- Try recognizing that just because you think some aspect of childrearing is important, right, good or superior to whatever your partner thinks, this doesn't mean that it's necessary, right or needed for your stepkids. Do your best to keep the big end goal in mind—having a happy life and helping everyone feel OK.

- Try relaxing (and lightening up). Get curious about new ways of doing things as you watch your partner parent. This may require that you process your feelings about his choices and that's a healthy way to honor your feelings while you're honoring his choices.

- Try refraining from using all those non-verbal clues, such as rolling your eyes, sighing or clearing your throat, to communicate your disagreement to your partner. This could be a big step for you. Take a different tactic—look for what he does right. Find ways to acknowledge when you agree with him and his choices. You might even create your own personal "high five"—it might help you express your support and help him to express his appreciation for that support.

- Withhold your opinion (to the best of your ability) until your partner asks you for it. This might be difficult initially or take a while, particularly if you've been offering unsolicited advice in the past. Hang in there. I practically needed to put duct tape over my mouth to stay quiet at first. Ha ha! It'll be satisfying for both of you when you realize and appreciate that neither of you is dreading nor bracing for these conversations. It's such a relief to be on the same side of stepfamily issues like you used to be.

- If applicable, get curious about why you might be so invested in doing things your way or being right. It's also important not to ask or expect your partner to prove his love for you by doing things your way. *Ouch!* These tendencies can be a bit embarrassing when you recognize them in yourself, so be compassionate with yourself when acknowledging and addressing past behaviors. You've been doing your best and now you have new information that gives you new ideas for the future.

- Try looking for more options if your current relationship dynamics cause stress and disconnection between you two. My experience tells me that if either a Stepmom or her partner feels uncomfortable, it's important to look deeper and figure out where your beliefs conflict. Like finding the prize at the end of a treasure hunt, it's exciting and satisfying when you uncover these answers.

Good Manners or Good Times?

Having stepkids without the greatest table manners isn't the end of the world—even if it's hard to watch. You can still model behaviors you believe in. Instead of correcting your stepkids, you can have fun catching them doings things the way you like and giving them a compliment or a little treat. Notice—and say something out loud—when you observe them being responsible and respectful. Positive reinforcement can impact children in remarkable ways, and it's a lot more fun than being the manners police or arguing with your stepkids and partner about rules and enforcement just because it's some standard you were forced to adhere to. Can you feel that difference? Modeling behaviors that you feel are important, plus catching and commenting on the successes, offers your stepkids truly positive emotional and self-esteem value even if you never hear about it.

Today's kids (and many parents) seem to have different, less structured attitudes about manners, etiquette and other things than what you may have experienced growing up. With the advent of smartphones and tablets, traditionally intimate family times—like meals and car rides—are now competing with or interrupted by news stories, music, videos, games, texts and other distractions. Our ever-present virtual connection to the outside world can hinder our connection to each other. In fact, the allure of technology also intensifies conflicts in intact families and now adds to the potential for greater childrearing differences between divorced parents as the kids grow older. Noted differences in the behaviors of today's kids can strike a dissonant emotional chord for a Stepmom raised in an environment where manners and rules were strictly enforced. How many fun family times have been cut short or missed completely because a stepkid wouldn't take his elbows off the table and refused to say please, chew with his mouth closed, put down his phone or take off his hat?

I'm not advocating any kind of rudeness or unhealthy habits. I'm just asking you to look at all the behaviors you may require or have corrected or criticized that have stunted spontaneous fun. Did this happen because you believe kids should do things your way, even at the expense of enjoying each other's company? Was it worth it? By the way, as an added bonus, it can be such a relief to set down the childrearing responsibilities—willing to give it a try? Even for one evening or weekend?

Important: I'm never advocating you become a Stepford Wife or *ever* allow yourself to be treated badly or disrespectfully. I have more to say about your side of things but just haven't gotten to that part yet. The His Kids: His Call strategy—plus whatever you need to do to safeguard your needs and pursue harmony in your life as a Stepmom—isn't simple, and let's just say I need lots of words to express it completely. Keep reading and I'll explain more.

Creating Peaceful, Healing Interactions

Have you ever felt that you ruined or lost out on happy family times because you made enforcing proper manners more important than happy times together? I know I have. Upon reflection, can you identify any beliefs you inherited and consciously or unconsciously imposed on your stepfamily that squashed happy times for no really good reason? This can be hard to admit so if it's true for you, remember to be gentle and kind to yourself. Maybe it's time to toss out some old child-created rules and make some new rules of your own. Buying into this concept opens lots of wonderful possibilities. If you're looking for some fun ways to enjoy time with your stepkids, two articles on the smoms.com public website offer you some creative, fun ideas for connecting with your stepkids.

I saw a sign once that said, "a truly loving mother chooses time with her kids over household chores and cleanliness." Maybe a Stepmom on a Mission chooses to make loving connections with her partner and stepkids more important than generations of inherited beliefs about what's right and wrong in childrearing. Are you open to this possibility? I'm not suggesting that you ever encourage harmful behaviors or habits—but do you really believe that, left to his own decisions, your partner would want his kids to grow up being irresponsible, rude, un-hygienic, disrespectful or otherwise unable to fend for themselves as good people? Do you think he would ever intentionally hurt or cripple his kids emotionally or socially? If your answer is *"yes"* then that's a matter for an important separate discussion. For the sake of this discussion, I'm going to assume your partner has his children's well-being as a top priority, and if you're willing to let go of controlling certain things, you can relax because you don't need to be involved in the childrearing and disciplining of your stepkids.

Changes Possible with His Kids: His Call

1. What if your number-one goal becomes helping your partner create the kind of family life that he wants for his kids, while also having the kind of intimate relationship the two of you want? How would you feel about that? What would have to change?

2. How different could it be for you if—instead of bracing for your comments, getting angry at you or defending himself over childrearing decisions—your partner eagerly wanted to hear your opinion because he valued it so much? Wouldn't that be lovely?

3. How much closer and more loving toward you would your partner be if he didn't feel like he was disappointing you? What if he didn't feel shamed and judged by you as bad, wrong or weak? Hint: remember how he felt toward you (and about himself) at the beginning of your relationship.

   Here's feedback I got from the husband of one SMOM I was working with on this issue. He told me, via his wife, that when she explained the idea of His Kids: His Call and told him how she was willing to change her approach to make things easier for him, for them, he felt deeply "known" and welled up with tears.

   He said the feeling reminded him of the scene at the end of the movie, "It's a Wonderful Life," when George Bailey is panicked and chased out of town by former friends who don't know him anymore. He desperately asks to wake up and moments later his friend Bert (the cop) recognizes him. In that moment, he feels the joy of being known and says, "You know me? You really know me!" He said her willingness to make these changes made him feel that same relief and joy. It was beginning of a new relationship for them, involving a lot less stress and a much deeper connection between them, that had already changed the course of their stepfamily life.

   You have the power to give your partner this gift without having to lose anything of true value. Yes, it's a big ask, I know. It means you have to do a lot of processing, reflection and soul-searching—*and* the benefits are win-win.

4. How wonderful would it be to feel like that closely connected, loving couple you were when you first got together, shared everything, felt supported and believed you could handle anything together, as a team? You have the power to recreate this with your partner.

Think of all the emotional energy you could free up and use for fun, positive things if you and your partner teamed up to consciously uncover beliefs that conflict. Together, you could support each other's needs in creative ways, allowing you to fully support your partner's beliefs about how to interact with his kids and their bio-mom. Think of the arguments you could avoid and the joyful, peaceful times you would spend together. *Ahhhhh!* This is such a worthy and attainable goal, and one you have control over—unlike trying to change other people.

Keep in mind that beliefs don't have to be wrong in order for you to change them or adopt new ones. It's about what is (and isn't) appropriate for you *now*, based on your unique personal situation. It's about continually reevaluating beliefs and being creative when a new or unexpected circumstance arises and when conflicts surface. It's about you and your partner finding ways—as a team—to contribute to achieving a shared goal that's better experienced together than apart. We Stepmoms can have a new mission. We can use our creative, loving, wise skills in new ways that increase the strength and longevity of stepfamily couples. There are many ways to use your enthusiasm to help your family. Rather than working hard to create a happy family dream in the future, what if you worked on feeling happy and closely connected with your partner right now, and from moment to moment?

Common Stepmom Wish: *"It would be amazing to feel like my partner was willing to help me stand up for my needs and protect my right to be respected by his kids so I could relax and feel welcome in my own home."*

Unlike all the other components of this approach, this is one area you can't implement by yourself. Hopefully, as you share some of these ideas with your partner, he may feel so supported, loved, relieved and maybe even excited that he begins to support you in new ways—perhaps by changing some of his own beliefs, views and behaviors.

After Implementing His Kids: His Call, a Stepmom Wrote to Me

"Dear Cathryn, it's been profound for us both. My husband says he feels more loved, respected and supported by me. He said that he now feels more protective of me and my feelings since I've been willing to defer to him to avoid so much stress. It was like untangling an invisible knot between us and discovering a new flow of feelings and energy that's now available for more positive and loving actions on his

part. He feels stronger and wiser and that there's finally a way to handle situations with his kids that allows him to feel good about his decisions AND stay connected to the woman he loves—me! He's told me several times how relieved he feels not to brace with "Here we go again" and be criticized and judged (by me) when handling difficult situations his ex-wife creates. By the way, your "sounds about right" idea has also really been great for us! Thanks for that too!

In doing his own work on his beliefs and reflecting on past situations, my husband surprised me and told me how sorry he is for all the times he didn't stand up for me—or himself. He felt so validated and really known when I acknowledged my part in the stress he was enduring all those years. His apologies and increased appreciation for my willingness to shift my priorities, making us most important, has been so broad that all kinds of wonderful things have changed between us. Thank you from both of us!"

It's always great to hear stories like this one. This SMOM's partner's willingness to self-reflect increased the benefits of her work. She got the ball rolling and it's always terrific when partners are willing to work together to step out of old patterns and into new, more loving ones.

You might even create a wish list of what changes or behaviors you'd like to see from your partner and bring it to your conversation when the timing feels right. Keep it close at hand and see what you two can work out together. This is definitely a synergistic process with a huge upside. Everyone has their own unique beliefs, values, emotional hot spots, pet peeves, personal needs, wishes and desires, and by using your imagination there's really no limit to the ideas or positive changes you and your partner can experience with this new strategy. All that matters is that the two of you agree and feel great about your new choices.

Beneficial Behaviors Your Partner Could Offer You

I've thought of seven ways your partner could possibly change *his* behaviors and choices, to benefit you, once he understands the benefits of you adopting the His Kids: His Call approach for him. You may think of more based on your unique life circumstances. That's great. Use these ideas to inspire you to encourage your partner to work with you. Make your own wishlist.

Benefit #1: If last-minute changes with your stepkids or their bio-mom's schedule have been a source of stress between you, your partner might agree to handle, to the best of his abilities, all consequences of these changes—particularly childcare emergencies. This will keep you from having to be on call, put in awkward situations with the bio-mom or negatively impacted in any way.

Benefit #2: If conflicting beliefs about the children's daily habits are a source of arguments between you, you could make a list of childrearing habits, manners, chores and consequences that you feel are absolutely critical. Ask your partner if there's *anything* on your list that he's willing to enforce/support with his kids going forward. If he picks 1 or 2 things to enforce with his kids, can you agree to let the other things go without any future nagging, pressuring, sighing or eye-rolling from you? Can you put your attention on where he supports you instead of where you differ? This is a half-full/half-empty moment of choice. Not right or wrong but in reality, paying attention to the places where you agree and he supports you feels much better.

Benefit #3: By implementing this strategy, you can expect your partner to become more relaxed and non-defensive, as fewer future situations related to the stepkids' behavior become an argument or ruin a potential good time. As a result of feeling supported, your partner is more likely to eventually solicit your opinion and feedback, giving you the ability to contribute to his childrearing approach. If the stepkids' behavior has negatively impacted you in a direct way, you can, as calmly as possible, thoroughly explain to your partner how and why it has done so. Ask him if he would be willing to stand up for you or in some way protect you from as much negative impact as possible. This is not about typical kid behavior but about overt acts of disrespect or abuse. Here's a guideline that's usually a surprising and effective eye-opener for your partner:

> If it's not OK for a neighborhood kid to treat you in a specific way,
> then it's NOT OK for his children to treat you that way, either.

Benefit #4: If you're feeling resentment, you and your partner could review and renegotiate new boundaries for your time, money, housekeeping or childcare-related duties so that he clearly understands what is (and is not) OK with you regarding his kids and their bio-mom.

If there are any current or past disagreements about something specific, perhaps based on a change you desire or an event, you can both agree to reflect on your individual motives for why you want what you do. Ask your partner to work with you to find a new way to help you feel emotionally and physically safe and respected in that situation. This is an excellent opportunity for creative problem-solving, which is something most Stepmoms on a Mission are very, very good at tackling.

Benefit #5: If your stepkids' bio-mom gives your partner problems regarding your participation in school or stepkid-related activities, your partner could agree to take the time to sit down calmly with you and 'fess up—to share his true fears, guilts, worries and feelings about each situation. This way, the two of you can figure out how to handle it all together. I've noticed that when our partners feel more supported by us, they are more willing to problem-solve and help us reduce our stress.

The personality of your stepkids' bio-mom will have a huge impact on how you and your partner handle each situation. This is a time to defer to your partner *and* to ask him to acknowledge any negative impact his ex-wife's behavior has on you. Ask your partner for lots of compassion and support. Ask him to help you find creative ways to feel better about deferring to his approach, especially when the results hurt your feelings in any way. It can be incredibly painful and enraging if you're unable to participate as much as you want in your stepkids' lives, especially if their bio-mom makes life miserable for you and your partner when you attempt to do so. It's so important to keep your relationship strategy in mind when this happens—heck, you can remind yourself of His Kids: His Call in all kinds of ways through post-its throughout the house, needlepoint, embroidery or tattoos—whatever it takes to help you remember it until it becomes a natural default, a new habit. When the pressure begins to build, remind each other that your connection as a couple and your individual well-being are paramount. With this strategy, the actions of an uncooperative bio-mom will not be able to destroy your connection, and you and your partner can handle any situation with minimum negative impact on your family. This can be tremendously liberating and empowering. This is a "win" for you and your partner when you decide to be unconcerned about what others think.

Note to a Stepmom feeling excluded: Yes, it's very unfair and hurtful—often infuriating beyond words—when you're denied "rights" to participate with your partner in your stepkids' public lives. It can feel even worse if the stepfather involved gets to be included because your partner is OK with his involvement. However, if your stepkids' bio-mom is adversarial, uncooperative or inclined to behave in narcissistic ways, it really is much more effective for you to concentrate on healing any triggered feelings, rather than taking a stand and showing up. The latter could force you and your partner to endure any additional melodrama and fury the bio-mom creates in response to your involvement. This is where your strategy to choose your well-being and connection with your partner over whatever seems right (according to your beliefs) is going to save you and your partner untold stress and relationship damage. I strongly urge you to see how it feels to focus on helping yourself feel better. See Section Six for more tips for dealing with uncooperative bio-moms.

Benefit #6: Your partner's willingness to share what he's *really* thinking, fearing and feeling will make a tremendous difference for the two of you. It will also help you both feel so much stronger as a couple. If defensiveness, blaming or judging each other has been an issue, see Section Three and Section Four of this book to help you and your partner work through sensitive relationship issues in loving, honest, productive ways.

Benefit #7: If you two just can't find a mutually satisfactory solution for a particular issue, ask your partner if he would be willing to join you in working with a professional to do so. The key is making sure you both hold the attitude of *"nobody's right/nobody's wrong and there's a solution out there somewhere that we both can feel good about."* This can be a new gold standard—a relationship covenant that will keep your creative juices, hope and love flowing, no matter what happens.

What else would you like to see change in your stepfamily situation and relationship? What would you like to get from your partner in exchange for offering him this supportive His Kids: His Call approach? You two have the ability, the right and the motivation to create a new, tailored map for yourselves. Whatever feels good for the two of you is all that's important. As a stepfamily, you can create your own relationship agreement. It's A-OK to step outside of any expected or typical family and relationship beliefs. Stepfamily dynamics are not like nuclear family dynamics, no matter how much someone tries to convince you of this, and tactics that work for nuclear families simply might not work for you. Hold your ground for the uniqueness of your situation. There's no need to be bound by any limitations espoused by society and generations of ancestors. Creating your own set of beliefs is a way for you and your partner to have a gloriously loving connection no matter the circumstances of your stepfamily situation.

Your Thoughts and Feelings?

Clearly the His Kids: His Call approach will present challenges and benefits to both you and your partner. I suppose the biggest issue is your willingness (or lack thereof) to let go of whatever beliefs you've been carrying with you—all in favor of crafting new empowering beliefs for yourself and a new reality with your partner. It's really profound (and wonderful) how drastically your feelings and your relationship can change when you're willing to see things in a new way and change your own beliefs.

I want to stress that I realize there are many reasons and ways to look at your life situations, your choices, your feelings and all the aspects of what you want and don't want. It can be monumentally difficult for a couple to nurture their relationship in a stepfamily, even when all the adults in the family get along and are willing to communicate and work together. The challenges you experience may trigger any and all unconscious childhood wounds you and your partner have brought into your relationship, which just adds to your stress. When you're faced with the additional complexities of difficult behaviors from your stepkids and their bio-mom, stepfamily life can present the hardest life situations you've ever faced. When you choose to implement His Kids: His Call, you and your partner will look at each situation and future choice differently—in a good way that makes you a stronger, more aware team.

Even after all we've been through as stepmothers, and maybe because of all this, I believe more than ever that personal transformation, emotional healing and increased insight are possible when we're willing to look for the lessons in all our challenges. Over the years, almost every Stepmom I've worked with has shared that she felt inexplicably drawn to her partner, and that she's perplexed by the space that has built up between them. The thing is, the one who touches us deeply and opens our hearts also has access to our wounds. Under stepfamily stress, you can end up hurting each other without meaning to in your efforts to protect yourself from the pain. As you become more and more conscious of how to help yourself and support each other, you can heal and grow stronger as you resolve each conflict in the complex relationship dynamic.

Stepfamily life can be outrageously difficult. It's unlike anything I experienced before—and maybe you too? Society has yet to find a supportive or instructive model for us, so we Stepmoms on a Mission are all out here working hard to make new maps. The deeply shared love you feel with your partner can help you navigate the rough waters you face as a stepfamily. Try His Kids: His Call, and make your loving connection with your partner and your well-being your highest priority. It can have so many positive ripple effects for both of you. When you're willing to work together as a team, set down your defensive patterns and compassionately help each other identify, honor, feel and heal, while forgiving your conflicting beliefs and blindspots, virtually nothing anyone else does, says or intends can put a wedge between you and your partner. You can become a solid, unbreakable team. That's the goal. That's the vision. That's our mission.

For stepmother reactions, questions and experiences on this topic, go to smoms.org/BonusChapters and click on the title "His Kids: His Call." See the complete list of additional chapters and follow-up discussions in Chapter 39.

A Stepmom's Relationship and Her Partner

Gracie Lu's Story

July 2016

I found SMOMS about two years into my marriage to my DH. Those first two years were the most stress-filled, horrible years—and if I'm to be honest, by the time I found smoms.org, I was desperate and we were quickly barreling toward a divorce. How I wish I had found this resource from the very beginning as it would have helped me better cope with the chaos that ensued after we got married. I seriously don't believe my marriage would have survived without the guidance, support and education provided by Cathryn and smoms.org.

I spent about two and a half years on the site, mostly just reading and not participating much, but felt so much better that I wasn't alone and that what I was feeling was normal for the situation. I took a break from the site for around two years and then re-joined under a new username in 2011 and began participating a lot. This is what I feel was the turning point for me. I've tried other sites dedicated to stepmother support and they just aren't the same. Smoms.org is truly a supportive, understanding, wonderful place that provides real solutions and support to stepmothers trying to navigate the stepfamily waters. I still browse other sites from time to time and am shocked at how women are attacked for sharing their true feelings—even if they aren't pretty. I know I can share anything with my fellow SMOMS and not be judged or treated harshly.

Reading Cathryn's articles has helped me tremendously and I am thrilled she is finally publishing this book. I swear I read her writings and think that she must be inside my head, pulling the thoughts out. They are THAT similar to my own thoughts and feelings. Over and over as I read them I'll find myself thinking "EXACTLY." Many times, I will print out the articles or read them aloud to my DH and we will discuss. This has helped not only our communication, but also helped DH to deal with his toxic ex in a way that causes us less drama and stress.

DH and I have been in and out of counseling since before we got married, but no counselor has helped us as much as Cathryn and smoms.org. I think very few counselors actually understand the real dynamics at play in stepfamily life, especially when an ex-spouse is openly hostile, uncooperative and using parental alienation tactics on the child(ren). All of the counselors we've seen have always focused on what's best for the child because we're the adults, and we're supposed to suck it up and deal with it. Sadly I think they just don't know what else to say.

Our Mission as SMOMS is to focus on creative problem-solving and taking care of ourselves. Yes, it's possible to take care of you without hurting the child(ren). I think the biggest thing I've learned is how to identify and make sure that my needs are being met. Self-care goes a long, long way when you're living in a stress-filled stepfamily.

I can never thank Cathryn and smoms.org enough for helping me make it through some of the most challenging times in my life. I'm happier now than I've ever been and the support and love I've gotten from them have made a huge difference in my life.

Gracie Lu
Stepmom since 2005
SMOM since 2011

Twenty

Nobody's Right/Nobody's Wrong
A Tactical Approach for Intimate Relationships

Ever feel like you and your partner spend way too much time in opposing corners of an uncomfortable relationship boxing ring, with some part of each of you feeling like you're opponents instead of partners? Have you felt desperate to be understood and supported by your partner, yet at the same time do you sincerely believe that if your partner would just see your side of things everything would be better? Lots of stepmothers tell me that they and their partners handle all non-stepkid and non-bio-mom problems beautifully as a relaxed, focused and loving team. This is why they're often upset and confounded about their inability to stay connected with and supportive of each other when it comes to responding to the actions of the stepkids and their bio-mom.

There are valid reasons for this difficulty among couples. Thankfully there are also ways to reduce and even eliminate the stressful feelings you and your partner experience when trying to resolve stepfamily-related issues. Working together in a new way allows you to remove emotional blinders and defensive blockages. This new approach, if you're open to trying it, gives you a way to access the power of your loving connection so you can see each other's points of view and appreciate any anger and pain caused by your stepfamily circumstances.

The key to staying on the same side with your partner as you resolve stepfamily issues is making new conscious decisions to become a competent team. How does it feel to imagine making an oath with your partner that starting today, you'll both agree to treat any stepfamily-related issue as a team of two conscious and loving adults, combining your skills, wisdom and talents?

A Loving Approach

After years of intense stepfamily-related stress, my husband and I realized we both needed a lot more compassion from each other. Sure, we'd listened to each other's words but for whatever reason we weren't feeling understood or supported enough by each other. We both needed more empathy and compassion, which we weren't giving each other for a bunch of valid reasons we couldn't seem to get past. Although we're two smart people who love each other, we just couldn't seem to get (or give) what we wanted and needed from each other when it came to stepfamily stuff. Oh, what a tangled web of thoughts, feelings, needs, beliefs, misunderstandings, emotional wounds and conflicting survival strategies.

One day many years ago, in the midst of an intense conversation, we had an "ah ha" moment at the very same time. In the conversations that followed this moment of awakening, we realized how powerfully healing it is to be able to share your deepest feelings and have the one you love the most listen and support you with deep empathy and loving compassion—it's like a magical emotional elixir.

In that moment our relationship started over again and we created what we call the "Nobody's Right/Nobody's Wrong—we won't give up, give in or settle until we find a mutually satisfying solution" approach to our relationship. Or "Nobody's Right/Nobody's Wrong" for short. The most important concept of this idea, and the biggest shift for a Stepmom and her partner, is to agree to look at any upsetting stepfamily situation as a "we" issue. No more you vs. me or *"my solution's more important or more right than your idea"* power struggles.

While this may sound easy enough, many stepfamily issues are complex and can trigger painful, enraging, fear-laden and strong feelings. Without intending to, couples can argue themselves into an oppositional (right/wrong) impasse without seeing any way back to each other. Each one can feel convinced the other person is being unreasonable, is wrong or doesn't care. They may sense the other is not courageous enough to take action, or that he/she is too controlling or maybe too stubborn to back down, even if doing so would make the other one feel better. This can be infuriating, isolating, confusing and painful beyond anything either one of them has ever experienced.

The new conscious team approach is more about an attitude than a technique, however there are a few pieces of homework and some ground rules that can be helpful. Your first assignment, if you choose to give this idea a try, is to look for patterns in your past disagreements. Here's an example that shows itself quite frequently: The Stepmom wants her partner to do something he doesn't want to do and he wants the Stepmom to stop doing, or not do, something she wants to do. This represents an unwinnable power struggle that can take a huge toll on your emotional connection and health, especially when it's repeated over time and becomes a well-worn "here-we-go-again" pattern. What repeated patterns of disagreements or conflicts in response to problems can you identify in your relationship? If you write them down it'll be easier to work on them as we go through some steps and questions.

Guidelines for This Approach

To be successful, you and your partner should do your best to make each other feel emotionally safe, respected, understood and supported. In order to get the most from this approach, choose to take the following actions together. You may want to copy these pages for your partner.

Guideline #1: Before you and your partner start conversations you expect will be tense, take a moment to appreciate any other stressors that your partner is dealing with so you can be as compassionate as possible for all he's going through. You can ask for and expect the same appreciation.

Stepmom Tip: If you suspect the issue you'd like to discuss is not a big deal for your partner, say some version of these words to him with as much love as you can muster in the moment: *"I know you may not be able to understand how upsetting this situation is to me, but I'm asking you to believe me when I say it's important to me. Would you please make time to give me your undivided attention and support? I could really use your help."* See Chapter 37, Tip #24 for more about this tip.

Guideline #2: Agree that neither of you will take any action without talking to the other one first. This is very important and can rebuild new levels of trust while reducing anxiety and collateral damage.

Guideline #3: Agree to suspend all blame and judgments toward each other—yes, all blame and judgements! Agree to deeply listen to each other's feelings and opinions before trying to discuss and solve any problems. Use the model of exemplary manners as a guideline.

Probably unnecessary, but just in case: This means no name calling, no cruel words and no destructive actions, no matter how angry or hurt either of you feels. The overarching goal is to agree to be kind (at least polite) to each other during this process. Remind each other to hate the problem but to love each other as you honor your feelings. Imagine pulling the issue out from between the two of you and then placing it across the room, in front of you both. This can make it easier to avoid defensiveness, help you see the issue more clearly and remind you that you're on the same side—looking for a creative and awesome solution that's acceptable to both of you.

Guideline #4: Promise each other you will not agree to any solution you don't fully believe is OK—ever again. This is important, especially if either of you has a pattern of giving in just to stop the conflict or avoid the stress.

Guideline #5: Agree that neither of you will shut down emotionally, clam up or walk away from this challenge for any reason. If you feel afraid or extremely angry, explain what's happening. If you can't find a mutually agreeable solution or you're feeling too tired, agree to take a break and reconvene another time to continue. Time outs are also a good thing if you reach an impasse or tempers flare.

Guideline #6: Cultivate the genuinely positive attitude of "Nobody's Right/Nobody's Wrong, we're so smart and creative and love each other so much we can figure this out together." Write it out, make a sign, do whatever you need to do to keep this new approach in mind.

Guideline #7: Whenever possible, deal with a given situation as soon as you can both give it your undivided attention—ideally within 24 hours. Important: keep these conversations out of your bedroom whenever possible. The expectation of privacy is also a must, even if you have to get logistically creative.

Guideline #8: Start your conversations with the heartfelt intention to bring your best adult selves and problem-solving skills to the table, and keep this promise to the best of your ability. If either of you slips into old patterns, take a breath, own it and start over again.

Guideline #9: Be sure you understand each other's priorities of needs and tolerances before you start trying to solve anything. This way, you can demonstrate a mutual respect for any differences in this area. A Stepmom and her partner may have conflicting needs and priorities when it comes to issues such as:

- Being included vs. being left out.
- Giving in to get along vs. insisting on taking a stand.
- Doing the right/fair thing vs. giving someone a pass.
- Avoiding conflicts at any cost vs. facing them head-on (at any cost).

See Chapter 18 for more specifics on handling conflicts and trauma as a loving team.

Guideline #10: If either of you finds yourself thinking, *"Here we go again…"* or *"If you'd just do what I say, everything would be OK,"* stop talking immediately, share your thoughts (if you wish), then consciously interrupt this well-worn, unloving, snowballing pattern. Substitute it with this new attitude: *"We're both upset and we want to handle this in a new way—as a team. Let's find a new way to help us both get what we need out of this situation."*

"Here we go again…" can be a powerful emotional response within your partner. He may also be thinking, based on past experiences, *"Here goes my night. I'm about to be pressured. This should be so simple but we keep having to deal with added stress and melodrama because you won't let things go."* This line of thinking is a slippery slope to martyrdom, self-pity and

blame for anyone—and these are all going to shut down the love between you and your partner, so watch for this reaction and do your best to stop when you notice it, interrupt it and stay open-minded to the possibility things can be different going forward.

Here's an excellent question either of you can pose at any time during an argument: *"What do we want to create here and going forward?"* When you're upset, it's easy to blame, judge, feel like a victim and say hurtful or angry things to each other. However, is that truly what you and your partner want to create from this argument? Hopefully not. You can interrupt hurtful, well-worn paths for dealing with stress by posing the question *"What do we want to create going forward?"* which brings it to your consciousness. Often, that is all that's needed to wake up (from reactive child-created behaviors) and get back into your adult selves.

Answers to this question can range, of course. Here are a few energy-changing, positive replies to a very powerful question you can ask each other: *"As a couple, what do we want to create going forward?"*

We want to solve this problem as a loving team.

We want to present (and truly be) a united front.

I want to feel like my feelings matter to you instead of you getting angry or defensive with me—what about you?

We want to find an answer we can both feel good about.

We want a solution that will not create more trauma or stress.

We want to solve this efficiently so we don't give away our power to the problem and so we can still have a great night/weekend together.

Guideline #11: If either of you starts to feel like you're not on the same team when discussing an issue, promise each other you'll speak up right away. This can help you get back on the same team before proceeding or saying something you'll regret. You may say something like this, *"You, I love. This situation, I hate. I'm on your side and I want you to be on my side. Let's take a breath, regroup and work together to resolve this problem as a team."*

At first these words may seem a bit fake but it's just a starting point—you'll find your own words with practice. If words are hard to come by, use the universal "timeout" hand signal or hold up a finger with a "give me a moment" reference. Do whatever you can to make your feelings known so you can make an adjustment, address whatever has just happened and get back to feeling like a team. See Chapters 21 and 22 to understand how defensiveness can interfere with a couple feeling on the same team. See smoms.org/BonusChapters for the chapter called "Six Sample Situations for Disarming Defensive Behaviors Between You and Your Partner."

Guideline #12: Acknowledge that every stepfamily thing is *not* necessarily truly an emergency, even if those around you may want you to feel that way—heck, even if that's your opinion because you're feeling so distraught—realize that a continual "hair's on fire" urgency can have a negative effect on your communications with your partner. One idea that works well is to introduce a scale of importance (1-10 or 1-100, for example) so you and your partner can put a number on a situation and appreciate your individual and combined priorities. This can help reduce compassion fatigue. This also helps you learn more about your partner and helps him learn about you so you can prioritize your action plans. See Section Four for more about how your partner might be feeling about dealing with stepfamily stress.

Guideline #13: If you or your partner experiences an urgency or anxiety when upsetting circumstances occur with the stepkids or their bio-mom, take responsibility for your vulnerable feelings and find healthy ways to calm and support yourself *before* you start this process. It's your responsibility to keep yourself in your conscious adult (vs. child) self. It's your partner's as well. Get the support you need so you can be your best adult self when you speak with your partner. This important step allows you and your partner to avoid unnecessary quarrels and to work together to create a well-thought-out, mutually agreed-upon choice as a fully functioning team. See Chapter 37, Tip #14 for an idea to help you get your partner's support while you're in the midst of a challenging situation.

Guideline #14: Respect each other's feelings with patience and kindness, even when impatience or frustration is knocking on your door. This is conscious love in action. Help each other become more aware of any child-created survival behaviors. Do your best to begin your team problem-solving as two wise adults who love each other and who find themselves facing outside sources of stress. Remind yourself that you're an unbeatable team when you work together. This positive encouragement spoken out loud can really make a difference. You may want to write all these phrases on notecards, like cue cards, to help yourself as you're learning this new way of handling stressful situations.

Guideline #15: Keep the big picture of your shared dreams and love for each other in mind. It's so easy to give away your power, time and attention as you two get caught up in the frustrations and daily melodrama that can be caused by other people's actions. To combat this drain on your life force, find ways to remind each other of what's important in your lives so you can keep a balanced perspective of what's happening around you.

For example, let's say you two want to have a happy, healthy life together, free from stress and with as few conflicts as possible. If you both agree on this goal, this may mean that giving in, letting go or ignoring certain situations is best for you as a couple. It's like creating a mission statement for your partnership.

Challenging Aspects of Nobody's Right/Nobody's Wrong

Anytime we're asked to change, there can be some natural resistance for all kinds of valid reasons. The more conscious you can be about the substance of any resistance and the details of what a change may ask of you, the better you will be able to succeed in your transition to a new way of thinking, feeling and behaving. You'll know you're on the right track if you find yourself wrestling with the issue or if you are trying hard to resist previous reactions.

Additional Thoughts

- Make the conscious choice to set aside any need to be right or the urge to get another to admit being wrong. This is understandable, yet almost always detrimental to an intimate relationship.

- Look for any conflicting or false beliefs that no longer serve you as an adult—without judging or shaming yourself or your partner. Chances are very good that both of you will realize you've been making decisions from beliefs and patterns from your past. For some it can be hard to admit, and getting defensive and shutting down has become a reflex. For others, it's a relief to understand the why of past behaviors. The good news about each discovery of a child-created, outdated belief and behavior pattern is that you can make new choices today—and everyday. It's one of the great things about being an adult.

- If you feel embarrassed, remorseful, angry or sad about the impact of your past choices, a heartfelt *"I'm sorry"* can be a remarkably healing gesture for you and your partner. It's also a cause for celebration because as you recognize these outdated behaviors and beliefs, you are liberated and free to make new choices. I encourage you to honor your feelings and then place your attention on the benefits of your good work on your future. See Chapter 2, Honoring vs. Shaming Your Feelings.

- Do your best to stay loving and open-hearted when feeling the urge to shut down and defend yourself. If you feel defensive, speak up so your partner will stop talking and assure you that you are safe. Take a deep breath and start listening when your heart is open. This is a conscious choice—do your best, over and over again as needed.

- Honor the ground rules and decision criteria you two establish—even when no solution seems apparent to either of you—and hold out for that mutually satisfactory solution.

It can save you and your partner so much time if you recognize old patterns and choose to do things differently, giving each other a clean slate and trying new ideas. This can also allow you to direct any charged-up emotional energy into finding solutions that could work for both of you. Adopting this approach requires you to help each other stay emotionally conscious, even under the pressures of personal and stepfamily issues. FYI, when I comment on being emotionally unconscious, I refer to anytime you slip back into childhood-created survival strategies that can't and won't lead you to the adult solutions your complex situations require. We all do it under stress until we realize we can interrupt this habit and make a new choice. Helping each other stay conscious (awake) can allow a couple to save time, energy and arguments, enabling them to stick together so they can get a lot done very efficiently.

If you decide to test out the Nobody's Right/Nobody's Wrong approach, you'll likely realize that in the past, you and your partner gave up on or stopped the problem-solving process too early—without a mutually acceptable solution. Going forward, when you begin a potentially stressful discussion, remind each other of your promise to work as a loving team. Refuse to stop working together until you find a solution that works for both of you. Something happens when you commit to being creative—your brainstorming inner genies seem to awaken. Plus, it's a fabulous feeling to be back on the same team with your partner. Here's something you can ask out loud: *"I bet there's a really good solution for this. Let's keep looking and find it."* This can help diffuse any defensiveness between you and your partner and activate the problem-solving parts of your brain, heart and gut.

Remember how, at the beginning of your relationship with your partner, you both felt you could handle anything as long as you were together? Stepfamily-related struggles are so intense that they can erode that powerful loving feeling. This is a terrible price to pay for a disconnect that's likely caused (to varying degrees) by others. As you two begin to find new solutions, you'll have the opportunity to realize that many of the painful situations you experience as adults also touch on emotional wounds each of you brought into the relationship from your childhood. This is not bad or wrong at all, it's this way in every romantic relationship. This can be hard to see at first, but once you both see the connection, it's much easier to support each other and have compassion for the emotions that are triggered by current events.

The Nobody's Right/Nobody's Wrong approach gives couples a chance to reframe each situation from a problem into a challenge they will solve together. It provides a chance for you to work together and to draw on the synergy of your talents and perspectives as you fortify the boundaries that protect your relationship. This approach can bring about tremendous results for you and your partner. Imagine how uplifting it would be to believe that future stepfamily issues will not tear you and your partner apart ever again. What a relief! What a worthy quest. Happily, it gets easier and even more exhilarating as your fear of conflict and judgment—and that of your partner—diminishes over time. With this change, solutions may come more quickly to you both without painful interactions or arguments.

Getting Started

Consider trying Nobody's Right/Nobody's Wrong the next time a stressful situation occurs. If that feeling of impending disconnect shows up, agree that either you or your partner will say some version of these sentences, *"Oh no. Here we go again trying to make each other wrong. Remember, nobody has to be right or wrong. I love you! Let's figure this out together."* Eventually you'll get good at this and you'll only need to say something quick like, *"Nobody's right or wrong here so let's get to work."*

Create a Safe Space for Sharing

1. Give this special processing time a name and honor it. Maybe you could call it the "Empathy Zone," "Team Time," "Safety Zone" or "Compassion Pow Wow." This is a private, sacred time when you and your partner agree to talk and listen with undivided attention and compassionate honesty so you can understand each other's feelings—*before* making any decisions or solving any problems.

2. The "Compassion Zone" is the time to express, explain and understand each other. It's *not* the time to problem-solve or to defend behaviors. There's plenty of time to work on solutions after the emotional charge has been released in the telling. First, make it an emotional discovery process where the two of you feel safe enough to put all your feelings out on the table with the goal of knowing each other more deeply because you want to. By understanding each other better, you're likely to find supporting each other much easier. When listening, you may want to ask clarifying questions to better understand something, and that's A-OK.

3. Do your best to create imaginary amnesia so you can let go of previous opinions and opposing positions. Imagine a clean slate. Consciously look for new ideas you hadn't thought of before.

4. Avoid telling the other what he/she should or shouldn't feel and instead accept his/her feelings as valid—whether or not you agree or even understand. Unlike what many guys I've worked with initially believe, it's *really* not necessary to understand why your partner is upset in order to offer comfort and support.

5. Resist the reflex to blame or interrupt each other. Give each other space for really listening and being heard.

6. Remember that listening and supporting each other does *not* mean you necessarily agree. I often hear that a partner resists offering support for fear he'll have to do something he doesn't agree with or want to do. Be sure to talk with your partner and *do agree* on this important issue.

7. This "Compassion Zone" is about doing your best to truly understand each other's feelings and nothing needs to be lost or given up in this process. If you feel that your needs are at risk by taking the time to listen and understand your partner's feelings, this may mean it's happened to you in the past. Be sure to talk about this fear and reassure each other that your goal is for both of you to have what you truly need.

8. During this special/sacred time together, decide who will talk first and who will listen first. Then swap roles. Let whoever feels most eager to talk first, go first. Whoever listens first needs to put themselves in a blame-free, judgment-free frame of mind. Your *only* job as the listener is to give your partner sincere, empathetic, non-defensive support and lovingkindness—like you would give a dear friend or even a stranger saying these same words.

    At first, it can be difficult to stay calm as you hear about the pain or anger your partner feels, especially if he believes your actions contributed to his suffering. It can be very hard to resist defending yourself and justifying your actions. I've found that listening without interrupting or defending yourself can feel a bit like having to watch your partner devour a plate full of delicious food while you sit there feeling like you're starving to death. However, you have a powerful choice here—you can choose to be impatient and to interrupt and defend yourself OR you can listen patiently because you love your partner and want him to get the nourishment he needs and because you trust your "plate of food" is only moments away. I recommend this latter attitude with great enthusiasm.

    When it's your turn to listen, just sit quietly and give him the safe space to express his feelings while you support him sincerely. Taking turns gives both of you the freedom, emotional relief and sense of being respected and treated fairly that's missing for a lot of couples who are under intense, complicated, stepfamily-related stress. It really does become easier to feel compassionate about your partner's feelings when you know he'll be doing, or already did, the same thing for you.

9. To help each of you feel a bit more relaxed about the sharing, agree to a time limit—10 or 20 minutes is usually enough, depending on the situation. Use the timer on your phone, giving yourself a 1 or 2-minute warning so you can focus and still have time to wrap up your thoughts.

Tip: After the first person talks and before the second person begins, try switching chairs to give this new ritual more weight and more meaning for you both. Designate a speaker's chair and the loving, empathetic listener's chair. You may only need to do this once or twice but it can be helpful, as it reminds you this is a new tactic and you're both learning together.

10. Hold each other's hands when you're in this "Compassion Zone" (or whatever you call it). Even though this can feel silly or be difficult—make and keep this promise to each other—hold hands to create a connection. Also, make sure you have the privacy and time to make this experience as effective as possible. Remember to do your best to find a comfortable place for this process that's *not your bedroom!*

11. Attentive listening is a treasured gift between partners. When listening to your partner, it's not about clamping your lips shut to prove you're not saying anything. It's about listening and, when appropriate, saying supportive, encouraging things like:

"I never looked at it that way."
"Thanks for sharing your feelings."
"I'm sorry you had to experience that."
"That makes sense to me."
"You did a great job."
"That must really hurt (or make you angry.)"

12. When it's your turn to talk and share your feelings, do your best to focus on what's happening now and how it impacts you in the present.

"Here's what happened and here's how I feel about it."
"When you did (or didn't do) this, here's how I interpreted it and this is how I felt."
"When she did x, I felt y."
"When this happens, I'm afraid that…"
"When you say [this or that], I'm assuming you mean [share your assumption]. Is this true?"
"Tell me more about that."

13. When you've both had a chance to share your feelings, take a moment for deep breaths, maybe even some hugs. Check in with each other. Do you feel that heart connection? Are you still angry/hurt or do you feel like you're on the same side?

Resist pushing forward into addressing the specific situation until you've found a way back to each other. Once you both understand and feel connected with each other, that's the time to move into working together to come up with a really good, creative, mutually acceptable solution. The mutual part is vital to the ultimate success of this approach.

If you and your partner have been under stress for a long time, you probably each have your own private emotional ledgers of past, unresolved issues. It's not necessary to resolve all your feelings the first time you have this compassionate exchange—that's way too much to ask of yourselves. Stick to the current issue. Another benefit of this work is you're likely to find that issues from the past get resolved through the process of addressing new situations. This is another reason that this approach alleviates so much stress between Stepmoms and their partners. For more detail, see Chapter 15 about resolving resentments from the past. You may also want to read a public-access article on smoms.org called "Are You Keeping an Emotional Ledger?"

14. Finally, plan something fun to follow these private sessions before or after you move into problem-solving mode, even if it's just taking a walk, listening to some upbeat songs or having a bite to eat to celebrate your teamwork. If it's been a particularly tough session, indulging in a nap, enjoying a movie or even setting aside chores and getting a good night's sleep can honor your accomplishments and set you both up for a good problem-solving session.

An Everyday Example of Seeking to Understand

When you're speaking from your heart, listening and then asking more questions can clear up hurtful misunderstandings and result in you both feeling closer to each other.

An actual example: A Stepmom and her partner are feeling a lot of tension due to stepfamily stress. The Stepmom decides to fix her signature dish (veal parmigiana) as a surprise for her partner and an expression of her love for him. When he gets home he doesn't comment on the yummy smell or react joyfully to her telling him what's for dinner. When he eats it, it's without joy nor a request for seconds. This Stepmom is disappointed, then hurt, then annoyed. By the time dinner is over she is hurt, angry and feeling resentful. While they spoke during dinner, neither talked about the food nor their feelings about it. In this case, a kind loving deed turned into a deeper wedge between them and neither of them knew what was happening.

The outcome of the evening could have been changed by either of them speaking up as soon as they felt upset or asking a question when they sensed the other was upset. If they'd been conscious there was something to learn from the tension, and willing to speak up and listen to each other, the Stepmom would've discovered that veal parmigiana was her partner's family's Sunday dinner—every single Sunday of his childhood. Those family dinners were tense and loud, often resulting in someone shouting and leaving the table. So not only was he sick of the dish, it also made his stomach turn from memories of all the emotional trauma. Her partner didn't say anything about not liking the dish because he knew she'd made a big effort for him and he didn't want to hurt her feelings. He was unaware of the responses she was looking for because he was doing his best to be polite.

Once they spoke up, asked questions and shared their true feelings, they both understood what was going on and were both relieved. Feelings were no longer hurt or angry and best of all, there was no more pretending. What creative solutions were discussed after they kissed and felt closer? The Stepmom made her veal for others when the urge struck her, was not upset her partner didn't want to eat it and joyfully agreed to learned how to make some of his favorite dishes, which he'd never asked her to do before. They had many future happy dinnertimes together where they both felt loved and appreciated. Happy ending. The resulting reduction of stress and cumulative positive impact of this safe-zone sharing, learning and changing for and with each other are tremendous and immeasurable. You can start with something this small and see for yourself.

Listen First—Problem-Solve Later

As you and your partner begin practicing this process together, there may be lots of accumulated feelings on both of your emotional ledgers. As I mentioned earlier, it may take Herculean efforts to avoid reacting or defending while the other is speaking, but it's worth it. It's such a relief to be heard, to have your feelings acknowledged and to be able to get loving support from each other. If you and your partner have been under stress for a while, it's possible you've both been missing out on each other's loving support. Many a Stepmom initially believes, in spite of the pain she's feeling, that no matter what her partner says or does, she's trying to do what's best and stand up for herself or her partner. While her intention is usually absolutely sincere, that kind of rigid or stubborn thinking can get in the way of moving forward as a team. Those days of power struggles between you and your partner can end with Nobody's Right/Nobody's Wrong.

Personal Story: The first time I was the listener in this process, I remember surprising myself and laughing as I told my husband I was imagining putting invisible duct tape over my mouth to ensure I would not interrupt him. Optimistic humor can be really helpful in this process. It's not about being perfect, just about being sincere in your efforts. I found myself relaxing as I concentrated on listening to him as if he were the most important person in the world. Then I chuckled again realizing he *is* the most important person in the world to me.

It's so much easier for me to listen with an open heart when I feel seen and truly heard. Although I know listening is important and do it quite well when working with others, I've also always been a natural talker. During this new process of consciously taking turns listening, I realized I hadn't been very good at giving my husband my full supportive attention. I continually interrupted him out of my own urgency for him to hear me. I was so eager to be heard that I forgot to return the favor. Well not anymore—at least not very often anymore. This approach gave us both a new way to give *and* get what we needed. It felt wonderful to spend time with my husband in this new, mutually created, safe place. Good news? It only gets better and better with practice.

Unexpected Bonus: Non-judgmental, non-defensive, open-hearted, loving empathy from the one you love can be so incredibly healing. Years of disagreements, resentments and hurts can be soothed in this safe space together. Many Stepmoms have told me that when they engaged in this process it was as if the pressure went out of the room and they and their partners could feel close and relaxed in each other's company for the first time in a long time. It's also quite common to cry when reconnecting with your partner in this way, releasing tears of relief and joy.

Another Unexpected Bonus: You will learn new things about each other when you both feel safe enough to share your deepest, most genuine feelings—even the ones you're ashamed of or that make you feel weak or afraid. When you and your partner feel safe to share, you help each other learn how to love each other even more deeply.

Creative Problem-Solving

After you've each had your turn to talk and listen, it's time to change gears and look at the situation as a team that is determined to find a solution. Since you've both shared your feelings, you're now in a newly empowered place—you understand all the pieces of the puzzle. Some solutions will be easily solved because you better understand and empathize with each other. Other problems will be more of a challenge and will take some thought and creativity. This is why pooling your gifts and talents—toward the same goal—works so well.

Uncompromising, creative problem-solving solutions sound like a terrific goal in theory, but what if you can't think of anything that works for both of you? Some issues are complex. Some are very emotionally charged. If you two can't find a mutually acceptable solution in the first hour of working on it, or if either of you feels tired, stop trying. Take a break and agree to come back to the issue later—it's OK. There's surprising power in a conscious pause. When you give yourself the time and space to let something marinate in your minds, it's really thrilling to see what comes up, particularly when you're both open to new ideas.

Sometimes the idea of this pause can be very stressful when conversations end abruptly or when partners are still entrenched in opposite corners. However, the Nobody's Right/Nobody's Wrong approach includes treating pauses and impasses with a very positive attitude. Imagine music from *Rocky* playing in the background and adopt a *"We can figure this out—we're smart people"* attitude. You're just creating room for new ideas to percolate to the surface. Sometimes it's important to sleep on your thoughts with mutual kindness in mind, refusing to settle and remaining open to all kinds of new options. Brilliance and creativity take as long as they take. From years of experience I can tell you that a solution will absolutely come to one or both of you—it really will—if you can stay open to new ideas and believe it's possible. The wait is worth it!

Practice with the Easier Issues

Experiment with Nobody's Right/Nobody's Wrong with a small (less charged) disagreement that's been lingering for a while. This way, you can build up some confidence and experiment in a space of nobody being made wrong in order to process and solve a problem. At the beginning, one of you may get frustrated thinking there's no way to find a solution that's OK for both of you. This is where optimism, determination, faith and patience are helpful.

It's important to remember this approach is not about being right or making each other wrong. Make the conscious decision to stop proving and testing each other's love. Stop any passive-aggressive patterns of taking pride in suffering for each other. These are all unconscious, unloving tactics that you and your partner do not need going forward. You may want to write out aspects of the Nobody's Right/Nobody's Wrong approach on a notecard. Like with any new process, there's a learning curve and a lot of well-worn habits that need your conscious, adult attention in order to change. Here's an affirmation that can serve as a reminder to you when emotions flare: *"Nobody's right or wrong—we deserve a solution that works for both of us and we're going to find it together."*

Yeah, But: *"What if one of us gets so angry that we can't recover our team spirit?"*

This is a good question. The answer will vary for couples based on how many unspoken emotions are in the backlog, so to speak. If you have this fear, there are a few things you can do. You can express your feelings about this. You two can agree to start with a minor issue, even one from the past, to begin to see the positive results of this process. You can also select a situation to work on and then agree that you'll each do some anger-releasing work prior to your conversation. There are many healthy ways to release anger. I can promise you that you will not forget what you were angry about just because you've moved some of the angry energy from the issue. As a team, the goal is to work together to achieve your common goals and to work through your feelings, perceptions and disagreements. As a member of your loving team, it's important you love yourself and your partner enough to take responsibility for the emotions and energy you bring to the team meeting.

This approach can work when you and your partner consciously choose to practice a new way of dealing with stepfamily pressures. Nobody's Right/Nobody's Wrong has a bit of structure yet it's really more about the loving, compassionate, optimistic attitude you both bring to the process. At first you may want to try it out as suggested above, and then customize it to make it your own process. Whatever keeps the two of you connected and on the same side of any challenge will feel much better than feeling disconnected, unheard and even unloved by each other. Aren't you tired of looking at your partner as the enemy when it comes to dealing with his kids and ex-wife?

In spite of whatever you've done in the past, nobody has to be wrong or right going forward. Today is a new day. With this new approach the judgments and blame can vanish, the relief for both of you can be immediate and your newly created solutions can bring you closer together no matter what others do or say. When you and your partner join forces to figure out how to best handle whatever the world brings your way, good things can come from stressful experiences. You will learn more about yourselves and you'll develop more awareness and skills to better support each other. Remember that you've agreed not to compromise or settle on a solution or plan until it's something truly acceptable for both of you. When you're on the same side, you're back into that wonderfully energizing zone where you can handle anything together.

A Stepmom's Relationship and Her Partner

Jackie's Story

July 2016

I've been a stepmother since 1998, when I married a man with a nine-year-old son. Our disagreements and arguments during those years centered around two things: my stepson and his bio-mom. One day in February 2000, after a particularly difficult day of disagreements, I was pretty much ready to call it quits. I was miserable. I felt misunderstood. None of my suggestions and observations about my stepson were particularly welcomed by my husband. I was tired of dealing with my stepson's bio-mom and I didn't know how to be an effective and loving stepmother. I was willing but it seemed like everything I tried caused more stress. There was nowhere to turn for help. None of my friends could relate to my particular stepmother problems, so I decided to go on the internet and see what advice I could find. I found Cathryn Bond Doyle's name and number and to my surprise read that she was starting a group for stepmothers—a support group of women just like me. Remarkably they were meeting only 60 minutes away. I had fortuitously found the answer to my prayers in Cathryn and her newly forming group called Stepmoms on a Mission.

I went to their first meeting quite soon after that and became one of the founding members of the group. We met every Wednesday night for two years. I can safely say that Cath and that group of wonderful, strong, trailblazing women saved my sanity and my marriage. Of course there was a lot of venting and crying—at first. We all needed a compassionate, understanding ear and a shoulder on which to cry. We helped each other validate and process our feelings. We realized we were starving to be heard and have our feelings honored but our husbands just didn't seem to know how to do that.

The predominant feature of Cath's support and advice was that she was positive and loving, always with the solutions coming from an understanding that we loved our husbands. Always asking, "What can we do to support our marriage without sacrificing our own integrity?" It's easy to remain in a place of emotional mudslinging and blame. But being stuck in that place is no fun and doesn't offer solutions to escape that pain. With our mission in mind,

Cath and our SMOMS group worked on new skills and found loving, creative and compassionate solutions that lifted us beyond the pain and made us stronger, wiser women as a result.

On a funny note: It only took a couple of months for our initially reluctant husbands to realize how helpful our SMOMS meetings were before they would start suggesting, "Shouldn't you call Cath or another sister SMOM for help with this? Please." Ha ha. Initially they were afraid we were going there to complain, but learned quickly that we were going because we wanted our marriages to survive the stress. That was an unexpected benefit we all welcomed.

After all these years, my stepson is now a 27-year-old young man, still somewhat wounded by divorce, but making his way in the world as an interesting, loving, and compassionate person—someone I now enjoy being around. We all have healed in ways that I didn't think possible that day in 2000, in the wee hours of the morning, when by magical chance I plucked Cathryn's name from the internet. We don't see each other much these days but when we do, Cath and I always marvel and feel grateful that we made it through all those difficult years. Mission accomplished.

Jackie
Stepmom since 1998
SMOM since the first meeting on March 1, 2000

Twenty-One

Understanding Defensiveness
Finding Compassion for the Defense Strategies
You and Your Partner Bring to the Relationship

In this chapter and the next, you will learn more about defensiveness and how to recognize and overcome this big obstacle to greater intimacy with your partner. This topic is broken into two chapters (plus a bonus chapter) because there's just so much material to cover. The overall goal of the material is to explain how to stop the damage caused by defensive behaviors so you and your partner can better love and support each other. As you embark on exploring this information, please make a promise to yourself to have patience and compassion.

I'm excited to share these ideas with you. Today is the day you may become aware of a lot of new emotional and relationship options. Being more conscious of your feelings and needs and taking more responsibility for your boundaries and actions will bring you more personal power and a greater sense of self. This is true even if the initial and temporary "pins and needles" phase of awakening to these ideas is a bit uncomfortable.

Please keep in mind that new insights can trigger resistance and fear. Resistance can take on a variety of voices and here are a few examples that might come up for you:

"What if I learn something that makes me feel more vulnerable or less powerful than I feel now?"

"What if I learn something about myself or my actions that embarrasses me or worse, that indicates I owe my partner an apology?"

"I'm doing fine, I don't need to learn anything more about this stuff."

Watch for the natural urge to resist giving up old patterns. If you find yourself wanting to roll your eyes at this chapter or stop reading entirely, please read Chapter 11 (about resistance) or the bonus chapter that addresses emotional resistance at smoms.org/BonusChapters. There's so much happiness and peace of mind waiting for us all when we acknowledge our resistance and choose to move forward anyway. These benefits await you.

Consider this affirmation: *"I welcome new ideas and skills that empower me. I have the courage, ability and resources to consider, adopt and implement new insights and options that serve my well-being."*

This statement is a wonderful reminder that the adult, wise woman you are now is conscious and able to make good choices, even if you feel nervous or afraid. My invitation to you is to be open-minded to exploring these new insights and options first, and then determine if they have any value to you and your unique life situation. Let's get started.

Defensive Emotional Armor

Emotional armor begins forming as soon as we're born. It's constructed from experiences of real pain, fear and anger. We all have it. It has kept us safe enough to get through childhood, through our teen years and to the present. For that reason, your uniquely formed defensive emotional armor deserves your appreciation. However, if you think about it, this personal defense system has also caused some (or a lot of) emotional stress and will continue to do so until you see it, understand it and realize that you have a choice to keep your defensive strategy in place or exchange it for a new system that can work better for you and your partner as adults and as a team.

The very fact that you can make new choices empowers you, your partner and your relationship in many important ways. Once you understand your options, you can retire your old armor with honor and begin to use more flexible, more spacious and more effective emotional strategies to keep yourself safe and give you that feeling of being empowered.

As most Stepmoms would agree, the Stepmom/divorced dad relationship is complicated to unprecedented degrees. Marriage is challenging enough, and having kids probably doubles or triples the challenges and potential stress for a couple. However, being members of a stepfamily unit can be exponentially more difficult. It can be devastating to couples who genuinely love each other because nothing prepares most of us for the situations we're likely to face. As Stepmoms on a Mission, we're taking the optimistic line of thinking and choosing to believe that our experiences and relationships present opportunities for tremendous personal growth and healing at a transformational level.

Is this process complex and difficult? Yes, it can be.

Is it worth the effort to work through the tangles of stress? Those of us who've made this journey believe it is—absolutely!

Being in an intimate relationship with a partner who has kids from a previous relationship stirs up issues that can touch on deeply personal, emotionally raw and vulnerable places. I believe that by being conscious of this, you can address and heal those tender spaces. It's like the emotional wounds are infected splinters and the Stepmom/divorced dad relationship keeps picking on them, as painful as they are, until they come to the surface so they can get your attention. I believe this dynamic, when ignored, is a major reason so many second and third marriages break up. It can be very, very difficult, as most of you reading this already know.

I believe the deep and powerful love you and your partner felt at the beginning of your relationship can, when drawn on by both parties, enable you to endure and overcome the relationship challenges you face. When you consciously choose to work with your pain, rage and fear while feeling supported and emboldened by the love you share with your partner, your life can change in wonderful ways. I know this to be true. I have lived through it and have watched many other SMOMS do the same in their lives.

How can you get to the good stuff in your relationship with all this stepfamily stress? It's about choosing to believe that you have the ability and willingness to use whatever's happening to you to become more mindful, stronger, more healed, wiser and more loving. So much of your success depends on your attitude about everything that's happening around and to you. A big part of this work is about understanding how you came to be the woman you are now so you can become your most empowered self—like how iron is forged, under tremendous heat, into the stronger and more flexible steel. When you replace self-criticism and harsh judgments with self-awareness and loving compassion, this can be a fascinating personal exploration. Let's start this adventure and step back to a time long before you fell in love with your partner.

Once upon a time, as you were growing up as a baby, then a child, then a teen and then a grown-up, you had to develop personal emotional armor to keep yourself safe from those who had varying degrees of control over you (literally) for most of your first 18 years, and emotionally for perhaps many more decades. While each of us has uniquely refined and designed emotional armor, there are some common elements shared by most everyone.

The Characteristics of Personal Armor

The make-up of your personal emotional armor impacts your life and worldview every day, depending on how healed and conscious you are (or aren't). It's made up of very natural and human behavioral tactics. We all have personal emotional armor. Yep, every one of us does. This armor is usually surprisingly heavy, often rigid or sharp, sometimes invisible, often camouflaged and generally energy-draining and disruptive to relationships under stress. In spite of its initial utility for us as children, our personal armor can also cause us to distort and misunderstand the actions and words of others, miss out on opportunities for more love and result in us having a negative impact on strangers, friends and loved ones.

Metaphorical Suit of Armor

Picture a medieval knight or warrior princess ready for battle, decked out in 100 lbs. of soldered metal encasing his or her body. This protective armor is heavy and awkward, requires a lot of energy to move around in and limits the wearer's range of motion. Making love while wearing it is nearly impossible.

> The knight and princess aren't bad or wrong to have that armor.
> It was the only thing available for protection at the time.
> Wearing it was considered a wise, life-saving choice when facing danger.
> The armor was better than nothing—having no armor was for fools.

This suit of armor protected them against dragons, crossbows and catapults, along with the many other weapons and dangers of the day. It was essential to have the armor to survive. The knight and princess used it to enable them to engage in battle, stay alive and reduce the threat of pain, injury and death. This is what armor does.

The emotional armor you've preserved and use today can also feel essential to your survival. However, if you think about it, you may have gotten some feedback about it or noticed more disadvantages than benefits when using the same survival strategies as an adult that you developed to defend yourself as a child. We've all paid a price for our outdated armor.

Using this original armor in your adult life has most assuredly caused others pain, whether you're aware of this or not. It has also prevented you from giving and getting more love. Not bad or wrong, just unconscious human behavior that can be changed.

Have you ever defended your own defenses? Ever rationalized whatever you do and the consequences, believing it's the only way, and the cost of staying safe and protecting yourself from mean people, disappointments, hurt feelings and other dangerous things in your world? This was all true when you were a child. But now you can ask yourself: *"Is using my armor from childhood the wisest, most efficient, most up-to-date way for me to keep my adult self emotionally safe and strong?"*

Until someone addresses this issue consciously, the answer is *"No."* When you're consciously on this journey, a compassionate answer is, *"Not anymore and I'm working on my new adult-created strategy as we speak."* That's the spirit! Today is a new day!

This important work is indeed a process. It requires you to practice adult compassion, creativity, curiosity, courage, patience and a willingness to keep trying new options and tactics. When you persevere, you can create a customized strategy that's right for you as a unique adult individual. No settling. No compromising. One size does *not* fit all.

I like to think of your adult, conscious awareness as your emotional force field, made up of a combination of strong boundaries, empowering beliefs and the commitment to staying as awake as possible so you can consciously make good choices from moment to moment.

Arriving at this awareness—and collecting the pieces that lead you there—is a bit like looking for that perfect outfit for an important occasion. You may embark on your journey by heading into a closet or clothing store believing the process will take you some time. You probably expect to reject a bunch of options but may get clearer about what you want in the process by discarding what you don't like. And when it comes to something like preparing for an occasion that really matters to you, you're likely OK with a plan that takes some time. You may tell yourself, *"Expending my time and energy is all part of the process. I'm not going to settle. I'm investing this effort because this is important to me. I'm willing to do what I have to do to get the right outfit."*

You may even find the perfect outfit in the very first place you look, but because you believe it's supposed to take a lot of time, you may keep looking, just to be sure. Humans can be silly like that sometimes—silly and driven by our beliefs—which is why all the time spent trying to uncover and understand our beliefs is so valuable.

When you can embrace the challenge to discover your existing defensive strategy and build something more suitable for the woman you are now with a patient, uncompromising approach, your exploration is that much smoother and more enjoyable. It's fun to design your own "anything" with a positive attitude and an open mind.

The good news is there are many adult, wise ways available for you to use to protect yourself. You just need to be willing to shed the old (awkward, outdated, limiting, punishing, draining, controlling and costly) armor and replace it with new forms of emotional protection that you can call on when you need them. This process can be invigorating—and if your partner is willing to join you on this journey, miracles may begin to show up almost immediately.

Factors Contributing to Armor

- Childhood emotional wounds not yet healed

- Childhood conditioning and survival strategies

- Personal beliefs and judgments (your Book of Beliefs)

- Fears and guilt

- Emotional projections and behaviors

- "Happy Family Dreams" about how life in a family is supposed to be

All these different issues can make it challenging to see current stepfamily and relationship situations accurately. It's kind of like having a dirty windshield with crooked wipers and a bunch of debris stuck in them while they move back and forth, distorting your view as you try to drive along the road. These factors can also act as camouflage, filters, detours and screens which keep you from seeing yourself, the world and your partner clearly. If you're unaware that you're wearing your emotional armor, you rarely think to question the accuracy of what you're perceiving. You may feel certain that you're seeing things as they truly are, but if you're unaware (unconscious) of your own emotional filters, there's room for all kinds of distortions. Not your fault but indeed your responsibility.

Fear Activates Defensiveness

When your armor is activated, in this case by your partner's behavior, you can feel betrayed by what you perceive as his intentions. You want to believe you're supposed to be safe with your partner, right? When your feelings (not feeling safe) conflict with what you believe you're supposed to feel (safe to share anything you wish with your partner), defensive alarms and behaviors are triggered. It's not that you don't love your partner—not at all. You get defensive because your armor is automatically activated by fear and your defensive shields go up. Once triggered, you'll try to protect yourself with your personal defensive behaviors, which are not aware that you're now following the advice of a child-created strategy. Rather than staying conscious to seek and receive the much-needed comfort of your partner's love, you may be unable or unwilling to give or get love in those defensive moments. As Ray Romano, in the TV show, "Everybody Loves Raymond" once said to his very cranky wife, *"You're just not huggable when you act that way."*

If asked or criticized as being defensive, are you quick to explain exactly why you're right to do what you're doing? Do you justify whatever you've just said or done without regard for your impact? These are both common reactions whenever we're being defensive. Sometimes, you may not understand what has happened to trigger your defenses and create a disconnect with your partner. Defensive behaviors can ricochet so quickly that before you know it, you've spent all kinds of time and energy arguing without knowing how to get out of it. This is a painful human dynamic. The key to making it stop is to become more conscious and skilled at recognizing when you or your partner become defensive. When you're willing, you can interrupt your own defensive patterns by simply saying the following as soon as you feel the shields activated for you or your partner:

"Oh my, I'm feeling defensive. I need a minute to regroup and figure out why."

"Honey, let's pause for a moment because it feels like you're being defensive and I really don't mean you any harm."

Once you realize what you're doing, you can compassionately make a new empowered choice—over and over again, as often as you need. This is one of the great things about becoming conscious of your behavior and making choices. Each time you interrupt your old habits, you can choose to do something more helpful. Perhaps you'll choose something else that'll actually help you feel safer and bring you true emotional safety in the form of new boundaries, skills and awareness of needs and emotional wounds that need your loving care. As you learn to recognize your armor has been activated and then immediately stop the conversation, you can spare yourself a lot of relationship damage and personal suffering.

When you become conscious that everyone carries emotional armor of some kind, you'll begin to see each other—and yourself—in new compassionate ways. As soon as you realize that you've engaged your armor, you can interrupt the reflexes and old habits and stop causing even more distress for yourself and those you're interacting with. You can stop old defensive tactics and take the time to help yourself (and your partner) better understand what fears or wounds just got triggered. You can figure out new and improved ways to support yourself and each other so you can get back to dealing with the real issue(s) at hand, but now in an open-hearted, loving way. It's really a powerful, efficient, beautiful thing, especially when your partner is willing to do this work with you.

Create an Empowered Force Field

It's never too late to replace old patterns with new ones. There's always a way to change a limiting or false belief or replace an ineffective boundary with something that's more effective and comfortable. For every adult, it's time to replace old outdated child-created defensive armor with a new adult-created defensive strategy. Healthy boundaries and beliefs are key ingredients for your newly empowered emotional force field. Figuring out what those healthy boundaries and beliefs are will become easier as you look to your resentments. They can be the map to your unmet needs, false beliefs and missing boundaries.

You can begin by watching for situations that activate the heavy armor for you, and your partner too. Keep in mind that whenever defensive armor is activated, it means some part of you (or your partner) is afraid of being hurt again, because of something in the past. It's a protective reflex that hopefully you can honor and have compassion for now that you know what's going on.

I hope you'll choose to awaken to the existence of your emotional armor. With this new information, it can be so much easier to be kind with yourself and your partner because you now know that defensive behaviors aren't trying to hurt anyone, just keep you safe. Going forward, when you notice an old pattern or defensive maneuver in yourself or your partner, you can speak about it with the enthusiasm of realizing that you're about to save each other pain and anger. It can be helpful to agree to remind each other that you want to help, love and support each other, even when either of you feels nervous, anxious, fearful or unsafe in anyway. Within the fortress of your loving relationship, you can create emotional and mental safety as a couple. What new behaviors come to mind that you and your partner might try with this new awareness and intention? This is the power of being aware and conscious in your adult self. Please share these chapters with your partner. From the feedback I've received over the years, my material has surprised and then interested lots of partners who initially resisted my work assuming I was *only* on the side of the Stepmom. Once they realize I'm cheering for you as a couple and that I try to represent their feelings and perspectives without bias toward the Stepmom, they're on board and eager to get to work. Remember, though, that even if you choose not to share this with your partner, you can help yourself quite a bit.

If your partner is not reading these chapters along with you, he's likely unaware of this issue or that there's another approach to painful arguments. Using the "Make It OK" concept (see Chapter 37, Tip #9), you can explain that you're learning this material and that it's new to you also. Learning together can be an exciting process and the lasting benefits can improve dramatically.

Can you see how your naturally accumulated defense tactics interfere with your ability to see each other clearly? You may not even know you have this defensive interference until you remove it and see things more accurately. This can be a very joyful and fascinating process. By understanding how your defensive strategies distort your view, you can discover how they interfere with your thinking—remove them from your windshield. By seeing and sensing things more accurately, you'll find you respond differently to what your partner says and does, hopefully with less anger and more curiosity and patience. You're also much more likely to stay in your adult self, even when under stress, which enables you to feel safer, even less defensive and more effective in handling the stressful circumstances—a very positive, self-supporting cycle. Instead of reacting defensively against your partner and hurting each other in the process of trying to protect yourselves, you can now focus on helping yourself and your partner feel safer while you deal with stepfamily issues as a team. If you and your partner can embrace this challenge together, there's so much to gain and there are amazing things to learn about each other.

See Chapter 18 for more about handling conflicts with your partner as a team.

For a chapter covering sample stepfamily situations, go to smoms.org/BonusChapters and click on "Six Sample Situations for Disarming Defensive Behavior Between You and Your Partner."

Twenty-Two

Stop Being Defensive with Each Other So You Can Listen and Talk Openheartedly

Romantic relationships can be amazing *and* extremely challenging. Add in an uncooperative bio-mom and some stepkids who feel entitled, maybe feeling guilty from a Loyalty War or remorseless about their impact on their dad and stepmother… and welcome to the complex world of the stepmotherhood that many women experience. While you can be eager and excited about making changes to improve your relationships, you may also feel resistant to dealing with change and emotional issues for all kinds of valid reasons. When people feel the need to protect themselves because of emotional vulnerabilities, they use defensive behaviors (consciously and unconsciously) to try to stop the feared incoming information and pain, and to separate themselves from the source of imagined danger. This self-protection tactic can create a disconnect between a Stepmom and her partner that ranges from moments of mild annoyance to deeply enraging, isolating pain.

When couples learn to avoid the triggering and fallout of defensive behaviors and instead create more space for mental/emotional safety and empathy between them, many problems are eliminated and many resentments simply dissolve. This shared emotional safety fortifies interpersonal connections and enables the couple to better understand and love each other while they deal with the stress of outside issues. This chapter is about learning more about defensiveness so you can interrupt or ideally stop it and save yourself from all the damage it can cause your relationships. It also offers several ideas for new ways of interacting with your partner when the impulse to raise your defensive armor occurs.

Why Cats Hiss: A True Story

Did you know that when a cat hisses it means the cat is afraid? Not angry. Not aggressive. Spitting is aggressive. Cats hiss to look bigger and as dangerous as possible when instinct tells them they are vulnerable, facing something new or in danger, and therefore in need of defending themselves. Without thinking, they take the offensive and do what they can to sound strong and brave with a good loud hiss. Isn't that interesting?

Knowing that hissing is a signal of fear (not anger) has changed my reaction when either of my cats hisses at something or someone. Now, when I hear a hiss, I become alert, gentle and compassionate, looking for ways to help my scared cat feel safe. It's easy to keep my heart open and not take offense, get angry or react inappropriately to a hiss now that I know what's happening in their minds. Because I love my cats, I want to help them, and this more accurate understanding brings out the natural caregiver in me.

Defensive behaviors are kind of like human hisses. Now that you know this, the next time your partner "hisses," you have a new choice. Being aware that if he exhibits defensive behavior it's due to him feeling afraid or unsure, even if he's not conscious of his fears or willing to admit them. Instead of reacting, you can now respond lovingly to soothe him and help him find a way to feel safer or remind him he's truly not at risk with you. This awareness and compassionate non-reactive approach can change a relationship profoundly. When you notice defensive behaviors in the future, you can do whatever you've done in the past *or* you can interrupt yourself or stop whatever you're doing or saying—take a deep breath and kindly say something like this to your partner:

> *"Honey, I love you. What's going on? What's happening to make you feel blamed, afraid or unsure right now? I want you to feel safe with me. Please talk to me."*

Can you imagine the avoided pain and arguments and the increased closeness that are possible when loving partners embrace this approach?

The dynamic between you and your partner will certainly be a factor in how easily you each drop your defensiveness and make the choice to be more open and loving when under stress. Being defensive is a lightning-fast reaction, even a habit for some, so it's going to be important to be patient with yourself and each other as you form new behaviors.

What's so good about defensive behaviors? Defensive behaviors are all about trying to create emotional, mental and physical safety. However, since defensive strategies were created long ago in childhood, they're based on what you've seen, what you've experienced and what seemed to work for you (based on your brain's abilities at the time) when painful, scary experiences occurred back then. Once you're a grown-up, most of these strategies just cause more pain and complicate situations by triggering the other person's defensive strategies. It can be a vicious cycle. Thankfully it only takes one person to step up as an adult, understand this behavior and break up the hurtful cycle with conscious new choices. That person can be you!

Triggers for Defensive Behaviors

- You may strike out, usually verbally, in anticipation of or in reaction against a perceived injustice or unfairness to you.

- You may try to divert attention away from something you don't like, something you fear or anything that upsets you that you don't want to talk about. We're all unique so the issues will be different but the fear of approaching pain, blame or shame is the common trigger.

- You may try to draw more attention to something specific when you don't feel like it has enough attention on its own or the other person is ignoring it.

- You may try to stop a conversation that makes you uncomfortable. This may involve distracting others from a specific issue or a proposed change.

- You may try to protect against some real or feared sense of vulnerability.

Are you aware of what triggers your defensive behaviors? This chapter is about becoming wiser in ways of short-circuiting your well-worn paths and patterns of destructive emotional defensiveness because they're not effective anymore—not because they're wrong. This is not criticizing the behaviors that have been used in the past. It's just about realizing there are better and more effective, loving ways to create true emotional safety for yourself and your partner. Everyone acts defensively so this isn't about judging or shaming yourself or your partner for this natural reflex and survival reaction. As human beings, sometimes we're conscious of what we're doing, sometimes not so much.

If you decide to test out these ideas to become more conscious of your defensive strategies, you can start giving and getting more of the loving support you deserve and want to provide. Through this process, you'll also be more equipped to share this same support with your partner whenever either of you feels afraid or anxious.

Think about this: Until you become conscious of your personal defense strategies and what triggers them, you're still defaulting to the defense strategies formulated by the 3-year-old or maybe the 6-year-old and even the 12-year-old child (and every age in between) you used to be. Yikes! This realization can be quite a jolt. I know it was for me. As surprising as it was, it was so interesting because it really made a lot of sense of my past behaviors. I find self-realization fascinating and I hope you can frame it that way also. If you've already started to realize some things about your own strategy that you want to change, good for you. You may want to jot them down so you'll remember.

Any surprise and embarrassment about the components of your personal defensive strategy will usually fade with reflection and compassion. It takes courage to wake up to unconscious choices, see yourself honestly and own your impact on others. Remember, you really needed your personal defense strategy at the time you created it. And it worked for you. You made it through everything and are here in the present day. Ideally you will make the choice to retire your old child-created strategy (with honor) to make room for something that better suits you today. The strategies you create to keep yourself safe will be very different now that you're a resourceful adult. Makes sense, right? Please review the following and decide if anything fits for you.

Defensive Behaviors

- Repeatedly explaining (defending) yourself and your point of view using logic, articles, examples, quotes, etc. You may use different words, but if you're feeling defensive, the tone is likely something like, *"Why can't you see the logic of what I'm saying?"* or *"This makes complete sense [you dummy], why can't you see that?"*

- Pleading, making tearful requests or throwing yourself (maybe desperately) at the mercy of your partner's judgment, *"I beg of you to please do this for me."* Whatever words you may use, this often last-resort approach can feel pathetic in hindsight, maybe even humiliating, disempowering and very childlike. It may also be a manipulation tactic—same behavior, different goal.

- Lashing out verbally in anger, sarcasm, hostile humor and other hurtful ways.

- Withdrawing or shutting down emotionally, ignoring the issue and repeatedly seeming to forget, avoid or deny the subject issue.

- Acting confused about or oblivious to the issue that's upsetting the other person. Refusing to give their upset any weight or merit, implying they're overreacting, over-sensitive or out of line.

- Assuming negative intentions about the words or actions of others, refusing to believe explanations, putting each other on the defensive and diverting the subject away from the one at hand. This can be crazy-making.

- Making judgments, declarations and proclamations with little or no regard for the impact on others. This is dictatorial, righteous and arrogant "better than or less than" behavior.

As you can see, none of these tactics is very loving or attractive, yet they do all have an impact. All of them were invented, witnessed or experienced in childhood. Everything you do when you're feeling defensive results from not knowing what else to do to help yourself. After these tactics are ingrained, you often aren't aware that you chose them to begin with and that you have other options at your disposal.

A Noble Intention: *"Going forward, I'm going to take responsibility for my emotional safety in new adult, wise ways that needn't hurt others in the process."*

Defensive Relationship Wedges

You may judge your partner in an attempt to stand up for your self-worth and your right to be heard. You may be trying to protect any triggered and exposed wounds caused by your own rage at feeling like you're losing your rights in the relationship and the new family unit. You might get defensive to numb the pain of not getting the expected and appropriate compassionate reaction and support from your partner. You might get defensive because your partner is calling you out on your controlling strategies and you don't want to admit he's got a point.

Your partner may judge you, the Stepmom, to defend himself against his fear of an approaching, imagined (or remembered) attack on his manhood. He may be engaging in this judgment to try to end the conversation and numb his fears, wounds and guilt. He may (consciously or unconsciously) be avoiding assuming certain responsibility, and judges your words or actions to numb his feelings and maintain this avoidance strategy.

When you are aware that there's an emotional battle going on but unconscious of the cause or cure, you and your partner are like a couple of emotional porcupines with all your quills at full attention. Both of you are scared, hurt or angry for not being hugged, understood, protected and loved while you continue to shoot quills at each other. In this state of heightened alert, neither you nor your partner is very huggable, right? More than likely, both of you are afraid and looking for support from each other while virtually preventing that reality from happening. See the dilemma? See how neither of you is trying to push each other away? It's just a reflex to stay safe that results in keeping you apart.

What Makes You Defensive?

Until you realize you have alternative ways to respond lovingly and wisely to your fears, your defenses will be triggered in any number of ways—it's a survival instinct.

More Triggers for Defensiveness

- Fearing punishment, shunning or retaliation for something you've said or done (or want to say or do).

- Feeling emotional pain or anticipating feeling hurt from a recent or old unhealed emotional wound that has just been poked or reopened.

- Feeling vulnerable because you're trying something new and still standing on shaky emotional ground. Fearing that you're going to "rock the relationship boat" and that the relationship might change in a bad way or not survive.

- Anticipating being criticized or actually feeling criticized when someone asks you to do something different from the way you're doing it today. This sensitivity to any form of criticism (constructive or punishing) usually results from real and painful childhood linkages between being corrected and truly being shamed, blamed, flawed and wrong as a child. It's a very tender place that needs to be healed. Until you do the work to heal the wound, it will be justification for defensive behaviors.

- Feeling unsure or conflicted about whether you have a right to do (or want) whatever you're wanting to change, resisting or planning to do (or not do).

- Feeling pressured to take a stand or state your opinion about something that is unsettled in your mind. It can also be an inner conflict between what you want and what you believe you should want or do. Dealing with this inner tension can also trigger defense strategies and resentment.

- Making and reacting defensively to negative assumptions without making the effort to check them out to see if they are true or not.

The Lawnmower Story

Here's an old story about how inner conflicts and self-talk can make you unnecessarily defensive. A guy is about to mow his lawn and as he pulls out his old yellow, worn out push mover (the kind without a motor), he remembers that his neighbor just bought a brand new rider mower.

He smiles and thinks to himself, *"Ah, that would be sweet. I could borrow his mower, finish the lawn and still have time for nine holes of golf with the boys. I'm going to go over and ask him if I can borrow it. He's a great guy. He's not using it. I bet he'd be happy to lend it to me. This is gonna be great."*

He happily puts away his old mower and heads over to his neighbor's home. While he's walking over there, he starts thinking to himself, *"Hmmm? This might be too good to be true. I wonder if he'll lend me that new mower. It IS brand new. I wonder if he'll let me use it. Would I let him use my new mower? I'm not sure. My other neighbor accused me of breaking his chainsaw but I would definitely take good care of this guy's mower. Doesn't he think I would take care of it?"*

Now, he's starting to get ticked off. He continues in the privacy of his own mind, *"I wonder if he thinks I can't be trusted with his new fancy, schmancy mower. What did I do to deserve that kind of attitude from him? That's not fair. He's a crappy neighbor."*

When he reaches the front door, his neighbor opens the door with a friendly smile and says, *"Hi there, pal."*

The first man, who started out excited at the thought of borrowing a mower and getting to play golf today, now scowls at his neighbor and says rudely, *"Keep your damn mower! I'm outta here."* Then he storms off, leaving his neighbor confused and upset. The end.

Can you see the conflict that brewed up within this man after he decided to go ask for what he wanted? See how he talked himself into and then out of being excited and able to have what he wanted because of a fear he *might* be rejected? Can you see how he changed his own mind because of his fear from past experiences? See how his demeanor changed from happy to angry and rude as a result of the conflict in his internal dialogue? See how the nice neighbor was treated and impacted when all he said was a cheerful, *"Hi there, pal"*?

What a shock this must have been for the neighbor. He isn't likely to lend the rude man anything in the future, which would serve as further reinforcement of the other's harsh judgments. For no good reason at all, an unfortunate rift may now have been created between these two men—and maybe their families, too—with the potential to last for a long, long time unless the first guy comes to his senses and apologizes for his mistake and rudeness. What a sad story… and one that happens quite a bit in our world.

As you've seen here, one man's (or woman's) unconscious inner conflict and aggressively defensive behavior can have lasting impact. You can stop this from happening in your own life when you're conscious enough to recognize and then address defensive behaviors. Think about any uncomfortable comparative experiences you may have had. What can you notice about your own defensive strategies?

Specific Stepmom Triggers

- Feeling you're not being heard or that your feelings are not being considered by others in decisions that impact you.

- If you have parents or an ex-spouse who are narcissistic or controlling in other ways, you will likely be very sensitive to decisions that feel unilateral to you. Any unhealed wounds from those previous relationships will be easily triggered by anything that feels controlling and that pays no regard to your feelings.

- Feeling you're being judged as bad, wrong or criticized in any way.

- Fearing you're about to be (or are being) asked to do something differently or be different than you are now. This fear is intensified if you're worried you may not be able to do (or be) this new thing correctly or successfully.

- Fearing that by being willing to do something new you're going to have to admit to being wrong in the past.

- Being unavoidably confronted with a painful truth you've been trying to ignore.

- Being "busted" about a real issue of needing to take more responsibility, while you're resisting stepping up and doing so. You may be avoiding this responsibility because of anticipated pain, shame or ineptness, or simply because you don't want to do something you're supposed to do.

- Assuming your partner is thinking or feeling something that hurts your feelings, but refusing to check it out—instead, you react to the negative assumption as if it were true. Negative assumptions are brutal and almost always wrong, yet the fear of them possibly being accurate may prevent you from asking about them.

- Feeling criticized, judged or shamed when someone asks you to change can be a huge trigger created from painful childhood, religious and cultural conditioning.

If you're inspired, take a moment to think about situations, thoughts and feelings that trigger your sense of defensiveness. What triggers you? This is valuable self-awareness.

Create/Uphold Strong Boundaries

When you put aside old defense tactics, you're going to want to replace them with conscious, healthy boundaries and some new communications skills and empowering beliefs. As you work on figuring out your true needs and feelings, you will find yourself in new emotional territory. This is a great adventure that can be terrifying and exhilarating at the same time—like the whitewater rafting trip I like to use as a metaphor for the sometimes tumultuous journey of a Stepmom.

As you work to become more empowered, you will inevitably realize that some of your own old beliefs and patterns need to change. Some of these changes will impact your partner and it's important to take responsibility for this impact.

If you're open to it, try sharing your ideas for change with your partner in the following ways. Ideally this will help you interact with him without either of you getting defensive.

- Take responsibility for your part in creating stressful interactions in the past. You may have noticed you've been following a repeating pattern or exhibiting a specific behavior in a given situation. As a participant in these situations, it's empowering to own your contributions to whatever has upset you. For example, you may find that you've been over-giving and then feeling resentful, not speaking your truth, not seeing situations clearly or relying on unconscious and conflicting beliefs and cultural programming that you now see are hurtful or limiting.

- Lovingly and patiently explain what you've learned about defensiveness. Specifically explain what you want to change in your behavior and that your goal is to avoid any hurtful misunderstandings in the future.

- If you discover that you need to make some changes in order to stop feeling defensive or resentful, be sure to take responsibility for your new choices and acknowledge the impact you believe these changes may have on your relationship. It's important to be honest about the potential impacts of any changes you will make so you can also build trust with your partner, instead of him feeling manipulated. Many Stepmoms support their partners by doing and handling many things for their stepkids. With this in mind, your partner may get concerned because he may indeed have to do more or do things differently as a result of any changes you may want/need to make. Expressing awareness and compassion for the impact of the changes you want to make goes a long way, making it easier for your partner to accept.

- Create a loving space to listen to your partner's feelings with empathy and compassion while maintaining an unwavering commitment to any change you've just explained. Learn more about his feelings and needs, then help him find ways to be OK with your decision or new plan of action. Sometimes he may need time to adjust. Give him the gift of time and get back to the conversation within 24 hours.

- Hold a steady commitment to yourself and your right to stand up for what you want, feel and need and for your desire to help your partner do the same thing in a mutually supportive way. If you feel you're standing on shaky ground, it's a call for courage. Hint: Mobilizing anger from the past can provide the energy you may need to take a stand in the present.

Fear Your Partner's Reactions?

What if you can't find the courage to speak up because you're afraid of your partner's potential defensive reactions? This complex situation can generate self-shaming, self-judging and harsh self-talk. This is cruel treatment of yourself so if you're feeling some fear about your partner's defensive behaviors, please replace your judgments with compassion and as much lovingkindness as you can muster.

Anyone raised by abusive, narcissistic or otherwise controlling parents are likely to carry the wounds of old rage, neglectful treatment and all kinds of painful memories from trying to stand up for yourself in the past. You may not even be aware of the wounds you carry from loved ones who were supposed to be kind to you, but instead hurt you in some way. This is nothing trivial. If this is true for you, these feelings need to be honored, supported and healed.

Support Yourself with This Process

1. Make a list of all the things you fear your partner might do in reaction to your new changes or boundaries. Do you fear he'll leave you? Stop loving you? Attack you physically? Lash out verbally? Withdraw from you? Judge you as selfish for trying to meet your needs when he feels his needs never get met? Write out every possible thing you're imagining.

2. Now look at each item on your list, one at a time. Ask yourself if this has actually happened or if you're imagining that it will happen. Ask yourself if you're projecting his reaction because you've experienced it in past relationships or if he has actually threatened you or done these things to you. Go through your list and gather as much information as you can about your feelings.

3. Now ask yourself this question about what you've learned about your list and all your feelings: *"Are these feelings coming from the child I used to be, from my previous relationship or from the adult woman I am today?"* All three are perfectly possible truths. The answers will vary and it could be that your feelings are coming from all three areas of your emotional world. Every answer is A-OK. It's about slowing down your process and learning more details about the sources and triggers of your feelings so you can support yourself in new ways.

4. Make a plan for implementing all the changes you want in your ever-increasingly empowered life. Make the decision to go forward in ways and steps that you feel you can handle. Speak to your partner about your list and

see how open he is to some of the other suggestions for ending defensiveness that have been covered in this chapter.

5. Get support from others for your plan. Look to people who've earned your trust, and who encourage you to have your needs met in your life. Depending on the results of your reflection on your list of fears, look into therapy for your emotional wounds and issues from your past. Every moment you spend learning more about yourself, your needs and your beliefs is valuable.

A Tough Relationship Question

If you're staying in a relationship that requires you to silence your voice and deny your own needs and rights—especially if you do so out of fear—gently ask yourself how you feel about choosing to stay in a relationship where you fear the one you love. Ask yourself, *"Why do I stay?"* Listen for your answers. Trust whatever comes to mind. Nothing you hear will be right or wrong. Everything you feel and think will be important. Look for beliefs and question their validity. Look for false beliefs and conditioning from the past that are imprisoning you now. This is a time to give these limiting beliefs your focused attention. What would you say to your best friend if she told you the exact same story? You deserve to be loved, happy, safe and respected. We all do. As the adult woman you are now, you really do have the ability to stand up for yourself. There are all kinds of resources you can draw upon to make this happen.

Important: If you fear for yourself at a level that is dangerous to your health, well-being or life, please get yourself someplace safe immediately—because your life is precious. This level of fear deserves a whole other level of action and attention beyond the scope of this chapter and my expertise.

Change Can Be Scary

Asserting new boundaries in a relationship means things are going to change. Sometimes one partner makes a change when the other partner wants to keep things the same. It's like a couple is dancing the foxtrot as a team for years and then one day, the woman decides she wants to do the cha-cha. It's sad for her if her partner doesn't want to do the cha-cha, doesn't know how to do it or refuses to learn how to do it. He's her dance partner and she loves him. However, she also feels strongly that she wants to do the cha-cha. How can she move forward lovingly? She can decide she wants to be mindful of and responsible for the impact of her new decision on her partner's dance life. This is a very loving approach.

If she learns why doing the cha-cha isn't an OK option for her partner, she has a chance to address this. There may not be any good reasons, from her perspective. She may have to learn more about his feelings to identify his resistance to her changes. In truly listening to her partner, she may realize that he has a point she didn't previously understand—with the new information, it now makes sense to her. In this case, it's very gracious and loving if she opens up to the possibility that there may be another option beyond the cha-cha that she hadn't considered—an option that makes both of them happy.

She might agree to look for a third solution by asking herself, *"How can we not do the foxtrot anymore and do something other than the cha-cha that pleases both of us?"* With both of their thinking caps on, she lets the creative problem-solving continue, this time as a couple working together with a lot more information and all the power of two creative minds.

With the common goal to find a mutually satisfying solution, you can be open to negotiating a plan while still holding to your new boundary or change, as long as it works for both of you. When doing this together, a Stepmom and partner are likely to feel empowered and closer because both are holding out for a mutually satisfactory solution, believing that it's out there, even if not clear—yet. Again, it goes back to being willing to believe that nobody has to be right or wrong, but both of you deserve to be happy.

Because of all the work I've done with the partners of stepmothers, I truly believe your partner wants to be considered, acknowledged and respected, just like you do. Your partner probably also wants to feel loved, supported and emotionally safe to be vulnerable with you, just like you do.

With this in mind, are you willing for your loving partnership to move to a new level of adult awareness and kindness, especially when under extreme stress? You can solve almost anything when you mutually embrace responsibility for the safety and well-being of the two of you as one couple, one team. Remember how you wholeheartedly believed this at the beginning of your relationship?

Many stepmothers know how it feels to be disregarded and to have the wishes, fears, mandates and manipulations of others imposed on them. It's an awful feeling. As an adult woman becoming more empowered each day, it's kind of you to stay mindful that your new boundaries might be upsetting for your partner. You can respect that and ask him to participate with you as a true teammate—on the same side. You can be empathetic about how your changes impact him and also willing to firmly stand up for any and all new boundaries and beliefs that are important for your well-being. This is the back-and-forth dance of intimacy.

As you're waking up and becoming more aware of your feelings, beliefs and needs, it's a magical, sometimes astonishing time. It can also be scary for both you and your partner. This fear of change, if present, is an indication of your experiences and beliefs about change. Do either of you hold a belief that change is bad or that change means losing something important? What are your beliefs about change?

Look for and explore these beliefs if fear comes up for you when you're taking a new stand with your partner.

- Do you believe that your loving relationship can survive changes in your behavior?

- Do you have a belief that taking a stand always results in a problem, rage or rejection?

- Do you have a belief that you have to comply with others or else be rejected? If you have one or more controlling or narcissistic parents, then you probably do, because it was true for you as a child.

- Can you believe that your relationship is something independent and separate from the way you and your partner interact within it? Many people don't see it that way and fear that if the behaviors change, the relationship will end.

I'm a fan of what I call the "Christmas Eve Theory of the Unknown." When I don't know what's going to happen or what change will bring, I think about how I have felt going to sleep each Christmas Eve as a child and even as an adult. I've never known what I'm going to get (or how things will change as a result), but it's always been good. As a result, I've chosen to believe good things will happen and I try to be optimistic when change occurs or the future is unknown. As my dad used to say, *"When you don't know whether something will be bad or good, choose good—it feels better."* It does feel better. It's also a decision to trust you can handle whatever actually occurs.

As an adult, I understand that every change is not going to be as fun as a Christmas gift. As an adult, I also believe I now have the ability and resources to handle whatever change comes my way. I believe I can find something positive and learn something valuable in whatever happens. These are beliefs that I've chosen to embrace. This is the power of a conscious mind. You can choose the beliefs you want to keep in your rulebook. When you're aware and awake, you can change any belief that no longer serves your well-being. It's your rulebook and it's easy to forget that you have the right to fill it with whatever you choose. What beliefs do you want to have about change and about your relationship's ability to handle change? What beliefs do you want to revise or delete altogether?

I believe your relationship is sacred, special and worth saving until you tell me otherwise. The circumstances of how you fell in love with your partner—and all that happened to make your paths cross in the first place—suggest that the universe really wanted the two of you to find each other so you could be in a situation so intense that your childhood survival strategies couldn't work for you anymore. This stress forces you both to look outside of your respective comfort zones so you can gain new insights to heal and deal with things you never imagined possible in new healthy, effective, wise, loving ways. The resulting wisdom, healing and new strengths allow you and your partner to experience deeper joy, intimacy and love in this lifetime—if you're both willing to do the work. It may not look like your initial Happy Family Dream but I believe that the love you first shared with your partner can sustain you through the tough times and lead you to something wonderful going forward.

Please see Chapter 18 for more about handling conflicts with your partner as a loving team.

Also see Chapter 21, Understanding Defensiveness.

For a chapter covering several sample conversations between a Stepmom and her partner that can reduce defensiveness for you both, go to smoms.org/BonusChapters and click on "Six Sample Situations for Disarming Defensive Behavior Between You and Your Partner."

Twenty-Three

Three Yucky Relationship Projections Possible Between You and Your Partner

Projecting qualities, attitudes, opinions and intentions onto other people is something we all do in our lives. It's human nature, and can be a default reaction when you're under stress or coming from a place of need, lack or fear. It's an unconscious choice until you put your attention on it and see what you're doing, giving yourself the ability to make new conscious choices to see people and situations as they truly are—free from your past experiences with others.

When you project feelings onto your partner, stepkids, their bio-mom or anyone else, it's like making assumptions about their intentions (almost always negative) and then reacting on these assumptions without checking them out or even realizing what you're doing. It's like stepping into a character in a play that feels familiar, powerful or disempowering but not knowing how to stop it or get out of the scene. When you project any kind of emotional intentions onto your partner, it stops you from feeling you're in an equal, adult, intimate relationship and puts you in a better-than or less-than, adult-to-child or child-to-adult dynamic. Positive projections aren't usually a problem but the negative ones are hurtful, frustrating, confusing and can snowball when neither the Stepmom nor her partner understands what's happening. The following is not a complete list of projections, just three of the most common and disruptive ones for Stepmoms.

Compassionate heads up: If you read something below and begin to feel queasy or defensive, take a deep breath and acknowledge your courage and openness. These projections are so common in intimate relationships, yet seem to be more intense in stepfamily situations. The good news is that seeing these projections puts you halfway (or further) toward ending them. Your conscious awareness will help you end or prevent projections going forward and this will enable you and your partner to avoid a lot of conflicts. With all the power struggles, stress and fear in a stepfamily situation, it can be such a relief to eliminate these projections with your partner.

Yucky Projection #1: Stepmom projects child onto her partner and, as a result treats him like a child.

Instead of feeling like an equal intimate partner, this Stepmom feels she's forced into the role of the bossy mother, and as a result projects child onto her partner (and then treats him like one). When this happens, her partner almost immediately feels the shift and may rebel by acting even more like a child by projecting mother onto the Stepmom.

In this emotional projection, a Stepmom treats her partner like he's a child, triggering the *"I'm in charge of you"* mothering behaviors instead of the loving, romantic, *"we're two adult partners"* behaviors. This dynamic can slip into place when a Stepmom believes her partner should be doing more than he's doing, or when her partner doesn't do what he says he will do. It's usually an unconscious, but very judgmental, angry shift into potentially harsh, unloving behaviors of the Stepmom's own mother, grandmothers or other women from her past. Thankfully this relationship projection can be quickly interrupted and ended by the Stepmom when she acknowledges this awful feeling and makes a new choice to step back into her adult self. If needed, she may say some version of the following to her partner to help them both snap out of the icky dynamic:

> *"I'm not your mother. I don't want to be your mother. I'm no longer going to play the role of your mother. It feels terrible and I'm sorry for treating you like a child. Going forward, I need you to step up and take responsibility for yourself. Going forward, I'm not going to nag, cover for or feel responsible for the impact of your actions or inactions. I want to be your adult, intimate partner. Will you please join me?"*

A Stepmom who's projecting child onto her partner begins treating her partner and sometimes her stepkids in controlling, unpleasant, judgmental, strict or cold ways that are similar to how she may have been treated when she was a child. It's called the negative introject. When the woman of the house feels she's losing control or losing her ability to run her home the way she wants to run it, or when she fears that her partner is not holding up his fair share of parenting duties (which perhaps she fears makes her look bad to others), she can unconsciously fall into this unattractive set of unloving, fear-based, controlling qualities to try to get her partner to change.

Ever feel like you're being your mother, but not in your favorite ways? Ever hear your mother's words coming out of your mouth when you promised yourself you would never be like her in that way? There are many healthy, adult ways to bring about changes without becoming your partner's fake-projected-mean-mom. Anytime you feel like your partner's mother, take a breath and then step back into your best adult self.

Yeah, But: *"If I don't step in and keep reminding my partner to do things, a lot of things will not get done and might cause problems or cost money. I hate wasting money and looking like we're not organized when it comes to my stepkids' school activities or when interacting with his ex-wife. How am I supposed to relax and sit back when his choices or lack of action have consequences I don't like?"*

These are valid and common feelings and fears worthy of your consideration. A Stepmom who feels like she needs to supervise her partner's chores or actions to avoid negative consequences probably has some experiences to justify her concerns. She may also be technically correct to be concerned. However, this scenario requires a conscious choice to interrupt the mother/child projection. The good news is you have the ability to stop this projection and turn your attention to your relationship in new ways. Make creating a healthy relationship with your partner more important than his chores and the consequences of his inactions. Let him be responsible for his choices like he was before you were around to handle and organize things.

It's important to let your partner know how you're going to be different in the future so he doesn't feel set up or surprised. You can tell him what you're happy to do as his supportive partner. Maybe you're only going to remind him once or maybe not at all about certain things. You can also tell him you're tired of feeling like a nag so whatever he does (or doesn't do) is going to be his responsibility, as well as handling any consequences. It's important to make a specific statement to draw a line in the sand so you can give him a way to succeed that frees you from responsibilities that aren't yours—not anymore. This is very liberating for both of you, even if you don't perceive it that way right away.

When a Stepmom has a partner who's behaving in child-like ways—perhaps projecting mother onto her or treating her disrespectfully like a forgetful or defiant child—it's likely *his* unconscious, child-created, survival-driven reaction to his own sense of disempowerment, stress or fear. If your partner projects mother onto you, it can unleash unprocessed mother rage or pain onto you. It's painful for him, too, and he will benefit from addressing these issues in a more conscious way. It's not fair to you, nor fun for either of you, and it's usually completely unconscious. Hopefully you can find it in your heart to have compassion for him. This behavior, if left unaddressed, sets up more power struggles between you and your partner. It's a distraction that prevents you from focusing on dealing with your stepkids or their bio-mom as wise adults. It's also very unlikely either of you will feel any sexual attraction for each other when this projection is taking place. This is another clue this projection is present.

Generally, neither of you is creating this mother-son dynamic on purpose. Sometimes a Stepmom may justify a harsh mothering tone and behavior because she's angry about her partner's lack of responsibility and truly believes it's the only way to get her partner to step up, do what's needed or act like the parent he's supposed to be. While that may appear to be the case, treating him like a child will rarely (if ever) motivate him to take more responsibility for his tasks or change in a good way. This presents another opportunity for a painful or passive-aggressive power struggle to grow into an awful experience for the couple. Thankfully either of you can stop this dynamic with awareness of what's happening. Treat each other like adults. Use your words, lovingly.

"I don't want to feel like your mother, I want to feel like your wife."

By discussing this possibility of emotional projection, you can help each other wake up and consciously become adults when you feel this yucky, control-based, intimacy-killing dynamic between you. Remember that you're both strong, resourceful adults capable of handling your situation as equal partners when you're awake and conscious of your adulthood. When the mother-son projection occurs, it's usually due to the extreme stress either or both of you are under. Things can get complicated but don't let that stop you from interrupting this projection. Do whatever you can, as quickly as you can, to remember the love and compassion you feel (or felt) for each other.

This stepfamily stuff is really hard for both of you. Another way to wake up from whatever you're both feeling is to imagine you're both at work dealing with this same situation—this often pulls the couple out of the projection. Another quick way to help you both wake up into your adult selves is to reminisce about a romantic experience or vacation, play your song, dance or talk about something funny that you shared in happier times.

Yucky Projection #2: Stepmom projects father onto her partner and therefore reverts to child-created strategies to get what she wants.

This is a similar—but reversed—projection from the first one, the Stepmom unknowingly reverts to feeling she's at the mercy of and less powerful than her partner. In this case, as if through a child's eyes, she projects father onto her partner.

When a Stepmom is anxious or under a lot of pressure—maybe she feels she's being treated cruelly by her stepkids or their bio-mom and has no control over her own well-being—she can unconsciously start treating her partner like her father. After all, her father was the man who had the power to help her and make things change when she was little. Or maybe she never had that ideal father, but always believed he would've helped her if she had been good enough. Maybe she unconsciously expects her partner to make up for any father-related hurt or perceived neglect she experienced. This projection can take many forms of behavior. A Stepmom may plead, argue, withdraw or try to charm her partner, all with the underlying, child-created beliefs that her partner is the one with the power and that she, like a child, has to persuade him because she's at the mercy of his decisions.

A Stepmom in this state of unconscious projection may also expect her partner to give her unconditional love to keep her safe from everyone, all the time, no matter what she does, at all costs, just like she believes an ideal father should do. This is an unfair expectation and too much for her to ask of an intimate partner. It denies her partner's needs as an equal adult in this partnership. It's unachievable and a no-win situation for both parties.

The remedy to this projection, as soon as you're aware it's happening, is to admit to yourself you're behaving in child-like ways (about a given situation) and that you're a resourceful, adult woman capable of standing up for yourself—even if you don't feel this way right now—in your stepfamily situation. Turn your attention to remembering how you feel when you're being your best self, maybe at work or when helping a friend. If you find yourself feeling like a child, at the mercy of another, out of control or disempowered by stepfamily situations, take a pause. It's a good time to step away from the situation until you can regain your sense of being a powerful, adult woman in a challenging situation.

It's important to know that even if your partner did every single unconditionally loving thing you asked him to do, it would not be enough to heal your child-created wounds. Our existing emotional wounds can make each of us like leaky buckets. We cannot be filled with love until we plug up those leaks, and plugging them (healing those wounds) is our individual responsibility. You can help yourself in new ways and feel better very successfully as soon as you acknowledge what's happening. If you realize you're looking to your partner as the one empowered to help you with your situation, wake up and use positive, empowering self-talk to remind yourself that you're capable of being an equal partner. With this regained wise awareness, you'll begin to see the situation more clearly as the adult you are today. You and your partner will both benefit from your awareness.

On the other hand, sometimes you may feel like the child because your partner is treating you like one or acting like a harsh, controlling father instead of a loving, equal partner. This is unfair and unkind to you. If your partner is being cold, bossy or dictatorial or if he's acting as if he's got the final word or is in charge of you and your actions, it's important to speak up right away.

"You're not my father, my master or my boss. So I'm asking you to stop treating me like a child, servant or employee. Please treat me with respect and as an equal partner. Let's be more conscious and be our best adult selves before we hurt each other further."

This dynamic can shift from a momentary projection to being abusive if your partner doesn't stop treating you in hurtful, disrespectful ways. Please seek help and support if your partner uses domination behavior to control you and your life. This is never ever OK.

Yucky Projection #3: Stepmom unknowingly projects mother onto her partner's ex-wife, (her kids' bio-mom) putting herself in an imagined but truly disempowered and enraging position of the child looking for her mother's approval, attention or acceptance.

This can be hard to see and very difficult to admit. It's also more common than you might think. Look at your reactions to the things she does (or doesn't do) that upset you. Check out your thoughts and feelings about your partner's ex-wife to see if you're seeking her approval or acceptance or if you care about her opinion of you. If this is the case, you may be projecting unhealed mother wounds onto her, which can trigger childhood emotional wounds you carry with you. This is common for Stepmoms who have unhealed childhood experiences of being rejected, abandoned or ignored by their mother. If you're unsure about whether or not you're projecting mother onto your partner's ex-wife, but you have those feelings toward her, talk with a trusted friend. She'll be able to help you see if this projection and disempowering behavior is happening for you. Seek out a trusted friend or another stepmother if you find yourself becoming anxious anytime your partner's ex-wife refuses to accept, like or get along with you or your plans.

It can be hard to recognize this projection because your stepkids' bio-mom may be at the top of the blended family pecking order, which is enraging on its own merit. When your partner's ex-wife refuses to treat you with respect or as a parenting ally, it will take conscious effort to resist falling into this emotionally triggering projection. It's liberating to wake up and stop it in its tracks. Once you do, it'll be a relief to you and your partner too. Once you regain your footing in your adult self, new solutions to previously stressful situations often come forth, as if out of the blue.

The remedy to this disempowering projection is awareness. She is *not* your mother. However, her power in this stepfamily situation could trigger this unconscious projection so be very compassionate with yourself. As soon as you realize you are feeling like you're at her mercy, stop and ask yourself if some part of you is projecting mother onto her. When you ask and answer that question, you can also remind yourself that whatever this woman does, says or thinks about you is none of your business. Yes, you are impacted by her behavior, but you don't have to be at the mercy of it. You can't control her actions—as difficult as that may be to accept. However, you do have full control over your own choices when you're consciously in your present, adult self.

If you find yourself unable to break out of any of these emotional projections or can't seem to make sense of the beliefs that are keeping you tangled in painful situations, it's a great time to work with a trusted therapist or consultant who's competent and confident to help you with these issues. The relief from the end of the tension between you and your partner can feel like a fresh start for you both. We don't want to feel nor be treated like a child and neither do our partners. There's tremendous healing and reclaimed power waiting for anyone willing to do this powerful work.

Section Four

A Stepmom's Partner

For some reason, guys generally seem more willing to do things differently when we phrase our request for a new agreement or a plan as a question and preface it with these two magic words: going forward. It seems to reduce the chances of triggering defensiveness or shame. Next time you want your partner to do something differently or in a new way, try starting with, *"Going forward will you please …?"* or *"Going forward, can we agree to…?"*

Serenity Now's Story

July 2016

I met and began dating my husband nearly a decade ago. He was divorced and had two young, adorable kids he shared joint custody of with their bio-mom. Soon there was a custody battle that went on for nearly two years, and there has been nearly constant drama from my oldest stepkid and her bio-mom. I found smoms.org about a year after meeting my husband in an effort to try to find help and make sense of the chaos I was living through. To my surprise, I found there were many ladies with very similar stories and problems like mine.

Cathryn helped me save my marriage and family. She understands the dynamics in stepfamilies, especially the difficulties, and has trained, developed and taught me the skills I needed to live happily within my stepfamily. My husband read a few of her essays relating to communication between us as partners, and he understood for the first time in years how I felt as a stepmother, going through the struggles I experienced with him, his kids, and the kids' hostile mom. It really helped him open up and begin to support me. From Cathryn, I learned to better understand how my husband felt, and how to kindly and lovingly advocate for my needs in our relationship and support my husband's needs as well.

I also became aware of how to lovingly detach at times from one or both of my stepkids, depending on the pressure they were under from their bio-mom to hate me. Most important of all, I learned how to take care of myself and love my husband and family, while maintaining healthy boundaries and my sanity, regardless of whatever chaos was happening around me. I continue to check in with SMOMS and use the skills Cathryn taught me regularly. My husband and I have grown so much closer and have learned how to support each other, thanks to SMOMS and Cathryn.

Serenity Now
Stepmom since 2008
SMOM since 2009

Twenty-Four

Emotional Callousing
Why Your Partner May Not Be Able to Understand What Upsets You

A Stepmom I was mentoring began talking one day about how difficult it was for her to watch her partner let his kids' rebellious (and in her mind, disrespectful) actions go without consequence or correction. The kids' behaviors were really upsetting her, she said, and her partner didn't even seem to react to them. While she spoke I could see that her emotions were ranging from annoyance to rage and even hatred. While we chatted, I introduced a concept I call "emotional callousing," a dynamic that can explain and bring about compassion for many bio-dad reactions to stressful stepfamily situations. As I explained the notion in more detail that day, I realized it could be helpful to all stepmothers.

I came up with emotional callousing to describe my sense of what happens to some divorced dads following years in a challenging marriage or with children who can be manipulative and even entitled. While callousing can become a coping mechanism, it can also provoke misunderstandings and arguments within couples, leading to false assumptions and a loss of closeness. Let's break this concept down and see if this will offer you and your partner some relief from any related confusion or frustration you might be experiencing.

First, let's start with the word "callous." I chose this word to be descriptive of a numbness caused due to repeated circumstances—it's not intended to imply anything negative or to be judgmental. The word can mean "hardened, unfeeling, thickened or unkind." Here I'm specifically referencing the physical metaphor of how bare, tender feet become calloused on rough terrain when repeatedly exposed to it over time.

As kids we would get to take off our school shoes when school was out and run around barefoot for most of the summer. Those first few days were a bit painful, but we knew that our tender feet just needed to toughen up a bit. When we'd go to the beach, the hot sand would bother us at first but after a couple of days—no problem. Somehow our feet magically adapted by creating layers of skin that were deadened (no nerves), providing us with insulation and creating pain-free protection from most surfaces that our feet encountered. The more often we walked or ran on rough surfaces, the bigger the callouses and the tougher our feet became. Unlike shoes, we were unable to voluntarily remove the callouses once they'd developed.

Some divorced dads have had a rough time with their previous partners. Many may have had difficult childhood experiences as well. Your partner may still be in active stress with his ex-partner or with his kids or even with you. He may even experience stress with all three sources simultaneously. This can be awful for a divorced dad who needs to protect himself from very real emotional pain. This is where his psyche's natural urge to self-protect may kick in—with emotional callousing—until he learns new ways to help himself deal with emotional pain.

Since emotional callousing occurs over time, your partner may have been dealing with upsetting situations for years or even decades, and hasn't yet been able to resolve or change very much. Instead, he may seek to survive and endure the pain, rage and fear that he believes he doesn't have any control over, or that he doesn't allow himself to feel or face. Divorced fathers have their own kind of emotional wounds that many Stepmoms can't easily recognize or understand. When you love a divorced dad, it's kind and loving to get curious and learn more about the challenges in his life, heart and mind that you may not be able to see without his help.

In the process of surviving his everyday life, your partner may have needed to develop emotional callouses to protect himself—just as our feet develop callouses without us doing anything consciously. While you understand and trust that the skin on the bottom of your feet will toughen up to protect you from challenging terrain, you may not imagine that people do the same thing emotionally to protect themselves from the actions of others and their potential negative impact. Emotional callousing is what naturally happens to your partner as he experiences rough emotional terrain over time. Some divorced dads appear to develop callouses to numb themselves from the sharp, judgmental and hurtful actions of their kids or ex-partners. They do this for their own protection and survival. They came into relationships with us with their callouses intact, even if unacknowledged. It's interesting to consider that while you may be frustrated that your partner isn't bothered by certain experiences that affect you deeply, these are likely the very experiences that caused him to form emotional callouses to begin with. In other words, there's every possibility that in the past, he *was* bothered by the same things that cause you distress today. Hmmm?

OK, enter the woman of his dreams. That's you. While you entered this relationship with your own emotional callouses, you may find you don't have them in place to insulate and protect you from rough stepfamily-related issues. You may discover that for some reason, your callouses don't protect you from certain situations in the same way your partner's callouses protect him. For example, while you may feel hurt when you're in conflict with your partner over childrearing issues, your partner may or may not be bothered in a similar way by this same situation. Over time, your wounds will close, a scab will form and, at some point, it will fall off. However, this process mysteriously leaves you with tender new emotional skin rather than a thick emotional callous. I don't know why this is the case with so many of us stepmothers. This fresh, unprotected skin can leave Stepmoms vulnerable to future hurtful and disrespectful actions and manipulations.

Is your partner dismayed and perhaps even annoyed that several repeated—and maybe even expected—stepfamily situations continue to trigger the same upsetting reactions in you? Why don't stepmothers develop callouses as they go through stressful experiences like their partners? Why don't stepmothers become numb to repeated challenging actions of their stepkids and their bio-moms? Why, unlike their partners, are stepmothers still negatively impacted after years of exposure to the same upsetting experiences? These are good questions that I continue to explore. For this next section, imagine a Stepmom is upset by something the bio-mom or stepkids have done, while her partner doesn't appear to be particularly bothered by it.

A Typical Misunderstanding

1. Stepmom gets upset and looks to her partner for his reaction. Stepmom wants her partner to validate her distress, be on her side and team up with her to create an action plan that addresses the situation.

2. Partner looks at Stepmom, communicating with a look or with words:

    "What's the big deal?"
    "Yep, there [the bio-mom/child] goes again."
    "It's not worth the effort to do anything because [the bio-mom/child] will only lash out worse if we do anything."
    "Sounds about right. Let it go, Honey, and forget about it."

3. Stepmom is now triggered by so many upsetting thoughts:

   "How could he allow this?"
   "If he really loved me, wouldn't he stand up for me?"
   "If he lets them get away with this, what's going to keep them from doing it again and again?"
   "We have to do something because this isn't right or fair!"
   "How can I respect someone who won't stand up for the right things?"

4. Stepmom urgently—and maybe even desperately—wants her partner to do something. Anything. Why? Because now she's equating her partner taking action with demonstrating support for her and vice versa—she sees his lack of action as a lack of support. While this is rarely true, it feels real to Stepmom in the absence of truly understanding what is going on.

5. Partner refuses to do anything. Or worse, he does something the Stepmom asks him to do and it causes more problems for all of them. Then he becomes angry at Stepmom and at himself because he feels he was pressured into doing something against his better judgment—which he was. It's a lose-lose, testing-and-proving situation for both Stepmom and her partner. If uninterrupted, this repeating pattern can cause real, deep, hard-to-heal problems between the couple.

6. Stepmom decides (makes an unloving negative assumption) that her partner's lack of action is evidence that he either doesn't care about her enough to take action or that he's siding with his kids or ex-wife over her. This is when Stepmom may also realize she feels very low on her partner's priority list. With this assumption, she feels more deeply hurt, enraged or even betrayed.

7. Stepmom becomes angry and tries—unsuccessfully—to talk her partner into any kind of action using all the logic, reason, pleading, articles, quotes and enticements she can unearth to convince him that action is the right thing. Stepmom finds it very difficult to let the situation go and move on.

8. Partner then gets annoyed at—or defensive with—Stepmom. The emotional distance and tension between Stepmom and her partner increases. He shifts from being lukewarm about the actions of his kids or their bio-mom to being angry at Stepmom, and now he may stubbornly defend his reasoning for doing nothing. A power struggle is now created (or strengthened) between a Stepmom and her partner.

Personal note to Stepmoms: It took me way too long to realize that the "doing nothing" strategy can often truly be the better option—which can be quite startling for us action-oriented Stepmoms. Be open to experimenting with doing nothing, potentially expanding your options.

9. The power struggle over the issue at hand, plus any other issues, can lead to more relationship damage between Stepmom and her partner. Nothing gets resolved but Stepmom and her partner are now more disconnected because of some situation that neither one of them caused. Both Stepmom and her partner believe they are absolutely right. They don't know how to bridge the gap without feeling they're giving in, making the situation worse or admitting they're wrong. From their viewpoints, it's a painful impasse.

A Stepmom from one of my workshops wrote to me about her experience with her partner:

"Dear Cathryn, when I finally figured out that something similar was going on in my own life, I was eager to make some new choices and changes. You suggested we start by slowing down our situation to see what's happening in between our words. This was an amazing experience. My partner and I were able to recognize thoughts and feelings that we sort of skipped over in our state of reacting. We learned a lot by truly listening to each other plead our cases in slowed down play-by-play commentary. During this consciously, very patient exchange something shifted, and in a flash of mutual empathy we saw and felt each other's pain.

While I was trying so hard to get my partner to understand what I was feeling, I realized I was blinded to his pain. I also realized that he had been at the mercy of painful situations for so long that he'd had to numb himself just to get by. Because he truly felt no emotional pain in the situations that bothered me the most, he found it impossible to believe I was really in pain until that moment. Wow! What a wonderful realization. It felt like we were back on the same team again. What a relief."

What kinds of insights and feelings can you expect to uncover when you and your partner slow down your process and share your thoughts and feelings, one at a time?

1. You may realize that what bothers you truly does not bother your partner at all.

2. Your partner may actually be flabbergasted that the repeated behaviors and situations in question still truly upset you after all this time. He may admit that he felt you were just being critical or over-reactive.

3. You may have felt hurt by your partner's apparent apathy, unable to comprehend that he really couldn't feel compassion for your pain—because he felt no pain.

4. Your partner may gain empathy for your feelings by listening with a more open heart. He may see all kinds of incorrect, never-expressed judgments and assumptions he'd been carrying about your actions and perceived underlying agendas. He may realize, after truly listening to you that his assumptions were wrong. This is an amazing moment to be relished.

5. You and your partner may have unspoken assumptions and disagreements related to differing religious, cultural and family "rules" that may never have occurred to you.

6. When you share your feelings openly with each other with the mutual intent to learn more, your partner is more likely to see the situation from your perspective and realize that you've been truly experiencing pain, fear and rage over issues that he was completely and totally unaffected by. This can be a healing moment for you and your partner.

7. Your partner could react by saying, *"Honey, how can this situation possibly still be hurting you? I don't understand it but I can see you're really in pain. I'm so sorry."*

8. A common Stepmom reaction to this new level of compassion and apology is to weep in the arms of her beloved. It feels so good to finally feel seen, heard and accepted by the one you love.

9. Any invisible barriers between you and your partner that have been caused by these misunderstandings will likely melt away. At a minimum they will most certainly decrease.

10. Once you have your partner's empathy, you will probably (maybe surprisingly) see these same situations in a new way. You'll see he was truly *not* impacted by the actions of others that so affected you. Your partner has superpowers that you didn't or couldn't envision or imagine.

11. You may reframe your partner's past actions and realize he wasn't ignoring you, he was just really not feeling negatively impacted by whatever was bothering you.

12. With both of you trying to survive the stress, you may realize that neither of you was able to have compassion for how the other was—or was not—feeling. When you and your partner realize you were experiencing the same situations very differently and quite authentically, the light bulbs of awareness can start turning on all around you. This is a really exciting adventure.

13. Questions you can begin asking each other when you feel this difference in reaction to something:

    "Does this situation bother you? Yes or no?"
    "How does that situation impact you?"
    "On a scale of 1 to 10, how upsetting is this for you?"
    "When this happened, what were you thinking and feeling?"
    "I see you're upset. How, exactly, can I best support you now?"

14. This new consciousness can shift your attentions from judging and blaming each other to focusing on learning more about each other's vulnerably tender and toughened numb places. It's common for a Stepmom who's unaware of the emotional callousing dynamic to judge her partner as weak or afraid for not responding as she wants him to, instead of trying harder to better understand his side of things. Occasionally I think of something that happened in my past with own my husband and I seek him out to apologize for not pausing to first understand what was happening for him. Forgiveness flows so much more naturally and easily with this shared empathy.

Do It Differently Going Forward

- You can begin to pay attention to the moment you feel tension or a sense of separation between you two, and agree to point it out right away before reacting.

- You can agree to check in with each other about how certain situations impact you, ideally at the moment something disruptive occurs.

- Going forward you can both agree to avoid making assumptions about how a situation impacts the other and just ask, then listen.

- It's so powerful if you can both agree to stay open-hearted instead of getting angry or shutting down in anticipation of an argument.

This is conscious relationship work. It takes some practice. Happily, each time either of you practices these tactics you'll learn more about each other. You'll learn about more ways to love each other when under stress. It's a mini-victory every time you or your partner call a "time out" before either of you says anything destructive or takes any hostile, hurtful or defensive action. This powerful choice to pause—even in your own thoughts and feelings—can avoid lots of stress and arguments.

Agreeing to pause, to ask questions and to listen compassionately before getting upset with each other is a way to stay connected, even when you and your partner have differing opinions about how to proceed. Why? Because it feels good to know you're going to take turns giving each other your attention (and your respect) for what's true for each of you—even though your truths may be different. It feels good to work together, bringing your different points of view to the same table, instead of battling or hiding out in opposite corners of that old familiar emotional boxing ring. Situations that had previously caused you to defend your differing opinions finally become a "we" problem. Once you and your partner realize the power and effectiveness of recognizing each other's unique numb and tender places, especially when dealing with situations caused by others, you'll wonder how you didn't see them sooner. It's possible you've both been trying so hard and yet hurting each other in your tactics simply because you didn't understand each other's true perspectives, beliefs and feelings.

While everyone is going to have emotional callouses for different things, when you realize these callouses and tender spots are very real, you can stop judging each other for having (or not having) them. Understanding where you and your partner have callouses and where they may be missing, exposing tender spots, can explain so much about your actions, inactions and past disagreements. Learning more about each other with mutual empathy and honest expression is a wonderful experience that builds trust and strengthens the love between you. It gives you and your partner greater compassion for each other and this can bring out the natural protective and supportive instincts in both of you.

Twenty-Five

Supporting Your Partner Through Divorce Guilt and Fears

A divorced dad doesn't have it easy. If he feels guilty about the impact of his divorce on his children, his actions and decisions will often reflect his guilty feelings in potentially frustrating, indirect and sometimes hurtful ways toward the woman he loves and lives with now. A stepmother is likely to become aware of divorce guilt very early in her relationship with her partner. In her attempt to provide support, she can be genuinely surprised that sometimes her help isn't perceived by her partner as a positive contribution to their relationship. As my mentor, Kit Carson told me often, "Help is not help unless perceived so by the recipient."

If your stepkids' bio-mom is not-so-cooperative to any degree, you may notice your partner flinching at text message alerts, incoming emails or ringing telephones. You may see him act in ways that appear irrational, defensive or emotionally driven. And these behaviors impact you as well as him—you will likely experience emotional pain yourself watching the one you love compromise (or seem to lose) his otherwise confident and sound judgment to appease his ex-wife and kids. This dynamic is particularly unnerving if the ex-wife is uncooperative or litigious, and if the children threaten him with the withdrawal of their love and attention. As an observer, you may feel angry or confused, and you may be disappointed in your partner or perceive him to be weak. Your first reaction may be to try to snap him out of it and lead him down, what you feel, is a stronger and more rational, action-oriented, get-results path.

Sadly, trying to coach your partner, while judging him as weak doesn't help him become stronger—it only shames him more, and can activate a defensive reaction because he doesn't know what else to do. His defensiveness will likely drive his self-esteem further into hiding and that can make him angry and even harder to reach. It doesn't bring you two closer which only adds to the stress you and your partner are already feeling.

This chapter (and this section) provides a practical, proven method to resolve stress and reduce arguments that can be caused by this dynamic. This approach can help you and your partner stay close and connected whenever the bio-mom or stepkids do something that triggers guilt and fear in your beloved. If your partner suffers from divorce guilt or fears, consider this approach. If his kids are manipulative or their mother is hostile, this approach won't change their behaviors, but it can help you and your partner stay close no matter what others do.

The Impact of Divorce Guilt

From all the descriptions I've heard, divorce guilt and fears are very sad, painful and often deeply wounding experiences for a divorced father. In addition to any feelings of guilt and fear, the shame, rage, humiliation and emotional exhaustion of the previous marriage and divorce process can really disable a guy—so much so that many men find it easier just to give in to (or go along with) their ex and kids, rather than do the inner work required to feel, deal and heal from the intense feelings and scary potential consequences. It's a logic-based decision about an emotional issue—common and understandable.

A man suffering from divorce guilt and fears can be reluctant to reveal his true feelings to himself, much less to the woman he loves, because it's just too painful. Often he can't figure out what good could come from it, so he buries the root of his feelings in denial, avoidance, hostility, defensiveness and other not-so-loving behaviors that can be misdirected toward his partner.

Divorce guilt manifests itself in lots of ways that can appear illogical, unreasonable and unfair. It can look like avoidance and forgetting, or possibly delayed decisions and reactions to events that seem clear-cut to the woman he loves now. Intensely contrasting opinions between a Stepmom and a divorced dad about how to best respond to a bio-mom or stepkids can cause tremendous pain and lasting resentments for both parties. That's not desirable, intentional or OK, so what can you do about it?

Ideally (remember when you read this next part that I started the sentence with the word ideally) as soon as a man realizes that he's being manipulated and controlled by his guilt and fears, he would seek insights and support from his partner, a therapist or a trusted guy friend. Ideally you would be supportive of this process. Working with his supportive sources, he'd get to the root of his fears and guilt, explore resolutions and create new collaborative action plans with you so he could feel like the strong, wise, loving, smart, sexy guy you fell in love with in the first place. Wouldn't that be wonderful?

Unfortunately, many men wait until they've been virtually destroyed financially or devastated emotionally before they'll seek help for these very real emotional wounds. And that's what they are—wounds (real, deep, complex and painful), many of which were likely sustained before these men even met, married and procreated with their ex-wives. An adversarial ex-partner may have added more of the same kinds of wounds, playing on the tender spots she grew to know when their relationship began. If your partner realizes this, it's likely enraging and humiliating to him. As a result, his survival strategy for emotional self-defense is in full force and can be very hard to break through. Sadly it can take the fear of losing his current partner before he gets a "wake-up call" and stops the madness that's been tormenting both him and his partner.

The ones who seek help give themselves, their children and their beloved (Stepmoms) a valuable, priceless gift. It's a gift that keeps on giving, especially if the stepkids and bio-mom have been and remain actively confrontational. The divorced dads who are willing to own their fearful, guilt-influenced choices now find themselves free and able to make new choices. The ones who refuse to acknowledge these choices present a bigger challenge for their stepmother partners.

If your partner is unwilling, for whatever reason, to take responsibility for his choices and get help with his guilt and fears, what can you do to help him? How can you be true to yourself, honor your feelings and beliefs *and* still support your partner when he makes decisions that seem so wrong, hurtful or even wimpy?

The following is a true story. This SMOM came to me for help about a resentment from the past over an issue of divorce fears. She just couldn't let it go, but wanted to resolve it. With her permission, I share the story as it actually happened between this SMOM and her husband. After you read about the situation, you'll read about another way they both imagined they could have handled it. Even though they were imagining this new approach 10 years after the actual event, this new mutually imagined, shared empathetic option led them to a much happier conclusion and the SMOM was able to let go of her resentment, and the emotional wedge between them—at long last. This new strategy can help you and your partner through similarly stressful situations. It can help you stay connected where you may have otherwise retreated to your opposite corners, each convinced you were right. It's a true and touching story that you and your partner can test out for yourselves if you have any resentments from past experiences.

A Stepmom Shares Her Experience

When my stepdaughter (SD) was in the third grade, her teacher was very kind to me from the first day of school. I'll always be grateful to her for that kindness. At the time my husband and his ex had 50-50 custody of SD. Our days were Monday, Tuesday and every other Friday through Sunday. We had an agreement with the bio-mom that my husband (DH) and I could do school things on our days and she would do them if they fell on her days. She was not willing to be in the same room with me and seemed to want to avoid DH except for teacher conferences. We were OK with that and had already honored it for over three years.

One day we got a notice about a class field trip. I was thrilled to see it was planned for a Tuesday. I was eligible and able to participate. Because so many parents wanted to go with the class as chaperones, they had a lottery system. I put my name in the drawing to go along. To my delight I won the lottery and was going to be one of the half-dozen adult chaperones.

When my SD came back to us Monday after school, she was already excited about the field trip the next day and then became even more so—be still my heart—when she learned I was coming along as a chaperone. It was one of the happiest afternoons we'd spent together.

Sometime before her Dad was due home for dinner, my stepdaughter wanted to call her mom to tell her about the field trip. I knew she would tell her I was going along. She was still too young to see the impact of this information on our lives. I tried to calm myself by reminding myself that the field trip was happening on our day as she went upstairs to speak with her bio-mom privately. She was only gone a few minutes. She came back and was still happy. It was unusual but I was willing for it to all work out OK.

An hour or so later my husband came home from work with a very odd look on his face. I wondered what had happened that day; he had a very stressful job. His daughter was so excited about the field trip that her enthusiasm and my joy sort of carried the evening. We put her to bed with her Dad's nightly storytime ritual and it continued to feel like a glorious day.

After my SD had been asleep for a while, I asked my DH what was troubling him when he came home. He quietly lowered the boom on me with a matter-of-fact tone of voice. My stepdaughter's bio-mom had called him at the office and told him that I was not allowed to go on the field trip. She told him, as a non-negotiable directive, that she was going in my place, as the rightful mother. He got the impression that if he didn't go along with her, she was going to make our lives more miserable and hurt our relationship with his daughter. Whatever she said, he believed her. He agreed to her demand while on the phone. He told me, quite mechanically, that because she was the mother and I was not, she was going along on the field trip. I was staying home.

A Stepmom's Partner

My emotional lights went out that night as if I was unplugged at a cellular level. I was in some sort of shock. In this case, I was certain the facts supported me. What was happening?

The stars had lined up so I could be involved:

- *It was during our time.*

- *It was the arrangement she had agreed to.*

- *We followed the agreement even when it benefitted her.*

- *Why didn't I have rights this time?*

The next morning, my husband got up with his daughter and took her to school. I was too crushed and heartbroken to put on a happy face for my stepdaughter. When she came home that afternoon she was very excited to tell me all about the trip and how she was so happy and surprised that her mother was there. I called upon all the strength I had to listen and smile at this child I loved like my own. I don't even remember if she asked me why I changed my plans.

The next week, when I saw the teacher again, she asked me what happened. I told her, and then she told me something that really surprised and touched me. She told me how sad she was for me. She told me she planned the field trip on a Tuesday and rigged the lottery drawing so I could go. I was so touched by her support and act of kindness. Even after all these years, I still thank her and tell her how much it meant to me, on the rare occasions I run into her in town.

We moved on to the next series of upsetting things with the bio-mom, but I've carried with me the hurt, rage and sense of betrayal from that field trip experience for all these years. At the drop of a hat, I can muster up all those hurt feelings. My husband has heard about the darn field trip so many times—I just can't seem to let it go. It's created a wedge in the intimacy between him and me. This wedge was reinforced many times whenever I paid the price of being excluded from events because of my husband's guilt and fear of his ex-wife's threats. I want to get past this but I just can't forget it. Some part of me doesn't want to let him off the hook. I feel so disregarded. What can I do? How can I apply your approaches to let go of this past resentment?"

Can you identify with this Stepmom? Do you have situations where your partner's guilt or fear has impacted you in upsetting ways? If so, I encourage you to think about an incident from your life, a past resentment, so while you're reading, you can imagine how you and your partner might process it in new ways and heal these old wounds once and for all.

What's another approach that allows Stepmom/DH couples to stay on the same side in these very difficult situations? How can she honor her partner's fears and guilt and perceive that her own feelings are being respected? What new choices could she try—or could they try as a couple—to better handle a scenario like this one? I worked with her to create a new imagined scenario for how both she and her husband could behave in different ways to help each other in what I call a "Nobody's Right/Nobody's Wrong" way. (See Chapter 20 for a thorough description of this approach.) Sharing with her permission, here's my recommended imagined process—a script for her thankfully willing husband—and what happened when she shared this with him. In addition to some other possibilities, I've also added some commentary at the end to point out the many things this Stepmom/DH couple did beautifully once this new option was discussed and more importantly imagined.

The Imagined Field Trip Story 2.0

Here's the script I wrote out for her, illustrating an imagined, revised version of what had happened following the bio-mom's phone call to her husband. We talked about it and she was very emotional just imagining this possibility. The Stepmom customized the script a bit and gave it to her husband, and he read his part that night. Together, they addressed this mutually painful situation—neither the Stepmom nor her partner had created it, but they were forced to deal with it and feel its effects for ten years. Now they owned its resolution. With the use of the script, they offered empathy to each other and attempted to grow through the experience. They did a beautiful job.

The story below picks up at the point of the husband arriving home that night. The rest is a revised sequence of events illustrating how things *could* have been different between the Stepmom and her partner. When he got home, in the new imagined version, he created the chance to talk with her *before* dinner. This would have given him the opportunity to unburden himself and explain the odd look on his face, among other benefits.

My Script for Her Husband

Stepmom's husband: *"Honey, SD's bio-mom has done it again. What I'm going to tell you is going to be very hurtful and difficult for you. I've thought about it since she called me at the office today and I want you to know I think I have an idea that might be OK with you. Please hear me out before you say anything."*

He would already be holding Stepmom's hand.

Stepmom's husband continues: *"As you probably know SD called her bio-mom about the field trip this afternoon and told her you were going. Bio-mom is now demanding to be the one to go on the field trip and she's threatened to make life even more difficult for us all if I don't let her go in your place. I believe her."*

Next critical difference in 2.0 version—He would be clearly upset and angry about the situation on Stepmom's behalf. His typically rational tone of voice, used when the situation first happened, felt cold to the Stepmom.

The script continues, as he expresses his own strong emotions about this situation. There's nothing blasé or monotone about this. He gives her the full emotional supportive force of his feelings (and imagines how his wife feels) about what's happened.

Stepmom's husband: *"Honey, this is absolutely wrong, unfair and despicable behavior. It's our time and you did nothing wrong by wanting to go with SD. But here's the thing—I feel afraid to force the issue and to encourage you to go as planned. We both know that bio-mom will carry out her threat. She's already made our lives stressful and things were just settling down into a routine. I admit it, I feel afraid of what she'll do and afraid that she'll poison my daughter against us so I agreed she could go instead of you. I'm so sorry."*

He'd now shift to a very loving, gentle tone.

Stepmom's husband: *"Thank you for hearing me out. Would you please listen one more minute to hear my plan? Then I want to hear everything you think and feel about this unfair situation."*

He's now being very tender and cautiously hopeful.

Stepmom's husband continues: *"What if you and I go see the teacher later this week and make plans to do an activity with SD's class? Just you, me and the class. We'll make it a special project. I know this isn't the same as going on the field trip with other mothers. I know you're paying the price. It's not fair at all and I hate it! I feel trapped and it sucks! I feel sickened when she does this to you and when she plays on my fears.*

Stepmom's husband with a very humbled gentle tone: *"It would mean so much to me if you were willing to be OK with this new plan. I'm so, so sorry for her negative impact on us and all the times she's been able to threaten us into doing what serves her at our expense. What do you think and how do you feel about this new idea? Can you find it in your heart to help me until I find a way to stand up to her without hurting our relationship with SD? Can you forgive me for being so afraid of her?"*

[End of scripted imagined version.]

A week or so later, this Stepmom reached out to me to share what happened after her husband read his part to her and they discussed it.

"Cathryn, it was amazing! I listened to my husband verbally react to the situation created by his ex 10 years ago but this time with compassion and being on my side. I have to say, I was changed by hearing those words and feeling his gentle, urgent caring for my feelings—yes, even though it was a script. I believe with all my heart that if he had originally responded that way when the situation first occurred, I would have responded the way I did just the other day, 10 years later. Yes, I would support him and his alternate plan.

My husband was a good sport and he performed your words to me beautifully. He surprised me by seeming so sincerely remorseful for his impact on me all those years ago. His anger at me was gone and he seemed so vulnerable and ashamed about his fears. Even though I already knew what he was going to say, after I heard him say those words to me, I flung myself into his arms and cried and cried and cried as if it had just happened the night before. It was a deep release of so much pain and loneliness. When he talked about his understanding of how the situation impacted me and then suggested a new plan to assuage some of my pain, the old hurt poured out of me until it was gone from my emotional and physical body. It was a huge wave of emotion, then it was gone.

It was an incredible experience. It felt amazing for him to finally understand and verbally acknowledge how unfair it was to me. As he shared his fears instead of defending them with logic, it opened my heart immediately. It was such a relief to hear him take responsibility for it being partially his stuff, instead of blaming me for causing this incident because I wanted to go on the field trip. It was exactly what I needed—for him to truly have empathy for how much I was hurt, denied and rejected because of his ex-wife's hold over him. Forgiveness flowed through us both so naturally that day. Let me say again, it was such a relief.

Just by hearing his voice saying those words, it was as if a clogged emotional drain inside me had been opened and all the pain and rage moved out of me. After ten long years I could finally let go of the resentment and all the other unprocessed, stored-up feelings I stubbornly held onto, as if waiting somewhat desperately for his non-defensive, authentic empathy and loving compassion. The moment arrived. It was an emotional miracle for me, my husband and our relationship. I can't thank you enough for your help."

Emotions are timeless. This is the good news for those of you willing to do this work. Can you see what was different about this new empathetic approach? Why did it change so much for both the Stepmom and her husband? In case this isn't evident in the Stepmom's story, I'm going to elaborate in the hope that you can apply this to your situations. Let me start with a question that might be on your mind right now.

Yeah, But: *"What if my partner isn't willing to admit his feelings, own his part in the situation and open up to me like hers did?"*

This is a valid question. Here's my heartfelt suggestion to you. Begin to treat your husband as if you understand just how painful his fear and guilt are for him. For those of you who are also bio-moms, you can certainly understand how scary it is to imagine losing the love of your child. If you can bring your compassion to him—even if he doesn't return the favor just yet—he's likely to feel the difference. I believe you'll feel the difference as well. Give it a try. Marianne Williamson says, "We need to bring to a situation that which we're looking for." In this Stepmom's case, she'll never know for sure how the original field trip story could've gone if she'd been more able to see, acknowledge and understand her husband's pain at the time. While she didn't do anything wrong in the original incident, if the imagined version had been true, it could have created a different outcome—eliminating any resentment.

While I can't say exactly how, I can tell you that new empathy for your partner's potential divorce fears and guilt will impact him positively. As you change, the people around you change. As you shift your focus and loving attention to staying connected to the partner you love, your needs for love, honor and respect will be met in new ways. I say this because I believe that your partner really does want to love you completely. He's just never had anyone teach him how to deal with so many complex emotional issues. The material in this book and your increased knowledge can fill that void.

The Stepmom's husband did many things differently through his new words, touches, looks and intentions that allowed this situation to be so healing for the Stepmom. His new approach included many tactics that helped her feel valued which enabled old resentments to dissolve.

1. This Stepmom's husband was willing to share his deepest fears and take responsibility for the impact of his decisions on their lives, and specifically on his wife and her feelings. He apologized for being defensive. Admitting, acknowledging and apologizing for these past behaviors is very powerful.

2. This Stepmom's husband took a risk and was willing to trust that Stepmom was not going to shame and judge him even more than she already had. He trusted she would not think less of him, even though he was feeling guilty and fearful of how his ex-wife and daughter could impact his ability to stand up for what he always knew, deep down, was the "right and fair thing." He admitted that their manipulations were very scary and he asked Stepmom to forgive him instead of judge him. Stepmom admitted she was guilty of judging him many times. She apologized to him sincerely. When we judge others, we hurt them. Sadly her husband has been hurt all those years by Stepmom's judgments, on top of his own pain. Stepmom was truly sorry and said so. He felt her remorse and was able to accept her apology.

3. This Stepmom's husband dropped his defenses and asked for Stepmom's help. Most of us will open our hearts to those asking for help. Instead of being defensive, angry or logical about his decisions, he was gentle, patient, open-hearted and honest. Her husband used to hide behind logic and would even call Stepmom over-sensitive. That never brought them closer but rather ended a lot of conversations, causing them to feel alone, unsupported and even more stressed.

4. This Stepmom's husband acknowledged Stepmom's pain and was tenderly supportive of her hurt feelings. He was loving and finally admitted that she had been punished unfairly because of his issues and his emotional baggage. That was really important to Stepmom.

5. This Stepmom's husband expressed how grateful he was that Stepmom was still willing to love him and his daughter, in spite of the not-so-kind bio-mom he had no choice but to bring into their lives.

6. This Stepmom's husband took the time and energy to come up with a creative option that really could be almost as fun as the field trip, and that would give Stepmom a chance to have a place and a role with the class. That kind of effort means a lot to many stepmothers.

This new offering of empathy is something that can change a relationship in a wonderful way, sometimes almost instantly. When a Stepmom and her partner realize that there are ways to be loving and safe together—no matter what anyone else says or does—intimacy grows, confidence soars and the relationship becomes stronger.

You and your partner can successfully work through the negative impact of situations and decisions caused by your partner's divorce guilt and fears. Old resentments can be resolved, digested and released. It starts with working together to share feelings in new ways and offering more non-defensive loving support. The new situations that crop up can now be handled very differently—more easily. Your partner's guilt and any fear he has of bio-mom actions can literally disappear and be replaced with a mutual commitment to a collaborative, creative approach that works for both Stepmom and her partner. It can take a little practice to figure this out, just like any new skill. It's worth every effort. May these ideas help you eliminate old resentments that come between you, saving you and your partner lots of pain and disconnectedness so you can get to a new level of closeness and strength together.

See Chapter 15, Resolving Resentments from Your Past.

For stepmother questions and experiences on this topic, go to smoms.org/BonusChapters and click on the title, "Supporting Your Partner Through Divorce Guilt and Fears." See the complete list of additional chapters and follow-up discussions in Chapter 39.

Twenty-Six

Your Partner's Relationship with His Ex-Wife Impacts Your Partner's Behavior
Learn More to Improve Your Relationship

When you and your partner made the commitment to become a couple, it was natural to focus on your relationship with each other. If your partner has children from a previous relationship, your relationship as a couple is naturally challenged and impacted by others in many additional ways. With some conscious effort, you can actually get good at riding out any emotional relationship storms by learning some things about your partner's relationship with his ex-wife. This extremely beneficial (yet often off-the-radar) exploration brings you a new level of understanding that you can use to make more effective strategic and tactical decisions as a team. This knowledge can also help you avoid being drawn into painful conflicts and unwinnable power struggles over any upsetting actions by your stepkids and their bio-mom. Need more reasons to consider doing this work? With these relationship insights and questions answered you'll be better prepared to fulfill more positive roles for your partner.

Your Partner Needs You

- Be a well-informed, emboldening, enthusiastic cheerleader—when he wants your support.

- Be a compassionate "safe place" sounding board—when he needs to vent.

- Be a wise, loving, confidence-boosting advisor—when he asks for your help.

Stepfamily stress can be overwhelming and even excruciating for a new couple, and even for couples who've been together for many years. One way to stay connected to your partner during any stressful situations with his ex-wife or kids is by looking at his pre-existing relationships with a detective's eye for details.

A Family of Origin

Because your partner and his ex-wife have "history" involving countless agreements (spoken and tacit), understood choices and behaviors, and power trade-offs, you and your partner are not able to start your relationship with a clean slate. If you bring children and an ex into the relationship, that adds more levels of complexity to your relationship dynamics outside of just you and your partner. Not a surprising statement. While some may try to address stepfamily challenges with the same approaches that work with families made of a couple with children that they share (birthed or adopted), I see it very differently. Let's review some of the issues that make handling stepfamily issues more complex and distinct from what I'm calling family of origin.

When a couple becomes a nuclear family by the birth of a child, both parents have already negotiated countless decisions and power allocations between them by living through a variety of life situations together over a period of time. They've resolved these conflicts and disagreements by way of discussions, trade-offs, compromises and other forms of verbal and non-verbal negotiating tactics, most often made when the relationship is in a loving, thoughtful, generous place. Agreements may be revised over time until well-worn paths are formed and understood by the couple. These mutually understood agreements may or may not be openly discussed. Documented, structured, signed agreements rarely exist in nuclear families. The couple may not be aware they're creating relationship rules—but the dynamics of their relationship expand from each experience in some form of mutually accepted resolution.

The couple's negotiations are private and whatever they decide is A-OK because they're likely the only two impacted. They make these agreements, big and small, generally without outsiders controlling, monitoring, judging or influencing their decisions. Rarely does anyone outside the couple openly discuss or criticize their private relationship, much less judge their choices as right or wrong, good or bad—except for maybe in-laws. Between friends and families, couples seem to respect other couples' relationship choices even if they don't understand or agree with them. It's a social norm.

The couple in the nuclear family has had the benefit of a learning curve and the time to get to know each other before children enter the picture and impact their relationship. After the first child or children are born, and as the newly expanded family of three (or more) encounters stressful life situations, the couple continues to learn about each other's needs, priorities, strengths, vulnerabilities and emotional wounds as they live through situations that they work out together—consciously or unspoken. As long as the couple is still sharing love, respect and the desire to help each other, they'll still be motivated to find a mutually agreeable solution to each challenge. If the couple's loving relationship breaks down, even pre-separation, parts of their mutually established set of agreements can also begin to break down. One or both partners may want a new agreement, plead for adherence to the old one or decide it's time to give up, give in or end the relationship.

A Stepfamily

The creation of a stepfamily is possible only after the original nuclear family experiences a major loss from divorce or the death of one parent. A stepfamily is created when one of the bio-parents falls in love again with a new mate and they decide to become a couple. Unless the Stepmom's new partner is widowed, the newly minted stepchildren now have a parenting team of 3-4 grown-ups who may not consider themselves willing teammates. Everyone in this new parenting team is now faced with the stress of unresolved issues originating from the broken nuclear family and the presence of new mates for either or both bio-parents. These people may not want to get along or be allies in caring for the children produced through the original couple's union. They may lack motivation to resolve conflicts. One or more parties may even experience motivation to create or amplify conflict. This is a breeding ground for intense resentments, rage, anxiety and confusion, and is hard on all the relationships involved. When the members of a newly formed parenting team choose to cooperate—even if just civilly—the Stepmom and any children involved are extremely lucky in immeasurable ways.

The new stepfamily begins without the valuable benefit of a child-free honeymoon and pre-parenting-responsibilities phase, as the original nuclear family likely did. The Stepmom and her new partner rarely have the luxury of time to work out a mutually evolved set of customized agreements between each other, much less with the stepchildren and their bio-mom, plus, if applicable the bio-mom's partner. That's a lot of new relationships and interactions all trying to find negotiated agreements without a socially approved, proven model to rely on. That's quite a difference from the way a couple becomes a nuclear family.

Being the Stepmom or bio-dad of a new stepfamily can feel exciting and full of possibilities. It can also feel chaotic and scary, a bit like being in the Wild West without any relationship laws, nor a single appointed sheriff to settle disputes fairly. The stepfamily couple grapples with the same daily life challenges that a couple in a simple nuclear family does. On top of that, they face the exponential difficulties caused by power struggles and any unresolved personal issues of the bio-parents, their children and stepparents combined. Problems are made worse when one or both of the divorced bio-parents are unwilling to work together to find new, mutually acceptable solutions that best serve the children involved. If either bio-parent feels wronged or vengeful toward their ex-spouse or a new stepparent, this makes it even harder for the new stepfamily to form loving and respectful connections. The euphoric joy and happy family dreams of the new couple can get shattered quickly, throwing the Stepmom and her bio-dad partner into excruciating and complicated relationship situations. It's a lot to handle for any new couple and for the stepkids, too—I know this may be a huge understatement for you.

A Common Power Hierarchy in Stepfamilies

- Bio-parents over Stepparents

- Bio-mom over Bio-dad

- Bio-mom speaks for Stepdad

- Bio-mom over Stepmom

- Bio-Dad over Stepmom

- Stepkids over Stepmom

From my experiences and observations from working with stepmothers and their families since 2000, the bio-mom is at the top of the power rankings. Even though bio-dads are gaining more parenting rights, the bio-moms generally still get their way and the benefit of the doubt, especially with pre-teen children. Stepdads rarely seem to contribute to stepfamily stress unless the bio-mom pressures him to get involved to prove his loyalty to her. The makeup of peaceful or conflicting situations among the bio-parents and stepparents is largely determined by the behavior and attitude of the stepkids' bio-mom. In other words, as has proven to be true in many stepfamilies I've known, "if the bio-mama of the stepkids ain't happy, nobody's happy." In fact, the most common, most strongly charged power struggles stem from a bio-mom's lack of willingness to get along with her ex-husband or her children's Stepmom. Ideally the bio-mom chooses to be cordial and cooperative with her equally cordial and cooperative ex-husband and his new mate. However, if the bio-mom is uncooperative then life's going to be that much more challenging for the Stepmom and her partner.

In my experience, bio-dads seem disinterested in power struggles with their kids' Stepdads. Stepfathers seem to rarely have an abundance of childcare-related responsibilities. A bio-dad also seems less likely to have a problem with or deny a stepfather (particularly if the stepfather is seen as decent and kind) from participating in his children's activities. However a bio-mom is more likely to have problems with a stepmother participating in her children's public lives. At Stepmoms on a Mission, we describe bio-moms in three categories: (1) kind, (2) civil and (3) hostile or uncooperative. It's not a judgmental viewpoint, but is simply descriptive of bio-mom's behaviors and makes a Stepmom's situation easier to understand—a form of shorthand.

From what I've noticed over the years, Stepmoms appear to be the least empowered and the most excluded of the 3-4 members of the stepchildren's parenting team, even though she often has significant responsibility for her stepkids' care when they're in her home. Unfortunately and infuriatingly, stepmothers are often denied a commensurate level of authority and inclusion when it comes to those same children in her care. When there's unequal authority, differing levels of respect offered by the bio-parents and a double standard for stepfather and stepmother participation in stepkids' events—particularly if this is due to the bio-mom's unwillingness to be kind or civil—the rage and pain a Stepmom may feel in her stepfamily situation can be off-the-charts difficult. All of this can bring up feelings a Stepmom isn't prepared for and doesn't know how to process. How could she prepare for something she never experienced and couldn't even imagine? Why can't we all get along?

Workplace Dynamics as a Model

If 3-4 adults found themselves required to work together in their day jobs, they would be expected by society to find ways to cope with each other. Moreover, they would do so with more dignity and respect than is often offered to stepmothers who join a parenting team, even if that team is made up of those same hypothetical people mentioned above. In workplace situations, co-workers who don't like each other are still expected to behave civilly to each other while at work. They communicate and behave (perform) as if they get along, regardless of how they feel deep down—usually. People at odds with each other at work find ways to minimize difficult interactions, contain each other's negative impact and maximize results because they all want to complete their assignments and deliver on their responsibilities. They do it to please their superiors and keep their jobs. If only members of a stepfamily-parenting team would embrace their relationships with each other with the same civility and cooperation—at least for the sake of their children's well-being. So, with all the above background in mind, what can a Stepmom learn from her partner's past relationship that will help them both going forward?

The Most Important Point of This Chapter

Exploring and learning as much as you can about your partner's past (and current) relationship with his ex-wife can help you better know your partner and improve your life together in countless ways. By increasing your compassion and creative support for each other—especially when dealing with the trauma caused by his ex-wife or kids—the conflicts with your partner will be significantly reduced or even become non-existent.

Typically a stepmother inherits the same power struggles that existed between her new partner and his ex-wife before the divorce. The importance of this relationship dynamic is easy to overlook, much to the detriment of the Stepmom and her partner. The crux of the issue is that power struggles among the Stepmom, her partner and his ex-wife can emerge strongly (and irrationally) when the Stepmom tries to assert her relationship strategies or change the bio-parents' pre-existing, pre-divorce, mutually agreed-upon relationship dynamics. So it is critical to discover and understand what you're dealing with, including your partner's expectations, those of his ex-wife and your own.

Meteorologists and Detectives—Who Knew?

This chapter invites you to be proactive and give meaning to the reality and challenges of your newly inherited relationships. You can do this by choosing to wear two new hats. First, I encourage you to think of yourself as a bio-mom meteorologist. With the help of your partner, you can gather information and become aware of the conditions for potential bio-mom storms. With this information, you can get good at predicting bad weather and learning how to prepare for—and survive—these storms.

In addition, you can become a relationship detective. To be adequately perceptive in this role, you'll need to be curious, open-minded and observant. Look for patterns and have confidence that you can find positive ways to deal with whatever you discover about your partner's pre-existing and present relationships with his kids and his ex-wife. Working with the realities you inherit allows you to handle stressful situations in wiser, more creative, eyes-wide-open ways without causing more damage through reactive behaviors. It's also more anxiety-reducing and energy-saving than striving to keep your blinders on or seeing your stepfamily situation through the understandably rose-colored glasses glasses of a woman newly in love.

Some stepmothers are so eager to get their lives started with their new partners that these investigative and weather-assessing relationship tactics never occur to them. Others may resist giving any attention to, or placing any value on, learning about their partners' previous relationships because they believe they already know enough and can change anything they don't like. It makes sense to want a clean slate with your partner. A stepmother may not want to spend much time thinking about the love (and "firsts") her partner shared with a woman who now causes her trouble, intimacy issues or heartache. These naïve or controlling approaches create an even greater potential for pain and rage and a lot of unnecessary tension between a Stepmom and her partner. If you haven't done your own investigative research for these or other reasons, don't worry—it's not too late.

Be a Relationship Detective

Clue #1: Look at how your partner treats you. Is he generally deferential to your wishes or does he demand his way or the highway? Is he creative or does he prefer the well-worn path? Open-minded or narrow-minded about new ideas or change? Generous or quid pro quo in his agreements? Does he return unacceptable food at a restaurant or does he endure it to avoid a potential conflict? Does he make plans for the two of you or defer to you? Does he "play nicely with others" or insist on his preferences? If he doesn't like something, does he suggest a solution, propose compromise or generally go along with your ideas, perhaps trying to make you happy or avoid stress with you? Does he keep a ledger of past angers or gift you with a clean slate each day? Does he tell you what he's feeling or do you have to rely on your non-verbal and mind-reading skills?

Clue #2: How do your answers above compare with how he treats his ex-wife now? Can you see similar patterns in his interactions with her? Where is it different? Ask him about anything that doesn't make sense to you. There are valid reasons for everything he does. This is true for all of us. Behavior has meaning. Listen carefully to his explanations. Learn about their previous negotiation style and how it has changed since they split so you can understand his choices. From this place of newfound compassion for what he's been doing and dealing with, you can now help him interact with her more effectively—*IF* he asks for your help. Whether or not he asks for your help the information you uncover will help you see things more clearly.

Clue #3: Observe the meaning and significance you give to your partner's behavior when he's interacting with you as compared to how he treats his ex-wife. Look for any double standards and judgments you may have when it pertains to his interactions with his ex-wife.

For example: If he's naturally deferential to your wishes and usually goes along with whatever you want, do you encourage this behavior with you but consider him weak or unmanly when he acts that way with his ex-wife?

If something like this is true for you, this is a good place to pause. What beliefs or expectations do you have about being his present partner, or about her no longer being his partner, that might conflict with what's happening or blind you to any double standards?

Clue #4: Accept the reality that your partner knows and understands his ex-wife better than you do. Your partner really can advise you about his ex-wife's attitudes, willingness to get along with you (or not), personality, and views on parenting. Has he been trying to convince you that she will not change her attitude about you but you won't believe him? Is he trying to convince you to do certain things to minimize or contain her negative impact on your lives but you refuse to accept it? Do you continue to think about (possibly obsess over) ways to control her and get her to do the right thing? Containing and controlling are two very different goals. One is self-care and the other is manipulation.

You can save yourself a lot of stress and arguments with your partner if you'll seek out and trust his opinion about how best to interact with his ex-wife and his kids. Yes, really! Listen deeply to what he says. Ask clarifying questions. After sharing your feelings about the situation and about what he's suggesting—so he can understand and validate your feelings—help yourself by taking his advice whenever you two are at an impasse. Even if you feel like you're losing a battle to win a war, this will enable you to stay connected with your partner—which is winning to me. How about you? He'll probably (hopefully) deeply appreciate your new levels of respect for his experiences and needs. If he's smart, he will also appreciate that you're sparing the two of you lots of added melodrama and stress.

If the situation with your stepkids or their bio-mom is denying you something you want/need or is upsetting you, this is also important to address. Look to your partner for compassionate support. Ask him to help you find new ways of helping you get whatever you're not getting from the situation. If the actions of his ex-wife or your partner's advice trigger strong anger, resentments, rage or pain for you, take those feelings very seriously. Resist any false beliefs or defensive strategies that try to convince you that taking a stand with the bio-mom is going to make you feel better. It's just not true based on all my years of working with stepmothers. However there is something you can do to stand up for yourself. Protect your feelings, dignity and self-respect by taking yourself off the power game board with your partner's ex-wife. Instead, put your energy into honoring your feelings in healthy, supportive ways. There are several chapters in this book that can help you do this work. When in doubt—and especially when your emotions are intense—take your partner's advice about how to handle current situations with his kids and their bio-mom. See Chapter 18 for ways to better support each other when strategies conflict. See Chapter 19 for more details about an approach called, "His Kids: His Call."

Clue #5: A Stepmom can mistakenly assume that divorce frees her partner from the previously established power, needs, fear and communication-related relationship dynamics that were pre-established with his ex-wife. If only this were true. While divorce clearly changes some things, many—maybe even most—interaction styles will remain the same. If, upon reflection, you discover this is true for your partner and his ex-wife, it will be helpful for you to take time to understand their usually unspoken relationship agreements and dynamics. Why do you want to do this? So you can help your partner to feel better understood, supported and more confident about a future that is different, more collaborative and less stressful with you. Your fresh eyes and outside perspective can give your partner creative, respectful and effective new ideas about ways to interact with his ex-wife that make him feel more empowered, less stressed, more connected to you and more peaceful. It's a gift to you both.

Clue #6: If your partner's ex-wife is in any way hostile toward your partner, give this attention right away. Realize and accept she knows his personality, his tender spots and all of his hot buttons. He knows that she knows how to hurt and manipulate him in the most devastating, shame-producing and emasculating ways because she's probably already done so in the past. He knows her tactics well. If/when he's brave enough to express his rage or fears and asks for your help, do your best to suspend your judgments, just as you'd like him to do whenever you express your own fears. By respecting his feelings as valid and supporting him in ways he needs, you model ways for him to return the favor when you need his validation and support. This is a healthy and endearing relationship skill.

Clue #7: It can be very challenging for your partner to stay conscious—meaning stay in his powerful adult self—anytime his ex-wife threatens to negatively impact his relationship with his kids or maybe his image or pocketbook. If this happens, your partner is going to need your support more than ever. Hopefully he will tell you what form that support takes—listening, talking, doing, not doing, distracting, etc. Mobilize any emotional energy and desire to help him in the form he requests. Trust him. Help him the way he wants to be helped!

Clue #8: Pay particular attention to how your stepkids behave when interacting with your partner, especially when your partner tells you, *"They're acting just like their mother."* These behaviors give you more insights about their mother and her childrearing values and behaviors. This will also reveal a lot about the pre-divorce family dynamics. Learn from watching them so you can better understand how to love your partner and help him with his kids. Judging his behavior and interactions with his kids will probably only shut him down emotionally and that separates you from each other and all your creative ideas.

Your partner may not be able to see any rude or disrespectful treatment he's been enduring from his kids. If you discover that he typically seeks to avoid conflict, this may help you understand how he could be blind (or now numb) to his children's negative behavior. Rather than ask him to throw himself into a parenting fire he's already experienced many times, request more details from him so you can help him minimize any pain and self-protect. With your love and support your partner can better understand his own feelings and even attempt new self-respecting tactics that can help him feel stronger around his children, no matter how they behave.

Clue #9: When you feel anxiety or tension stirring between you and your partner about how to handle a situation involving his ex-wife—stop talking immediately. Pause. Interrupt the natural urge to argue for your opinion. Instead get curious, ask your partner more questions and seek to learn more about his viewpoint, feelings and past relationships.

"How did you handle this when you two were together?"

"How did you handle it when you were first separated?"

"In the past when this happened, what upset you the most?"

"What would you like to do differently going forward?"

"I think we may have different priorities here. What's most important to you?"

"I really want to know how you feel and what you need from me. You already know how I feel. Together let's make a plan that honors us both. OK?"

As easy and tempting as it can be to express strong opinions, especially when you're angry or afraid, no one likes to be shamed or judged. It's particularly difficult to feel judged by your partner when you're under stress and looking for support, kindness and compassion. Be aware of your feelings and your partner's feelings as best you can. The choice to bring your wise, loving perspective to whatever you observe generates a lot of benefits for both of you. Remember to make it a high priority to process your reactions to whatever feels uncomfortable to you *outside* the realm of interacting with the stepkids or their bio-mom. Their behavior is probably going to stir up stuff for you—personal, important emotional stuff that you can turn into more skills and greater strengths if you're willing to look deeper. See Chapter 9 for specific ways you can choose to take advantage of the emotional energy generated by stepfamily stress.

A Crossroads Decision

A Stepmom who tries to change, fix or ignore the well-worn relationship dynamics between her partner and his ex-wife will experience more relationship stress than a Stepmom who understands their history and works consciously with the reality she has inherited. If these relationship dynamics are left undiscussed, your partner may expect your blind loyalty and support for anything around his kids and ex-wife—he may believe that's what a "good wife/partner" should do. He may expect this without ever discussing this with you, assuming you agree. You may believe and expect the same from him. Have you two ever talked about this belief or issue? These undiscussed beliefs and unexplored emotional territory can unintentionally and unknowingly sabotage the strength of your connection. You can fix that with a good calm conversation each time this tension shows up for you.

Stress between you and your partner may start as arguments because the realities—and the unconscious expectations and assumptions your partner had formed in his past relationship—may conflict with your desires for your new relationship with him. Perhaps neither of you has been taught how to recognize and settle these differences—that's normal. If you're both in the dark about your differences and how to handle them, this can lead to a confusing, painful power struggle and a battleground for judging and blaming each other. On top of it all, it can be lonely and sometimes scary to realize how much another person (not you or your partner) and her behavior can impact your loving connection with your partner and your daily sense of well-being.

Most Stepmom/bio-dad couples have never been taught to discuss the bio-dad's past relationships and what those could mean to him today. Couples starting out without inheriting kids from previous relationships don't need to have the conversations or skills I'm suggesting here. Their shared wisdom and tactics evolve over time in ways that please them both. You and your partner are in a different situation. Becoming a stepfamily is like buying and completely renovating a pre-fab house that was already partially designed and built by others—without your input.

Lovingkindness for yourself, your partner and your situation will help throughout this process—let's face it, it will help anytime with just about anything. You and your partner can become wiser and less vulnerable to being hooked into an argument today, simply by recognizing there are things to learn, discuss, create and do differently to reduce arguments and build a more empowered, loving intimate partnership. When the pre-existing relationship between your partner and his ex-wife is consciously explored and understood, you and your partner can be consistently supportive of each other's feelings with the shared goal of handling stepfamily issues together. In this way, you can stand calmly and competently with your partner, and together you can weather any relationship storms caused by his ex-wife or children. Imagine your life without this stress. What can you do with all the reclaimed energy, time and happiness?

Twenty-Seven

Empathy for Your Partner
Stepfamily Stress from Your Partner's Perspective

It can be easy to lose touch with what's happening for your partner when you're under so much stress in your own life. You don't fail to see his perspective on purpose. It's common to lose empathy and compassion for your partner when the intense levels of anger, pain, anxiety and rage you're feeling put you in survival mode. In this state, you may be blind to things he's experiencing that you would normally see and respond to more lovingly than you may be presently. This is human nature and completely understandable. However, if you lose that loving feeling for your partner, an invisible connection can be severed or shredded. When this happens, both you and he can feel painfully alone, unsupported and betrayed. You may even begin to look at each other as enemies. Yikes!

Many times, I've been surprised and disappointed at my inability to see past my own defenses. On top of that, I've found myself unwilling and unable to offer my husband the very empathy I wanted so desperately from him. It's my goal to help you get beyond barriers like this one, and it's the goal of this book to help you and your partner weather the storms of stepfamily life as an ever-stronger loving team. With this in mind, I ask that you review the information below to see if there are any places where you could practice more empathy and compassion for your partner's feelings. If you find yourself reading these things and feeling too hurt or angry, or if it doesn't feel safe to open your heart to your partner at this time, honor that and be very gentle with yourself. This chapter will be here when the time is right for you.

Over the years, I've collected a list of thoughts, feelings, beliefs and perspectives that divorced fathers feel are important but that often escape their partners' awareness, acknowledgement or sympathy. This list can serve as enlightening, exploratory discussion points for you and your partner if it feels like there's a mysterious invisible wall between you. When Stepmom/bio-dad couples feel that they're each deeply known and supported, nothing from the outside can break their connection. I hope this chapter opens new pathways for mutual lovingkindness to flow between you and your partner.

1. Your Partner's Divorce Experiences

How's your partner really doing? His divorce may be the most painful, challenging, enraging situation he's ever experienced. When children are involved, a marriage may end but the relationship between the bio-parents does not. This can complicate the healing and recovery process as both parties are not free to move on completely. If either party is looking for revenge, validation, justice or punitive compensation, the divorce process can become a bloody battleground of grievances and power struggles.

The entire divorce process is likely to bring up a lot of feelings for your partner. One moment he may be furious with his former spouse. Another moment he might feel strong and generous. And yet another he might feel like a failure, ashamed or guilty for the impact his divorce has on his kids. The financial aspect of the divorce, plus any regular work-related pressure, can magnify his stress. This combination can do major damage to his confidence and self-esteem.

Your partner, like many bio-dads, may be unprepared for the emotional turmoil he experiences when dealing with competing power struggles among an ex-spouse, kids and now a new partner—you. All this negative stress can also collide with his passionate excitement about a relationship with you. Your partner has a very full emotional plate—trying to heal from the emotional impacts that led to his divorce, re-adjusting the dynamics of his relationship with his ex and other friends, and perhaps feeling unsure of how to best help his kids *and* build and navigate a relationship with you. Complicate this scenario with an openly angry ex-spouse or defiant kids and this is an unfathomable emotional nightmare for your partner. It's a lot for anyone to process and handle.

You can help your partner feel less defensive, more supported and more confident that he can get through to a new place. Start by lovingly expressing your awareness of his challenges. Create a safe space for your partner to share his pain and fear—this is a priceless and loving gift you can give him. Offer him your empathy and compassion while knowing you also have the right to be supported in the same way. These approaches will help you both weather any difficult circumstances you may face together. See Section Three for chapters about improving your relationship.

2. The Often-Overlooked Pressure of Spinning Plates

Generally speaking, men learn to compartmentalize their work life from family life, while many women carry their emotions into all areas of their lives. While a man might want to come home to a space to relax, regroup and unwind from work, a stressed-out Stepmom may look at his presence at home as the time to talk through, work through and figure out how to address stepfamily issues. This allows for very little or no peaceful, safe space for a stressed-out guy to rejuvenate with the woman he loves. Can you help your partner create some emotional downtime and breathing space between himself, his ex and his kids? See Chapter 37, Tip #7, for a proven and practical suggestion for creating a stress-free zone.

If you and/or your partner deal with stressful situations outside the stepfamily purview (like with work, elderly parents, etc.), it can make a big difference to acknowledge the impact this stress has on each of you and to help each other find daily rejuvenation. It's amazing and wonderful how helpful and healing it can be to say to each other, *"Honey, I just want you to know that I see you're dealing with a lot of spinning plates and you're doing a great job in a tough situation. How can I best help you? What do you need from me?"*

Many a partner has told me that his Stepmom partner seems oblivious (to varying degrees) to the impact of his stress at work and to his possible need for emotional support. These men have said that their partners act as if their priority as a couple should be to spend time talking about stepfamily problems. The urgency and lack of compassion—even harshness—that a Stepmom may have for her partner's job-related stress is usually not intentional, but an indication that the Stepmom is experiencing emotional tunnel vision and not handling things from her wise, adult perspective. Instead, she may be acting from the disempowered, angry, hurt perspective of her child-self. If this one-sided sense of urgency and lack of compassion for your partner's stress is prolonged, he may end up feeling resentful and alone—as if he has no choice but to remain the sane, stoic, un-emotional one and ignore his own feelings until his partner feels better. This is a lonely, painful, enraging place for a divorced father who is also under stress and longing to feel known, supported and loved.

I've also learned that sometimes our partners just want to come home, relax and talk with us about happy things that have *nothing* to do with their ex-wives or kids. It can be overwhelming and sometimes even debilitating for either partner to have no place or time to be free of stepfamily stress. This is really about the perception of compassion between partners, rather than a direct reflection of reality. We Stepmoms know how important it is to feel acknowledged for our feelings, pain and rage yet somehow it's common for stepmothers to overlook this need/wish from their partners. Upon reflection, if you realize there's room for you to be more empathetic and make time to hear about and nourish your partner's feelings, you can simply begin to share the giving and receiving of attention more consciously. This can make a world of difference to your partner.

3. Few Men Seek Support

Another aspect of your partner's emotional life that may not be on your radar screen is that many men do not talk to anyone about their personal problems or stresses no matter how bad it gets. Your partner's feelings may be so overwhelming or embarrassing to him that he might even turn down the chance for effective and genuine peer support. Guys just don't seem to feel manly discussing their feelings with other guys. Socially they've been conditioned with a set of man rules that are geared to have them *not* talk about, ask about or admit feelings to other guys. They fear being judged as weak even when this kind of conversation and camaraderie would help them. It makes it much harder for our partners to process their feelings and get fresh ideas. Between 2000 and 2005, in those first years of the SMOMS support group meetings I ran in New Jersey, we tried several times to get our partners to agree to attend a meeting with each other so they could help each other feel acknowledged, like we did. Every single time they initially agreed—vaguely—but never attended or even met each other over all those years.

Married men generally have only one emotional support channel—their wives. If you're not there for your partner, ideally as a non-judgmental outlet and source of insight and support, your partner may be left to deal with all the complex feelings, in all the areas of his world, alone. Because women are often more comfortable getting and giving emotional support in all kinds of ways, it's easy to overlook how difficult it could be for your partner to not have this support. Your partner's emotional life could very well be a closed system and you're likely the only outlet available to him. Hopefully remembering the sacred role you can play in your partner's life can make it easier for you to pause and look at his emotional situation with greater empathy and patience. He will feel the shift. Hopefully he'll also express his appreciation and, more importantly, share his feelings with you.

If your partner has been without your patient, compassionate support for a while, he may have some hurt and anger to express when you first reconnect with him in this way. Take a moment to reflect on how you felt before you found support for your feelings as a Stepmom. Remind yourself how you feel when your partner doesn't give you support. With these perspectives in mind, I encourage you to find gentle and empathetic ways to help your partner safely air his upset feelings so you can move on together in a new, closer way.

4. Men May Have Rarely Experienced Empathy Toward Them

Without the experience of giving and getting empathy, men learn to endure—they find other ways to cope with their feelings. Consider that your partner may not have grown up getting compassion when he was afraid, stressed or dealing with difficult people and situations as a child. Many men have been raised in a culture that allows for little sympathy for whatever upsets them emotionally. They were taught not to cry (seen as weakness) and to "tough it out" or "grit your teeth" or "be a man." Because of this, their skill and capacity for tolerating (not feeling and processing) emotional pain is often quite high. To survive their childhoods and emotional stress they had to learn to endure. At some point, they may have even stopped expecting or seeking empathy and compassion because the pain of not receiving it was just too much. They were wired to seek a solution rather than to share the pain of others. They learned to re-direct their emotional energy toward thinking (not feeling) about whatever needs to be fixed.

These coping skills serve them well in their work life. Men are generally overtly rewarded for being able to handle stress stoically. As a result, men can base their self-esteem and "manliness" on their ability to endure and hold it together as they disregard their feelings—just as they were taught in childhood and as was likely reinforced in adolescence. Growing up without experiencing the benefits of empathy and compassion can make it harder for your partner to appreciate how positive and impactful those gifts really are. He has probably spent his life trying to endure without this emotional support. This means that a lot of his unprocessed emotions may not have been acknowledged, validated or processed because no one taught him how. He may never have been guided to lovingly explore his emotions, particularly his negative ones. Does your partner have the space with you to process his feelings (including fear and grief) without being judged as weak? What can you do to help your partner honor his feelings as you teach him how to honor yours?

After decades of repressing their feelings to be viewed as "the Man" and without knowing how important empathy and compassion can be, your partner may already be near his endurance threshold for emotional stress when you come into his life. While your partner may feel competent with his skill set at work, his self-esteem and self-image can become eroded, even shattered, when he realizes his survival tools aren't successfully managing the conflicts and power struggles with his ex-wife, with his kids and with you.

Naturally, it would be hard for our partners to offer us something they've had to go without all their lives. They may even resent us demanding compassion if they feel we don't offer it to them. The infusion of your attention, lovingkindness, empathy and support, which may have come more naturally at the beginning of your relationship, is a chance for you to help your partner in positive, palpable ways. Modeling empathy is one of the gifts you can give your partner. If your compassion lessens when you're under stress, your partner may not understand how to ask for it—instead, he may feel abandoned without understanding what he has lost. This is painful for him and the relationship. Thankfully this is something you can do something about.

5. Competing Priorities

This discussion may open you up to new levels of empathy for your partner. Sharing this information and maybe this chapter with your partner and getting his perspective may also help him see you and your feelings in a new, more loving light.

There are many ways couples are blinded to the conflicts that cause pain in stepfamily situations. Recognizing that men and women (generally speaking) have different hierarchies of values and priorities of needs is a good place to begin your mutual investigations. Have you talked with your partner about what needs are most important to him? Are you aware of your priorities regarding the urgency of issues? Men and women are typically different in how they prioritize what's important to them in relationships, including (again, generally) the need to be included, to be heard, to avoid conflicts, to do the right thing, to seek peace at all costs and to have equal rights. Reflecting on past conflicts like a post-game analysis can help you identify where your needs conflict.

The Stepmoms I've worked with are generally looking to be heard, to be included, to feel confident about their rightful place in their home and to feel their giving and receiving are balanced and valued in their lives with their partner. Stepmoms often feel that trying to get others to do the right thing, enforcing justice and insisting on rule compliance are worth all the emotional, financial and energetic investments—and even worth the stress created between them and their partners.

The partners of Stepmoms that I've worked with typically see it differently. They place a higher value on having a peaceful life and are willing (and even eager) to do whatever it takes to avoid conflicts with their ex-wife, their kids and the woman they love now—you! The partners of Stepmoms are often less interested in justice and more motivated to concede to their ex-wife so they can avoid conflicts, look like the good guy and have more happy moments in their current marriage.

Think about the times you and your partner have clashed over his response to the latest actions of your stepkids or their bio-mom and you'll likely see conflicts in your individual priorities. These differences can explain much of the stress and many of the disagreements you two experience together. It may be obvious when you're examining these conflicts in hindsight, yet so easy to miss in the heat of the situation. It's easier to find solutions that honor each other's needs—as a team—when you're both clear about each other's priorities and work together to find creative compromises that lead to a mutually agreeable plan. Chapter 18 was written to describe these conflicts and teach you how you can resolve them as a loving team.

6. Compassion and Conflict Fatigue

One of the most painful relationship experiences for a Stepmom is feeling that she doesn't have the compassionate support of her partner when it comes to the impact his kids and their bio-mom have on her life. She may feel her partner is siding with "them" and against her. She may perceive that her partner is being impatient with her or trivializing her feelings, when this is actually not true. Common complaints from Stepmoms include, *"How can he say he loves me and do what he's doing?"* and *"If he loved me, he would side with me or do what I ask."* These statements are understandable and yet detrimental to a loving partnership. If you feel you need to make comments like these, this may indicate your partner is suffering from what I describe as compassion or conflict fatigue. You may be suffering from the same thing if you've invested a lot of time and energy in trying to help everyone else deal with the divorce so you can get on with your happy family dream life.

I've learned our partners often feel these same things about us, even if they can't articulate it or understand their own discomfort. When a Stepmom and her partner are suffering from this emotional phenomenon, it makes for some lonely, painful and angry moments. To make things worse, these moments are scary because they are hard to define and address, and therefore hard to prevent. The following is designed to probe your partner's potential perspectives, but could also apply to you. Discussing the scenarios below with your partner can lead to productive, healing experiences that break down defensive barriers, particularly when you agree to listen to each other open-heartedly. If you find yourself feeling defensive, please honor that feeling and see the chapters about defensiveness before delving into more conversations. See Chapters 21 and 22 in this book and an additional chapter at smoms.org/BonusChapters called "Six Sample Situations for Disarming Defensive Behaviors Between You and Your Partner."

Stepfamily Scenarios

- Is it possible your partner can't muster the compassion you want from him because you're treating all the things your stepkids and their bio-mom do as a five-alarm fire?

- Could your partner feel angry or enraged because no matter how hard he tries to support you, you're still upset at him for not supporting you correctly—or enough?

- Could your partner feel the pain of despair because you're angry at him for not being able to prevent the problems with his kids or ex-wife? Why do you expect him to be able to control his ex-wife or kids?

- Could you be unfairly projecting superhero onto him, expecting him to make all your pain and stress go away? It's one thing for your partner to deal with relationship stress, but when he feels like all he's doing is disappointing you and failing—in spite of investing enormous energy to try to please you—it can lead to depression and despair.

- Could he feel sad, betrayed and even ashamed because he believes he has lost his biggest supporter and fan—you?

- Could your partner feel hopeless about living the life he wants—a life that's aligned with his needs and values? Is he unable to create it because of your needs, those of his kids and those of his ex-wife? This kind of stress can destroy a man's self-image, especially if you now see him as a failure in spite of all his efforts.

- Does your partner feel he knows how to deal with his ex-partner in a way that will minimize her negative impact on your lives, but you're not supporting him in this?

- Could he feel dismissed, betrayed or enraged by your insistence that you know how to handle his ex-wife better than he does, even after many experiences that show your tactics create more conflicts or stress among you, your partner and his ex-wife?

- Could your partner find it difficult to be compassionate—and maybe even feel angry at you— because he believes that many (most?) of the situations that upset you could have been avoided if you'd just taken his advice about dealing with his ex-wife and kids in the first place? Ouch! I know this was a big one for me. See Chapter 19 for more about this issue.

- Could he be furious with you because he believes many of the issues that upset you could have been handled in a more straightforward manner (or just ignored or overlooked) without becoming a throw-down or blow-up conflict with you, his kids and/or his ex-wife?

This is an issue worthy of sincere reflection. Stepmoms reflecting on this often admit that their partners are correct about this issue, yet they can't accept this or change until they get clear about their own sense of urgency for justice and the priorities for the couple. It's a tactics-vs.-strategy kind of situation worthy of more discussion with your partner. See Chapter 20.

- Could your partner be feeling disregarded, blamed and judged (as weak) by you for how he reacts to the actions of his kids and their bio-mom?

- Could your partner be feeling rage or despair because he perceives that his former *and* current partner both refuse to respect his needs, opinions and feelings?

- Could he feel powerless and hopeless? Does he feel he'll never be able to end all the conflict, be an excellent father and spend his time and energy having a happy life with you?

- Could he be scared at the passing thought that he would be better off alone? Does he want to stop the excruciating and perhaps emasculating conflicts stemming from his relationships with his ex-wife and kids? Does he want to avoid the painful, dream-shattering arguments with you but doesn't know how?

7. Wired to Serve and Eager to Please

I've been told a man often feels like he's been hardwired to please the one he loves. He wants to give his partner whatever she wants and derives a lot of self-esteem from being able to make his partner happy. A guy wants to be his partner's champion, her hero—the man of her dreams. This is likely how he feels when he first gets together with his new partner. It's a powerful, passionate, healing feeling. However, sometimes an ex-wife or a Stepmom pressure a guy to do something that he doesn't agree with in order to prove his love. The women may put him in a lose-lose situation when they are at odds with each other, expecting him to pick a side or pay the painful price. When this happens, he may feel tremendous internal pressure, and emotional rage and pain. He can feel abandoned by his new partner, blackmailed by his kids and tormented by his ex-wife. His desire to support his new partner can, come with a painful price tag that's easy for a stressed-out Stepmom to overlook (or diminish) as unimportant because her focus is solely on getting what she wants. This is extremely hurtful (provoking sadness, anger and despair) to many partners.

As mentioned earlier, when a woman first comes into a divorced father's life, she becomes his best friend, lover and greatest fan. A newbie Stepmom's initial unconditional support is often the magic elixir needed to mobilize her partner to action. However, if the stepkids and/or their bio-mom do something that conflicts with the beliefs, needs or wishes of the Stepmom, and if her new partner doesn't behave the way she wants him to, she can unwittingly become the blaming public, play-by-play announcer to her new partner. A Stepmom's shift from being fully supportive of her partner to being his personal critic can elicit shame, embarrassment and despair. The emotional energy this creates in her partner can be misdirected to acts of overt or passive anger toward a number of targets, including the Stepmom herself and other people in his life or his career, leaving both partners lonelier, angrier and less empathetic toward each other. This is a place where more conscious awareness and lovingkindness between partners can dramatically and quickly reduce stress and pave the way for reconnection.

Conflict between a Stepmom and the stepkids' bio-mom can blind the Stepmom to the needs, rights and feelings of the bio-dad. She may think she's fighting nobly for the rights of her partner and stepkids, all the while unaware of the pain and damage she's causing her partner and their relationship. So the challenge is this: how can a Stepmom be empathetic and supportive in this situation when she feels at risk or upset? So many uncomfortable issues can be avoided if a Stepmom is willing to empower her partner to follow his own guidance about how to deal with his kids and their bio-mom. Yes, you read that correctly! Further, when the circumstances of his choices impact the Stepmom in any negative way, this is the moment for the couple to go into serious, creative, problem-solving mode as a team. Rather than trying to change the stepkids or bio-mom, they'll feel closer and get better results if they immediately get focused on helping each other find ways to feel better and safe. When the Stepmom stops trying to get relief by changing the stepkids and bio-mom and instead turns to her beloved partner for loving support, many profoundly healing things can happen for them as a couple.

8. What Would Your Partner Do?

You can save yourself a lot of stress and damage control by asking yourself, *"What would [your partner's name] do?"*—and be sure to ask it before doing anything in reaction to a stepfamily situation that involves your stepkids or their bio-mom. When anything happens that upsets you, push in the proverbial clutch before you say or do anything. You know your partner pretty well, maybe very well at this point. When you can stay conscious enough to ask yourself what your partner would want you to do, you're going to get answers. Put your initial emotions or tactical ideas aside. Then make the choice to draw on your knowledge of your partner's values, needs, opinions and approaches. Part of you may not love the answers you get, but I can almost guarantee that if you listen to those answers, you will avoid a lot of stress and tension between you and your beloved. Even though it's hard to measure the value of the *absence* of potential tensions, this represents real anger, pain, time and energy saved.

If you're unsure about what your partner would do, do nothing—yet. If you find yourself furious, process your anger in healthy ways *before* you talk to your partner. No worries, you won't forget how you're feeling just because you've moved a nuclear bomb of anger or channeled a river of hurt, sadness or fear. I call it "the power of the pause" and giving yourself some time before acting rarely causes a problem. If you choose to support your partner by repeatedly handling stressful situations the way he would, or the way he's asked you to, he will hopefully appreciate your support—ideally with words and lots of heartfelt, loving actions. Over time, he will feel the relief and eventually stop bracing for the next daily report and argument. This will make things so much more relaxed between you—and you can become an even closer, stronger team with this strategy.

A Gift Beyond Measure

What else can you do to support your partner so he feels you understand the stress he's experiencing? If your partner's ex-wife happens to be uncooperative, it is a very good start to acknowledge that this can put your partner in a horrible, complex, unwinnable power struggle. Viewing the actions of an uncooperative bio-mom as an uncontrollable approaching storm—instead of looking at her as someone to try to control or change—enables you and your partner to work together to contain any potential damage by drawing on your combined strengths, resources and talents. You're especially powerful when you tap into the compassionate love you and your partner know is possible between you.

You and your partner fell in love yet somewhere along the way, you may have found your relationship negatively impacted by the actions of your stepkids or their bio-mom. At the beginning, mutual empathy and compassionate support came easily. However, the real gift of love to each other is vowing to offer and seek continued empathy and support for all the feelings that are generated by the actions of others. Find ways to create a safe space for each of you to openly share your feelings. This can make a huge and immediate difference for your relationship. Come up with a code word or phrase (even a non-verbal gesture) that's honored, used as shorthand and clearly understood to mean something like this:

> *"Honey, I need your compassion right now because I'm hurting. Will you please give me your full attention and listen to me without judging or blaming me so I can move through these feelings and be ready to work on a solution with you?"*

Whether you call it an empathic zone, a compassionate pow wow, a marriage meeting or simply a time out, pick some words and find a way to make time for this important relationship magic. Giving your partner more empathy and compassion takes conscious intention, attention, patience and time. The benefits of greater empathy for your partner are not guaranteed, but through all my experiences, I've seen that the rewards are lasting, positive and worth the effort.

For an additional chapter that offers your partner some ideas for ways to better support you, go to smoms.org/BonusChapters and click on "Twenty-Three Tips for the Partners of Stepmoms."

Section Five

A Stepmom and Her Stepkids

Children are, by nature, disempowered from birth. Their very survival is outside of their hands. They are fully at the mercy and impact (positive and negative) of their caregivers. Children of divorce are additionally disempowered by circumstances and rarely have anyone in their lives consciously capable of helping them process, heal and learn from their additional levels of rage, pain and fears.

Stepmothers can fill this often undetected need. As a Stepmom *you* are uniquely positioned to make a huge positive impact on the lives of your stepchildren. You can be that reliable, wise, loving, compassionate person who gives each stepchild the gift of being seen as a unique and valued individual. You can give them the experience of feeling respected and having a safe emotional space to express their true feelings. You can offer them kind and non-judgmental guidance and you can model healthy boundaries and strategies for becoming happier and stronger, without manipulating or controlling others, in spite of challenging life circumstances.

Stepmoms on a Mission

Robin's Story

August 2016

When I met my DH, he was in the middle of a volatile divorce. Bio-mom was trying to destroy him financially and personally. Her biggest offense was trying to use their daughter to gain custody, and doing everything from making up lies about him to attempting to get their daughter to say that Daddy hurt her. All was tossed out, but that didn't stop her from trying.

When my stepdaughter's bio-mom found out about me, things got worse. Imagine how heartbreaking it was to have a six-year-old tell me she hated me because mommy hates me. At that point her mom had not met me yet. We were dealing with a severe case of parental alienation. Bio-mom used her own daughter to try and sabotage my relationship with DH and push me out of the picture. Then, once the divorce was final and she had done enough damage, bio-mom moved out of state, leaving my DH with primary custody. This triggered more emotional and behavioral problems with my stepdaughter.

Now we were dealing with abandonment issues on top of the alienation. I suddenly had this big red target on my back and became the primary one my stepdaughter blamed for all her problems. In her mind, mommy was perfect and would come back if only she could get me to leave, or she could get her dad to kick me out. I also had my own daughter to worry about, who was eight when DH and I met. My stepdaughter often took out some of her issues on my daughter. Up until then I had successfully sheltered my daughter from the majority of the drama from my divorce and was worried about how all of this would affect her.

Despite all the drama and stress, I fell hard and fast for DH. I knew he was the one I wanted to spend my life with and I wanted this to work for all of us. So I started scouring the internet for articles and blogs about co-parenting and blended families. That's when I stumbled onto smoms.org. I joined the group and started reading others' stories. I was amazed at how similar some of their stories were. It was such a relief to know that I wasn't alone. I quickly became an active member and my life was forever changed. Cathryn and the other members of the group have helped me through some of our toughest times. They were there to help me through some common mistakes I made in the early days of learning how to navigate the world of being a stepmother. They were there to help celebrate my triumphs. They were there to give me advice, support, understanding, validation, and virtual shoulders to cry on. Without Cathryn, her workshops, and the ladies I've met on smoms.org, our family probably wouldn't have survived the first few years. They were my first real support system and are still my primary go-to spot. I've been supporting newbie members of our group more and more—helping me realize just how much I've learned and what a positive difference it makes to share our compassion and experiences with each other.

Our family dynamic now? We're not the Brady Bunch, that's for sure, but we're pretty darn awesome. My stepdaughter is now 13. She no longer hates me and actually thinks I'm pretty cool. We have our ups and downs but get along pretty well. Am I her "mom"? No. She has a mom and I have to respect that—but we're friends and sometimes, I even make parental decisions. She and my daughter, who is now 15, get along quite well and often act very much like sisters. Our house is calmer, less stressful, and happier. We have definitely "blended."

Robin
Stepmom since 2009
SMOM since 2010

January 2018 Update:

Just as this book was going to the publisher for formatting, Robin told me some wonderful news. She has just completed the first legal steps in the process of formally adopting her stepdaughter. Now 15 years old, her stepdaughter has grown to love her Stepmom in ever-increasing ways and is excited about being adopted by her Stepmom. Robin realizes once this happens she will no longer be a Stepmom but a proud mom of two wonderful daughters. What a journey she and her family have traveled since 2009. Her sister SMOMS are cheering for them all and the new happy family dreams they are creating together. The adoption is expected to be formalized this summer.

Twenty-Eight

The Loyalty Wars
When Stepkids Feel Stressed About Loving Their Stepmom

Almost every Stepmom I've met and worked with over the years started out wanting to have a great relationship with her new stepkids. It was all part of the happy family dream of a joyful new life with her partner. However, sometimes the friction between a Stepmom and her stepkids' bio-mom creates a rift between an enthusiastic well-meaning Stepmom and her stepkids resulting in some stepchildren experiencing what I call the Loyalty Wars. This is a bit different from parental alienation, which is the result of one parent's campaign against the other parent.

The Loyalty Wars arise when a bio-mom doesn't want her children to have a positive, caring relationship with their Stepmom. The stepkids feel stress because they get the message from their bio-mom that she will be hurt or angry if they care about their Stepmom. From experience, they learn (and now fear) they will be punished if they express (or dare to feel) any affection for their Stepmom.

In addition, stepkids learn their bio-mom will give them more of the love and attention they crave from her when they openly talk about the details of—and their dislike for—their stepmother and any aspect of life at their father's house. Directly or indirectly, these children are taught that enjoying time with their Stepmom would make them disloyal to their bio-mom. So when they have a kind, loving Stepmom who wants to connect with them when they're at dad's house, this creates a real dilemma for the kids. Even though it's impossible to know exactly what goes on in the bio-mom's house, the comments, actions and moods of your stepkids can indicate if they're experiencing an internal Loyalty War. If your stepkids don't feel free to have a positive relationship (or happy times) with you or openly express love for you, they may treat you badly at times because it's the only way they know how to relieve their fear and anxiety.

In the movie *Stepmom,* the young boy tries to prove his loyalty to his mother over his stepmother by saying, *"I'll hate her if you want me to, Mom."* He is willing to hate his stepmother—someone he obviously likes and cares for—just to please his bio-mom, and he says so in a sincere effort to prove his love for his mother and to help her feel better.

This is a painful and emotionally cruel circumstance for any stepchild. To make things even worse, it is well beyond a child's ability to process, prevent or resolve. Until an adult becomes conscious of the situation and chooses to help them, these stepkids are going to have to help themselves in the only ways their child-brains understand—by lashing out, tap dancing or shutting down. The emotional pressure will likely cause them to behave in angry and hurtful ways. Ironically, their negative behavior is usually directed toward the ones who are *not* perpetuating the conflict. Stepkids are put under tremendous stress by any hard-to-prove and impossible-to-escape manipulation from their bio-mom to push her children away from their stepmother. It can be difficult to recognize what's happening. And it is absolutely infuriating, completely unfair, heartbreaking to witness and even more difficult to accept that as stepmothers, we can't stop this situation. Why not? Because we have zero control over the behavior of our stepchildren's bio-mom.

Not having the power to control a bio-mom's behavior is a circumstance that stepmothers and their stepkids share. Recognizing this commonality with your stepkids and becoming conscious of the Loyalty Wars that impact all of you may help you have more compassion for them—and yourself. Thankfully, when you understand the loyalty power struggle a bio-mom may have established for her kids, you can do several things to reduce the negative impact on your stepkids. Understanding this situation can also free you from a lot of suffering and help you take your stepkids' actions less personally.

I'm writing this from the perspective of a stepmother and with the assumption that you're an ever-more-conscious and dedicated stepmother yourself. I can't speak to situations where the bio-dad is perpetuating a battle against the stepdad—I've never come across that situation. What I do know is that when a bio-mom is unwilling to behave (or at least perform) in a responsible way, accepting and talking positively (or at least civilly) to her children about their stepmother and life at dad's, an often-overlooked emotional Loyalty War can break out in the hearts and minds of the stepkids.

It doesn't take two parties to create a disturbance of this magnitude. The Stepmom may be sincerely trying her best and have no idea about what's going on. When the bio-mom denies her kids her blessing to have positive feelings and interactions with their Stepmom, this impedes their ability to enjoy a warm fulfilling stepchild-stepmother relationship. Sometimes the bio-mom reinforces this denial by threatening to withhold her love if she thinks her children care about their Stepmom. Kids may even sense this dynamic from their bio-mom without ever hearing a word spoken.

If your stepkids have a bio-mom who has been not-so-nice, openly uncooperative or outrightly adversarial toward you, you're probably dealing with many issues at once, and this particular relationship dynamic may elude you—at least at first. The Loyalty Wars involve a complicated tangle of emotions and relationships so please cut yourself some slack and be very compassionate with yourself if you didn't understand this before now.

The younger your stepkids are when you come into their lives, the more vulnerable they are to loyalty conflicts and guilty feelings because chances are good you've grown to know, like and even love each other over time. You may not be able to identify any loyalty-related internal conflicts in your stepkids until you know what to look for. The stress your stepkids feel is very difficult for them to understand and overcome because biological mothers have an almost unbreakable emotional connection with, and invisible—yet palpable—power over their children. This truth can be a hard thing to accept. Yet once you accept it, you can begin to make changes in *your* actions that reduce your stepkids' stress and help them get off the emotional battlefield.

It's well known that the biological and energetic connection between mother and child is so strong that words aren't even needed for a not-so-cooperative bio-mom to declare a Loyalty War on her children's stepmother. This places the children in an emotional tug-of-war with painful consequences, no matter what the kids may do or say. This is such a tragic and unfair situation. A bio-mom who requires her children to prove their love for her by not loving someone else is being unkind and selfish, with serious negative impact. This is noteworthy. Whether an uncooperative bio-mom uses words or not, she has ways to make her point very clear, even to very young kids. Children learn quickly that they pay a painful price for defying their bio-mom in any way. Stepchildren caught in the Loyalty Wars can't take a stand for their rights to love anyone they want to, in this case their Stepmom, until they believe they're strong enough to endure the feared or experienced wrath and potential shunning of their own mother—if they ever reach that point. In the meantime, children will often do whatever it takes to prove to their mother that they don't care for their stepmother, both to get their mother's loving attention and to avoid her punishments. If this issue extends to the bio-mom pressuring the children to push their father away too, then parental alienation issues and damages are now also in the works. Again, the Loyalty War I'm going to focus on here is initiated by a bio-mom unwilling for her kids to have a loving connection with their Stepmom.

On the positive side, the bio-moms who process their feelings about divorce and their children's stepmothers in healthy ways are honored and appreciated by Stepmoms on a Mission. Stepmothers whose stepchildren have civil or kind bio-moms are fortunate in immeasurable ways. There are plenty of thoughtful and responsible bio-moms out there. Many Stepmoms on a Mission are also divorced bio-moms whose own children have a stepmother. These bio-moms are committed to working through (and taking responsibility for) their feelings privately because they want their bio-kids to have as many loving adults in their lives as possible. All the kids with kind and civil bio-moms are very lucky indeed, and have won the parental lottery. It's all chance since there's very little, if anything, that both children and stepmothers can do about the attitude and actions of the bio-moms in their lives.

The Attitude of Bio-Moms

The ugly side of competition between women who "share" relationships with the same man or children is certainly a common dynamic that transcends stepfamily issues. However, you can save yourself a lot of hassles if you notice and accept the behaviors of your partner's ex-wife early on, resisting the urge to believe you can change her. If she is angry about the divorce, feels she has been wronged or acts determined to get revenge, then she has a full plate of stresses that may not make her an ideal candidate for being a parenting ally. This may be further compounded if she is worried about her financial security or about being a single parent.

Some bio-moms are OK with their kids having a terrific relationship with their dad and their Stepmom. Others are not, and they may do things to destroy their kids' connection with their dad and/or Stepmom. Some bio-moms have an acceptable working relationship with their ex-husband (your partner) until another woman comes into the picture, and then things change for the worse—a little or a lot. Sometimes a bio-mom is truly focused on the well-being of her children, doing everything she can to shield them from her upsetting emotions about you or the divorce because she wants to help them through their pain and the adjustments in their lives. However, sometimes a bio-mom, for whatever reasons, stops being cooperative and begins to act in hostile and not-so-cooperative ways when her ex-husband (your partner) starts a new relationship with you. Although this may not be entirely shocking, it can be disappointing and noteworthy when it happens to you.

I'm bringing this up because I want you to recall the attitude of your stepkids' bio-mom when you first arrived on the scene as the new Stepmom—married or not. How did she react to your presence? Did her interactions with your partner change in any way? Did she make any statements or demands about your role in her kids' lives? Was she willing to get along with you or not? How did she treat you?

To Do—or Not To Do?

A common, understandable mistake many newbie stepmothers make (in their enthusiasm for a happy stepfamily) is thinking that any negative behaviors from a bio-mom will lessen over time or that the bio-mom can become kinder or more civil once she sees the Stepmom's acts of kindness and respect. A bio-mom may indeed change her behavior over time, positively or negatively, but it's not likely to be because of anything you do. There are exceptions, happily, but if there's a Loyalty War going on for your stepkids, chances are that your efforts to get along will only cause the bio-mom to be more uncooperative. I know this isn't what you want to hear. So, what can you do to improve your situation?

Be willing to listen to and believe your partner when he tells you about his ex-wife. Ask your partner to help you clearly recognize and fully understand the current attitude/behaviors of your stepkids' bio-mom. Process your feelings about the reality you've inherited. Then turn your attention to something you can control. Work with your partner and start planning your life, making your choices and accepting the bio-mom's behavior as an unchangeable fact of your stepfamily situation. From a conscious, awake state of mind as a talented, savvy, adult woman, you can work with the facts to contain any negative impact from the bio-mom and maintain your well-being, helping your stepkids in the process. Embracing your reality as early as possible will save you unfathomable stress and immeasurable energy, pain and anger. You can make all the respectful gestures you'd like and treat the bio-mom with kindness and compassion for her situation (and you should do this because it's who you are) but this will not likely impact the actions of a bio-mom who is determined to not get along with you. See Chapter 33.

To take back your power and positively influence any Loyalty-War situation you identify (and which you've inherited, not caused), you first have to recognize what's happening. Once you do, you'll probably feel a new wave of compassion for your stepkids—no matter how badly they may have behaved toward you. You may also find that your heart opens up (even more) to your stepkids, especially if you've already grown to care for them.

You may surprise yourself by feeling a newfound compassion for the bio-mom when you stop to realize that the divorce is costing her time with her kids. If you have your own kids, this may be even easier to understand. If you're a mother-by-marriage (a Stepmom without bio-kids of your own) you may want to choose to suspend any judgments and take a moment to imagine how you might feel if she had partial custody of your beloved pets. Oh my! This analogy usually helps Stepmoms without their own bio-kids have a bit more compassion for the feelings of an uncooperative bio-mom.

Still, if you're being ignored or treated unkindly, you will feel additional waves of anger at the unfairness of the situation and the negative impact on your life—even if you're trying hard to be compassionate with her and with yourself. This is all completely understandable. Sometimes emotions aren't singular or stand-alone. You can have compassion *and* resentment. You can be empathetic *and* furious. Do your best to make room for whatever emotions show themselves. For your own well-being and sanity, these intense feelings need to be honored and processed in healthy ways. Please help yourself by first doing this work in the emotional realm so you don't have to get physically sick. For right now let's focus on your stepkids and how you can help free them from this painful, emotional, unwinnable power struggle.

Observe Your Stepkids

Behavior #1: Your stepkids may feel the need to compare anything you do or that happens at dad's by commenting on how the same issue is handled by bio-mom or is experienced at their bio-mom's. The stepchildren's comparisons almost always make the bio-mom's choices and possessions as good as—or better than—yours and dad's so the kids can feel they're being loyal to their bio-mom. See Chapter 37, Tip #21 for ideas.

Behavior #2: Your stepchildren may suddenly express the need to call or text their bio-mom and connect with her *"right now"* in the middle of a happy family moment at dad's or with you. They may feel guilty when having so much fun and then suddenly realize they're not thinking about their bio-mom in their moments of joy. The only thing they may know to do to reduce their guilt, anxiety or fear of getting in trouble is to stop the fun, contact their bio-mom immediately and report to her what's happening. Maybe she'll be happy about it and let them continue—and maybe not. The young ones naturally desire their bio-mom's approval for having fun. The tweens and teens may discover they can start lying to their bio-mom to save them from punishment and to allow them to enjoy their Stepmom and time at dad's. But until they understand this survival tactic, they may reach out in the midst of a happy time to try to calm their anxiety.

When they interrupt a joyful time with you or at their dad's, they may feel they're saving themselves some future punishment from their bio-mom. Maybe they believe they'll score some points and get extra attention or rewards from their bio-mom for trying to ruin—or at least stall—the happy moments with you and at dad's. Sometimes the urge to call their bio-mom relieves the stress of being grilled for details when they go back to her house. As annoying as it is, not allowing the call or text can generate genuine fear and anxiety, especially in young, pre-teen stepkids.

Suggested response to their actions: Let them make the call or send the text. Do your best to be relaxed and casual about it. View it like they are calling an official time-out or as if they were excusing themselves to go to the bathroom—no big deal. When they return, chances are good they'll be a bit subdued so you're going to have to be wise, caring and creative about how to proceed to prevent bio-mom's impact from ruining your good times. Making your stepkids wrong or taking your frustrations out on them when they're unconsciously just trying to ease their internal pressure only creates more emotional shrapnel. As the adult, you will ideally process your feelings privately and in healthy ways out of your stepkids' sight. You can interrupt the cycle and reduce the stress for you and your stepkids with your new awareness of (and response to) what's happening.

Behavior #3: Your stepchildren may suddenly feel reluctant to be openly happy or to joyfully participate in fun activities they've previously enjoyed. Your stepkids may express some version of *"My mom might not like it,"* or *"My mom said she wanted to be the first one to do this with me,"* or *"My mom told me doing this was stupid or wrong."* One stepchild, age 10, told her Stepmom she couldn't participate in any future Christmas rituals with her dad and stepmother because it upset her mom too much to think of her child doing those things without her. This is so sad for the child and her dad and Stepmom.

FYI: This behavior is actually an early form of martyrdom-in-training. It's martyr-like for stepkids to deny themselves pleasure and fun while they are with their dad, just to prove their love and loyalty to the bio-mom. However, remembering that your stepkids are likely just trying to avoid being punished can make it easier to be compassionate and patient with them. When your stepchildren are dealing with an uncooperative bio-mom, they can feel powerless and may use whatever they know to gain favor with her so they can minimize their emotional stress. It can be a huge relief to your stepkids when you recognize this behavior. By your actions, you can help them see they're not trapped between being happy with you and dad (making bio-mom angry with them) and being angry and unhappy with you (making bio-mom happy with them). This is an act of true lovingkindness on your part.

You can help your stepkids find new options—even if they never understand how you're helping them. Their little baby/child-brains aren't capable of forming alternatives. Whatever they are doing is the best they can conjure. Even as teens, children rarely find a healthy pathway through this problem without outside help. Offering your help is one tremendously unselfish life-impacting gift a Stepmom on a Mission can give her stepkids.

Behavior #4: Your stepchildren may pick fights and cause arguments right before returning to their bio-mom's to make it easier to leave you and their dad. It also gives them "material" to genuinely complain about to bio-mom in exchange for her attention. This tactic is often a result of an uncooperative bio-mom showing her kids that they'll get her love and approval for as long as they have anything negative to say about you or their dad. The bio-mom may have also shown the kids (perhaps never having said a word) that they can expect a negative, neutral or shunning reaction from her when they share a happy Stepmom or dad story.

If you notice disruptive behavior occurring among your stepkids right before they leave your house, you can resist taking the bait and instead be as patient and empathetic as possible. The best and easier way to avoid (or at least temper) this issue and minimize the stress for all of you is to create exchanges with an interim place (and time) in between being at either parent's home. For example, use the school day, a playdate, a team sporting event or other activity to avoid the direct bio-mom/dad exchange.

Behavior #5: Your stepchildren may seem annoyed or hesitant to answer your questions about his/her time away from your home. Your stepkids may even ask you to stop asking them about their time at their bio-mom's because it feels like too much pressure to remember all the details. This is not them trying to be mean to you. If their bio-mom has told them not to share certain things, or anything, about their life with her, your questions may put the stepkids under a lot of stress (between a rock and a hard place) as they struggle to anticipate what you will ask, to try to keep secrets to avoid getting in trouble or feeling disloyal to their bio-mom.

If you sense this may be an issue, even if your stepkids have not said anything about it to you, ask them if they'd prefer you not ask them about their lives with their bio-mom. Experience with this has been pretty consistent—*"yes please stop asking us."* If possible, release them from having to keep secrets about life at your home. By offering this freedom and asking them what they want, you demonstrate respect for their feelings. You can continue to show them you care and switch your question to, *"How are you?"* whenever they return from time with their bio-mom. In this way, you show them you're interested *and* you give them control over what they share without causing them to feel any pressure to be a double agent. It's certainly tempting to want to know what's going on when your stepkids are with their bio-mom, but as an adult, it's merciful, respectful and kind to help your stepkids feel they can relax and be themselves when they're with you.

Age Impacts Their Vulnerability

The Loyalty Wars seem to be particularly impactful and effective (for the bio-mom) with children around the ages 4-13. At some point, a stepchild will figure out what's going on but not usually during these important years. When they're older, their frustration, anger and reactions to the situation may become more correctly and effectively focused (toward their bio-mom) even if they don't know how to change things once they understand what's happening—if they ever do. In the meantime, they learn ways to survive, express their anger and numb the pain. At some point they may enter the game as an active player. They may choose to manage their mother by learning they're now free to have a great time with dad and Stepmom and then make up tales of woe when talking with their bio-mom in order to get her attention, approval and maybe permission from her to do things or get things from her. If your stepkids have an uncooperative bio-mom who behaves in ways that lead you to believe she might be suffering from narcissism, borderline personality disorder, bi-polar disorder or other mental-health or personality disorders, you can teach your stepkids emotional and behavioral survival tactics, for their own well-being, when the timing and their maturity is right. See Chapters 35 and 36 for more about dealing with continually uncooperative bio-moms.

Some stepkids will remain trapped indefinitely by the Loyalty Wars and won't figure out how to have relationships with both their bio-mom and Stepmom. When they choose to avoid the pain of bio-mom's rejection by rejecting their Stepmom, they may never be able to understand or admit what they've missed out on by not being free to connect with their Stepmom. This is tragic and much too common in stepfamilies that are under stress from uncooperative bio-moms. Parental alienation can grow out of this dynamic, sadly often resulting in stepkids looking at their dad as just a source of money. Unless or until the stepkids see what their bio-mom is doing, they're at the mercy of her treatment. This Loyalty War rarely ends until children grow strong enough to call out their mother on any of her hurtful behavior, realizing that they can indeed survive her anger or rejection and want to feel free to love both parents and their Stepmom (and Stepdad). In the meantime, a Stepmom has an opportunity to play an important role in her stepkids' lives. There are things you can do to help your stepkids if they're experiencing this difficult circumstance.

What You Can Do?

Suggestion #1: You can recognize and accept the conflict for what it is and respond to it as a wise, loving adult. Trying to get someone to get along, play fair or do the right thing—particularly when they've shown repeatedly that they're not interested in doing so—is a losing battle and a huge energy drain on you and your relationships. Knowing what you now know, you can make the conscious choice to direct all your efforts and energy toward what you can do to help the stepkids. For the sake of your sanity and your stepkids' well-being, make the choice to accept that the bio-mom is who she is. See Chapters 18, 19 and Sections Four and Five for more support with this often difficult yet always empowering decision.

Suggestion #2: You can choose to take *nothing* personally. Once you realize that your stepkids are being asked, expected, manipulated or threatened to pick their bio-mom over you, compassion for your stepkids will likely flow freely. Whether your partner keeps trying to get the bio-mom to behave or you both choose to let go of trying to change the bio-mom's actions and instead focus on helping the stepkids, you can help the children feel more freedom and relief when they're at their dad's and with you. Initially, this can be a difficult and painful choice for you because it probably means not doing as many things as you would genuinely like to do with your stepkids. It's also difficult to be treated badly by children so desperate for their bio-mom's love. This is not your fault. You may have to make the choice *"to do or not to do"* from one moment to the next. That's OK. Thankfully you can choose where you put your attention over and over again as needed. You can also find many other ways to love and care for your stepkids that do not trigger an emotional tug of war between you and their bio-mom—with the kids feeling pulled apart in the middle. It's just about being conscious of what's happening and then being willing to look for responsible and creative options.

Suggestion #3: Take the high road and step away from the invisible power struggle with bio-mom. You can choose to take the more self-protective and honorable path. You have the power to resist the understandable urge to counter-attack any actions she may make. This urge is not a bad thing, it's human nature. It may make it easier to stop reacting to the bio-mom when you realize that getting "hooked" by her actions and reacting outwardly to her behaviors only make things worse. Sad and true. When you react to sticky issues or even increase your involvement and activities with your stepkids, you can make the stepkids feel like they're caught in an emotional ping pong game where they feel batted around, out of control and hurt—in spite of your good intentions. The reality is they're right about this situation. They *are* trapped—powerless and therefore furious about it at varying levels of consciousness. You have the ability to end this war for them, you really do! As an adult woman (meaning you are consciously staying out of old survival or defensive strategies) you have healthy ways to process your rage and grief about your unchangeable reality. I encourage you to honor all your feelings, get lots of support for what you're going through *and* help your stepkids. They may never know what you're doing. They may never thank you for your help. However, they will feel an immediate, very tangible emotional relief—the proverbial breath of new, "it's OK-to-relax," fresh air. Ahhhh! See Chapter 16 for an approach for dealing with unchangeable stepfamily realities.

Brace yourself for this next suggestion—

Suggestion #4: Give your stepkids the attention they want even when they're referring to their bio-mom. By focusing on their natural need for attention and your inner peace instead of the subject matter at hand, you too can find relief, even when they're talking about, comparing you to or blatantly appeasing someone who is causing you pain. You can give your stepkids a true gift of your loving attention by choosing to ignore any annoyance and instead to help build their sense of self-worth.

Your Stepkids Might Say:

> "My mom puts bacon in my grilled cheese."
> "My mom got a big promotion at work."
> "My mom is younger than you."
> "My mom says chiropractors are wackos."
> "My mom puts apples in her dressing, not sausage like you."

Sometimes, these comments can be deeply upsetting in ways that are difficult to describe until you understand your stepkids' underlying motives for sharing with you. Usually they're not trying to make you angry—unless their bio-mom feeds them lines to say to you. In this case ignoring them is a "win" for you because you didn't give the jabs any attention. They're usually just trying to get your attention and your approval. Really—hear me out on this one! If they get attention from their bio-mom by talking about you, they may see that as the only way to get your attention—talking about her. Children need attention. They need mirrors to help them learn about themselves and they will choose negative attention over zero attention. Knowing this and assuming you want to help your stepkids develop a healthy sense of self, you can look at anything they say about their bio-mom and life with her as requests to be seen. They're just children needing loving attention without always knowing how to go about it.

Going forward, rather than gritting your teeth when your stepkids mention their bio-mom, or resentfully explaining to a child your choice of car or your family recipes or any other of the many comparisons they may bring up, try this—say, "How about that." It works! It also saves you a lot of stress and the anxiety of anticipating their comments because now you have a pithy, almost fun, healthy and kind response. While you can't control what the kids say (and they know that), you can control your responses and what you say.

Stepkids are unconsciously looking for their own emotional antidote for their internal stress. When they can say something good about their bio-mom and get attention from you (positive or negative), they feel they don't have to feel badly about it. They feel they're not going to get in trouble with bio-mom if a sibling overhears and tattles on them. As a matter of fact, some stepkids will even get kudos from their bio-mom by reporting that they said something positive about her to their Stepmom. Can you see how your stepkids may just be trying to survive the uncontrollable conditions of life with their uncooperative bio-mom?

As you can give your stepkids *positive, cheerful* support for their observations, be they about their bio-mom's world, school or anything else, the stepkids will feel acknowledged, respected, valued and happy. They will relax more and you'll probably see their delight as well. This might seem fake at first but an enthusiastic (not sarcastic) "how about that" in response to whatever they say really does seem to satisfy their need to be seen and, if necessary, to make their bio-mom bigger than you in their loyalty-war-conscious minds. Feeling seen, they're usually OK to move on to other things, especially if you're willing to give them your positive attention. Your response, "how about that," can also free them from feeling guilty that they're having a good time with you. You're giving them the loving attention they're looking for without exacting a conditional, uncomfortable price from them. The long-term emotional benefit of this strategy is that it models a new way of loving and being loved. It shows stepkids another way of being mothered and being a mother. There's really no way to measure the value of this gift to your stepkids—and to their future children. See Chapter 37, Tip #21 for more about the benefits and uses of the "how about that" response.

Suggestion #5: You can protect your relationship with your stepkids by recognizing what's happening and backing off whenever you observe that your participation is causing them emotional stress. I realize that this suggestion is going to bump up against genuine feelings of *"that's not fair"* or *"I love my stepkids. I want to go the recital, etc.,"* and very strong understandable beliefs like *"I have a right to be involved."* I get it and you're right in my way of seeing things. However, as adults we have more resources and sophisticated options than your stepkids, so this is me urging you to do what you can to help your stepchildren (because they can't help themselves), then get the help you need to process whatever you're feeling.

The conscious choice to remove yourself from some stepkid activities helps you disengage from any energetic competition with your stepkids' bio-mom. With your withdrawal from the loyalty-war dynamic, you give your stepkids a dose of lovingkindness. Your stepkids are very likely going to feel and be visibly relieved when they perceive you withdrawing from any unspoken, emotional power struggles with their bio-mom. They'll feel better even if they don't understand exactly why. We're often told by experts to "put the kids first." Well, this is a priceless and positive opportunity for putting your feelings aside for the moment and helping your stepkids feel as comfortable and unstressed as possible. Again, because you're an adult, you can later find healthy ways to take care of your own, equally important and valid feelings.

If being at the same events with their bio-mom causes your stepkids stress, this is another place where stepping back is an act of truly unselfish love. If the bio-mom makes her own children feel badly about acknowledging or hanging out with you in public, it will ease their pressure when you stop interacting with them in public or maybe even stop attending public events altogether. Yes, you're right. This is another hard-to-hear (or read) suggestion. One SMOM taught her stepkids how to wink at her after they told her they'd gotten in trouble when their bio-mom saw them waving at her at a basketball game. Sadly the winking only lasted a couple of months until the bio-mom saw one of them winking and figured out it was a signal to the Stepmom. The stepkids got in trouble when they admitted they did this to their bio-mom—and never did it again.

I know that even pondering the idea of not doing as much with your stepkids in public may activate deep issues of unfairness. You may feel rejected and left out. You may feel angry. Still, based on the experiences of many stepmothers, withdrawing can be a truly loving gift to your stepkids, even as hard as it is for you. At some point your stepkids understand you have the ability to help them. They realize your presence is causing them pain and that they don't have the capability to help themselves in this situation. Sometimes your stepkids are at the mercy of your choices—or said in another way, sometimes you have the power to relieve your stepkids of stress they have no other way to stop.

If this is your situation, it's time to get creative and tend to your well-being. Consider looking for other ways to be involved even if you're not physically present. You or your partner could videotape things or use technology like Skype or FaceTime when it makes sense. It's much easier nowadays to find ways to witness events if not physically present. Thank goodness! You may want to explain to your stepchildren that you're staying away because their bio-mom isn't comfortable with your presence at the event—this way they know it's not that you don't want to be there. This can be a bit tricky depending on the personality of your stepkids' bio-mom, so check with your partner about how to explain the reason for your absence. I believe kids can sense the truth. I like the word "uncomfortable" because it's not judgmental or blaming, just descriptive and true.

Depending on your stepkids' ages, you can explain to them that since your desire, as their Stepmom, is to make things less stressful for them, you're going to step back for now. You can ask them to share all the details when they return to your home—if they want to. This gives them a chance to remember and re-live fun times with a devoted audience—or not—but either way you're giving *them* the power of choice. Stepmothers faced with uncooperative bio-moms can find themselves having to miss out on some important stepkids' events, and that really hurts! On the other hand, you are doing something that takes courage for the good of children you care about, and that feels empowering. Sometimes you may even have to defend yourself and stand up for your rights to participate with your stepkids and partner—or worse, deal with outright lies. If this is the case for you, taking care of your own feelings in healthy ways is a loving thing for you to do for your family and can keep you from feeling resentful toward your stepkids or your partner.

Suggestion #6: You can take the pressure off your marriage and stop expecting your partner to do something to mitigate his children's loyalty pressures if he isn't already inclined to do so. Unfortunately it's not against the law to do what many uncooperative bio-moms do. And remember, bio-moms—both friendly and uncooperative—have been controlling their kids verbally and non-verbally forever. We need to choose to look for healthy ways to contain and manage any negative impact that uncooperative bio-mom behaviors may have. It's also impossible to prove destructive loyalty pressure and sometimes even parental alienation without getting the stepkids in the middle. Just keep in mind that if you back away and begin to support your stepkids in new, non-competing ways, as difficult as you may find this to be, they feel the positive difference immediately. You'll see the change in them even if they can't express it.

When Doing Less Helps More

Imagine a Stepmom has been joyfully and generously engaging with her stepkids, eager for a mutually happy relationship. As a result of this Stepmom's effort to connect, her stepkids find themselves growing to care about her and soaking up her lovingkindness, particularly in areas and ways that their own bio-mom is not giving them love and attention. Things are going well between this Stepmom and her stepkids. They are connected and happy. The next day or the next visit—POW! Out of the blue, the stepkids act angry and cold to their stepmother and treat her as if she's the enemy. Or maybe they demonstrate a more passive and annoyed lack of interest in their Stepmom. This surprising evidence of a festering Loyalty War can manifest in several ways.

Loyalty War Symptoms

- After a period of family fun with your stepkids, they become angry in a sudden, almost Jeckyl/Hyde kind of way and refuse to interact with you, implying you've done something to upset them. They can't explain their anger or behavior because they don't really understand it either.

- Shortly after doing something loving or thoughtful or after you've gone out of your way to help your stepkids by filling a mothering role you know they've not had (or can't get) from their own mother, the stepkids wake up the next day or return from time with bio-mom acting cold or overtly angry toward you without being able to give you a reason why.

- After a calm, happy visit or two where you felt particularly close to your stepkids through giving them lots of undivided attention, time and effort on a specific project (perhaps you created a happy memory with them), one or more of your stepkids gets really angry at you for no apparent reason, breaking your loving connection without explanation or any interest in reconnecting with you.

Emotional Dilemma—My Theory

The painful disconnect between a Stepmom and any of her stepkids can be heartbreaking, frustrating and confusing. Below is my take on what's happening. Full disclosure: I have no formal study or clinical trial to corroborate my theory. That said, I've had dozens, maybe hundreds of Stepmoms over the years confirm this same experience *and* the success of the tactics I'm about to suggest.

When a Stepmom treats her stepkids with authentic, unconditional, loving attention and does things for them that her stepkids might wish their own mother would do, it seems to set off an inner, impossible-to-process alarm of hurt (anger and sadness) in the stepkids. This may not affect all stepkids in the same way or even at all. It may happen at different times or ages. I believe the children get angry because they suddenly have new thoughts that upset and confuse them. *"How can a woman not related to me possibly treat me more kindly than my own mother?" "How come she's doing this with me (or for me) when my own mother won't?"* As a result of these unwelcome inner queries, they may feel confused, angry or even furious—a lot of intense emotions stirred up.

Sometimes, when stepkids realize how much they love their Stepmom, their warm feelings are followed by a deep anxiety-producing wave of guilt. This is especially true if they believe their bio-mom isn't going to approve and will somehow find out about their disloyalty and punish them. While their anger may actually be at their bio-mom, children often can't admit this and don't know how to process their anger, or they don't feel safe getting angry at their own bio-mom, fearing her rejection. So instead, they lash out at their Stepmom, finding it much easier to believe she's the one causing their internal distress. In a way, they're correct.

They may be thinking that if their Stepmom would just stop doing things that made them feel close to her (which triggers their guilt), they'd feel better—well, actually just less guilty. Problem seemingly solved. In the stepkids' minds, the Stepmom's lovingkindness for them, their love for her and now any newly realized anger at their bio-mom causes the stepkids uncomfortable feelings on varying levels of awareness, depending on their emotional maturity.

To endure their stress, the stepkids may believe the answer is to stay angrier than they are sad—in a situation where part of them knows they're powerless. They can't allow themselves to admit (or feel) the full impact of anxiety and fear they endure so they lash out at their Stepmom instead of their bio-mom. The choice to get angry (instead of feeling sad) makes them feel a bit more in control of their lives, even if just for a few moments. They will also usually minimize or deny their pain over losing connection with their Stepmom and rationalize their anger to stay numb to pain they don't know how to handle any other way. This tangle of feelings can be caused by:

- Their instinctive longing/need to be loved by their own mother.

- The desire to be seen and mothered in a loving way.

- The guilt, shame or self-blame they feel at enjoying love from their stepmother.

- Their rage at feeling forced to choose between bio-mom and Stepmom instead of having the freedom to love (and be loved by) both of them.

The intensity and complexity of all these strong emotions is just too much for most children to process so they do the best they can to survive. The only thing their baby/child brains can think of to stop their internal anxiety and pressure is to direct their emotional energy toward being angry at their Stepmom—the disposable parent. *Ouch!*

By getting angry at you, they feel the relief of moving the too-big-for-me-to-handle energy of fear and anger, eliminating their guilt and telling themselves (hoping really) they'll get some appreciation and more love from their bio-mom. Poor dears! That's a lot of feelings to deal with as a child.

It may help you feel less hurt about your stepkids' decisions to lash out at you if you remember that children usually lash out at the "parent" whose love they believe can withstand their antics. If you see this outburst of anger happening after a period of happiness and affection between you and your stepkids, it will now make more sense to you. Hopefully, by understanding their dilemma, having compassion for their stress and reminding yourself that they're just children trapped in a complex and painful situation, you won't take their actions to heart or get upset with them.

Heartbreaking True Story

A SMOM working through this issue in one of my workshops shared the story of what brought her nine-year-old stepson's Loyalty War issue to her attention. She realized he was feeling the pain and conflict of loving both his bio-mom and his Stepmom. This is her story, paraphrased from my notes and used with her permission.

One morning, after a fun week with his dad and Stepmom and while preparing to return to his bio-mom, he must have recognized his painful dilemma. While his Stepmom was chatting away helping load his backpack, her stepson became suddenly still. With alligator tears flowing, he looked his Stepmom in the eyes and said quietly, *"My life would be so much easier if you weren't in it."* In a moment of profound, shared understanding, she hugged tightly the child she loved, then suggested to her husband that he be the one to take his son back to the bio-mom's house. It was a transformational moment for this Stepmom and thankfully she realized what was happening.

This child wasn't trying to be mean, just stating a sad truth for both of them. Upon hearing his words, the Stepmom knew she had to back away from the child she'd grown to love because she had the power to help in a significant way. From that point forward, she stayed away from most public events and looked for ways to connect with her stepson that didn't trigger disloyalty or guilt. While the stepchild may never know the price she lovingly paid to ease his pain and stress, she knows she did the kind thing—the right thing for the child's well-being. It took her a while to process her own grief and rage about this situation. She did her work to help herself and to avoid resenting her stepson so they could maintain as loving a connection as possible.

Helping Your Stepkids

As an awake, adult woman, you have the opportunity to make an unselfish choice for the well-being of your stepkids—as a loving Stepmom, rather than as a victim of circumstances—even when it hurts your feelings. You have the power to make this choice because you are aware of what's happening and know how to help yourself. It's a bit like the King Solomon story in the Bible, only in this circumstance, it's the stepmother who makes the more loving choice to prevent her stepkids from feeling emotionally cut in two.

You can reduce your stepkids' pain and suffering by first understanding the situation, recognizing through observation that they may be experiencing stress. Then, you can do less for and with them. *Ouch, again!* Wherever their bio-mom might see and feel competition with you, you can resist the natural urge to display your happiness, pride and other parental feelings when it comes to your stepkids. This may mean not posting as many pictures (or any) on social media, not sharing the happy family stories in the annual holiday cards, not talking about the details of the fun you and the stepkids had with their dad, or avoiding situations where others may unintentionally say things to the stepkids (or worse to the bio-mom) that make them feel guilty (and perhaps be punished) for loving you.

In essence, you're downplaying the outward and public expression of your connection with your own stepchildren to help them feel less anxious about being punished by their bio-mom and less guilty about how they feel. It's a bit like keeping your relationship with your stepkids a secret. Isn't it odd to realize that you can actually make it easier for your stepkids to get along with you by doing fewer nice things for and with them? It's a real head-scratcher at first, that's why it's hard to figure out and even harder to know what to do about it. Now that you see this from an expanded viewpoint with new context, you may reflect on your stepkids' past actions in new ways that are much less hurtful than believing they're rejecting you.

Just think—you can help your stepkids manage their complex emotions and reduce the stress of their life circumstances by changing your actions. That's a Stepmom superpower! When you reduce the overtness of your expressions of love for them, it assuages and maybe even eliminates their anxiety, fear of punishment and guilt. By reducing opportunities for them to compare the actions of you and their bio-mom, you and your stepkids can share more calm, pleasant times together because their emotions are less jubilant and therefore less likely to trigger a sense of disloyalty.

It's about looking for new ways to love, do for and be with them that aren't overtly about mothering. This can take a bit of creativity since mothering is often a Stepmom's default role and responsibility. It's about consciously choosing to give more meaning to the benefits your stepchildren reap from your mindful attention and lovingkindness, and assigning less significance to the stuff and activities you may be sharing with them now. Reflecting on your history with your stepchildren will give you all the evidence you need to understand their possible Loyalty War triggers. Each child will have different triggers because they have different needs due to their respective ages, personalities and relationships with their bio-mom. Evidence of a Loyalty War is usually easy to spot once you understand what to look for in each situation.

This next recommendation can be challenging and eventually fun once you work through your own grief—at every opportunity find ways to give credit to anything or anyone *other than you* for any shared joyful experiences. This can enable and extend your happy times by helping your stepkids not see a given event as a bio-mom vs. Stepmom thing—therefore avoiding triggering their guilt, anger, fear of being punished or need to be angry at you. For example, you can say great things about (and bring their attention to) some aspect of the movie you just saw, the pool you swam in, the coolness of their new shirt, the fun your parents create for everyone when they visit, the exciting results of sports activities they played in, attended or just watched, or the neighborhood block party you all attended, recognizing all these events as the cause for the joy your stepkids are feeling at any particular time. *You* know what you did, even if you're quiet about claiming any credit. Hopefully, your partner will adore you even more for your significant contribution to his kids' emotional well-being. By using this diversionary tactic, you make it possible for your stepkids to be with you during all these fun times because they can attribute their happiness to other things. And these may very well be things that their bio-mom has not made them feel guilty for enjoying. Can you see this loophole in the loyalty-war power struggle?

If you handle things the way I suggest, these tactics may initially seem harsh, outrageous, unfair and maybe even mean or wrong—even in spite of all the benefits they can have for your stepkids. These proposed approaches present you with both a tremendous emotional challenge and a significant healing, learning and growth opportunity. I understand that the very idea of choosing to help your stepkids by reducing the public, loving, happy activities you share with them may initially make you angry, sad or resentful. This is especially true in a situation where your rights, authority and roles may already be adversely affected by an uncooperative bio-mom. As you are helping your stepkids (or even pondering the possibility) you may experience an almost overwhelming sense of raging feelings. It makes complete sense. Hopefully, after you've thought about these recommendations for a bit and vigorously processed your feelings from a new elevated perspective, this all makes sense and may even explain a lot of previous stepkids' behaviors.

Your new choices are certainly going to stir up some feelings and more than likely some unhealed emotional wounds from your past that you may (or may not) be aware you're carrying. I can also tell you that if you're facing this or any other stressful situation in your stepfamily life, you can use *every single feeling that you have to become more self-aware, stronger, more healed and more empowered*—if you're willing to do this emotion-processing work. It will be easier to handle your feelings, making these loving choices (and their impact) much more doable. You'll see you how your new choices can generate new levels of self-esteem and self-respect if you have support. Implementing these actions for the good of your stepkids, while helping yourself work through your own feelings, is not only responsible but also admirable, with potentially life-changing benefits for you, your partner and stepkids.

Delightful, Potential Benefits

Following these suggestions can also lead you, your partner and your stepkids to have a lot more fun together, even if you don't talk about it as much. Ever been in a severe storm where plans are ruined, everyone has to help prepare and maybe the power goes out? Have you discovered that in these situations, when you work together it turns out to be a fun, memorable adventure shared by all? Your new interactions with your stepkids can have the same kind of surprisingly happy result. You can achieve this result for yourself with a positive attitude, an open heart, some creativity, the desire to take care of your stepkids and a healthy dose of self-care.

As you shift your attention away from trying to get an uncooperative bio-mom to behave as a mature, civil, cordial adult to end any Loyalty Wars, and instead devote your attention to helping your stepkids feel less guilty, fearful, anxious and angry, a new peacefulness can blossom in your home. It's a gift to show your stepkids that when they're at dad's house it's OK with you that they love their bio-mom *and* dad *and* Stepmom *and* Stepdad and anyone else. You can model generous lovingkindness without saying a word or doing a thing. Kids feel this genuine kind of love. You want to be able to look back on your actions and choices as a stepmother and feel proud of yourself, right? This is one of those Stepmom choices you can feel good about immediately. Recognizing a Loyalty War in your stepkids' lives and adopting this approach to help them can also unearth any difficult and bruised feelings you may have that need to be healed and released—bringing you more short and long-term benefits.

Grown-up stepkids have told me that when Stepmoms do as I suggest, many stepkids notice, feel and appreciate it more than they're aware of, or can even express, until years or decades later. You're more likely to receive gratitude when your own stepkids become adults. While receiving gratitude is terrific when it happens, it isn't the ultimate goal. Embracing the strategies I've outlined in this chapter is a kind, compassionate and responsible way to help your stepkids deal with emotional stress and anxiety—whether or not your efforts are noticed or appreciated.

It's also important (necessary really) to honor the impact this same stress has on your own body and emotional realm by making sure you compensate yourself with extreme self-care, healthy emotion-processing rituals, creative problem-solving sessions and lots and lots of support. You can't end the Loyalty Wars. You can, however, make loving and wise choices that can substantially reduce the negative impact on stepchildren caught in the emotional crossfire between an uncooperative bio-mom and loving, conscious Stepmom.

Twenty-Nine

Ever Get Angry When Your Stepkids Get Away with Things? Discover the Reasons for Your Strong Reactions

Differing opinions about childrearing between you and your partner are to be expected and many things will be worked out over time. However, have you ever noticed that sometimes your stepkids will do something you don't like or agree with and then out of the blue—POW!—an unexpected wave of rage pours through you that seems disproportionate to the situation, even to you? When this happens, it's extremely beneficial if you can hit the internal "pause" button on your voice and actions so you can take time to reflect on what just happened. Chapter 9 presents the general principle of what's happening when situations in our present trigger seemingly over-the-top reactions. This chapter covers the specifics of how to apply this wisdom to the emotional upheaval that can be caused by particular situations with your stepkids.

Time spent understanding exactly what triggers such strong waves of emotions can save you a lot of future pain and help you understand a lot about your past behaviors. This pause can also prevent you from creating more stress in your relationships. It gives you a valuable opportunity to recognize and heal your childhood wounds. Realizing and claiming greater empowerment is only one benefit of this work. We all have childhood wounds—every single human being. The key is to choose to become aware of them so you can help yourself *and* respond to your present situations in more calm and effective ways.

When your stepkids get what you didn't get as a child—or what you don't have now—intense emotions can surge through you. Why is that?

Upsetting Reactions

- Have you ever felt a jolt of bitterness shoot through you as you watch or hear your stepkids receiving all sorts of compliments, privileges and material things? Do you feel this way if they are being given opportunities and experiences even when they behave badly or do nothing to deserve rewards?

- Have you ever felt stunned at the rudeness your stepkids are allowed to get away with when talking with you or either of their parents?

- Does the fact that your stepkids get stuff without having to earn it ever stick in your craw or make you feel like you want to scream or have a little (or big) temper tantrum?

- Do you ever secretly hope your stepkids will get in trouble for doing something bad and then shift into rage when they get caught but nothing happens?

- Have you ever felt a burst of excitement when you catch your stepkids doing something they shouldn't be doing, only to get criticized or rebuked by your partner (or stepkids or their bio-mom) for pointing it out in the first place?

- Have you ever noticed yourself becoming cold, hostile or harsh toward your stepkids when they refuse to go along with your "house rules"?

This stuff can be crazy-making. Although your feelings may not be pretty or something you like to admit, most stepmothers have experienced them to some degree. This intense sense of unfairness, plus the pain, fear and rage that are triggered, come from an unconscious emotional comparison of their childhood and your own. Stepmothers seem to be triggered more deeply when their stepkids are involved because they are not their own children. No matter how much you've come to love your stepkids, you're most likely not bonded to them the way bio-parents are and society reminds us of this often.

This combination of circumstances can make the impact of your stepkids' actions gut wrenching and emotionally charged beyond logic. If you factor in the actions or inactions of a partner mired in divorce guilt, the emotional impact on you can be overwhelming. Judging yourself for feeling whatever you're feeling isn't going to help—not ever. No amount of self-judgment will shift, heal or resolve your feelings. Temporarily numb them? Yes. But never heal them. It's about becoming compassionately aware that you've been triggered or hooked by a situation. Once you're conscious of this you can choose to suspend all outward actions and get curious about your feelings and how to help yourself feel better. This is an amazing awareness that creates a space for transformative personal insights.

When you judge something or someone, all that energy gets locked up—sort of frozen in place. Although it can be tempting to judge yourself or others because being numb feels better than the pain, it's not healthy or helpful. Also, it's not always the actual activity or situation that's upsetting. Ever notice that another child can do whatever your stepkids do and you would not only not care at all, but would happily fix things, comfort them or go with the flow? Why is this?

Helping Yourself

Could it be that your stepkids sometimes fail to treat you with the same basic manners and respect you watch them offer a stranger, teacher or friend's parent? It's helpful to look into your own upbringing and experiences to help you have compassion for the part of you who's upset when you notice these things. Next time this happens, take a moment to breathe and recognize, *"Hey, something deeper than this present situation is happening right now."* Take time to reflect—before reacting—so you can identify the issue being triggered. This is the key. It's extremely helpful and healing to take that detouring thought process. What can you do about this sort of thing so you can remain your loving, adult self no matter what your stepkids do?

The following four specific Stepmom/Stepkids examples offer some ideas for ways to get past, over and through your upsetting reactions in a new way that can lead you to more empowerment.

Stepmom/Stepkids Example #1

Your elementary school-aged stepkid loses his/her new raincoat (or lunch box or backpack, etc.) twice in the first month of school. One or both of the parents rush to get another new raincoat without any consequences, chores or efforts required from the stepkid who repeatedly loses the item. You may feel upset by this, "free pass." You may think, *"no big deal"* or find this consequence-free scenario infuriating.

If you didn't have an unlimited supply of things when you were a kid, or if you were given consequences every time you lost or broke things, this situation will likely upset you. Imagine yourself as "the child you used to be," watching your stepkids repeatedly getting away with this carelessness, while you were punished or shamed in some way. Doesn't it make sense that your younger self would feel upset? The way to work with these feelings is by learning how to separate the feelings you're having now (in response to the present situation) from similar feelings (from your past) which are surfacing now because they are so like much like your present feelings. Emotions are timeless and so any of those feelings that never got processed and released will come to you, through you—in an instant.

Stepmoms who have their own bio-kids often talk about how upsetting it is for their own children to watch their step-siblings get away with things they would never get away with. However, since "the child you used to be" isn't physical, it may never occur to you or you may not understand (or believe) that those feelings could still be alive and real after all this time. In these situations you're likely to discover that they are very real and surprisingly strong emotions at that. Being willing to explore your feelings gives you a chance to help yourself, learn about yourself and spare yourself a lot of future distress.

Here's a SMOM's story from one of my workshops. Once she decided to get curious about the possibilities, she turned her attention away from reacting to her stepkids' behavior and toward her own feelings.

"When I realized that much of my anger and hurt came from my own childhood stuff—stuff I brought into the relationship—I was caught up short, yet it made sense to me. I found some quiet time then shut my eyes and invited an imaginary younger version of me to come sit with me and tell me what she was thinking and feeling about whatever was going on at the time. Since this was all happening in my imagination, I invited this young me to climb up in my lap.

The first time I did this, I asked her what she needed from me. Boy oh boy did I get a surprise! This little me, in my imagination, was about five years old. She was incredibly upset. I was really amazed at how real all of this felt. I encouraged her to talk to me. After she told me all about her anger, which I could obviously relate to and understand, her tears came—then my tears. The wave of tears was followed by a deep exhale and then she looked at me for some major TLC. The tears I shed were real. The rest of it was all in my imagination yet I felt very different afterwards. I've done this countless times since this first experience and each time, a different younger me seems to show up with more information and feelings that no one acknowledged at the time I first experienced them.

It wasn't a weird thing or even scary, it was profound for me. After that experience, I became aware that I was less triggered when others got away with things. What a relief."

This is a very common experience for Stepmoms engaging in this work. It's so easy to become so focused on your stepkids and their well-being, that you can end up unknowingly ignoring how your own younger self might be feeling. Being ignored is painful in and of itself. Being ignored when also feeling hurt or afraid is infuriating.

Instead, you need to be willing to acknowledge and help your younger selves. Yes, all of them—you as a child, a teen, a young adult, a newbie Stepmom and even the you from before you acquired this book. You can do this work for yourself anytime you have a few moments to yourself to go into your imagination and give your feelings your loving attention and compassion. You can start having these inner dialogues whenever you feel that surge of unfairness and rage. You can start by gently and lovingly saying reassuring and supportive things to yourself, imagining a younger you looking to you for compassion and support. Perhaps say something like this to yourself, in a very patient and kind tone.

"I can see why this situation would be upsetting for you. What exactly does it feel like to you? Tell me what this situation reminded you of from your life. I'll listen and totally be on your side. You can count on me."

When Stepmoms I work with try this technique, they almost always remember new memories and realize, much to the surprise of many, that the feelings triggered by their stepkids today feel just like their feelings from sometime in their childhoods. Many times these feelings were from experiences when they were the same age as the stepkid whose behavior triggered them. This correlation has proven startling, fascinating *and* profoundly healing. Why? Because it helps you get to the core of these upsetting feelings so you can process and release them. That's the goal and relief is your reward.

What might "the child you used to be" desire from you?

- She may want you to pay more attention to *her* needs.

- She may want to be heard by someone who genuinely wants to support her—and that could be you.

- She may want her feelings to be respected and acknowledged as valid instead of tolerated, judged or disregarded like the first time she experienced them.

- She may want your unconditional loving attention.

- She may want you to seem (be) truly happy to spend time with her.

Giving this younger you a voice, even when only in your imagination, is a huge step in shifting how you'll view whatever your stepkids do or say. Why? Because somehow when you have honored and supported your younger self, the actions of other children don't generate rage, jealousy or nearly as much upset. Really! If you begin looking at the things your stepkids do that upset you as valuable clues to finding out more about your own unhealed stuff, it can one day result in you sending them a silent "thanks for the clue" and then getting busy helping yourself. Going forward, let their father deal with them while you start paying attention to your feelings in this new way. Before you go thinking I'm nuts, give it a try and see what happens in your imagination. According to feedback from clients and workshop attendees over the years, this has been one of the most profoundly insightful, helpful and empowering practices to add to your emotion-processing skill set.

Stepmom/Stepkids Example #2

Your stepkids speaks rudely to you or to his/her father and there are no consequences or even corrections made for this behavior. This could be upsetting to you or no big deal. What could be happening if it is upsetting to you? It wouldn't occur to many Stepmoms to speak to their parents—much less another adult—in the ways many kids of today are talking with their parents. Many, dare I say most, women dealt with their disempowered rage in childhood by creating beliefs that one day, when they were adults, kids would have to speak to them with respect or there'd be heck to pay, just like when they were kids. Can you relate to this coping strategy?

When your stepkids speak rudely or disrespectfully to their parents or you and then either get away with it and are uncorrected or their transgressions are ignored, a younger version of you may rise up and say with or without words yet with strong emotions, something like this:

> "Wait a gosh darn minute! This is wrong and something should be done here. This is not the way children speak to adults. This makes me furious and I want someone to do something about my anger!"

If their father doesn't react the way you believe he should, your inner child or teen, who was most likely threatened into behaving and punished if misbehaved—starts to balk at the injustice through your feelings. Unless you're conscious of this additional source of your own emotional energy, you're likely to just get angry and try to get your partner to do something. If you lash out or blow up in anger, you may feel badly. You may be judged and criticized for over-reacting. I want to assure you that the anger you feel is real but can feel obscured by the present situation and your lack of understanding about what's happening. Hopefully you will be more compassionate with yourself the next time something triggers your anger.

Ever noticed how when something feels unfair, it can strike a very intense energy chord in you? Becoming aware that present situations can tap into past memories can help you respond to present situations more wisely and process your feelings in more compassionate productive ways. Instead of unconsciously using the situation as an avenue to spew out rage or anger (getting you nowhere, healing nothing in your emotional life and often causing damage to your relationships) you can now stop yourself and get clear on what was then and what's now before reacting or saying a word. This is a powerful moment of consciousness awareness. This is you being an empowered adult. It feels great!

Note to Self: This awareness and new strategy can really avoid a lot of stress and reduce your need for damage control with your partner. It's also a great way to turn a previously upsetting situation into a chance for you to heal from past wounds you didn't even know you had. I've heard this feedback from so many Stepmoms. Being aware of these two separate sets of feelings (those from then and now) really helps you see the actions of your stepkids in a new more insight-filled light. Oh you may still be annoyed or upset about what they do, but it will feel less charged, like how you'd feel if a neighbor kid behaved in that way.

The questions below can help you glean personal insights about what's happening when your stepkids are rude or misbehave. Learning how to separate and identify the true source of your feelings changes so much in so many good ways. You can help yourself by reflecting on specific situations that have enraged you in the past. Think about one of those times now and ask yourself:

1. Were your stepkids speaking to you directly or did you observe or just hear about their behavior?

2. If they spoke directly to you, did you speak up for yourself, saying, "*This is not OK with me*" or did you stay quiet, now feeling mistreated and upset they got away with something? If you stayed quiet, what was your reasoning? Was it a fear choice or a growth choice?

3. What can you do to make yourself feel better once your feelings are triggered? Yes, right this minute—what can you do or say to yourself to help yourself feel more respected, acknowledged, at peace and loved by YOU?

4. What specific new boundaries and consequences for future occurrences can you create for those situations that happen directly to you? How likely is your partner to support these new boundaries and consequences? If he won't, what can you do, what actions can you take to avoid or spare yourself from any future negative impact?

If you're lucky, your partner will support your right to avoid feeling hurt or disrespected by his kids. If he thinks you're making a big deal over nothing or if he feels that since he needs to endure disrespectful treatment you should too, that's a bit more difficult. If he asks you to endure because he fears losing the love of his children, that's another tough row to hoe. It's now going to be up to you to decide what you will (and won't) accept from your stepkids. Thankfully, using your creativity and focusing on yourself, you really can find ways to take their behavior less personally. Letting go of being the manners police in your home and deciding to stop agonizing over how your stepkids speak to their father are two choices that you can make to significantly reduce the stress between you and your partner. These are clearly two of those easier-said-than-done suggestions. The good news is, you're going to discover very quickly that it's worth the initial effort and gets easier with practice and processing.

Stepmom/Stepkids Example #3

You want to keep all the boots in the laundry room or the back packs off the floor, food out of the bedrooms, etc. but the stepkids are disregarding your wishes and your partner tells you that you're too controlling. Your partner allows his kids to disregard your house rules and instead permits them to leave their boots, books and dishes wherever they want them to without any consequences or corrections. That could upset a stepmother who feels like she should have some authority in her own home. Or perhaps you're OK with this situation.

What's happening here is similar to Example #2 above. Did you grow up being told that when you got a house of your own, you could set the rules? Did you believe this would be true? Do you still believe it should be true? If you're like many women, you distracted yourself from some of your natural teenage rage, thereby shoving this energy into your unconscious, by telling yourself that one day, when you had your own home, you'd have the power to determine what was and was not OK. Your home = your rules. My guess is that this is true for most non-stepmother women running households today. Women who aren't stepmothers may have a hard time understanding your feelings because they *are in charge* of the house rules and consequences of the children they care for.

The possibility below can help non-stepmother friends, family members and partners of Stepmoms have more compassion for your feelings by putting things in terms they might experience. I suggest you ask them:

> *"How would you feel if a neighborhood kid (the age of one of your stepkids) came into your home and spoke rudely to you, disregarded your polite requests or took your things without your permission and then, in spite of the way they treated you, you were expected to feed, shop for, chauffeur and care for them—all with a smile?"*

Non-stepmothers seem to have a hard time understanding how this feels, not because they're trying to be unsupportive but because they have no reference. Sharing this example might help your partner or family be more supportive of your feelings. Being judged for your feelings or having no support can feel unfair, as if you are truly powerless in a place that was supposed to be your domain, under your house rules. You can end up feeling like a servant in your own home—a home that was supposed to be a safe haven for you but is not at this time or under certain conditions.

First things first—it's absolutely critical to get clear on your personal beliefs. Being aware of your beliefs about any given situation can be a great source of understanding about why you react as you do. The more aware you can become of your "inner rules," the more you can understand your responses and where there's a conflict. A conflict between what's happening and what you believe should happen is a source of anger that will lead to resentment, if it is left unaddressed. See Section Two.

In all cases, the anger is a clue that some inner emotional boundary or belief is being violated. Anxiety is an indication that you're anticipating a future boundary violation. You can use these feelings as alerts and give your own feelings priority *before* taking any action on your present situation. Without this awareness, you're likely to put your attention on other people and this only makes some part of you feel more ignored and enraged. Why? Because whether you're conscious of it or not, focusing on others means you've abandoned yourself again, believing falsely that the solution to your well-being lies with getting others to change. See Chapter 8 for more about the formation of beliefs and their pivotal impact on your choices and feelings.

Children absolutely need others to help them resolve most of their upsetting circumstances. It makes sense that a child would believe that she needs others to help her solve a problem or help her feel better. However, you aren't a child anymore, you're an adult, savvy, smart woman. Realizing you might still carry a belief that others are responsible for making you feel better can now give you motivation to replace your child-created survival beliefs with new adult-created beliefs. How about believing that you are competent and responsible for helping yourself? The good news is that you're absolutely capable—resourceful and creative too. It's sort of amazing when you feel the shift into your empowered self. It's also fascinating how quickly your feelings will change and new ideas will occur to you when you own your newly realized permission and power to help yourself.

Stepmom/Stepkids Example #4

You believe there are some table manners that are appropriate or required for dinnertime but your stepkids are able to get away with behaviors that you feel are unacceptable or ruin the meal for you and your family.

You just want your stepkids to learn to behave well in public yet you're unable (unauthorized and unsupported by your partner) to get them to comply with your requests at home. It can sometimes feel like you're trapped in the twilight zone when you and your partner argue over enforcing something you consider basic table manners.

You want your stepkids to grow up to be polite, thoughtful, kind and loving people. When they're in your home and you're caring for them, you may feel it's your duty, role, job, responsibility, etc. to help them learn, right? When you're not supported or listened to by the stepkids or your partner on topics you feel are important, it can be generate feelings that range from frustrating to extremely infuriating.

Have you ever felt afraid or anxious about speaking up or taking action in response to the behaviors of your stepkids? Do you fear that if you don't teach your stepkids good manners, they may not learn the things you believe all children should learn? Do you believe it's your job to correct them? This belief is common and having it in your "book of personal beliefs" can trigger inner tension, plus self-judgment that you're not doing your job as a good stepmother if you let bad manners go unaddressed. This can be an upsetting issue. When your stepkids' parents don't seem to be teaching their bio-kids what you believe are good manners, you may end up feeling even more responsible. How can you feel like a good stepmother when there are children in the house who are unwilling to respond with respect to your requests for basic kindness and manners? What if you hold your own bio-kids to manners that your stepkids aren't expected to comply with?

Recognizing the impact of your beliefs and your childhood experiences on your present reactions to your stepkids' behaviors is a big step. Identifying the specific conflicts between your beliefs and your realities can help you better understand how to support yourself. It allows you to choose your battles. It gives you more insights and hopefully self-compassion so you can find more ways to maintain your kind nature and happy personality no matter what your stepkids do or say.

Working with your partner to identify your differing needs and conflicting beliefs in relation to your stepkids' actions is a very good use of your time. This thoughtful exploration can make any disagreements easier to understand and work through. It's easier to have compassion for each other when you both understand the reasons you want whatever you want regarding the stepkids. As I've written throughout this book, there are darn good reasons for all of your feelings, beliefs and behaviors. Know this is true—even if you don't *yet* know what they are or understand them. When there's a conflict between you and your partner about beliefs and needs, it's time for some creative brainstorming that honors these upsetting conflicting situations. See Chapter 18 for more about this topic.

The process is a lot more enjoyable when a Stepmom and her partner can look at any conflicting, upsetting situations as "we" problems, and not just a stepmother issue. My goal is to help Stepmoms and their partners find a process that enables them to get to a peaceful place of reconnection. Recognizing, understanding and respecting the conflicts in their underlying beliefs and feelings about difficult situations is a healthy path toward this goal.

If you're thinking that working with your intense emotions, triggered by the actions of your stepkids is much easier said than done, you're right—but only at first. As you practice and become more conscious of your needs and beliefs, you won't become triggered as much when the stepkids get away with things or act out in anger. Going forward, when something they do does hook you, you can use the experience to learn something important about yourself. This is turning lemons into profoundly valuable lemonade. While you can't control your stepkids' actions, it's always helpful to remember you have complete control over how you respond to them.

Going forward with this information, you can now understand that your stepkids' actions and their attempts to rebel and lash out at you are a result of their own anger toward their life situations. They are disempowered children—truly out of control of much of their lives. This out-of-control reality is actually something that stepmothers and stepkids share in several aspects of their lives. Realizing this shared circumstance can help you have more compassion for them and for yourself. Thankfully you have one huge advantage over your stepkids—as a conscious adult you have much greater resources, life experiences, support and wisdom enabling you to create new solutions that allow you to preserve your well-being no matter how others behave.

For more information about this topic, go to smoms.org/BonusChapters and click on the title "When Stepkids Manipulate Their Fathers (or Try)." See the complete list of additional chapters and follow-up discussions in Chapter 39.

Thirty

Caring For vs. Catering To Your Stepkids

In your enthusiasm for welcoming stepkids into your life, you can end up making choices that you later regret or that backfire on you and cause you stress. This chapter takes a compassionate look at the potential negative impact of your eagerness to create a happy new life with your stepkids. Being more aware of the motivation and impact of your urges to serve and please your new stepkids can help you make more conscious choices to avoid feeling resentful—or worse, like the family servant.

As a woman in love, it's natural to want to do everything you can for your new partner and stepkids. It's also imperative to take care of yourself. You know the adage, "put on your oxygen mask first so you can then help others," don't you? With waves of enthusiasm, passion and dreams of a happy future flowing through you at the beginning of your journey as a stepmother, you can find yourself full of all kinds of energy for your stepkids and no need for reciprocation. By making wise choices about how to use this energy now, you can save yourself lots of resentment and hurt feelings in the future. If you already feel exhausted and resentful, you can learn why and do something about it.

It's natural to want your stepkids to like you. You probably also want them to be happy when they're in your home. This chapter is about a painful pitfall that many stepmothers fall into quite unintentionally. It's when you do too much for your stepkids. At first, you strive to do things because you have compassion for what they're going through—as they adjust to a new way of life and in most cases, continue to deal with the pain of their parents' divorce. At first you may have lots of energy for the tasks at hand and may help everyone in every way you can—because you're capable and want to. However, sometimes, over time, it can become draining if the stepkids don't appreciate your efforts, return the kindness or at the very least say thank you.

If your partner doesn't acknowledge your contributions, seeds of resentment may start sprouting very quickly. You can start feeling like an unpaid, disrespected nanny or maid, working for ungrateful stepkids and an oblivious partner. This is an all-too-common and terrible feeling for any stepmother trying her best to create a happy family. Whether you're at the beginning of your relationship or have been a stepmother for years, there's always time to make new, wiser choices and learn from your past behaviors and previous choices. Thank goodness!

A Straightforward Question: Before doing *anything* for the stepkids, ask yourself, *"Can I do this without expecting any appreciation in return?"*

If the answer is *"Yes,"* go for it, feeling happy and generous.

If the answer is *"No,"* stop yourself, even if in mid-sentence or action.

Get curious about your urge to do things for your stepkids. Get clear about your expectations of them. Look at all the little extra things you're doing for them. You may even want to take a moment now and jot these things down. It can be helpful and sometimes shocking to see the list in writing. If you notice, like so many of us have, that you're really doing a lot more for them than they are doing for you, consider a new approach which can avoid potential resentments and help you find a balance between the value of the energy you give and receive. For most newbie Stepmoms it means making a mindful decision to reduce your doing for your stepkids. One place to start is by continuing to do the things you're (now consciously) willing to do over the long-term course of your relationship. Begin to pay attention to your feelings about the stepkids' reactions and responses to the things you do. Give yourself permission to honor your feelings about the exchange of your giving and whatever you receive. Claim your power to change your mind and make new choices to find the balance that dissolves resentments.

Becoming aware of the natural, initial urge to pamper the stepkids to try to create a "Happy Family" is a big step into awareness. The value to you comes from doing things more consciously. Doing things because you feel you have to in order to be a good stepmother is another source of resentment, so it's important and helpful to honestly reflect on your motives and expectations. The chapters in Section Three explain varying aspects of resentment and how to process it in healthy ways.

Becoming conscious of your urge to do *before* you act gives you a newfound ability to think about the consequences. Giving yourself permission to *not* do some of the nice things you're capable of doing—without guilt and while maintaining your self-respect—will make a difference in how much you do and how good you feel in the short and long run. If part of you is thinking, "Not me, I love doing all this stuff," please read on with as much curiosity as you can muster.

Redirect Your Enthusiasm

Try this idea. The next time you have any extra energy to do things for your stepkids, turn your attention to yourself and your partner. When in doubt, do something for yourself. You'll be glad you did and the stepkids won't notice or miss a thing.

When your creativity and enthusiasm (compulsion?) for giving to (and doing for) others gets the better of you, you can end up regretting your actions and unintentionally contributing to the creation of spoiled and entitled stepkids. It's hard to say how much entitlement is a symptom of the kids of today's generation and how much is produced through the divorce of their parents. Either way, ungrateful, manipulative or entitled behavior isn't very kind, fun to be around or attractive.

Catering Can Backfire

Here's a story from an eager-beaver Stepmom waking up to her part in this pattern. She writes:

> *"When my stepdaughter came into my life, she was four years old and still loved baths. It was a calming, nightly ritual with her dad. She loved to talk about her day while in a tub of suds. Besides provisioning the bathroom with all kinds of fun soaps, toys and other bath-time goodies, I decided to treat her to something I'd experienced at a spa. I put a big, plush towel—her "special towel"—in the dryer for a few minutes before she was ready to come out of the tub. With a shout from her dad, I brought this freshly warmed, soft towel to the bathroom door. Her dad wrapped her up in the towel. She really loved that! Who wouldn't? I did it joyfully quite often. It made me feel included in the bedtime ritual. I felt like it was a nice thing to do for the sweet girl. It felt good until two things happened in the same week that made me rethink my actions.*

First, her bio-mom complained vehemently to my partner that her daughter was asking her to do that "heated towel thing" when she was with her. Bio-mom didn't want to. She blamed me for causing this problem for her. And she was right. I did cause her that annoyance with her own child. I did something my stepdaughter liked and she wanted it from her bio-mom, too. I didn't cause the bio-mom this irritation intentionally. I thought I was doing a nice thing for my stepdaughter. Are you beginning to see the problem?

Secondly, and more importantly, one time I didn't do it for her after a bath and she threw a hissy fit. She also pouted for the rest of the evening. Whoa! That was quite a moment of realization. In hindsight, I wished I'd given my actions more thought. I also wished I'd transferred that lesson learned to other activities in our lives. The heated towel could have become a special treat but instead it died a sad death in our home.

Over the first few years, I made many of these mistakes. My acts of kindness went from initially appreciated treats to expected entitlements in my stepdaughter's mind. To top it off, her father and I were punished by her bad behavior or withdrawal of love if she didn't get her special treats each and every time she wanted them. The two child psychologists we consulted intermittently had a hay day with this situation."

The goal is to catch yourself if you feel the urge to cater to your stepkids out of your desire to make them happy, avert a temper tantrum, encourage them to like you more or just because you are in the mood for some fun. There are plenty of ways to demonstrate that you care for your stepkids without indulging them. The reality is you may be trying too hard. If you're ready to stop trying so hard and are looking for some ideas, see Chapter 31. The good news? As soon as you're aware of this potential problem, it can be easily avoided or resolved and you'll find yourself feeling better. The bottomline is this—make decisions and choices about what you do for your stepkids with the guideline that your contributions should be sustainable, enjoyable for both parties and appreciated. Save treats and special acts of attention for special occasions and family rituals.

Another Warning Sign: If you find you're neglecting other areas of your life because too much energy and time is focused on the stepkids, you may be doing what I call "over-giving." It's another call to pause and reevaluate your actions. Anytime you feel resentful, this is a clue that you need to pay attention to how you're feeling, what you're doing and what you're expecting in return so you can make some new choices that result in a positive change. Chapter 10 explains the behavior of over-giving.

Becoming more aware of why you're doing whatever you're doing for your stepkids can help you make choices with minimal negative impact. Making self-honoring, wise choices that don't result in you feeling resentful is a good way to reduce your present stress and avoid future stress, which also reduces anxiety. Take a look at what you're doing now and at what you have done that has caused you stress. Rethink choices that might lead you down the potentially martyred pathway of feeling unappreciated and resentful. Whenever possible, redirect your energy, time and attention to supporting yourself and your partner. There is a way to care for your stepkids without catering to them. The unexpected benefit is modeling kindness, self-respect and healthy boundaries for these children one day at a time.

Jersey99's Story

July 2016

I was at my wit's end when I found SMOMS. I did a search for a stepparent support group, and found smoms.org to be the most relevant, nonjudgmental and easy-to-navigate site. When I read some of the posts, I suddenly realized I was not alone.

I have one son who is 26 now. When we all decided to move in together, he was just entering the tenth grade. Fortunately, I never had many issues with him—he was involved in sports, which kept him out of trouble, and he was surrounded by very well-grounded friends and coaches who were amazing role models. He's a college graduate and is now living in Vancouver, Canada, working in a career he loves. My son is my reminder that I am capable of being an effective, competent and loving parent.

I became a stepmother about 10 years ago. I thought I knew what I was getting myself into because my husband (DH) and I had been together for over five years by then. I had known my stepdaughter (SD) just about as long as I had known him, and I had helped him settle her in when he became a single dad. My DH had taken custody of her when she was about eight. Her mother could not keep a stable home or job and could not get her to school on a regular basis. My DH was notified by the school's truancy officer after she could not get my stepdaughter's mother to get SD to school more often. On average, my stepdaughter missed more than 28 days of school from pre-K to half of third grade, and she attended pre-K twice.

My SD spent the next six years using our home as a hotel while she went to school, and then running off to her mother's on the weekends. Her mother got her a cell phone so they could stay bonded at the hip at all times. It quickly turned into us against them. SD was only living with us because her father wouldn't give her back to her mother, and we were the bad guys for attempting to give her boundaries and structure.

To make a long story short, in December of her senior year of high school, SD moved out and emancipated herself from her father. She moved in with her drug-addicted, unemployed boyfriend and his parents. She then went through a series of really bad decisions to include not graduating high school, getting pregnant on purpose, covering herself with really bad tattoos, and then finally ending up homeless with a baby. After two months of moving from friend's house to friend's house, we took her back in. It was just the right thing to do.

That's where we are now. SD and her baby have lived with us for over two years. It has not been easy. While she does not make stupid life-changing decisions anymore (mostly because we won't allow it), it's not the optimal situation for my DH and me. There are few single mothers who have it better than SD has it. She and her child live under our roof, in the same room together. I cannot predict when she will move out on her own, or if that will ever happen.

What I have had to come to terms with, and what Cathryn and the other SMOMS at smoms.org have helped me do, is to not blame myself for who my SD has grown to be. She lived in my house and I thought if I could just live by example, she would grow to be a strong, independent woman. Instead, she did just the opposite. Even with "family meetings" and almost two years of family therapy, the best she can come up with is, "I thought I would have my own family."

My SD is a grown-up but is still living with us, and I still need to be part of a stepmothers' support group. There's no other group of women who can even remotely understand the issues I have or the total impact of having a stepchild in my life. I've had to come to terms that being a stepmother is a life-long commitment that does not magically end when the child turns eighteen.

Stepmoms on a Mission was, and still is, the support group I've needed to help me understand what I was experiencing and why it was happening, and to give me the specific support I needed at the time I was feeling the worst. Unlike other websites I found, the group is totally non-judgmental. There were some frustrating times when I knew I was behaving badly. Even when I would angrily describe exactly what I did, and then spend way too many words justifying why I did it, Cathryn would help me understand more about my own feelings and options.

Every time I wrote in, Cathryn and my sister SMOMS would respond back with nothing but unconditional compassionate support and all kinds of recommendations of how I could make the situation better for me. This is why I have actively stayed with Cathryn's site for the past ten years and plan to continue as a loyal member. In the last year, I realized that I've really learned a lot because I find myself helping and supporting the new stepmothers who find their way to smoms.org.

Jersey99
Stepmom since 2006
SMOM since 2006

Thirty-One

The "Stop Trying So Hard and Start Lovingly Ignoring Your Stepkids" Plan

What can you do when you've already tried everything you can think of and your stepkids still don't want to connect with you? Or they treat you with apathy or disrespect? Here's a potentially radical, sanity-saving idea to implement. When you've tried everything else and failed—step out of the power struggle with your stepkids and do your best to *not* connect with them. Here's the key to success—do this with an open-hearted, neutral (perhaps even cheerful), non-hostile attitude. You'll discover that the benefits of greater peace of mind and other surprisingly good things can come about if you're willing to experiment with not trying so hard.

One of the qualities most Stepmoms on a Mission share is an initial genuine desire to connect with their stepkids. Another quality is a sustained willingness to exert energy, in spite of any related stress and emotional pain, to achieve a goal. Right from the start, most are willing to try, try harder and try again to make a loving and respectful connection with the children of their new partner. At the beginning, many believe they can make a difference and help with childrearing. Many stepmothers do whatever they can think of to help their stepkids feel welcome, safe, loved and valued while they're in her home. But for some stepmothers, after years of trying and failing to create (or maintain) a positive relationship with their stepkids, there comes a moment of dreaded realization, *"Oh my! I can't think of anything more to do. My efforts are creating more pain for me than I want to (or can) handle. Now what?"* If this is familiar to you, you may have fallen into an emotionally tangled situation, rampant with fears, false beliefs, guilt, manipulation and pain that just can't be resolved with more love and more trying.

Hopefully you never experience these moments of despair. But if it's circling your inner thoughts or you're already feeling this way, *not* connecting is an option that may work for you. It's founded on a basic truth that a healthy, happy relationship cannot be accomplished with the efforts of only one person—that person makes up only 50% of the equation. It can be hard to acknowledge that some people (like uncooperative bio-moms and some stepkids) may actually *not* want the relationship with you to work well, or at all. With that in mind, there are no guarantees that what I'm about to describe will improve your connection with your stepkids. It will help you feel better and can significantly lessen the stress between you and your partner. Experimenting with this approach and customizing it based on your experiences can reduce incoming pain and the negative impact you may feel if your stepkids act out hurtfully toward you. It will also give you a chance to recover and reclaim that joyful, enthusiastic, happy loving adult woman you used to be. It *may* result in an improved connection with your stepkids, too, but that's up to them.

To be clear right up front, if you've reached this point, you haven't done anything wrong to feel the way you feel. Distancing yourself emotionally from your stepkids and exploring your own needs doesn't make you wicked, evil, cold or cruel. Although we can all understand how that stepmother stereotype was born though, can't we? When something goes wrong or doesn't work, many of us immediately go to work to fix things. Many of us learn in childhood that if we can make something our fault, or our responsibility, we can feel more in control and therefore hopeful about making changes to achieve a successful outcome.

Why is that? Because we know we can count on ourselves to keep trying. We can't always say the same about others. There's often an underlying fear that if we give up, all is lost. So to avoid facing defeat, we take our bumps and bruises, withdraw to regroup and try again. I call this the cycle of a frustrated Stepmom. By now, you know whether or not this chapter is going to be of any help to you. If you can relate to any of this, grab a cup of something soothing, get comfortable and open up to another possible way of dealing with your stepkids.

How It Works

Imagine withdrawing your attention, energy and expectations for a response from your stepkids in a loving, non-hostile way. Perhaps you're no longer going to start conversations with them, ask them how they are first or initiate contact (hugs, high fives) with them as you used to do. It can mean you decide to stop volunteering to be their concierge, nanny, chauffeur, mother-figure, pal, buddy, banker, personal assistant or maid. It may sound far-fetched, but this approach can actually help you reclaim the power you may have unknowingly given to your stepkids. Reclaiming power is always a good thing.

An important element of this approach being effective, vs. manipulative or cruel, is that you want to be calm, patient and loving without expressing anger, resentment or hostility while you're testing out this new way of being around them. Hostility is anger that's generated from feeling pain. It's real, and when we feel hostile it deserves our attention so it can be acknowledged, processed and released. Most people can sense hostility, and it often evokes some kind of reaction that's not positive. Check out the article on smoms.org called "Hostility is NOT Fine!" if you want to learn more about the causes, dynamics and alternatives to feeling hostile.

Wanting to once again feel kind and relaxed around your stepkids—especially if you've been experiencing a great deal of pain, anxiety and anger—can be enough to motivate you to choose a new approach with them. However, this new tactic is not about repressing or suppressing your sadness. It's about making new choices that honor your needs and feelings above your need to connect with your stepkids. The impact of this decision on your stepkids is going to vary tremendously based on their age, their personalities and your history with them. Your partner may experience the benefits of less stress between you and his kids. He may also find himself with more childcare-related chores (and therefore potentially additional stress) as a result of you implementing this approach. This possible impact can make changes a little scary. Experiences of many Stepmoms demonstrate that sticking with this plan and explaining your feelings and rationale to your partner can make things so much better in the long run. Your partner plays a role in how successful this strategy can be for all of you but thankfully, his support is not required. The more you two can work together, the faster you'll feel better and the sooner your stress with be reduced.

Once you understand the objectives and dynamics of this idea, you can customize a version specific to yourself and your situation. Try things. Experiment and see what happens and how you are feeling. Make your plan exactly what feels best for you. Ideally, share your intentions with your partner and hopefully you'll feel and be supported. Hopefully, too, your partner knows and acknowledges at least some of what you've been going through. Whether your partner can understand or not, it's also highly likely that his actions, inactions and reactions may also be a part of the stress you've been experiencing. A new plan may give him hope once he adjusts to any impact on him.

This approach could also make your partner uneasy because some part of him is going to realize that the less you do, the more he's going to have to do. He's probably right. Consider telling him that he needs to be the "go-to" person for his children in all situations—at least for the time-being. Stay strong with all new boundaries. Test out your new plan and seek out all the support you need.

Reclaim Your Well-Being

Idea #1: Resist the urge to ask them about their day when they return to your home (from school, activities, their bio-mom's house, etc.) Just look up and smile at them, creating a space for them to talk to you. If they say something first, reply with a brief, cordial, warm greeting then return your attention to whatever you were doing when they arrived.

Idea #2: Resist initiating conversations with them. Stop asking yes/no questions if you realize you're just trying to engage with them. You can still be your smiling happy self but remind yourself that they are the same kids who upset you in the past. If they want to talk with you, super—you'll respond happily as your authentic self. If they want to be silent, decide that it's A-OK with you as you continue doing whatever you were doing when your paths crossed.

Idea #3: Give up on being the manners police. Sigh! Give that job to your partner or just let it go as a matter of self-care. This can be a tough one for stepmothers who hold the belief that it's their job to teach everyone in the house proper manners. If your partner does not share your beliefs about the importance of certain manners or doesn't want your help in teaching and upholding them, accept his wishes, revise your beliefs and move on to other things—they *are* his kids.

Ugh! I know that initially (or forever) this can really be hard to accept. Even harder when you have bio-kids and feel you do have the authority to impose, expect and enforce certain behaviors with them. This situation requires a new way of looking at manners so there can be peace in your home. Ask your partner what manners are important to him and let go of the rest. Choosing to say nothing, when you observe an "infraction" makes a dramatic statement about your new approach to stepmothering. Decide to look at this as an experiment, make your peace of mind and well-being are more important than most house rules—for right now, anyway. One day at a time.

Idea #4: Stop volunteering to help your stepkids with projects, homework, shopping, etc. If they ask you to do so, calmly and cheerfully suggest they talk with their dad. If they keep after you to help them as you had in the past, take a deep breath, smile and tell them that you simply don't want to do X or Y for them today—no other reason is needed. Again, tell them that they need to help themselves or go ask their dad. The key is to stay calm and open-hearted. Smile to yourself knowing that you're trying a new approach to reclaim your power and to no longer be tormented, disrespected, ignored or otherwise upset by them. Remind yourself you have a right to determine and manage your own time and energy.

Idea #5: Make arrangements for other people to take care of any stepkid-related chores and activities you normally handle for them. If you know that your partner will not be able to handle something, get creative. Ask for help from other moms, relatives, friends and resources. If potential helpers ask you why you need them, tell them something important, and personal, has come up and you need their assistance. No need to share any more than that. Really! Sometimes saying less is more effective. Personally, I resisted the "saying less" concept for a long time but it's proven to be helpful quite often in all areas of my life.

Idea #6: Release all expectations of getting any kind of attention from your stepkids. Do the best you can and catch yourself if you find yourself feeling hurt or disappointed. Resist reaching out to them for any kind of physical contact. Stepkids are often very aware of their passive-aggressive ability to hurt and to manipulate adults. You may have even told them how their actions impact you, hoping their understanding would lead to change, while actually making yourself even more vulnerable. Sometimes stepkids feel powerful by not giving you the connection they know you want. They're powerless over so many things, and their Stepmom can often become their outlet for misdirected rage and control. This is sad whenever it is true.

Idea #7: Give your stepkids the space and permission to not connect with you at all. Step off the old game board. Have them see that you're happy with no contact *and* happy if they decide to talk with or even hug you. If they want to talk or hug, talk and hug them back. The key is to resist the urge to reach out first, which gives them the ability to reject, hurt, disappoint, ignore or disrespect you. Show them by your pleasant, calm, happy demeanor that you're A-OK either way. Show them that whether or not they reach out to you, you're not going to chase them anymore. It's now their choice to engage with you or not.

Idea #8: *"The best way to get someone's attention is to ignore them."* My mentor, Kit also taught me this and it can be downright amazing to watch this in action.

With these new tactics, you're reclaiming your adult right to choose to engage your time and energy with people who are kind and polite to you. With this strategy, you're *showing* them, which is more powerful than words, that you're no longer going to be there to do things for them unless they choose to treat you with respect—and hopefully kindness. You're also showing them that you can be happy without interacting with them. Children sense when they're losing power over someone and will often increase their attempts to connect to get their sense of power back. Be aware of possible manipulations so you can smile and resist the urge to serve them unless you truly want to. Ideally, going forward, this will always your conscious choice.

This approach may shock your stepkids—it's hard to predict. You can still love them from across the room. You can still wish them well while their dad handles the latest crisis. You can choose to respond to their polite requests and conversations. You can also kindly tell them you're busy doing something else and they need to find their dad. Remember, there's no need to explain your choices. Daydreaming as you look out the window is doing something. Remember that your precious, finite life force is your responsibility and worthy of being well-managed and respected. Welcome to the world of *"I'm in charge of doing whatever I want, for whom and when. I'm no longer at the mercy of anyone who isn't nice to me."*

Can you feel the surge of energy—maybe even some joy—while envisioning this possible reality? This imagined new future of calm, everyday joy may also bring you to tears if you've been under extreme stress for a while. Freedom from the oppression and impact of unkind and unconscious people is indeed a relief. With this approach, you're about to reclaim freedom from anticipating future experiences of being hurt, enraged, left out, ignored, disrespected and dishonored while still being in your relationship with your stepkids. It's just going to be a different relationship. This option gives you back your power. It can help you become a wiser version of the strong, energetic, loving woman you were when you first became a stepmother.

Prepare for Stepkids' Reactions

In some cases, stepkids have felt in charge and may have played, consciously or not, on your desire for everyone to get along. Those days can be history with your new awareness. The tyranny of their control over your well-being is about to be challenged and overthrown. When you choose to believe that you have the right to make your happiness, well-being and relationship with your partner more important than connecting with your stepchildren, your life can change in many positive ways—almost immediately in some ways.

As you focus your efforts and attention on taking back the reins of control over your own happiness, you're going to stop doing a lot of things you used to do. You will do some things differently. And hopefully you will start doing more for yourself and with your partner. You're reclaiming your right to choose how you spend your time. As the late Dr. Wayne Dyer used to say, *"We teach people how to treat us."* Why and how did we become so blinded to, and willing to give up on, our own needs and rights when we became stepmothers?

After trying so hard for so long and for all the right reasons, can you be open to the possibility that the other characters in your life's play are showing you, with their actions, that it's time to stop trying so hard and do things differently?

Let's review four common reactions to the "Stop Trying So Hard and Start Lovingly Ignoring Your Stepkids" plan. Remember the choices your stepkids make will be influenced by their personalities, their bio-moms, their ages and their relationship history with you. It's also possible that some stepkids may employ all four reactions in varying sequences. Watching for these reactions can make this approach feel like it's part of a field test or experiment—one that you have the ability to tweak as you wish.

Reaction #1: Your stepkids may sincerely try to reconnect in reaction to your withdrawn attention. This should be palpable for you if it's sincere. At these times, it's a chance for you to "catch them doing it right" and give them your loving attention and encouragement. Resist the urge to go overboard in appreciation. Be yourself. Show them that they can get your attention when they're being sincere, kind or even just polite to you.

Reaction #2: Your stepkids may try to guilt, anger or manipulate you into returning to your old ways, only to revert to their old ways once they feel things are back to the way they want them. Unpredictable behavior can make people anxious. Their sense of control may be threatened. If this happens to you, and you feel your stepkids are trying to manipulate you, just smile—as best you can—at their tactics. Stay strong and aware. You have a right to act as you choose. Sometimes eager-beaver stepmothers can forget this basic truth—this very important belief.

Reaction #3: Your stepkids may act thrilled at your withdrawal, making sure everyone knows how happy they are about your new decisions. It's the *"you can't fire me, I quit"* reaction popular with teenagers. This is their attempt to continue to feel powerful and to have others think it was their decision. If their reaction hurts your feelings, bring even more compassion and kindness to yourself. Seek TLC from your partner, trusted friends and other stepmothers. It hurts to be manipulated. Watching their behavior from a new level of conscious awareness can initially be difficult because you may see more clearly how you've been treated in the past. Please make time to process your feelings about your experiences so you can release them and give yourself (and your stepkids) a clean slate going forward.

Reaction #4: Your stepkids may become even more aggressive and angry at you for not being there to serve their every need. They may use guilt or judgments. They may use melodrama and accusations. They're likely to try all kinds of things to get you to chase after them, help them and try to connect with them, only to get what they want and create another chance to reject you. Watch out for last minute requests and so-called emergencies where you are used to being the one that comes to their rescue. Listen for things like: *"Where's my permission slip? What happened to my new backpack? I need cookies for tomorrow."* Or, from a clever teenage stepdaughter trying to hook her stepmother into a conversation, *"I can't believe what my mom said about you."* Be aware of manipulation tactics so you can avoid falling prey to them. Do your best to take nothing personally. This can be initially difficult but really does get easier. Seek out all the support you need.

Since stepkids lack control in so many areas of their lives, treating you like you're their maid and the disposable parent is one place where they can find a sense of control. Smiling calmly, knowingly and compassionately while not engaging with them is a powerful way to be your new self around them.

Reaction #5: Your stepkids may behave as if they don't even notice or care whether you interact with them or not. That's usually only an initial reaction, yet it may provide some relief for them, especially the boys. Since we can't read their minds, the key here is to be neutral about their behavior and remain cheerfully true to yourself.

When children figure out a way to ease their emotional pain and then things change (you removing yourself as a receptacle of their emotions), it can send another wave of rage (sense of disempowerment) though them that they rarely have guidance or support for handling. If you see this angry behavior arising, the best you can do is remove yourself from their company, stay aware and have compassion for them without feeling responsible for filling in any gaps they complain about. You can encourage their father to step in and help them gain new emotion-processing skills. Be aware that both your stepkids and your partner may do whatever they can, intentionally or not, to "hook" you back into old patterns of serving them. Stay strong and be the observer of whatever occurs. You are free!

Awakening to the Need for This Plan

A SMOM wrote to me about an experience she had with her stepson that taught her she needed to adopt this radical approach:

> *"I was surprised and heartbroken when I realized how easily I'd been manipulated. [My stepson] knew how much I loved him and wanted to be a happy part of his life. However, I'd shown him, unknowingly, that he could treat me badly, like a doormat in hindsight, and that I'd keep coming back again and again to try to create a happy connection with him. The grief and anger came soon after the shock of realizing what was happening. Then I woke up one day and realized I was ready to change. Thank you for giving me insight about what to do. What a difference it's made for us all. I am not longer annoying my stepson with repeated requests for connection and he is no longer hurting my feelings with what I experience as disrespectful behaviors. I have a lot more time for me now."*

If you choose to step back and *not* connect with one or more of your stepkids, you're going to become more aware of your own emotional needs and wounds from your past and childhood. Why? Because you're no longer distracting yourself with the goal of connecting with your stepkids. This is a chance for you to gain profound insight and healing—if you're willing and curious about that kind of thing. If you're not interested in doing this personal growth work, you may just reap the immediate benefits of no longer being upset by your stepkids and instead having more time to focus on you, your partner and your lives together.

If not getting a hug or kind words from your stepkids breaks your heart, hug yourself and say really nice things to yourself with the full force of your own lovingkindness. If your stepkids minimize you when you try to talk with them and then you feel hurt or angry, turn your attention inward and talk with yourself the way you would comfort a child who'd just been treated that way. See Chapter 29, Ever Get Angry When Your Stepkids Get Away with Things?, if your stepchildren refuse to comply with the rules and behaviors you had to live with as a child and that makes you furious. You can learn so much about yourself by watching how you react to your life experiences as a Stepmom. I look at these situations as potential emotional gold mines of insights and healing waiting us all.

So there it is. What do you think and feel about this idea for your situation? Know that resistances and questions are important indicators—they tell you there's something of value to learn about yourself, and some part of your psyche is trying to get your attention. It's possible to have a happy life with your partner even if you don't have the relationship you'd like with your stepkids. You just need to be willing to accept some differences between your new reality and the fairy tale you'd first imagined when you and your partner fell in love. When you stop trying so hard to connect with your stepkids, you may also find that your time with your partner is much more relaxed and pleasant. You may discover that your new liberating and self-respecting choices and boundaries give you newfound optimism, happiness, time and energy. Another lasting benefit of this approach is that anytime your stepkids want to connect with you in kind ways—even just polite ways—you're more likely to have the ability and willingness to start up a new kind of relationship.

For a follow-up discussion of this chapter, go to smoms.org/BonusChapters and click on chapter titled "Stop Trying So Hard and Start Lovingly Ignoring Your Stepkids."

Section Six

A Stepmom Dealing with Her Stepkids' Uncooperative Bio-mom

Grant me the serenity to accept the things I cannot change;
the courage to change the things I can;
and the wisdom to know the difference.

~ Partial Serenity Prayer
Reinhold Niebuhr

Diane's Story

July 2016

Before I found smoms.org, I felt frustrated, angry, emotionally spent and discouraged. After being involved with the SMOMS community through local meetings and online, I learned that I was not alone. I found comfort in knowing about other stepparents who were experiencing similar situations with their stepchildren and the ex-spouses. I learned coping mechanisms, new approaches to recurring situations and the importance of self-care. I also learned how to be neutral and move forward. Cathryn and smoms.org are most helpful to a stepmother who wants to move past the anger and resentment stages and engage with her stepchildren, the ex-spouse and husband in more positive ways.

The most important takeaway for me with this great group and with Cathryn's direction is that I know how to set boundaries that have helped me move forward. I did not remain perpetually stalled at anger and resentment. Fourteen years later, when something I can't control goes awry, I still hear Cathryn's voice in my head saying, "That sounds about right," and that voice helps me let it go. When I'm in a situation where I can either get angry and upset and lash out or take a deep breath and tell myself that I get to choose how this plays out, I now choose to prioritize the health of my marriage, my family and my own feelings. I know that the work I did with this group early on along my stepmother path has helped me grow.

Most recently, my oldest stepdaughter was married. When the wedding planning began in earnest, I felt myself defaulting to a negative place where I was going to dread every future interaction with the ex and her family and even financial discussions with my husband. I consciously decided that I wanted "our" daughter and her future husband to enjoy every minute of the journey without any worry about awkward situations or anyone behaving badly. If there was going to be drama, I wanted to be sure that neither my husband nor I were going to be associated with it.

A Stepmom Dealing with Her Stepkids' Uncooperative Bio-mom

I gave my stepdaughter license to exclude me from any event that she wanted to be special with her mom (dress shopping, invitation selection, etc.), and I told her that it would be impossible to hurt my feelings. My expectations were only to be invited to the shower and wedding. The rest was up to her, and her decisions should be made without any guilt. A weight was lifted off my shoulders. I knew that my conscious choice set the boundaries for my own emotional well-being. The wonderful consequence was that by stepping back and giving our daughter (my SD) that freedom, she was appreciative and actually included me in events along with her mother. It was awkward at first, but we moved past it. If you had told me 14 years ago that I would text my husband's ex directly and be her Facebook friend, I would have laughed bitterly.

When my own stepmother was alive, I was blessed to be able to tell her how much of a positive role model she was for me. When things get bumpy, I try to remember that the issue will be resolved, one way or another. I want my stepdaughters and husband to look back and remember that even though I made mistakes and even when I had really wanted to behave otherwise, I always had the peace of our family unit as my priority

Diane
Stepmom since 2002
SMOM since 2002

PS: I think one of your chapters of your book should be called "Baby Steps"—where we cautiously stand up and commit to moving one foot in front of the other. There will be times we fall right on our rumps, but we have enough padding that the hurt is more to our ego than physical pain, and we know that if we can move one or two steps, even more are possible.

Thirty-Two

"Sounds About Right"
Use This Approach When Bio-mom's Actions Upset You

If your stepkids' bio-mom chooses to behave in unkind, uncivil or uncooperative ways, she can have negative impact on your daily life even if you never see or interact with her directly. (I'm sure this isn't news to you—just setting the stage.) It's human nature to have feelings about this and to try to counter any efforts she makes to interfere with your life. It's also common to spend countless hours urgently trying to persuade your partner to stand up to his ex-wife in any number of ways so you can feel better. Rarely do these counter-controlling tactics motivate her to seek a pleasant alliance. Your efforts, in reaction to her actions, use a lot of your time and energy that could otherwise be used in positive, productive ways. If you're a Stepmom who has strong feelings about the importance of fairness, rule-following and the need for justice, you might even find yourself a bit obsessed with trying to compel your stepkids' bio-mom to be kind or civil for the good of the stepkids. Isn't everyone supposed to do what's best for the stepkids?

This chapter is for a Stepmom who unfortunately inherits stepkids with a bio-mom who's unwilling to get along. It describes a liberating attitude you and your partner can embrace to minimize the negative impact of a not-so-cooperative bio-mom. What you're about to learn only works if you're willing to make a new conscious choice (sometimes over and over again). This choice can preserve your energy and well-being, as well as dramatically reduce stress between you and your partner—all worthy benefits.

If you and your partner have been struggling with the actions of an uncooperative bio-mom for a while, it can be painful to acknowledge all the time you've lost to stress. If you're in the middle of this stress now, it can be hard to think of anything but trying to get the stepkids' bio-mom to "behave." Your frustrations are totally understandable. For the sake of your own sanity, I'm asking you to open up to the possibility that there's another way to respond to anything your stepkids' bio-mom does, writes and says. To avoid the suspense, here it is in a nutshell: the next time she does something upsetting, take a deep breath and say to yourself, *"Sounds about right."* This conscious attitude offers you a healthy emotional escape hatch from being repeatedly and negatively impacted by her choices.

Sometimes stepmothers find themselves having to deal with the negative impact of their stepkids' bio-mom's uncooperative words and actions—these can include anything that's outside of the realm of kind, cordial, fair or civil. The behaviors can be curt or annoying on one end of the spectrum and excruciating and enraging on the other. Any upsetting behaviors she displays can cause you to lose precious hours and days to stress and conflict. You may find yourself in long, drawn-out arguments with your partner about the impacts of her actions and how you (or, more likely, he) should respond. The often-resisted, hard-to-hear reality is that the bio-mom's actions can't be controlled. You can try, but you'll never succeed—not in the long run. Not even the courts can force her to change who she is or what she values.

Even though the wise, logical part of you may know there's nothing you can do about the bio-mom's actions, they can still be very upsetting, and sometimes all-consuming. It may not be possible to ignore them. Do you have a false belief that there's a way to control her—or at least to shape her behavior in some clever way? If so, that false belief can keep you trapped (or hooked) into trying over and over again. Ultimately, it's accepting the truth that other people can't successfully be controlled—at least not without damage and more negative consequences—that can move you to open your mind, even just a crack, to the possibility of another approach.

So how can you help yourself? What do you have control over? How can you help yourself in a new way when the stepkids' bio-mom does something that upsets you, and perhaps upsets your partner also? Next time something happens try the "sounds about right" approach. You probably get how it works, but it's worth breaking down the process.

Implementation

1. Respond to whatever she does by pausing—do *nothing* for a few seconds. This pause will help you interrupt any old, well-worn reactionary or defensive patterns.

2. Do something to release energy in new ways—take a deep breath, sigh heavily, roll your eyes, stomp your feet or shake your hands or head.

3. Say *"sounds about right"* matter-of-factly to yourself—out loud if possible.

4. If absolutely necessary, have a brief conversation with your partner to address anything logistical that needs attention. Stay on topic (*"just the facts Ma'am"*) and refuse to lose precious time complaining or commiserating. Make it your goal to handle whatever needs handling within the span of a TV commercial break, or set a timer for 5 minutes. Have some fun with it and try to beat the buzzer. Then share a high five with your partner—reclaiming power and freedom is worth a celebration.

5. Once you acknowledge the bio-mom's action and make a plan (if needed), choose to either return to whatever you were doing before she grabbed your attention *or*, if any part of you needs to regroup and feel better, do something that comforts you right away.

Choosing to *not* think about the bio-mom or the situation, and instead putting your attention and energy into what you want to do—something that's positive—is a vitally important step in this process. Redirecting your attention to your needs—instead of giving away your power and attention to think about her actions—creates a new emotional fork in the road that you and your partner can take, a detour to avoid many current and future problems. Practicing this new approach with your partner, another stepmother or a trusted friend works great because it's about creating a new habitual response. Doing this with your partner can be delightfully euphoric. Why? Because you two can make an empowering declaration together. Imagine how it would feel to enthusiastically share this sentiment with your beloved: *"We're not going to give away our time and energy to the drama of the stepkids' bio-mom any more than is absolutely necessary."* At first this can be easier said than done. You might feel some resistance to this approach, as it means disengaging from melodramatic situations, ego-tempting power struggles and other control strategies. You may feel like you're giving in to the unacceptable actions of another by not fighting back. I get that resistance and have provided you with more details and "Yeah, Buts" a little later in this chapter. It's good to notice them. Please jot down your "Yeah, Buts."

A few years ago, two SMOMS wrote extraordinarily similar posts on the smoms.org forum. In both cases, the stepmothers had bio-moms in their lives who had disregarded agreements and made them and their respective partners feel like the bad guys to the stepkids. While these bio-moms' actions may not have garnered compassion from your non-Stepmom friends, every Stepmom who's experienced similar situations will understand how upsetting they can be—even beyond logic and reason. Getting two posts on the same issue within a couple of days of each other felt noteworthy, so I introduced "sounds about right" to the group in my responses.

I've included both of my replies below, in the hopes they will help you see new ways to feel powerful, and only minimally impacted if your stepkids' bio-mom does something unfair, unthoughtful, unexpected or unkind. Some stepmothers are taught, or feel pressured, to endure this kind of stress to prove they love their partners. Sometimes either out of frustration or due to her nature, a stepmother will take no prisoners and act out as she pleases, believing she has a right to take a stand no matter the cost to herself, her partner or her stepkids. Other stepmothers avoid direct contact with their stepkids' bio-mom but look to their partners to stand up for them because they believe that's what their partners should do. "Sounds about right" is another option that can become more effective and appealing than any of these. Deciding you can make a choice liberates you, improves your well-being and makes you feel more empowered immediately, even before anything changes in your outer world.

Stepmom's Post on Our Forum

SMOM1 wrote to me that she felt helpless, and that she'd run out of options. Her stepkids' bio-mom was acting in ways that really upset her and was causing a lot of stress between her and her partner.

My Reply to Her and Now You

Hi. This is a good time to take a deep breath, physically shake out as much anger as you can (justified as it is) and say out loud, "sounds about right." You know that statement is accurate. You probably have a lot of energy moving through you so here's something you can do—make a new choice. After you say, "sounds about right," gently and firmly escort your attention back to whatever you were doing before you got the upsetting news. If you need a bit of self-care to settle yourself, do something else that makes you feel better and then return to your activities. Initially this can be tough—like trying to pry your eyes away from a traffic accident. Thankfully, making that choice gets much easier once you realize it helps you feel so much better.

From what I understand about your stepkids' bio-mom, she seems to repeatedly find ways to rob you of your peace of mind. Given that this is repeated behavior and you can't stop her (darn it), are you willing to try something new? How would it feel to pull your thoughts and energy away from whatever she did and refocus your attention on something that gives you pleasure, energy, support and happiness?

In the early days when the original group of SMOMS was meeting weekly in my office, we put a TV remote on the coffee table for each meeting. Whenever we were trying to help a member of the group redirect her attention, someone would grab the remote, point it at her and click it to symbolize the suggestion to go to another topic. We acknowledged the other figurative TV channels were still playing even after we'd moved on to a new one. We also realized that by changing the channel, we were no longer having to watch what we didn't want to see anymore, and that we were choosing not to be impacted by whatever was playing on the other channels. Somehow the metaphor worked for us.

If the mental "change the channel" maneuver was embraced (it's always a personal choice), the SMOM was then encouraged to start talking about something else—anything that she loved, dreamed about, aspired to, was interested in—until her mood and her state of well-being were restored. When the SMOM was willing to let go of the upsetting event and think about something else, this approach worked very well, and quickly. When she resisted letting go, the approach was less effective, but we then knew to lead her through deeper conversations about the situation to give her more attention and compassion until her resistance eased up. I can assure you, it feels wonderful to take back control of your time and attention.

Feeling Resistance?

Makes sense to me. I resisted it for years so the goal of this chapter is to save you some time. Why might you feel hesitant to let things go and divert your attention, even if it could make you feel better? Maybe your resist because if you accepted this premise, you'd have to give up the "secondary gain" of the situation. What's a Secondary Gain?

- Feeling that you're right (she's wrong)

- Feeling "better than" the bio-mom

- Feeling satisfied that you've won (she lost)

- Celebrating you're finally in control of her (she's at your mercy now)

In the end, that "gain" only represents a temporary "cheap hit of power." It can feel good because judging and over-thinking numbs emotional pain or obscures fear. While you may actually feel better for a few minutes, you have to keep thinking or talking about that same subject to maintain that superior feeling. This can take up a lot of your time. It can be an awful feeling when you realize just how much time, attention and energy you've been giving to her, without anything actually being fixed or changed. For many SMOMS, recognizing that tremendous waste of time and energy serves as a wake-up call that motivates them to change. How about you?

Perhaps you look at implementing the "change the channel" idea as admitting defeat, giving in or letting your stepkids' bio-mom get away with lousy, unfair or destructive choices. I hear you. To me, this is a half-full/half-empty situation—both perspectives have validity, but which one makes you feel better? Since I want you to feel better, I recommend you reclaim your attention and choose to step off an unwinnable game board. The game, you see, is very costly and there are very few rewards for your efforts. If your stepkids' bio-mom is vindictive and if she learns—via your stepkids, for example—that she's making your life miserable with her actions, doesn't *she* win if you let her choices squash your happiness and drive a wedge between you and your partner? By stepping off the game board, you can choose to see yourself as winning, as you're no longer losing huge chunks of your life feeling upset about things you can't change or arguing with your partner. By making this empowered choice, you're in charge of your time and happiness.

My mentor, the late Kit Carson, taught me this "sounds about right" approach in 1996, my first year as a stepmother. I was using our precious time together talking about my stepfamily frustrations instead of focusing on the new skills I wanted to learn from him. Ugh! After listening for a while, he stopped me and said, *"Kiddo, wake up and reclaim your power. Your empowered choice is to not give away any more of your power, time and attention."* For some reason I kept forgetting this great advice until years later when it finally, thankfully sunk in and I was able to embrace it wholeheartedly. He also taught me, *"People change for two reasons: to avoid pain or to seek pleasure."* I wanted both so I finally incorporated "sounds about right" into my daily life and Kit's sage advice still rings in my ear.

What About You, Dear Stepmom?

Be aware of the allure and the temptation of spending time on her "channel" (continuing the TV remote metaphor). Pay attention to see if you indulge in moments of feeling "better than" after your stepkids' bio-mom does something. You may begin to see a pattern. You're likely more susceptible to spending your time and attention thinking about or reacting to the bio-mom (or to anyone else who upsets you, for that matter) when you're not feeling good about yourself or your situation, or when you don't know what else to do to improve things.

Getting upset or angry isn't a bad thing, it's a human thing. It's not wrong. It's understandable. However, *staying* angry is just a painful, usually unproductive way to drain your time and energy. When you realize how much time, energy and peacefulness you're giving up to upsetting stepfamily situations, instead of to your life and goals, you're probably going to be angry. Redirecting the emotional energy stirred up by your situation toward positive actions is a healthy benefit and the intention of anger.

Anger tells you when a boundary has been violated and it generates energy for you to make some changes. It tells you that something needs your attention. When you focus on the person causing the anger, this is a form of self-abandonment—which unwittingly causes more anger. Anger is trying to tell you that you need to be alert and bring your attention to what you need ASAP. As Karla McLaren says in her book, *The Language of Emotions*, anger asks you to look at what needs to be restored and protected. When you look at getting angry as a red flag to wake up, you can take a breath and become very present and conscious of your feelings—in that moment. When you do this you're less likely to be lured into old behaviors or be distracted from focusing on your own well-being. Bringing yourself back into the present, as the adult you are now, feels really good, even if nothing has yet changed. The situation is immediately better because you're awake, aware of all your resources and no longer feeling at the mercy of bio-mom's repetitive actions. This choice allows you to stay focused on yourself so you can give your attention to what you (and your partner) need, want, have to do, etc.

Imagine what your life could be like now, if every moment that you've already spent thinking about your stepkids' bio-mom were refocused on you and your life plan? This can certainly be applied to anyone whose now predictable behavior repeatedly upsets you. I was humbled when pondering this possibility in my own life, and thinking about it kept me motivated to get good at "sounds about right." I became determined to learn from my mentor's wise recommendation and create stronger emotional and mental boundaries than I had in the past.

- How would your life be different if you were able to take in the event, then confidently think "sounds about right" and get right back to your life without any negative impact?

- How does it sound to you to avoid extended arguments with your partner by addressing things in 5-15 minutes?

Can you see how reacting to the bio-mom's antics by taking a deep breath, making a silly face, rolling your eyes or shaking your head (whatever), and then calmly saying *"sounds about right"* alone, with a friend, with a sister SMOM or with your partner makes *you* the winner? Imagine the freedom—it's yours for the taking. Consider the amount of time and energy that would be freed up in the future if bio-mom's upsetting actions no longer negatively impacted your day for more than a few moments.

Talk about winning and having control over your well-being! This is a triumph for any Stepmom and her partner. With that said, I recognize that not everything your stepkids' bio-mom does is going to warrant just a "sounds about right" and a redirection of energy. Some of her actions may require all of your attention. Still, by paying attention to your reactions to her behaviors no matter what's going on, you can catch yourself before spinning off to blame and complain your time away. You can choose to hold on to your well-being. If you're game, try this and see how much better you feel, right away. Imagine how much personal stress, grief and tension with your partner can be avoided in the future if you adopt this approach.

Offering you this new approach is NOT about making you wrong for being upset—not at all. It's upsetting whenever we feel disregarded, our boundaries are violated or someone doesn't play by the rules. Using "sounds about right" and averting your attention is just one way to stop giving away your power and avoid letting the actions of others drain your emotional time and energy. You'll want to honor and process any negative feelings you experience, just not in ways that cause more stress.

You may experience several types of relief—even a sense of freedom—upon using the "sounds about right" approach. This will happen when you first successfully think or say "sounds about right" and then return to whatever you were doing before you learned of the bio-mom's upsetting action. It will also happen when you realize the approach works and you've kept your attention and energy from being sucked away to a dark place. You and your partner will probably be elated when you realize you've saved your night or your weekend and avoided tremendous stress between you. You've now freed up time and energy to spend in the ways you choose, and retained your power and connection to your partner. Ahhhh!

That said, you may also find that by not choosing that strong, numbing sense of "better than," you might feel sad, grief-stricken or hurt—feelings that may not have gotten your attention until now because you were distracted by feeling angry and judgmental. If this happens for you, it's helpful to just pause and take a few breaths. Get curious. Choose to interrupt any harsh judgments and instead be compassionate and patient with yourself. Check in with your feelings.

Ask yourself these questions:

> "How do I really feel—right now?"

> "What thoughts are coming up for me?"

> "What do I need right now to feel better, safer, more loved, less left out?"

> "What feelings is this situation bringing up that reminds me of something from my childhood?"

You're likely to get some clear answers and maybe even discover some emotional wounds or hot buttons that need your loving attention. You can learn valuable information about yourself by reflecting on whatever comes up for you and giving yourself attention. The more hot buttons and wounds you can identify and heal within yourself, the less likely you are to be hooked, fooled or manipulated by anyone. Doing this work will help you reclaim so much emotional power—power that may have been slowly drained, stolen and given away since the beginning of your stepmother journey. And this is likely power you've been giving away all your life. SMOM1, thanks for sharing what happened today.

[End of my reply to SMOM1]

Another Stepmom Too Angry—Now What?

SMOM2 wrote this to me: *"My SD11 (stepdaughter, age 11) came home from her bio-mom's this week with new Ugg Boots... The ironic thing about that is bio-mom just told us that she couldn't pay her half of medical bills ($600) for SD's broken arm because she didn't have the money. Hmm? Seems like she had enough for $150 boots. It may not sound like a big deal but I was furious that she did something like this, again. How can I feel empowered when I'm just feeling angry?"*

My Reply to Her and Now to You

Let me start off and say with gusto, this kind of thing is indeed infuriating! But to help you feel better and learn something from this situation, let's slow things down and look for some insights and new choices.

First Response: If it works for you to handle this by taking a deep breath and saying to yourself, "sounds about right" before moving on to something that feels good—terrific! You've freed yourself. Nice Job! You may want to let your husband know what happened or talk about it later. You may learn from this situation and decide to do something different in the future, etc. With the "sounds about right" approach, you can continue with your day feeling good about yourself and what you're doing. This is one way to avoid giving your power away to an uncooperative bio-mom.

Yeah, But: *"What if I'm not ready or open to that option at this time when reacting to this particular situation?"*

If you can't let it go with an initial "sounds about right" response, it means there's more emotional energy here to explore. Your feelings want more attention. Okay, let's honor that and try another alternative to the well-worn path of a ruined day, stress and a potential argument with your partner who keeps telling you to ignore her and to "let it go."

Finding Relief

Step #1: Process as Much Anger as You Can—First Things First

- See the article about processing anger on smoms.org for a description of an anger letter process.

- Find a place where you can scream for a few moments. This is a way to honor the anger and rage that are trying to flow out of your energy field, body and mind.

- Last year one of our SMOMS found a "Dammit Doll" on Amazon. They are quite affordable and transportable. Give a dammit doll, bought or homemade, a few (or a lot of) whacks on the edge of a counter. It may surprise you how much better you can feel after moving that anger.

- Go somewhere you can sit down for a few minutes, maybe the bathroom. Close your eyes, picture yourself outdoors somewhere and imagine screaming and shouting and thrashing around for a few moments—yes, in your imagination.

- Perhaps you'd prefer to imagine you're a fire-breathing dragon and see the flames emitting from you with great ferocity.

- Maybe you want to imagine being in an interrogation room, facing bio-mom and saying everything you've always wanted to say but couldn't, can't or didn't. See her immobilized by two bodyguards holding her at a safe distance. Know these visualizations aren't going to hurt her.

- As they say on the TV show *Grey's Anatomy*, "dance it out" or flap your arms and shake it off, like geese do instinctively to free themselves of tension after a conflict. It's all about moving your anger out of your physical and emotional bodies.

Any of these tactics can feel very satisfying. It's difficult to describe but you'll know it when you feel it. Taking this intentional action brings a physical relief that makes it possible for you to relax. This work, even via your imagination, is surprisingly impactful—as hard as that might be to believe. Why? Because there's no difference in your subconscious mind between recalling an actual memory and imagining the very same thing. Isn't that interesting? That's why fantasies are so powerful. That's why worrying about negative futures is genuinely so stressful. Use this truth to help yourself get the anger out of your body and feel better. You may think doing this work in your imagination wouldn't be very satisfying. Try this and see for yourself. There's very little to lose and lots to gain.

The thing about infuriating situations is that they often pull on (and play off of) a cumulative list of upsetting situations that have yet to be processed. Have you noticed that? The major cause of rage is likely the realization that you feel out of control of your life, that you can't control the actions of another or that you feel you have no value or options. Whenever you feel powerless or valueless, unprocessed rage spews forth. This is why little kids and senior citizens can get so upset whenever they can't control their own life situations and activities. They're aware they can't help themselves. But you *can* help yourself in your situation if you're willing to add some new emotion-processing skills to your collection.

Step #2: Pay Attention to Your Thoughts and Feelings

Decide to have compassion for yourself no matter what you're thinking and feeling. It's a conscious, self-caring choice to pull away from harsh, impatient and critical negative self-talk. Once you make the choice to be patient and kind with yourself, perhaps by imagining how you would support your best friend in the same situation, ask yourself, *"What can I do to help myself right now?"* Yes, keep your attention on yourself.

Asking this question will trigger a variety of options related to your own personality, preferences, experiences and current circumstances. Once you've released the anger that was triggered, checking in with what you need offers you the possibility of receiving comfort and support. This is so important. Whenever your anger is experienced but ignored, or when it's misdirected to produce blame, judgments, self-pity or other defensive tactics, it's almost impossible for you to identify or acknowledge your genuine thoughts and feelings.

Review this list of self-comforting choices that take anywhere from 5-30 minutes. They may be brief, but they can change the rest of your day:

- Grab a cup of your favorite coffee, tea or water.

- Count to 10, 100 or 1000.

- Breathe mindfully for 5-15 minutes.

- Seek encouragement from a friend who supports the "sounds about right" theory.

- Go for a brisk walk or run in nature.

- Meditate and be open to ideas and guidance.

- Listen, sing or dance to a song that invigorates you.

- Watch or listen to something that makes you laugh. (This will keep you out of self-pity.)

- Write a post on smoms.org or in your journal.

- Play with a baby or pet.

- Be productive and knock a couple of quick chores off your to-do list.

- Help someone else with one of their chores.

- Perform a random act of kindness.

- Get outside in the sunlight so you can turn your face to the sun.

- Plan a future surprise for a loved one.

- Plan your next party, vacation or birthday.

It's important to do something (anything) that keeps your attention on you. Do something that helps you feel more like your wise, adult self. This step is often overlooked because the old well-worn path of expressing anger pushes you to take action, do something, lash outward or react to whatever the other person has done. When you take time to do something for yourself, things turn out better in the short and long run.

Step #3: Use What You've Learned to Plan and Prepare

Once you've released some anger and given yourself some lovingkindness, hopefully you will feel calmer and ready to make some changes going forward. Now it's time to put on your creative thinking cap. Take some time to write down or type out any repeating and predictable actions of your stepkids' bio-mom that have triggered, hooked or upset you in the past. These can include both big things (like not following the co-parenting agreement or major false accusations made against you in public) or little things (like tardiness for exchanges, not passing along school notices or returning clothing, refusing to reply to questions about the parenting schedule or failing to pay for her share).

Write out everything you can think of because there's lots to be learned from this list. When you have your list, reflect on how you've handled these situations in the past. Now, imagine a "do over" and think about all the new ways you can react to the situations, with the primary goal of trying to reduce any negative impact on you, your partner and your stepkids. Start with the simple phrase "sounds about right." Chances are good that this will adequately address many situations on your list—yahoo! For the rest, start brainstorming and see what comes to mind.

Creative Example #1: If it upsets you when the bio-mom is late for pick-ups, create a new game with your stepkids or partner that makes it fun to wait whenever she's late. Play it only when waiting to keep it fresh. Turn her behaviors into a chance for some fun. This shouldn't include badmouthing her for being late in front of the stepkids—it would simply be a way to pass the time in a positive, fun way. Nowadays, smartphones fill this gap for many but to assuage any anger, turn her delay into something that benefits you.

Creative Example #2: If she doesn't return clothes or other items that your stepkids bring to her house, pick up some clothes or other items to which you have no attachment. Send them off to their bio-mom's house without caring if you ever see those things again. Consciously reclaim your power over the bio-mom's ability to dampen your day by not returning things. The more creative choices, the better. The more choices, the more empowered you will feel, and the faster the rage will dissipate. Use the energy of any anger or rage to make your list of new options. Make your goal to feel good instead of to get her to do things correctly—this can be a strangely difficult decision. See Chapter 37, Tip #15.

Still Not Convinced?

Even if you're not sold on the effectiveness of this idea yet, make your list anyway. If she does things that you're convinced are impossible to prepare for, write them down and then see how many possible responses you can imagine, even in hindsight. If you're stumped for ideas, ask a trusted friend or your partner, as long as this won't cause an argument. Use the energy of your anger to do something constructive for your well-being. Include all the choices you can think of—even the far-fetched ones. Why? Because they're choices too, right? The more choices you have, the more powerful you'll feel.

Is there something big on your list? This situation is worthy of even more creative brainstorming. The key thing is to actually write down every possible option. Look at them, imagine them, talk about them. Be creative and consider every good, bad, outrageous, silly, risky, harsh, clever, complex, simple, savvy and ridiculous option you can muster up. Once you've identified your preferred choices, consider making a "final answer" ritual out of shredding, burning or flushing your lists. Alternatively, you can lock your list away somewhere and consult it as needed.

The Benefits and Related Tactics

There's a big upside to identifying what upsets you, creating a list of options and then choosing a new future response to whatever happens. This process can result in you gaining new insights and motivate you to learn new skills. It can help you become wiser and more capable of responding to whatever happens to you. By being more aware of how you're triggered, you're not likely to be blindsided by whatever happens—at least not for very long, not anymore. Any unexpected acts of hostility or control will no longer rob you of your well-being. You can relax, knowing you have a fall-back approach that works for you in the short and long term. This is going to save you, your partner and your relationship a lot of stressful hours, days and even weeks.

Further, when you interrupt your urge to react to upsetting behaviors and instead choose to write them off with "sounds about right," you avoid the stress of the current incident *and* prevent additional conflicts and painful disruptions in your life. Think about your past experiences. When you've acted in anger or lashed out in the past in reaction to the bio-mom's behavior, did this lead to additional upsetting behaviors or escalations from her—and perhaps even from others? Remember, while you can't change her, and you can't change others, you can change *you*—and this makes all the difference.

The "sounds about right" approach can also help you and your partner become closer, making you feel more supported by him. Um, really? How does this happen? Well, embracing "sounds about right" can significantly reduce the need for many tense conversations between you and your partner about his kids' bio-mom. When you're willing to let the bio-mom's actions roll off your emotional back, it makes it easier to remain your loving self and you give the gift of a calm connection to your partner that he can enjoy every day. This can be a huge relief to your partner who, by the way, almost always wants to be on your side. Right now, he may feel trapped or imprisoned without a way out—stuck between what you want, what his kids want, what their bio-mom wants, what he wants and what he thinks is right. That's a lot of pressure you can virtually eliminate from his life—from your lives.

When your partner can relax and no longer reflexively brace for any collateral damage caused by your reaction to his ex-wife, he'll likely be extremely appreciative of you. He knows what you're up against, and he'll learn that you've now chosen a tactic to reduce conflict and stress between you. His increased gratitude can magnify his desire and willingness to support you and take a stand on your behalf when you ask for his intervention in the future.

When you respond to your stepkids' bio-mom's actions with some form of "sounds about right," you and your partner are free! The time you previously spent trying to get the bio-mom to see your point of view or to stop doing what she's doing—plus any efforts to get even with her—can now be refocused on your own well-being and your loving connection with your partner. It's empowering to realize that although you can't control what the bio-mom does (or anyone else, for that matter), you now have a way to contain her negative impact and protect your connection with your partner. See all the chapters in Section

Three for more specifics on reducing stress with your partner. See Section Four to gain insights on your partner's potential perspective.

For stepmother reactions, questions and experiences with this topic, go to smoms.org/BonusChapters and click on the title "Sounds About Right." See the complete list of additional chapters and follow-up discussions in Chapter 39.

Courtney's Story

August 2016

Before I found SMOMS, I was feeling discouraged and drained by my efforts to create peace in my life regardless of the actions of my stepkids' hostile mom. After finding SMOMS and working with Cathryn, I changed. I learned how to focus on my needs, find goals for my family that were within my husband's and my control, and use negative situations I continued to be faced with for my own personal growth.

Over the last five years I've taken a few workshops with Cathryn and worked with her privately as well. I've cried many tears during our sessions. Not so much from the pain and fear—although that was surely present—but more out of the relief of finally feeling known by someone who has been through this and who can teach me how to find my own power in my personal situations. Working with Cathryn, I learned that my stepchildren's bio-mom was acting in narcissistic ways. It made so much sense.

While learning specific ways to lessen the bio-mom's impact on us, we discovered a lot more about ourselves and our own emotional triggers in the process. It was like learning a whole new skill set. We "woke up," as Cathryn calls it. My husband and I also learned new ways to help his kids as they faced all the stresses of having a hostile bio-mom.

We've been having great successes by creating fun family rituals and holding regular family meetings. It's given us the ability to give my stepkids a voice in their lives and some choices they actually have control over. We've gotten them involved in many family decisions like vacations and extracurricular activities. It's been fun. While we've come to realize we have no control over what their bio-mom does and says to others, when my stepkids are with us, we make sure they feel seen, heard, respected and loved as unique and cherished individuals.

A Stepmom Dealing with Her Stepkids' Uncooperative Bio-mom

For the first few years we were continually reacting to all the chaos their bio-mom kept causing us all. But with the tools Cathryn has given us, the insights we've gained about ourselves and the compassionate ongoing support of so many amazing SMOMS from the site, we're feeling empowered and excited about our lives as a family. We've given up a few battles that used to hook us, yet we've definitely won the war because now WE now decide how much time and attention to give to her antics. It's very liberating and a huge relief.

The actions of my stepkids' bio-mom have not improved since I found SMOMS. But the work I've done with Cathryn has made my life, my marriage, and my relationships better.

Courtney
Stepmom since 2009
SMOM Since 2011

Thirty-Three

When Your Stepkids' Bio-mom Doesn't Want to Get Along with You

When your stepkids' bio-mom refuses to get along with you, it can be frustrating or downright infuriating. It's one thing to be treated with a cold shoulder, but it's another to be rejected, left out, judged or falsely accused of any wrong-doing. While rude behaviors are annoying, more severe experiences can trigger deeper pain and rage that most of us aren't taught how to handle. With honorable intentions, a Stepmom can unknowingly get emotionally hooked or triggered by the circumstances and end up giving away tremendous amounts of her personal power, time, energy and even self-esteem to the mother of her stepkids. The more hostile a bio-mom is toward a Stepmom, the more negative impact the Stepmom is likely to experience. This type of situation can be crazy-making and cause a lot of stress in your relationship with your partner until you're aware of what's happening and realize you can make new choices to help yourself.

Even if a Stepmom is as kind, respectful and accommodating as possible, there may come a moment when she finally realizes there's nothing she can do to convince an uncooperative bio-mom to get along. No matter what efforts or concessions the Stepmom offers, she may see that this situation won't ever change. As if new to the party, a Stepmom may think, *"Don't divorced parents want to find a way to work together for the benefit of their children? Aren't the kids supposed to be more important than any issues between the bio-parents and stepparents?"* Unfortunately for some stepmothers, the answer can be no. Some parents are not willing to put their kids' well-being ahead of their own personal feelings. Oh, the mental, emotional and physical energy expended (wasted?) believing that the goal of everyone getting along was achievable—if you could just find the magic solution. It can be difficult to accept that there's nothing you can do. It can also be demoralizing to imagine a lifetime of dealing with an uncooperative bio-mom. This is particularly tough for a Stepmom who tries to do her part to create a healthy alliance with her inherited stepkids and their bio-mom.

Of course, not all bio-moms are difficult, and many are friendly, warm and welcoming. Uncooperative bio-moms, however, can range from being cold or dismissive with you to treating you like an enemy she's determined to destroy at any cost to her own children. If you've been living with a vengeful bio-mom who displays extreme anger, you may find that only other Stepmoms in your situation can truly understand what you're going through. Seek out their support and compassion. To truly let in that a bio-mom could be so mean-spirited, cruel, narcissistic and unconcerned about her impact can be jolting to a well-meaning, eager-beaver, enthusiastic Stepmom with a "glass half-full, everyone has good inside them somewhere" attitude. It can be mind-blowing and devastating to interact with someone who behaves as if she's willing to do long-term emotional damage to her own children and who purposefully avoids following rules or agreements and insists on being contrary, even at the expense of truth, facts, written promises and common goodness. It can be difficult yet it's so important to see the reality of your situation so you can adjust your approach.

Reflecting on your situation can be a real eye-opener, especially if you've worked hard to understand all the bio-mom behaviors you've experienced. A stepmother may cling to the goal of getting along with her stepkids' bio-mom, consciously or not, ignoring feedback, innuendo or actual statements from the bio-mom. She may fight off grieving her lack of connection with her stepkids or their bio-mom by doing, trying and doing some more. A Stepmom may resist giving up, quitting and accepting her reality because she believes if she stops trying, the happy blended family dream will die and life will be unbearable. What's left if the dream dies? What's it going to be like if the bio-mom won't get along with you and your partner, plus convinces her children they can't love you, while you and your partner disagree over how to handle it all? This lack of positive options is scary and can keep you trying much longer than is good for you and your relationships.

Stuck on Getting Along?

Getting clear on your answer to that question is personal growth gold—it can be really insightful, surprising and sometimes even a bit embarrassing or humbling. It's important to be very gentle with yourself because chances are high you've taken a lot of emotional shrapnel in the name of getting along.

- Are you convinced you need bio-mom's blessing or acceptance to have a positive Stepmom experience?

- Are you trying to get bio-mom's approval because her rejection is not only unfair but upsetting and undeserved?

- Do you feel you're comparing yourself to or competing with bio-mom to see who can be the best mothering figure to the stepkids?

- Do you feel that getting along (or not) is making a statement to the world about your ability to connect with others or be a good Stepmom?

- Does not having a good relationship with bio-mom feel like a failure to you—and therefore an unacceptable outcome?

- Do you feel left out of your new family and believe that if the bio-mom accepts you, your role is more secure?

- Do you strive for an acknowledged, equal position in your new family so you can stand up for any unfairnesses between the bio-parents and make a difference?

- Do you feel having a positive, productive, respectful relationship with the bio-mom is the "right" thing to do for the stepkids so you're trying to convince your partner and his ex-wife they should all get along?

- If you look at your own past, when did you have these same feelings growing up? Did you have parents who didn't get along? Did you feel rejected by your own mother? These three questions can be more impactful than you may imagine.

Extreme honesty with yourself, in response to these questions, will help you see what may compel you to keep trying to get along with your stepkids' bio-mom, even when all the signs read that it's not going to happen. Whatever you discover about your motives or emotional hooks is worthy of more self-reflection so that you can better support yourself going forward. Self-compassion combined with your insights can lead you to feel stronger in your present role and heal old emotional wounds, while helping you understand your vulnerabilities and become wiser and better able to love your partner. Lots of good can come from the lessons we experience as stepmothers, such as emotional healing, increased self-care skills and a closer relationship with our partners. Believe it or not (yet), while you've potentially experienced your interactions with your stepkids and their bio-mom as a dangerous minefield, they can also be used as a treasure map and lead to your personal empowerment. Our interactions with them bring to our consciousness any past emotional relationship turmoil that is still active and unprocessed within us.

If there comes a time to let it finally sink in that a happy family relationship with your stepkids' bio-mom isn't going to happen, a Stepmom may realize—perhaps for the first time—that the bio-mom *never* gave her any indication that she wanted a cordial or civil relationship with her. Have you ever asked your partner how he felt about you and his ex-wife getting along? An enthusiastic Stepmom often tries to get along with her stepkids' bio-mom because she can't imagine how their lives would work without getting along. Reflecting back, she may also realize she's been blinded by a desire to create a happy stepfamily dream. She may have found it incomprehensible that any bio-mom would really *not ever* want to work out any conflicts with her kids' dad or stepmother. Who wouldn't want peace over conflict? This question may reflect your own wishes and sincere willingness but not necessarily anyone else's viewpoint. Surprisingly, it's a liberating wake-up call when a Stepmom finally opens her eyes to see the reality of her situation and then, if applicable, the futility of her "get along" goal with her stepkids' bio-mom.

Mustering Compassion

When you believe or know that your stepkids' bio-mom's actions are responsible for some (or a lot) of your stress, it can be very challenging to feel any compassion for her. Even Stepmoms with their own bio-kids have told me that while they would prefer to relate to, and even find common ground with, their stepkids' bio-mom as fellow bio-moms, it's really difficult to stay open to that when their stepkids' bio-mom acts in hostile and uncooperative ways, especially over a period of time.

For a Stepmom who inherits an uncooperative bio-mom, and who doesn't have bio-kids herself, it can feel nearly impossible to have compassion for the bio-mom. It could also make this Stepmom angry if I ask her to consider finding even a sliver of space for holding compassion for the bio-mom who's causing her so much pain or anger. Why bother trying to have compassion for your stepkids' bio-mom if you believe she's the reason for your stress? Because when you're able to muster any compassion for another person, you're coming from your empowered adult self and not the grown-up version of the wounded child you used to be. When you feel compassion you can still self-protect, still minimize or contain any negative impact and still find ways to problem-solve with your partner. Also, with this compassion, you will see you can make choices and handle your feelings from a wiser, more authentically "you" state of mind.

When working with a Stepmom who's willing but can't seem to feel any compassion for the mother of her stepkids, I ask her to consider how she'd feel if her stepkids' bio-mom had partial custody of her most beloved pet. A loud "gasp!" is often her first reaction and then, after a moment or two, she begins to think about how upsetting it would be to have another woman (non-friend) caring for her pets without having any control over how she treated them. Yikes!! Yes, this could be horrible and scary for most pet lovers.

To be clear, having compassion for your stepkids' bio-mom doesn't excuse any of her negative impact, nor does it mean you should allow or endure hurtful treatment or stressful experiences. Choosing to find compassion for another person benefits you because it can free you from the consuming and harmful (to you) effects of vengeful and jealous thinking. This can help you be your best self when handling stepfamily challenges.

Because I support and consult with stepmothers who are usually under extreme stress at first, I've heard lots of stories about the actions of not-so-kind bio-moms. As a matter of fact, when we SMOMS hear or read about kind and civil bio-moms on our site, we cheer for that Stepmom—it's kind of a sympathetic joyful moment that feels good for Stepmoms who aren't so lucky. With the wide spectrum of bio-mom personalities and circumstances, there are still some common feelings that are understandably difficult (to varying degrees) for bio-moms to handle. Could your stepkids' bio-mom feel out of control? Is being in control important to her as she tries to feel safe? Could she be feeling fearful, and is this leading to more controlling behaviors on her part (that are rarely win-win)? Could she be overwhelmed or bitter at having to handle her kids on her own? Is she perhaps worried about finances? Is she frustrated that she's on her own and she sees her partner having your support? Is it possible that she didn't want the divorce and faces the grief of losing her family dreams? Does she believe that being divorced damages her image? Could she maybe hate the fact that you now potentially know her bug-a-boos and secrets from the past?

Sometimes Stepmoms arrive on the scene when both bio-parents are still feeling wounded and battle weary from months (or years) of stress between them. Now, this former couple may find themselves unprepared for the new complicated dynamics of stepfamily life. Like wounded and frightened animals who strike out of fear, some bio-moms know no other way to respond to stress. Your stepkids' bio-mom may have no source of support or perhaps zero interest in processing her feelings in conscious ways so she can become wiser.

I'm not sharing all this to create sympathy for any bio-moms who are causing you extreme duress, but rather to help you step out of your own trauma, even if just for a few moments, to see the entire situation from a 10,000-foot perspective.

Please be assured that having compassion for another human being never implies nor necessitates your agreement. It's not a "hall pass" for bad behavior but it can help you understand more about why that person is doing whatever she's doing. Asking you to have just a bit of compassion for your stepkids' bio-mom is definitely not about letting down your guard, lowering any healthy boundaries or making yourself vulnerable in any way! It's just that the benefits to *you* of holding a sliver of compassion for her can enable you to be a wiser (not nicer), more creative and empowered human being as you handle your stepfamily situations—regardless of her actions. She's got all kinds of reasons to justify her actions and you never have to try to change her mind. You can just be more prepared to handle her actions when you keep even the teeniest bit of compassion for her in your consciousness.

When Nothing Works, There's a Reason

If your stepkids have a bio-mom who doesn't want them to get along with or interact with you during public stepkid events, it won't matter how kind, fair or helpful you and your partner behave toward her—she's likely to try to keep the conflict and stress alive. Your overt attempts to play nicely with the bio-mom may drive her to become even more uncooperative. There are many reasons she might be angry or feel unwilling to get along with you. She may be annoyed you don't seem to heed her spoken or unspoken messages, *"Back away from me and my children! Know your place! You're not welcome in my life! I'm never going to give you what you want and get along with you—not ever!"* Sometimes an uncooperative bio-mom will even distort your kind or respectful gestures until she believes she has legitimate grievances against you. Maybe she believes you're interfering with her right to motherhood, or stealing or denying her happy memories. She may complain about you to judges, school officials, therapists, neighbors, your partner and/or your stepkids.

If your stepkids' bio-mom is vengeful in any way, you can become a target for misplaced rage. The desire to destroy happiness for you and your partner can become her new goal/pastime/obsession. A hostile or uncooperative bio-mom may justify not getting along because she feels wronged by you or your partner. It can be tempting to try to identify the roots of her animosity, but it's not productive or helpful for your well-being. Really! In spite of what some part of you may believe, remember that trying to compel, convince or control her to get along will result in you giving away tremendous power, time and energy. You may never know the truth about her motives or actions. The important thing for your happiness, well-being and relationship with your partner is to accept that there's nothing you can do to change her mind about getting along with you. The sooner you accept her rejection, the sooner you free yourself from a lot of stress and anxiety and the sooner you and your partner can stop arguing about how to deal with her.

Accepting the Unacceptable

Waking up to this truth can also bring up self-critical judgments and feelings of humiliation or rage about how naïve and "played" you may feel. Realizing you didn't fail, but simply never had the ability to change her mind, will hopefully make it easier for you to have compassion for yourself. You may feel hurt about the loss of a future in which you've invested a lot of time and energy. On the bright side, seeing the truth about your stepfamily situation is like being freed from a stubborn, expansive log jam that was never going to clear up.

Before rushing into the specifics of a new game plan, you'll have some grief and rage to process when you accept that your initial happy blended family dream won't happen. In addition to your grief over lost future dreams, you may feel some remorse for the stress caused between you and your partner in your pursuit of getting along with bio-mom, especially if he's been trying to convince you to stop trying. You'll probably have some feelings about all the painful interactions you've endured with your partner—all for the good of the failed cause.

Even though your partner is bound to feel relieved at your realization, he may also have some feelings to express. If you're lucky, he'll share and process his feelings so you can both be free of the negative impact of your sincere efforts. Sometimes we owe our partners an apology for the negative impact (on him) of being blinded by our own dreams—this is a very healing gesture in a relationship. Giving each other empathy and forgiveness for *why* you did whatever you did goes a long way toward dissolving any barriers that have been built up from your quest to get along with bio-mom.

Once your emotions are processed and your losses mourned, you'll start to feel more like yourself again. What a relief! With your new attitude, your happiness is no longer at the mercy of your stepkids' bio-mom. You can now choose to accept your situation or continue to resist reality. I vote for accepting your situation—you? When you choose to look at your stepkids' bio-mom's behavior as unchangeable, like the weather, you can now redirect your energy elsewhere. You could, for example, focus on making you and your partner as happy as possible. I call this choice "empowered acceptance" because it's about consciously accepting what is and believing you can find ways to successfully deal with any unchangeable realities in your life. This is empowerment. Chapter 16 covers this concept in more detail.

Helping Yourself

Once your empowered acceptance settles in, you may find yourself daydreaming about the peaceful and happy experiences you can create for your life. Yes, the new dream will be different from your original happy family dream. It will involve redirecting your energy and attention toward actions you *can* implement and that don't involve or require the cooperation of your stepkids' bio-mom. If she chooses to cooperate at any time, this can be viewed as a bonus. Your updated dream will likely bring about changes in your interactions and relationships with your stepkids and their bio-mom. The ages and personalities of your stepkids will all need to be factored in as you imagine a new life. Your new plan will incorporate the realities of your life situation *and* outline goals and wonderful futures you and your partner can create together.

You can draw a line in the sand and proclaim something like this: *"Starting today I refuse to give my stepkids' bio-mom any more of my time, attention and energy."* You can honor your feelings about the past and get clear about how your experiences have impacted you—an important part of recovery. It's important to reflect on what you've been through and how your choices, actions and reactions to bio-mom's refusal to get along have affected you, your partner and your stepkids. At some point in this process, you'll probably find yourself feeling ready, maybe even eager, to think about new goals and plans for your future that do not include trying to win over your stepkids' bio-mom. This is a liberating and invigorating moment.

Finally accepting you have zero control over your stepkids' bio-mom's behavior is an important milestone that can change your life. It's liberating to stop trying to change her. Instead, looking at ways to contain her negative impact is thankfully something you and your partner can do successfully. If you're on the verge of accepting this situation in your life, use lots of supportive self-talk and be courageous. Know that accepting this reality is important for your personal growth, well-being and maybe even your sanity. Plus, it can dramatically improve your relationship with your partner. If, after reading all this, you realize that your stepkids' bio-mom is actually pretty good compared to what some may be experiencing, maybe additional reflection can help you feel a bit better about your situation. That's OK too!

Resist the Urge to Control

Whether due to exhaustion or realizing you have better options, the choice to stop trying to get along with your stepkids' bio-mom offers you a doorway to freedom, joy, relief and a closer connection with your partner. Letting go of your "get along" goal also gives you newfound time to create a lot of new positive opportunities for your life. The key decision to make is this one: stop trying to control or convince bio-mom to change her attitude about you and instead accept her behavior so you can start focusing on containing her negative impact and protecting yourself, your partner and your stepkids and any indirect impact on your own children, if you have any.

Sometimes you can discover new creative and effective ways of dealing with a not-so-kind bio-mom by thinking about how you'd handle the same kind of personality/behaviors in a work colleague or a disagreeable boss. Yes, there are power issues and differences if someone is a peer vs. a boss, yet thinking about how you might deal with her if she were a work associate can automatically shift you into wise adult mode. Looking for solutions from this adult, strong, capable foundation feels *much* better than feeling you're trapped or at the mercy of someone. Don't believe me? Fair enough. Pick a single situation and adjust the circumstances enough to make it a plausible workplace scenario. Now list some ways you could handle it and see what comes to mind. This process can result in out-of-the-blue ideas and a reconnection with your true strengths.

Another analogy that may be effective is this: imagine your stepkids' bio-mom is like an approaching storm. Think about how you'd handle an unstoppable, unchangeable reality. Doing this can shift some of your feelings. In addition, you may come up with new ideas for how to contain any potentially destructive impact on you and your partner, with the bonus of feeling confident in your ability to do so. When Hurricane Sandy was approaching the New Jersey shore many years ago, it's a pretty safe bet that no one spent time or energy trying to control it, stop it, change it or convince it to go somewhere else. Sure, New Jersey is a very nice state and didn't deserve any damage, but that meant nothing to the storm, did it? No one felt the approaching storm was launching a personal attack—it was just something that happened, and in order for residents in its path to stay safe and be as prepared and comfortable as possible, immediate adult decisions, actions and use of resources were required.

In response to the reality of the approaching stormy weather, men and women sprang into all kinds of creative actions with the motivation and confidence that they could keep themselves safe in the storm. How does it feel to imagine responding to the current and potential actions of your stepkids' bio-mom as if she were bad weather and you have the ability to keep yourself safe? When you're dealing with weather, your adult self sort of kicks in. Can you feel yourself—a competent, creative and strong woman—mobilizing in creative, smart, efficient ways to stay safe in your stepfamily situations?

The make-up and intentions of your actions change when you realize it's up to you to protect yourself. Your actions will be more effective and it will be much easier for you to work with your partner when you agree that the goal is to preserve yourselves emotionally, mentally, financially and physically from the approaching storm. Can this approach really work for a Stepmom with an uncooperative bio-mom? Yes! I've seen countless situations where a Stepmom's shift of intention goes from control/change to contain/self-protect with positive (sometimes miraculous) results for the Stepmom and her partner—even if the bio-mom never changes. When you're feeling like your wise, adult self, you'll see that creative, empowering and self-respecting ideas begin to flow quite naturally. These new tactics can keep you and your relationship safe from future bio-mom storms.

Whether you've been in the role of stepmother for ten months or ten years, remind yourself you have the power to change your strategy anytime, and as many times as you want. When you see what you're dealing with (and with whom!), you're free to create a new game plan each and every day if you want to. Seeing your stepkids' bio-mom situation as it truly is, instead of how you wish it could be, enables you, your partner and your stepkids to have a much more peaceful experience together.

Realistic, Self-Supporting Goals

- Intentionally assess the situation with as much objective perspective as possible.

- Listen to and heed your partner's recommendations whenever you can.

- Make your family's happiness and your well-being a high priority.

- Look at feelings stirred up by the actions of your stepkids' bio-mom as clues to discovering your unhealed emotional wounds. Then turn your attention to helping and healing yourself.

- Check in to make sure you're not projecting "mother" onto this bio-mom. See Chapter 23 for comments about three emotional projections common to stepmothers.

- Identify any conflicting needs, beliefs and values with your partner so you can be on the same side of whatever stress the bio-mom causes you.

When you can do all these things, you will find yourself in a very different emotional world. Your new world is one where you are so busy becoming wiser, more healed, stronger and more skilled, that getting along with your stepkids' bio-mom becomes a "nice to have" for your happiness—but not necessary. At the risk of seeming overly dramatic, I suggest that embracing this approach puts you in the empowered driver's seat of your own life.

Making the choice to accept what is and knowing you can find new ways to build a happy life—whatever the weather or bio-mom forecast—also helps you stay out of victimhood, martyrdom and self-pity. Reminding yourself that you're talented, wise and strong enough to handle whatever life brings your way enables you to reclaim more of your power and create your own life experiences, regardless of whatever reality you've inherited. The overall change? Give up trying to control her and find more ways to contain any negative impact and self-protect from the actions (or inactions) of an uncooperative bio-mom. Once you have your strategies and tactics in place, you and your partner can both turn your energy and attention to enjoying your time together as a united loving team.

There are several articles on public section of smoms.org about controlling others if you're interested in this issue. Also see the article "Testing and Proving Love" on smoms.org.

For two follow-up chapters with reactions and discussions on this topic, go to smoms.org/BonusChapters and click on the titles "When Bio-mom Doesn't Want to Get Along" and "Raging at the Injustice of Bio-mom Actions." See the complete list of additional chapters and follow-up discussions in Chapter 39.

A Stepmom Dealing with Her Stepkids' Uncooperative Bio-mom

Diana's Story

August 2016

From the first day I met my husband and we shared our stories, he was completely open and honest about the difficulties he was going through with his ex. It was an extremely high-conflict divorce, and had been since day one. Literally. One day, he had kissed her goodbye in the morning as he left for work, said "I'll see you tonight," and later that afternoon, police walked in to where he worked and arrested him, walking him out in handcuffs. He was never allowed back into his home again.

He spent eight months fighting criminal charges that the Crown withdrew (we're in Canada) at the preliminary hearing, after her testimony. In the meantime, she had filed for divorce, gone to court (despite telling him they would mediate and her lawyer had made a mistake that she would get changed), got full custody of their two daughters, child support in an amount that was outrageous for his income and spousal support that she didn't actually qualify for. I can't believe how fast she got it done. Of course, he didn't understand or realize any of that at the time. He was just gobsmacked.

And she continued to have him arrested. We figure that she realized that if it worked once, it would probably keep working. And she was right. Our lawyer told us it happens so often now, that they call it "separation by arrest." It often happens to men in positions of power: police, firemen, lawyers. In the end, she'd had him arrested four times by the time I met him. He was 15 months into it at that point.

The fifth time he was arrested was a week after I met him. He'd been on the phone with his youngest daughter, at his mother's place, trying to make arrangements to see her the next day. She said she would have to ask mommy. It pushed him past his 5:30 p.m. "curfew." Next thing he knew, police were at his mother's house looking to arrest him. His ex had called the police when his daughter asked mommy if she could see her father. He ended up in jail for three months, over Christmas, waiting for his case to be heard.

We had planned to fight all of the charges, but he needed surgery and he was only going to be able to get it properly if he was out of jail. The judge suggested he plead guilty to breaching his recognizance and get out with time served and one year probation. He agreed—however, an assistant Crown attorney, a woman just back from maternity leave in a department of men, was looking to make her mark with the "abusive" man and insisted on a three-year probation period if he was allowed to visit his mother's home in the same hometown where his ex and daughters lived. It was absolutely crazy. I had sat for three months, every month, at every court hearing for him, watching as drug dealers were allowed to walk out of the court room with nothing. Yet here he was being held accountable in a way that made absolutely no sense, by a woman who claimed to be a victim over and over again to anybody that would listen, because she believed it would get her the house, the kids, the car, the investments and everything else. It very nearly did.

The system is broken and definitely veers in favour of women. And I say that as a woman. I was still going through my divorce when I met my husband. And I couldn't believe how discriminatory the system is toward women and against men. I've been with my husband seven years this year, and we've spent five of those in court. The first two were spent getting the original court ruling overturned by the initial judge who realized she had been lied to. Bio-mom tried another two times to get him arrested, but we kept paperwork on us at all times, faxed it to the main police station and the police told her she had no grounds. Even still, she would tell the girls she was going to get their father arrested if he showed up to pick them up. They would call us crying, begging us to pick them up down the street, around the corner, so that mommy wouldn't call the cops.

It was a never-ending battle. My mother says it took over my life. I was 44 years old when I met my husband, newly single after being with my ex since I was 19, married for half my life. I didn't have any children of my own. I ran my own award-winning consulting business from my home. I was a successful, together, "with-it" woman who owned her own beautiful home, had the opportunity to travel, be involved and do things. All of a sudden, I was up to my eyebrows in muck. I was trying to find documents that my husband no longer had access to because his ex had them all, fighting for custody of two girls, 12 and 13. By this time, their mother had moved a boyfriend half her age into their house, claiming he was just a friend, and we were hearing from neighbours that parties were going on till the wee hours of the morning while the girls were there. Bio-mom was demanding more money, while our calculations showed my husband had probably already overpaid by $25,000. We were trying to figure out how to literally keep the girls safe with a mother who smokes up daily, and doesn't respond to calls from the school when her daughter doesn't attend or hand in assignments. (The school had resorted to calling me instead.) And we live an hour away, by choice, because of the need to keep some distance between us and the craziness.

In the midst of all this turmoil, I did what I always do—I researched and went looking for help. I needed any kind of information to educate me and help me to better handle all the crap I was dealing with. And I found smoms.org. I lurked for almost a year I think. Just kind of lingered on the edges. Read others' stories. Was amazed at the similarities and thought, "Holy Cow. It's not just me. I'm not alone."

But I think it was when Cathryn posted about Narcissistic Personality Disorder (NPD) and about the book, "The Wizard of Oz and Other Narcissists" by Eleanor D. Payson, that I was motivated to actually sign up because I wanted to start posting and getting more involved. The need to share, to talk, to be heard...it resonated with me. We had just finished the first set of parenting and financial agreements, and finished with court, we thought—naïvely as it turned out—and what Cathryn was writing about sounded so much like what we had gone through. I immediately went online and ordered Payson's book. And then other books. I remember lying in bed, reading at 2 a.m. with my husband beside me and just wanting to shake him awake to say, this is it. This is what we've been dealing with. How narcissists have to prove to the world that they aren't the ones with the problem, so they set out to systematically destroy the other person and to take everything away. Wow! If we'd only known sooner, it might have made things easier. Or we might have changed the way we dealt with things.

At the very least, it finally allowed me to understand what was going on. And I could explain it to my husband. How his ex could lie on all her court documents. How she could lie to all kinds of people and have them believing her. Even when we presented document after document, refuting what she was saying, she still steadfastly stood by her lies. But even more damaging were the lies she would tell the girls. And all the damage she had done to them along the way that they won't even realize until they are much older.

I was part of the very first workshops that Cathryn offered. Her Resentment Workshop helped me to learn to breathe again—to figure out how to put my survival gear on when hurricanes swept through my house every other weekend when the girls came. That's what it felt like. They blew in like a hurricane, swept through leaving a wrath of destruction in their path, and then went back to their mother's, leaving me feeling like I was barely standing sometimes. Usually because dealing with them meant having to deal with an extremely hostile bio-mom—one that we actually had no direct contact with except through the court-ordered online Family Wizard program. The amount of resentment I had was immense after dealing with years of injustice in the courts, because of this woman, who continued to act like she was doing everything right and in the best interests of her daughters, even as she continued to lie and make life difficult. I used to tell my husband that I didn't hate my controlling, abusive ex and my divorce as much as I hated his ex and his divorce.

Working with Cathryn on the phone and through the workshops helped me to find my way through this darkness. It's an ongoing journey and I often pull out my notes. I also met some sister SMOMS who have become very dear friends as a result of taking these classes together first, then by just talking on the phone. Opening up and sharing with one another the challenges you have as a SMOM is so necessary to survive this journey; there is really no one else that will understand what you're going through, not even your husband or partner. No one gets it like another SMOM.

Working with Cathryn taught me it's OK and necessary to set boundaries. The classes themselves were a challenge because I kept getting interrupted by the girls or my husband, even though I reminded them that I had a class that night. I even had one of them pick up the phone and start dialing it while I was on my class call. Hello?? Cathryn's teachings helped me to rethink the situation. Every class after that and in similar situations now, I run around the house and collect every phone extension and bring them into my office with me right before the call time. I then put up on my glass office door a black-out curtain I made especially for these times that signals "do not even THINK about disturbing me." And I put up a sign on the outside of the door, "On a Conference Call. Do Not Knock or Disturb. I'm Not Home." I have heard feet approach...and then leave.

Three years ago, my husband and I got married in a beautiful backyard wedding at our home. But even as we were planning this wonderful occasion, we were dealing with an incredibly stressful time, because our youngest daughter had decided to come live with us. She had tried the year before, but her mother made it too difficult for her to leave. After almost failing every one of her first-semester subjects in ninth grade, she realized she needed to live with us if she wanted to be a success in the future. So, she made the difficult transition and we were thrown back into having to go to court again, because nothing could be handled civilly. And nine months later, after being incredibly difficult with us, blaming us for her mother's situation and her own, and not speaking to us for three months, her older sister realized that she needed to move in with us as well. Through it all, my sister SMOMS and Cathryn were there, offering support and words of encouragement and reminding me that it's not me. I'm not the problem.

So, now both girls live with us. The younger one is doing extremely well. She has grabbed the challenge of going after what she wants for herself and her life and is doing wonderful things, winning awards, doing well at school and in the community. This is why as Stepmoms on a Mission we fight for our stepkids and our lives and the families we're building. Her sister, unfortunately, has done the opposite. It has been a never-ending litany of excuses and reasons for why she can't achieve what she sets out to do and soon abandons, including failing out of two different college programs this year. It breaks my heart because I see the glimmers of goodness, the ability to be successful, and yet the damage from the foundation gaps of the six very formative years with her mother is immense and I'm worried she won't overcome it—at least not anytime soon. And the toll it is taking on our family in the meantime is immense.

It's SMOMS and Cathryn who have kept me sane through the entire process over the past five years. Although that's been a matter of opinion at various points—whether I've stayed sane. It's a tough journey to be on, this choosing to be a stepmother. And choosing to be a SMOM, a Stepmom on a Mission—actually trying to make an impact and a difference and to have a real role in the lives of stepchildren—is even harder. You don't really understand what you are getting into, you can't. You've never experienced anything like this before. It's a truly soul-sucking experience. Most of us on SMOMS have landed here because we're in extreme situations and we need to feel connected, because it becomes so isolating. You feel so alone. And it's not of your making. You're living with the outcome of someone else's poor life choices and it is impacting every facet of your life. And you need support and resources to help you every day and there aren't very many out there. SMOMS was the one community I found that has helped me to learn, to grow, to keep it together, to make wonderful new friends and to grow stronger in my marriage. Without it, I don't think I would have survived. I can't imagine my life without SMOMS.

Diana
Stepmom Since 2009
SMOM since 2011

Thirty-Four

Feeling Hatred?
Redirect These Intense Feelings to Reclaim Your Power

Almost everyone has felt hatred for someone or something in their lifetime. If you're a stepmother experiencing repeated stressful situations with your stepkids or their bio-mom, then chances are high you've experienced moments of hatred for them and their impact on you. Hatred is defined by Webster's dictionary as "passionate dislike; detestation." It can rob you of your joy, enthusiasm, energy and a lot of other good things you like about yourself and your life. Hatred is a powerful emotion that most people don't know how to channel, learn from or process in healthy ways. Rather than process and release this powerful feeling, it's much more common to avoid, deny or distract yourself from it. Maybe you cry, lash out, misdirect it, numb yourself or cover up whatever you're feeling—which only throws all the emotional energy under the carpet of your psyche and it stays there, often being tripped over, waiting to be cleaned up and removed.

These common reactions rarely help you become more self-aware, feel more powerful or improve the circumstances causing these feelings. So what's a Stepmom on a Mission to do with her hatred? How can you stay open-minded, non-defensive, creative and compassionate when this feeling is present? How can you make sense of your hatred when you know you can't control the people causing it? Why do so many circumstances and events generate hatred in stepmothers, even when they may be judged as merely annoying by others?

In a nutshell, uncooperative bio-moms, challenging stepkids and hesitant-to-act partners can cause Stepmoms to experience new levels of hatred because their actions tap into a warehouse of similar feelings from our past that we've not yet processed.

On a philosophical note, I also believe many of us had such strong initial connections with our partners because their emotional baggage can potentially provide us with life-changing growth and healing opportunities. The opposite is also true—our baggage provides similar learning opportunities for our partners. When our connection with another is deep, this connection—and the intensity of our love for each other—stirs up other feelings as well. Consider for a moment that the actions that drive you to feel hatred have a higher purpose that serves your well-being. Embracing this idea can change your perspective when things upset you. When you believe this, it's also helpful to do your best to protect the love you and your partner share from the impact of others' actions. How would it feel to use whatever others do to become wiser, stronger and closer to your partner? This represents a massive lemons-to-lemonade quest which, if you take on the challenge, you'll discover is well worth the effort in many ways.

This chapter offers you insights and options so you can use the intense energy of any hatred you may feel to benefit you in ways you may never have imagined. As you do this work, you'll see the role everyone in your stepfamily situation plays in your waking-up, empowerment process. As unlikely as this may sound to you now, you may very well discover that their actions and the unchangeable realities in your stepfamily life motivate you to discover feelings and strengths you didn't know you had. Choosing to grow from whatever is happening in your life can motivate you to consciously reclaim power you'd lost, particularly as you learn new ways to respond to previously upsetting situations. You'll be able to change your responses to stressful experiences—both new and repeated ones—if you're willing to invest in some self-reflection, curiosity, courage and creativity.

Whether you're a stepmother or not, and regardless of your life situation, anytime you feel hatred it's a chance to release it from your emotional body. Furthermore, I believe that the person who activates your hatred is really kind of doing you a favor—when you're conscious enough to see what's happening. Why? Because you—like virtually everyone—have unconscious warehouses of emotions looking to be acknowledged, processed and released. Sometimes, because of strong survival strategies, your circumstances need to get so excruciatingly painful and enraging that you bust out of the well-honed, child-created, defensive survival strategies and false beliefs that you may stubbornly defend and cling to—whether you're aware of this intention or not. As you've read in other chapters, these same patterns keep you emotionally imprisoned in (or repeating) hurtful relationship dynamics until you wake up to what's happening.

Learning how to process and free yourself from old, upsetting feelings and limiting beliefs has many benefits. It can reduce your fear, rage and anxieties—especially the possibly scarier ones you numb with over-giving and resentment. As I write this, I'm assuming you're open to the possibility of learning new skills so you can free yourself from any hatred and transform that energy into something that makes you feel calmer, stronger, safer and more competent.

My Perspective on Hatred

- Hatred is on the extreme end of the anger spectrum.

- Hatred is crystallized rage that has nowhere else to go. It's like a lion circling its cage, trapped. It's too powerful to freeze or numb in place, and it has to move.

- When the energy of hatred doesn't move, it becomes self-poisoning.

- Hatred is the sensation of wanting and needing to annihilate, to destroy and to make something or someone no longer exist in your life.

- It's vital to acknowledge feeling hatred—without judgment and with compassion—so you can work with it.

- Indulging in how you might act on your hatred gives you brief moments of feeling powerful. These temporary, false feelings of strength drain you of precious time and energy.

- Hatred often leads to obsessive thinking. You feel hatred when you don't feel like you have any recourse, so you may use thinking to distract yourself from your pain and fears. If you feel relief, you believe you have to keep thinking about the situation in order to keep the pain and rage under control. When you stop thinking the hatred resurfaces, so you numb it with more thinking. This cycle can go on and on.

Anytime you interrupt a vicious cycle, it will free up the energy. Obsessive thinking *can* be stopped by interrupting this closed cycle and giving the energy a new place to move. The mere act of acknowledging that you're feeling hatred opens an emotional window and lets in fresh air. Once you realize what you're doing, you're in a new position to process it consciously—obsessive thinking is no longer needed.

Hatred is the intense desire to annihilate something or someone, but since you're not going to physically annihilate anyone, how about if you find effective ways to eliminate others' negative impact on you and in your life? Rather than pushing away or ignoring your desire to destroy a person, what about annihilating his/her ability to hurt or anger you in any way? How about completely destroying his/her ability to cause stress between you and your partner? These are attainable and desirable goals. If this sounds good to you, start to use your imagination, your creativity and practical skills to think of ways to destroy the negative impact anyone you hate has on your life. You can do this by making changes in the way you interact with this person or react to anything they do. While the following tactics work with anyone you may feel hatred toward, we'll expand on some specifics for uncooperative bio-moms.

Process Your Hatred

1. Stop yourself as soon as you recognize feeling hatred. Say out loud, *"I'm feeling hatred right now."* Naming the emotion is an important step and skill.

2. Stop thinking about the situation in that moment. Stop talking. Just breathe for a moment to consciously interrupt any old patterns and remember you have lots of new options to help yourself—even if you don't know what they are yet. Stopping in your tracks can save you a lot of collateral relationship damage.

3. Be compassionate with yourself—as if your best friend were sharing the exact same feelings with you. Give yourself the empathetic understanding and freedom of expression that you and perhaps "the child you used to be" didn't have but deserves. Express to yourself (in a mirror would be great), *"This stinks. This is wrong, unfair, etc."* Be your own validating advocate and support yourself and how you feel. Refrain from judging, denying or disregarding your feelings. Give yourself this much-needed attention. When you ignore this step (consciously or unconsciously) and put your attention on the source of your hatred, you're actually abandoning yourself—which leaves parts of you feeling vulnerable and hurt.

4. Acknowledge the desire to annihilate your "hate partner." This is a term Karla McLaren uses in her work with emotions. She says when you hate someone it keeps you energetically connected to them. Yuck! If you choose to believe this, it may bring on nausea initially, but then most likely motivate you to free yourself from the impact of anyone you hate. The reality of how much time you

may have spent thinking about your hate partner (in this case potentially your stepkids' bio-mom) can be embarrassing and even more motivation for learning new skills.

Karla goes on to say that the hate partner's actions bring the unconscious energy of your old rage to your attention so you can feel it and process it completely—therefore releasing the energy from your unconscious warehouses of emotions. She says that once you do this work, the person who once generated so much hatred becomes much smaller in your world. Yahoo! This is both an incentive and a reward for your efforts.

5. Next, shift your focus to looking for practical, specific ways to annihilate the *impact* your hate partner has on you. You have complete control over this goal. Even if nothing comes to mind right away, promise yourself that you will do some brainstorming until you find some new options.

6. Identify your beliefs about hatred.

    - Do you hold any childhood beliefs that it's impossible to resolve hatred within yourself—meaning without taking action against that source of hatred?

    - Do you believe that the only way to stop feeling hatred is to somehow intimidate, control or avoid the person you hate?

    - Do you believe that you, as the adult woman you are today, have the ability and resources to free yourself from the impact of this hated person's behaviors? If not, are you willing to establish a new belief that says you are capable of acquiring these skills?

The reality is that the child you used to be did *not* have the ability to help herself in similar situations. The child you used to be was truly disempowered and at the mercy of people she loved and hated along the way—you are not. It's helpful to remind yourself that there are new things you can learn to do to help yourself. Again, this is true even if you don't yet know what they are. This is important, and can help you break up obsessive thinking. What a relief! You can also prevent compulsive, anxiety-based action and painful bouts of despair when you give yourself an alternative task.

Annihilate the Impact of a Bio-mom

Tactic #1: Give yourself permission to imagine all kinds of crazy, fantastic, maybe even science-fiction, "you're never going to do it but it feels sooo good to think about it" ridiculous options for getting rid of your stepkids' bio-mom's *impact* on you and your partner. Use your imagination. Talk with a trusted, creative friend. This conversation alone can move a lot of emotional energy. If you haven't tried this option yet, just give it five minutes of genuine imagination and see how you feel. It's very liberating. You'll feel better afterward because you've helped the emotional energy move out of your body with your thoughts and intentions.

Tactic #2: If your partner is willing, take turns sharing your feelings and your wishes about how things could be different in the situations that cause you to feel hatred. Not to give or get permission, but as an emotional relationship practice. Take turns giving each other lots of empathy. I call this safe space and time "the Empathic (or Compassion) Zone." This tactic can diffuse a lot of energy when both of you suspend all judgments and defensiveness. Yes, this is a brainstorming time that honors every feeling and idea as valid—even if only for the time you're discussing it. Having your feelings acknowledged by the one you love is a powerful way to move your emotional energy. It's also a wonderful way to help you and your partner genuinely re-experience a deep, supportive closeness that can become lost during extended stressful times.

Tactic #3: Make new choices about how important an uncooperative bio-mom is going to be to you. You have the freedom to think about her in many different ways. For example:

- Stop caring about what you imagine she thinks about you.

- Stop caring what she says about you. Explain the truth only if needed to defend yourself legally, socially or with those you love.

- Going forward, stop caring if she likes or includes you. As the saying goes, what she thinks of you is none of your business.

- Stop trying to get along if she's made it clear she's not interested.

- Stop giving her actions your time, attention and energy unless they directly impact you.

- Stop monitoring her rule-breaking behavior. It only drags your attention away from your own happy life. Sadly, in many situations no amount of proof, complaints or presentation of the facts will get an uncooperative bio-mom to change or hold her accountable.

Tactic #4: There are many new choices you can make about how you behave when it comes to her and her actions. Be creative, put aside your old beliefs about what you "should" do. Take actions that make you feel better and enhance your well-being.

- Refuse to pretend that everything is hunky-dory when you see her. You can be civil, no more is needed.

- Avoid interacting with her whenever possible.

- No more answering the door when she comes to your home.

- No more listening to her voicemails or reading her emails or text messages.

- No more overseeing the making or purchasing of her Mother's Day or birthday gifts with the stepkids (unless you want to).

- Most importantly, declare a moratorium on arguing with your partner about her behavior. If you can't avoid discussions, put a time limit on the conversations—10-15 minutes is usually enough time to make logistical decisions as a couple.

The good news is that you can make all these choices to eliminate her negative impact on your life. What else can you stop doing that enables her actions to have negative impact on you? These options will save you many fruitless, lost, angry, upsetting hours of your valuable time and untold arguments with your partner. While all these ideas have worked for others and can work for you too, what resistance might arise?

Yeah, But: *"What if that's not enough and I still feel angry and filled with hatred?"*

Chances are high that if you take these steps you'll feel some immediate relief and then realize there's more emotion here than a reaction to the present situation. This is true for many stepmothers—not wrong or stupid, just part of being human. The intensity of the energy can be just the tip of your emotional iceberg. The majority of the energy represents accumulated, unprocessed rage, pain and hatred that you brought into your relationship from your past. When this unprocessed emotional energy is surfacing—maybe blasting—through you, it's because your present circumstances have generated emotions that align with unacknowledged feelings from your past. It's like having all the tumblers line up in a padlock, letting the unconscious emotions flow through to your conscious mind. When you can acknowledge—even if just privately to yourself—that most of what you're feeling comes from your past, it's much easier to stop blaming others and get to work on helping yourself. This is another empowered choice that brings great benefits.

If you to want to track back to the source of your anger, which has turned to rage and then to hatred, ask yourself how you were feeling right before you felt the hatred. In order to do this, you'll want to slow down your thoughts and feelings so you can identify them in sequence. This takes a bit of focus at first but it's worth the effort. Your well-being and relationship with your partner are certainly worth it. Hint: It will be some form of disempowerment, boundary violation or denial of your value. Did you feel unheard, disrespected or unloved? Were you perhaps feeling disregarded, ignored or mistreated? Take time to think and feel about this.

Work with the Child You Used to Be

Once you identify the specific thought that preceded your feelings of hatred, ask yourself another question: *"When was the first time I can remember feeling like this?"* Go back through your life experiences until you get to the youngest age when you can recall a similar feeling. It's amazing how memories will surface as you begin looking for them. When you can give yourself 20-30 minutes of uninterrupted time, use your imagination to give that younger version of you your complete loving attention so she can express her hatred and rage. Then you can begin to see (and distinguish) the difference between your feelings about the present situation and feelings stored from the past. See the step-by-step process at the end of Chapter 9. There's also another example of a Stepmom going through this process with anger triggered by the actions of her stepkids in Chapter 29.

As I've written elsewhere in this book, the teachings of Dr. Alice Miller in her book, *The Drama of the Gifted Child,* explain how memories and feelings can flow into your conscious mind through the doorway of your imagination, and that they've been stuffed in your unconscious—unseen and unacknowledged for since birth. When you make contact in your imagination, then memory, with any younger version of yourself, there are bound to be tears of relief for finally feeling supported. Maybe there will be sadness, too, for feeling so badly and so alone for so long. It's a tender healing moment of release and palpable relief.

Do your best to allow the emotions to course through you without any judgment. Rest assured they'll subside naturally for you and the younger versions of you. Once the sadness passes, you'll probably feel the energy moving again, but now in an invigorating way—it's hard to describe, but you'll know it. Then you'll be able to give that younger you a lot more compassion and love going forward. It's a very liberating and powerful healing experience you can give to yourself.

In Chapters 35 and 36, I describe an imaginary, energetic beekeeper's suit that acts as protective energetic emotional gear when you're around anyone you feel might emotionally "sting" or upset you. While I present this concept as helpful when dealing with uncooperative, hostile or narcissistically behaving people anywhere in your life, it can prove handy for all sorts of toxic situations. It's powerful to imagine this because by doing so, you're more likely to stay conscious and in your adult self. This makes you less vulnerable to others and wiser in your responses to whatever occurs.

Keep your beekeeper's suit on at all times around anyone you feel might treat you in cruel, manipulative, draining or narcissistic ways. You can imagine it as your forcefield, your invisible protective fencing—sustainably fueled by your anger—to protect you from anyone trying to harm you or hurt your feelings. Some people are just oblivious or unconcerned about their impact, and others are more intentional. The good news is that regardless of others' awareness or intentions, you can learn how to render any incoming actions as harmless, giving you more confidence and ease around anyone. This is another conscious Stepmom superpower.

Reclaim Your Power

Here's something that may startle you. When you hate someone, even for very good reasons, you're giving them some of your power. They can't use it, but you can't either. Some part of you knows you're more vulnerable to their negative impact when you're hating them because your attention is on them instead of on holding your boundaries. Here are some ways to take back your power from uncooperative, manipulative or even narcissistically behaving bio-moms, stepkids and any other upsetting people in your life.

1. Give yourself permission to make that person less important in your life. Imagine her (or him) as a tiny person talking to you in that teeny tiny voice of a three-inch creature who's no longer a threat to your well-being.

2. Keep reminding yourself that you can help yourself without needing her (or anyone) to change. With your new awareness, you can create options and make new plans that will eliminate/annihilate her negative impact on you and your life. Even if you don't know exactly what they are yet, keep thinking about it—you'll get better and better at this with practice. Seek a trusted friend for new ideas if you feel stumped.

3. Look for any choices, beliefs and patterns in your own behavior that may be sustaining feelings of hatred, maybe even mutual hatred between you and another. By being willing, and having the courage, to look honestly at your contribution to situations that generate feelings of hatred within you, you give yourself the chance to discover more about yourself. This new information makes it possible for you to see ways to interrupt the previously "unconscious compulsion to repeat" behaviors that have kept you engaged with another. The good news about this is you're always free to change your own behaviors. You can make new choices and when you do, circumstances will change around you.

4. Spend your valuable time, energy and attention on yourself (and your family) with lots of lovingkindness and compassion. Chances are you've been giving the object of your hatred your attention for a while, so it may take some time to break the habit and create a new focus of attention. Anytime you find yourself thinking about this person—stop, just stop yourself. Then make a new choice to think about something else.

5. When hearing or thinking about something this person does that upsets you or makes you feel hatred, ask yourself, *"How important do I want to make this in my life today?"* Look at your daily life as a pie chart and decide how much of it to apportion to the actions of that person. Make the slice as small as you can.

6. Ask yourself, *"What would be more interesting to think about now?"* or *"What would make me feel better in this moment?"*

7. Remember your priorities in life and make a choice to put that person far down your list.

When feeling hatred for someone who's acting in uncooperative or even narcissistic ways, what are some choices?

- Futile Options: You can ask them to change their behavior by giving them your feedback. (This will not work when the person refuses to change.)

- Frustrating and Risky Option: Try to get your partner to handle things so you feel better. (This rarely works unless your partner is inspired to take action. It's also likely to cause a lot of stress between you.)

- Surefire Way to Feel More Powerful Option: Take your focus away from that person and imagine yourself much bigger than anything she could throw at you.

Here's a visual metaphor that has been helpful to many: Imagine that the hated person will always throw twigs at you, it's just their nature. When you feel you're like a small, vulnerable kitten, the sticks injure you and can even devastate your world. Now change the visual and imagine that you're a Clydesdale instead of a kitten. She can continue to throw those same sticks at you but now they're just an annoyance. As a powerful Clydesdale, you can easily ignore the sticks or brush them away and continue with your day. You'll still see the sticks and feel them but they will not hurt or distract you from your life and well-being.

8. Make your own well-being your #1 priority. (I know I suggest this a lot—it's so important and so easily overlooked when stressed.) Choose to make it more important than any happy family fantasy, need for approval, need for justice or desire to connect that may have been fueling your actions in the past. This new choice can be the positive avenue for your energy going forward.

Hatred and resentment are valid and common feelings brought on by the stresses stepmothers face when stepkids, their bio-mom or even their partners are unkind, unfair or cruel in any way. The encouraging news is that these feelings have a lot to teach you about how you can honor and help yourself in new, more effective, healthy ways. When you make the choice to look at your hatred with curiosity and compassion, you'll free up a lot of trapped emotional energy. You'll feel better, less reactive, stronger and more alive. Once this hatred-related energy is acknowledged, consciously redirected elsewhere and then released and moved out of your energetic forcefield, you'll be able to witness and handle the antics of others with greater awareness, wisdom and a sense of calm competence.

For reactions, questions and experiences on this topic, go to smoms.org/BonusChapters to find two follow-up chapters. Click on "Feeling Hatred and Hating It" and "Raging at the Injustice of Bio-mom Actions." See the complete list of additional chapters and follow-up discussions in Chapter 39.

Pandora's Relief's Story

June 2016

I found smoms.org when I was still just dating my husband. I was 26 years old and had met a man with an eight-year-old girl who was born when he was still in high school. To say the least, I had no experience with children, much less one that old. While we had an instant bond and my then-boyfriend and I were a near-perfect match, the mother of my stepdaughter had other ideas about whether my husband deserved ongoing happiness.

As a licensed clinical social worker and mental health therapist, I had enough shoulds/oughts in my head to fill my own book. I thought I knew enough to get through these situations. Even with a license to practice therapy, I found myself often confounded and sometimes shocked by the audacity and snowballing negative impact a hostile bio-mom can have on her ex, her kids and the new Stepmom in the picture.

It took Cathryn, her workshops and the other SMOMS of our smoms.org group to help me see that no matter how correct, kind, fair or eager I was to create a positive stepfamily situation, a hostile bio-mom is going to do everything in her power to wreak havoc on my partner and me. If a bio-mom has any features of Narcissistic Personality Disorder (NPD), her children will also be left in the wake of this pain. Cathryn also helped me wake up to this fact—stepkids are innocent victims, too.

Your presence in their lives, and theirs in yours, will require a unique set of skills. Until you live it, it's almost impossible to imagine what you'll need or how you can feel. By the way, the non-judgmental, compassionate support from other women in my situation was a huge benefit of being a member of smoms.org.

I can say that now, five years later, the hostility from my stepdaughter's mother has only increased and we've been through the ringer. Cathryn and my friends at smoms.org supported me through two unfortunate court battles and constant upheavals until my husband and I finally learned the secrets—insulating our marriage, protecting our family life, embracing empowered acceptance of the unchangeable facts of our life and learning strategic deescalation and disengagement techniques.

Working with Cathryn can ensure your success in what really can be a battlefield—stepfamily life. Thankfully she's translated her insights and experiences into teachable skills. I pushed back many times, wanting to know the reasons behind her concepts and suggestions. I found her patient explanations made good sense to me and allowed me to customize them to fit my personal style.

Being a Stepmom with a hostile bio-mom and challenging in-laws has changed me. In addition to feeling more calm and confident to handle whatever drama is created by others, I've tapped into a new source of inner strength and courage. Cathryn calls this becoming a "non-reactive warrior."

My story is hardly unique, but our voices as Stepmoms subject to hostile bio-mom treatment remain mostly silenced. I believe that as a result of Cathryn's work and advocacy, we are becoming more empowered and less silent. I know I'll be passing along my newfound wisdom to my own clients, hoping to help them as Cathryn has helped me. We SMOMS are truly Stepmoms on an important mission.

If you're considering marrying someone with children, you can't afford not to have the information in this book or Cathryn's help. Save yourself a lot of time, heartache and stress and learn from someone who's been through what you're now facing. Should you be lucky enough to have a kind or civil bio-parent on the other side, you'll still learn invaluable techniques for how to manage all the other things that come along with blending a family.

Pandora's Relief
Stepmom since 2011
SMOM since 2012

Thirty-Five

Is Your Stepkids' Bio-mom Consistently Uncooperative? Shifting Your Attitude and Approach Brings Relief

The most common reason women seek out smoms.org is that they're looking for effective ways to deal with the stress they experience with their stepkids' bio-mom and to minimize the problems this causes in their lives. Bio-moms and Stepmoms (and their partners) can find themselves tangled up in all kinds of big and small, overt and covert, unwinnable power struggles that can cause devastating results for everyone involved. This can potentially be one of the most emotionally, financially and physically draining, enraging and painful relationships a Stepmom has ever been forced to handle.

This chapter is intended to support a Stepmom who is looking for new approaches for dealing with bio-mom conflict, and particularly when the bio-mom acts out toward her in not-so-kind, not-so-civil, hurtful or hostile ways. Whether your stepkids' bio-mom's actions range from annoying and unfair to completely outrageous and destructive, I've chosen to describe them as simply "uncooperative." This word is descriptive of behavior only, covers a broad spectrum of possible impacts and makes no judgments about the bio-mom herself.

In the 18-month process of preparing the chapters for this book, I've done a lot of soul searching about how to be empathetic, helpful, fair and respectful to every Stepmom in this very difficult situation with a bio-mom. It's easy for a Stepmom to get caught up (or overwhelmed) in the understandable rage, pain, grief and despair she may be feeling. Since my mission is to help you find your power within your life situation (which is unique and probably complex), I've decided to stay away from psychological labels. I will not be referring to any form of mental illness or emotional disorder such as borderline, narcissism (NPD), depression, etc. when referring to any stepkids' bio-moms because I don't know anything about your situation and the people in it.

Being divorced and in a stepfamily situation can be an excruciating experience for everyone involved—for any number of reasons. Occasionally even the most well-meaning person loses her temper or composure. When working with a stepmother privately, I'm able to understand her situation and make specific suggestions, as I did with the SMOMS whose stories are included in this book. But since I don't know your situation, let's focus on how you can better manage the impact of someone who is unwilling to be cooperative—for whatever reason.

I've also found it can be a distraction (costing you time and energy) to label the stepkids' bio-mom for behaviors that may (or may not) be limited to certain situations. As tempting as it can be to diagnose, blame and judge the bio-mom's motives or emotional state of mind—even when you're right—it's proven unnecessary for getting you to a more peaceful state of well-being. This chapter is not about changing your stepkids' bio-mom. It is about reducing, and ideally eliminating, any negative impact she has on you. It's about changing the way you (and your partner) respond to her behaviors with the over-arching goal of you and your partner feeling confident and connected as you deal with stepfamily stress caused by your stepkids' uncooperative bio-mom.

If you're a fortunate Stepmom whose stepkids' bio-mom is usually willing to get along, normally treats you with respect and is generally kind or just polite toward you, this chapter may only serve to make you aware of how fortunate you are in your stepfamily situation. It'll be here should you ever need it in the future.

Things Change When You Change

Are you willing to look at your relationship with your stepkids' bio-mom in a new way? Perhaps you've been trying to outsmart, win over, control or cajole her so you can feel less stress. Maybe she displays what seems to be a lack of commitment to resolve issues, making it impossible for you and her to find an acceptable, peaceful way forward. Now, I'd like you to step back and try something different for the sake of your everyday happiness. As an added bonus, this can help you protect and strengthen your relationship with your partner. I'm guessing you've already tried a lot of tactics so what could I possibly offer you? What can you do differently to help yourself? You can make the conscious, empowered choice to step off the stepfamily game board of "control or be controlled" with your stepkids' bio-mom. Yes, I'm asking you to consider backing away from strategies and actions that may be justified by your need for justice and inflamed by conflicting beliefs about what's "right."

I've been reading and listening to thousands of Stepmoms share their stories since 2000. In doing so I have noticed several characteristics that consistently uncooperative bio-moms share. Working with these common traits and with the help of some wise therapists and consultants, I've developed tactics Stepmoms can use when dealing with a woman we shall now refer to as an uncooperative bio-mom. Since your stepkids are her offspring, you may see some similarities in their actions. Please know that the following insights and skills can significantly reduce the negative impact of any bio-mom or stepchild who's unwilling to get along with you for any reason.

If you're like most of the Stepmoms on a Mission I've worked with over the years, you'll recognize (even if reluctantly) that there's a wise part of you who already knows you have zero control over her behavior. Still, there's another part of you that urges you—sometimes compels you—to stay in the old game, often at great personal expense to you and your family. Whatever the feelings or motivation of your stepkids' bio-mom, if she's acting in consistently uncooperative ways and impacting you in negative ways, these new approaches and responses to her upsetting behaviors can build your confidence, reduce your anxiety and help you feel like your pre-stepmother happy competent self each time she contacts your partner. Implementing these tactics can also enable you and your partner to stay "on the same side" of any stepfamily issue. This may sound too good to be true right now because of all you've been through—I get that. I understand. I also know these approaches can bring about tremendous changes, for the better. The good news is you have 100% control over implementing them.

The following insights offer observations and explanations for why your stepkids' bio-mom may choose to be uncooperative. I recognize it's not always easy for bio-moms to have to make space for stepmothers in their children's lives because so many of my clients are also bio-moms whose children have a stepmother. My intention is to bring compassion and more awareness for all members of a stepfamily. I share these ideas not so you can use them to try to change, control or cure her, but so you can better understand how your past (and future) choices may be perceived by her and potentially upset, provoke, trigger and aggravate her uncooperative actions. Once you have this information, I will recommend ways you can adjust (not concede) your interactions with her so you and your partner can avoid future stress with her and between you two.

Characteristics of the Uncooperative

Insight #1. An uncooperative bio-mom is rarely logical or rational when it comes to her children and stepfamily matters. She may disregard the rules whenever she doesn't like them, act as if she writes her own rules and even violate the existing ones already agreed to, perhaps using the excuse that as the bio-mom it's her right to do so when it comes to her children. Since men often share the beliefs (consciously or not) that a bio-mom does indeed have the final say about her children, this can make decisions and situations challenging for the Stepmom and her partner. Rarely does anyone grow up being taught and therefore believing that a Stepmom has any rights in her own stepfamily life situations.

Insight #2: An uncooperative bio-mom may act as if she's unconcerned about her impact on others—even choosing to behave in ways that have clear negative impact on her children, relatives and past or current lovers.

Insight #3: An uncooperative bio-mom may make choices that indicate her public image is a high priority. She may behave in ways that seem like attempts to earn her "Mother of the Year" at school, in the community or at church events but make choices privately that would not earn her this award from your perspective.

Insight #4: An uncooperative bio-mom may demonstrate a strong desire to win on all stepfamily issues, perhaps expressing this entitlement because she's the one and only bio-mom of the children. She may rarely agree to win-win suggestions and opportunities unless she can publicly take credit for a win-win solution. If she benefits from others watching her grant your partner (or you) permission for an everyone-wins solution, she may be more likely to agree to it—at least for the moment. This can be hard to understand by those who seek a fair-for-all solution.

An uncooperative bio-mom may act upset if she feels you and your partner win anything or get what you want because she may see that as her losing—which may not be OK with her—based on her reactions. For an uncooperative bio-mom to agree to almost anything, she may need to believe she wins *and* your partner (or you) lose. This is an extremely valuable insight to incorporate in negotiations and decisions with an uncooperative bio-mom. Whenever you or your lawyers present any agreements or plans, always stress how she benefits and what you are most unhappy about but willing to agree to, to gain her agreement and for the good of her children.

Insight #5: An uncooperative bio-mom may reject, react negatively to or get defensive about any written or verbal comment that could possibly be construed as criticism or an indication that she has made a mistake. This makes it challenging (or nearly impossible) when she doesn't follow an agreement and you're trying to hold her accountable for her actions or problem-solve a situation. Her reactions to being corrected or criticized in any way may take the form of illogical actions that intend to invalidate, undermine or discredit whomever she sees as the source of criticism. When confronted with facts proving any wrong-doing or error, she may become unpredictable. In extreme cases, she could break into scary flashes of rage that can escalate to include acts of destruction and even violence toward you and your partner. She may justify these actions or refuse to acknowledge them, no matter the facts, and find a way to convince herself and anyone interested that the problem is you, not her. Alternatively, she may start up a whole separate complaint or completely ignore the issue as if it didn't happen, which can be downright crazy-making until you understand it's just a tactic—conscious or not—to assert her sense of power over you and your partner.

Insight #6: An uncooperative bio-mom may ask you or your partner to do something first before she'll fulfill her part of the agreement. Once your side of the agreement has been completed or fulfilled and before she fulfills her part, she may change her mind and not abide by an agreement (for all kinds of reasons). She may portray this "you first" approach to try to get you (hook you) into proving your good faith. Whenever you can, resist the bait and do your best to craft an agreement that makes both parties take action at the same time.

Insight #7: An uncooperative bio-mom can be an Oscar-winning actor. She may be very smart and clever, skilled as a master manipulator with persuasive verbal skills and charm, particularly with school, legal and medical professionals. She may portray herself as right or as a blameless victim of circumstances, making you and your partner out to be the bad guys. Being aware of this tactic can help prevent you from being fooled or drawn into a defensive no-win situation. It can also motivate you to be as forthright as appropriate with outside authorities. Your awareness of these potential tactics can give you the ability to see her actions as a "sounds about right" event whenever possible, therefore saving you and your partner precious time and energy. See Chapter 32 for an explanation of the "Sounds About Right" approach.

Insight #8: An uncooperative bio-mom may act afraid or anxious when you and your partner share the same social territory with her—like school, church, work, friends and/or community. Why? You may never know for sure or even have the chance to assuage her anxiety, but if it's the case, you'll likely hear about it or see actions that prove this to be true. She may fear you'll tell stories about her. She may fear losing status as her kids' mother. She may take an aggressive stance by spreading untruths or personally embarrassing stories about you or your partner to ease her fears about the uncontrollable. She may distort situations to make you and your partner look like the "bad guys." She may have no problem, and be extremely good at, making things up to serve her purposes.

Insight #9: An uncooperative bio-mom may only back down or back off from the overt public accusations if she believes you and your partner will stay quiet, stay away, go away or go along with her every command and acknowledge her ability to control your life or stepfamily family circumstances. It's important to realize that these issues are not (repeat—are *not*) about the truth or facts of your situation but about this uncooperative bio-mom's perceptions of the situation. This may mean that you and your partner need to do a bit of acting to reduce the stress of your situation with the uncooperative bio-mom.

Insight #10: An uncooperative bio-mom may need to continually convince herself that she's in charge of your stepfamily situation. If this is true, a bio-mom can prove this to herself by taking actions to try to provoke a reaction from her ex, her kids and even you. Sometimes it's her only overt measuring stick for her degree of control (and resulting emotional safety). Her sense of having control over others and being right may be her only pathway to feeling safe, then good—criteria needed so she can relax. When she's relaxed she's less likely to cause you and your partner as many, or any, problems.

Beware: When things are going smoothly between both sides of a stepfamily for a while, an uncooperative bio-mom may create a problem, out of the blue, just to make sure she's still in charge. One way for her to prove to herself that she's in control is to confirm her ability to upset you, your partner and even her own kids.

Insight #11: When it comes to control issues, sometimes an uncooperative bio-mom may have the conscious goal to feel in charge of the situation by disrupting any of the win-win, happy family dreams her ex (your partner) and his new lover (you) may have. Why? It's impossible to know precisely what she's thinking or feeling but common motivations are revenge, anger, grief and fear. Fear because your partner, and now you, know the truth about her life, her history and her flaws, which can be excruciating to some uncooperative bio-moms. She may blame you for the divorce. She may believe she's been treated unfairly. She may feel that you've ruined her life. Or she may be upset because she believes you and your partner are having the joyful, carefree life and relationship experiences with her children that she may feel belong exclusively to her—the bio-mother.

Insight #12: An uncooperative bio-mom may insist that she should be in charge of setting the pace and timing of all events involving her children. If she feels she's being rushed or delayed she may act unhappy or refuse to participate when anyone else is controlling the timing of a situation. Why? Because it smacks of someone else being in charge—sort of an emotional kryptonite for the bio-mom if she values being in control.

Insight #13: When angry, afraid or upset, an uncooperative bio-mom may lash out or act out in hurtful ways, wanting to emotionally "sting" you with her customized set of uncooperative behaviors. The issues of fair/unfair, right/wrong and good/bad may appear to be irrelevant to some uncooperative bio-moms.

Many Benefits to Reap

It can be very helpful—and a lot less stressful for you—if you're willing to make the choice to look at her behaviors, attitudes and choices as if she's coming from a foreign culture you don't understand. Interacting with an extremely uncooperative bio-mom can cause a Stepmom to experience previously unfathomed levels of obsessive thinking, rejection, resentment, hatred, over-giving, over-trying, exhaustion and incredibly painful interactions with her partner, who often wants peace at any price. See Chapters 18 and 19 and Section Four for more about this conflict of needs and how to resolve your differences with your partner.

Now that you have this information, each experience with an uncooperative bio-mom can be viewed as a half-empty, half-full moment of choice for a Stepmom on a Mission. It's not about right or wrong but about making choices that make you feel better about yourself—or not. It's a powerful choice to turn your attention away from what's wrong with the bio-mom (or her actions) and instead look toward opportunities for greater self-awareness and self-care. Consider mastering more effective skills with each upsetting incident. It really does feel much better to look at any negative impact from an uncooperative bio-mom as an opportunity to become more conscious of your limiting beliefs (so you can change them) and to become more aware of your emotional tender spots (so you can learn how to help yourself in powerful ways). It's a terrific feeling to avoid past tension with your partner. It's fun to dazzle and congratulate yourself with your skills and talents as you rise to the challenge of staying calm as you begin to handle previously upsetting stepfamily situations in new, competent, effective ways.

A Stepmom interacting with an uncooperative bio-mom may find it impossible to believe anyone could behave as she does and continue to get away with it. In addition to these painful feelings, and perhaps not knowing how to process her feelings with her partner, a Stepmom may dread feeling at the mercy of an uncooperative bio-mom for decades to come. Watching how an uncooperative bio-mom's behavior impacts her children (your stepkids) can be another very upsetting situation for a Stepmom. If you can relate to this nightmarish situation, what can you and your partner do differently to feel better? The good news is that there are many effective tactics you can implement to contain or reduce the negative impact of your stepkids' bio-mom. With new enthusiasm and skills you can learn to protect yourself, your relationship with your partner and perhaps even your relationship with your stepkids.

Become a Non-Reactive Warrior Stepmom

I learned the term "non-reactive warrior" from therapist Eleanor Payson, L.M.S.W., the author of *The Wizard of Oz and Other Narcissists*. She used the term in her "Healthy Self" workshop in 2012 to describe a desirable mindset and strategy for anyone dealing with a person exhibiting narcissistic behaviors. I found many similarities between certain uncooperative bio-mom behaviors and the characteristics of narcissism. I decided to customize Eleanor's non-reactive warrior model for stepmothers to see if it could reduce the drama, trauma and stress experienced when dealing with an uncooperative bio-mom. In 2013, I presented the concept of a non-reactive Stepmom warrior in several SMOM workshops, on our support forums and in private sessions with Stepmoms. The feedback was consistently positive with stories of immediately successful and lasting results. Eleanor and I have had many discussions about this and I am so grateful to her for her past and continuing support of my work with Stepmoms.

The whole concept of doing less to help yourself more can be initially unsettling, especially to anyone who is used to taking action to solve anything, believing that the best way to fix or change things is by doing more and trying harder. This approach of non-reacting is going to challenge those beliefs, so be aware of any resistance and look for the valuable insights that await you. Adding this new approach and skillset to your repertoire of responses can be a liberating change and a huge boost to your confidence and effective dealings with any uncooperative behaviors.

Non-Reactive Warrior Qualities

Quality #1: A non-reactive warrior Stepmom who feels stressed refrains from taking action, contacting or speaking to an uncooperative bio-mom, particularly in response to anything the uncooperative bio-mom does. This is not withholding, avoiding or denying. It's making a conscious choice to resist reacting (in the present moment) for the good of the cause—your well-being and relationship with your partner. It takes more energy than you might think to interrupt a lifelong belief and pattern of doing. You may think that *not* taking action is cowardly—many people judge inaction in this negative way. However, with an uncooperative bio-mom who can feed off of your actions and reactions, it's a more powerful response—most of the time. This can be hard to believe so try it for yourself. It's tremendously effective, avoids many arguments with your partner and can reduce the need for you to deal with additional reactions from an uncooperative bio-mom.

Quality #2: A non-reactive warrior Stepmom adopts a *"No expectations, no violations"* approach when dealing with an uncooperative bio-mom. This is something else Eleanor Payson points out in her book and workshops. Her approach initially requires mindfulness, and then becomes a stress-relieving habit. It means becoming aware of and resisting the temptation to expect an uncooperative bio-mom to do (or not do) anything, such as be on time, follow through on what she says or behave in certain ways toward you and your stepkids. With this in mind, it's very helpful to create Plan B's for every occasion and interaction involving your stepkids so you're ready with an acceptable alternative if something comes up from the bio-mom. This is a very effective anxiety- and stress-reducing tactic and gives you a new way to use any of your newly restrained energy.

Quality #3: A non-reactive warrior Stepmom manages an uncooperative bio-mom without manipulating her. When you're managing someone, you're looking for ways to handle things to a mutually beneficial conclusion. You're taking the known capabilities and feelings of the uncooperative bio-mom into consideration. This approach requires creativity, compassion, resolve and focus. No one likes to be manipulated. When you're manipulating others you're forcing or tricking people in a hurtful or deceptive way into taking actions that serve you and/or hurt them. I refuse to engage in or endorse any form of manipulation. There are always honorable and ethical ways to protect yourself and you're about to learn about them here and in Chapter 36.

Quality #4: To be clear, a non-reactive warrior Stepmom does less, not more. For example? You can choose to talk less, write less, respond less quickly, worry less, imagine fewer bad things, offer fewer explanations, give out less (or better yet no) unsolicited advice and offer to do as little as possible when interacting with an uncooperative bio-mom.

Quality #5: A non-reactive warrior Stepmom honors and learns from whatever she's feeling. She notices her urge to want to keep doing so she can isolate false beliefs and change them to more empowering beliefs. See Chapter 10 if you have discovered you believe that the best way to fix, react, change or address anything is by taking action. Sometimes doing less really is more effective. I personally resisted this truth for way too long. Give it a try and decide for yourself based on your experiences.

Examine Your Beliefs

Below are examples of beliefs (conscious or unconscious) that can keep you entangled and engaged with an uncooperative bio-mom. Beliefs are so strong that many times you'll act on them even when you know from experience how she'll probably behave, and when you suspect there will be collateral damage to address.

Beliefs That Compel Action

"If I stop trying, I'm a quitter and that's a bad thing." (False, but many were taught this is true.)

"If I stop expecting good things, only bad things will happen." (False.)

"I gotta figure out this uncooperative bio-mom so I can get her to change and so I can finally be safe, feel better, etc." (Partially true but not in the way most of us believe.)

"If I stop trying to create a happy family, my dream will die and she'll win—and that's incredibly unfair." (Partially true, partially false. This assumes there's only one happy family dream to have and requires more discussion.)

Resistances to Becoming Non-Reactive Warrior

Reason #1: You may believe the *only* way to deal with an uncooperative bio-mom is to interact with her directly or indirectly through your partner. This mindset engages a competition of sorts. You may also believe you're smart enough to figure out how to make any situation work. Yes, you're probably smart enough, but this belief can lead to continuous controlling choices and an urgency to engage so you can win and cause her to lose. It's sort of confidence on steroids.

One key to uncover about interacting with an uncooperative bio-mom is to realize it's not about our intelligence, confidence, courage or willingness to effort or confront. It's about realizing that the uncooperative bio-mom is *not* interested in resolution with you. Nope! She may just be trying to keep you and your partner entangled in trauma. You may find yourself selectively forgetting all the past failed attempts to resolve things with her. It can be hard to accept, yet so important to realize that a consistently uncooperative bio-mom is actually fueled by (fed, enjoys, gets a kick out of) your failed efforts.

Reason #2: Have you noticed how the desire to beat her, to get her to do the right thing, to keep from losing to her and to stand up for fairness (or for your partner) can overtake your sense of wisdom, self-care and perspective—even when you're exhausted? Ever feel the compulsion to control her at the expense of your own well-being and relationship with your partner? If so, you have a lot of company at Stepmoms on a Mission. We truly get it and understand how you feel. We also know how good it feels to override those urges and become a non-reactive Stepmom.

Reason #3: You may feel too angry, resentful, anxious or scared of the possible consequences her actions may cause to believe that not doing something—anything—could possibly help your situation. This is what an uncooperative bio-mom is counting on. As crazy as this next suggestion may seem, please give it a try. The next time your partner suggests you two do nothing or ignore something the uncooperative bio-mom does, listen to him and do nothing! Yep, you read that right. He knows her. He's had to find ways to survive dealing with her. He knows what sets her off and can usually predict her negative responses to many of your reasonable, fair, healthy, but doomed-to-fail-with-this-woman suggestions.

While this can initially be difficult for "eager-beaver" stepmothers to accept, you will avoid so much stress if you will make the empowered choice to trust your partner and follow his lead on when to act and when to be non-reactive. This is a powerful and wise choice. It is not giving in, and it is not giving up. It's choosing something that serves your best interests. Just try it when you're in the mood for a new kind of victory. See Chapters 19 and 26 for more about how better understanding your partner's experience with his previous partner can help you reduce your stress.

Reason #4: The issue of justice (or true injustice) seems to be one of the strongest, most emotionally charged compulsions driving a stepmother to action—even when past experiences and an angry partner urge, even plead with her to stop. The actions and negative impact of an uncooperative bio-mom can sometimes be hurtful, unkind, expensive, enraging and upsetting in ways almost beyond words. When the actions of an uncooperative bio-mom are unfair, breaking an agreement or rules, it's not right or fair that she get away with them—but it happens a lot.

If you choose the non-reactive approach, you will have more time and energy to become more aware, more healed, more skilled, closer to your partner and more empowered to protect your well-being. Even if you're still a bit skeptical, open your mind—even if only a teeny tiny bit—to the possibility that these field-tested and Stepmom-approved tactics are worth a try in your situation. From my experiences with others, chances are very high you'll get good results immediately, even if that result is just the avoidance of some trauma—something that's hard to measure but very positive for you and your partner.

Non-Reactive Warrior Tactics

Tactic #1: Imagine you can put on an invisible energetic beekeeper suit (like an emotional forcefield!) when you're dealing with an uncooperative bio-mom. Beekeepers understand that bees sting when fearful and agitated so they use tools and behaviors to keep themselves safe from the impact of the stings. Knowing they're safe from the pain, beekeepers are calmer and more relaxed around the bees. This calmness also makes the bees less likely to sting. It's an excellent cycle that begins with your wise self-protection.

Tactic #2: Remember "No expectations, no violations" when making plans or participating in an event with an uncooperative bio-mom. It's so tempting to keep trying and hoping that you can compel, reason with, bully or manipulate the uncooperative bio-mom to do what's right, fair and legal. Why? Because most of us were forced to behave as kids with the same tactics. It's also tempting to assume there's gotta be a way to force her to accept the consequences of—and take responsibility for—her actions. Take a moment to reflect on past situations involving this uncooperative bio-mom to help yourself see where you're vulnerable to being hooked into action, blinded by your own need to act. Also think about when you've found yourself trying to control or judge your partner so he will take the action you want him to. There are valuable insights in this self-reflective work.

Tactic #3: Be logical when dealing with your stepkids' bio-mom. Stop wasting time and energy on emotional pleas for fairness, honesty or rule-following—even "for the good of the children"—when interacting with the uncooperative bio-mom. Instead, focus on the facts and make rational, direct requests. Emotional pleas often feed an uncooperative bio-mom's desire to strike out and draw pleasure from NOT giving you or your partner what you want. It's a bit vampiric, energetically. An uncooperative bio-mom may believe she's more powerful when she can get your attention and drain you of your energy. Avoid "feeling" words wherever possible. Write out what you want to communicate and then delete all the emotional words. Just the facts ma'am is a good policy.

Tactic #4: An uncooperative bio-mom may be deeply attached to money and may try to get more or pay less—perhaps in an effort to win, to feel she's safe, to punish your partner, to deprive you of something and/or to control circumstances. At every opportunity, offer less than you're prepared to give or ask for more than you need, not because you're being cheap or withholding a fair settlement, but so the uncooperative bio-mom can feel powerful by rejecting your offers, lowering her costs and denying you money. Remember this is about her perception of believing you feel you've lost. I know this can seem strange or silly, and it would be when you're dealing with cooperative folks, but it may be necessary in your situation.

Tactic #5: Brush up on your acting skills. Whenever possible, give her the impression that she's causing you to suffer or is robbing you of some anticipated joy or satisfaction. If your stepkids' bio-mom believes you or your partner did her wrong, she may derive pleasure causing you and your partner pain. The facts of the situation are irrelevant. If an uncooperative bio-mom believes her ex-husband (or you) has caused her pain, embarrassment or financial insecurity, she may have endless energy to get what she feels is her just reward or revenge. It's very sad for everyone involved.

Incorporate the impression that you're "suffering" in your written and verbal communications. A common and often disastrous tactic is to act like you're unaffected by an uncooperative bio-mom. This choice often compels the uncooperative bio-mom to escalate her trauma-causing antics until she feels she's in control by seeing (or hearing about) you and your partner suffering. Instead, again for your own benefits, try the opposite approach. Consider giving her the impression that you're upset (or at least not happy) whenever possible. It may seem weak, but if the goal is to reduce her stinging and stressful actions, this can be a winning formula.

Tactic #6: To the best of your ability, resist reacting or replying to any verbal or written barbs directed at you or your partner. Remember that if at first an uncooperative bio-mom doesn't succeed in getting a reaction, she may try, try again and again. With her intimate understanding of your partner, she can be very effective at "hooking" him and you, so consciously *not* reacting is your most powerful move. Even if you have to put imaginary duct tape over your mouth, step away from the door/phone/keyboard and agree not to send, say or do anything until you've cooled off. The less you react to her, the better—really! This is only hard at first. Once you realize all the avoided relationship damage, it's much easier and even fun sometimes. Why? Because you feel the relief of keeping your power in a situation where, in the past, you've given it away in exchange for the false hope of a fair or win-win resolution.

Tactic #7: Whenever possible, avoid publicly confronting an uncooperative bio-mom with facts that prove her wrong. Yes, it seems counter intuitive and that's the point. Dealing with an uncooperative bio-mom is not like dealing with a much appreciated civil or kind bio-mom. It's a natural tendency to feel powerful when the facts prove your point. However, with an uncooperative bio-mom who can't/won't accept ever being wrong or embarrassed, a public display of how she is wrong can unleash varying degrees of rage and exhausting retaliation attempts. Use those facts only when absolutely necessary and explore having others present the materials whenever possible. While you may win a battle by sharing your truth, you'll also trigger a potentially relentless obsession within her to get even in another area of your lives. Why? Because she may feel she has to make you lose to feel she's won. Depending where she is on the spectrum of caring (or not) about right/wrong, and whether she's concerned by any potentially negative impacts to others, her tactics could be downright scary.

Tactic #8: Do your best to give the uncooperative bio-mom choices—*all* of which are OK with you and your partner. Do this so the uncooperative bio-mom has choices and can feel like she is in charge (she actually will be) while telling herself you're also at the mercy of her choice. If you act the part effectively and manage to give her the impression that one (or more) choice is worse for you, she's very likely to do whatever she feels will cause you the most suffering or rob you of the most joy or peace of mind. This managing strategy feels like (and is) a superpower once you realize how well it works. It also works very well with uncooperative stepkids.

Tactic #9: When talking with an uncooperative bio-mom, write the goal of any conversation on paper in front of you to help you can stay focused. While it may seem silly at first, this can be a helpful tool because distraction is often a well-honed uncooperative bio-mom skill. No matter what she says to get off-topic, you can calmly repeat the following, *"That's a topic for another time. The point of this conversation is [insert your topic.]"* Then read your written words to her and return to the subject. Interrupt and repeat as often as needed. This tactic saves time and stress.

Sometimes this tactic enrages the uncooperative bio-mom. If this happens, imagine "shields up," as they used to say on Star Trek, and remain as non-reactive as you can. Let her words and emotional impact fly right past you. If you feel compelled to do something, honor that urge in a new way—take notes, take a walk, hold hands with your partner, take deep breaths and do whatever you can to support yourself until the present storm passes. If you're in public place, excuse yourself to the ladies room and breathe deeply, do jumping jacks or scream silently in your head to release that energy in a healthy way.

Tactic #10: Avoid the uncooperative bio-mom's social circle as much as you can. This can be a tough one—even heartbreaking to accept—particularly if you really enjoy and want to be involved with your stepkids' school or sporting events. And while stepping back is a powerful, trauma-reducing tactic, you may also find you need to honor your grief and rage at the potential losses to you, your partner and your stepkids. Take good care of yourself in productive, healthy ways. Creative problem-solving can offer a soothing antidote for the loss of face-to-face experiences.

Tactic #11: Take back your power as a conscious, non-reactive warrior Stepmom. Acknowledge the power you have in no longer being hooked, triggered or robbed of your well-being by the actions of others. Exercise your right to push in the clutch and refuse to speak, act or make decisions under pressure. Even though an uncooperative bio-mom may not like it, you and your partner have the right to resist being forced into making a decision under any time pressure or melodramatic circumstances. If you give the uncooperative bio-mom a time/date when you commit to getting back to her and then follow through, she will often feel she's still controlling you. Ironic, isn't it?

The right to take your time in responding to her requests or actions is one tactic often overlooked or avoided, particularly if you fear it will cause an uncooperative bio-mom to become angry or cause more problems for you. Recognizing potential manipulations like this one can hopefully help you take your power back and make decisions on your own timetable. Give yourself time to make a well thought-out and conscious choice that's best for you and your situation. This is not a counter-controlling maneuver, but rather a tactic that honors what you need.

Take Several Deep Breaths

I want to acknowledge that just imagining doing some of these things can stir up strong and intense emotions for you, especially if you've been treated badly and unfairly for a while. By all means, honor all your feelings. Write them down and talk about them with a trusted friend, a sister SMOM or a therapist. There's a lot of information in this book and support for you on smoms.org. There's so much value in understanding exactly (and more about) whatever you're feeling so you can stay conscious, compassionate with yourself and empowered—no matter what other people choose to do.

The attitudes, actions and responses of an uncooperative bio-mom are much easier to work with once you understand some of the motives that may be driving her choices.

Learning the common triggers and her possible needs can help you manage her with more compassion and effectiveness, and may reduce the stress for all of you—including the uncooperative bio-mom. As mentioned earlier, be open to learning from your partner and seeing him as a valuable resource about his ex-partner. Gather insights in ways that enable him to feel he's being valued and helpful.

If you've been a stepmother for a while, there are likely to be lots of unhealed emotional wounds from the history of your relationship with this uncooperative bio-mom. These aren't trivial, simple to solve, easy to handle or something that most non-stepmothers can relate to. Thankfully, the tactics here can work to reduce the negative impact an uncooperative bio-mom has on you, your partner and your daily life. Be patient and gentle with yourself and your partner, as this is a complex dynamic that takes some practice to manage. Happily, chances are excellent that you'll feel and see results very quickly. My final plea to you: whenever you feel the urge to act and your partner feels it's important not to act, put on your non-reactive warrior outfit, trust him and go do something else with your precious time and energy.

Full Disclosure: I became such a fan of Eleanor Payson's work, from studying *The Wizard of Oz and Other Narcissists,* attending her workshop and working with her personally, that one day I proposed narrating her book so it could be available as an audiobook. To my delight and honor, she said yes, and it's available on audible.com. You can listen to Chapter One on my website for free, with Eleanor's permission. See cbdoyle.com/narration.php.

If you recognize a majority of these uncooperative behaviors in anyone in your life, please check out Eleanor's book, workshops and consultation options at eleanorpayson.com.

If you notice these uncooperative behaviors in either of your parents, take a look at the book *Trapped in the Mirror* by Elan Golomb. It's another groundbreaking book that has been profoundly helpful for many stepmothers with uncooperative bio-moms. You see, one reason an uncooperative bio-mom is able to get under a Stepmom's skin so much, is that it touches on emotional wounds from childhood she never imagined possible.

For more about the impact of bio-mom actions on stepfamily life, go to smoms.org/BonusChapters and click on the chapter title "Raging at the Injustice of Bio-mom Actions."

A Stepmom Dealing with Her Stepkids' Uncooperative Bio-mom

Christine's Story

July 2016

Back in 2013, I was a newlywed. Interestingly enough, I met my husband online from a dating website. After a year of dating, we moved in together and a year after that, got married. What he told me back then was something like, "My ex and I get along ok, but it's not like we're high-fiving." We both had been previously married; he had two daughters and I had three. I guess my expectations of motherhood at that time were that moms love their kids, and despite not being with their dad anymore, they want to do what's best for the kids. My divorce had a brief period of upheaval, but since then, I think both my girls' father and I try to do what's in the best interests of our children. So I guess that's what I understood from his "high-fiving" comment. Was I ever wrong.

I'm not one to let go easily and I was always waiting for the storm to be over. To this day it continues, unfortunately. Back in 2013, I was alone. Things were happening that I could not understand. It was pretty obvious to me that I was not welcomed as a stepmother, and bio-mom's jealousy and insecurities kept coming up in subtle and direct ways. My husband consistently got emails, texts, and phone calls belittling him and telling him I have no part in their daughters' lives. This woman's behavior totally went against my logic and notion that children come first. She regularly threatens us with legal action (harassment, slander, court) and in my opinion, carries a lot of narcissistic traits.

I went online to find support. I wanted to read anything I could get my hands on about step-parenting and conflict resolution. Some websites focused a lot on "bio-bashing" and although all stepmothers need a good vent once in a while, I wanted to find a solution and to find like-minded people. So, I joined Stepmoms on a Mission at smoms.org. I was nervous to post at first and spent the first few weeks reading others' posts and Cathryn's articles. I instantly felt connected to this cyber space. I had finally found someone who understood what was going on and also wanted to approach situations in a productive way. Cathryn gets it. She has spent years working on her own stepmother-related issues and really understands the challenges we face. Her articles inspire me to do and be better. I have also met other amazing women who I'm proud to call true friends. They are my SMOM family and so supportive.

Choosing to live as a blended family already has its challenges, but when you add to the mix a person who acts narcissistic and behaves in ways that are not in the best interests of her children, it's almost impossible to have a successful relationship with your spouse and his children. With Cathryn's wisdom and the resources she has provided, it is possible and can actually be enjoyable.

I cannot say enough about how Cathryn approaches step-parenting and relationships in general. With the tools she has provided, I feel so much more equipped to manage the nearly impossible circumstances thrown my way by a woman who literally hates every ounce of me and the role I play in her kids' and my husband's lives.

My husband and I have saved ourselves a lot of stress now that we understand his ex-wife's crazy-making antics. I'm also better prepared to support my stepdaughters. They are deeply affected by their bio-mom's actions and helping them feel good about themselves as they navigate the Loyalty Wars is important to me.

Although step-parenting is the basis of her help, Cathryn's approach undoubtedly helps in all relationships—especially the relationship you have with yourself. I'm truly indebted to have found Stepmoms on a Mission and the woman who created this support forum.

Christine
Stepmom since 2012
SMOM since 2013

Thirty-Six

Managing an Uncooperative Bio-mom (and Stepkids)
Reduce Stress Almost Immediately

People who are intentionally and consistently uncooperative are often experts at manipulating others. They frequently suck the joy and energy out of a room whenever the attention is not on or controlled by them. If your stepkids or their bio-mom want to disrupt peaceful events and relationships in a stepfamily situation, they can have serious negative impact on you and your partner. Thankfully, there are several things you can do to preserve your well-being and reduce the stress in your daily life by managing the uncooperative people you encounter. Using wisdom and skills while resisting the natural temptation of rage, control or manipulation can enable you to keep yourself feeling strong and secure. In Chapter 35, I explain ways to understand and respond to the negative impact of dealing with an uncooperative bio-mom. This chapter is about specific tactical approaches you and your partner can implement to preserve your well-being in spite of uncooperative behaviors.

Because my work is all about supporting Stepmoms under stress, I've had the chance to develop and test responses to countless actions and reactions of uncooperative bio-moms. Through my studies with various experts, I've discovered that many behaviors displayed by consistently uncooperative bio-moms—including those bio-moms of many SMOMS I've worked with—fit into the description of narcissistic behaviors. Over these past several years, we've had tremendous success applying the wisdom that's effective for dealing with narcissistic behaviors (referred to as NPD by members of the site) to dealing with uncooperative bio-moms, as described in this and the previous chapter. Since most of us aren't qualified to officially diagnose anyone as a narcissist, and more importantly because it's not necessary to label anyone in this way in order to help a Stepmom with her situation, I will refer to the people in your world who act, from your perspective, in narcissistic ways as "uncooperative." While we can't "cure" consistently uncooperative bio-moms—or anyone else for that matter—we can learn ways to manage their negative impact and reduce their urges to cause stress for you and your partner.

Holidays and special events for your stepkids can create stepfamily situations that put you and your partner in the same physical space with their bio-mom. If there's tension between you and the bio-mom, school plays, birthdays, teacher conferences, doctor appointments, etc., can generate varying degrees of anxiety for you and even painful disagreements with your partner. If the bio-mom is openly hostile and uncooperative (unwilling to be kind or civil to you), these situations can be especially difficult. In order to strengthen your confidence and build some new skills, let's go over some proven and practical things you can do when dealing with an uncooperative bio-mom or even one or more of your stepkids to reduce the conflicts and at the same time strengthening your own well-being.

Action #1: Feel like Your Best Self

When have you felt terrific about yourself? The next time you're in the presence of the uncooperative person, make a conscious effort to feel like you did when you were your most relaxed, confident, adult, loving self. Make this your #1 goal. If you only do one thing to help reduce your stepfamily stress, this is the thing to do. How do you know if you're awake and empowered as your adult self—or not? Think about a time when you felt you were the pinnacle of amazing, talented, loving, happy and/or smart.

- A career event where you looked great and felt confident.

- A creative problem-solving situation you resolved using your own brilliance.

- A social occasion where you really felt great about yourself.

- When you supported a dear friend and knew you were giving wise advice—that worked.

Think of a specific moment when you felt terrific and lock in the feelings of that moment. Give that moment a name, like it's a snapshot, to help you recall those feelings quickly. Maybe you felt like your best self when you were "PTA Me" or "Board Meeting Me" or "Camping Trip Me" or "Christmas Eve 2010 Me."

Whenever you feel unsteady or start to feel upset or anxious around this uncooperative person, ask yourself, *"Am I feeling present right now? Am I feeling like my best self?"* If possible, find a mirror and some privacy, look into your own eyes and talk to yourself gently. Help yourself remember feeling like that amazing self you've been before and can be in this moment. Can you reclaim that feeling of being supremely calm and capable? Have you slipped into a not-so-adult-like, child-you-used-to-be pattern? That can easily happen anytime we become stressed, frightened or worried. Why? Because it's a default, a well-worn path, a habitual reflex when our emotional or physical safety is threatened. No worries. Everyone does it—until they don't. Stay as aware as you can and be supportive of yourself. It's not bad or wrong to slip into old patterns—it's just what people do as they're learning. You'll continue to revert to those patterns until you interrupt them and remind yourself that you're now a wise adult capable of keeping yourself safe and handling whatever situation you face. Note that I didn't say perfect, just wise enough to see what's happening and then choose to become your best self.

What can you do to help yourself remember to be awake as your amazing adult self? When I'm in situations that put me at risk of going unconscious (slipping back into child-created patterns) I wear a simple, inexpensive, colorful beaded ring on my right index finger. I'm left-handed so it doesn't interfere with anything. The ring gets my attention because I don't usually wear anything on my index finger and I can see it in my peripheral vision most of the time. You could wear a charm bracelet or earrings that jingle to get your attention—even a rubber band on your wrist will do the trick. Anything to remind you to be in the present moment as your best self will help. Amy Cuddy has written an inspiring book about the subject of staying present and in your power. It's called *Presence: Bringing Your Boldest Self to Your Biggest Challenges.* I highly recommend it. You might recognize her name and TED Talk about power-posing. Check it out if you're looking for more ways to feel powerful in each moment.

Whatever you can do to slow yourself down and remember to stay present will reduce the negative impact of anyone treating you in hurtful, unfair or upsetting ways. Why? Because when you're consciously aware of being your capable adult self, you can see manipulations more clearly, adjust and hold your boundaries more firmly, and choose to not give your power (time, energy, attention) to the uncooperative bio-mom, stepkids or any of their actions. It's liberating.

Action #2: Resist the Urge to Connect

Intentionally uncooperative people are masters (conscious or not) at energy draining. This tactic makes them feel safer and they thrive on the power they have to influence and reject others. Next time you're aware of your desire to engage with your uncooperative stepkids or their uncooperative bio-mom, interrupt that urge and stop yourself, even if you are in the middle of a sentence. Examples of this are urges to ask a question, start a conversation, solicit an opinion or seek any sort of acknowledgement, agreement, emotional validation or support from the uncooperative person. Once someone has shown they're not interested in getting along, you can become wiser and recognize that when you reach out to connect, you set yourself up to be "stung" by hurtful or rejecting words and actions.

If you think back to upsetting experiences with other uncooperative people in your life, chances are very high that you were the one who initiated the encounter. Are you usually the one who reaches out to connect with others? Once you see this behavior, you have complete control over this choice going forward. Gently remind yourself that the urge to reach out doesn't make you stupid or wrong—it's natural to want to be seen and respected and to connect. Gently acknowledge that part of you who wants to reach out and take a firm stance that this urge is *not* in your best interest, in spite of what you may believe or were taught in the past. Being as non-reactive as possible is a good strategy in this situation. Celebrate each successful choice point of not reaching out. It gets easier as you break old habits and feel the relief you're giving yourself.

Note to Self Going Forward: *"When I become aware of the urge to start an interaction with an uncooperative stepchild or their bio-mom, I'm going to stop myself and take a moment to breathe."* Yep, even if you're in the middle of a sentence, just interrupt yourself, start to cough and maybe excuse yourself to get a drink of water. I promise you that this will save you many upsetting experiences and emotional stings and daggers. Each time you stop yourself, be sure to give yourself a pat on your back, a high five into the mirror, positive self-talk and other encouraging feedback. You might even challenge yourself and give yourself a prize for each time you resist an urge to connect.

Action #3: Give Yourself What You Want from Her/Them

Think about the last time you tried to connect with an uncooperative person in your life. Slow down your thoughts and find the moment, in your memory, right before you reached out to connect with them. See if you can figure out what personal needs, reactions or feelings you were hoping to get from the experience of interacting with them. Keep reflecting on this situation until you realize, *"ahhhh, I was hoping they would say or do…"* There are specific emotional needs or beliefs there (yes, every time) or you wouldn't do it.

Once you're clear on what needs or feelings you're looking for, use your creative skills and find other ways to create those same desired feelings or meet those needs yourself or with trusted others.

This is healthy self-reliance and personal power. This is being awake and aware that, as a competent adult woman, you are responsible for and capable of creating your own well-being. When you were a kid, you needed others in your life to give you what you needed to survive. It was true then, but it's not true now. Knowing this is true—I mean really knowing this deep down—and then choosing to believe you are now capable of taking care of your own needs brings you to an empowered state of conscious awareness and immediate access to all your adult resources. As the awake, wise woman you are now, you have the ability to give yourself whatever you need. What might you need? What can you do for yourself, right now? Nothing is too grand or too simple. What comes to your mind?

Here are some Stepmom-specific examples of human emotional needs that can drive you to initiate connection with an uncooperative bio-mom or stepkids, plus ideas for what you can do to help yourself fulfill those needs.

- You may need a hug, a smile or some kind of acknowledgment you're being seen as part of this stepfamily.

  Help Yourself: Go to a bathroom mirror and look deeply into your own eyes. Acknowledge yourself lovingly like you would do to a beloved child or pet. Tell yourself how terrific you are today—yes, say it out loud if possible. Talk about your amazing gifts and talents. If that's not comfortable or effective, reach out to a loved one. Text a friend you can trust to give you that feedback when you need it. Remember that amazing you—your best-self moment from the past—and believe yourself. Smile at yourself while looking directly into your eyes (not at your hips or waistline or wrinkles or anything else you may judge as not fabulous) and see yourself as part of your family.

- You may need to experience a happy memory of a special stepfamily event. Since many uncooperative bio-moms can't tolerate a win-win stepfamily situation, they often sabotage situations they know you hope will be successful and enjoyable. Whether an uncooperative bio-mom or stepchild ruins an event by causing a problem consciously or unconsciously, it has a very real impact on you and others.

Help Yourself: Make plans that you can enjoy without her. Make alternative plans for every shared event so that if the uncooperative person interferes with the original plans, you can take a breath and smile inside, knowing you have other options she can't ruin. Your creativity is a powerful ally in this circumstance. Works like a charm.

- You may need to have your opinion respected by the uncooperative bio-mom or stepkids. Unfortunately, this understandable desire/need is not likely to materialize unless the uncooperative person needs something from you, in which case she may turn on the charm and pretend she respects you in order to get her way. Realize that the uncooperative person is not likely to give you the kind of genuine emotional connection that you want. Why not? There are countless reasons and one of the common ones is that she may draw a sense of power from watching you try to connect and then rejecting or denying you.

    Help Yourself: Respect *yourself* with your thoughts, words and deeds. Make your opinion of yourself more important to you than the opinion anyone else has of you. Yes, you may want to read that sentence again. *Make your own opinion of yourself more important than the opinion anyone else has of you.* Happily, this is something you also have complete control over. Be your own best friend in the presence of an uncooperative bio-mom or stepchild. Whatever she does, talk to yourself as if your best friend were right there beside you. Maybe your real best friend can be there with you.

Draw confidence from the realization that you're more awake than ever before and quite capable of handling this situation. Remind yourself you're A-OK honoring and respecting yourself. Honor any sadness and rage that come up about your situation as you implement this liberating approach of self-empowerment. Process any grief and anger in healthy, private ways with trusted people in your life. In the present moment, respect yourself enough to deny an uncooperative person any power over you—don't let any disrespectful actions or apparent lack of interest in you matter at all.

Action #4: Make Your Well-Being More Important than Their Bad Behavior

Uncooperative bio-moms (and uncooperative stepkids) can have a way of "hooking" your attention, pushing your buttons and zapping your energy. You can free yourself from the clever emotional hooks of an uncooperative person by consciously choosing to make your own well-being your highest priority. Take their actions off your emotional radar. Make your own well-being more important than getting along with anyone. This will shift your attention, actions and choices.

You may want to write out your goals and priorities on post-it notes so you see them throughout the day. Maybe it feels right to tell your partner you're refocusing your attention away from the uncooperative bio-mom or stepkids. Initially you'll probably need to gently remind each other of this new goal when you're making decisions together. Since many uncooperative people need to believe they're in control, they'll often increase their attempts to get your attention if you're not reacting in predictable ways. Be aware of this tactic. You can smile as you watch the uncooperative person turn on the charm, create drama or break agreements in an attempt to get your attention—all to try to prove to herself she can disrupt your well-being, feel good about that impact and amp up her sense of control.

How This Works in Life

Imagine you're having a good time after a school concert, and you decide to invite the uncooperative bio-mom to join you for ice cream and make a happy blended-stepfamily memory. She refuses, walks away or misbehaves, blaming you for upsetting her. First lesson: don't make any more suggestions like that to her! Seriously, learn (and adjust) following each experience. Rather than spending any time and energy trying to figure out a new way for you to invite her in an acceptable way, recognize (accept) that she's not likely to ever allow you to create what you want—for everyone to get along. Can you see this dynamic?

If you've found yourself being blamed for ruining a public, shared, stepfamily event because you wanted everyone to be together, promise yourself that next time you will do your absolute best to stop yourself from saying or doing anything to bring you all together—even if your compulsion to plead or demand is strong. Allow her to do whatever she will (or won't) do and shift your attention to yourself. Look to yourself to feel better. Ask yourself, *"What can I do to make this event as pleasant for ME as possible?"* With this new question, all kinds of new options present themselves. Make a conscious choice that gives you the strongest sense of peace and joy. Give yourself permission to leave the situation alone, to remove yourself or to observe the uncooperative bio-mom (or stepchild) not participate. By backing off, you're claiming your power. When the uncooperative person walks away or chooses not to participate, she may actually be doing you a favor by sparing everyone potential drama.

Choose to ignore bad manners. If the uncooperative bio-mom or stepchild acts out in an attempt to garner attention and cause drama, let it go—remember "sounds about right" in Chapter 32? Smile knowing that you're giving yourself a gift of well-being and peace, potentially saving yourself and your partner hours of stress and trauma. Does giving your well-being top priority make you feel selfish or odd to you? Many of us were conditioned as children to do for others and to do the right thing, no matter how those choices impacted us personally. If you find yourself feeling selfish, rude or mean when you're taking care of yourself as top priority, there are some false child-created beliefs you'll want to uncover and change ASAP.

As Dr. Phil would say, *"How's that working for you?"* Even if just for the holidays or a special occasion, give yourself permission to make your well-being the most important criterion for your decisions and responses to others. It's your responsibility as an adult woman to look after yourself. Thankfully, you have the skills to do it. The real question is: are you willing to? Claim your power to choose to take care of yourself.

Action #5: Feed an Uncooperative Bio-mom's Need for Genuine Attention (this also works beautifully with most stepkids)

You can take assertive action to reduce an uncooperative person's urge to behave in ways that upset you by consciously feeding her with the energy of your attention. Initially and understandably this advice can invoke varying degrees of *"No freakin' way"* reactions. I ask you to take a breath and consider this option for certain circumstances for one important reason—because it works. The benefit to you, to others involved and to your overall well-being are well worth it. Test it out and see for yourself.

- Give her compliments when they are sincere.

- Give her choices and defer to her wishes, feeding her need to feel in control.

- Give her choices to reject. It's helpful if you are OK with anything she chooses, and you may want to indicate you prefer one over the others. (She will likely reject the one you appear to favor and choose the one she thinks you want the least.) This approach requires a bit of acting.

- Acknowledge her presence—look her in the eyes, compliment her on her clothing, looks or hair, and do/say anything that lets her know she's being seen as a unique person.

- Applaud her actions when appropriate, no matter how small or expected.

- Agree with her wherever you possibly can. No matter how trivial—she'll likely to soak it up, feel better and be less likely to strike out at you and your partner.

- If your very presence makes this interaction possible, stay out of her way and encourage your partner to offer these doses of sincere attention. This is a good way to be an effective team with your partner instead of feeling left out or at odds with him.

This is effective, to varying degrees, on uncooperative people of all ages. Giving an uncooperative person genuine doses of compassionate attention *before* she gets scared or feels angry, out of control or disempowered can satiate her neediness and stave off her urge for drama-creating, negative, energy-draining behaviors.

This works so well it can feel like magic (good) or manipulation (not so good). Since I refuse to teach or use anything that manipulates others, I had a lengthy conversation with therapist and author Eleanor Payson about this important issue. After our conversation, we agreed to call this tactic "managing" someone. She explained the reason this tactic is not manipulation is that we're not intending or causing anyone harm, nor disregarding their free-will during or after these interactions. It's a win-win tactic so most uncooperative bio-moms may not even acknowledge it, but it's highly likely that she'll be disarmed by it in some way that is better for you and your partner.

If you implement this tactic before, during and after social gatherings, chances are good you can decrease the chances of her acting out for attention or negative impact. When you're doing this, you're managing any possible emotional wounds in a way that can soothe her deeply. It's a compassionate action that benefits everyone. But again, don't let on because remember, most uncooperative bio-moms won't go along with win-win circumstances, plans or agreements.

Action #6: Imagine a Force Field Surrounding You

Imagine wearing an invisible, energetic beekeeper's suit around anyone who displays uncooperative behaviors. Review the previous chapter for greater details. In short, bees sting when agitated or frightened. When beekeepers are around bees, they consciously behave in ways that will not frighten or threaten the bees. In addition, thanks to their protective suits, beekeepers are able to be calm and safe, and therefore feel confident and relaxed around the bees. Ultimately, this keeps the bees calmer too, causing them to sting less.

You can be safe from the pain of an emotional sting by realizing you now have the ability to minimize stinging behaviors and survive rogue stings. You also have the wisdom and consciousness to be aware of some reasons why uncooperative people do what they do. This can make it easier to take their actions less personally and be less upset by them. Think about how calm and wise you feel when you watch a child in a grocery store try to manipulate a mother into getting something, but the mom sees what's happening and thwarts the efforts kindly and firmly. Or think about how clever you feel when watching a movie and you see one person trying to seduce, goad or trick another person into doing something for them. When you're wise to the con, you're not a victim.

When you know what to look for and you're in your awake, adult state of mind, the actions of an uncooperative bio-mom or stepkid will cause less anxiety and stress for you and your partner. When you imagine being in your energetic beekeeper's suit or forcefield, you're giving yourself the imagined confidence, safety and space to realize that uncooperative people, like bees, often sting when they're afraid. Uncooperative bio-moms and stepkids cause others stress when they're angry, made to feel wrong, faced with facts proving their misconduct or want to regain a sense of control. You can't always stop the stinging behavior, but you can stop the sting from causing you as much (or any) emotional pain—thanks to your conscious awareness.

Imagine how you would respond if an uncooperative person acted out and "stung" your best friend. A stinging behavior never has the same hurtful impact once you're aware of the situation. You'd probably say something like, *"Oh my goodness. There she goes again. You OK?"* or *"Sounds about right. Need anything?"* You would give your best friend your compassionate attention. You wouldn't focus on the bee, right? You would know that the uncooperative person's actions are not about your best friend, but rather are all about the uncooperative person and her own painful or raging emotions. Now imagine this same scenario, replacing your best friend with yourself, and start to offer yourself this same type of empathy, support and confident reassurance. This knowledge and self-support are powerful.

―――

Action #7: Avoid a Win-Win Backlash—Be Prepared

Because uncooperative bio-moms and stepkids often find it difficult to see you winning in situations they're involved with—unless they can take credit for it in some way—it's very helpful to be prepared for an aftershock from anything that the uncooperative person might possibly interpret as win-win.

One common mistake well-meaning Stepmoms and their partners make when interacting with an uncooperative bio-mom is striving for a win-win, fair and mutually beneficial solution, agreement or plan. This win-win approach is understandable and popular with lawyers, judges, therapists and teachers. Win-win situations, which are great for willing-to-cooperate people, can be experienced like emotional nails on a chalkboard for an uncooperative bio-mom. This is important to keep in mind and to address in all negotiations.

So what can you do? First watch for win-win situations, public events and stepkid-related experiences that involve you, your partner and your stepkids' bio-mom. While many stepmothers seek to create and highly value happy public social events where dad, bio-mom and stepparents are all included, get along and give all the kids involved a happy time, some uncooperative bio-moms will look at this pleasant experience as if she lost this round. Why? Because she may believe you're winning if you achieve your goal. If this bothers her, she'll likely find herself unexplainably obsessed with finding something wrong, picking a fight, bringing up something from the past or future, changing plans—basically anything that will hopefully cause you, your partner or stepkids some upset and stress. After tracking this theory with SMOMS who attended one of my workshops in 2013, it's amazing how often this happens. Being aware of this win-win backlash and consciously taking action to avoid it has no downside. In fact, it can have a big upside for you and your partner—peaceful silence from an uncooperative bio-mom after a pleasant shared social event.

What can you do after a win-win experience with an uncooperative bio-mom? As soon as possible after the win-win event, do, say or write something to her that will give her the sense that you're upset. Indicate that you feel you've lost in some way, acquiescing to her desires or begrudgingly admitting she can have her way about this or that at your expense. Yes, this requires a bit of acting—but it is acting for the good of all involved, with no harm intended for anyone. Usually there's some outstanding plan or decision that couples can use—at least that's what I've seen work so far.

Win-Win Backlash Examples

Example #1: Give the uncooperative bio-mom the sense that you're giving in on something she wants, which makes her feel she's winning. This will help her relax. It may benefit you and your partner to prepare for this in advance. As you're leaving the event, have your partner bring up something that the bio-mom wants and give the impression that you two are upset about it but are resigned to accept it. Explain that (sigh) you will go along with her demand because she's the bio-mom—music to her unconscious ears. *"We're disappointed that we can't have the kids on this day or time, but we realize that this was the original agreement."*

Example #2: Give her the sense that she's granting you something that makes her feel in control of your life in some way. Ask her for a favor or a special change in plans. Pick something that you and your partner are actually OK not getting, in case she needs to feel better by denying you. Sometimes an uncooperative bio-mom will agree to granting a favor because it gives her the sense that she's the all-powerful one giving you something. If it scores her "Mother of the Year" points with her kids, the community or neighbors, this will also feed any need she has to be seen as a great bio-mom. This sense of importance will very often soothe her. In the end, she may grant you the favor or reject it—either way, she still feels in control and so can therefore relax.

After something goes very well with the bio-mom and stepkids, you and your partner may want to do something sooner rather than later—perhaps on your way out of the event or in an email shortly afterward. This proactive step will ease the uncooperative bio-mom's unconscious tension and help distract her from the win-win experience she may irrationally detest. I realize this must seem a bit looney, but it has actually proven very effective and can reduce the crazy-making actions of an uncooperative bio-mom. It can dramatically reduce the unexpected incoming trauma as well. The best thing to do is try whatever feels right to you and your unique circumstances. Remember to trust your partner's sense of the bio-mom's reactions even if it doesn't make sense to you.

Knowing that you can implement this management strategy can have another benefit. As these tactics will quiet the urge for an uncooperative bio-mom to sting and lash out, implementing them can also reduce levels of your own anxiety—conscious or not—of waiting for the next jolt or sting to come your way. It's hard to put a price on this benefit. It can actually feel good to acknowledge you have used an ethical, non-manipulative, compassionate approach to minimize potential problems with an uncooperative bio-mom.

If any of these suggestions strike you as inauthentic or manipulative, consider first whether they're hurting anyone in any way. These actions can actually be comforting to the uncooperative bio-mom or stepkids and spare future stress and pain. Remember if it's win-win—shhhhh—keep it to yourself. Remember to appear to lose so she can feel she has won. I repeat myself again, as this is a vital part of the successful strategy for consciously managing any uncooperative people in your life.

These tactics work with parents, siblings, friends, neighbors and co-workers as well as with stepkids and bio-moms. The sooner you find ways to stand confidently in your conscious, wise, empowered adult self whenever you have to deal with a consistently uncooperative person, the sooner you and your partner can also relax. May these suggestions give you and your partner some new things to try and a dose of hope in your ability to create trauma-free stepfamily social experiences.

See Chapter 35 for more about understanding how to deal with uncooperative bio-moms and stepkids.

Section Seven

Stepfamily Tips, Closing Comments and Additional Materials

As my mentor, Kit Carson said to me often, *"Nothing changes until you do, Kiddo."*

Thirty-Seven

Thirty-One Tips to Improve Your Well-Being and Stepfamily Relationships

Tip #1: Cue Cards for Your Partner—An Effective Way to Teach Him What You Need to Hear

The cue card approach was conceived as a spontaneous attempt at humor when my husband and I were having a very stressful conversation one day. It ended up teaching us both how helpful it can be for him to offer a compassionate comment when I'm telling him about something that upsets me. Experience has since shown me that this kind of interaction can work miracles for Stepmoms and their partners. The next time your partner doesn't seem to know what to say, ask him to read a cue card you've written. Here's how we discovered this straightforward, funny and effective tactic that makes you feel closer to your partner during times that could otherwise be stressful.

After the first couple of weekly Stepmoms on a Mission meetings in 2000, where we stepmothers all gave and received much-needed support and acknowledgement from each other, we also realized that we were emotionally starved for compassion, patience, empathy and support from our partners when we were talking to them about something involving their children or ex-wife. Each of us had experienced great relief when exchanging stories and empathetic support, reinforcing the power of recognition and feedback. As we came back from our meetings noticeably calmer and optimistic, our partners began telling us they felt relieved we were all part of a support group. Many women had partners who feared our meetings might heighten the tension between the couples but that was never the case. Our partners were relieved and happy we were getting the support we wanted from other stepmothers instead of being angry at them for not supporting us in the way we wanted.

While this was good and all true, at some level I still felt I needed more compassion and empathy from my own husband. Hmmm? What to do?

Now imagine that a whole bunch of stuff happens in my stepfamily life. When, in mid-story, my husband still hadn't reacted as I'd hoped he would to what I was saying about my feelings or the situation, I calmly (or maybe just exhaustedly) found myself saying:

> *"It would mean so much to me if you would acknowledge the impact these things are having on me OR at least acknowledge that I'm having feelings about what happened. Showing understanding and empathy doesn't mean you agree with me, nor that you have to do anything about it. I just want you to suspend your judgments and acknowledge my feelings—because I'm upset. OK?"*

I was unexpectedly calm with this request and he heard me in a new way. He said he was sorry and that he didn't realize how much his lack of empathetic verbal responses was affecting me. He admitted that sometimes he just didn't know what to say so he stayed quiet. He focused more on the content and issues to solve than on my feelings about each incident. Maybe it's a guy thing or just his extremely well-developed listening and problem-solving skills. His new awareness was much appreciated and I found my anger and hurt diffused quite a bit just from his new responses.

Suddenly I got (what I thought was) this great idea. I explained it to him right then and there. I told him I was going to write out some cue cards for him. All he had to do was read them out loud whenever I held one up in front of me. He said nothing and waited patiently as I ran off to collect paper and pen.

Cue Cards for My Husband

> *"What can I do to help you feel better?"*
> *"I'm so sorry this happened."*
> *"That's a terrific solution. Let's try that."*
> *"I know this is difficult."*
> *"That's incredibly unfair!"*
> *"That must've been really hard for you!"*
> *"You're amazing to put up with this!"*
> *"I totally understand why you're upset."*

"That would make me angry too!"
"Thanks for all the things you do for us."

Can you imagine how great it would be to hear those words from your partner (particularly if stated sincerely) when you're under stress? If your partner already offers these comments, this is a chance for you to realize how lucky you are in this area. My husband, being a good sport, was willing to give the cue cards a try and did a great job. After the first couple of cards, we starting laughing so hard I had trouble even speaking as I kept thinking of more things I would love to hear him say. Then I said to him, *"Even though I know you're only saying these things because you're reading them, it feels incredible to hear those words in your voice."* It was really quite surprising how positively impactful this exercise was for me. We kept going. I continued to share my feelings as we laughed and laughed, which is always a great relationship healer.

A few days after this initial conversation, I began to tell my husband about something that upset me. Remembering the cue card idea but not having anything to write on at the moment, I started out the conversation by saying, *"Please pretend I'm holding up a single cue card that says, 'I can understand how you feel.' I'd like you to say that after I tell you what's happened."* He agreed. We were both kind of chuckling as I began to relate the story. This amusing approach was new for us and surprisingly enjoyable. Whenever I paused to breathe or end a sentence and when he thought is was appropriate, he said, *"I can understand how you feel."*

The shift in the dynamic between us was wonderful—and priceless. I felt like we were on the same side, even though the subject matter often created stress. The anticipated stress, the energy toward rehearsed conversations and the internal bracing for a potential conflict were drastically reduced and I felt much better *before* any plan for a response was even suggested. This cue card idea generated compassion from my husband that not only felt great but changed how I felt about whatever happened. Using the cue cards, even imaginary ones, was oddly comforting and always funny. It really did feel wonderful to have him listening to me and not being neutral or defensive—or jumping ahead toward a solution.

Responding this way to me was a new skill for him. I've found that anytime we can introduce something new that helps us relax and connect—particularly if it's something new to both of us—we both become all the more willing to try it out. With the introduction of the cue cards, the stress that had been part of many conversations between my husband and me was now replaced with a new and much sought after, *"we're in this together and we'll figure something out"* attitude. Sure, we still had some disagreements about possible solutions, but from that day forward we realized we could save ourselves a lot of stress by taking time to acknowledge each other's feelings *before* we started trying to solve the problem. Doing this helped us feel more like a team whenever we needed to face a situation and find a solution. This was a loving shift welcomed by us both.

Get creative and make your own cards. You may find—like we did—that whether you have actual physical cards or just imagine them, this tactic can help you and your partner move through stressful situations much more quickly while also becoming even closer to each other.

Follow-up Note: Several months after our first cue card experience, I was starting to tell my husband something. He stopped me mid-sentence and with a smile asked, *"Before you continue, are there any specific cue cards needed today?"* We both laughed and were reminded how important it is to empathize with each other during difficult times before a solution is even discussed. While I don't use physical cue cards anymore, we do mention them if either of us feels we might need, or do need, more compassion from each other before moving on.

Tip #2: Refer to Your Partner's Ex-Wife as the Stepkids' Mother (or Mom)

Instead of referring to the bio-mom of your stepkids by her first name, as your partner's ex or by any other name, agree (with your partner) that you'll both refer to her only as the *"stepkids' mom"* or *"my daughter's mom"* or *"the kids' mom"* or "[insert the stepkid's name] *mom."* This change packs a surprisingly positive punch by redefining her connection to you all and by reducing the negative emotional charge either of you might feel when hearing her name. It also eliminates the ongoing reminder that your partner was once in an intimate relationship with her.

Tip #3: Ten Ways to Feel More Loved by Each Other

With each new day comes the chance for an emotional clean slate and a new beginning with your partner. With that in mind, here's something that can bring you and your beloved a bit closer—just for fun or when you're feeling disconnected. If you and your partner are feeling stressed, give it a try. For those of you who've been around smoms.org, you'll recognize it as a tried-and-true tactic.

This is a way to make you and your partner feel more loving and loved. All you need are two index cards, a pen and the willingness to think about what makes you feel loved and happy. Intrigued?

Fill out one index card like this:

Ten things [insert your partner's name] can say or do to make [insert your name] feel loved.

1.
2.
3.
4.
5.
6.
7.
8.
9.
10.

Now comes the fun part. Put on your thinking cap and imagine all the little fun, romantic, practical, silly and sweet things that your partner could do or say that would result in you smiling and feeling less tense, more loved and more connected.

The secret to this working is that the ten items need to be simple, doable gestures that you're willing to receive as offerings of love from your partner. This will give him confidence that there are at least ten things he can to do whenever he doesn't know what to do, even if it's just a peace-offering. These are meant to be words, actions and things that feed your heart and soul.

Examples:

- Put your arms around me, for no reason, and tell me you love me.

- Cheerfully do extra chores without being asked, such as make the bed, empty the dishwasher, fold the laundry, etc.

- Join me when I walk the dog just because you want to be with me.

- Tell me about happy times you remember from when we were dating.

- Leave me an unexpected note somewhere.

- Call me during the day just because you want to connect.

- Tell me about something I did for you that made you feel closer to me so I can do it over and over again.

- Come around and open the car door for me or carry me over the threshold or do anything that smacks of a romantic comedy.

What would be on your list? (Buy me chocolates, maybe?) This exercise is meant to be easy and fun. Once you've filled out your index card to give to your partner, prepare an index card for him to fill out for you.

His card would look like this:

Ten things [insert your name] can do or say to make [insert your partner's name] feel loved.

1.
2.
3.
4.
5.
6.
7.
8.
9.
10.

Once the index cards are prepared, think about how and when to present them to your partner. Here's where your creativity can make it fun for both of you. If it's a new exercise for him, you might tell him about it, give him his card to complete and ask that you exchange completed cards at the time of your choosing. If your partner is shy or hesitant, you can also give him your completed one so he's not afraid of filling in his own incorrectly. There are all kinds of ways to do this—use your imagination!

With all the stress in our life situations, this can be a source of humor, relief and much-needed reconnection.

Tip #4: The Power of One Thing
Submitted by Nichole, SMOM since 2004

We had a problem with dividing the chores at our house. Everything seemed to tumble back onto me. I'm not a big believer in lists because different members of the family have different workloads on different days. If someone has something on their list but it doesn't need to be done that day or if they can't get to their list because they have too much homework, it's more trouble than it's worth to sort out what's fair.

Here's what has been working for us so far: I call it "the power of one thing."

Everyone has to do ONE thing, each day, to contribute to the common good of the family. At the end of the day, if any kid is asked, or asks herself, "What did I do today to contribute my one thing?" and the answer is, "Nothing," she'd better get off her duff and do something today or else she will have to do TWO things tomorrow. If she has a big day coming up and won't have time for even one thing, she can plan ahead by doing two things the day before.

We have four girls living with us full time who visit with other parents on weekends. So one thing times four children, multiplied by five days per week—that's twenty things getting done each week! Ironically they hardly notice they're doing it. The one thing doesn't have to be a big thing.

Examples

- Empty the trash cans
- Hose off the patio

- Pull weeds

- Empty the dishwasher

- Sweep or vacuum just one floor

- Water the plants

- Move a load of laundry from the washing machine to the dryer

At first I gave them an assortment of options but I wanted them to learn to identify what needed to be done to run a household and take their own actions. They're doing a good job of that now and I don't need to spell out the tasks so much anymore.

The children are now taking some ownership in the management of the household. I've learned that breaking the choices down into tiny manageable pieces has helped. It has really relieved a lot of pressure from me too.

Tip #5: A Satisfying Response to the Accusation, "You're Not My Mother!"

When people are angry and don't know what to do to maintain their power, they often resort to accusations that are intended to stop the conversation. This overt action makes them feel powerful instead of afraid, vulnerable or weak. That's human nature.

When stepkids don't like something we stepmothers may say to them, ask of them, demand of them or discipline them for, some stepkids may shout out, *"You can't do X! You're not my mom!"*

For those of us trying hard to do the right thing for these stepkids by giving them so much of our energy, attention, money, time and care, this can feel like a stab in the heart. Logically we know we're not their bio-moms—yet until we're resolved and at peace with this, that comment, delivered with a biting tone, can be hurtful and upsetting.

Since we can't control what comes out of their mouths, let's be ready with a new response.

Here's a proven, empowering, diffusing and sometimes even funny way to respond the next time one of your stepkids shouts *"You're not my mom!"* at you:

1. Stop whatever you're doing or saying.

2. Look at them with as much of a smile as you can.

3. Say calmly and with confidence, *"You're absolutely right!"*

4. Use an upbeat tone of voice as if they correctly answered a question you just asked them.

5. Say nothing more, looking at them in the eyes, curious to hear what they will say next.

Pulling this off may require a bit of acting on your part. However, once you do this (and you may only have to do this once), your stepkids may understand he or she is "busted" with this retort. The Stepmoms I know who have used this technique have reported they've not heard *"You're not my mother!"* again from the same stepchild.

Your calm, non-defensive validation of the true statement that you're not their bio-mom takes all the bite out of your stepkids' intended delivery and gives you, the wise, adult woman in the room, a chance to breathe and get as consciously awake as possible.

By addressing the comment in this way, you give your stepkids some kudos for speaking the truth. You're happily (vs. bitterly or devastatingly) verifying their understanding of the situation without any other reaction and a gap is created in their tantrum. It can be fascinating to watch. Something in their faux-powerful-word-weapon-dispenser has failed them in that moment. Your past reactions to this declarative attempt to hurt you may have ranged from fury to laughter, depending on many circumstances. This new reaction is a great way to stand in your power, interrupt a tense situation and spare yourself some emotional stab wounds.

Variations from Other Stepmoms

Alternate Response #1: *"You're right—and your eyes are brown."* Smile. The stepkid stopped in her tracks and looked at her stepmother with a "what the heck" look. Stepmom smiled again and said, *"Both are true, right? However, I'm not sure what me not being your mom has to do with what we're talking about now."*

Alternate Response #2: *"You're right. You're not my child either. However, what does that have to do with what we're talking about?"*

Alternate Response #3: *"You're correct."* Smile, look back and wait for the stepkid to say more.

This is an empowered approach because it does a few things at the same time:

- It gives you a chance to catch your stepkid saying something true and correct. At times, depending on your situation, you may find it difficult to find anything good to say about their behavior.

- It gives you two a chance to agree on something that you can smile about as a fact. You may even look sort of confused that he or she is deciding to shout out this fact when you're talking about something else. One SMOM replied, *"Yes, and today is Wednesday! What's up?"*

- By choosing to respond to the stepkid's outburst with a calm, cheerful acknowledgement that they're speaking the truth, it breaks the attack-defend verbal cycle. Being ready for this biting retort but not taking the hit is a powerful way to stay in your adult self.

- The fact that your stepkid used it on you tells you that he/she has run out of logic or leverage, so may be trying to stop the conversation or hurt your feelings with statements of fact to feel powerful. Rather than take the bait, embrace the statement and watch how it changes things.

The reality is you're not their bio-mom, you're their Stepmom. This is a fact that you can't change. However, you don't need to deny or make excuses for this truth. It feels much better to acknowledge it, move on and be your best self around your stepkids no matter what happens or what they say to you.

Tip #6: Pause Before Doing Anything for Your Stepkids

There's such power in taking a moment to pause and reflect before you do or say anything. And tremendous freedom and joy will likely flow when you give yourself permission to not give or do something! Decide to pause before you do anything for anyone and ask yourself a question:

> *"Can I do this without any expectation of getting anything specific in return for my act of giving? Am I giving for the joy of being able to express my true nature in this situation?"*

Bringing your honest, conscious attention to this question may lead you to some interesting replies. You may find yourself answering anything from *"Absolutely yes!"* to *"Heck no!"*

If you can pause—even for a moment—to get clear on why you're giving or doing for others, you're likely to discover you have a lot more choices than you'd initially thought. These new choices include not doing, not giving and not feeling badly about it. That's a bonus.

If you feel it's possible that you may be over-giving and would like to better understand this urge, please read Chapter 10 for more about this very important, popular and draining pattern for sincere and dedicated stepmothers.

Tip #7: Create Stress-Free Zones with Your Partner

Once you try this idea, I bet you'll say to yourself, *"Why didn't we think of this ages ago?"* The bio-mom-free, stepkid-free zone (or Stress-Free Zone for short) is a designated time when you and your partner agree that there will be no conversations whatsoever about the stepkids or their bio-mom. It's a sacred time period that's devoted to talking about anything else. This is not a tactic to avoid conversation—just a way to give yourselves much-needed emotional breaks from stress that can suck up every ounce of life force.

Implementation Ideas

- On a non-stepkids weekend, schedule up to an hour on Friday evening after work for talking about anything that needs to be addressed about the stepkids and their bio-mom. Then agree to be in the Stress-Free Zone until Monday morning. Plan some fun things for you and your partner during the rest of the weekend.

- Take turns planning a special romantic evening or day together as a couple. During this special time, promise each other there will be zero conversations about anything relating to the stepkids or their bio-mom. This can initially be challenging so stay vigilant, forgive any slip-ups and have a fabulous time together.

- Limit your conversations about the stepkids and their bio-mom to 30 minutes or less, unless there's some kind of true emergency. Set a timer if you have to. Challenge yourselves to stick to it. Be concise, efficient and effective with your time, as if you were both in a work situation. Finish up and agree to spend the rest of the evening in the Stress-Free Zone, focusing on making each other feel happy and loved.

- Select one or two day a week for your Stress-Free Zone. Make it a sacred commitment and relish the time together.

- Give each other the ability to declare a spontaneous Stress-Free Zone. This can be for an hour, for the morning or whatever the two of you agree upon.

- Create a Stress-Free Zone for yourself. It can be absolutely exhausting to have an uncooperative bio-mom and/or challenging stepkids. And it can be such a recharging experience if you'll give yourself a break from time to time. You can promise yourself that you'll get back to whatever situations need attention. I promise you, you'll remember anything that's going on. Whatever you can do to reclaim some peaceful, rejuvenation time for yourself will feel very good and help you and your interactions with others in many good ways.

Implementation Challenges

- Talking about ways to get the bio-mom and stepkids to shape up, be better, follow the rules or stop interfering with your happiness can become a bit of a mental obsession for us Stepmoms. Ask yourself if you have a belief that talking about something is the only way to make it change or deal with it. Do you believe that changing things is the only way to find relief?

- Sometimes talking with your partner about his kids and their bio-mom feels like the only way you can get his attention. It can be very lonely being a Stepmom when your partner has an uncooperative ex or challenging kids. Your partner may also feel sick and tired of talking about the same things and his impatience can make you feel even sadder and more isolated. The key here is that if you realize that you've been using your troubles to get your partner's attention, you can find other things to share that give you two a chance to connect on something other than the stepkids and their bio-mom.

- It can be hard to feel lovey-dovey with your partner if you're feeling angry, hurt, anxious or ignored about something that's going on with the stepkids and their bio-mom. This makes perfect sense and yet—when you make the conscious decision to reclaim your power and not let anyone steal away your precious time together—something can shift within you. The Stress-Free Zone can become a mutually enjoyed, nourishing time for you and your partner.

Here's a hint for how to recapture the loving feeling: Think about some of the most romantic dates you and your partner have shared. Think about the music, the food and the romance and bring it up in conversation with your partner, out of the blue. Memories are powerful emotional triggers, and in this case, in a very good way. Tip #17 explains how to use memories to connect with your partner in more detail.

Tip #8: Learn to say "NO"
From EvilStepmom, Stepmom since 2002 and SMOM since 2008

"NO." Note the capital letters and the period. It's a complete sentence all by itself. It doesn't require any further explanation or justification. Any time someone gets you to keep talking after you've said *"No,"* they're hoping to get you to change from *"No"* to *"Maybe"* and ultimately to *"Yes."* Don't let that happen anymore.

Quite a few of us SMOMS are pleasers. We don't like to disappoint others—but at what cost? We cannot and should not do everything. Say *"No"* once in a while. Notice how the world doesn't stop turning. Smile.

Tip #9: "Make It OK" for Your Partner to Change His Mind

Inspired by Christopher "Kit" Carson, Cathryn's mentor from 1984 until his death in 2012

Introducing new ideas or changes to anyone can be met with resistance and even stubbornness. Nagging or repeating ourselves can just feel controlling and result in our partners digging in their heels and refusing to consider our ideas, which is frustrating to both parties. Next time you want to share something new or ask for a change, try this tactic because it's effective and respectful.

Make it OK for your partner to change his mind and accept new information or advice. You can do this by telling him something new while making it clear that you know he had no way of previously knowing this information. By clarifying that he had no way of knowing what you're about to tell him, the information won't likely activate any defensive reactions. By contrast, his defenses could be triggered when he feels he's being made wrong or seems stupid, or when he feels embarrassed for not already knowing something he believes he should know.

Reading this book is something new for both of you so it's probable (and logical) that your partner has no way of knowing much of what I suggest for you two. Sharing what you're now learning in this book, which he has not read, can make it OK for him to listen to you with an open mind and ideally curiosity, without any sense he should know it already. Since it's new information, both of you can recognize you have a *new* chance to make a *new* decision or form a *new* opinion about something—without feeling defensive or dumb or made to feel wrong.

When you're getting past your partner's defenses and making it comfortable for him to change his mind or behavior, you may hear something like this:

> *"Hmm? That's interesting new information. If you'd told me this earlier (or if I had known this back then), I probably would've handled things differently. Now that we know about this new idea, I believe we should re-think this decision. I'm willing to change things going forward. What else have you learned?"*

Whether you've known the information for ages or have just learned it, no one likes to feel wrong, stupid or uninformed. Making it OK for people to change their minds is a kind and effective way to helping people embrace new information.

Tip #10: Ask Your Stepkids If They Want You to Clarify You're Their Stepmom

If you "inherit" any young stepkids, you're bound to be mistaken as their bio-mom when you're out and about with them. At any age, you and your stepkids may be mistaken as mother/child, especially if you seem to be enjoying each other's company. While some may not bother to correct the honest mistaken assumption, it's very respectful to ask your stepkids what they prefer—do they want you to correct anyone who makes a comment about you being their mom or would they prefer you just ignore the comment and allow the assumption?

Whenever this happened to me, I always spoke up to clarify because this is what my stepson wanted. I would simply say, *"I'm not his mom, I'm his lucky stepmother!"* Then I would smile and we'd move on. Stepkids have little control over most aspects of their new stepfamily life situation. I've gotten a lot of positive feedback that this choice is one that stepkids appreciate being offered. What do your stepkids want you to do in this situation?

Tip #11: Get a Letter for Authority with Your Stepkids

Submitted by Rachel, Stepmom since 2000, SMOM since 2002

This tip can be surprisingly helpful for women in the role of stepmother, whether you're legally married to the father of your stepkids or not. It can be written, copied and signed in less than 30 minutes and save you countless potentially upsetting, inconvenient, humiliating and enraging experiences with public and school-related officials. Once your partner makes a general statement about giving you his permission to be his representative in his absence, you can also be specific. This is a non-legal, generalized example of a letter:

"To whom it may concern, [insert name of Stepmom] has my permission to pick up my children [insert their names] from school, collect them at the school nurse's office if they're sick on my custody days, pick them up from sporting events, talk with any school officials about their educational plan and performance at school and speak for me if I'm unreachable. Signed, [insert your partner's name.]"

If you're having any issues with an uncooperative bio-mom, my guess is you'll know exactly what to include. While it can be more detailed, there are many stories of this brief statement being enough. Once you have the copies, give them to the school principal, the teachers, the school nurse, the children's doctor's office, the sports coaches, the scout troop leaders and any adult who may hesitate to release the stepkids to you, share information about them or take instructions from you about their welfare. Consider carrying a laminated copy with you in your car and purse and maybe a photo on your smart phone as well.

Hopefully you'll never need this kind of official authorization, yet being prepared can ease your mind, strengthen your sense of being included by your partner and, if needed, help lend clarity to anyone questioning your right to take care of the stepkids. So often we're responsible for the stepkids but denied any real authority. This is one way to do something about this issue.

This single piece of paper can empower you in many ways and it can also inflame the situation if you're dealing with a hostile or vengeful bio-mom. Customize any of these tips to suit your personality and situation.

Legal Note: Check out the rules for your state if you're concerned so you can confirm this letter would stand up for your right to interact publicly with your stepkids. Depending on your situation, a letter signed by your partner may be enough. Others have gone the notary route. Depending on the situation, you may also require additional documentation to speak to a doctor or seek medical care for a stepchild. Please do whatever gives you and your partner a sense of confidence that you will have the authority required to assist your stepkids when you're needed.

Tip #12: Think Big Picture
Submitted by Post Office Face, Stepmom since 2009, SMOM since 2011

The biggest lesson my husband and I have learned in our stepfamily situation is to decide together what we want for the long term vs. the short term. Keep reminding yourselves to keep your attention on what's best for you, your marriage and your family.

So many things come up on a stepmother journey when it includes an uncooperative bio-mom. Early on, your days could be spent dealing with situations created by the bio-mom, trying to get her to change, trying to get others in the situation to change, etc. But, when you have an established idea of what your end goals are, it gives you a way to decide where to step back, where to act and how to react.

Many times for us, this has meant letting go and choosing to ignore bad behavior by the bio-mom. This choice has left us more time for what we both agree is really important to us, such as:

- Staying married and connected to one another in a loving, supportive relationship.

- Maintaining a good relationship with the stepkids, regardless of anything bio-mom or others do or say. Most of my stepkids' life will be as adults and we want them to continue to feel loved by us, heard and supported and to continue to want to spend time with us as grown-ups.

Tip #13: R-E-S-P-E-C-T
Submitted by EvilStepmom, Stepmom since 2002 and SMOM since 2008

In some form or another, many of us were taught The Golden Rule as children: "Do unto others as you would have done to you." My husband (DH) and I taught respect in our home as a core value. To be honest, if everyone treated everyone else with respect, any issues that came up would be minor, wouldn't they?

A basic tenant is: If whatever the other person says or does to you makes you feel bad, it's disrespectful.

- A teen who rolls their eyes at you—disrespectful.

- A spouse who asks with a "tone" why you did X—disrespectful.

- A parent who demands a child do something and doesn't thank that child for their compliance—disrespectful.

- Nagging—disrespectful.

- Intentionally doing something that your spouse has asked you not to do—disrespectful.

- Backtalk—obviously disrespectful.

- Expecting someone else to clean up your mess—disrespectful.

- Expecting someone else to cook your meals for you, without ANY contribution by you in the prep or the cleanup—disrespectful.

We do not permit disrespect in our home. Not from anyone. Not toward anyone. The boys are addressed as "gentlemen." As in, *"Gentlemen, it's time for dinner. Please wash up."* Note the word "please." If we're expecting our kids and stepkids to use "please" and "thank you," they should hear it from us. We should be saying it MORE than they do.

If DH has for the zillionth time done something that I've asked him not to do, I'll say, *"DH, can I ask you a favor? Can you please not do X?"*

The boys are permitted to share their opinions on something, and even disagree with us, so long as it's done in a respectful tone. We do NOT argue with any of the children. We have the final say, but they do get to share their opinions. It may or may not change the outcome—but they have a voice. At bio-mom's this does not happen. Arguments and screaming happens. Snarky tones of voice? Nope. Not permitted.

The boys are now grown—19 and 22 years old. They're both very respectful toward us, but not so much toward bio-mom and her DH. Even she has commented about that. The tone in that house is sarcastic, snarky and loud. The kids are permitted to argue and backtalk and speak in a demeaning manner to their mother, who will do the same toward them and her DH. My stepsons' bio-mom is a yeller. She would routinely scream at DH or her sons, or really whomever, until she got her way. She tried to scream at me once. Once.

Because I respect myself enough to not allow someone to disrespect me like that, I calmly told her four times that I wasn't going to listen to her yell at me. When she continued, I hung up. She NEVER tried that on me again. I do try to respect the fact that she is the boys' mother. I try not to do something that I know will upset her, but if it means trading my own self-worth for hers—not gonna happen. So, if you're finding yourself being resentful because you're overworked cooking, cleaning, dragging kids everywhere—could it be that you're resentful because you're being disrespected? Maybe.

Think about how you interact with your spouse—can you speak to each other about your issues without it turning into a scream fest?

Think about HOW you are communicating. Do you or your spouse have a "tone" when voicing your requests? Try it without the tone. See what happens.

If you are feeling overworked and resentful, think about exactly what is making you feel this way, and try to address it in a calm manner with your partner at a time when tensions aren't sky high. Think about your delivery. Ask yourself, *"Is my tone likely to put them on edge?"* and *"How can I impart my information so that it's heard instead of putting the other person on the defensive?"*

Respect. A little goes a long way. Off my soapbox now.

Tip #14: Establish a Secret Support Code with Your Partner

Identify a word or combination of words that you and your partner can use to signal to each other that you're feeling emotionally stressed. Choose something you can use in front of the stepkids, and anyone else for that matter. As a stepmother there are likely to be many times when everything is going along nicely and you're feeling calm and confident—and then POW, out of the blue, something happens or someone says something that triggers your anger or hooks an emotional wound to some degree of discomfort. Your reaction can range from annoyance to infuriating rage and it can strike in a flash or after a slow simmer.

Maybe your partner doesn't notice your distress. Maybe it's because he doesn't feel it or is not bothered by whatever is happening. If your partner does notice your sudden distress, it can be confounding to him. It can leave him unsure of what to do and he might even do nothing or turn away just when you need connection the most.

Your reactions can trigger your partner's defenses, so now you may be left distressed and feeling very alone. This can add to your pain, anger and sense of being rejected, left out or abandoned—and sometimes feelings are admittedly disproportionate to the present circumstances. It's a painful, snowballing pattern. Implementing the secret support code can help you both in many of these situations, and help you stay emotionally connected through whatever you're feeling, no matter what the stepkids or their bio-mom does.

Using Your Secret Code

Pick a word or phrase to use as your secret code and share it with your partner.

Ask your partner to agree that when you use this code, you're asking for emotional compassion, support, attention and lovingkindness in any form he can offer, right at that moment. It's an emotional, private 911 call out to your beloved.

Ask your partner to agree that support will be offered subtlety, so as not to draw attention. It should also be offered lovingly, even if the cause of your stress is unclear at that moment. The goal of your partner's action is connection, support and solidarity without judgment.

In return for this support, you agree to explain what happened at the earliest possible private moment. Why? So you two can learn from it—not judge or defend against the situation. This is very important. When you're both feeling calm, that's the time to do some creative problem-solving for the future.

My Personal Experience

My code was "cup of tea." I'm a tea drinker and everyone in my life knows this. I ended up using the code phrase in several different ways.

"I'm going to fix myself a cup of tea, want one?"
"Excuse me, I'm going to go get a cup of tea. Be right back."
"I had the best cup of tea today. Really unusual flavor."

It was an easy thing to fit into conversations. My husband understood my message and honored his promise so I was able to say it in ever-increasingly relaxed tones. The first few times I said it I think my teeth were clenched because I was concentrating on interrupting old behaviors. After the first couple of times, and knowing I had this support as an option, it was quite easy.

Over the years, I got clearer about the things that triggered my distress. My husband began to help me catch myself even before I realized I was getting tense. In those cases he would say to me, *"Sweetie, can I get you a cup of tea?"* Once, he said, *"Would you please go get me a cup of tea?"* I was a little startled when he used the phrase, then I realized he was trying to get me out of the room so I could regroup emotionally—which I did. It works like a charm.

The idea was born at one of the early weekly meetings of Stepmoms on a Mission. It feels good to know you share a special, private way to get support when you're under stress. A secret support word or phrase can give you and your partner a new way to stay more connected and reduce the stress between the two of you so you can focus your combined attention on your circumstances.

Tip #15: When the Bio-mom Doesn't Return Stepkids' Clothes—Try This

Submitted by StepMomma123, Stepmom since 2011, SMOM since 2013

Free yourself from the power struggle with the bio-mom over returning clothes by providing an expendable wardrobe for your stepkids. This is something I do to help us cope with how bio-mom behaves regarding their clothes and to save some aggravation. It may not seem like much, but for me it has made a world of difference.

My stepson is four, going on five. So he's not at or near the point where he keeps track of his own clothing, nor does he do his own laundry. His bio-mom is also extremely disorganized. Over the years this has made for headaches for DH and me when we've sent my stepson to the bio-mom's house in new or nice or expensive clothing. The items basically disappear into a black hole, not to be seen by us again until my stepson has outgrown them or they've become damaged in some way. So to save myself and DH the aggravation, I now do a couple of things:

First we do our best to send my stepson back to bio-mom's in the clothes he was wearing when she sent him to us, usually an outfit belonging to her. Of course, we wash it first.

Second, I have stockpiled yard-sale and store-clearance clothes to send him back in. I will buy these clothes a year or two in advance if they're the right price, condition, style, etc. I find it so much easier to just not care about whether something I spent 50¢ or $1.00 or whatever on ever comes back to us or not, or if it gets damaged.

And if bio-mom is hoarding these clothes for my stepson to wear while at her home, then we've provided decent clothing for him to have there and feel better that he's not wearing the tattered and torn, too-small clothes that she might otherwise be putting him in.

We still do buy him new, nice clothes—we just reserve them primarily for the times he'll be with us, and then we can make sure they're taken care of and not lost, etc.

PS: Some Stepmoms have shared that putting labels in the clothes increases the chances of them being returned. However, if your stepkids' bio-mom is uncooperative, it may inflame the situation so use your own judgement.

Tip #16: Create a Calm Re-Entry Ritual When Stepkids Come to Your Home

You may have noticed that when the stepkids come back to the home you share with their father, it can be, well, uncomfortable. Maybe it's hectic, awkward or stressful among members of the family, just to name a few possible sensations. Experience has taught us that by delaying all talk about scheduling issues, plans for the future and any questions about their activities at their bio-mom's, we have significantly reduced any tension and improved the rest of the day or evening for everyone.

While this can be difficult at first, give this idea a try. Resist the urge to jump right in with all the questions and news, and choose instead to stay quiet about the logistical and informational stuff. The main benefit of this approach is it gives everyone a chance to settle in gently (at their own pace) before regular household life resumes again. How could this work, practically speaking? There are many possible re-entry circumstances so you'll want to tweak and test things out to find what works best for you and your family.

How It Could Work in Your Life

The most important component: Hold off on making any announcements about plans or asking questions when your stepkids first come back to your house—20 minutes is usually enough time.

When they return, exchange happy greetings and let the stepkids initiate additional conversation (or not). Then in a relaxed, calm way, busy yourself with other things. This gives the kids a few minutes of unstructured time to do their own thing without any orders, chores or questions. At first it can seem a bit awkward because so many families are in rush—plan—rush mode. However, if you do this you may discover what so many of us did—the positive change and the improved moods of all the kids involved for the rest of the evening was apparent immediately.

Many of us noticed that within a few minutes our stepkids would come to us on their own to ask questions about our plans or share their activities from when they were with their bio-mom. This was a much more relaxed and fun way to begin their time with us. We were often surprised by how much more our stepkids shared with us when we gave them control over the timing and conversation. I'm now convinced that this is because they had some quiet time to get their own bearings at the very beginning of their visit.

You want your stepkids to know you care, and you may not realize that questions and enthusiasm for sharing your plans can feel like stress to them. It can feel to them like they're being overpowered, controlled or at risk of giving a wrong answer. The younger ones often don't feel like they have the freedom not to answer your questions. If they're teens, not answering is an opportunity to rebel (assert their sense of power) against any sense of feeling controlled and can also sadly disconnect the stepkids from you or their dad. Giving them a little space at the beginning of each visit and the choice to start up a conversation (or not) can set a new respectful, positive tone for your time together right from the start.

Tip #17: Reminisce About Loving Times with Your Partner

In a nutshell, make the effort to talk about wonderful experiences from the early days with your partner to remember and reconnect with that "we can do anything together" feeling.

This has been a popular approach when the relationship between a Stepmom and her partner feels caught in an impasse, perhaps due to the emotional impacts of dealing with stepkids, their bio-mom or other life stress. It's a powerful way to remember the love that can often get buried under differing opinions, hurt feelings and the pain of feeling disconnected and powerless.

Here's how it works: Scan your memory for a favorite dating experience when you and your partner felt those passionate, expansive, closely connected, wonderful feelings for each other. Now think about and talk about as many details as you can from that situation.

- What was the occasion?

- What did you eat? See? Do? Feel?

- What music did you listen to? Dance to? Romance to?

- What did you talk and laugh about?

- What did you dream about?

As you do this, you're likely to feel a warm sense of your heart opening up to some pretty nice feelings that hopefully put a smile on your face. This is a great sign.

Once you have the memories back, think about how you can share them with your partner. It can be as simple and effective as bringing it up in conversation. *"Honey, today I was thinking about that time we* [fill in the blank]. *What do you remember from that time?"*

Once you bring up the memory, you can do any number of things:

- Simply spend time together talking about the memory.

- Ask your partner for his favorite memory from the early days.

- Play a song from that experience.

- Suggest dinner at that same or a similar place.

- Serve or order in some of the same foods.

- Wear a special outfit.

- Pull out the photos.

- Print up a favorite photo and put it on the fridge or surprise him with it in some way.

This is where creative thinking skills come in very handy. If you're willing to try this, it can be lots of fun for both of you. It can break through the invisible (yet palpable!) emotional wall that might be present between you and your beloved.

To be clear, this tip is not about manipulation. I will never, ever recommend nor endorse manipulations because they always diminish the "other." This approach is about choosing to reach past your own defenses and into your heart—through what can be weeks, months, even years of stress—to remember and put your attention on the very real feelings of the passionate expansive love that brought so many Stepmoms and their partners together.

Reminiscing with your partner about the very real times you shared and the way you felt when you fell in love can be a powerful way to dissolve layers of defenses in a loving, honest, kind way.

Tip #18: A Third Alternative to Right/Wrong and Good/Bad Judgments

You can save yourself, your partner and your stepkids a lot of emotional stress by offering your stepkids a comfortable way to avoid comparing life at their two homes. Teaching stepkids a positive, new way to think about the differences between their divorced parents' lives is a tremendously kind thing to do for them. Giving them a third choice of "different" instead of either right/wrong or good/bad can also drastically reduce the loyalty conflicts many stepkids feel when there's tension between their divorced parents or between their bio-mom and their stepmother.

Most of us have found ourselves being scolded or judged by our stepkids with comments like, *"My mom does X this way, you're doing it wrong!"* Until children are taught something else, they're most likely going to think there are only two choices. Good or bad. Right or wrong. Healthy or unhealthy. Better than or less than.

This limited, absolute, win-or-lose, black-and-white thinking is sadly very common. It's also very judgmental, and therefore hurtful and annoying, to be repeatedly told that you're on the bad or wrong side by a child you have inherited, are taking care of and have even grown to care about.

What's the Third Alternative?

Are you tired of hearing about how wrong you are because you do so many things differently from your stepkids' bio-mom? It's so important to resist criticizing their bio-mom even though it can be difficult to stay quiet. Sometimes stepkids seem uptight, almost panicky, if you're doing something different from their bio-mom. Many Stepmoms have reported very good results using this ice cream example and approach. The next time one of your stepkids tells you you're doing something wrong (or badly) try using this example:

Stepmom to stepkids: *"I have a question for you. When you and your friends go to get ice cream, you each order the flavors you like best, right?"*

Stepkids: *"Um, yeah."*

Stepmom to stepkids: *"When you get chocolate chip mint and your friend gets vanilla, do you think your friend is wrong because it's not the same flavor that you like? Do you think your friend is somehow bad because she gets a different flavor than you get?"*

Stepkids: *"No."*

Stepmom: *"Can you and your friend get different flavors and both be OK?"*

Stepkids: *"Yes."* (At this point, they may roll their eyes. Of course the answer's yes, right?)

Stepmom: *"Well, this is how you can look at lot of things in life. We all have different favorite things. There are many ways to do things. Sometimes it doesn't have to be about right or wrong. Sometimes things are just different, like different flavors of ice cream. Can you see how it's OK to do things in different ways without anyone needing to be right or wrong, good or bad? Your father and I would like you to think about how things can simply be different—and not right or wrong."*

Feedback from a Stepmom after speaking to her two pre-teen stepkids:

> *"Cathryn, they seemed to completely get this explanation. They both nodded yes, then were ready to move on to something else. Later that night at dinner, I asked my stepdaughter (10 years old) if she wanted ketchup or mustard on her hotdog. She got a smile on her face. I could see a light bulb go on and then she said, 'It's not about ketchup or mustard being right or wrong, is it? I'll take both because they're just different, right?'"*

Comments about the differences between your stepkids' parents' two homes can be opportunities to teach your stepkids that judging people's choices can be hurtful. No one wants to be wrong. You can teach your stepkids that there's more than one way to be right and that choices can be different and equally OK. Encourage your stepkids to think about what they like and want and what they would choose so they each know that even when their choices are not like yours, they are not wrong—just different.

When stepkids no longer get a reaction from you when they point out the differences between their parents' homes, and when you make it OK for there to be differences without judgments, you're probably going to find that they curb their comparisons. With your new approach, you can be relaxed even when they do compare.

For more about the impact of judging, plus what you can choose differently, see "Feeling Judgmental?" on smoms.org.

Tip #19: Responding to "You're Being Over-Sensitive!"

"You're being over-sensitive" is a judgmental statement that can be used to hurt someone's feelings and end a conversation. When used against you, it can stop you in your tracks. It's sometimes used when someone doesn't know what else to say or feels criticized (or maybe even busted) by your comments. It can also be used to distract you from the current topic by triggering defensive explanations or pleadings that lead to, well, no place good.

I've been called over-sensitive for as far back as I can remember—and never took it as a compliment of my empathic skills. I've never really known what to say in reply to that declaration. Each time someone has said this to me, particularly in tones that were dismissive, hostile, judgmental or even trying to shame me, I was indeed in a very emotional state. Who's to say when sensitive crosses the line into over-sensitive? That question prompted an idea.

Next time anyone says to you, *"You're being over-sensitive"* or *"You're too reactive,"* try this:

1. Pause and take a deep thoughtful breath. This step alone is very powerful.

2. Say as calmly and curiously as you can, *"Hmmm? How would a normally sensitive person respond to this situation?"* or *"How would a normally reactive person respond?"*

3. Then look into the eyes of the speaker and stay quiet, waiting for a reply.

I've been prepared, almost excited, for anyone to call me over-sensitive since 2007 when this new option occurred to me. Guess what? No one has said it to me since I've had this great response ready. Isn't that cool?

Knowing you have a right to feel whatever you're feeling and that now you have a reply to this hurtful attempt to judge or side-track the conversation, you will feel more empowered in your interactions. You may find yourself feeling more confident about whatever you're saying because you're no longer afraid of being shut down by this criticism. It's sort of like having a new superpower at the ready. I was taught that the definition of power is the ability and willingness to act. Having this response ready empowers you on many levels.

The feedback I've gotten from SMOMS who have used this response ranges quite a bit. It has varied from the other party (often a partner) laughing outright (getting the point and breaking the anger between them) to stomping away or stopping to ponder this question and not coming up with an answer. Some people see the point right away, while others get it after some contemplation. Sadly a few others have escalated the defensive strategies by countering with more unkind statements. If this happens, I hope you'll stop the conversation by extending your hand (palm forward) and saying, *"That's not OK!"*

There's no telling what the reaction will be to your new calm, confident response. Almost every story I've heard has been positive and has led to more meaningful conversations. What is certain is that you will no longer be vulnerable to this distraction tactic. You will not silence yourself out of fear of being judged as over-sensitive, and you will not be hooked into needlessly defending yourself. Knowing you have a response can help you can stay focused on whatever topic you want to discuss. May you feel ready and willing to use your new reply.

Tip #20: Complain Consciously

Concept from Karla McLaren, Author of *The Language of Emotions* and *Energetic Boundaries*.

This idea really impressed me and I've found it extremely helpful so I wanted to share it with you. I wrote the following from memory, paraphrasing Karla's work. I've included some things from my experiences, including positive stories from SMOMS that support its effectiveness.

As human beings, there are times when we're feeling and acting annoyed, ticked-off, cranky or in a bad mood for any number of reasons, or no known reason at all. When you feel this way, it's very helpful to give yourself a practical tactic for releasing this very real emotional energy. One way to do this is to give yourself the permission, the privacy and the time to complain about how you're feeling. It's excellent (and much more effective) if you can do this with true vim and vigor.

How Conscious Complaining Works

Find some private space and time, maybe a mirror in the car or the bathroom or bedroom. A good session of conscious complaining need take only 5-10 minutes and it can last 20 minutes if you have a lot built-up feelings to express. Limit your session to 20 minutes.

Officially start your session by saying out loud, *"Right now I'm going to start complaining."* Yes, say it out loud so you can engage more parts of your brain and more senses.

During this private time, give yourself permission to be as petty, as crude, as outrageous as you want. Know you aren't going to hurt anyone. The goal is to put into words all the annoying, angry feelings that are bouncing around inside your mind and your body.

You're honoring all those feelings when you to do this. You often unknowingly magnify your feelings by telling yourself that you shouldn't feel as you do. You hurt yourself by judging your feelings as unkind or telling yourself you don't have any rights to feel x, y or z. In these private, special-purpose times, the goal is to empty your internal complaint box right down to the silliest teeny things. Listen to yourself intently. Acknowledge yourself and your feelings when looking into your eyes.

Be focused and stay on topic. Keep asking yourself, *"What else?"* After a few minutes, it's tempting to move into problem-solving mode. Resist this urge and repeat your complaint(s) if you run out of new things to say. There's time for fixing things after you complete this session.

Again, remember (and it's worth stressing here), this is not a time for explaining or solving anything. This is an important boundary for this practice. Problem-solving can come later. This is a very specific time to search your mind for anything that's annoying or bothering you. This is a time to give these feelings your full attention and compassion.

There's time for setting or upholding new boundaries *after* you've finished the complaining session. Stay focused on the complaining for 10-20 minutes. Note: It can be tempting to stop before you feel that true sensation of being ready to stop. Ideally, it's time to end a complaining session when you experience a visceral readiness to move on. This is kind of like the sensation of naturally waking up from a nap. Ahhhhh!

When you're ready to stop, officially close your complaining session by saying something like this, out loud. *"I'm finished complaining for now, and now I'm going to go do something fun or nice for myself."* Then go do something nice or fun or kind for yourself, even if it's just a huge smile to that lovely you in the mirror and a pat on your back or a hug for yourself!

Option: Do this with a friend. If you want to do a mutual conscious complaining session with a trusted friend, that's great. Agree to keep asking each other, *"What else? What else?"* for the designated complaining time. Remember no problem-solving, just complaints and supportive responses.

Yeah, But: *"Won't that make me more upset?"*

Some people think so, but it's not been the case for me or anyone else I've worked with. This concern often comes from the false belief that putting your feelings into words makes them somehow more real. This belief silences us and keeps all that angry, unhappy energy trapped in our bodies or shoved into our unconscious. There's a saying that's motivating to me: "Emotional energy denied doubles in force." Holy moly! If this is true, this is another good reason to move frustrations out of your heart, head and body before they can hurt you or others in indirect ways. Let your emotional energy flow out of you as you give voice to your feelings. Consciously complain and give yourself lots of validation. This is a freedom that you can give to yourself.

From experience I can say confidently that you'll feel much less cranky afterwards. I think this is because you're validating, expressing and listening to your authentic feelings. While you may really want and deserve validation and compassion from others, are you open to the possibility that you have the power to give all this to yourself? How empowering would it be to get to the point where validation from others is a bonus, not a requirement?

If you're compassionate with yourself, you won't judge yourself. Ideally, you won't make yourself bad or wrong for whatever you're feeling. It's a priceless gift to give yourself the benefit of your loving attention and compassion.

Here's another benefit from consciously complaining: you often learn more about yourself. This is where the magical "ah ha's" can happen. While you may think you're upset for a certain reason, talking about it out loud somehow activates a wise part of yourself. It's very common to gain personal insights in these sessions. *"Oh my goodness!"* is a common reaction to realizing what's really upsetting you.

Willing to give it a try? This is one of those things that might provoke a sarcastic, "Yeah, I'll get right on that." You might even dismiss it outright. I hope you'll push through that resistance and try it yourself. All you've got to lose is a few minutes and at least you'll be clearer about your complaint(s). What you've got to gain has tremendous potential value to you, your life and the rest of your day.

Tip #21: Reframe the Comments Your Stepkids Make About Their Bio-mom

Most stepmothers know how annoying it is to be in the middle of a happy family moment, only to have her stepkids say something about their bio-mom. *"My mom makes pancakes into animals."* (Yours are round.) Or *"My mom has a new car and it has a DVD player in it for me."* (You and your partner are driving the same cars you had when you met.) Or *"My mom's engagement ring has 17 diamonds in it. Too bad yours only has three."* You get the point.

Initially—sometimes through gritted teeth—we can usually muster a few responses like, *"That's nice!"* and *"Isn't that interesting!"* When we're feeling good about life, we can often be truly A-OK with whatever bio-mom comment is tossed into the conversation. However, if you've inherited a hostile, narcissistically inclined, or even just a not-so-cooperative bio-mom, there comes a time when anything the stepkids say about their bio-mom can stir up sudden waves of rage, hatred or emotional pain within you. Some SMOMS have reported unexpectedly losing their tempers after years of holding their tongues. This only makes them feel worse. At a certain point, repetitive stress makes it hard to say anything positive.

Helping Yourself

Thankfully you have the ability to change the meaning and significance you give to anything. You can make the conscious choice to shift the meaning and intention of the comments your stepkids make about their bio-mom. Initially you may think they say these things with a passive-aggressive intent to hurt you, assuage their guilt because they're having fun or prove they love their mom more than they do you. This may (or may not) be true. However, if you're willing to consciously choose to look at their comments about their bio-mom as a call for your attention and a plea for you to see them as unique individuals, their comments have a different impact—not a bad one anymore. Really!

What if talking about their bio-mom is the only thing they feel they have to bring to the conversation or situation? What if, at some level, it's the only way they know how to get attention because they've learned at their bio-mom's that talking about you gets them her full attention? Children need attention and rarely care if it's positive or negative.

There's a new way you can respond to your stepkids' comments. The next time one of your stepkids says something about their bio-mom, reply, *"How about that!"* or say with a cheerful, curious tone, *"Is that right?"* Here's more about this idea:

- Choose to hear the comments in a new way—as if the child is actually saying, *"I'm looking for someone to see me as a worthy, unique human being and I don't know how to ask for the kind of attention I really need. So I'm just going to say something about my mom because I want/need some attention and don't know any other way to get it."*

- Make the conscious decision to overlook the content about the bio-mom and instead pivot right into giving this child or teen a dose of your powerful attention and lovingkindness.

- Follow up whatever they just said with a "How about that!" and then a question that gives your stepkid a chance to talk about themselves, express their opinion and share a special moment with you.

Example #1: Younger Stepchild

Stepchild to Stepmom: *"My mom makes her chili with white beans, not yucky kidney beans like you use."*

Stepmom smiles and says calmly: *"How about that."*

Stepmom pivots the subject away from bio-mom and to focusing on the stepchild. *"What's your favorite thing to cook/bake?"* After asking the question, she stops whatever she's doing, if possible, and gives her full attention to her stepchild. Most kids will begin chatting away, usually oblivious to the initial bio-mom comment or to the change of topic. Watch them bask in your kind attention.

Example #2: Stepchild with Attitude

Stepchild to Stepmom: *"My mom always lets me eat whatever I want for dinner."*

Stepmom takes a deep breath and says with a smile: *"Is that right?"* or *"How about that."*

Stepmom pivots the subject to focusing on the stepchild. *"Hmmm? If you were trapped on a deserted island for a week, what 3-4 things would you want to bring to eat?"* Or perhaps, *"What are your 10 favorite things to eat?"*

Activating your stepkids' imaginations is an excellent way to engage with them. As they realize someone is asking them for *their* opinion and actually listening to them, most will continue talking. When this happens, a stepmother is likely to learn a lot about her stepkids as she validates the uniqueness of each child. This validation is one of the most important benefits of these interactions.

Example #3: Teen Stepchild

Because most teens are ramped up with their thoughts and feelings (not to mention hormones), an effective response to anything they say about their bio-mom can be something like this:

Calm, conscious Stepmom: "How about *that. It sounds* _____[good or bad, nice or awful, whatever is appropriate for whatever they've said]." Then the Stepmom shifts the focus (and her attention) to the stepchild, asking a follow-up question to learn more about the stepchild's opinions and feelings.

"What do you think about that?"

"If you were making that choice, what would you do?"

"How would you handle things if that happened to you?"

"What do you like/dislike most about this situation?"

The goal is to respond to whatever the stepchild has said about the bio-mom with an acknowledgment of their statement. Everyone likes to be acknowledged, right? Next, consciously redirect the focus of the conversation to your stepkids by asking a question about them and their opinions, preferences, wishes, etc. Listen until they stop talking—or until you have to go to sleep. Ha ha!

Potential Benefits

- It can tremendously reduce or even neutralize any emotional jolt you may feel when stepkids talk about their bio-mom. With this new approach you no longer need to brace yourself emotionally or defensively when the stepkids return from time with their bio-mom.

- You can take back your power. With this awareness and your conscious choice, you have the power to transform any incoming bio-mom comment into a chance to affirm the stepkids' value.

- You create room for a potentially fun learning moment or even happy shared memory with each conversation.

- It gives you something positive to say and do, helping you avoid feeling hurt, compared to, left out or shut down by any future *"My mom…"* comments from stepkids. This is so liberating. It's hard to measure the value of anxiety you don't yet feel, but having a positive reaction at the ready sure can help you relax.

- Your partner can relax a little, or a lot, knowing that the comments his kids make no longer have the power to upset you, ruin an evening or cause tension between you two as a couple.

If you're not convinced, just give it a try. For many Stepmoms on a Mission, this conscious choice to see all bio-mom comments as a stepkid's unwitting request for some attention is a welcome relief to the old reaction. It gives you a chance to be your best self. It also gives you a chance to feel good about your positive impact and even to make a magic moment with your stepkids. It's actually an underutilized Stepmom superpower!

Tip #22: Use an Email Program to Communicate with Bio-mom
Submitted by PR Queen, Stepmom since 2009, SMOM Since 2011

We use Family Wizard to communicate with bio-mom and reduce our stress. Because the divorce was so high conflict, we actually have a court order that stipulates *all* communication is to be through this third-party website service. It costs each party $99 per year. And there's the option for one party to pay for both parties. I know of lawyers who pay for it for their clients.

Family Wizard is wonderful. It's made up of an email service, an online calendar tracker, an invoice payment platform, a journal and many more features. It really is awesome. We get a message from it whenever an email has been posted by bio-mom, and we can then go in to review and answer it. And all documents can become court documents. It also allows a provision for lawyers and judges to go in and see the documents.

The stepkids can go into the platform to view the calendars it contains so they can see for themselves what's going on. For instance, I go in and post the entire year of which weekends belong to whom, where the holidays are, which breaks are where, etc. I then color code it all.

The system allows someone like a stepmother or stepfather to be in there as well. However, bio-mom has knocked me out twice now. Apparently, because the system is originally designed to serve as a communication tool between the parents, the service will allow her to do that. So I just go back in as my husband.

A lot of testimonials say Family Wizard has cut down on the really nasty language used by different spouses. It didn't do this in our case, but we then had bio-mom's comments on record and actually used a lot of the emails in court documents.

The best part of this is that there's absolutely no intrusion by bio-mom communications into our daily lives and we get to control when we check messages. Now, just to be honest, my stomach still rolls when we go in to look at what she has written, but it certainly is better than having her email us non-stop.

Tip #23: Encourage Yourself with a "Nice Job!"

Concept from Elan Golomb, PhD, Author of *Trapped in the Mirror*

This idea came from a conversation I had with Elan in 2016. After I reviewed with her some of my self-comforting ideas for specific Stepmom situations, she told me how stunned she was about situations where the expectations of stepmother responsibility were so high, yet not matched by equal appreciation or authority. She offered me this quick and simple way to encourage and soothe yourself. Several of us tried this before I posted the idea on smoms.org and we all got a kick out of how good we felt when giving ourselves this tactic of self-support.

Here it is: Next time you do something nice for anyone, complete a task, solve a problem or take action to avoid a problem, physically pat yourself on the back and say something like this to yourself—using your name—for a mere 15 seconds:

"*Nice job* [your name]*! Really good work,* [your name]*!*" Then reach your hand across your body and pat, pat, pat your own shoulder as you smile at yourself in a mirror. Even if you can't actually see yourself physically, you can smile anyway.

Engage Your Senses

1. Look yourself in the eye whenever you can, even if you have to walk over to a mirror or excuse yourself to go to the bathroom. This allows you to see and be seen.

2. Speak the words out loud. You can say a lot in 15 seconds. Try it and see. Speaking out loud engages the part of your brain that has to form the words, as well as your sense of hearing.

3. Physically reach across yourself and pat your back with genuine feeling. To touch and be touched triggers positive reactions in your brain chemistry. This is good for your well-being.

Why This Works

When you use this approach to self-comfort, your brain chemistry is changed. (Real science, not hocus-pocus.) When you choose to consciously acknowledge yourself, you're also honoring all the younger versions of yourself who aren't feeling seen or thanked or appreciated from the past.

We all know how good it feels to be lovingly acknowledged and genuinely praised by others. Surprisingly, it also feels great to be seen, appreciated and praised by ourselves. When we do this for ourselves, it can make the praise of others more like frosting on our own emotional cake. We can give ourselves something we may have thought only valid if it came from others. (A false belief.) This is an empowering realization and skill to add to your personal self-care practices.

The power of your own touch is often undervalued yet super effective when you use it consciously. The content of the words helps the part of you longing for appreciation. The kind tone of your voice soaks right into your hungry heart. That's why speaking supportively out loud is even better than thinking things, because you engage your hearing, not just your thoughts. It seems silly that most of us haven't been taught this important skill. Sadly, many of us are taught instead that this kind of self-supporting self-talk is arrogant, shameful and wrong. It's time for a new belief. We certainly have a right to appreciate, support and feel good about ourselves.

And the good news? As a present, wise, adult woman, you can give yourself permission to try this technique and see how you feel. Implementing this technique makes you conscious of how many kind, good, responsible, skilled things you do in a single day. It can help you realize that before you started looking for the things you did well, you may have been giving more attention to your flaws or to what you believe you lack. Giving yourself pats on your own back feels surprisingly good and can have a palpable positive impact on you and your attitude. If your partner wants to join you in this exercise, that can be a lot of fun also.

Short and Sweet Comments

"That was a super nice thing you did for him. Well done, [your name]."

"Wow that was hard, but you (looking at yourself) *did a great job,* [your name].*"*

"You're so generous [your name]. *Not many people could have pulled that off so well."*

"[Your name], that was really thoughtful of you. I'm impressed."

"With all you have on your plate, you still helped her. Way to go, [your name].*"*

Try it! See if it makes sense for you. See how you can give yourself that which you're wanting from others. There's no reason to make them quick. If you have the time and space, say good things about yourself as long as you want to. How will you know to stop? You may find yourself starting to laugh. Ding, ding, ding! Yet another benefit! Laughter triggers a release of feel-good endorphins into your bloodstream. There's nothing like a good bout of laughter to reduce stress and brighten a day.

At a minimum, all it takes is your conscious choice and a few seconds of privacy. Ideally you do this every time you look at yourself in the bathroom or car rearview mirror! You can begin to feel better no matter what's going on or who is around you. You can share this with your family and have some fun with it. There are many things we stepmothers can't control in our life situations. Giving yourself more support, more kudos and recognition for all that you do is thankfully something you can control. "Nice job!"

Tip #24: Ask Your Partner for His TLC

When your stepfamily situation is fraught with trauma, difficult stepkids or an unhappy bio-mom, the constant or continual pressures can overwhelm your partner and cause you to feel that he has lost his patience and compassion for how you're feeling. This is a difficult dynamic for both you and him.

The next time you want to get your partner's full loving and compassionate attention instead of bracing for an argument or defending your feelings, try either of these opening lines:

"Honey, I know what I'm about to say may seem silly or unimportant to you, given all the stress you're under at work and with all this stepfamily stuff. However, I really need to be heard and want to feel loved by you for a few minutes, can you do that for me?"

"Sweetheart, I know that what I'm about to talk about is no big deal to you. However, it would really mean a lot to me if you could give me your attention and listen. No problem-solving right now, OK? For whatever reasons, what I want to talk about IS important to me and I sure could use a few minutes of your full loving attention—please?"

Both of these requests acknowledge that whatever you're about to say next may be overly dramatic, a repeated complaint or even trivial in your partner's eyes. By starting the conversation with either of these requests, you're showing him you can see his side of things. You're giving him the empathy he may need but that he might not know how to ask for from you. It also lets him know that you're aware you're asking him for time and attention even though he has a lot of other things to think about. It shows him you're not looking for an argument but for a powerful and valued dose of his TLC—something that means so much to you.

Since it is more than likely that your partner truly wants to support you and wants to feel good that he can help you in a meaningful way, these initial requests can pave a new way for you to get what you need—his loving compassion about whatever is bothering or upsetting you. It also gives him a heads up that he has a chance to succeed in supporting the woman he loves. It's not magic, exactly, but it can come pretty close if you and your partner are feeling on edge or emotionally exhausted from dealing with so much stepfamily stress.

See the chapters in Section Four, "A Stepmom's Partner," for more insights into your partner's potential perspectives, plus ways to better understand him so the two of you can feel closer even under stepfamily stress.

Tip #25: Give Your Stepkids Some Genuine, Positive Power

All children are disempowered by starting out life completely dependent on others. Children of divorce may experience this feeling to an extreme. In addition, they may see that some of their friends don't need to adjust to two different sets of households or move between Mom's and Dad's. It can be overwhelming to have to deal with new people and rules, and they may believe their friends have a stable, simpler (happier?) life like they used to have. Now they may feel thrust into a complex situation and can feel doubly disempowered through the behavior and choices of their bio-parents. Feeling disempowered is enraging at any age. The antidote to this awful feeling starts with believing that feeling powerful is possible. Then you can choose empowerment and find creative ways to make choices that impact your well-being, safety and happiness. This is what you can teach your stepkids right after you reassure yourself of this truth in your own life.

As a stepmother, you can help shift some of the disempowered rage your stepkids feel by giving them the power to make some decisions when they're with you and their dad. The gift of this newfound power can impact their daily lives in so many positive ways. When stepkids feel happier and more empowered, their improved moods can have a positive impact on the entire family. Giving your stepkids—or really any person—the power of choice is effective no matter how small or trivial the choices seem. This helps them feel (and be) seen, heard and respected for their uniqueness. This also enables them to have some control over their own life and meeting their needs.

If you're up for it, take some time to look at your stepkids' lives through their young eyes. No matter what their ages, you and your partner were that age once, which means you have some experiences to draw on. Look for power you can bestow on them. There are endless options appropriate for your stepkids' ages and personalities.

Most kids will feel better, more excited, more determined and some kids may become super-serious immediately after receiving more power to make decisions. Teens may balk or even act resistant at first, however, the results can still be very positive. The impact of the kids' new contributions can also be a source of fun and create shared family memories for all.

Just for fun, and to get your creative juices flowing, below are a few suggestions for you and your partner to consider. While some of these may seem like no big deal to you as adults, it's important to realize that having control over almost anything will feel very good to most children and teenagers.

Important: As you read the following ideas and think of your own ideas, you may hear your mom's or dad's voice in your head saying something like, *"That's ridiculous!"* or *"Who has time for that?"* or *"What if they pick something dumb, ugly, silly or…wrong?"* You may also imagine yourself with a pouty lip and arms crossed over your chest saying, *"I didn't get to do that, so they can't either! Hmph!"* If you hear anything negative in your head, choose to hit the mental mute button and give your ideas a try anyway. We SMOMS have had tremendous and consistent, widespread success with this approach over the years.

Choices for Younger Stepkids

- Appoint one child as "Parking Prince or Princess" and let them direct you to the best parking place each time they're in the car with you. Suspend your urge to make suggestions or correct them. Be patient and watch them search for their idea of the best parking spot. The goal is that they get to choose and you happily take their suggestions, giving them appreciation and a sense of importance and true value to the family.

- Give the stepkids coupons to use whenever they want special treats or privileges, based solely on their choice. These are *not* performance-based rewards. They are more like personal presents they can claim as they wish. You can impose expiration dates or extend the time period of their value.

- Give a stepchild the ability to choose colors for items you're buying. You can offer this choice for paper towels, tissues, plastic bags, napkins, cups, scents, flavors, fruits or cereals, for example, as long as you're OK with whatever they could choose from. Even presenting a choice of *"Do you want this or that?"* can be amazingly uplifting for a child. Match their enthusiasm so they know whatever they choose is A-OK with you. This is not a teaching moment nor a moment to impose your tastes on your stepkids. This is an opportunity for them to express their uniqueness and preferences.

- Make a stepchild the honorary "Dinner Captain," who officially begins dinner by talking about their day first—with no time limit—capturing everyone's undivided attention. You and your partner may need to help enforce this one, and you should give all the children a turn. Depending on how many children are at your dinner table, you can assign a weeknight to a specific child so this is a repeating family ritual. Please include yourself and your partner in this ritual. It will help the kids all feel more equal since some may be used to being (or feeling) excluded.

- Give the stepkids the power to determine family game night activities—within your boundaries and permission. Providing a selection of acceptable options is a great way to make their choice always a good one.

- Let the stepkids pick out their own pajamas, undies, bedding, toothpaste, shampoo, toothbrushes, towels, etc. Since these things aren't public, you can give your stepkids the power to exercise their own tastes, no matter how they differ from yours. Are you hearing that harsh voice? If so…mute! This can be really fun for everyone and a fabulous balm for children who may feel controlled by the world.

- Let the stepkids arrange the cereal cupboards, the coat closets or the refrigerator and have them explain their organizational strategies to you. This can be interesting and even hilarious while also serving to complete some helpful chores.

Choices for Tweens and Teens

- Pick one night a week for a stepchild to plan the dinner menu. Depending on their age, they could help you shop for it or prepare the meal. Pretend each stepkid has a "café night" where they have a budget for food so the meal can be purchased, cooked or ordered in.

- Let a stepchild organize a family spring cleaning chore list and suggest assignments for your review before implementation. This is an excellent way to build their planning skills. Give them the ability and incentive to manage this as they see fit, with your watchful veto power. Chores could include cleaning or organizing the garage, basement, etc. This is not about giving them all the chores to do themselves, but rather asking them to manage a family activity in which everyone participates. Have a surprise planned once all the work is done to commemorate the accomplishment. Perhaps allow the stepkid who did the organizing to also choose the components of the after party.

- This idea is good if you have more than one teen in the house: Give them a timetable and a budget, then empower them to do the research and propose a family weekend or mini-vacation. Ask them to present you with at least two options that meet your criteria of cost, timeline, geography, etc. Have them present the options to you and your partner first, to give you all a chance to make any adjustments before presenting them to the whole family. The overarching goal is to help the stepkids genuinely feel good about themselves, appreciate their own value and create some fun in their lives—fun that they have chosen to share with you and their dad.

- Give your stepkids permission to arrange their bedrooms any way they want to, and maybe even paint the walls any color(s) they wish! When it comes to their rooms, free them from as many "shoulds" as you possibly can. Be aware this may bring up feelings from your childhood. Note these feelings and deal with them outside of the environment you're trying to create for your stepkids. Help them create a safe space for themselves and learn how to enjoy it. Remember how you felt as a teen and remind yourself that you can always close their door.

- Empower siblings with the ability to barter their chores without your involvement. Leave the responsibility for successful completion with the original child. Watching siblings nag each other to get things completed is much more fun than doing the nagging. Offer rewards and awards for every week or month that everything is completed. Catching people doing things right is contagious and very enjoyable.

- Impose this new rule in your home: *"If you have a problem and want your father's or my help, be ready to explain the problem AND three possible solutions you've thought of that will solve it. If you don't have three ideas for a solution, we're going to ask you to come back when you do."* I learned this when I worked for IBM (a hundred years ago). My manager told me he would only make time to hear about my problems if I brought in three suggested solutions and a plan for implementing each one. He also told me if I did this work in advance, he would do everything he could to approve at least one of my ideas so the problem could be solved my way. It's very motivating for some personalities and a wonderful life lesson for personal responsibility.

Helping children claim their power is a great act of kindness and compassion. Having the ability to give another human being a greater sense of themselves and their power, plus a chance to express their uniqueness through choices, is an amazing responsibility and honor. As good as this type of exercise can be for the stepkids, it could also bring up some old, not-so-good feelings from your own childhood and your partner's as well. Does that seem odd or make sense to you?

Granting your stepkids power and options that you didn't have when you were kids can bring up a lot of strong emotions that may seem disproportionate to the situation. This is a clue that there's something for you to heal. This is completely normal and healthy, and it presents a chance for you to do some healing work. When you're conscious of what's happening and how you're feeling, you can help yourself. When you're aware this is happening, separate your childhood feelings from the present situation with your stepkids. This conscious awareness is key. When you honor your feelings and process them consciously, you'll find this whole approach very empowering and liberating for your stepkids and yourself. Another win-win tactic for Stepmoms on a Mission.

See Chapters 9 and 29 for more on how to help yourself deal with any feelings that arise from stepfamily situations.

Tip #26: A Mistake Allowance—Help Kids Enjoy Learning

Growing up, my father explained something he called a "mistake allowance." It came into play whenever he needed to teach my sister or me something new.

Mistake Allowance Process

1. Before we were about to learn a new skill (for example, in sports or a game), assemble something or try something we hadn't done before, my father would announce a number for the mistake allowance. For example: Learning a board game = 15 mistakes, baking a cake with mom = 8 mistakes, mastering a new tennis serve = 200 mistakes, learning how to drive a manual transmission = 500 mistakes. As we got older and the tasks became more complex, the number got higher, and that made sense to us.

2. The agreement was that we would not get upset with ourselves or my father until *after* we had exceeded the number of mistakes allowed for each new project or task. Guess what? None of us can remember *ever* exceeding the mistake allowance. Learning new things from my dad was always fun and rewarding because we enjoyed the learning process. Through this game, I learned to be patient with myself (and others) when facing new situations. The mistake allowance changes the dynamic of learning new things, combats the fears of making a mistake and virtually eliminates the frustrations of perfectionism and self-hate.

3. When I did make a mistake, it was framed as no big deal—just part of the learning process—and it didn't lead to self-judgment, temper tantrums, impatience or

shame. After I made a mistake, I'd note it, learn from it, refocus and get busy trying again. I learned very quickly that mistakes are normal and expected for everyone, and that learning a new skill takes time and effort (and, of course, mistakes!) This approach made the experience of learning about progressing toward the goal instead of about failing, fearing criticism or being perfect.

Every one of life's journeys involves learning new things and making mistakes, and introducing the mistake allowance in your life or the life of any kids in your care can eliminate a lot of frustration and tears. Take the pressure off everyone and make it a game they will always win. The mistake allowance is a way to help you cultivate compassion, patience and positive self-talk for your stepkids—and for yourself.

Tip #27: Lessen Your Power Struggles with Teenage Stepkids

To save you and your partner a lot of stress, get off the "power struggle" game board with your teenage stepkids and instead model conscious, adult behaviors that build self-respect for all. Society seems to accept that the teenage years need to be filled with all kinds of drama, trauma and struggles. What I've learned is that the more consciously in our adult selves we can be while interacting with our teenage stepkids, the better things go for everyone in the family. We stepmothers can also learn a lot of valuable things about ourselves in the process of finding new ways to interact with our teenage stepkids.

Two Proven Resources to Improve Your Interactions with Teens

Resource #1: Read the fabulous book, *Get Out of My Life, but First Could You Drive Me and Cheryl to the Mall* by Dr. Anthony E. Wolf. This funny, pragmatic, insight-filled book is worth its weight in gold. The chapters are first broken down into topics. Then the author writes a section on each topic to point out the specifics for girls and boys, illuminating fascinating differences.

The most common initial reaction to the book is, *"It's like he's been living with us."* While there are many good books out there for parenting teens, this one feels like it was written for stepfamily couples. I've been meaning to send a thank-you note to the author and tell him how much we appreciate him at smoms.org.

Resource #2: If you're interested in reading more about ways to respond to rude teen stepkids, check out the interview I conducted years ago with a local therapist who has expertise in adolescent behavior. The interview is featured on smoms.org and is called "Dealing with Disrespectful Teenagers." FYI, the therapist I interviewed is a stepmother and a bio-mom who had several adolescent stepkids and bio-kids at home at the time of the interview.

As soon as you realize you're engaged in a power struggle with a teenager, your partner or anyone else, do whatever you can to step out of it. Consider that power struggles are like an energetic game of Tug of War. Think of all that time and effort expended by both sides trying to get the other side to cave in, give up or lose. Next time you feel that tug, I invite you to consciously let go of the rope (ideally in a gentle way). This frees up your energy to find creative solutions to address the source of the conflict. Power struggles never resolve anything. Exploring alternative ways that focus on helping the teens identify their feelings, needs and finding a solution—instead of determining who has the most power—benefits both sides.

When you remember that you're a conscious adult, you are less likely to be lured into a power struggle with a teenage stepkid. It's so easy to awaken the teen you used to be and all the unprocessed feelings from your teenage years. Remaining in your adult self enables you to stay awake and have access to your wisdom and resources. In this state of consciousness, you're more likely to see the futility in a power struggle and the benefits of shifting your attention toward exploring feelings and discovering creative solutions that will work for all parties involved.

Tip #28: Honor and Process Your Anger

Stepmothers often have many opportunities to get really, really good at mastering the art of processing anger in healthy ways and upholding self-respecting boundaries. Many have partners who suffer from divorce-related guilt and fears and who have experienced emotional callousing through interacting with uncooperative ex-partners and challenging children. Both Stepmoms and their partners can struggle with anger and how to express it in productive ways. If this anger causes them to lash out at each other, the resulting conflict can wreak havoc on even the closest couples.

The true function of anger is to point out where your personal boundaries are being violated and to provide you with the energy to stop the intrusion, enabling to you create and uphold new, more effective boundaries. However, somewhere over the centuries, people began using anger to justify and rationalize lashing outward, retaliating and punishing others who have angered them. Many people believe that the proper reaction to being angered or enraged is to punish others or get others to change. Sadly, focusing on this goal neither stops nor corrects the boundary violation that caused the anger to arise in the first place.

When you direct the surging energy of your anger toward another person, you're unknowingly leaving yourself more exposed and less protected. Some part of you realizes this, feels vulnerable and experiences even more rage from the sense of powerlessness. Feeling trapped or at risk of being hurt, you may lash out instinctively or withdraw inward to fume. Television, movies, society and many cultures perpetuate and rationalize this well-worn set of reactions.

The bad news about reacting to anger by lashing out is that it causes more harm to your relationships and exacerbates your problems. This leaves all parties involved depleted, wounded and sometimes plotting their next move to get revenge or justice. People don't typically lash out intentionally or consciously—they do it because it's all they know or because they know of no healthy alternative that feels as satisfying in the moment. This tip is intended to give you a couple of things to think about before you take any action or say anything to others the next time you feel angry.

Next time you feel any form of anger, do your best to push your inner pause/mute button. Give yourself some attention instead of lashing out in reaction to whatever (or whomever) has angered you—reflect on your feelings instead of mentally designing your action plan. Stay with your feelings, even if you have to excuse yourself politely from the room, end the conversation or step away from the keyboard. Rather than just counting to 100 while day dreaming, use this time-tested pause to learn something about your needs and how to help yourself.

Figure out the source of your emotional energy.

1. Is your anger related to what has just occurred? Sometimes it is. Sometimes not as much as you think. Usually the source is more complex, and not related to a single situation.

2. Are you angry because the present situation is tapping into old, unprocessed, angry feelings from your past? Feeling disproportionately angry about something that has just happened is a good indicator that this is happening. Not bad or wrong, just human nature and noteworthy.

3. Are you getting angry and expressing that anger as a calm, competent adult? Or does your reaction feel more like a reflex, maybe resembling how one of your parents got angry at you as a child? Are you expressing your anger in a way you imagined your parents would have expressed theirs if you had done whatever someone has just done to you? The behavior and demands of rude or entitled stepkids can elicit this unconscious reaction. Why? One reason is you find yourself in a parenting role of someone else's children. The often-undefined role and responsibilities of a stepmother may trigger a lot of unexpected reactions. See Chapter 9 to explore this experience in more depth.

Make a decision to help yourself first—and deal with the offender later. Yep, this is another variation of the oxygen-mask instructions you receive on airplanes. In order to do this, you have to be conscious enough to resist old habits and apply new choices. This is much easier said than done. That said, it's incredibly helpful and gets much easier with practice.

There are darn good reasons why you feel any form of anger. Once you figure out what those reasons are, you can help yourself with the full support of your adult skills, resources and creative wisdom. It can feel like a whole new way of interacting with others. It can change everything about the way you feel when interacting with your partner about the stepkids and their bio-mom. It's an empowering way to benefit from every upsetting experience you have. This is being a Stepmom on a Mission.

Consider making the conscious choice to use your anger as an emotional alert system that can now trigger two courses of action—one potentially destructive and one productive. You can choose to look outward or inward. You can lash out or reflect on your feelings. I challenge you to look inward the next time you feel angry—before you do or say anything in response to a perceived violation. There's always time to do whatever you used to do, so what's the downside of trying this out and seeing how it feels?

This approach is all about what you decide to do for your own well-being, and the benefits can spill over onto the people around you. This tip encourages you to honor your feelings and to look inward at what you can change to feel more respected and emotionally safe around others. It's about choosing to stay with your feelings—even when you feel compelled to expend your energy on punishing others for making you angry (like you may have done as a child).

You have the power—and the responsibility—to help yourself. If you embrace this work with confidence, self-respect and a healthy curiosity, then solutions will pour through you.

It's like tapping into a vein of emotional gold. When you're hurt or angered, it's easy-peasy to fall back into old patterns of believing that your emotional safety is the responsibility of others, for example your partner. However, it's much more satisfying to wake up to your options and realize that as a conscious, wise, capable, smart, loving, adult woman, you can help yourself and be loving and respectful with your words and actions no matter what others are doing or saying.

Honoring your anger instead of shaming, blaming or judging yourself or the cause of your anger is an opportunity to transform your annoyance, anger, rage, resentments and hatred into more self-awareness, more effective boundaries, better self-care and all kinds of other good things. You can interrupt old well-worn pathways of behavior that don't serve you anymore, and it's through conscious choice that you can achieve this. It's not about being perfect. It's about being aware and responsible—and willing. The next time you feel anger rise up within you, may you test out new ideas about how to process your anger and uphold good, strong boundaries as you make anger your newly appointed emotional body guard.

On smoms.org, under Cathryn's Articles, there's an article about processing your anger called "The Anger Letter."

Beverly Engel has many wise and wonderful books to support your personal growth and healing. She has a terrific and practical book devoted to this topic called *Honor Your Anger*.

Anne Katherine has two fabulous and thought-provoking books about setting boundaries that I also highly recommend. They're called *Boundaries* and *Where to Draw the Line*.

Tip #29: Remember a Moment of Feeling Like Your Best Self!

Even though this concept is explained in Chapter 36, it's so important I've made it a free-standing tip to increase the odds that you'll see it. Stepmothers in challenging situations can experience previously unfathomable stressors, emotions and reactions. When we're under extreme stress, we're likely to resort to the survival strategies that we created as children and fine-tuned as adolescents. These enable us to defend, protect and try to control our lives—unconscious reactions that occur within all of us. They're not bad or wrong, just human.

The bad news about this reality is that when you're making assessments and decisions from your now-outdated but once-successful childhood-created set of beliefs and strategies, you're not able to see the present circumstances as clearly. You're much more perceptive and effective when being your best—that is, your most resourceful, creative, loving, compassionate *adult* self.

Important: When you're operating unconsciously from your childhood survival strategies, you're likely to feel powerless, defensive, controlling, anxious, bitter, fearful, at the mercy of others, disregarded and unappreciated. You may feel like your world will somehow fall apart if you can't get someone else to start or stop doing this or that. Upon conscious reflection you may see that you felt this same way when you were a child.

The good news is that as soon as you become aware that you're behaving like your much younger, truly disempowered self, your awareness expands and your previously unconscious feelings and choices flow into your conscious minds naturally. This is actually an excellent thing about this process. Your intention to understand yourself brings unconscious things to your conscious mind. When you're conscious, you have the power to make all kinds of new choices.

From a "half-full" point of view, being a Stepmom gives you the opportunity to stumble across and encounter many of your unhealed, emotional, childhood wounds. When you become conscious of them, you also realize that you're the one who is uniquely qualified to help yourself in ways no one else ever did or could. You can become empowered to grow and evolve in wondrous ways. This can be a unique opportunity to reap previously unimaginable benefits.

When you're upset, it can be profoundly impactful to pause before doing anything and ask yourself, *"Am I being my best adult self right now? What's going on for me?"* Through this type of reflection you can step back into your adult self very quickly—like you would if your best friend were asking for your help. You can also see that you have two main choices: stick with your old child-created strategies or create new adult strategies that are customized to your present circumstances.

I'm going to assume that you want to choose to establish new, adult-created strategies. You can reassure yourself that you'll work with your childhood stuff after you've addressed your current dilemma. Keeping this promise to "the child you used to be" is as important as keeping a promise to any other child in your life. So be sure to go back and discover the power and insights trapped in those newly unearthed feelings. This is an important way to honor and support yourself.

But how can you tell if you're being your best, adult, wise self when you're under stress? The best way that I've found to calibrate whether you're thinking, feeling and acting from your present, adult, awake, wise self is to remember a specific time when you felt super smart, confident, competent, beautiful, wise and full of loving energy and hope. Lock in the feelings from that moment so you can compare and contrast them with how you're feeling in any given situation.

Think back to your recent past—say, in the last 5-10 years. Consider how you felt when you:

- Completed that big project or got that degree.

- Attended that New Year's Eve party when you felt like a million bucks.

- Accomplished an important personal goal.

- Were recognized by others for an accomplishment.

- Figured out how to solve a complex problem and it worked.

- Fell deeply in love with your partner and believed all things were possible.

- Helped your friend or family member through a difficult time and, in doing so successfully, felt wise, strong and capable of handling just about anything.

If possible, find a picture of that event and put copies where you'll see them to help you remember that "Best Self" feeling. When you tap into the energy, confidence and self-awareness you experienced at that time, you can better recognize when you're not being the best version of yourself. This is very important. It's a time to be compassionate and honest with yourself. In these moments of conscious awareness, when you wake up and recognize that you're acting from your childhood-strategy playbook, you can gently make another conscious choice. It's not about being perfect, just about continually checking in and stepping into your adult best self any time you slip into your child self.

From this moment of conscious choice, things can change immediately. Whether you take a deep breath or take a time out, you'll likely return to your adult self when that's your intention. When you can choose to get grounded in your best adult self, you can address any situation as the responsible, loving, adult woman you are now, not the brave child you used to be. While this may initially seem like no big deal, I urge you to reflect on past traumas to see how differently you might have responded as your best adult self. Not so you'll feel badly, but so you'll see the stress you can avoid and the wise solutions that are easier to see when you're awake. I have found this to be very effective and motivating—maybe you will too.

This conscious choice can radically change your life as a stepmother. You can compassionately and patiently remind yourself that being a stepmother can be difficult beyond words. You can take your time. You can think about things and talk to other stepmothers about your situation to get compassion from others who know how you feel. You can work with your beloved partner in new, non-defensive ways to creatively and powerfully handle whatever the stepkids and their bio-mom throw at you and feel good about yourself. You can work as the loving couple who started this journey together.

Standing in the adult shoes of the amazing woman you are today, you'll see that sometimes there's more work you can do to help yourself, your partner and all the kids involved in your family life. As scary as that can be, it's good to see things as clearly as possible. It's also invigorating to believe that the energy you expend to solve a daily problem will help you heal something from your past. When you heal core emotional wounds, you'll respond differently to all future situations. That makes the work well worth it, I can assure you. So, remember a time when you felt like your best self so you can consciously access all of your many adult talents, resources and energy reserves to find ways to create a joyful life with your partner.

Tip #30: Rituals and Traditions to Honor All Family Members
Submitted by Post Office Face, Stepmom since 2009, SMOM since 2011

Building and keeping a sense of family and togetherness can be difficult for stepfamilies. This can become even harder when one parent speaks badly to the kids about their other parent and family life in the other home. In spite of encountering that situation ourselves, we've had a lot of success in our stepfamily by building an environment where all of the kids feel seen, loved and accepted and where we truly are a family.

Here are some things I feel have had a positive impact:

1. Every week we do something we call "accolades." This is when each person says something nice or something they like about another person in the family. We go around the table giving everyone a chance to say something nice about each other every week.

2. At the end of every weekend or extended visit we do "I likes." Everyone goes around the table and says something they liked about the weekend or the week—whatever amount of time the stepkids were here. Some things are bigger and some are smaller. Everyone has a good time remembering fun times we had together. It feels good to put our attention on the good things.

3. We have all sorts of family rituals around holidays including half birthdays, birthdays, Christmas, Stepfamily Day, our wedding anniversary, Halloween, Easter, etc. Some are big and some are small, and each one gives us lots of good memories of celebrating together and having fun.

4. Every week we have a family meeting:

    - We start with the accolades (see item #1).

    - We go over what's coming up that week to plan logistics.

    - We talk about upcoming agenda items.

    - We go through anything that happened that week that anyone would like to share.

Agenda Items? We keep a board on the fridge where anyone can write something they want to talk about as a family, such as something to share, an issue to resolve, a special request, etc.

Because all three kids are invited to write on it (in addition to my husband and me), we've had some silly conversations as well as serious ones where we've brainstormed to find a solution to an issue or request. It's been great to see how well the kids do in creative problem-solving challenges. They often happily surprise us with their ideas.

Although the items we deal with are real, the best, most important thing about our family meetings is that we hold them as a family. Everyone knows we can talk about things, big and small, and work together to figure things out.

My Additional Thoughts

When we stepmothers enter the picture, there are now potentially three sets of holiday traditions, beliefs, "rules" and favorites. It's common to hear the stepkids say, "At Mom's we do it this way" or "Why can't we do it like we used to when were a real family?" Stepmothers usually want to share and enjoy some of the traditions and rituals that they grew up loving. Multiple traditions around the major holidays can cause competition and stress. I mean how many different kinds of stuffing can you put in one turkey?

One way to turn this stress into more fun is to invent some new things that you, your partner and all the kids in your home can do that no one has done before. Start some new traditions of your own. This makes it a shared adventure. Ask them all for new ideas. Planning for these new rituals can give all the children involved a voice in family activities. Most importantly, this approach helps everyone stay in the present moment, instead of only triggering grief for a past they had no part in ending.

What can you do? Put on your festive invisible creative-thinking caps. Stop competing with the past or the bio-mom. It's so healing, not to mention a huge relief for everyone, when you, your partner and the kids can just have fun without any guilt or grief issues invoked in your activities.

For many ideas, see the two-part article on smoms.org called "Connecting with your Stepkids."

Tip #31: Bring Compassion to Yourself

Make the conscious choice to be extremely kind, non-judgmental, patient and compassionate with yourself for as many moments as you can, every single day. Acknowledge to yourself that being a stepmother can be incredibly difficult. Be aware of your inner self-talk. Anytime you realize that you're being unkind or not-so-compassionate to yourself, simply say, *"Hey, I deserve compassion. Being a SMOM is hard and I deserve my support."* Choose your own words as a gentle reminder. No more inner harshness.

Once you're aware of negative self-talk, mute any negative thoughts. This is a choice. This can happen instantly. Resist the urge to shame or judge yourself. Shift your thinking by talking to yourself with the same kindness you would naturally give to your best friend, beloved child or pet. Yes, sometimes we need to calibrate kindness in different ways.

There may be many reasons to not be kind and compassionate with yourself but there are *no good* reasons. I've saved this tip for last because I believe it's the single most important and positively impactful thing every stepmother in every situation can do to help herself. It's great to get support from our partners, friends, family, etc., but despite what we've been taught, that kind of support is not essential for our well-being. We can change our experience of daily life in immeasurable, wonderful ways when we realize it's possible to help ourselves—we can choose to be the recipient of our own lovingkindness.

You may want to read the article in the public articles section of smoms.org called "Negative Self-Talk: Why Do We Torture Ourselves."

See Chapter 2 for an expanded explanation of honoring your feelings. Also go to smoms.org/BonusChapters for follow-up conversations about this topic and click on "Honoring vs. Shaming Your Feelings."

Thirty-Eight

Closing Comments
Do You Want to Be Right or Happy?

Ask yourself: *"Do I want to be right or happy?"* Sure, like most people, you may want to be both, but in intimate and loving relationships sometimes you have to choose. As you've likely learned, it's kinder to choose happiness, because standing firm for what you believe is right (and judging the other as wrong) can sometimes negatively impact your connection to a loved one. When time allows, it's very important to honor the feelings that come up when deferring to happiness—sometimes it's more intense than other times. Then investigate your needs and beliefs about the topic, along with the meaning and significance you place on being right. Why bother looking into the thoughts, feelings, needs and beliefs that caused you to have to choose between right and happy? Because I can promise you, with decades of experiences in my own life and with countless Stepmoms, that you'll learn valuable information that will make you wiser, more loving and more self-aware, and even happier as a woman, as a Stepmom and as part of a couple. Really!

Choosing Happiness...

With a Child: Think about the last time a child asked you to witness one of his/her newest accomplishments—let's imagine a 5-year-old little girl has set the entire dinner table as a big surprise for you. You see the excitement and anticipation of shared joy in her eyes as you're pulled over to the table with your own eyes covered. As you open your eyes and survey the table, you immediately notice that the spoons are placed between the knives and the plates and your dish towels are folded into giant triangles by each place setting. What do you do, as the child looks to you expecting your support? Do you immediately point out her mistakes or do you praise her efforts, her good intentions and all the things she has done correctly? Because of varying childhood experiences, the answer is sadly not clear cut for some. However, hopefully you'll agree that the loving response in that moment is to express your appreciation and admiration for the child's gesture. You know that those spoons and your real napkins will find their way to their rightful places on the table another day.

With Your Partner: When you and your partner first got together, chances are very good that no matter what his kids or their bio-mom did, you were probably flexible about plans, gracious about helping wherever you could and very supportive of him and his decisions—even when you realized you might have handled things a bit differently if they were your own kids or ex-spouse. You stayed focused on being an amazing supporter, lover and cheerleader, and it felt good when your partner counted on you. Like many of us, you may have felt like a bubbly fountain of energy overflowing with love. As a Stepmom on a Mission, you probably also brought enthusiasm, compassion, optimism and creativity to your partner's life—and he most likely accepted your contributions, soaking them up appreciatively. These good intentions and your genuine desire to do whatever it takes to be there for each other kept you both feeling closely connected. You were convinced that together, you two could find ways to deal with whatever stepfamily circumstances surfaced.

In both of these scenarios, you likely chose to be happily connected with your loved ones when you could have chosen to make them wrong. I believe you made that loving choice because your heart was full. You were not feeling fear or neediness. You chose happiness in the moment, confident things could be fixed, corrected, addressed or adjusted as needed, all in good time. In those moments, you felt good about your role in these relationships. You saw an opportunity to be loving (a.k.a. happy) and you took it—and everyone felt good.

Over time and because you're reading this now, you and your partner have probably lived through many stressful stepfamily events that may have highlighted any differing childrearing approaches and conflicting strategies. Maybe you've had to navigate potentially traumatic stepfamily issues such as custody and co-parenting conflicts with your stepkids' bio-mom, challenges with your stepkids and more. If your circumstances are (and have been) particularly difficult, you and your partner may have had to deal with previously unimaginable feelings of rage, sadness and harsh judgments—much of this sadly directed toward each other. Perhaps you are at the end of your emotional ropes! Worst of all, you may be at odds with each other with no clear-cut pathway back to those early days of sharing a deeply loving connection.

You may feel unsupported and drained on many levels, and maybe even shell-shocked by ongoing stepfamily experiences, many of which neither you nor your partner caused. Anxiety and defensiveness may have replaced your enthusiasm and connectedness from the early days together. What happened to your closeness? Short answer: somewhere along the way, and most likely unintentionally, the energy exchange between your partner and you changed. Instead of both of you flowing loving support *toward* each other (strengthening your connection), you found yourselves expecting unconditional support *from* each other. As a result, each of you has probably experienced hurt feelings when you haven't gotten what you wanted from each other (weakening the connection). Unless a couple becomes aware of what's happening in this complex dynamic, an invisible wedge begins to grow between their hearts. This can trigger a painful chain reaction of thoughts, feelings and behaviors.

When a couple disagrees or discovers they have very different beliefs about the "right" course of action, they will often unconsciously turn away from their upsetting feelings (too painful) and instead hang out in their thoughts (where there is no pain). Without realizing it, with this choice they deny their own happiness, disconnect with each other and instead choose the hurtful but numbing benefits of judging each other. This doesn't happen because the Stepmom and her partner don't love each other. It occurs because they've not been taught how to resolve their differences *while* keeping their hearts open to each other.

The good news is that through reading the chapters in this book and examining your own experiences and beliefs, you can learn how you and your partner can stay openly loving—even when you disagree. Yes, even when you feel furious or betrayed by behaviors or circumstances. With these new skills, you and your partner can learn more about yourselves and become emotionally self-reliant, which will prepare you to better support each other. Believe it or not, you two can actually become closer by working through whatever your stepkids or their bio-mom throw at you. Honest! Many of the SMOMS stories in this book attest to this counter-intuitive truth!

So in closing, dear Stepmom, the next time something happens and you feel your heart start to harden, your sense of "rightness" ramp up and your defensive shields rise, create a new pathway forward with your beloved partner:

1. Pause for a moment, interrupting yourself if necessary.

2. Take a couple of deep breaths.

3. Remember the powerful love you share with your partner.

4. Choose to keep your heart open to your partner—you're a terrific team.

5. Imagine you and your partner encircled by an invisible forcefield and then place the upsetting feelings and situations outside of your circle—see it as separate from your relationship.

6. Believe there's a solution to every problem, emotional wound or disagreement either of you faces.

7. Trust that you'll find better options (and probably more quickly, although speed is not the goal) when you work together as a united, loving couple.

The words from Carrie Underwood's song, *The Champion*, really sum up the strengths of any couple who work together as a conscious team—"invincible, unbreakable, unstoppable, unshakeable." That's my wish for all Stepmom/DH couples.

Your journey as a Stepmom on a Mission begins when you're willing to believe that things can be different, and that lasting relief (and joy with your partner) is really possible, no matter what happens. There are answers for all your questions, even if you haven't found them yet. With your determination to explore your feelings and learn new skills, there's really no limit to the positive changes you can create in your life. While there is still work to be done to improve society's perception of the role and importance of stepmothers in today's family life, remember—you are not alone! We SMOMS really do get what you're going through. We're in this together and we're making new maps that will serve us (and future Stepmoms) going forward.

Putting this instruction manual together has taken a lot longer than I thought—and a lot more words than I imagined. In the process of reliving so many experiences and SMOMS stories, I came face to face with another unexpected (and welcomed) batch of new personal insights. I'm so excited to be able to share what I've learned with you and to help you on your own journey as you exchange outdated beliefs and behaviors for new insights, skills and a greater sense of your authentic power as a woman in the role of Stepmom.

I wish you relief, happiness, lots of "ah ha" moments and miracles galore with your beloved. If there's anyway I can support you or if you want to share your experiences, please reach out so we can connect as sister Stepmoms on a Mission.

Thirty-Nine

Bonus Materials at smoms.org/BonusChapters

There is just too much information to put in one book, so I have created a bonus section at www.smoms.org/BonusChapters for readers like you. (No password is required.) There, you will find six additional chapters containing new information and follow-up material for eleven chapters from this printed book. Because I have shared some early drafts of this book's content on smoms.org over the past 16 years and have had many related discussions on the smoms.org forum, I'm delighted to share excerpts of these discussions, including real SMOM reactions, questions and experiences related to my suggestions. I hope you'll find it valuable and thought-provoking.

For your reference, the bonus material is listed below. Note that all contributors' names have been replaced with "SMOM1, SMOM2…" to protect their privacy.

Bonus Chapters

1. Honoring and Supporting Feelings of Sadness
2. Understanding Emotional Resistance: Why You Might Resist Increasing Your Self-Awareness
3. Your Three States of Consciousness (Brief Explanation)
4. The Personal Growth Process: Why It's Painful in the Short Run and Still Worth It
5. Six Sample Situations for Disarming Defensive Behavior Between You and Your Partner
6. Twenty-Three Tips for the Partner of a Stepmom

Follow-Up Discussions About Chapters from This Book

7. Honoring vs. Shaming Your Feelings (Follow-up to Chapter 2)
8. Boundaries vs. Blockages (Follow-up to Chapter 4)
9. Over-Giving (Follow-up to Chapter 10)
10. His Kids: His Call (Follow-up to Chapter 19)
11. Supporting your Partner through Divorce Guilt and Fears (Follow-up to Chapter 25)
12. When Stepkids Manipulate Their Father (or Try) (Follow-up to Section Five)
13. The "Stop Trying So Hard and Start Lovingly Ignoring Your Stepkids" Plan (Follow-up to Chapter 31)
14. Sounds About Right (Follow-up to Chapter 32)
15. When Bio-mom Won't Get Along (Follow-up to Chapter 33)
16. Feeling Hatred and Hating It! (Follow-up to Chapter 34)
17. Raging at the Injustice of Bio-mom Actions (Follow-up to Section Six)

Forty

Cathryn's Public Articles on smoms.org

Stepmom Self-Awareness and Empowerment

- Connecting with Your Stepkids-Part 1

- Connecting with Your Stepkids-Part 2

- Dealing with Disrespectful Teenagers: An Interview

- Feeling Powerless? A Compilation from Posts from the Past

- Handling the Holidays: Choice and Creativity Can Save the Day

- Hostility Is Not "FINE" But It's Real

- If…Stuff Happens…You Might Be a Frustrated Stepmom

- Marry a Man with Kids: Compilation from Posts from the Past

- Resentment Case Study

- Shift Your Perspective to Reduce Emotional Pain

- The Anger Letter: One Way to Move this Powerful Emotion

General Self-Awareness

- Are You Keeping an Emotional Ledger?

- At the End of Your Emotional Rope?

- Boundaries for Nice People-Part 1 (What's Going On?)

- Boundaries for Nice People-Part 2 (Tactics)

- Choices: Are Yours Based on Fear or Courage?

- Comforting Ourselves Is More than Self-Care

- Controlling Others: Understand Our Motivation and Our Options

- Express Your Expectations and Assumptions

- Feeling Judgmental? Understand Why and Our Options

- Hostility Is Not "FINE" but It's Real

- Negative Self-Talk: Why Do We Torture Ourselves?

- Over-Functioning: A Natural Pitfall for Caring People

- Self-Pity: Understand It and Help Yourself in New Ways

- Selling New Ideas: Improving Your People Skills

- Shift Your Thoughts from "Bad and Wrong" to Ineffective to Improve Relationships

- Stop Being Controlled by Others: Take a New Stand

- Testing and Proving Love: A Damaging Response to Fear

- The Gift of Receiving: A Priceless Act of Kindness

- Turn Frustrations into Positive Actions

- What's Your Mental and Emotional Processing Style?

- When You End a Relationship

- When Your Loving Relationship Ends

This is the list as of February 2018. The articles available to the public may change over time with occasional additions and deletions.

Forty-One

About the Author

Cathryn Bond Doyle has spent decades studying and teaching about self-awareness, embracing change and creative problem-solving in human behavior and relationships. After graduating from the University of Hartford in 1978 with a business degree in Management, she became a marketing representative at IBM selling computer systems to financial institutions. Her expertise in new retail banking products led her to go work for a bank as Director of Electronic Banking for First Connecticut Bancorp in 1980, overseeing the installation of online branch teller systems and ATM machines at the 3-bank holding company. While at the bank, she set international consumer usage levels for ATMs and debit card acceptance, nearly twice the national and international averages at the time. She began speaking around the country about her unique consumer and employee training programs, and then went out on her own in 1984 to establish an international speaking and consulting career in retail banking.

Cathryn began speaking at regional, national and international banking conferences in the U.S., Canada, Great Britain and Mexico and was a speaker at seven annual European self-service banking conferences in Edinburgh, Scotland. She lived in England for 12 months between 1994-1995, working for several banks and building societies. She also made several training videos for banks, shared ATM networks and MasterCard. The common theme of her work was helping people overcome their fear of change and improving staff communications and customer service skills in comfortable ways.

In 1996, Cathryn became a stepmother and her focus and life goals changed almost immediately. In the process of settling into her new role, with a 5-year-old stepson living with her half the time, she found herself dealing with the unknowns and complexities of new relationships. Much to her surprise, she learned quickly that her previous training and experience didn't help her handle the stepfamily traumas she was experiencing. In her quest for greater understanding, less stress, a closer connection with her husband and a chance to care for (and get to know) her new stepson, she shut down most of her consulting practice and went to work on gaining new skills to improve her responses and approaches to stepfamily situations.

Cathryn started a stepmothers' support group, Stepmoms on a Mission (SMOMS), in 2000. This face-to-face group of women met weekly for two years and then became a monthly meeting and an online community when she created the smoms.org website and forum in 2002. During these two years, she also authored a monthly relationship column and hosted a bulletin board for phenomenalwomen.com, the second largest website supporting women at the time. Through these experiences and beyond, she discovered that many of the new lessons she was learning in her own stepfamily life were also helpful for other stepmothers. Together, she and her sister SMOMS worked to increase their self-awareness and skill sets, heal their personal emotional "hot spots," build stronger relationships with their partners and become their most empowered selves. This represented a dramatic shift in Cathryn's career plans and one she remains passionate about continuing.

From 2007-2014, Cathryn invested a tremendous amount of time, money and energy to work with various experts so she could learn more about dynamics related to families, couples, the impact of our upbringing on our adult behaviors, beliefs and power struggles so she could find answers. As a result of this effort, she has developed new approaches and skills specifically designed to help women feel strong and confident in their role as stepmothers while also improving their relationships with their partners and stepkids.

For the first thirteen years of her work with stepmothers, Cathryn offered all of her personal, group and website support services for free to every stepmother who sought her help. This included providing access to her website community forums and her many articles, training workshops and private consultations as requested. In 2013, feeling she was prepared and had acquired enough knowledge and field experience, she was ready to, once again, "hang out her consulting shingle." She began offering paid website memberships, workshops and private consultation services to Stepmoms (and, when asked, to their partners), while continuing to provide a large body of written support materials for free to the public. This book represents the beginning of the next phase of Cathryn's work helping Stepmoms and their partners, plus her work with therapists who want to better assist their clients dealing with stepmother-related issues.

When Cathryn is not working with Stepmoms, studying or writing to share what she has learned, she's enjoying time with her family and friends, working on a quilt for someone she loves, or cheering on her favorite Philadelphia sports teams with her husband—they're huge Flyers (hockey) and Eagles (football) fans!

You can reach Cathryn at cathryn@smoms.org or P.O. Box 7, Medford, NJ 08055.